A DICTIONARY
OF THE EUROPEAN UNION

A DICTIONARY
OF THE EUROPEAN UNION

DAVID PHINNEMORE AND LEE McGOWAN

SIXTH EDITION

Routledge
Taylor & Francis Group

LONDON AND NEW YORK

337.14203
PHI

Sixth edition published 2013
by Routledge
2 Park Square, Milton Park, Abingdon, Oxon OX14 4RN

Simultaneously published in the USA and Canada
by Routledge
711 Third Avenue, New York NY 10017

Routledge is an imprint of the Taylor & Francis Group, an informa business

First published 2002

British Library Cataloguing in Publication Data
A catalogue record for this book is available from the British Library

Library of Congress Cataloging in Publication Data
A catalog record for this book has been requested

ISBN: 978-1-85743-683-9 (hbk)
ISBN: 978-0-203-79695-5 (ebk)

Typeset in 10.5 on 12 pt Bembo
by Taylor & Francis Books

Editor: Imogen Gladman
Senior Editor: Juliet Love
Editorial Director: Paul Kelly

MIX
Paper from
responsible sources
FSC   FSC® C013056
www.fsc.org

Printed and bound in Great Britain by
TJ International Ltd, Padstow, Cornwall

Foreword

A DICTIONARY OF THE EUROPEAN UNION aims to give a comprehensive overview of the development and current status of the European Union. The journey from European Communities to European Union has been a long one; there have been many arguments and difficulties, but also co-operation and enlargement. Information on a variety of European issues is here brought together to give the reader a wide range of facts and background knowledge on the European Union. Thus, this Dictionary includes entries on the history of the European Union and the issues and personalities of importance to its development, as well as on current achievements, debates, concepts, programmes and people.

Most entries in the Dictionary will point the reader towards other relevant entries by means of cross-references. These cross-references within entries will be found in bold type, to denote the existence of a separate entry. However, it should be noted that the potential number of highlights precludes putting in bold those terms that are used in almost every entry. Thus, European Communities, European Union, the names of current member states, etc. are not highlighted, unless the authors deem it necessary to further understanding for the reader to be pointed towards such entries. For the purposes of alphabetization, words such as 'and', 'of', 'the', etc. have been ignored.

The reader should be aware of the difference between the terms European Union, European Community and European Communities. The European Communities were established by three separate treaties, with, from 1967, common institutions. The name of one community, the European Economic Community, was formally changed to the European Community from 1993; thus, when referring to the Treaty of Rome alone after 1993, European Community (EC) is used in the singular. Referring to the three communities from their conception onwards, the Dictionary uses European Communities (EC) in the plural. The European Union, consisting of three inter-related pillars until their unification under the Treaty of Lisbon in 2009, came into existence in 1993. Thus, with respect to the period 1993–2009, the supranational pillar of the European Union continues to be known in this book as the European Communities (EC), while references to the European Union as a whole, also including the two intergovernmental pillars, use European Union (EU).

January 2013

The Authors

Lee McGowan is Senior Lecturer in European Studies at the School of Politics, International Studies and Philosophy, Queen's University Belfast, Northern Ireland, where his teaching interests focus primarily on the politics and policy-making processes of the European Union (EU). His research interests concentrate largely on the political dimension of EU competition policy; relations between the devolved institutions of Northern Ireland and the EU; and Euroscepticism. He has published widely in leading journals such as the *Journal of Common Market Studies*, *Journal of Contemporary European Studies*, *Journal of European Public Policy*, *Journal of European Integration*, *Governance*, *European Journal of Political Research*, *Public Administration*, and *Regional and Federal Studies*. His latest book explores *The Anti-Trust Revolution in Europe* (Edward Elgar, 2010), while other publications include *Competition Policy in the European Union* (jointly authored with Michelle Cini, Palgrave, 2009) and *The Radical Right in Germany: 1870 to the Present* (Longman, 2003).

David Phinnemore is Professor of European Politics at the School of Politics, International Studies and Philosophy, Queen's University Belfast, Northern Ireland and Visiting Professor at the College of Europe, Bruges, Belgium. He teaches courses on contemporary Europe, European Union (EU) institutions, the enlargement of the EU, and EU external relations. His research interests include EU enlargement, treaty reform and the position of Romania within European integration processes. Among his most recent publications are *Reflections on European Integration: 50 Years of the Treaty of Rome* (edited with Alex Warleigh-Lack, Palgrave, 2009), *Romania and the European Union* (jointly authored with Dimitris Papadimitriou, Routledge, 2008) and, co-authored in each case with Clive Church, *Understanding the European Constitution* (Routledge, 2006) and *The Penguin Guide to the European Treaties* (Penguin, 2002). Among his other publications are articles in *European Foreign Affairs Review*, *Journal of Common Market Studies*, *Journal of European Integration*, *Journal of Southern Europe and the Balkans*, *Journal of Southeast European and Black Sea Studies* and *Revue d'études comparatives est-ouest*.

Abbreviations

AIDS	acquired immunodeficiency syndrome
bn	billion
e.g.	exempli gratia (for example)
etc.	et cetera
i.e.	id est (that is to say)
m.	million
UK	United Kingdom
US	United States
USA	United States of America
USSR	Union of Soviet Socialist Republics
v	versus

Acknowledgements

The authors and editors of this book gratefully acknowledge work previously carried out by Professor Derek Urwin and, subsequently, by Professor Urwin assisted by Linda M. Stevenson. These contributors provided the A–Z section for early editions of *The European Union Encyclopedia and Directory*, and their text has subsequently been extensively updated and expanded by the current authors.

A

À LA CARTE EUROPE is a term related to concepts of differentiated integration. Effectively it suggests that European Union (EU) member states should be able to pick and choose which programmes and policies they wish to adopt and participate in. Opponents of the concept argue that the reality of any such development would create a considerable amount of disarray and confusion, undermine solidarity and almost certainly make the EU unmanageable. Nevertheless, the idea is not infrequently espoused by some member states as a means of showing their opposition towards certain priorities. The **opt-out** secured by the United Kingdom at the **Maastricht summit** of the **European Council** in December 1991 on **economic and monetary union** is an example of an *à la carte* approach towards EU integration.

ABATEMENT is the term used to describe the annually calculated 'rebate' that the United Kingdom received from the European Communities' **budget** following an agreement reached in 1984 at the **Fontainebleau summit** of the **European Council**. In recent years, the United Kingdom has come under increasing pressure to accept a reduction in the 'rebate', as the European Union (EU) seeks to meet the challenges of financing **enlargement**. There was a growing demand from other member states, most notably France, for an end to the United Kingdom's rebate as part of the new multi-annual financial package for 2006–13. The issue rose to the top of European Council deliberations in June 2005, when the British Government refused to consider contemplating the rebate issue unless France agreed to review the financing of the **common agricultural policy**. The meeting was reportedly one of the most acrimonious in the EU's history, and the British Government rejected the efforts of the Luxembourg presidency to broker an agreement. After several months a deal was finally reached at a meeting of the European Council in mid-December 2005, whereby the United Kingdom agreed to a reduction in the rebate. Under this deal, £1,000m. a year was to be cut from the United Kingdom's rebate in order to invest in the future prosperity of Eastern Europe. The role of the German Chancellor, **Angela Merkel**, was critical in securing overall agreement, especially from Poland.

ABSTENTION: See **Constructive Abstention**

ACCESSION CRITERIA, often referred to as the **Copenhagen criteria**, were adopted by the **Copenhagen summit** of the **European Council** in June 1993, when the European Community committed itself to admitting the countries of **Central and Eastern Europe** (CEE). Accession was, however, to depend on the **candidate countries** meeting the following criteria: having stable institutions guaranteeing democracy, the rule of law, **human rights** and protection of minorities; possessing a functioning market economy and the capacity to cope with the competitive pressures of the **internal market**; and having the ability to take on the obligations of membership, including adherence to the aims of the European Union (EU), notably political, economic and monetary union. In 1995 the Madrid **summit** of the European Council added a further criterion: that the countries seeking membership should possess the administrative capacity to implement the *acquis communautaire*. Formally, countries in the **Western Balkans** also have to pursue regional co-operation before they can be admitted to the EU. In addition, states are required to have made every effort to resolve any outstanding border disputes and other related issues. This was agreed in 1999, with a particular view to the division of Cyprus being resolved before **Turkey** could join the EU. Since the **enlargements** of the EU in 2004 and 2007 there has been a noticeable tightening of the criteria. The EU has also placed increased emphasis on its own **integration capacity**. This has led to justifiable claims that accession to the EU is becoming more difficult.

ACCESSION NEGOTIATIONS need to be completed before **applicant countries** can join the European Union (EU). They are conducted on a bilateral basis, with the **European Commission** co-ordinating the position of the EU's member states. The last 14 years or so has seen the EU engaged in an unprecedented number of accession negotiations, beginning with Cyprus and five Central and Eastern European countries (the Czech Republic, Estonia, Hungary, Poland and Slovenia), often referred to as the '**Luxembourg group**', in 1998. Two years later, in 2000, the EU opened accession negotiations with the so-called '**Helsinki group**' (Bulgaria, Latvia, Lithuania, Malta, Romania and Slovakia). Negotiations with those applicant countries meeting the **accession criteria**—the Luxembourg group plus Latvia, Lithuania, Malta and Slovakia—were concluded at the **Copenhagen summit** of the **European Council** held on 12–13 December 2002. The **Accession Treaty** was then signed on 16 April 2003. Following **ratification** of the Accession Treaty, the 10 countries joined the EU on 1 May 2004. The following month, Bulgaria concluded its accession negotiations with the EU. Romania followed suit in December 2004, and an Accession Treaty was signed on 25 April 2005. Bulgaria and Romania joined the EU on 1 January 2007. Accession negotiations with **Croatia** and **Turkey** were opened on 4 October 2005. Progress in the negotiations with Turkey has proved to be particularly slow, partly because the EU insists on certain benchmarks being met before negotiations are opened and partly owing to political opposition, notably from France, to the prospect of Turkish membership of the EU. Negotiations with Croatia were completed in 2011. Of the current applicants, the EU opened accession negotiations with **Iceland** on 27 July 2010 and with **Montenegro** on 29 June 2012.

ACCESSION PARTNERSHIPS were first adopted by the European Union (EU) for **applicant countries** from **Central and Eastern Europe** in 1998 and were designed to assist them in meeting the **accession criteria** and preparing themselves for membership of the EU. They list priority areas for legal adaptation and administrative reform in the countries concerned and for EU financial assistance through the former **instrument for structural policies for pre-accession** (ISPA), **Phare** and **Sapard** programmes (which were replaced in January 2007 by the **instrument for pre-accession assistance**). Accession partnerships have since been adopted for **Turkey**, **Croatia** and **the former Yugoslav republic of Macedonia**. Similar in purpose and content, although precursors to accession partnerships, **European partnerships** have been developed for other countries of the **Western Balkans** seeking membership of the EU.

ACCESSION TREATY see **Treaty of Accession**

ACCOUNTABILITY has been a major concern of the European Union (EU) since the early 1990s, as the EU's institutions have been perceived to be increasingly remote from the people. Although the EU has a democratically elected **European Parliament**, which has seen its powers increased, it continues to suffer from a growing **democratic deficit**, with citizens feeling that decision-makers in **Brussels** are unaccountable. In response, the EU has sought to promote greater **transparency** and **openness**. It has also sought to increase monitoring of the activities of the **European Commission** and to ensure tighter financial control over the **budget**.

ACP STATES is the collective title of those African, Caribbean and Pacific developing countries that entered into an **association agreement** with the European Communities (EC) under Articles 182–188 of the **Treaty of Rome** (now Articles 198–204 of the **Treaty on the Functioning of the European Union**) 'to further the interests and prosperity of the inhabitants of these countries and territories in order to lead them to the economic, social and cultural development to which they aspire'. The provisions were originally directed towards the colonies and ex-colonies of the **Six**, and were finalized in the **Yaoundé Conventions** of 1963 and 1969. With the successive rounds of **enlargement**, ex-colonies of new member states have joined the arrangement, which from 1975 was regulated by the **Lomé Convention**; this was replaced in 2000 by the **Cotonou Agreement** and, from 2008, by bilateral **economic**

partnership agreements (EPAs). The original 18 participants were known collectively as the Associated African States and Madagascar. The present title was adopted in 1975 and 79 states signed the Cotonou Agreement. ACP States have traditionally been allowed duty free entry to the European Union market for most of their products on a non-reciprocal basis, and are also eligible to receive both grants from the **European Development Fund** and low-interest loans from the **European Investment Bank**. Preferential treatment for ACP States has caused friction between the EC and members of the **World Trade Organization** (WTO), especially the **USA**, which has long objected to the preferential treatment given to **banana** producers in Caribbean states. Indeed, the EPAs are a response to a WTO ruling that the Cotonou Agreement was not WTO-compatible. (See also **Development aid** and **OCTs**.)

ACQUIS COMMUNAUTAIRE is a phrase that collectively describes all the secondary **legislation** of the European Community (EC) passed under the provisions of the **founding treaties** and their subsequent amendments. It covers all the **directives**, **decisions** and **regulations** adopted by the EC/EU. States that apply for EU membership have to accept the *acquis communautaire*.

ACQUIS POLITIQUE is a phrase describing all the **decisions** and **resolutions** adopted by the member states of the European Union (EU) in the field of foreign policy. It is also used in a broader sense to describe the principles and goals underpinning the activities of the EU.

The **ACTION COMMITTEE FOR A UNITED STATES OF EUROPE** was an interest group established by **Jean Monnet** in 1955 following the failure of the **European Defence Community**. Monnet created it as a selective group of political and trade union leaders who would work for closer European unity, and it contributed to the ideas and pressures that led to the formation of the **European Economic Community**. After 1958, it continued to argue for more intensive integration involving as many European countries as possible. It was led by Monnet until 1975, but after the 1960s it became a less prominent organization.

ADDITIONALITY is a principle applied to the allocation of money from the **European Regional Development Fund** (ERDF). It means that ERDF funding is additional to that provided by local and national authorities. The principle is designed to ensure that member states contribute to the financing of infrastructural projects.

KONRAD ADENAUER (1876–1967) was the first Chancellor (1949–63) of the Federal Republic of Germany (FRG, West Germany). He believed strongly in European co-operation and integration, based in particular upon reconciliation between France and Germany. In 1945 he emerged from retirement, eventually to become the leader of the Christian Democratic Union (CDU). He led the German delegation to the **Congress of Europe** at The Hague in 1948. As Chancellor, he also directed the FRG's foreign affairs. His foreign policy, known as a 'policy of strength', had two main objectives: the rehabilitation and the reunification of Germany. For Adenauer, the FRG had to work to be accepted by its Western neighbours as an equal and trustworthy partner in both Western co-operative endeavours and security measures in an alliance against the **USSR**. The recovery of the FRG and the policy of strength were aimed in the longer term at German reunification. Adenauer supported all European co-operative developments from the Congress of Europe through to the establishment of the **European Economic Community**. After 1958, he formed a close relationship with President **Charles de Gaulle** of France, with whom he was an architect of the 1963 **Treaty of Friendship** (Elysée Treaty) between the two countries. This treaty established much closer cultural, economic and political ties between both states and became the basis of the Franco-German axis that later came to dominate many of the developments and activities of the European Communities.

ADONNINO REPORTS: See **Committee for a People's Europe**

ADVISORY COMMITTEE FOR THE CO-ORDINATION OF FRAUD PREVENTION (Cocolaf) has responsibility for co-ordinating action by the member states and the **European Commission** to combat fraud affecting the financial interests of the EU.

ADVISORY COMMITTEES are bodies that advise the **European Commission** on problems and issues in specific areas. They are part of the world of **comitology**. More than 200 such committees exist and include advisory committees on food, consumer products, health and environmental risks, and equal opportunities. The membership of each committee is drawn from experts and professionals in the relevant area.

ADVOCATES-GENERAL: See **Court of Justice**

The *AETR* **JUDGMENT**, sometimes referred to by its English equivalent— the *ERTA* Judgment—was a 1971 ruling by the **Court of Justice**, which established the important principle that, where the European Communities (EC) have an explicit internal competence, they also have a parallel external competence. Its implication was that in such areas of competence, member states could not act independently of the EC. Where a member state entered into an international agreement that conflicted with EC law, the latter took precedence over any obligation arising from the agreement.

AFRICAN, CARIBBEAN AND PACIFIC STATES: See **ACP States**

The **AFRICAN UNION** (AU) was established on 9 July 2002 as the successor organization to the Organization of African Unity (OAU). The idea of forming such a body was conceived by the former leader of Libya, Col Muammar al-Qaddafi, and aspired to 'an integrated, prosperous and peaceful Africa, driven by its own citizens and representing a dynamic force in the global arena'. The AU is very loosely modelled on the structures of the **European Union** and includes an Assembly, an Executive Council, a Commission, a Pan-African Parliament (established in March 2004) and an African Court of Justice. The AU comprises 54 African states (with **Morocco** as the only all-African state not to be a member). South Sudan became the AU's 54th member in 2011. The AU's broad aims are: to accelerate the political and socio-economic integration of the African continent; to promote and defend common positions on key issues that are vital to the states in Africa; to pursue peace and security in Africa; and to work towards the creation and development of democratic institutions, good governance systems and human rights across the continent. In accordance with these goals, a number of member states have been suspended from the AU— Madagascar in 2009 as a result of the political crisis in that country, and Mali and Guinea-Bissau in 2012 following the *coups d'état* in these two states. The AU's secretariat is based in Addis Ababa, Ethiopia. Following the example of the EU, the AU aims to create an African Economic Community and to introduce a single African currency by 2023. However, the Union recognizes the need to resolve conflicts on the continent and inaugurated a Peace and Security Council in 2004, to act as a decision-making body for the prevention, management and resolution of disputes among its members.

AGENDA 2000 was an **enlargement** strategy developed by the **European Commission** in 1997 following a request from the **European Council**. Its objectives were to strengthen growth, **competitiveness** and **employment**; to reform agriculture and structural policies; and to expand the membership of the European Union (EU) eastwards, to include 10 countries from **Central and Eastern Europe** (CEE). The report comprised three sections: the first covered measures to strengthen and reform policies, in particular the **common agricultural policy** and economic and social **cohesion** (see **cohesion policy**); the second contained recommendations for preparing the EU for enlargement; and the third proposed a new financial framework, covering 2000–06. Also published as part of Agenda 2000 were the Commission's *avis* on the membership applications from the 10 CEE countries. In these, the Commission assessed the extent to which the applicants had met the **accession criteria**. A report on the status of Cyprus was also included.

AGRICULTURAL POLICY: See **Common Agricultural Policy**

AIR TRANSPORT POLICY was slow to develop towards a level that met the **competition policy** requirements of the European Communities (EC). The airline industry has been dominated by an international **cartel**, the International Air Transport Association (IATA), and by a series of intergovernmental agreements. The emphasis of these was upon the mutual protection by governments of state-owned airlines, their pricing arrangements and access to scheduled routes. The result was an absence of competition, and some of the highest air fares in the world, in terms of cost per kilometre. Before 1986, **European Commission** initiatives were restricted to technical matters relating to, for example, co-operation on accident procedures and noise emissions. Challenges to the government-supported IATA structure were largely left to small, independent airlines.

In April 1986 the **Court of Justice** ruled in the *Nouvelles Frontières* case that EC competition policy also applied to air transport. The European Commission immediately threatened legal action against 10 European airlines unless they substantially modified their price-fixing arrangements. Simultaneously, it sought to persuade the member states to opt for more liberal policies. In April 1987 the airlines indicated that they would comply with the Commission's demands. Subsequently, progress was positive, but slow. A number of Commission proposals relating to discount fares, competition on established routes, the rights of prospective new competitors and the establishment of new scheduled routes were implemented in January 1988. These measures also gave the Commission substantial investigatory powers.

In anticipation of the introduction of the **internal market**, and partly because many state-owned airlines were substantial money-losers, governments began to accept a greater degree of private ownership and capital, and also to urge the consolidation of their national companies as a way of warding off foreign competition in a more competitive market. Matters were complicated by the fact that the major carriers, to meet the conditions of the internal market and world developments in air transport, began to seek closer and more formal collaboration, which in turn threatened the survival of smaller, independent airlines. However, airline agreements and co-operative arrangements were subject to Commission approval and the EC's **merger policy**. The acceptance of liberalization also varied from one country to another. Full liberalization of the market took place in 1997, when restrictions on European airlines within the European Union (EU) were removed, with the result that airlines were able to operate domestic air services in EU countries other than their own. In 2002 the European Commission adopted proposals for the creation of a European Aviation Safety Agency (EASA), as an independent organization within the

EC; the EASA began operating in September 2003. Meanwhile, in October 2001 the Commission adopted proposals for a Single European Sky (SES), which aimed to establish a single legislative framework for aviation in the EU. Accordingly, a first legislative package, SES I, was adopted by the European Parliament and the Council in March 2004. Revised SES regulations, incorporating improvements aimed at addressing environmental challenges and fuel cost efficiency, were adopted in June 2008, as the Single European Sky second package, SES-II.

AIRBUS is one of the successes of European industrial co-operation. Founded in 1967 as a consortium of European aircraft manufacturers, Airbus aimed to design and build large passenger aircraft that could compete with Boeing, the large US corporation. Since 1992, Airbus' share of the large civil aircraft market has grown steadily, from over 30% to more than one-half by 2004, and its future successes seemed assured with the launch of the new double-decker-style aircraft (Airbus A380) in 2005. This new plane was specifically designed to carry 525–853 passengers (depending on the aircraft's class configuration) and has been marketed to fly to a series of hub international airports. It appeared set to revolutionize the nature of air travel in much the same way that the jumbo jet did some 40 years previously. However, Boeing met the challenge by building a smaller plane, able to land in smaller airports.

Airbus comprises four partners: British Aerospace, Construcciones Aeronáuticas SA (CASA) of Spain, Daimler-Benz Aerospace of Germany and Aérospatiale of France. Each of the four partners specializes in producing different parts of the aircraft. Boeing, however, complained about the massive government **subsidies** channelled into Airbus in order to make it viable, and labelled such activity as constituting nothing less than unfair competition. Tension was particularly acute in the 1980s, until a bilateral agreement on civil aircraft, which capped government support for new aircraft, was reached in June 1992. Nevertheless, relations remained tense, as was evident in the European Union's (EU) total opposition to the planned merger between Boeing and McDonnell Douglas in 1997. This merger aimed to create the world's largest aerospace and defence company. Airbus would be the only other major competitor. The **European Commission** raised concerns about the potential dominance in the world market of this new company, and threatened to oppose the merger and to impound Boeing aircraft if they landed on EU soil. The **USA** saw EU **competition policy** as another unfair means to protect Airbus.

Fears of a trade war between the EU and the USA grew, and the sensitivity of the issue also led to intervention by the US President, Bill Clinton. The issue was only resolved when the Commission sanctioned a merger, providing that many of the clauses that would have tied Boeing customers to the new company for 20 years were removed. In an effort to make Airbus more competitive and more efficient, it was transformed in 1999 into a limited company;

it became a single integrated operating company in 2001. Tensions between Airbus and Boeing over the degree of subsidies supporting the activities of both companies became a frequent feature of the EU/US trade discussions. In October 2004 both companies launched the largest trade dispute in the short history of the **World Trade Organization** (WTO). However, aware of the economic repercussions of any damaging ruling against them, both parties agreed in January 2005 to return to the negotiating table in an effort to consider how to cut subsidies. A renewed bitter dispute erupted between both companies in May 2005, centred on the failure of both Airbus and Boeing to agree on the level of subsidies, which led both sides to revive their charges before the WTO. The Europeans resent what they see as illegal subsidies that focus on the way in which Boeing is facilitated through a number of military contracts and tax breaks, while the Americans resent the aid being given in the construction of the new A380. It seems highly unlikely that subsidies will ever disappear altogether and both sides are certain to complain about unfair competitive advantages for some time to come.

Airbus continues to mount a serious challenge to Boeing. The ongoing competition between the two international giants continued to intensify, with the launch of a newly designed A350 in July 2006. The decision to redesign the A350 followed scant interest in the product and criticism about the initial design. The long-haul, mid-sized plane was to compete directly with the Boeing 787 Dreamliner (which entered commercial service in October 2011). It was anticipated that the new A350 would commence services in the second half of 2014. There are other problems: doubts, for example, were raised at the beginning of 2010 over whether any further progress could be made in the production of Airbus's A400M Atlas military transport aircraft—which was already over budget—without a significant financial contribution from European Governments. The member states themselves were divided over the issue, but they could not risk abandoning the venture as it would open the way for an alternative aircraft (the C-17) from Boeing. At July 2012 the A400M was undergoing flight testing and Airbus was expected to deliver the first of the new military aircraft in early 2013.

ALBANIA concluded a trade and co-operation agreement with the **European Community** in 1992 that held out the prospect of negotiating an **association agreement**. Progress towards such a goal was hampered in the 1990s by domestic political and economic instability in Albania. In 1999, however, the country became part of the **stabilization and association process** that the European Union (EU) launched in the aftermath of the **Kosovo** crisis. This led to assistance under the former **CARDS** programme, and the possibility of opening negotiations on a **stabilization and association agreement** (SAA). Albania is keen to become a member of the EU, a point recognized at a summit of the **European Council**, held in Feira, Portugal in 2000, when Albania, along with other countries in the **Western Balkans**, was confirmed as a **potential candidate state**. In 2003 EU membership clearly remained a priority for the Albanian Government. Although negotiations on an SAA were opened in February of that year, effectively representing Albania's first step towards eventual EU membership, the then Commission President, **Romano Prodi**, asserted that substantial problems remained which required serious consideration by the authorities in Tirana before any real progress could be made by Albania towards the acquisition of full EU membership. These included suppressing criminal activities and showing evidence of solid economic progress. A **European partnership** was adopted in 2004, however, and negotiations on the SAA were eventually concluded in February 2006. Albania also began to receive pre-accession financial assistance under the new **instrument for pre-accession assistance**, with €213m. allocated for the period 2007–09. A new European partnership was adopted in 2008, the same year that an EU-Albania agreement on visa facilitation, signed in 2007, entered into force. This was followed by the entry into force of the SAA on 1 April 2009, the same day that the country joined the **North Atlantic Treaty Organization**, and Albania's integration with the EU entered a new phase. Further confirmation of this came with the submission of an application for EU membership on 28 April 2009. The Commission's **opinion** in November 2010 was critical of the political situation in the country and of the Government's faltering record on reform; the Commission reached a similar conclusion a year later. In October 2012 the Commission recommended that the European Council give Albania **candidate status**, provided that further reform of the judiciary and public administration were undertaken in advance of legislative elections in 2013.

ALDE: See **Group of the Alliance of Liberals and Democrats for Europe** (ALDE)

ALE: See **European Free Alliance**

ALGERIA: See **Maghreb States**

ALLIANCE OF LIBERALS AND DEMOCRATS FOR EUROPE (ALDE): See **Group of the Alliance of Liberals and Democrats for Europe** (ALDE)

JOAQUÍN ALMUNIA (1948–) is a European Commissioner who holds responsibility for the Competition portfolio under the **Barroso** II Commission (2010–14). Almunía has also been appointed as one of the Commission's four Vice-Presidents following a highly distinguished career in politics. He is a Spanish national, born in Bilbao, and studied law and economics at university before opting to lecture briefly in employment and security law. He became an active trade unionist and joined the Spanish socialist party in 1974. He was elected to parliament (*cortes*) in 1979 and rapidly rose through the ranks to become Minister of Employment and Social Security (1982–86) and then Minister of Public Administration (1986–91). He became leader of the Spanish socialist party in 1997 following the resignation of **Felipe González**, but left office after the party's poor performance in the 2000 general election. He was appointed to the **Prodi** Commission in April 2004 before being re-appointed in November 2004 as a Commissioner under the first Barroso Commission, in which he held the portfolio of Economic and Monetary Affairs (2004–09).

ALTENER stands for Alternative Energy, an initiative relating to the development of new and renewable energy resources (RES) (see **electricity**). It was established in 1993 and its objectives were to make such resources competitive, to eliminate barriers to their marketability, and to develop public awareness about their availability and virtues. The 1997 **White Paper** laid down a clear strategy of doubling the proportion of RES in the European Union's gross domestic energy consumption from 6% in 1997 to 12% in 2010. The Altener II programme (1998–2002) was launched in 1998, but little progress had been made towards the objectives by 2001. The **European Commission** remained optimistic, however, and in September 2001 a directive was adopted by the **European Council** and the **European Parliament** on the production of electricity and RES. This aimed to increase a reliance on RES by advocating greater use of 'green' electricity. Altener III was incorporated into the **Intelligent Energy-Europe** programme.

AMS is the acronym for Aggregate Measure of Support, the calculation of the costs to taxpayers and consumers of both the domestic farm support and the export subsidies provided by the **common agricultural policy** (CAP).

AMSTERDAM TREATY: See **Treaty of Amsterdam**

The **ANDEAN COMMUNITY OF NATIONS** (Comunidad Andina— CAN), formerly the Andean Pact, comprises five South American countries: Bolivia, Colombia, Ecuador, Peru and Venezuela. The community is based on a **customs union**, and formal ties with the **European Community** date back to agreements on bilateral trade and aid signed in 1983 and 1986. Since then, co-operation has developed both on a European Union (EU)-Andean Community basis and within the context of the EU's developing relations with **South and Central America**. Following a series of declarations in 1996, a new institutional framework for relations was developed, with dialogue focusing particularly on drugs. Funds amounting to more than €400m. were allocated by the EU to co-operation with the Andean Community for the period

2002–06. In December 2002 the EU and CAN signed a political dialogue and co-operation agreement and have since pursued, with mixed success, negotiations on more comprehensive forms of association and trade liberalization. Co-operation has been expanded and its priorities now include social cohesion, regional economic integration and the fight against illegal drugs. A sixth EU–CAN summit was held in Madrid, Spain, in May 2010.

LÁSZLÓ ANDOR (1966–) is one of the 27 Commissioners of the **Barroso II Commission** (2010–14), in which he has responsibility for Employment, Social Affairs and Inclusion. László Andor was born in Hungary and studied economics in Budapest, Washington, DC, USA and Manchester, United Kingdom. After graduating he became a lecturer and an adviser on economic issues for the Hungarian parliament and more recently the Hungarian Government. He was appointed as a member of the Board of Directors of the **European Bank for Reconstruction and Development** in 2005.

ANIMAL WELFARE is a growing area of European Union (EU) responsibility and aims to address issues surrounding the keeping of millions of animals for economic purposes (for example, farming) across Europe. The **European Commission** regards animals as sentient beings and seeks to ensure that they do not encounter avoidable pain or suffering. The Commission is working towards establishing minimum welfare requirements for all those who keep animals (including pet owners). The Commission adopted its first animal welfare strategy in 2006—an Action Plan on the Protection and Welfare of Animals (2006–10). A new four-year, improved strategy was adopted in January 2012 and was to run until the end of 2015. The **Treaty on the Functioning of the European Union** reaffirms a number of fundamental principles regarding animal welfare (first introduced under the **Treaty of Amsterdam**) that should be respected. Article 13 states that 'in formulating and implementing the Union's agriculture, fisheries, transport, internal market, research and technological development and space policies, the Union and the Member States shall... pay full regard to the welfare requirements of animals, while respecting the legislative or administrative customs of the Member States'.

The **ANNUAL REPORT** is a general report on the activities of the European Union (EU) and the member states. It is published annually in all EU languages and is submitted to the **European Parliament**.

ANTICI GROUP is the name given to the personal assistants of the Permanent Representatives (see **Permanent Representation**) in **Brussels**. It has no formal status, but functions as an integral and important part of the structure of the **Committee of Permanent Representatives**, and is consulted by the presidency on work programmes and procedures.

ANTI-DUMPING: See **Dumping**

The **ANTI-FRAUD OFFICE** (OLAF), an independent office within the **European Commission**, has, since June 1999, been responsible for combating fraud against the European Union (EU) **budget**, corruption and serious misconduct within the EU institutions, as well as transnational organized crime and any fraud or illegal activity prejudicial to the budget. OLAF was established in April 1999 and replaced UCLAF (the Task Force for the Co-ordination of Fraud Prevention), created in 1988. In contrast to its predecessor, OLAF is empowered to examine the management and the financing of all of the EU's institutions (not just the European Commission). The Director of OLAF is appointed by agreement between the **European Parliament**, the Commission and the **Council of the European Union**, and OLAF can bring cases before the Courts and can also authorize any investigation that it deems necessary. OLAF has completed some 3,500 case investigations since 1999, which have enabled the retrieval of a total of around €1,100m. for the EU budget. In 2011 alone, OLAF was involved in 463 investigations and recovered some €691m.

ANTI-TRUST: See **Competition Policy**

The **APPLICANT COUNTRIES**, in order of application for membership of the European Union (EU), are: **Turkey** (14 April 1987), **Croatia** (21 February 2003), **the former Yugoslav republic of Macedonia**—FYRM (22 March 2004), **Montenegro** (15 December 2008), **Albania** (28 April 2009), **Iceland** (16 July 2009) and **Serbia** (22 December 2009). Other countries have also signalled their intention to apply for EU membership at some point in the future. These include **Moldova** and **Ukraine**. **Switzerland** has applied for membership, but its application was frozen by the Swiss Government following popular rejection of Swiss participation in the **European Economic Area** in 1992.

Of the current applicant countries, Croatia, the FYRM, Montenegro, Serbia and Turkey are formally **candidate countries**, Serbia having had the status conferred on it most recently by the **European Council** on 1 March 2012. Iceland is also regarded as a candidate, although this status has never been formally conferred on the country. Of the candidates, Croatia and Turkey opened **accession negotiations** in October 2005, Iceland in July 2010 and Montenegro in June 2012. The FYRM and Serbia are awaiting the opening of accession negotiations. Albania has been told that further reforms are needed before candidate status can be conferred.

APPROXIMATION is a term used to describe the process of removing undesired or unwarranted differences in national **legislation** within the context of the **internal market**. Proposals for approximation come from the **European Commission**, but must be approved by the **Council of the**

European Union. Approximation can involve not only member states, but also non-member countries.

'ARAB SPRING' is the term coined to describe the popular uprisings that took place across the Middle East from December 2010. A series of large-scale demonstrations in Tunisia followed the self-immolation of a young Tunisian man in protest at state restrictions in mid-December 2010, and led President Zine al-Abidine Ben Ali to flee the country in mid-January 2011. A number of regional governments were subsequently overthrown, and there was widespread and ongoing civil conflict in Syria.

In late February 2011, at a Senior Officials' meeting to discuss the unrest in the Middle East, **the High Representative for Foreign Affairs and Security Policy** and Vice-President of the **European Commission**, **Catherine Ashton** (EU), identified the need for the European Union to respond in three ways: by helping to develop 'deep democracy', through a process of political reform, democratic elections, institution-building, measures to combat corruption, and support for the independent judiciary and civil society; through economic development; and by facilitating the movement of people and of communications, while avoiding mass migration. In June Ashton established a new Task Force for the Southern Mediterranean, which aimed to combine expertise from the **European External Action Service**, the Commission, the **European Investment Bank**, the **European Bank for Reconstruction and Development** and other international financial institutions to act as a focal point for assistance to countries in North Africa experiencing political transformation. The Council appointed an EU Special Representative for the Southern Mediterranean in July, who was to strengthen the EU's political role in North Africa and the Middle East, to ensure the coherence of EU actions in relation to the region and to support the transition to democracy in the EU's southern neighbourhood. In late September the Commission agreed to new economic support for the Middle East. The Support for Partnership Reform and Inclusive Growth (SPRING) programme was to be allocated a budget of €350m. in additional funds for 2011–12, and was to provide support on a so-called more-for-more basis to those countries that demonstrated progress in implementing democratic reforms. The Civil Society Facility was to be established, with a budget of €26.4m., with the objective of strengthening the capacity of civil society to promote reform and increase public accountability. By December 2011 the European Commission had provided funds amounting to some €80.5m. to help the refugee crisis in North Africa, while EU member states had provided a further €73.0m.

ARC: See **Rainbow Group**

Creating an **AREA OF FREEDOM, SECURITY AND JUSTICE** was a goal inserted into the **Treaty of Rome** by the **Treaty of Amsterdam**. It involves co-operation in many of the areas previously dealt with under Pillar III of the European Union (EU), the third **pillar** covering **justice and home affairs (JHA)**. The Treaty of Amsterdam transferred the issues of asylum, immigration and judicial co-operation in civil matters from this third pillar into the European Community pillar, leaving the more sensitive issues of police and judicial co-operation in criminal matters in a newly renamed pillar 3, **Police and Judical Cooperation in Criminal Matters (PJCCM)**. Hence, an emphasis on assuring the **freedom of movement** of persons is accompanied by measures governing external border controls, asylum, immigration and the prevention and combating of crime. How to realize the area of freedom, security and justice was the principal focus of the **Tampere summit** in 1999, which produced a five-year action programme focused on progress towards a common EU asylum and migration policy, mutual recognition of judicial decisions, and enhanced cross-border co-operation against crime, including with non-member states. Subsequently, a second action plan—the Hague Action Plan—was adopted in 2004. It was followed by the **Stockholm Programme** in December 2009. The Treaty of Lisbon abolished the pillar structure and brought all JHA and PJCCM issues back together under the Area of Freedom, Security and Justice. It also enabled the **European Parliament** and the **European Court** to wield greater influence regarding these issues.

ARIANE is the name of a series of European civilian rockets that have been taking satellites into space since the late 1970s. The Ariane project, originally conceived as a French-designed rocket-launcher, became Western Europe's second attempt successfully to design commercial rockets to compete with their American and Soviet counterparts. The Ariane project was partly funded by loans from the **European Investment Bank**. In 1980 the **European Space Agency** (ESA) established the Ariane space company (Arianespace) to market the launcher commercially. Its facilities were made available to all, and Arianespace has 24 shareholders from 10 European states, with France the largest by far. The company has been involved in a regular programme of launches, putting satellites in space since 1979. Over time the rockets have been adapted and re-designed to allow for greater efficiency and capacity. The latest version is the Ariane 5-ECA, which was first launched in May 2007. The 200th rocket lifted off from Arianespace's base in Kourou in French Guiana in February 2011.

An **ARTICLE** is the basic clause or unit of a European treaty. It may be subdivided into paragraphs.

ARTICLE 36 COMMITTEE, formerly the K.4 Committee, and also known as CATS, was established by the **Treaty on European Union**. Its role is primarily to co-ordinate European Union **police and judicial co-operation in criminal matters**. In addition, the Committee is expected to provide the

Council of the European Union with opinions and assist in the preparation of the Council's discussions, along with the **Committee of Permanent Representatives**. It was planned to re-assess the role of this committee following the creation of a new **Council standing committee on internal security (COSI)** by the **Treaty of Lisbon**.

ARTICLE 352 (formerly **Article 308**) allows the European Union, in the absence of any explicit powers and acting by **unanimity**, to take 'appropriate measures' to achieve a particular Treaty objective.

ASEAN: See **Association of Southeast Asian Nations**

CATHERINE ASHTON (Baroness Ashton of Upholland, 1956–) is the United Kingdom's European Commissioner. She has been a Labour Party member of the House of Lords since 1999 and prior to her appointment in **Brussels** served as Parliamentary Under-Secretary in the Department of Education and Skills (2001–04), the Department of Constitutional Affairs (2004–06) and the Ministry of Justice (2007–08). As Commissioner, although Ashton was generally regarded as having made little impact on the wider public, she won widespread support in Brussels for her handling of the portfolio and her competence. Ashton emerged in the latter half of 2009 as an initially unlikely-seeming choice for the newly enlarged post of foreign policy chief, the High Representative of the Union for Foreign Affairs and Security Policy, under the **Treaty of Lisbon**. She easily secured the endorsement of the **European Council** and thus occupies one of the most high-profile positions within the entire European Union (EU) institutional architecture, where she both sits in the Council and is one of the Vice-Presidents of the Commission. She has been responsible for developing a single coherent strategy for EU foreign policy and also for managing the **European External Action Service**, which has a staff of more than 1,600. She is one of seven females within the **Barroso** II Commission and is one of the most senior women in the British Labour Party.

ASIA has not been the subject of a co-ordinated **regional policy** by the European Communities (EC), although most Asian countries participate in the **Generalized System of Preferences**, and the EU has developed links with the **Association of Southeast Asian Nations** (ASEAN). In addition, there are **co-operation agreements** with several Asian countries, while others have been the subjects of separate economic and development accords. India is the largest single recipient of EU aid among developing countries.

ASIA–PACIFIC ECONOMIC CO-OPERATION (APEC): See **Association of Southeast Asian Nations**

ASSIZES (or Conferences of the Parliaments) are consultative meetings of representatives of **national parliaments** designed to improve awareness of and support for the integration process.

ASSOCIATION AGREEMENTS have been concluded by the European Communities (EC) with numerous countries both within Europe and beyond. Agreements concluded with the latter include the **Lomé Convention** and the **Cotonou Agreement**. Within Europe, association agreements were initially drawn up only with countries aspiring to but as yet insufficiently developed economically for membership. Hence, those with Greece (1961) and **Turkey** (1963) envisaged the creation of a customs union with the EC as well as co-operation in a wide variety of areas. Later agreements with Malta (1971) and Cyprus (1972) were, by contrast, far less ambitious, restricting themselves to little more than the creation of a free trade area, although they too involved the establishment of a series of bodies (e.g. an Association Council and an Association Committee) to oversee the operation of the Association. Since the early 1990s an increasing number of association agreements have been concluded with European countries. These include the formation of a **European Economic Area** with the member states of the **European Free Trade Association** (EFTA), **Europe agreements** with the countries of **Central and Eastern Europe**, and the **stabilization and association agreements** with countries in the **Western Balkans**. Association agreements were subsequently envisaged for the Eastern European countries covered by the EU's Eastern partnership, such as **Ukraine** (which initialled an association agreement with the European Union— EU—in March 2012).

The **ASSOCIATION OF SOUTHEAST ASIAN NATIONS** (ASEAN), when formed in 1967, comprised Indonesia, Malaysia, the Philippines, Singapore and Thailand. Brunei and Viet Nam joined in 1984 and 1995 respectively, with Myanmar and Laos joining in 1997. Cambodia became a member of ASEAN in 1999. The Association's main purpose today is to promote free trade between its member states and other members of the Asia-Pacific Economic Co-operation (APEC) organization, which includes Australia, **Japan**, **Russia** and the People's Republic of China among its 21 members. Relations with the European Union (EU) date back to the early 1970s and include a **co-operation agreement** signed in 1980, although at times development of relations has been hampered by concerns over alleged **human rights** abuses in certain ASEAN countries, notably Indonesia. In 1997, a 'new dynamic' to EU-ASEAN relations was launched with a view to increasing co-operation and encouraging greater collaboration in business and trade. Ten years later, in 2007, the first EU-ASEAN summit took place in Singapore. This endorsed a Plan of Action to implement an Enhanced Partnership covering political and security co-operation as well as co-operation on economic, energy, environmental

17

and socio-cultural issues. A second EU-ASEAN summit was held in Brunei in April 2012.

An **ASYLUM POLICY** did not exist for the European Communities (EC) before 1989, although matters relating to asylum had been discussed more informally within the **TREVI** process. The collapse of communism in **Central and Eastern Europe** and fears, which were especially pronounced in Germany, that there would be a dramatic increase in the number of immigrants to the EC from the east, combined with greater immigration pressures from non-European sources, led to demands for more formal arrangements. The member states, except Denmark, signed the **Dublin Convention on Asylum** in June 1990. Partly in response to growing unrest in the **USSR** and **Yugoslavia**, the member states agreed in June 1991 to establish a Quick Reaction Consultation Centre to deal with sudden and large-scale immigration pressures. After 1991 asylum procedures were generally tightened, and grants of asylum more restricted. More recently, the **Treaty of Amsterdam** established a timetable within which member states had to establish common rules relating to both their **asylum** and **immigration policies**. Asylum and immigration policies were principal issues raised at the **Tampere summit** of the **European Council** in 1999, which urged the creation of a Common European Asylum System (CEAS). Since then the asylum issue has been a high priority for the European Union (EU) and there has been growing recognition of the need for increased European co-operation in this area. During a first phase of activity (1999–2005) the EU established the CEAS and succeeded in passing a number of legislative acts that sought to harmonize minimum standards in the area of asylum, covering such issues as reception conditions for asylum seekers, qualifications for becoming a refugee and asylum procedures. Agreement was also reached on the 'Dublin' regulation that determined (when difficulties arose) which state actually held responsibility for dealing with asylum cases. As a means of further developing policy, the **Commission** produced a **Green Paper** on Asylum policy in 2007 and adopted its Policy Plan on Asylum in June 2008. The current priorities of the CEAS are: making refinements to the existing legislation regarding reception and asylum procedures to secure further alignment; the creation of a European Support Office to facilitate European co-operation; and finding means to provide greater solidarity and responsibility among member states on asylum policy. The Commission hoped to complete the establishment of the CEAS by the end of 2012.

ATLANTIC ALLIANCE is a popular alternative name for the **North Atlantic Treaty Organization** (NATO).

The **ATLANTIC ARC COMMISSION** is an intergovernmental association of regional authorities from those regions of the European Union (EU) that border the Atlantic, including islands located in this ocean and any other regions with close economic and cultural ties with areas bordering the Atlantic. It was founded in 1989 and has as its main objective securing EU funding for infrastructural developments for the poorer, more peripheral areas of the EU.

ATMOSPHERIC POLLUTION was a central element of European Communities initiatives in the field of **environment policy** from the mid-1980s. Regulations governing automobile emissions were introduced in 1985 and 1987, though the extent of improvement was hindered by disagreements between the member states. There was also a series of **directives** on industrial pollution, especially the discharge of sulphur dioxide and chlorofluorocarbons (CFCs) into the atmosphere, with CFCs due to be totally banned by 1997. The European Union (EU) agreed in 1997 to curb emissions of six 'greenhouse' gases by 8%, in comparison to 1990 levels, by 2008–12. The Clean Air for Europe (CAFE) programme began in 2001, aiming to co-ordinate the collection of scientific and technical data necessary for policy-making in this area. As part of the EU's Sixth Environmental Action Plan, adopted in 2002, the EU aimed to bring about, *inter alia*, by 2020: a 47% reduction in the erosion of life expectancy owing to exposure to particulate matter and a 10% reduction in acute mortality resulting from ozone exposure. In April 2009 the Council adopted new climate change legislation, committing EU member states to reducing carbon dioxide emissions by 20% in 2013–20, compared with emissions levels in 1990. The Council also agreed to increase the use of renewable energy sources to 20% (10% for transport energy consumption) by 2020, and to increase energy efficiency by 20% by the same date. An Emissions Trading System (ETS) was launched in January 2005, which obliges companies that exceed their agreed carbon dioxide emissions to buy extra allowances from more efficient companies or incur considerable fines.

AUDIOVISUAL POLICY dates from the 1980s and activity in the audiovisual sector comprises two broad aspects. The first focuses mainly on industry sector considerations that centre on efforts to ensure the standardization of the systems used in the member states to broadcast programmes by satellite and cable. The first directive on this specific issue was approved in 1986. Later, in 1989, objectives were defined for the development of high-definition television (HDTV). Then, in 1991, a single standard for high-definition television production and financial support for a programme of co-operation between the businesses concerned were introduced. There is also a legal dimension to audiovisual policy and this centred on the Television without Frontiers directive, which was adopted in 1989 and amended in 1997. This directive sought to provide a harmonized framework in order to promote the free movement, production and distribution of European television programmes. To this end, common rules were agreed on advertising, sponsorship, the protection of minors and the right of reply. Interestingly, this directive also introduced distribution quotas, thus requiring TV channels to reserve, whenever possible, more than one-half of their transmission time for European productions. An updated Television without Frontiers directive, renamed the Audiovisual Media Services without Frontiers directive, was adopted by the European Parliament in November 2007.

The European audiovisual market continues to face a series of hurdles: continuing language barriers which prevent the free movement of programmes; an unwieldy decision-making process which generally requires unanimity; and the need to make considerable investment to anticipate technological developments, which requires international alliances and/or mergers. It is important to stress that the development of European Union (EU) audiovisual policy must respect certain interests and priorities, such as competition rules (especially regarding state aid—see **subsidies**), the rules on intellectual property and the principles of public service.

Furthermore, since 1991 the Community MEDIA programme (measures to promote the development of the audiovisual industry—see **Media policy**) has been supporting the European audiovisual industry by encouraging the development and distribution of European works. It also finances schemes to improve the training of professionals in the sector. The **MEDIA 2007** Programme (2007–13), which followed on from MEDIA II (1996–2000) and Media Plus (2000–05), had a budget of €755m.

AUSTRIA for many years felt unable to consider European Communities (EC) membership because of its neutral status and the terms of the Austrian State Treaty of 1955, which ended the Allied military occupation of the country. It did, however, become a founder member of the **European Free Trade Association** (EFTA) in 1960, despite the disapproval of the **USSR**, which had been a party to the 1955 Treaty. Austria requested a special arrangement with the EC, and exploratory talks began in 1964. Subsequent negotiations were vetoed in 1967 by the Italian Government. Hence, it was not until **enlargement** was included on the agenda of the EC that Austria concluded a **free trade agreement** with the EC, in 1972. Given its large volume of trade with the EC, especially with the Federal Republic of Germany, in the late 1980s Austria began to fear that its economy would suffer from the establishment of the **internal market**, unless it was party to the process. It supported the attempt by EFTA to reach a general agreement with the EC, but soon broke ranks with its EFTA partners to apply formally for EC membership in July 1989, arguing that membership was not, in fact, precluded by the 1955 State Treaty. While the EC indicated that action on the application was unlikely until after 1992, the collapse of communism in **Central and Eastern Europe**, the successful completion of the **European Economic Area** talks and the decision by most of the other EFTA states to seek EC membership led to early progress being made. Negotiations on terms of entry began in 1993 and the terms were endorsed by a popular referendum in June

1994. Austria's membership of the European Union (EU) was effective from 1 January 1995 (Finland and Sweden also joined on the same date). Adapting to membership was a relatively smooth process, although Austria was forced to endure a period of diplomatic isolation in 2000 when the far-right Freedom Party led by Jörg Haider entered briefly into coalition government. The Austrian Government found itself isolated in mid-2005 when it strongly resisted the opening of accession negotiations with **Turkey**. Austria eventually agreed to remove all obstacles to the opening of talks with Turkey, provided that accession negotiations could commence with **Croatia**. However, Austrian attitudes towards Turkish accession to the EU remain somewhat mixed, and even as recently as May 2011 the Austrian Vice-Chancellor and Federal Minister of European and International Affairs favoured forging a special relationship with Turkey over Turkish membership of the EU.

AVIS is the term applied to the opinion issued by the **European Commission** on the acceptability of a country's formal application for membership of the European Union.

B

BALKANS: See **Western Balkans**

BALTIC STATES: See **Estonia**; **Latvia**; **Lithuania**

BANANAS were the cause of a trade dispute between the European Union (EU) and the **USA** throughout the 1990s. The EU's banana regime had always been strongly contested as it granted preferential access to British and French markets to banana producers in their former colonies among the **ACP** (African, Caribbean and Pacific) **States**. The EU banana trade regime (BTR) antagonized the Government of the USA as it restricted access for US producers. With the support of several Central American producers, an appeal was made by the USA to the **World Trade Organization** (WTO) disputes settlement panel against this apparent discrimination. The WTO backed the US complaint and forced the EU to reconsider its BTR. Although a majority of EU member states wanted to abolish the BTR, a minority, including France and the United Kingdom, wished to defend it. Efforts to enlarge the quota for Central American producers were rejected by the USA in 1999 and heralded the imposition of substantial tariffs on a range of British and French goods entering the US market. This trade war was resolved in April 2001 when a resolution was reached between the EU and the USA, which agreed a transition to a tariff-only system by 2006. Despite this, in June 2007 the USA again raised allegations at the WTO that EU treatment of Latin American banana producers was unfair, citing the continued existence of a 'discriminatory' tariff quota. In December 2009, after much deliberation, the EU-Latin American Bananas Agreement finally sought to end the 20-year dispute between the EU and Latin America over the former's preferential treatment of the ACP states. In the agreement, the EU opted to reduce its tariffs and the Latin American states pledged to abandon all disputes over bananas before the WTO. It was hoped that the agreement would bring greater stability to the banana market.

The **BANK FOR INTERNATIONAL SETTLEMENTS** (BIS) is a joint venture, originally of European national central banks, established in 1930 as an aid to the resolution of the problem of German reparations. After 1945 it extended its activities and membership to include, among others, Canada,

Japan and the **USA**. In 2000 it held deposits for some 120 international financial institutions and central banks world-wide, managing some 7% of the world's foreign exchange reserves. Based in Basel, **Switzerland**, it has served as the headquarters of the **Committee of the Governors of the Central Banks**, and has acted on behalf of the European Communities as their agent for the **European Monetary Co-operation Fund** (EMCF). By working closely with the International Monetary Fund (IMF), BIS provides a forum for the co-ordination of international monetary policy.

BARBER PROTOCOL is the name given informally to a **protocol** introduced by the **Treaty on European Union** intended to clarify the remuneration criteria contained within Article 141 of the **Treaty of Rome** (now Article 157 of the **Treaty on the Functioning of the European Union**) regarding equal pay for equal work by men and women. It restricts the definition of remuneration by largely excluding benefits under occupational social security schemes, and has been interpreted as meaning that the **Court of Justice** has a more limited ability to clarify its own judgments. The protocol results from political pressures and financial expediency.

The **BARCELONA DECLARATION** of November 1995 launched the **Euro-Mediterranean partnership** and, in doing so, committed the signatories to the establishment of a **Euro-Mediterranean Economic Area** (EMEA). The signatories were the European Union and the so-called MED-12 states: Algeria, Cyprus, Egypt, Israel, Jordan, Lebanon, Malta, **Morocco**, Palestinian Authority (now Palestinian Autonomous Areas), Syria, Tunisia and **Turkey**. (See also **Barcelona Process** and **Union for the Mediterranean**.)

The **BARCELONA PROCESS**, initiated in 1995, was designed to promote closer ties between the European Union (EU) and the so-called MED-12 states of the Mediterranean (Algeria, Cyprus, Egypt, Israel, Jordan, Lebanon, Malta, **Morocco**, Palestinian Authority—now Palestinian Autonomous Areas, Syria, Tunisia and **Turkey**). Forming the central element of the EU's **Mediterranean Policy**, it was initiated by the **Barcelona Declaration** of 1995, and subsequently came to form part of the **European neighbourhood policy**. In July 2008 a new, but rather vague, multilateral partnership, the **Union for the Mediterranean**, was created; the Union comprised the 27 EU member states and 16 Mediterranean partner countries from North Africa, the Middle East and the Balkans.

MICHEL BARNIER (1951–) is one of the 27 European Commissioners in the Barroso II Commission (2010–14). Barnier was born in the Rhônes-Alpes region of France and studied business at the École Superieure de Commerce in Paris (graduating in 1972) before entering the world of politics. He was elected to the French National Assembly in 1978 at the age of 27 and, as a member of **Jacques Chirac**'s Rassemblement pour la République (RPR), became a member of the French Council of Ministers for the first time in 1993 as Minister of the Environment. He became Secretary of State for European Affairs following Chirac's successful presidential bid in 1995. Barnier was appointed to the **Romano Prodi** Commission (1999–2004) in 1999 and took responsibility for **regional policy**, but was recalled to Paris to become French Minister of Foreign Affairs in March 2004. However, his tenure in this post was brief and he was replaced in June 2005. He was elected Vice-President of the **European People's Party** (EPP) in the **European Parliament** in 2006 and rejoined the French Council of Ministers (following the election of **Nicolas Sarkozy** as President) as Minister of Agriculture. His experience of Europe and European affairs was by this stage quite considerable and led to his nomination as the French choice for Commissioner in the Barroso II Commission, where he now has responsibility (for some commentators, rather controversially) for the internal market and services.

The **BARRE PLAN** was one of the alternative strategies for **economic and monetary union** that was advanced after the 1969 **Hague summit**. Prepared by Raymond Barre, who was the French Minister of Economy and Finance in 1976–78, and written at the request of the **European Commission**, it was supported by Belgium as well as France. It favoured a monetarist approach to union with the immediate introduction of fixed exchange rates. This tactic, it argued, would enforce a **convergence** and **harmonization** of the economic policies of the member states. The alternative argument, an economic approach, was expounded in the Schiller Plan. (See also **Optimum currency area**; **Werner Report**.)

JOSÉ MANUEL DURÃO BARROSO (1956–) was chosen as the new Commission President-designate by the **European Council** on 29 June 2004. Barroso's background was in European affairs: after a law degree in Lisbon, Portugal, he went on to take a diploma in European Studies and a Master's degree, both at the University of Geneva, Switzerland. Barroso initially held academic posts before moving into politics. He was elected (and re-elected five times) as a member of the Portuguese parliament in 1985 as a member of the Social Democratic Party. He served as chairman of the parliament's Foreign Affairs Committee in 1995 and went on to act as both State Secretary for Foreign Affairs and Minister for Foreign Affairs before becoming Prime Minister of Portugal in April 2002. His nomination as **European Commission** President was universally endorsed by his peers in the European Council and his candidacy was endorsed by the **European Parliament** (EP) on 22 July 2004. Barroso's appointment was confirmed with a majority of 413 out of 711 votes cast. There were 251 votes against, 44 abstentions and three spoiled ballots. He had firm support from the centre-right groups and liberals, but was opposed by many members of the Socialist group as well as the Greens, the far left and the **Eurosceptics**. It should be noted that the **Socialist Group in the European Parliament** (PSE) voted by a large majority to reject Barroso's nomination, largely as a result of his neo-liberal views.

Barroso took up his posting as the new Commission President on 1 November 2004. Barroso was determined from the outset to take charge of the **agenda** and was committed to making economic reform the hallmark of his presidency. To this end he carefully distributed Commission portfolios and placed responsibility for the principal economic reforms (trade, competition and the **internal market**) in the hands of reform-minded countries (the United Kingdom—**Peter Mandelson**, the Netherlands—**Neelie Kroes** and Ireland—**Charlie McCreevy**). Nevertheless, his aspirations were dented almost immediately by a series of events that encompassed the dilution of the Lisbon agenda, the rejection of the **Treaty establishing a Constitution for Europe** in both France and the Netherlands, increased concerns in some national capitals over the economic direction in which the EU was heading, and the debate on EU funding in mid-2005. Barroso emerged as a more competent and `media-savvy' President than his two immediate predecessors. Barroso was keen to renew his position as Commission President for a further five years and formally announced his candidacy in June 2009 following the outcome of the EP elections. The victory for the centre-right within the new seventh EP meant that the European Council was looking for a candidate from the centre-right and opted to reappoint the incumbent (who was the only candidate) for a second term. The EP approved Barroso's second term in office in September 2009 by a vote of 382 to 219; there were 117 abstentions. Barroso was the first Commission President to be reappointed since **Jacques Delors**. Barroso announced agreement on a new **Europe 2020** strategy (as an extension of the **Lisbon 2010 agenda**) in March 2010.

BASIC PRICE: See **Target Price**

BATTLEGROUPS have been created as part of the EU's commitment, following the development of the **European Rapid Reaction Force**, to equip itself with the military capacity to fulfil the **Petersburg tasks** set out in the **Treaty on European Union** and pursue its **European security and defence policy** (notably the **European security strategy**). The battlegroups, usually drawing on personnel from a coalition of member states and often with niche capabilities, each consist of up to 1,500 personnel deployable within 5–10 days.

BELGIUM is a constitutional monarchy under the current King Albert II and dates its origins to 1830. It emerged as one of the pioneers of European integration after 1945. It is part of the **Benelux** Economic Union, and a founder member of the European Communities (EC). Belgian governments have been consistent supporters of the European Union (EU) integration process and all have regarded economic integration as only a step towards a political union. In the 1960s Belgium was strongly in favour of **enlargement**, especially the admission of the United Kingdom. After the mid-1980s it believed that neither the **Single European Act** nor the **Treaty on European Union** (TEU) had been sufficiently far-reaching, and was critical of states such as the United Kingdom and Denmark that were reluctant to accept fully the political implications of integration. However, it has at times been wary of a too forceful Franco-German leadership in the EC; this was a further reason for it to favour a strengthening of the EC's supranational institutions. Belgium was one of the first member states to ratify the TEU. It has, overall, been a net beneficiary of EC membership, not least perhaps in terms of the employment possibilities that membership has created in **Brussels**: the fact that the city is the institutional heart of the EU means that Belgium has developed almost a proprietorial interest in the organization. However, the formal decentralization of the state on linguistic lines, which was concluded in 1993, along with an expensive social security system, imposed heavy public sector costs and raised initial doubts as to whether the country could meet the **convergence criteria** set by the TEU for **economic and monetary union** (EMU). In the end, the criteria were relaxed sufficiently for Belgium to be declared eligible for EMU membership, and the country entered as one of the first wave of 11 states in January 1999.

Belgium remains one of the EU's most enthusiastic members and maintains that a flexible approach to EU integration should be adopted so as to enable a central core of states to integrate faster than others, if they so desire. In contrast, Belgium's internal political scene is much more complex and divides along linguistic lines that see two main communities within the state, each with its own political parties, newspapers and television networks. An inconclusive general election in June 2007 prevented agreement on the formation of a new federal government as divisions intensified between the two main communities within Belgium, the French-speaking Walloons and the Flemish-speaking population. After six months without a government, an emergency coalition Government was established in December under the temporary leadership of (outgoing) Guy Verhofstadt. Yves Leterme became the new Belgian Prime Minister in March 2008, ending some nine months of political impasse. The new Government pledged to bring forward plans for a major restructuring of the state, particularly in terms of devolving greater powers to the two main parts of Belgium. This was a controversial agenda as increasing rivalry between the French-speaking Walloons and the Flemish-speaking population in recent years seriously threatens the long-term survival of the Belgian state. Leterme resigned as Prime Minister amid allegations that he had tried to influence a court decision on the breakup of one of Belgium's major banks (Fortis). He was replaced by a fellow Christian Democrat, **Herman Van Rompuy**, in December 2008, but became Prime Minister for a second time when Van Rompuy was appointed President of the European Council in December

2009. Ongoing tensions, primarily over language issues and rights within Belgium between the Flemish and the Walloons, led to the collapse of the Government and Leterme's resignation as Prime Minister in April 2010. The domestic difficulties were not resolved in the subsequent legislative elections (of 9 June) and were the backdrop to Belgium assuming responsibility for the EU's six-month rotating presidency in July. In the absence of an agreement on the formation of a new government, Leterme continued to serve as the head of what was widely viewed as an ineffective administration. After 541 days of political deadlock, a new government, headed by the francophone socialist Elio Di Rupo, finally took office on 6 December 2011.

The **BELGO-LUXEMBOURG ECONOMIC UNION** (BLEU) is primarily a **customs union**, but in many ways a complete economic union, between Belgium and Luxembourg. The BLEU agreement dates from 1921 and led to the removal of frontier controls between the two states from May 1922. Although originally scheduled to last for some 50 years, the agreement has been renewed every 10 years since 1971. In 1944 the customs union element was extended with the creation of **Benelux**, although BLEU still exists within Benelux. As a result of the BLEU agreement, both countries hold their gold and foreign exchange reserves in common, while many financial, trade and other statistics for Belgium and Luxembourg are recorded together.

BENCHMARKING is an increasingly familiar part of current European Union (EU) vocabulary. It involves the use of comparison (from the perspective of a member state or an EU institution) with other states or organizations (for example, with regard to issues such as pension reform or employment practices) with the aim of improving one's own performance by learning from the experience of others.

BENELUX is the commonly used shortened name of the Benelux Economic Union, an economic grouping of Belgium, the Netherlands and Luxembourg within the broader economic structure of the EU. It was formed by the exiled Governments of the three states in 1944, and a Benelux Customs Union was formally established in January 1948. Ten years later a new treaty of economic union was signed in The Hague and came into operation in January 1960. As this treaty was due to expire in 2010, a new legal framework (known as the Treaty revising the Treaty establishing the Benelux Economic Union) was signed on 17 June 2008. The most recent treaty has no fixed expiry date, and the name of the Benelux Economic Union was changed to the Benelux Union, to reflect the wide scope of the union. Benelux survives within the EC because the **Treaty of Rome** permits the existence of internal regional groupings of states, as long as these conform to its own stipulated goals. (See also **Belgo-Luxembourg Economic Union—BLEU**.)

BEP: See **Biotech**

BERLAYMONT is the name of the large 13-storey building in **Brussels** that was purpose-built in 1969 to house the **European Commission** and its administrative personnel, although not all Commission employees based in the city worked in the building. Berlaymont became a shorthand term often used to describe the Commission and the administrative structures of the European Communities, and has sometimes been employed in a derogatory sense to refer to bureaucratization. In 1991 the building had to be evacuated for substantial renovations because large quantities of asbestos had been used in the original construction. The staff was relocated to a number of adjacent buildings, with the Commissioners moving initially into the Breydel building. The renovation and futuristic makeover of this vast star-shaped building, measuring 230,000 sq m (which critics dubbed the 'Berlaymonster'), took 13 years to complete. The building opened again for business in November 2004. After renovation, the Commission opted in 2002 to buy the building from the Belgian State for €553m. by means of a 27-year annuity. Structural problems remain, and the building was damaged in a major fire in May 2009.

The **BERLIN DECLARATION** was adopted at an informal gathering of the **European Council** on the 50th anniversary of the signing of the **Treaties of Rome**, on 25 March 2007. It offered a formal statement on the achievements and purposes of the European Union and paved the way for negotiations on a mandate for an **intergovernmental conference**, which resulted in the **Treaty of Lisbon**.

SILVIO BERLUSCONI (1936–) was reported to be the richest man in Italy in 2008. Berlusconi, who controls a huge media empire and owns AC Milan football club, has been a central factor in Italian politics for much of the last decade or so and has often brought a degree of colour and controversy to European politics and the **European Council**. After a term in office as Prime Minister of Italy in the 1990s he was sworn in for a second term in May 2001, after his Forza Italia party secured agreement on a centre-right coalition government with parties including the National Alliance and the Northern League. Berlusconi also assumed the position of Minister of Foreign Affairs and quickly antagonized fellow European Union (EU) leaders with the adoption of a much more sceptical position towards European integration, which ran contrary to the stance taken by all Italian governments since 1945.

In the second half of 2003 Italy assumed the presidency of the EU and, accordingly, Berlusconi became responsible for representing the EU on the world stage and, importantly, for chairing the **European Council** when it met in the Italian capital, Rome, in December. Berlusconi's reputation and authority as an international statesman were questioned from the outset of the

Italian presidency and he did not escape criticism when the 15 member states and the 10 **candidate** states failed to reach an agreement on a constitutional treaty for the EU. Confronted with turmoil and dissent within his government coalition following disappointing results in a number of local elections, Berlusconi tendered his resignation to Italian President Carlo Ciampi in April 2005. Ciampi resisted this move and asked Berlusconi just two days later to form a new government rather than opt to hold new elections. Berlusconi agreed and formed a new coalition government (the 60th in the history of the modern Italian republic) on 21 April. Berlusconi's political fortunes did not improve and he encountered mounting criticism and growing pressure prior to the national elections in April 2006. His personal standing had been damaged by a number of scandals, including his participation in several court cases where it was alleged that he had been involved with corrupt business practices. Italy's involvement in Iraq had further tarnished his image, as had some of his more infamous public pronouncements, but it was the ailing Italian economy that really damaged his popularity. Berlusconi was narrowly defeated by a left-wing coalition under the leadership of **Romano Prodi** at the national elections in April 2006, but only resigned as Prime Minister following the rejection by the Italian courts of his challenge to have some of the results overturned.

Berlusconi underwent successful heart surgery in December 2007. Although a number of fraud charges against Berlusconi and his acquaintances were dropped by the Italian courts in January 2007, he continued to face accusations of perverting the course of justice by paying for favourable testimonies in earlier corruption trials. Berlusconi had always protested his innocence, and was acquitted of all charges against him by Italy's highest court in October 2007. In the following month he pledged to create a new centre-right political party in Italy and was determined to maintain an active presence in Italian politics. He achieved both aims by launching his long-planned new centre-right People of Freedom Party (PDL)—which merged his own Forza Italia party and the right-wing National Alliance which had been led by Gianfranco Fini—and winning the 2008 elections. He successfully defeated his rival Walther Veltroni's left-wing party in April 2008 to become Italian Prime Minister for the third time. His notoriety was heightened by the media's continuing fascination with his much publicized personal life, his fortune and a vast array of often risqué comments about individuals and other world leaders. Although Berlusconi was a highly controversial figure in terms of both European and Italian politics, he remained a very popular politician among many of his compatriots. His party performed well in the 2009 **European Parliament** elections and his coalition scored impressive regional election results in March 2010 (winning six out of 13 regions).

In May 2011 his candidates performed badly in local elections across Italy and, most notably, his party lost control of Milan for the first time in nearly two decades. This particular result was a setback for Berlusconi, especially given that he had urged voters to use the election as a referendum on his Government. Meanwhile, in April a new court case was opened against Berlusconi, who was charged with abuse of power and sexual misdemeanours; if convicted, he risked a prison sentence. With the Italian economy experiencing a deepening crisis and having lost his parliamentary majority, Berlusconi resigned as Prime Minister in mid-November 2011. In late October 2012 Berlusconi received a custodial sentence for tax fraud; his lawyers intended to launch an appeal.

BICS: See **Business and Innovation Centres**

BIOTECH (Biotechnology) is an area in which the European Union has been promoting research and development policy since the mid-1980s. In 1985 the Biotechnology Action Programme (BAP) was established as part of the new emphasis on the importance of **research and technological development** (RTD) **policy**. BAP succeeded the 1982–86 Biomolecular Engineering Programme (BEP), sponsoring collaborative research and training between industry and research institutions across the whole field of biotechnology. The original programme was concluded in 1989, but its work and objectives were incorporated into the subsequent Bridge programme of 1990, which also later changed its name to Biotech. This was superseded by the **quality of life and management of living resources programme** in 1999. A Life Patent directive on biotechnology was adopted in 1997 in an attempt to harmonize rules on gene patenting.

In the context of the Lisbon strategy (see **Lisbon agenda**), in February 2002 the Commission presented a communication setting out a strategic vision for life sciences and biotechnology up to 2010, and proposing how to address ethical issues, following a broad public consultation.

In 2007 the Commission carried out a mid-term review of the progress made since 2002, and examining the economic, social and environmental impact of biotechnology, in order to enable it to draw up proposed revisions to its strategy for Europe on life sciences and biotechnology.

Europe had some 1,836 dedicated biotechnology companies in 2009, compared with the USA's 1,754. However, European companies are smaller, employ fewer people (49,060 compared with 128,200 in 2009), are much less well capitalized, and have far fewer biotechnology products in development.

BLACK MONDAY has become synonymous with a meeting of European Communities ministers of foreign affairs on 30 September 1991. At this meeting an ambitious draft of a potential treaty on political union, submitted by the Dutch presidency as part of the deliberations of the **intergovernmental conference** charged with drawing up the **Treaty on European Union** (TEU), was rejected by almost all other national delegations. Only Belgium accepted the draft. This was an embarrassing rebuke to the Netherlands and to the most enthusiastic supporters of deeper integration. The dismissal of the Dutch text and of the Netherlands' efforts to promote a unitary structure for the European Union essentially paved the way for the **pillar** structure that was enshrined in the TEU at Maastricht in December 1991.

BLACK WEDNESDAY is a popular term used to describe the international speculation against currencies in the **exchange-rate mechanism** (ERM) in September 1992. The ensuing crisis, largely fuelled by uncertainty over the fate of the **Treaty on European Union**, saw the suspension of the British pound sterling and the Italian lira from the ERM. The speculation that returned the following year, almost causing the collapse of the ERM, exposed weaknesses in the ERM and threatened the intentions of the European Union to establish **economic and monetary union** by 1999. Several countries were forced to devalue their currencies, and hence the fluctuation rules in the **European Monetary System** were made more flexible.

ANTHONY (TONY) BLAIR (1953–) became Labour Prime Minister of the United Kingdom in 1997, following almost two decades of Conservative government in that country, and was re-elected to a second term of office in June 2001 and to a third in May 2005. In terms of European policy, he proved much more favourably disposed towards the European Union (EU) than his two immediate predecessors, **Margaret Thatcher** and **John Major**. He agreed to subscribe to the content of the **Social Protocol**, and by implication the Charter of Fundamental Social Rights (see **Social Charter**). He was also instrumental in the final deliberations of the **intergovernmental conference** that led to the **Treaty of Nice** in December 2000. While promoting the completion of the **internal market** and **enlargement** of the EU, Blair insisted that the United Kingdom remain outside full **economic and monetary union** until the country had met the United Kingdom Treasury's five economic tests. Although at that time Blair favoured British membership of the **euro**, this could only take place if endorsed by the British public in a referendum, early enthusiasm for which evaporated. Blair's decision in March 2003 actively to participate in the US-led war against Iraq, with the aim of bringing down the regime of the Iraqi President, Saddam Hussain, opened up fissures in relations with EU heads of government (most notably with **Jacques Chirac** of France) and ensured that moves towards a **common defence policy** became even more problematic. Crucially, the decision to send British troops into Iraq also weakened Blair's reputation on the Continent.

Interestingly, and in line with his immediate predecessors, in 2005 Blair began to find himself at odds with his European counterparts and especially President Chirac, as was evident over the extended debate over the issue of a British rebate. The United Kingdom, once again, found itself in a minority of one. The British presidency in the latter half of 2005 offered the potential for Blair to reassert a vision for the development of the EU, but it proved a rather lacklustre affair. Positively, it secured the opening of accession negotiations with **Turkey** and reached a deal on the future funding of the EU. However, this agreement was labelled domestically by Blair's opponents as either a surrender or a disappointment. Blair's relationships with his fellow leaders had clearly deteriorated significantly since the United Kingdom had last held the presidency in 1998.

After 10 years in office Tony Blair resigned as Prime Minister on 27 June 2007. He was succeeded by **Gordon Brown**. Blair's European legacy remains somewhat mixed. Although he had successes in such areas as promoting greater European co-operation, particularly in the area of security, and was always a strong advocate of the EC's eastern **enlargement**, his premiership attracted some early criticism for his failure to pursue euro adoption and his indecision over, and failure to explain the abortive **Treaty establishing a Constitution for Europe** to an increasingly Eurosceptic British public. On his resignation, Blair deliberately exited the British political scene and became a Special Envoy to the **Middle East** on behalf of the Quartet of the EU, **Russia**, the **United Nations** and the **USA**. Any aspirations to stand as a candidate for the newly created position of **President of the European Council** effectively ended when **Angela Merkel** and **Nicholas Sarkozy** indicated their preference for the Belgian Prime Minister, **Herman Van Rompuy**.

BLEU: See **Belgo-Luxembourg Economic Union**

BLOCK EXEMPTIONS is a term that refers to those categories of agreements under EU **competition policy** between the EU member states and other states that, as stipulated by the **European Commission**, are exempted from the general prohibition of restrictive trade agreements. Under these, specific economic sectors are exempted from the general provisions relating to competition policy for a period of up to 10 years, after which time they need to be renewed or they lapse. Although such exemptions were initially designed as a means to allow the EC competition authorities greater time to investigate more pressing cases, the Commission is rather cautious about allowing too many block exemptions, and they are granted only rarely. The first, covering exclusive dealing agreements, came into force in 1967 and the second in 1972. They have been applied, for example, to patent licences, specialization agreements, research and development agreements, and motor vehicle distribution and servicing agreements. Block exemptions provide some legal certainty for firms and have benefited small and medium-sized enterprises (SMEs) in particular. There is even evidence that company lawyers draft their agreements using the block exemption regulations as a starting point in order to ensure that they satisfy the Commission guidelines. As both policy statements and enforcement tools, they exclude the application of competition law for certain types of agreement (e.g. liner shipping agreements) and provide a delineation between law-abiding and illegal practice. There remain less well-defined areas where the competition rules *might* apply, but the regulations also take these into consideration and make allowances for agreements that are not clear-cut. However, if there is any doubt, firms are wise to pursue the more conventional individual exemption route. This applies when firms draft or alter their agreements to include provisions that are not covered by the block exemption. Block exemption regulations are frequently renewed and updated so as to take on board the latest data. There are currently eight block exemption regulations in operation. These cover agreements in the areas of transport, maritime transport, specialization agreements, research and development agreements, motor vehicles/distribution of cars, insurance, technology transfer and air transport.

The **BLUE FLAG** is a voluntary eco-label that is awarded annually to bathing beaches and marinas in 46 countries around the world that meet strict standards of water quality and environmental management. The idea of the Blue Flag originated in France and the scheme was presented to the **European Commission** by the Foundation for Environmental Education in Europe (FEEE) in 1987 as part of the 'European Year of the Environment'. The programme is run by the non-governmental organization, which was renamed the Foundation for Environmental Education (FEE) in 2000 to reflect the global nature of the scheme. The Blue Flag concept is a core aspect of the EU's **environment policy** and specifically the EU water framework directive. A total of 3,849 beaches and marinas were awarded a Blue Flag in 2011. Information on the recipients of the award is published every year in June.

The **BOLKESTEIN DIRECTIVE** or, officially, the Directive on Services in the Internal Market, prompted a great deal of debate and controversy in various European Union (EU) countries, and especially Belgium, France, Germany and Italy, in the first half of 2005. The directive was put together by Frits Bolkestein, the former Commissioner for the Internal Market, and aimed to establish a single market for services within the EU. Services are a rapidly growing sector and account for around 70% of EU economic activity. The directive contained changes to the EU services market, which can be summarized under two fundamental principles. The first principle focused on the 'freedom of establishment' and sought to ensure that any company or individual who provided a service in one EU member state should be allowed to provide it in all EU member states. The second was the 'country of origin' principle. This sought to establish that if goods were produced in one EU member state, then it was legitimate and acceptable to sell such goods in other EU member states. In short, the Services Directive sought to remove the administrative and legal barriers that prevented firms from offering their services in other countries. The directive presented a radical vision and certainly could have had a wide-reaching impact in the EU services sector. Services that were covered included, for example, car hire, estate agencies, advice from architects, social care and environmental services. Trade unions argued that such changes would culminate in **social**

dumping practices, as rules in Eastern European countries were often less rigid than in Western Europe. The Commission maintained that the directive would create 600,000 jobs, stimulate economic growth and provide greater choice for consumers. Critics feared, however, that the directive would unleash unwelcome competition between workers in different parts of the EU, reduce income levels and lower standards of social and environmental protection. These fears, combined with concerns about the dangers of companies opting to relocate to low-cost economies, led to a series of mass protests, which culminated in a 100,000-strong march through **Brussels**, Belgium, in opposition to this directive in March 2005.

The pressure of public opinion led the **European Council** (and especially France) effectively to postpone the directive in late March 2005 by calling for alterations before it could be considered. There can be little doubt that this example of liberalization fed into the discussions on the **Treaty establishing a Constitution for Europe** in France. The Services Directive was approved by the **European Parliament** (EP) at its first reading in February 2006. However, in effect the directive had been diluted, and excluded a number of services such as broadcasting, postal services, gambling and audiovisual services. The **European Commission** pledged to take the EP's views into account before producing an amended proposal in April 2006, which would serve as a basis for a second reading in the EP. After substantial amendments (including for example the exclusion of public and private healthcare and social services), the directive was finally adopted in December 2006 by the EP and European Council, and came into force in December 2009.

BNP: See **British National Party**

BOSNIA AND HERZEGOVINA declared its independence from **Yugoslavia** in 1992 only to become the focus of a ferocious civil war which lasted until 1995, when the Dayton Peace Accords, marking an agreement to end the war, were signed. Since then the government of the country has been overseen by the Office of the High Representative of the International Community (which was created under the agreement) and by the Special Representative of the European Union (between 2002 and 2011 these two positions were held concurrently by the same person), with initially a NATO-led force (IFOR) and, since December 2004, a European Union (EU) peace-keeping force (EUFOR), seeking to maintain peace and stability. Relations with the EU since 1999 have developed, albeit slowly, in the context of the **stabilization and association process** (SAP). A Road Map initially detailed a catalogue of essential measures that would have to be adopted in the country before the feasibility of concluding a **stabilization and association agreement** (SAA) could be explored. Appropriate measures were eventually taken, with negotiations on an SAA opening on 25 January 2006. These were closed in December 2007 and the agreement was eventually signed in June 2008, following the implementation of further reform of the police, public broadcasting and public administration and an improvement in the country's co-operation with the International Criminal Tribunal for the Former Yugoslavia. However, failure to carry out further reform, including that of the country's Constitution, meant that the SAA had still not entered into force at late 2012.

Along with the other countries in the **Western Balkans**, Bosnia and Herzegovina was granted the status of **potential candidate** in 2000. The country also has a **European partnership** arrangement with the EU. This was first adopted in 2004 and has subsequently been revised, with a new European partnership being adopted in February 2008. This followed a **European Commission** progress report on Bosnia and Herzegovina, which noted the deceleration of political reforms, limited progress with economic reforms, that state institutions continued to be compromised by ethnic division and that the country had yet to assume full ownership of its own governance .The report, however, records the EU's continued commitment to supporting reform, noting that pre-accession financial assistance to the country was being provided under the new **instrument for pre–accession assistance**, with €226m. allocated for 2007–09. Subsequent reports have raised similar concerns. Financial assistance continues to be provided, with the allocation for 2012 being €107.8m. Although Bosnia and Herzegovina had planned to submit an application for EU membership by the end of 2010, no application had been submitted by late 2012.

BOVINE SPONGIFORM ENCEPHALOPATHY (BSE) or, as it is more widely known, 'mad cow disease', became an issue for the European Union (EU) in early 1996 following a public announcement made by the British Government about the possible connection between BSE and a new variant of Creutzfeldt-Jakob disease (a degenerative and ultimately deadly brain disease) in humans. Several British scientists had long believed that there was a link between the two diseases that originated in feeding offal (the remains of sheep and cattle) to cattle, and that the disease was now being passed to humans following their consumption of BSE-infected beef. The British Government had persistently denied the link, and its belated recognition of that possibility sparked public alarm about the safety of eating diseased beef, both in the United Kingdom and across Europe. The fact that **John Major**'s Government had not consulted its EU partners prior to its announcement only made matters worse. The **European Commission** responded by banning the import of all British beef into the EU, as did the Governments of both the **USA** and Australia. The British agricultural community was plunged into crisis as its export markets suddenly disappeared and sales of beef in the United Kingdom fell dramatically. Major responded by introducing a 'no co-operation agreement' with the EU that effectively meant blocking all proposals (even those supported by the British Government) that were subject to unanimity in the **Council of the European Union**. At the same time many cattle herds were slaughtered on suspicion of infection. The crisis came to an end in June 1996 when the **European Council**

approved a plan to have the ban on British beef gradually lifted once each sector was given the all-clear by the Commission's Scientific Veterinary Committee. The episode was investigated by the **European Parliament**, which in a 1997 report was openly critical of the Commission's handling of the crisis, and in particular accused the Commission of placing farmers' interests above those of consumers. Despite the lifting of the ban on British beef, some states, notably France, continued to refuse to import British beef, which led to legal action being brought against the French Government before the European Courts. Exports of British beef to France finally resumed in 2002.

WILLY BRANDT (1913–92) was Chancellor of the Federal Republic of Germany (FRG—West Germany) from 1969 to 1974. His major interest was foreign policy, and his greatest achievement as Chancellor was the series of agreements, known collectively as **Ostpolitik**, negotiated between the FRG and the states of Eastern Europe, as well as with the **USSR**. All sought to develop closer economic, political and humanitarian links between West Germany and the countries of **Central and Eastern Europe**. In reorientating West German foreign policy away from Westpolitik and the 'policy of strength' pursued by **Konrad Adenauer** and his successors, Brandt was concerned to emphasize that this in no way represented a diminution of the FRG's commitment to the European Communities (EC) and to other Western organizations, such as the **North Atlantic Treaty Organization** (NATO). Nevertheless, Brandt's policy aroused extreme hostility among the leadership of the Christian Democratic opposition in West Germany. While Brandt was not averse to EC plans for further economic and political integration, he tended to think of Europe on a broader scale, an attitude instilled by his long exile in Scandinavia after 1933, which, he said, had taught him to think of himself as a European. Hence he supported the principle of **enlargement**, and argued with President Georges Pompidou of France that the French position on enlargement, or specifically on the membership of the United Kingdom, should be reversed. Equally, while supporting further integration, he was sceptical towards proposals that either were too expensive or had not been costed properly, and was highly critical of assumptions by other member states that the extra costs would be borne by the FRG. For example, he opposed the creation of the **European Regional Development Fund** and was particularly concerned with the budget and spending patterns of the **common agricultural policy**, a position that was resented by France and other EC states. In early 1974 Brandt resigned from office following a political scandal concerning one of his personal assistants who was discovered to be a spy working for the East German regime.

BRETTON WOODS in New Hampshire, **USA**, was the location and name of an agreement, made in 1944 by several Western countries, on the introduction of a new international monetary system based upon fixed exchange rates, and backed by two reserve currencies, the US dollar and British pound sterling. The intention was to make currencies convertible on current account, so facilitating multilateral trade and reducing the need for disruptive devaluations. The system experienced a number of problems in the late 1940s, and did not become fully operational until 1958. In the 1960s the fixed exchange-rate system, especially the two reserve currencies, came under increasing pressure. The agreement effectively disintegrated in 1971, when the USA unilaterally suspended dollar convertibility against gold. The Smithsonian Agreement and the European **Snake** were efforts to salvage some advantage from the failure of the Bretton Woods agreement since, despite the benefits that floating currencies may have held for governments, the consequent currency fluctuations adversely affected international monetary stability. The **European Monetary System** (EMS) of 1979 was an attempt by the European Communities to stabilize currency fluctuations by introducing a modified exchange-rate system that would replicate what were believed to have been the virtues of Bretton Woods.

BRITAIN: See **United Kingdom**

The **BRITISH NATIONAL PARTY** (BNP) has emerged as the leading and most successful party on the **far right** of the British political scene since 1945. The election of two BNP candidates as **Members of the European Parliament** (MEPs) at the **European Parliament** (EP) elections of June 2009 was greeted with universal condemnation by the mainstream political parties in the United Kingdom, but the event signified success for the BNP's electoral strategy. Although the party was founded in 1982 and has sporadically contested national and local elections since 1983, it only really began to make a serious inroad into British political life over the last decade or so, under its current leader Nick Griffin (1999–). It is the party's policy aspirations that have attracted the particular scorn of other parties. It may have moderated its anti-Semitism of the 1980s, but this strand of thought is still present, and members of the BNP have been accused of promoting Holocaust denial revisionism. In recent years the BNP has opted to focus its energies on portraying an anti-Islam message and made much political capital out of the London bombings in July 2005. While denying that it is a racist party, it very much espouses an anti-immigration view, and seeks the voluntary repatriation of all non-white immigrants within the United Kingdom. The party leadership makes much of the need to give British jobs to British workers and demands the withdrawal of the United Kingdom from the European Union (EU). The BNP has slowly been making inroads into local politics and managed to have a number of county and district councillors (some 58 in 2009) elected throughout England and Wales; however, by May 2012 the number of BNP councillors had fallen to only three. The party's share of the vote at national elections has been small (it attracted 0.7% of the vote in 2005 and 1.9% in 2010), but the 2009 EP elections propelled it (with 6.3% of the votes cast and two MEPs— Nick Griffin and Andrew Brons) directly into the media spotlight. Interestingly, its percentage of the vote in 2009 was smaller than that for the 2004 EP elections, but a lower rate of participation and the collapse of the Labour Party's vote benefited the BNP. The BNP was determined to develop links with other far-right parties within the EP and managed to foster a closer working relationship, especially with the French Front National and the Hungarian Jobbik party, through the creation of a new Alliance of European National Movements. Although this alliance cannot be recognized as a political group within the EP (as it does not meet the necessary numbers—25 MEPs—or have sufficient transnational membership, as members must come from at least seven EU member states), it may still be entitled to some funding as a pan-European bloc. This new and very loose alliance rejects all attempts to create a European 'superstate', advocates strong, pro-family policies and seeks to fight against the destructive effects of globalization.

LEON BRITTAN (1939–), now Baron Brittan of Spennithorne, was perhaps one of the most influential Commissioners in the history of the European Union. Prior to joining the **European Commission**, Brittan had held senior positions in Conservative governments of the United Kingdom during 1979–86. He was appointed to the European Commission as one of two British nominees in 1989. He was made one of the six Vice-Presidents of the Commission, and given the two important portfolios of **Competition Policy** and Financial Institutions. He therefore had a large part of the responsibility for ensuring that the European Communities (EC) reached their target of completing and implementing the **internal market**. His vigorous enforcement of EC competition policy made him a highly successful and much respected Commissioner, but his command of the competition brief along with his ultra-liberal credentials and commitment to free trade led to disagreements with his colleagues, and in particular with the President of the Commission, **Jacques Delors**. However, he also had policy disagreements with his former party leader, **Margaret Thatcher**, on several occasions. In particular, he believed that the United Kingdom should become a full member of the **European Monetary System** (EMS). In 1993–94, no longer a Vice-President of the Commission, he held the portfolios of Trade Policy and External Economic Relations, with responsibility for territories that included Eastern Europe and the **Commonwealth of Independent States** (CIS). Brittan was keen to succeed Delors as President, but the timing was not right for a British incumbent, nor was there a desire among several member states for a formidable personality at the helm of the Commission. When a new Commission took office under the presidency of **Jacques Santer** in 1995, Brittan was once again appointed as one of the Vice-Presidents, now numbering only two; however, his responsibilities were reduced to Multilateral Trade and Relations with the Developed World. His final term in the Commission ended prematurely following the mass resignation of the Santer team in 1999.

BROADCASTING: See **Cultural Policy**; **European Broadcasting Union**; **Media Policy**

GORDON BROWN (1951–) succeeded **Tony Blair** as British Prime Minister on 27 June 2007. Prior to assuming his position as the head of the British Government, Brown had spent the previous 10 years as arguably one of the most able, and longest serving, Chancellors of the Exchequer, in which post he had effectively controlled the direction of British economic policy. During his tenure he had thwarted Blair's plans of seeking to join the **euro** and became involved in a series of disputes with his fellow European finance ministers over issues such as the **United Kingdom Budget Rebate**, European taxation and general economic policy direction. His arrival in power coincided with attempts to rejuvenate the **Treaty establishing a Constitution for Europe,** which led to the **Treaty of Lisbon**. His first seven months in power demonstrated a reluctance to enter the European arena. His decision to arrive in Lisbon several hours after the formal signing of the new treaty by his peers (in October 2007) caused a degree of bewilderment and for many commentators provided an apt illustration of the United Kingdom's continuing lack of engagement. Indeed, he only made his first official visit to **Brussels** in October 2007. At home, he steadfastly resisted calls for a referendum on the Treaty of Lisbon and successfully steered it through both chambers of the Houses of Parliament in mid-2008. Thereafter his premiership was buffeted by the impact and aftershocks of the 'credit crunch', doubts among some of his colleagues about his abilities to do the job of Prime Minister, and a scandal over MPs' expenses that erupted in May 2009. All are deemed to have contributed to the disastrous results for the Labour Party at the June 2009 European Parliament elections, when the Labour Party finished third behind **David Cameron**'s Conservatives and the UK Independence Party (UKIP) and became the second party in Wales and Scotland. A series of ministerial resignations just before and after the European poll in 2009 certainly dented Brown's authority, and his poll ratings slipped. Nevertheless, in the last year of the third Labour administration (2005–10) it was noticeable how Brown sought to utilize the European Union as a vehicle to rally support among his fellow leaders and to help overcome the global economic crisis. His successful profile on the international stage was not replicated at home, and in May 2010 Brown led the Labour Party to its second worst defeat in a British general election, before duly resigning as Prime Minister.

BRUGES GROUP was the name given to a group of anti-European Union British Conservative Party politicians who formed the Campaign for a Europe of Sovereign States in 1988. The campaign was inspired by a speech made by the British Prime Minister, **Margaret Thatcher**, at the College of Europe in Bruges, Belgium, in September, in which she attacked the **European Commission** and its efforts to impose what she regarded as a bureaucratic and unrepresentative centralization upon the European Communities at the expense of national **sovereignty**. The major concern of the group (which, although often associated with the Conservative Party, is in fact an all-party think tank) was primarily domestic British party politics and it helped fuel the growing force of Euroscepticism (see **Eurosceptics**). Its members were particularly vocal at the time of the **ratification** of the **Treaty on European Union** in the early 1990s, but since then the group has had a very low profile, and has had no real impact, within and outside the United Kingdom.

BRUSSELS is the capital city of Belgium, with a population of some 1m. Brussels is also home to the executive and administrative branches of the European Union (EU). In addition to being the location of the **European Commission** and the Secretariat of the **Council of the European Union**, it also houses the offices of both the **Committee of the Regions** and the **European Economic and Social Committee**. The **European Parliament** has much of its staff in this city and the majority of its committee meetings take place in its new Brussels headquarters. In addition, all the national representations of the member states reside in Brussels, as do representations of many regions (e.g. the German Länder) and sub-national authorities (e.g. the Northern Ireland Executive Office in Brussels and Scotland Europa), which have premises near the EU institutions. Moreover, Brussels has attracted the attention of a variety of public, private and voluntary organizations that either own or rent offices in the city in the hope of being able to influence policy development and EU **decision-making**. Finally, Brussels has also been the home of the **North Atlantic Treaty Organization** (NATO) since 1967. The concentration of EU institutions in the city has meant that the name 'Brussels' has often been used as a term to describe the EU and its decision-making bodies. Suggestions have been made that Brussels, as it functions in many ways as a capital-elect of the EU, should be given a special status similar to that accorded to Canberra (Australian Capital Territory) or Washington (DC, **USA**).

BRUSSELS, TREATY OF: See **Treaty of Brussels**

'BRUSSELSIZATION' a term that is associated with the evolution of the European Union's (EU) **common foreign and security policy** established under Pillar II of the **Treaty on European Union** in 1993. Although the EU's supranational powers are highly marginalized in this policy area, there is a growing sense that this policy's development is being determined to a greater extent than ever in **Brussels** by a number of Pillar II working groups. Since the days of **European political co-operation** in the 1970s and the 1980s, working groups have played an instrumental role in EU foreign policy business. There are an estimated 20 in existence and they exchange information on issues ranging from landmines to the **Organization for Security and Co-operation**

in Europe (OSCE). Foreign policy may still remain firmly under the control of the national governments, but since the **Maastricht summit** it has become increasingly apparent that more authority and expertise on Pillar II questions has shifted from member states to their national delegations (**Permanent Representations**) in Brussels, which collaborate with the working groups. In other words, the process of 'Brusselsization' ensures that a substantial amount of information on foreign policy is exchanged between the national delegations, and more so than between any other sovereign states in any other international organization.

BSE: See **Bovine Spongiform Encephalopathy**

The **BUDGET** has always proved to be a source of controversy, first for the European Communities (EC) and then for the European Union (EU). When the **European Economic Community** was established in 1957, it was agreed that its budget would be financed by national contributions from the member states, the contribution of each state to be determined by its gross national product (GNP). This was the standard means for financing international organizations such as the **United Nations**. The **European Commission** regarded the EC as being a different type of organization, however, and since the mid-1960s has sought access to its own revenue sources. In 1970 the original **six** member states in the **Treaty of Luxembourg** decided that national contributions would be progressively phased out by 1975, to be replaced by a system of EC **own resources**, that is, funds that originate in the member states but are the property of the EC. In other words, the amount of money that is available to the EU is determined by an agreement among the member states. It was generally assumed at the outset that the contributions and the receipts would more or less balance. This has not been the case, and the budget has been a politically sensitive issue. However, the European Commission states that the financial contributions made by EU countries to the EU budget are **distributed equitably**, so that each country contributes a percentage of its value-added tax (VAT), together with 1% of its gross national income.

Revenue comes from two main additional sources, as the EU receives levies on imports of sugar, and **customs duties** from outside the EU. In addition, fines imposed by the Commission for infringements of EC **competition policy** were added to the budget, and in recent years accounted for approximately 1% to 2% of the entire budget. The now defunct **European Coal and Steel Community** (ECSC) retained its own budget, which was financed by a direct levy upon coal and steel enterprises within the EU. The **Treaty on European Union** formally recognized that the EC have their own sources of revenue, stipulating that there must be sufficient own resources to cover all agreed expenditure.

The annual spending plans of the EU are determined after lengthy negotiations between the **Council** and the **European Parliament**. The budget process consists of five stages. A preliminary draft budget is prepared by the Commission for presentation to the **Council of the European Union** no later than 1 September of the year before the one during which the budget is to be implemented. The Council can then accept or amend the draft: it has tended invariably to reduce the total amount of proposed expenditure. By 5 October the Council must have agreed, by a qualified majority (see **Qualified Majority Voting**), upon a draft budget and have sent it to the **European Parliament** (EP). The EP enjoys 'power of the purse' with regard to the budget and has 45 days in which to consider the draft. Prior to the entry into force of the **Treaty of Lisbon**, on those items that represented compulsory expenditure, the EP was only able to suggest modifications to the Council's proposals; the EP has since gained co-decision over the entire budget. On **non-compulsory expenditure**, it is free to amend the draft budget, albeit only within a general limit previously defined by the Council. Once its deliberations are complete, the revised budget returns to the Council, which may reject the EP's changes. When the proposed modifications to compulsory expenditure do not entail an overall increase in expenditure, a qualified majority vote is needed in the Council; when an increase is involved, a positive majority in the Council is required for rejection.

In cases where the Council decides to reject EP amendments to non-compulsory expenditure, the two institutions are obliged to enter into a conciliation procedure to seek a compromise. The final revised document is then returned to the EP for adoption. For the budget to be rejected by the EP a two-thirds' majority of the recorded votes must be against adoption, and this qualified majority must also constitute an overall majority of the total EP membership. If the EP votes against adoption, the net effect is that the EU does not have a budget for the new calendar year, and expenditure is restricted each month to one-12th of the budget approved for the previous year. This restriction remains in force until a new budget can be approved. The EP rejected the budget in 1979 and 1984, but each time it ultimately accepted a version that was only marginally different from the one it had refused to adopt. Since 1993 the budget has been the subject of an inter-institutional agreement that seeks to inject greater budgetary discipline and to improve budgetary procedures between the Council, the Commission and the EP. This 1993 agreement was judged a success and was renewed in 1998.

Fraud remains a significant problem and it is estimated that between 2% and 10% of the budget becomes subject to fraudulent financial claims, primarily from the operation of the CAP. The **Treaty of Amsterdam** introduced measures to protect against fraud and misuse of EU finances. It also provided for greater scrutiny of agricultural expenditure. The **Court of Auditors** was to have an enhanced role in ensuring that the budget was not being misspent.

Discussions for the current financial perspective (running from 2007 to 2013) began in earnest at the end of 2004 and proved to be heavily contentious. The difficulties centred on the overall level of spending and the breakdown between the various headings of expenditure. The Commission, with the support of some of the smaller EU states, had been keen to maintain the existing level of 1.24% of GNP to determine the overall size of the budget. However, the net contributors to the budget (Germany, Sweden, the Netherlands and the United Kingdom) wanted to limit spending to 1% of GNP. The final agreement was to be determined by the member state governments and was capped at 1.05%. The British rebate and reform of the CAP formed part of the negotiations and discussions, but both proved extremely contentious. In the 2000s the issue of EU financing became more controversial than at any time since the early 1980s. For example, discussions between the EU member states stalled in June 2005 at a meeting of the **European Council**, as the United Kingdom refused to give way on its rebate unless the French Government showed willingness to engage in serious CAP reform. The ramifications of this frosty meeting endured for the remainder of 2005, with the French and British Governments in conflict over how best to finance the 2004 enlargement to the advantage of the new entrants. President **Chirac** insisted on an end to the British rebate while **Blair** resisted and tried to make a direct link with the future reform of the CAP. The United Kingdom came under increasing pressure from the other member states to reach an agreement on the budget and to recognize that the United Kingdom was no longer in a position to need the maintenance of the rebate. EU leaders finally secured an agreement for the new financial perspective (2007–13) of €862,400m. This figure corresponds to 1.05% of EU GNP, and although it represents an increase from an earlier proposal of 1.03%, falls far below the Commission's hopes (1.24%). The overall figure was also lower than the amount (€883,000m.) that the European Parliament had requested. As part of the overall agreement the United Kingdom agreed to relinquish approximately €10,500m. over this period in return for serious consideration of a farm subsidy reduction in 2008. The leaders of the member states praised Blair for his decision on the rebate, which it was generally agreed had prevented another major crisis for the EU. The leaders of the states from **Central and Eastern Europe** expressed their satisfaction at the outcome, particularly the Polish Prime Minister, Kazimierz Marcinkiewicz, who secured an additional €4,000m. in aid. Overall aid to the new member states was capped at €157,000m. Farm and rural development remained the biggest item of expenditure and accounts for €292,000m. Time would tell how member states came to view the revised budget agreement.

The Commission published a **Green Paper** in September 2007 that was designed to initiate a wide-ranging debate on the future shape and focus of the EU budget. It was intended to identify priority targets for expenditure and to consider the best ways of securing the revenue stream. As part of its reform agenda, the Commission also aimed to include discussion of such principles as equity, stability, simplicity, administrative cost effectiveness and financial autonomy and sufficiency as core elements of future budgetary policy-making. On 15 December 2010 the European Parliament approved the EU budget for 2011. This was the first budget adopted under the new rules provided for by the **Treaty of Lisbon** and amounted to some €141,900m. The budget was made up from the following sources: 76% stemmed directly from the gross national income (GNI) contributions; 11% came from VAT receipts; 12% from customs duties and sugar levies; and, finally, some 1% came from unspent monies from the previous year and from fines imposed on companies for breaching the **competition policy** rules. The largest part of the budget (some €64,500m.) was directed towards sustainable growth, including competitiveness and cohesion. Of this amount, €13,500m. were targeted towards competitiveness (such as education and training, transport and energy networks). Most of the money, some €51,000m., under this heading was allocated towards cohesion, where the EU attempts to assist its least-developed regions; the monies are channelled through the **ERDF**, the **ESF** and the **Cohesion Fund**. Agriculture (under the title of natural resources) still represented a substantial part of the overall budget and accounted for €42,900m., with an additional €14,400m. aimed at rural development. Together, agriculture, rural development, competitiveness and cohesion consumed the major part of the EU 2011 budget (some 90%), but money was also directed towards other areas; for example, €1,800m. went to the **European Neighbourhood Policy** under the European Neighbourhood and Partnership Instrument (ENPI), which promotes good governance and social and economic development; €1,600m. to pre-accession assistance states under the Instrument for pre-Accession Assistance (ISPA); €2,600m. to humanitarian aid and human rights; some €825m. to help people affected by natural disasters; €612m. to reinforce measures against illegal immigration; €134m. to combat crime and terrorism; and €168m. to support the European film industry and crossborder co-operation. Just under 6% of the entire budget was to be used for the financing and running of the EU institutions, primarily the Commission. On 1 December 2011 the European Parliament endorsed the EU budget for 2012: of the total projected expenditure of €147,200m., sustainable growth accounted for €67,500m. (competitiveness €14,700m., cohesion €52,700m.), natural resources €60,000m. and administration €8,300m. (Commission €3,300m.).

BULGARIA is one of the 10 Central and Eastern European countries that applied for European Union (EU) membership in the 1990s, submitting its formal application in 1995. Prior to this it had signed a **Europe agreement** with the European Communities in 1993, which entered into force in 1995. The **European Commission**'s report on the applicant countries of July 1997, entitled **Agenda 2000**, proposed that **accession negotiations** with Bulgaria should be deferred, owing to the limited measures undertaken with regard to economic reform and the degree of political instability experienced in the early to mid-1990s. Although the country had almost fulfilled the political criteria for membership, the report stated that investment was still needed in the areas of environment, transport, energy, home affairs, justice and agriculture. Bulgaria was thus not a participant in the first round of accession negotiations that began in March 1998. However, greater political stability under Prime Minister Ivan

Kostov (elected in 1997) helped Bulgaria's image, and the country was included in the second round of negotiations that commenced in 2000. The country continued to make steady progress under Prime Minister Simeon Saxe-Coburg Gotha (formerly King Simeon II), although difficulties still persisted over specific economic targets and the EU's demands for the early closure of the obsolete reactors at the controversial Kozloduy nuclear plant. The Bulgarian Government made a decisive move towards achieving the latter in December 2002 when it closed two of the reactors and announced its intention to shut down a further two by the end of 2006. The final negotiating chapters were closed in June 2004, and in April 2005 a **Treaty of Accession** was signed. This was ratified by the Bulgarian parliament on 11 May 2005, with 230 MPs voting in favour and two against. Bulgaria joined the EU on 1 January 2007 alongside Romania. As with Romania, Bulgaria has been subjected to post-accession monitoring by the Commission of progress in compliance with judicial reform and anti-corruption measures. This has resulted in further demands for action to be taken in these areas.

The **BUNDESBANK** is the central bank of the Federal Republic of Germany, and was established in 1957. It is unusual as a national central bank because of its substantial autonomy from government. Because of the importance of the German economy and the strength of its currency, the Bank has had a substantial influence upon Western European economic policy and activity, and was the core of the **European Monetary System**. The Bundesbank's central policy concern was to fight inflation in West Germany. However, this obsession with price stability as the core policy objective in turn affected other European economies, which experienced rising unemployment and weaker economic growth. This was particularly the case in France by the late 1980s, and was a prime motivating factor behind the French Prime Minister Edouard Balladur's pursuit of **economic and monetary union** (EMU). By the early 1990s, the heavy financial strains of the German reunification process only fortified the Bundesbank's priorities of controlling domestic inflation and maintaining high interest rates, and led to further political controversy in 1992–93, when these domestic objectives took precedence over policies that other member states believed the Bank should have adopted in order to preserve the **exchange-rate mechanism** (ERM). The problem with the Bundesbank's policy was external, in that other countries, with weaker currencies, had to match the level of German interest rates if they wished to stay in the ERM. This adversely affected their own economies, while exposing them to market speculation on the grounds that their currency values were artificially high. The Bundesbank and a majority of the German electorate remained unenthusiastic about the notion of EMU and feared that any new currency would be less stable than the Deutsche Mark. The decision for Germany to embark on the EMU project was, however, politically driven and decided. With the establishment of the **euro** and the **European Central Bank** (ECB), the direct influence of the Bundesbank over European finance policy inevitably declined.

The **BUREAU** or Executive Committee is an essential part of the organization of the **European Parliament**. The Bureau comprises the President, Vice-Presidents, Quaestors and potentially others, and focuses its activities on both political and administrative matters.

BUSINESS AND INNOVATION CENTRES (BICs) were launched by the **European Commission** in 1984 to encourage diversification of activity by small enterprises, and to help establish new small companies in innovative areas of activity and production. Their role today is very much to promote regional development. By 2008 there were 155 BICs (full members) in the 27 member states, in addition to 75 associate members. (See also **European Business and Innovation Centre Network**.)

BUSINESSEUROPE was until January 2007 known as the **Union of Industrial and Employers' Confederations of Europe** (UNICE), a transnational federation of employers' associations. It is one of the earliest (founded in 1958) and most influential of the pressure groups (see **Interest groups**; **Lobbying**) operating in **Brussels**. BUSINESSEUROPE represents the interests of industry as a whole, and is a confederation comprising national federations of major business associations from across Europe. For example, it includes the Confederation of British Industry and the Irish Business and Employers' Confederation, as well as groups from the largest states such as the German Confederation for Industry (Bundesverband der Deutschen Industrie) and the smallest states such as the Malta Confederation of Industry. In 2012 there were 41 members from 35 countries, including the European Union countries, the **European Economic Area** countries, and some Central and Eastern European countries. BUSINESSEUROPE plays both an informal and a formal role in European public affairs. On an informal level, its representatives meet **European Commission** officials on an almost daily basis, and on a more formal level it is frequently asked for its views on policy initiatives. Its priorities centre on market **liberalization** and **deregulation**. It remains much more unenthusiastic, however, about initiatives in the area of social policy. BUSINESSEUROPE has as one of its objectives the promotion and elaboration 'of an industrial policy in a European spirit', which is qualified by the statement that it 'should mainly consist in taking into consideration the industrial imperatives in the various policies of the European Communities and not become an instrument of intervention'. BUSINESSEUROPE has therefore tended to oppose measures such as the proposed **Company Law Statute**, which threatened to place restraints upon its members, although on occasions its impact on the European Communities was weakened by differences of interest among both its economic and its national components. BUSINESSEUROPE operates as one of the Commission's **social partners** alongside the **European Trade Union Confederation**. The organization's activities can be grouped under six principal headings. These strive to release entrepreneurial energy; to promote innovation; to liberate the **internal market** of 27+; to improve the functioning of the labour market; to make **environmental policy** more effective and efficient; and to foster international trade and investment.

BUTTER MOUNTAIN is a term that has become part of European Union (EU) folklore. It is a phrase, usually of derision, popularly employed to symbolize one of the consequences of the price guarantee scheme of the **common agricultural policy** (CAP), the intervention purchasing by the European Community (EC) of agricultural produce, either when the market price fell below the predetermined EC level or when over-production occurred. EC practice was to store the surplus for an indefinite period, until either price levels rose or, more commonly, a decision was taken to sell the surplus at discounted prices to non-EC countries. CAP over-production was most pronounced in dairy farming, and the butter surplus was one of the first to come to popular attention. Limits were placed upon production **subsidies** in dairy farming in 1984 with the introduction of milk quotas, after which the demand upon CAP financial resources made by milk products fell by one-third. Further restrictions were imposed in 1988 with the introduction of **stabilizers**. These measures have substantially reduced such phenomena. (See also **Wine Lake**.)

JERZY BUZEK (1940–) was elected as the new President of the **European Parliament** (EP) in July 2009 and, at the age of 69, became the first politician from the former Soviet bloc to hold this position. A Polish national, he has been active in politics since the 1970s. He served as Prime Minister of Poland from 1997 to 2001. Buzek served his term as EP President and was succeeded in January 2012 by **Martin Schulz**.

C

CABINET is the name given to the group of personal advisers and aides attached to each Commissioner within the **European Commission**. Its purpose is to provide the Commissioner with political and policy advice, as well as liaising with other groups within the European Union and speaking for the Commissioner in meetings of officials.

CABOTAGE is the system whereby transport providers may offer services in the domestic market of another member state. As part of the European Communities' (EC) **road transport** policy, the Council of Ministers (see **Council of the European Union**) agreed in 1993 on measures including a common tax system for heavy goods vehicles using EC roads, which led to full liberalization of road *cabotage* by 1998. Since then efforts have focused on promoting *cabotage* on the rail network and within shipping.

DAVID CAMERON (1966–) was elected as the leader of the United Kingdom's Conservative Party in December 2005. He first entered parliament in 2001 and his rise was meteoric. He comes from the growing Eurosceptic wing of the party and, after his election, he was very critical of **Tony Blair**, especially his handling of the United Kingdom rebate issue. During his campaign for the leadership Cameron promised to withdraw the party's **Members of the European Parliament** (MEPs) from the ranks of the **European People's Party** (EPP) within the **European Parliament** (EP). Cameron repeatedly expressed his determination on this issue following his election in the face of strong opposition from some British Conservative MEPs, who argued that such a move would reduce the party's influence in the EP. This seemed likely, and **Angela Merkel** expressed her reservations about the implementation of such a measure by the Conservative Party leader. Nevertheless, in July 2006 Cameron unveiled plans for a new centre-right grouping in the EP, and signed a joint declaration with Mirek Topolanek, the leader of the Civic Democrat Party in the Czech Republic (while acknowledging that any change would not happen for several years). At a joint press conference both men hailed the planned group as a strong new voice for change, optimism and hope. However, little progress was made, as the continuing sensitivity of Europe for many within the Conservative Party rank and file has ensured that pronouncements on matters related to the European Union (EU) are relatively rare. None the less,

Cameron has made the occasional foray into EU concerns, as, for example, in March 2007 when he set out his vision for the EU. He identified three main areas for future EU concern and development, namely globalization, global warming and global poverty. Opposed to the **Treaty of Lisbon** and committed to a British referendum on it, Cameron was swift to urge the abandonment of **ratification** following the Irish 'no' to the treaty in June 2008. Prior to the EP elections in June 2009, Cameron returned to his opposition to Conservative MEPs sitting within the **EPP** group and increased his determination to create a new political grouping within the EP for those Conservative MEPs elected in 2009 if he could find suitable like-minded allies. Following the outcome of these elections, on 22 June 2009 Cameron unveiled his new European alliance—the **European Conservatives and Reformists Group**. This group currently comprises 25 British Conservative MEPs and one Ulster Unionist, meaning that the British Conservative Party accounts for nearly 50% of the group's total membership of 52. Cameron's pledge to hold a referendum in the United Kingdom on the Treaty of Lisbon was dropped once the treaty had been ratified and came into force in December 2009. Nevertheless, Cameron clearly recognized that the Europe issue remained contentious within some of the ranks of the Conservative Party and pledged to renegotiate a number of aspects of the EU treaties (especially social and employment issues) if the Conservatives won the 2010 British general election. Critics argued that any such move was almost certain to alienate the other EU member states and to reinforce the United Kingdom's position as a reluctant member. Cameron won a majority of the votes at the 2010 general election, but the Conservative Party did not win enough to secure a majority of the seats within the House of Commons; this result produced a 'hung parliament' for the first time since 1974. To resolve the political impasse, Cameron opted to enter into a coalition government with the Liberal Democrats, and he became Prime Minister on 10 May 2010. The coalition with the pro-EU Liberal Democrats was expected to dilute the much more abrasive tone towards the EU that many Conservative supporters may have wanted. Nevertheless, the new British leader quickly stated that he was not interested in any new treaty and was not prepared to hand over any more power to 'Brussels'. In November the Cameron-led Government introduced an 'EU Bill', which required increased parliamentary and, in several cases, popular approval of further treaty amendments and decisions concerning the United Kingdom's position within the EU (for example, with regard to euro membership). The bill received royal assent in July 2011. Referenda, therefore, appear set to become an integral feature of the country's continued membership of the EU. In an attempt to dampen dissent among his backbench colleagues and to dent the growing popularity of the **UK Independence Party** in marginal parliamentary seats Cameron expressed his view in June 2012 that a referendum on the United Kingdom's relationship with the EU would happen at some point in the future but he did not indicate when. The EU question may yet prove to be one of the issues that threaten to create serious tensions at the heart of the coalition Government.

CANDIDATE COUNTRIES was the term adopted by the Helsinki summit of the **European Council** in December 1999 to refer to those countries involved in **accession negotiations** launched in February 2000. At the time, the term covered the 10 **applicant countries** from **Central and Eastern Europe**, Cyprus, Malta and **Turkey**. With the **enlargement** of the European Union (EU) on 1 May 2004 and 1 January 2007, the number was reduced to three: Turkey, **Croatia** (granted candidate status in June 2004) and **the former Yugoslav republic of Macedonia** (December 2005). Since then, Montenegro (December 2010) and Serbia (March 2012) have also been granted candidate status; Iceland is also referred to as a 'candidate'. In addition to adopting the term 'candidate countries', the European Council in 2000 introduced the term **potential candidate state** to describe countries in the **Western Balkans** that aspire to membership.

CAP: See **Common Agricultural Policy**

CARBON TAX is the name of a proposed **energy tax** that was under consideration by the **European Commission** from 1991. Part of the campaign to reduce **atmospheric pollution**, it was a key element of the European Communities' (EC) efforts to develop an **energy policy** that would be closely linked to EC **environment policy**. The tax would involve a levy on petroleum produced within the European Union (EU) as well as upon the fuel and carbon content of all non-renewable fuel. The tax was seen as part of the EU's acceptance of the agreement at the **United Nations** Framework Convention on Climate Change, held in Rio de Janeiro, Brazil, in 1992, to stabilize carbon dioxide emissions at 1990 levels by the end of the century. The proposal found support among the traditional 'leader' member states on environmental policy (the Netherlands, Germany and Denmark), which sought EU-wide measures to match taxes already in place at the national level, but it provoked strong opposition from the poorer member states, as well as from energy-intensive industries. The Commission published details of its proposal for a carbon tax in 1992, but supporters of the carbon tax ultimately gave way to their opponents at the 1994 **Essen summit**. The issue continues to resurface, however, particularly as some member states have since adopted such a tax at the domestic level (Austria, Ireland, Denmark, Finland, the Netherlands and Sweden). An Emissions Trading System (ETS) was launched in January 2005, which obliges companies that exceed agreed carbon dioxide emissions to buy extra allowances from more efficient companies or incur considerable fines.

CARDS (Community Assistance for Reconstruction, Development and Stabilization) was the financial assistance programme dedicated to the **Western Balkans** as part of the **stabilization and association process** launched in 1999. It replaced the OBNOVA programme and involved total funding to the region of €4,560m. for the period 2000–06. From 1 January 2007 CARDS was replaced by the **instrument for pre-accession assistance**.

CARTELS: See: **Competition Policy**; **Transport Policy**

CARTOON is another name for the European Association of Animation Film. It is based in **Brussels** and is linked to the MEDIA programme (see **Media policy**).

CASE LAW: See **Court of Justice**; **Law**; **Legislation**

CASSIS DE DIJON is the popular name of an important ruling (Rewe-Zentral AG v Bundesmonopolverwaltung für Branntwein) by the **Court of Justice**. The Court ruled in 1979 that, where a product is manufactured and legally on sale in one member state, another member state cannot prohibit its import and sale, except on grounds of its constituting a risk to public health. The product in question was a French fruit liqueur, whose importer into the Federal Republic of Germany (West Germany) had appealed to the Court of Justice against a decision by the German courts to ban its import. The West German case rested on the argument that, under the national spirits monopoly, potable spirits had to contain at least 25% by volume of wine spirits to be marketable in the country: the product in question, *Cassis de Dijon*, had less than 20% by volume of wine spirits. In rejecting the West German argument, the Court delivered a decisive legal precedent for the European Communities (EC) in its affirmation of the unconstitutionality of national legislation and technical regulations in relation to intra-EC trade. It enabled the **European Commission** to develop the principle of **mutual recognition** as an important instrument of **harmonization** and the development of the **internal market**. The ruling was subsequently applied to a wide range of products, and its essence was formally incorporated into the **Treaty of Rome**.

CCBE: See **Council of the Bars and Law Societies of Europe.**

CCP: See **Common Commercial Policy**

CCT: See **Common External Tariff**

CDP: See **Common Defence Policy**

The **CECCHINI REPORT** of 1988 gave the **European Commission** powerful ammunition in its quest to introduce a range of practical measures that would ensure the effective operation of the **internal market** by 1992. Requested by the Commission, the report was compiled by a committee of experts under the chairmanship of Paolo Cecchini, and published in 16 large volumes, with a summary presentation also published as *The European Challenge 1992—The Benefits of a Single Community*. The committee consulted both economic and financial data collections and analyses, as well as other official and academic studies. It also interviewed some 11,000 companies across the European Communities (EC). The result was an extensive listing and costing of the obstacles—national practices, regulations and standards—that prevented the realization of the objective of **freedom of movement** contained in the **Treaty of Rome**. The report concluded that the cost of these obstacles was about €200,000m., or some 5% of the EC gross domestic product. Although it was accepted by the EC, not all authorities agreed with its findings.

CEDEFOP: See **European Centre for the Development of Vocational Training**

CEE: See **Central and Eastern Europe**

CELAD: See **European Committee to Combat Drugs**

CELEX stands for Communitatis Europae Lex, an inter-institutional database for European Union (EU) law, compiled by the **Legal Service** of the **European Commission**. Established in 1971, it contains details of, and provides an information service on, treaties, legal agreements resulting from the external relationships of the EU, all secondary **legislation**, case-law and **Court of Justice** rulings, and questions and answers in the **European Parliament**.

CEN is the acronym of the European Committee for Standardization (Comité Européen de Normalisation), a body of experts based in **Brussels** that was established in 1961 to assist in the advancement of the **industrial policy** and research and development policy of the European Communities. Funded by the **European Commission**, it was given a general remit to prepare European standards across a whole range of products, processes and appliances, as well as in the field of **information technology**. The variety of systems of national standards employed by the member states was believed to be a barrier to the effective **implementation** of the **internal market**. A number of the smaller states were concerned that the process of integrating the national standards would be dominated by France, Germany and the United Kingdom, which collectively produced some 85% of the national standards. Around 2,000 subjects have been covered by CEN. The field of electrotechnical standardization is the brief of a parallel committee, the European Committee for Electrotechnical Standardization (**CENELEC**).

CENELEC, the European Committee for Electrotechnical Standardization (Comité Européen de Normalisation Électrotechnique), is an expert body based in **Brussels** and funded by the **European Commission**, the role of which is to prepare European technical standards across a range of products and appliances as well as in the field of **information technology**. Its work is regarded as important for both the research and development policy and the **industrial policy** of the European Union. Its work is similar to that of the European Committee for Standardization (**CEN**).

CENTRAL AMERICA: See **South and Central America**

CENTRAL AND EASTERN EUROPE (CEE), as far as the European Union is concerned, comprises 10 countries: Bulgaria, the Czech Republic, Estonia, Hungary, Latvia, Lithuania, Poland, Romania, Slovakia and Slovenia.

The **CENTRAL EUROPEAN FREE TRADE AREA** (CEFTA) agreement entered into force in 1993, agreed on by the so-called **Visegrad group** of countries (Czechoslovakia—now the Czech Republic and Slovakia—along with Hungary and Poland), with Slovenia and Romania joining them in 1996 and 1997, respectively. Bulgaria joined the association in 1999, followed by **Croatia** in 2003 and **the former Yugoslav republic of Macedonia** (FYRM) in 2006. The agreement led to the establishment of free trade in industrial goods between the nine countries. While free trade is an important goal in itself, the main purpose behind CEFTA has always been to facilitate integration with the European Union (EU) and enhance the prospects of the participant countries obtaining EU membership. Indeed, five of CEFTA's members joined the EU on 1 May 2004, and two more on 1 January 2007, thus reducing the membership of CEFTA to just two countries, Croatia and the FYRM. In December 2006 CEFTA was therefore extended to include **Albania**, **Bosnia and Herzegovina**, **Moldova**, **Montenegro, Serbia** and the United Nations Interim Administration Mission in Kosovo (UNMIK) on behalf of **Kosovo**.

CERIF stands for Common European Research Information Format. It is a facility established in 1991 to enable the member states to exchange information on research projects as a prelude to a planned network of European research databases.

CERN is the acronym of the European Organization for Nuclear Research, a transnational research institution founded in 1954 and based in Geneva,

Switzerland. CERN is a pure, as opposed to an applied, research institute, focusing upon the theoretical basis of nuclear and particle physics. Twenty European nations, including 18 member states of the European Union, are members, and the **European Commission** acts as an observer. CERN maintains links with the **European Atomic Energy Community**.

CET: See **Common External Tariff**

CFP: See **Common Fisheries Policy**

CFR: See **Charter of Fundamental Rights**

CFSP: See **Common Foreign and Security Policy**

CG: Coalition des Gauches—See **Left Unity**

The **CHANNEL TUNNEL** rail link between France and the United Kingdom was not a European Communities project. However, funding for the road and rail links to the tunnel was provided by the **European Regional Development Fund** because the project was widely regarded as an important contribution to an integrated European transport system (see **transport policy**). Some assistance for the tunnel itself came in the form of a loan from the **European Investment Bank**. The Channel Tunnel Treaty was signed in February 1986, and completion was scheduled for June 1993. Although the first engine to pass completely through the tunnel did so on schedule, technical problems and rising costs prevented the tunnel from becoming fully operational until late 1994. The tunnel has made a significant impact as a means of facilitating the shipment of goods, became a major source of controversy between the United Kingdom and France over the latter's policing of entry points to the tunnel, which became a principal means by which immigrants gained illegal entry into the United Kingdom. The tunnel was a technical feat of modern engineering, but its operating company, Eurotunnel, experienced severe financial difficulties, and was compelled to reduce its prices in an attempt to win back travellers who had been lost to cheaper ferries and, more significantly, to the budget airlines. In 2007 the company embarked on a major debt reduction plan in an effort to avoid bankruptcy; as a result of the consequent restructuring, the company recorded annual net profits in the late 2000s.

CHAPTER is the term denoting a subdivision of a **Title** in a European Treaty. A Chapter may in turn be subdivided into **Sections**.

CHARTER FOR A NEW EUROPE: See **Charter of Paris for a New Europe**

The **CHARTER OF FUNDAMENTAL RIGHTS** (CFR) was proclaimed by the Presidents of the **European Commission**, the **Council of the European Union** and the **European Parliament** at the Nice summit of the **European Council** in December 2000. Since then it has been included as Part II of the **Treaty establishing a Constitution for Europe**. It should not be confused with either the **European Convention on Human Rights** (ECHR) adopted by the **Council of Europe** in 1950 or the **Charter of Fundamental Social Rights of Workers**, otherwise known as the Social Charter, adopted in 1989. These two documents did, however, inspire some of the content of the CFR. Its existence owes much to the increased awareness of fundamental rights within the European Union (EU) and the desire of the EU to promote such, whether internally through, for example, **citizenship**, or externally through the **common foreign and security policy**.

The text of the CFR comprises seven chapters covering Dignity, Freedoms, Equality, Solidarity, Citizen's Rights, Justice and General Provisions. These contain a total of 54 **articles** setting out individual rights such as those to life, liberty and freedom, education, non-discrimination, good administration, and a fair trial. As such, therefore, it presents in a single document the existing rights and freedoms enjoyed by EU citizens whether through the **European treaties** or through the ECHR or the Social Charter. Indeed, no new rights were created. All the same, the member states were not willing at the time to make the CFR a legally binding document. However, they accepted the proposal of the **European Convention** to include it in the Treaty establishing a Constitution for Europe. This was only possible, however, after a number of additional clauses had been inserted clarifying the interpretation and application of the rights contained in the CFR. Further clarifications and a partial **opt-out** for the United Kingdom were negotiated as part of the **intergovernmental conference** of 2007 that led to agreement on the **Treaty of Lisbon** which, upon **ratification**, made the CFR legally binding on the member states and the EU's institutions when implementing EU law. As part of this process, the CFR was duly signed and proclaimed again by the Presidents of the European Commission, the Council of the European Union and the European Parliament on 12 December 2007.

CHARTER OF FUNDAMENTAL SOCIAL RIGHTS OF WORKERS is the official title of the original document that later became known as the Social Charter. It originated in the review of progress towards the target of completing the **internal market** by the end of 1992, in which the **European Council** referred to the equal importance of developing the social aspects of the single market. The **European Commission** subsequently drew up a set of proposals for the introduction of a European Communities (EC) charter of fundamental social rights. A modified version of these proposals was approved by the European Council at its Strasbourg summit in December 1989, although British opposition meant that only 11 of the 12 member states signed the document. Thereafter, the Social Charter figured prominently in the discussions leading up to the **Treaty on European Union**, but persistent British opposition prevented it from being included in the treaty. Instead a Social Chapter, complete with an **opt-out** arrangement for the United Kingdom, was agreed allowing the 11 to proceed with measures, notably on health and safety and worker consultation, to implement the Charter. The Labour Government elected to power in the United Kingdom in May 1997 agreed to sign the Charter shortly after taking office. Following this, the **Treaty of Amsterdam** removed the opt-out clause and incorporated the Social Chapter in the revised **Treaty of Rome**.

Essentially, the Charter set out to codify in general terms what the EC had already begun to do in the social sector, as well as introducing some new proposals. In emphasizing that the single internal market must benefit workers as well as employers, the Charter set out a code of practice that dealt with living and working conditions, **freedom of movement** of labour, collective bargaining, training, **equal opportunities**, gender equality, measures to protect underprivileged groups, and safety and health protection. Much of this was already the subject of EC **directives** and **regulations**. The Commission wanted a further **harmonization** of practices that would bring them to the level of the best national practices currently in existence, and stressed the appropriateness of EC action where the desired goals could be more easily achieved at the EC, rather than the national, level. Since the Charter's adoption, many of the rights of workers contained in it have been incorporated into the **Charter of Fundamental Rights** proclaimed in 2000.

The **CHARTER OF PARIS FOR A NEW EUROPE**, often referred to simply as the Charter of Paris, was a document signed at the meeting of the Conference on Security and Co-operation in Europe (see **Organization for Security and Co-operation in Europe**) in Paris in November 1990. The signatories, including the European Communities' member states, declared that 'the era of confrontation and division in Europe has ended', and committed themselves to the promotion and defence of democracy, **human rights** and a free market economy. The Charter has often been held to mark the formal end of the **Cold War**.

CHASSE GARDÉE is a phrase ('protected competition') that has been employed within the European Union (EU) by opponents of too great a movement towards free trade. It refers to a belief that the EU's ability to survive economically in the context of international competition depends upon the provision of a protected domestic market for EU companies.

JACQUES CHIRAC (1932–) became the President of France in 1995 and embarked on his second term of office in May 2002 after a resounding victory over Jean-Marie Le Pen, the leader of the extreme right-wing Front National. Chirac studied administration and graduated from the élite Ecole Nationale d'Administration (ENA) prior to working in the Cour des Comptes (the highly prestigious French audit office) before entering politics. Thereafter he rapidly emerged as one of France's most prominent political figures on the Gaullist right in the late 20th century, serving as mayor of Paris from 1977 to 1995 and Prime Minister, firstly under **Valéry Giscard d'Estaing** from 1974 until his resignation in 1976, and later under **François Mitterrand** from 1986 to 1988. The latter marked the first period of *cohabitation,* where a socialist president was compelled to work with a right-of-centre prime minister following separate presidential and parliamentary elections. Chirac's election to the French presidency in 1995 raised some concerns in Germany with respect to his more relaxed approach to European Union (EU) affairs, but Chirac quickly conformed with the approach adopted by his immediate predecessors in the Elysée Palace. Chirac's strong opposition to the **Iraq War** in 2003 fortified his popularity at home and transformed him into one of Europe's most respected leaders. His popularity began to decline, however, owing to the trial of his protégé and former Prime Minister, Alain Juppé. Juppé was found guilty of allowing party employees from Chirac's Rassemblement pour la République to be placed on the payroll of Paris City Hall when Chirac was mayor (1977–95) and Juppé was its finance director. Juppé received an 18-month suspended sentence and was banned from holding public office for 10 years. Chirac stood loyally behind Juppé, but some began to question his own involvement in the affair. As President, Chirac was immune from any indictment or sentencing. His decision to stage a referendum on the **Treaty establishing a Constitution for Europe** in May 2005 was unnecessary and, in retrospect, a miscalculation. The outcome of the French 'no' vote undermined his authority and his subsequent skirmishes with British Prime Minister **Tony Blair** over the EU **budget** throughout 2005 weakened Chirac's position both at home and abroad. However, arguably more lasting damage was inflicted upon Chirac in relation to Paris' bid to host the Olympic Games in 2012. Chirac made several comments on the eve of the International Olympic Committee's vote that almost certainly irretrievably damaged the French campaign, including blaming the United Kingdom for the BSE crisis. Paris lost the bid to the British capital, London. Chirac had considered running for a third term as President, but growing unpopularity persuaded him that it was better to stand down in favour of a new generation. Chirac's term in the Elysée Palace came to an end in May 2007 when he was succeeded by **Nicolas Sarkozy**.

CHRISTIAN DEMOCRATIC GROUP: See **Group of the European People's Party (Christian Democrats) and European Democrats**

WINSTON CHURCHILL (1874–1965) made an important contribution to European developments after 1945. Before the Second World War, he had on several occasions expressed a belief in the value and necessity of European unity. As the charismatic Prime Minister of the United Kingdom during the war, he became a symbol to all those who sought the post-war construction of an integrated Europe, in part because of his offer to France in 1940 of a Franco-British Union. Churchill returned to the theme of a united Europe throughout the war. Although his premiership ended in 1945, he continued to urge integration. While delivering a major speech in Zürich, **Switzerland**, in 1946, he argued that it was imperative to establish a United States of Europe. He supported the **International Committee of the Movements for European Unity**, and acted as General President of the sessions of the 1948 **Congress of Europe**. After the Congress he became one of the patrons of the **European Movement**. However, notwithstanding his offer to France in 1940, Churchill did not see the United Kingdom as being part of an integrated Europe. That was to be a continental integration, built around reconciliation between France and Germany, which, he said in 1946, 'must take the lead together'. Upon his return as Prime Minister in 1951, his European policy did not differ from that of the previous Labour Government. He believed that the United Kingdom should act as a transatlantic link between Europe and the **USA**. He was not willing to consider British involvement in anything other than limited intergovernmental co-operation, and during his premiership the United Kingdom refrained from participation in the developments being pursued by the Europe of the **Six**.

DACIAN CIOLOŞ (1969–) is one of the Commissioners in the Barroso II Commission (2010–14). He is a Romanian national, who studied agriculture and agricultural development programmes at the Universities of Cluj, Romania, Rennes, France and Montpellier, France. His expertise and interest in agriculture was furthered in his professional career from his time as an intern at the Directorate-General for Agriculture in the late 1990s to his role as adviser to the Romanian Minister for Agriculture in 2005–07. His background has equipped him well for his post in **Brussels**, where he has been given responsibility for the agriculture and rural development portfolio.

CIS: See **Commonwealth of Independent States**

CITIZENS' RIGHTS are determined and guaranteed by the provisions of the **Treaty of Rome** and others of the **European treaties**. However, the treaties only deal with rights in terms of general principles and in specific, mainly economic, areas. A second source of citizens' rights, again only in specific areas, has been the rulings of the **Court of Justice** in the context of its interpretation of the treaties. These cases have been concerned primarily with the principle of equality between citizens within one member state, especially for minority groups. In the 1980s the European Communities (EC) began to emphasize citizens' rights as part of their promotion of awareness of, and loyalty to, the EC at the level of the individual. This was one of the objectives of the 1984 **Committee for a People's Europe**, but **implementation** of its proposals was slow. The **Treaty on European Union** attempted to expand the rights already enjoyed by individuals into a broader notion of **citizenship**. The **Treaty of Amsterdam** continued to build on this idea, and focused further attention on the citizen's rights. A new **Article** permits the **Council of the European Union** to take action, by unanimity, in cases of **discrimination** based on sex, race, ethnic origin, religion or belief, disability, age or sexual orientation. Member states signing the treaty also agreed to eliminate inequalities between men and women; to protect citizens against misuse of data held by EC institutions; and to maintain and establish co-operation in areas of public health, the environment and sustainability, and development and consumer protection. The Treaty of Amsterdam, moreover, incorporated the **protocol** on social policy (see **Charter of Fundamental Social Rights of Workers**) into the revised Treaty of Rome. At Nice, in December 2000, the rights of citizens were once again on the agenda with the proclamation of the **Charter of Fundamental Rights**, which contains a section dedicated to citizens' rights.

CITIZENSHIP is a concept that remained undeveloped within the European Communities (EC) until the **intergovernmental conferences** of 1991 that preceded the **Maastricht summit**. While certain individual rights were provided by the **Treaty of Rome**, they were based essentially upon the economic objectives set by the treaty. While these rights were strengthened by rulings of the **Court of Justice**, they were limited in number and scope, and did not in any way provide a condition of citizenship. This lacuna in EC thinking was directly addressed by the **Treaty on European Union** (TEU), which attempted to formalize and develop the concept of citizenship beyond the economic rights of workers. The aim of introducing and defining European Union (EU) citizenship was part of the ambition to make the EU more democratic and to instil identity with, and commitment to, the EU in its inhabitants. However, it was not totally clear what citizenship was or what it involved. There were no references to the duties of citizens and, since the EU did not at the time have **legal personality**, citizenship appeared to lie within the EC **pillar**, which was the only part of the EU in which the Court of Justice, as the guarantor of rights, had jurisdiction. With the **Treaty of Lisbon** the situation has changed. The EU now has legal personality. In addition, the TEU reaffirmed that **sovereignty** rested with the member states, thus accepting that questions of nationality and citizenship should be decided at the national level. Even though EU citizenship is therefore indirect, its establishment was not accepted unanimously. There were fears, particularly among

Eurosceptics, that the introduction of a formalized citizenship would be used by the European institutions to reduce further the freedom of the states, with the long-term aim of EU citizenship superseding national citizenship. Under the 2006 **budget**, citizenship emerged as a new, albeit very small, category of expenditure. Initiatives under this heading included efforts to combat health threats from animal diseases such as bird flu, **BSE** and foot and mouth disease.

CIVIL PROTECTION is a new area of European Union (EU) competence, contained in the **Treaty of Lisbon**. It envisages the EU encouraging co-operation between member states to improve the effectiveness of systems for preventing and protecting against natural or man-made disasters within the EU.

NICK CLEGG (1967–) became Deputy Prime Minister of the **United Kingdom** and Lord President of the Council in May 2010 after he took his party, the Liberal Democrats, into a full coalition with **David Cameron**'s Conservative Party. The formation of a coalition Government was unexpected and is the first of its kind since 1945 in the United Kingdom; it is also the first time that the Liberal Democrats have sat in government since the 1920s. The coalition was the product of an indecisive general election. One of the most noticeable differences between the Liberal Democrats and the Conservatives centres on their attitudes towards the European Union (EU). The former have always been ready to cement and build relations with their European counter-parts and have supported European integration, whereas the Conservatives have become increasingly Eurosceptic over the last two decades. Clegg studied social anthropology at Cambridge and took a Masters at the College of Europe in Bruges, Belgium. He speaks four European languages and is well versed in EU affairs. Prior to becoming a member of the British parliament in 2005, he sat in the European Parliament from 1999 to 2004 and in the mid-1990s worked for the European Commission, where he was involved in developing aid pro-grammes for **Russia** and the former territories of the USSR. In his current position he was expected to attempt to restrain any efforts by his Conservative partners to develop a more bellicose position towards the EU. However, at mid-2012 his influence appeared to be weakening given the growing clamour among Conservative party members for a referendum on the United King-dom's relationship with the EU and Cameron's view that such a referendum was unavoidable in the future.

CMEA: See **Council for Mutual Economic Assistance**

CN: See **Combined Nomenclature**

COAL: See **ECSC**

COALITION DES GAUCHES: See **Left Unity**

COCOLAF: See **Advisory Committee for the Co-ordination of Fraud Prevention**

The **CO-DECISION PROCEDURE** is the European Unions' main decision-making procedure. It was introduced by the **Treaty on European Union** (TEU), being later simplified by the **Treaty of Amsterdam**, and requires all **legislation** adopted under the procedure to be approved by both the **Council of the European Union** and the **European Parliament**. Where the two institutions are initially unable to approve legislation, a **Conciliation Committee** is held. The co-decision procedure is used to adopt legislation in an increasing number of policy areas (e.g. the **internal market**, **social policy**, **transport policy** and **environmental policy**), although it does not apply to certain principal areas, such as the **Common Agricultural Policy**, which is still governed by the **consultation procedure**, and matters of **economic and monetary union**, which are decided by the **co-operation procedure** introduced by the **Single European Act** of 1987. The **Treaty establishing a Constitution for Europe** envisaged the co-decision procedure being renamed the 'ordinary legislative procedure'. The **Treaty of Lisbon** copies this example and, in renaming the procedure, also further extends the areas in which co-decision will be utilized, notably to include decisions relating to the Common Agricultural Policy.

The **COHESION FUND** was established by the **Treaty on European Union** (TEU) in 1993 as part of the European Communities' cohesion policy. It is a financial instrument available to finance transport infrastructure and environmental programmes in member states with a gross national product (GNP) per head of less than 90% of the European Union (EU) average. The Fund was not designated as a structural fund, but was linked directly to the move towards **economic and monetary union** (EMU) and was designed to ease the fiscal problems experienced by the poorer member states as they tried to meet the excessive deficit criteria for EMU membership. Originally, only the four poorest countries in the EU-15—Spain, Greece, Portugal and Ireland—were eligible for support from the Fund. Member state governments agreed to support this fund with annual commitment appropriations amounting to €2,615m. for each of the first four years, €2,515m. for 2004 and 2005, and, finally, €2,510m. for 2006. If a member state became ineligible it was always intended that the available resources would be reduced accordingly. Exactly how the overall resources of the Fund are allocated among the member states is determined by a series of criteria that takes into account member state population and area, overall GNP per head and socio-economic factors. The original financial allocation provided Spain with 61.0%–63.5% of the fund; Greece with

16%–18%; Ireland with 2%–6%; and Portugal with 16%–18%. It should be noted that the total amount that member states can receive from the Cohesion Fund each year (including any monies under structural funds) should not exceed 4% of their gross domestic product (GDP). In 2006 the Cohesion Fund was substantially increased to provide €6,000m. for some 200 environment and transport projects to assist the regions in the less prosperous member states to meet and comply with environmental standards. At 2005 the EU member states eligible for financial assistance from the Cohesion Fund were Greece, Portugal, Spain, Cyprus, the Czech Republic, Estonia, Hungary, Latvia, Lithuania, Malta, Poland, Slovakia and Slovenia. Spain was eligible for a phase-out fund only. With this exception, all these states, plus Bulgaria and Romania, are eligible to receive financial support from the Cohesion Fund for the current financial perspective that runs from 2007 to 2013. Under the heading of Cohesion: Creating an Inclusive Economy, some €31,400m. has been allocated to investments that seek to modernize and diversify economic structures throughout the EU's least-developed regions. The Commission aimed to rebuild or improve some 25,000 km of new roads and over 7,000 km of railways by 2013. In order to enable people to train in new skills, some €10,900m. was allocated to the **European Social Fund**.

COHESION POLICY: See **Structural and Cohesion Funds**

COLD WAR is a term that was first used in the late 1940s to describe the competition and tension that arose soon after the end of the Second World War, especially in Europe, between the **USSR** and its East European satellites on the one side and the **USA** and its Western associates on the other. Relations between the two sides were definitely frozen by 1948, as illustrated by the Berlin Airlift (1948–49), with the imposition of Soviet hegemony over Eastern Europe being matched by a series of US commitments to Western Europe through the Truman Doctrine, the **Marshall Plan** and the **North Atlantic Treaty Organization** (NATO). The Cold War made impossible the pan-European alliance envisaged by some in the immediate aftermath of the Second World War, and ensured that any movement towards integration would be confined to Western Europe. It further strengthened US support for European integration. The fear of Soviet intentions also gave a powerful impetus within Western Europe to efforts at collaboration and integration for the sake of self-preservation, and to the feeling that the Federal Republic of Germany (West Germany), itself a product of the Cold War, must be thoroughly integrated with the rest of Western Europe. The US military protection guaranteed by NATO allowed the European Communities (EC) to develop without having to be overly concerned with political and defence requirements. However, the EC's later attempts, in the 1970s, to develop **European political co-operation** (EPC) were in part a response to the bipolarity engendered by the Cold War and the result of a desire to secure a distinctive Western European voice within it. While the necessity of preserving the US commitment limited the extent of EPC to the political and economic aspects of security, the end of the Cold War (as marked by the signing of the **Charter of Paris** in 1990) meant that the EC could feel less reliant upon US views, and less obliged to take account of them, and begin to consider developing their own **common foreign and security policy**. The Cold War between the superpowers shaped and provided the backdrop to European political and security developments for over 40 years, and on occasions it seemed that the rivalries, as seen during the Cuban Missile Crisis in 1962, the Soviet invasion of Afghanistan in 1979 and the deployment of US cruise missiles in West Germany in the early 1980s, would lead to war. Ultimately the economic and political costs of the Cold War led both the Americans under Ronald Reagan and the Soviets under Mikhail Gorbachev to re-evaluate their positions. It caused the latter to commence his policies of *perestroika* (reform) and *glasnost* (openness), which gave rise to the 'revolutions' in Eastern Europe in the second half of 1989, the breaching of the Berlin Wall and the fall from power of Eastern Europe's communist systems. The USSR was not immune to these processes and began to fragment in 1991. Its collapse signalled the end of the Cold War.

COLUMBUS is the **European Space Agency**'s research laboratory that forms part of the international space station. Originally linked to the Hermes space shuttle project, the project to produce Columbus began in 1988. Columbus launched on 7 February 2008, and had an anticipated 10-year lifespan.

COM DOCUMENTS are part of the official working documents of the **European Commission**. They are documents prepared by the **Directorates-General** and submitted to the **Secretariat-General** for placement on the agenda of Commission meetings. They consist of proposals for **legislation**, policy discussion papers, and reports on the implementation of policies.

COMBINED NOMENCLATURE (CN) is the goods nomenclature created by the European Communities. Established in 1988, it replaced two previous systems: the **common external tariff** (CET) nomenclature and the Nomenclature of Goods for the External Trade Statistics of the Community and Statistics of Trade between member states (NIMEXE). The CN is published in the *Official Journal of the European Union* (OJ), and is updated annually.

COMECON: See **Council for Mutual Economic Assistance**

COMENIUS forms part of the European Union (EU)'s **Lifelong Learning Programme** (2007–13) and is a European Commission-sponsored support initiative that seeks to foster greater contacts between schools (from pre-school, through primary school and up to secondary school level) across the EU. It was estimated that some 3m. pupils would take part in joint educational activities by 2010. The scheme is designed to help young people and their teachers better to appreciate and understand European cultures, languages and values as well as providing some important life skills for personal development and future employment. The programme is also open to local authorities, parents' associations, **non-governmental organizations** and teacher-training institutes. Comenius aims to enhance the quality of teaching and strengthen its European dimension by facilitating both pupil and teacher mobility between schools throughout the EU. As part of its ethos, Comenius also emphasizes issues such as multi-cultural education, support for disadvantaged groups, countering under-achievement at school and preventing exclusion. See **Socrates**.

COMEXT is a databank of external trade statistics produced by the Statistical Office of the European Union (**Eurostat**).

COMITEXTIL: The Co-ordinating Committee for the Textile Industries in the EEC

COMITOLOGY: See **Committee Procedure**

COMMISSION: See **European Commission**

COMMISSION OF THE EUROPEAN UNION is the official title of the **European Commission**.

COMMISSION PRESIDENT: See **European Commission**

COMMISSIONER: See **European Commission**

COMMITTEE FOR A PEOPLE'S EUROPE is the name of a committee established by the **European Council** at the June 1984 **Fontainebleau summit** 'to suggest ways of strengthening the identity of the Community at the individual level and of improving the image of the Community among the national populations'. The Committee was composed of personal representatives of the heads of government, and was chaired by Pietro Adonnino, a **Member of the European Parliament** (MEP) for Italy. The Committee produced two reports, often referred to as the **Adonnino Reports**. Both contained a series of recommendations based on the Committee's brief, as well as proposals for measures to improve the rights and freedoms of European

Communities (EC) citizens, and both were approved in principle by the European Council.

The first report was submitted in March 1985. It recommended the immediate **implementation** of a number of specific measures relating to the simplification of border crossing formalities, duty-free allowances, tax exemption for books and magazines, the taxation of trans-frontier workers, rights of residence, and the reciprocal recognition of equivalent diplomas and other forms of professional qualifications. Several of these proposals were incorporated into the longer second report presented in June 1985. This report listed longer-term targets relating to **citizens' rights, cultural policy**, youth exchange schemes and education policy, **sport** and strengthening the image of Europe. It urged, for example, greater use to be made of the **European anthem, European flag** and **European passport**, as well as the introduction of special postage stamps. Legislative proposals on most of the Committee's recommendations were drafted by the **European Commission** in 1986 and 1987. Some of the proposals with direct relevance to the **internal market** were incorporated into the **Single European Act**, which also referred to social justice. The more political and general rights were eventually to be incorporated into those provisions of the **Treaty on European Union** that related to **citizenship**; others were the theme of specific EC programmes. People's Europe was not so much a programme as a set of unco-ordinated initiatives. The fact that over one-half of European Union (EU) citizens surveyed claimed never to have considered themselves European indicates that in some ways the People's Europe concept has had little effect on national identity. The **Treaty of Amsterdam** further emphasized the desire of the EU to move closer to the people by introducing new social measures. These included measures to combat unemployment, to extend **citizens' rights**, to expand the role of the **European Parliament**, and to encourage greater involvement of **national parliaments**; measures that emphasize the principle of **subsidiarity**; and measures making public access to information relating to the European institutions easier, with a view to ensuring greater **openness** and **accountability** within the EU.

The **COMMITTEE OF PROFESSIONAL AGRICULTURAL ORGANIZATIONS IN THE EUROPEAN UNION** (COPA) is based in **Brussels** and is a transnational federation of farming unions and associations, which supplements the activities of the national agricultural unions by lobbying in the various institutions of the European Union for farming interests. Its influence has been far in excess of the importance of farmers in European society and to the economy. The nature of the **common agricultural policy** (CAP) has meant that in lobbying the **European Commission** and the national governments, COPA has effectively engaged in annual wage negotiations for the farming sector, and has opposed proposals for limiting the CAP.

COMMITTEE OF THE GOVERNORS OF THE CENTRAL BANKS was a body established in 1964. It was essentially a consultative body, charged with overseeing and commenting on monetary developments. However, because it consisted of the heads of the central banks of the member states, its opinions had considerable influence. It provided technical and managerial advice and assistance for the operation of the **European Monetary System**, and was central to the planning and institutional development of **economic and monetary union** (EMU) from January 1999. The Committee elected its own President on an annual basis, without any principle of rotation by state. It met on a monthly basis at the headquarters of the **Bank for International Settlements** in Basel, **Switzerland**. The Committee ceased to exist on the establishment of the **European Monetary Institute** in January 1994 (the start of stage two of EMU), although the governors of the central banks of the member states were to play an important role in the Governing Council of the **European Central Bank** and in the **European System of Central Banks**.

The **COMMITTEE OF PERMANENT REPRESENTATIVES** (COR-EPER) consists formally of the heads of the delegation, or **Permanent Representation**, that each member state maintains in **Brussels**, but the term COREPER is also used to refer to the totality of the delegations and their various committees and subcommittees. The members of COREPER, the Permanent Representatives, have senior ambassadorial status. COREPER's task, which expanded enormously as the European Communities (EC) extended the range and volume of their activities, acts as both service agent and 'gatekeeper' for the **Council of the European Union**. Supported by diplomatic and bureaucratic personnel, it prepares the agenda for Council meetings. If the members of COREPER, who receive their instructions from their own national capitals, are able to reach unanimous agreement on a particular issue, the proposal is given an 'A' category on the Council agenda. This means that the proposal is approved by the Council without discussion. Where COREPER finds it impossible to reach a consensus, the issue is referred back for discussion and possible resolution. More generally, COREPER holds frequent meetings to review and consider the details of all proposals for EC **legislation**, in order to seek a common position acceptable to all national governments, upon which it could make recommendations to the Council of the European Union.

The workload of COREPER increased to the extent that the Permanent Representatives do not always attend its meetings. Much agenda evaluation is now handled by deputies, who meet as COREPER I, while the ambassadors' committee is known as COREPER II. By tradition, COREPER does not discuss agricultural questions: these are the province of the **Special Committee on Agriculture**. The centrality of COREPER to the decision-making process of the EC has been the subject of much criticism, notably from the **European Parliament**, particularly on the grounds that it both reinforces the role of national governments and lacks **accountability** within the EC institutional framework. However, its existence was given formal recognition in the **Treaty on European Union**: previously, its authority was based only on the Rules of Procedure of the Council of the European Union.

The **COMMITTEE OF THE REGIONS** (CoR) was established by the **Treaty on European Union** (TEU), thereby formalizing a grouping that had emerged in the late 1980s. It was recognition of the fact that many regional political authorities in the European Communities (EC) had established their own liaison offices in **Brussels**. It was intended, in keeping with the principle of **subsidiarity**, to involve representatives of elected local and regional authorities in EC decision-making in an advisory capacity. Since the European Union (EU) was enlarged to 27 member states on 1 January 2007, the Committee has comprised 344 members appointed by the Council to five-year terms on the proposals of member state governments and an equal number of alternates; it elects its own officers. The current President of the Committee of the Regions is Ramón Luis Valcárcel Siso (the President of the Spanish region of Murcia), who was appointed to a two-and-a-half-year term in July 2012 in succession to Mercedes Bresso. The Bureau is the ruling body of the CoR and comprises some 60 members—the President, the First Vice-President, the 27 vice-Presidents (i.e. one member from each member state), the presidents of the four CoR political groups and 27 other members. In general, the Bureau meets on seven occasions throughout the year and is responsible for drawing up the Committee's annual work programme.

The **European Commission**, the **Council of the European Union** and, after 2009, the **European Parliament** must consult the CoR as directed by the treaties or when they believe an opinion from it would be useful. The areas upon which the Committee must, according to the Treaty on European Union, be consulted are: economic and social cohesion; **Trans-European Networks** in the areas of transport, telecommunications and energy; public health; education and youth; and culture. It was also given the right to issue opinions on matters that have been referred to the **European Economic and Social Committee** (ECOSOC), where it feels regional issues are involved. The regions represented by the Committee's members do not correspond rigidly to any single level of **Nomenclature of Territorial Units for Statistics** (NUTS) regions.

Under the terms of the **Treaty of Amsterdam**, the range of areas on which the Committee must be consulted was extended to include aspects of employment policy, **social policy**, **environmental policy** and vocational training. None the less, the CoR's impact has been relatively modest. It has proved difficult to maintain a common purpose in a committee with such a disparate membership (ranging in depth and significance from local councillors in the United Kingdom to the premiers of the German *Länder*). Instead, many regions have opted to utilize the CoR as simply another avenue to pursue their particular interests and gain access to the European Communities' decision-makers. The **Treaty of Nice** in February 2001 established an overall ceiling of

350 for CoR membership. Significantly, the Treaty of Nice linked membership of the CoR to holding a regional or local authority mandate, with membership of the CoR lapsing simultaneously with the ending of an elected mandate. The final declaration of a Committee conference convened in Salamanca, Spain, in September 2001 included a proposal that the Committee be given the status of an institution in its own right, with the power to bring cases of alleged infringement of subsidiarity before the **Court of Justice**. With the coming into force of the **Treaty of Lisbon** on 1 December 2009 the role of the CoR was further strengthened. The treaty obliged the Commission to consult with local and regional authorities across the EU and also with the CoR. This ensures that both local and regional representatives are actively involved at a very early stage of policy proposals and pre-legislation activities. The Treaty of Lisbon also added other policy areas to the CoR's remit. These included: civil protection, climate change, energy and services of general interest. For the very first time, the Treaty of Lisbon stipulates that the CoR must be consulted by the European Parliament.

COMMITTEE OF THREE WISE MEN is the popular title of a body established in 1978 by the **European Council**, following a proposal by President **Valéry Giscard d'Estaing** of France that the Council should launch a further review of the operation of the institutional machinery of the European Communities (EC), even though the Council had not discussed the **Tindemans Report** of 1976, which covered the same theme. The committee consisted of three senior politicians: Barend Biesheuvel of the Netherlands, Edmund Dell of the United Kingdom and Robert Marjolin of France, whose task it was to investigate the EC institutions with a view to suggesting amendments to augment their effectiveness, and to consider progress towards European union. The group reported back to the European Council in 1979, commenting adversely on the negative role of the Council of Ministers (see **Council of the European Union**), concluding that the **European Commission** should be reorganized and endowed with more authority, and that **qualified majority voting** should be more widely applied in the Council of Ministers. Although the European Council welcomed the report, no action was taken on its recommendations.

COMMITTEE PROCEDURE: or 'comitology', is a name given to the process of decision-making and its scrutiny within committees of the **European Commission**. It describes a process whereby the Commission consults with a series of specialist advisory and other committees when seeking to draft and implement European Union (EU) law. Under Article 291 of the **Treaty on the Functioning of the European Union**, it is the task of the Commission to implement legislation. The nature of the committees, which are made up of national bureaucrats, technical experts and representatives of interest groups, varies: some are management committees, with executive powers, while others are only advisory. The latter do, however, allow access to decision-making and can be highly influential.

There were previously three types of committee, namely the **advisory committees**, the management committees and the regulatory committees. A fourth, the regulatory and scrutiny committee, was created in 2006. All have different powers when it comes to decision-making. All are chaired by the Commission and enable the Commission to establish a dialogue with national administrations before adopting implementation measures. The Commission ensures that they reflect as far as possible the situation in each country in question.

Procedures that govern relations between the Commission and the committees are based on models set out in a Council Decision (Comitology Decision) of 13 July 1987. However, this initial decision was modernized by the Council Decision of 28 June 1999, to take into account treaty changes and the enhanced powers of the **European Parliament** (EP) under co-decision, and also to respond to increasing criticism that the system was too complicated.

The 1999 Decision ensured that the EP could watch over the implementation of legislative instruments adopted under the **co-decision procedure**. In cases where **legislation** came under this procedure, the EP could express its disapproval of measures proposed by the Commission or, where appropriate, by the Council, which, in the EP's opinion, go beyond the implementing powers provided for in the legislation.

Lastly, several innovations in the latest council decision enhance the **transparency** of the committee system to the benefit of the EP and the general public: committee documents were to be more readily accessible to the citizen (the arrangements are the same as those applying to Commission documents); committee documents were also to be recorded in a public register; and, since 2000, the Commission has published an annual report giving a summary of committee activities during the previous year.

In 2006 (following years of complaint from the EP) the committee procedure underwent significant reform, when it placed the EP and the Council on an equal footing. This decision was the outcome of an initiative of the EP's Constitutional Affairs Committee (and its *rapporteur*, the former Labour MEP Richard Corbett) and was agreed under the Austrian presidency (of 2006). The EP was given the right to block individual Commission comitology decisions where the original legislation was adopted by both the EP and the Council under the **co-decision procedure**. This newer Regulatory Procedure with Scrutiny was another major development for the EP, but it occurred only under co-decision and when powers had been conferred upon the Commission to implement measures, and was subject to a strict timetable.

Pressure for reform of the comitology procedure intensified as critics argued that it was too complicated. Following the terms of Article 290 of the **Treaty of Lisbon**, new rules were introduced from 1 March 2010 (and agreed by the **Council** in February 2011) to change how this procedure worked and effectively further enhanced the role of both the Commission and the EP. Under the previous system, member state governments were able to block a Commission proposal by a simple majority. The new procedure only allows member state governments to do so if they can reach a qualified majority. The new regulation also confers a right of scrutiny on both the EP and the Council. These institutions can now inform the Commission at any time if they believe the Commission has exceeded its powers. The Commission is then obliged to review the draft act and decide whether to maintain it, amend it or withdraw it. In short, the Commission is obliged to respond to objections, although these are not commonplace.

The **COMMON AGRICULTURAL POLICY** (CAP) is one of the obligations imposed on the European Communities (EC) by the **Treaty of Rome**. It represents one of the oldest and most established European Union (EU) policy responsibilities. Agriculture has long been deemed a special area of economic activity. Rural areas make up over 90% of the EU's territory and account for approximately 50% of its population. Enlargement from the **Twenty-Five** brought an extra 4m. farmers into the EU, increasing the total farming population to some 7m. The enlargement process also added a further 38m. ha of land to the 130m. ha that existed in the **Fifteen**. Agriculture and forestry are the main land users and play a fundamental role in the management of natural resources in rural areas and in determining the rural landscape. The Commission argues that agriculture makes an important contribution to the EU's overall prosperity and estimates that the agri-food sector (including beverages) accounts for some 14% of total EU manufacturing output. None the less, the CAP remains an issue of controversy and its future is one that clearly divides the member states. To understand the ongoing demands for reform it is necessary to appreciate the reasons why governments intervene in agriculture, why agriculture became an EU competence and also the way in which this system was put into operation. It is also important to stress that the CAP has changed fundamentally from the mid-1980s, as old subsidies were replaced by a new rhetoric, advancing a more market-driven solution.

After much disagreement and protracted bargaining, the original **Six** members of the EC agreed, in January 1962, on the principles of a common market for agriculture based upon five objectives set down in Article 33 of the Treaty of Rome (now Article 39 of the **Treaty on the Functioning of the European Union**): an increase in agricultural productivity; a fair standard of living for the agricultural community; stabilized markets; guaranteed regular supplies of agricultural products; and a guarantee of reasonable prices to consumers. The 1962 agreement was an interim arrangement due to expire at the end of 1965, and the need for the EC to finalize the financial arrangements concerning the reform of agriculture in the various member states was one factor contributing to the **empty chair crisis**. In 1968 the framework for the CAP was described in detail in the **Mansholt Plan**. However, only a diluted version of the Plan was finally adopted by the Council of Ministers (see **Council of the European Union**) in 1972.

The CAP was established with three main components: a single market for agricultural products, with common prices; community preference with a **common external tariff** (CET) and levies on agricultural imports from outside the EC; and common financial solidarity or responsibility. A further element, the development of which remained at a very basic stage, was the restructuring of European agriculture.

Common prices for agricultural products were introduced between 1962 and 1967. The increasing volatility of exchange rates in the late 1960s that heralded the breakdown of the **Bretton Woods** agreement made it increasingly difficult to maintain a common price structure, except by artificial means. The solution was the adoption of artificial **green currencies**, with the difference in value between green rates (the original common prices) and real rates prevailing on the money markets being covered by **monetary compensatory amounts** (MCAs). In the 1980s the **European Commission** came to favour the abolition of green currencies, but this was resisted by several member states. It was agreed that MCAs were to be eliminated by 1989, but continued resistance preserved them until 1993.

The core of the CAP is the guaranteed price system, administered through the **European Agricultural Guarantee Fund** (EAGF), which replaced the European Agricultural Guidance and Guarantee Fund in 2007. Prices are determined each year by the EU agricultural ministers who, because of pressure from national interests and bodies such as the **Committee of Professional Agricultural Organizations in the European Union** (COPA), have tended to set the common prices at high levels, which, in the last resort, have been determined more by political pressure and compromise than by any form of rational economic calculation. Two basic prices are set each year. The first is a **target price** for each product covered by the price support mechanism; the other, set at a slightly lower level, is the **intervention price** below which the market price is not allowed to fall. EC prices fixed under the CAP have invariably been higher than those prevailing on world markets.

The guaranteed price system stimulated over-production. Early attempts at reform, most notably the 1968 Mansholt Plan, which sought to reduce the number of farmers within the then EEC, failed to make any progress. Many small and inefficient farmers remained active and put added pressure on limited resources as over-production became the norm. Until the system was modified, under the guarantee system, farmers' incomes rose the more they produced. Over-production incurred no penalty. The surplus produce was bought at the fixed prices, and stored. This is the origin of the accumulation of huge stocks of produce, such as the **butter mountain** and the **wine lake**, the storage of which also came to consume large amounts of EC expenditure. The highest levels of over-production occurred in dairy farming, which, although producing only one-fifth of EC total agricultural produce, had by 1980 come to absorb some two-fifths of CAP financial support. Cereal and sugar cultivators were other major over-producers. After 1985, these products were treated more severely in the annual reviews of guaranteed prices, in an attempt to reduce the levels of production.

In addition to protecting farmers within the EU, the CAP helps European agriculture to compete on world markets. It guarantees the payment of export subsidies or **restitutions**, whereby exporters of EU agricultural produce receive refunds to cover the difference between the lower prices at which they must sell on the world markets and the high EU prices at which they must purchase produce. During the 1970s and the 1980s, higher agricultural prices, as determined by the **Council**, encouraged over-production and moves to more intensive farming, which had a negative impact on the environment, failed to improve the incomes of the smallest farmers and consumed ever more of the EEC's limited **budget**.

The price support mechanism is administered through the EAGF. This operates in four different ways, which together cover almost the whole of the EU agricultural output. The majority of produce has enjoyed full CAP protection, with guaranteed support and sale prices, and with intervention buying if market prices fall below the levels fixed in the annual review. Some 25% of production, including eggs, poultry, pork, quality wines and some minor cereals, fruit and vegetables, is protected only against lower-priced imports. Most remaining products have enjoyed direct **subsidies** to strike a balance between consumer prices and adequate income for the affected EU farmers. In the case of oilseed, where variable import duties apply, the CAP has operated a system of **deficiency payments** to cover the difference between the guaranteed price for the EU producer and the world price. Finally, a very small amount of produce, mainly cottonseed, flax, hemp and hops, is covered by a flat rate of aid based upon the quantity produced or the number of hectares planted.

The domination of the guaranteed price system has meant that, of the original aims of the Treaty of Rome, the CAP has greatly improved agricultural production, self-sufficiency and prosperity. This, however, has been at the expense of the fifth aim. The fact that the farm support prices of the CAP have invariably been higher than world market prices has led to greater costs for the consumer, not only directly through higher prices, but also indirectly, because of the demands made by the CAP on the EU budget. The CAP consumes almost one-half of the annual budget, and of this amount some 95% has been taken up by the guarantee system.

The CAP has been unpopular with non-EU countries. The **USA** and other efficient and traditional exporters of food have been critical of its protectionist nature, as well as of the practice of **dumping** its stored surplus produce at reduced prices, which, they argue, distorts world trade. There is also a widespread opinion among developing countries that EU agricultural policy is detrimental to an effective development of their own agriculture. Internal criticism of the CAP has been less marked, except in the United Kingdom, where the costs of the CAP are seen as being directly related to the level of its own net budget contribution; this has been the consequence in part of its own agricultural structure and its policy of importing large quantities of food from outside the EU.

By the early 1980s the European Commission had accepted the need for restraints on agricultural expenditure, firstly because it was rising at a much faster rate than the **own resources** of the EC could bear, and secondly because its financial appetite, consuming over two-thirds of the EC budget, effectively prevented the development of other EC policies. In the mid-1980s the cost of the CAP was spiralling out of control, which was one of the reasons why member state governments were compelled to consider CAP reform. After much argument, it was agreed at the 1984 **Fontainebleau summit** that CAP expenditure should increase at a lower rate than that of the budget as a whole. International currency instability over the next few years frustrated this objective, although **guarantee thresholds** and **quota restrictions** were introduced for some products in 1984 and 1986, and in 1988 it was agreed to introduce **stabilizers** for most products. It was also agreed in 1988 that the future annual growth of agricultural expenditure should not exceed 74% of the increase in total gross national product (GNP) of the EC member states. While these measures contributed to a reduction in the share of the budget consumed by the CAP, in the early 1990s the problem intensified again with the re-emergence of surpluses and because CAP protectionism had become a major issue which threatened to prevent a satisfactory conclusion to the **Uruguay Round** negotiations on international trade. In June 1992 the Commission made a political breakthrough when it agreed on a new programme of reforms which involved a further reduction of guaranteed prices for some products, a shift from subsidies for production to income support for producers, a considerable extension of **set-aside schemes**, the encouragement of less intensive and more environmentally friendly farming methods, and opportunities for early retirement. These were reflected in the Commission's forward budget planning for 1993–99, which anticipated the CAP share of the budget falling from 54% to 46%.

Moreover, in March 1999 reforms to the CAP were agreed by the **European Council** in Berlin. The European leaders were conscious that they needed to reach a deal before the next wave of **enlargement**. Certain intervention prices (for example, for cereals and beef) were to be lowered in stages, although intervention prices for dairy produce were not to be lowered until 2005. The aim of the reforms was to limit spending on the CAP while supporting farmers with direct income support. However, the accord reached did not go as far as the pro-reform member states (which included Denmark, Sweden and the United Kingdom) wished, and exceeded budgetary stabilization limits. However, the source of the problem remained to be tackled—and would entail a radical overhaul of agricultural policy and a changed political climate. This was especially necessary by the end of the 1990s, as the eastward expansion of the EU from 2004 incorporated states with large agricultural sectors, by Western European standards, which were generally inefficient.

The **Agenda 2000** programme aimed to reshape the CAP and prepare the rural sectors of the EU for enlargement and integration. Greater emphasis was to be placed on the integration of agricultural policy within the broader socio-economic context of rural areas, and the development of a coherent rural policy. From the late 1990s, multifunctionality emerged as one of the principal concepts in the operations of the CAP.

According to the then Agriculture Commissioner, Franz Fischler, the criticisms of the CAP in 2003 were a sign of the widening gap between the positions of farmers and of civil society. Urgent action was needed to restore mutual understanding between both parties. Civil society is justified in supporting a CAP that provides incentives for producing what people want and not what attracts the highest subsidies. In addition, opinion polls consistently confirmed that people wanted healthy, good-quality food, together with a healthy environment and a viably managed landscape.

In 2002 the European Commission tabled a mid-term review of the CAP, which expressed the opinion that public expenditure for the farming sector must be better justified. Besides supporting farming incomes, the CAP must yield more in return with respect to food quality, the preservation of the environment, **animal welfare**, landscapes, cultural heritage, and the furthering of social enhancement and equity. The review aimed to free farmers from excessive bureaucracy, encouraging them to produce at high standards for the highest market return rather than for the sake of the maximum possible subsidy. According to the Commission, the review would ensure better value for money for European consumers and taxpayers.

To achieve these goals the Commission proposed: to cut the link between production and direct payments; to make those payments conditional on the appliance and maintenance of environmental, food safety, animal welfare and occupational safety standards; to increase EU support for rural development; to introduce a new farming audit system; and to adopt new rural development measures to improve quality production, food safety and animal welfare and to cover the cost of the farming audit.

As for the market policy that remained an essential pillar of the CAP, the Commission proposed to bring to a close the process of cereal reforms, notably with a 5% reduction in the intervention price and a new border protection system. Like all previous reforms of the CAP (e.g. the Mansholt Plan in 1968 and the MacSharry Plan in 1991—see **Ray MacSharry**), these radical proposals had to be approved by the member states. At a meeting of EU ministers of agriculture in Luxembourg in June 2003, agreement was reached on what amounted to a fundamental reform of the CAP, and spending levels were determined for 2007 to 2013. The compromise agreement was ratified by the Council of the European Union and the accession states in September. Production-linked subsidies were to be replaced by a Single Farm Payment, and linked to environmental, food safety and animal welfare standards. Obligatory decoupling was only partial for beef, cereal and mutton, with production still accounting for as much as 25% of payments for cereals and as much as 40% for beef. Overall, however, 90% of payments would no longer be linked to production. The agreement contained a commitment to reduce all payments above €5,000 a year by 3% in 2005, by 4% in 2006 and by 5% in 2007. Increased resources were to be directed towards rural development projects, protecting the environment and improvements to food quality; organic farmers and those offering high-quality produce with special guarantees were to receive grants of up to €3,000 a year for five years. Under the principle of 'modulation', an increasing percentage of direct farm subsidies was retained by individual member states to finance rural development measures. The equivalent of at least 80% of the funds gathered in each member state (90% in Germany) was to be spent in that country. Implementation of the CAP reforms agreed in June 2003 commenced on 1 January 2005.

Meanwhile, in April 2004 the EU Council of Ministers of Agriculture reached agreement for CAP reform of the olive oil, cotton, hops and tobacco sectors. The principle of decoupling aid from production was to be extended to these commodities. A significant share of the existing production-linked payments was to be transferred to the Single Farm Payment (which was provided independently of production), although production-linked subsidies were permitted of up to 60% for tobacco, 40% for olive oil, 35% for cotton and 25% for hops. Moreover, full decoupling in the tobacco sector was to be introduced progressively over the four years to 2010 and rural development aid was to finance conversion to other crops in tobacco-producing areas. The remaining production aid for olive oil was to be directed at maintaining olive groves with environmental or social value.

In September 2006 the European Court of Justice annulled the CAP provisions on cotton, proposing a slightly revised reform of the support scheme in November 2007. The new proposal maintained the support arrangements agreed in 2004 (i.e. production-linked subsidies of up to 35%), but provided for additional funding for support measures in cotton-producing regions and the creation of a 'label of origin' to enhance the promotion of EU cotton.

The EU finally agreed on reforms to the sugar industry in November 2005, following a **World Trade Organization (WTO)** ruling earlier in the year (after an action brought by Brazil, Australia and Thailand) that the current level of subsidy breached legal limits. In 2005 the EU sugar sector was still characterized by large subsidies, high internal prices, and imports by African, Caribbean and Pacific (ACP) countries on favourable terms under quotas. The EU produced large surpluses of sugar, which were disposed of on the world market to the detriment of more competitive producers, notably developing countries. The reforms, which were implemented from July 2006, included the gradual reduction of the internal EU market price (which was three times the international price for the commodity in 2005) by 36% by 2009, and direct aid payments of €6,300m. over the four years of the phased introduction of the reforms to EU sugar producers as compensation. The proposals were criticized by **non-governmental organizations** (NGOs), as they would not help create a sustainable international sugar market, and by ACP countries, which claimed the measures would adversely affect their economies. A fundamental element in the reform of the EU sugar sector was the establishment of a restructuring fund, financed by sugar producers, to ease the transition to greater competitiveness. The objective was to remove a total of some 6m. metric tons of sugar quota during the four-year reform period. Amendments to the sugar-restructuring scheme were adopted in October 2007 in an attempt to encourage greater participation, and, by the conclusion of the reform period, in early 2009, some 5.8m. tons of sugar quota had been renounced.

At the Doha round of the WTO in Hong Kong in December 2005, agreement was reached on the elimination of export subsidies on farm goods by the end of 2013. This represented a concession by the EU but was three years later than the date sought by the USA and developing countries. A new regulation laying down specific rules concerning the fruit and vegetables sector was adopted in September 2007 and entered into force in January 2008. Notable reforms included: the integration of the sector into the Single Farm Payment scheme; the requirement that producer organizations allocate at least 10% of their annual expenditure to environmental concerns; an increase in EU funding for the promotion of fruit and vegetable consumption and for organic production; and the abolition of export subsidies for fruit and vegetables. In April 2008 agriculture ministers adopted a new regulation on the reform of the wine sector. The regulation provided, *inter alia*, for the inclusion of the sector in the Single Farm Payment scheme, while distillation subsidies were to be gradually withdrawn by 2012, releasing funds for measures such as wine promotion in third countries and the modernization of vineyards and cellars. In addition, the regulation provided for the introduction of a voluntary scheme, under which wine producers were to receive subsidies over a three-year period, with the aim of removing surplus and uncompetitive wine from the market.

In May 2008 the European Commission proposed a number of regulations to reform and simplify the CAP further in 2009–13, including additional reductions in production-linked payments and increased funding for rural development. In November 2008 the European Council reached agreement on the proposed reforms, which: raised the rate of decoupling in those countries that maintained the link between subsidy and production; provided for reform of the dairy sector; abolished the set-aside scheme from 2009; and provided for payments to farms qualifying for subsidies of at least €5,000 a year to be reduced gradually, so that by 2012 10% of funds (compared with the existing 5%) would be transferred to the rural development budget (large-scale farms would be required to transfer a greater proportion of funds). Milk quotas were to be increased by 1% per year in 2009–13, before their eventual expiry in 2015.

As a result of a severe decline in dairy prices from 2008, in June 2009 the Commissioner for Agriculture and Rural Development established a High Level Experts' Group on Milk (HLG), comprising representatives of the 27 EU member states, and chaired by the Director-General for Agriculture and Rural Development. The HLG sought to identify medium- and long-term measures for stabilizing the market and incomes, and increasing transparency, given the expiry of milk quotas from 1 April 2015. The HLG held 10 meetings between October 2009 and June 2010, and identified significant problems in the supply chain. In late September 2010 its proposals for addressing the problems were endorsed by the Council's presidency. The Dairy Package was formally approved by the European Parliament in February 2012 and was to remain in effect until mid-2020.

On 18 November 2010 the European Commission launched the consultation process on further reform of the CAP with the adoption of a communication entitled 'The CAP towards 2020: meeting the food, natural resources and territorial challenges of the future', based on the results of large-scale public debate on the issue of CAP reform, which were summarized at a conference held in Brussels in July 2010. The Commission aimed to draw up legislative proposals during 2011 targeted at simplifying the CAP from 2014, while ensuring greater transparency, and the long-term sustainability, competitiveness and diversity of the agricultural sector. The two existing pillars of the CAP, comprising direct annual payments and market measures, on the one hand, and flexible rural development measures, on the other, were to be retained. The existing, two-tier system of direct payments was to be reviewed, removing the CAP's reliance on outdated reference criteria, calculated on production volumes in 2000–02, prior to the expansion of the EU. There were also plans to introduce a 'green' component to reward environmental competitiveness. In addition, the Commission sought to counter the effects of climate change and to cushion the impact of volatility in the prices of raw agricultural materials. On 12 October 2011 the Commission presented its full set of legal proposals that were designed not only to make the CAP a more competitive and sustainable economic system but also to assist the continued vibrancy of rural areas. The proposals were passed to the European Parliament and the Council for consideration. However, this is to be a lengthy process and final decisions on the proposals are not expected until towards the end of 2013 (with the intention that the new arrangements come into force from 1 January 2014).

COMMON CARRIER LEGISLATION refers to European Union **legislation** that requires transmission systems to carry energy between any third-party supplier and the consumer at a reasonable tariff.

The **COMMON COMMERCIAL POLICY** (CCP) is at the core of European Union (EU) external relations and has been in place since the **customs union** of the European Communities (EC) was established in the late 1960s. It is the aim of the CCP under Article 206 of the **Treaty on the Functioning of the European Union (TFEU)** to contribute to the harmonious development of world trade, to work for the progressive abolition of restrictions in international trade and on foreign direct investment and to secure the lowering of customs duties. The CCP results from EU competence to regulate non-member state access to the single European market. The CCP therefore confers on the EC, via Article 133 of the **Treaty of Rome** (now Article 207 of the **TFEU**), so-called 'treaty-making powers'. This means that tariff and trade agreements are no longer conducted by the member states, but by the EU. Agreements are negotiated by the **European Commission** under the supervision of the **Article 207 Committee (formerly 133 Committee)** and formally adopted by the Council of Ministers (see **Council of the European Union**), by a **qualified majority** and by the **European Parliament** (EP). Indeed, it is the European Commission that represents the EU and its member states in both bilateral and multilateral trade negotiations, such as those conducted within the framework of the former **General Agreement on Tariffs and Trade** (GATT) and the **World Trade Organization**. Member states will have a presence at these meetings but the Commission is the body that is heavily involved in discussions. It conducts its negotiations in consultation with the Article 207 Committee, the members of which are determined by the Council. The Commission must report at regular intervals to this Committee and to the EP on the progress of negotiations. In those policy areas where the EU holds exclusive responsibility (e.g. agriculture and fisheries) the Commission negotiates directly on behalf of the Council. External trade policy is identified as one of the EU's exclusive competences under the **Treaty of Lisbon**. The Lisbon Treaty is also significant because under its terms (Article 207 of the TFEU) both the **European Parliament** and the Council using the **ordinary legislative procedure** now adopt the measures defining the framework for implementing the CCP. Most agreements involve granting non-member states preferential access to the customs union and **internal market** through an increase in or abolition of quotas, or a lowering of the **common external tariff**. However, GATT rules dictated that most agreements must involve the creation of a free trade area or a customs union within a reasonable period of time and cover substantially all goods. This is true of various **free trade agreements** concluded on the basis of Article 207 (formerly 133) and trade arrangements contained in **association agreements**. Traditionally, the CCP has covered mainly trade in goods, although the EU has tended to be highly protective of its own agricultural markets and therefore access here has been less liberal. With the **Treaty of Nice**, the coverage of the CCP was extended to include trade in services. In this area and the commercial aspects of intellectual property, the Council acts (under Article 207) by **unanimity**. It also acts unanimously in relation to trade in cultural and audiovisual services, in the area of social, educational and health services, and in relation to transport agreements.

COMMON CUSTOMS TARIFF (CCT): See **Common External Tariff**

COMMON DEFENCE, perhaps in the form of a common European army, is a long-term aspiration of the European Union and is asserted in the **Treaty on European Union** as the extension of a **common defence policy**.

A **COMMON DEFENCE POLICY** (CDP) has been the goal of the European Union (EU) since the **Treaty on European Union** was signed in 1992. Originally, it was to be pursued as an extension of the **common foreign and security policy** and in co-operation with **Western European Union**, although the gradual transfer of this organization's functions to the EU since the late 1990s has meant that the CDP is being developed very much within the framework of the EU, notably as part of the **Common Security and Defence Policy**.

The **COMMON EXTERNAL TARIFF** (CET), also known as the common customs tariff (CCT), is a term that refers to an essential element of any **customs union**, and an integral part of the **Treaty of Rome**. A common external tariff, imposed on goods entering any member state from outside the European Union (EU), was first introduced in the early 1960s, based on an average of the customs levies previously exacted by the member states, although with some downward adjustment. Since then the CET has been further lowered from around 10% to less than 5%, in accordance with the EU's acceptance of decisions on tariff barriers and international trade as part of the former **General Agreement on Tariffs and Trade**. Certain exceptions are permitted. The **Council of the European Union** may reduce or waive the CET for a member state where domestic production of the goods being imported cannot meet demand. The **European Commission** may do the same where there is a general shortage of that product within the EU.

The **COMMON FISHERIES POLICY** (CFP) was provided for by the **Treaty of Rome**. The first proposals for a CFP were not, however, made until 1966, and it was not until 1970 that the **Six** committed themselves to such a policy. The Council of Ministers (see **Council of the European Union**) adopted a limited scheme according to the principle of free access for all European Union (EU) fishermen within EU waters. The scheme, modelled on the principles of the **common agricultural policy** (CAP), envisaged price support mechanisms and protection for the EC market, with measures to ensure equal competition within the market, modernization of the industry, and **harmonization**, if necessary by intervention, of national policies.

These proposals were adopted by the Six at the same time that they were negotiating terms of entry to the EC with Denmark, Ireland, **Norway** and the United Kingdom. All the applicant states had important fishing interests, and the EC plan was, to some extent, perceived and resented by those states as a stratagem to rush through a common policy that, while it might benefit the Six, did not necessarily take into account their own interests. The fisheries issue is widely believed to have been a factor in the Norwegian rejection of membership, at the referendum of 1972. The EC eventually negotiated a compromise agreement with the other three applicant states, whereby each member state could, as an interim measure until 1982, restrict entry within a zone of six nautical miles (11.1 km) around its shores, or 12 miles in certain areas, to fishing vessels that had traditionally operated within those limits.

The scheme never worked satisfactorily, either in terms of national interests or in encouraging the preservation of fishing stocks. A major disruptive factor was the extension in the 1970s by many countries bordering the Atlantic Ocean, but particularly by **Iceland**, of an exclusive fishing zone to 200 nautical miles, an action that was subsequently endorsed by the **United Nations** Convention on the Law of the Sea. Deep-sea vessels from the EC were excluded from many of their traditional fishing grounds. They were obliged, if they were not to be forced out of business, to concentrate in EC waters. While the EC also adopted a 200-mile limit in 1977, this did little to obviate the fierce competition within the zone between national fleets, and the inevitable overfishing that followed.

After much disagreement, a common fisheries policy was adopted in 1983. Its two central elements related to access to stocks and their preservation. As far as access was concerned, it endorsed the principle of all waters being open to all EC fishermen within a 200-mile limit of EC shores (which is inevitably less in the Baltic and Mediterranean Seas). However, individual member states were permitted to retain an exclusion zone of up to 12 miles, within which fishing rights were restricted to their own fleets, and to vessels from other member states that hitherto had possessed traditional rights of access.

The central concept of conservation is the **total allowable catch** (TAC). Each year the Council of the European Union agrees on TACs for different species. The TAC is the total amount of that species permitted to be caught in EU waters, and each member state is allotted a quota within each TAC, often only after long and acrimonious bargaining. The operation of the TAC system through the surveillance and inspection policies and practices of the member states is monitored by a body of inspectors answerable to the **European Commission**. However, problems of verification and enforcement have persisted. Other conservation measures not only relate to the extent of fishing in certain areas, governed by the system of EC licences, but also regulate the size of fish that may be caught, and the type and size of mesh that may be used. Any member state may introduce further conservation measures within its own zone, as long as these do not discriminate against other vessels from the EU.

Other CFP provisions are modelled on the CAP. Guide prices for all categories of fish are set annually by the Council of the European Union. The EC provides compensation for catches that have to be withdrawn from the market, setting a withdrawal price of between 70% and 90% of the guide price. If both guide and withdrawal prices are higher than world prices, a system of refunds to exporters applies, along the lines of CAP **restitutions**, to maintain the income of the fishing industry. By contrast, when catches in the EU are insufficient to meet market demands, customs duties on imports can be suspended. By the early 1990s quota controls and limited stocks had fallen below demand, with the shortfall being made up by imports. The volume of cheaper imports deflated price levels, obliging the EU to introduce a system of minimum prices in 1993.

The European Commission has also set common marketing standards and principles on, for example, the size, weight, quality and packaging of fish. The **implementation** of these standards is the responsibility of the member states, but they are monitored regularly by the Commission. The CFP was also charged with providing some limited financial assistance to the industry to help with the modernization and restructuring of fishing fleets, but the funds available to it have been very modest, rather less than 1% of the EC **budget**. The basic problem faced by the CFP is that the objective of reducing overfishing and preserving fish stocks has tended to increase the relative capacity of the fishing fleet, and reductions in capacity have been strenuously resisted by member states. In 1991 the Council of Ministers introduced the first of a series of measures intended to address this problem, and in late 1992 it agreed to establish a **Financial Instrument for Fisheries Guidance** (FIFG) as part of the **structural funds**. The FIFG was replaced by the **European Fisheries Fund** (EFF) in January 2007. In 1996, following some controversy over the Commission's proposals to reduce the number of fishing vessels, and the British Government's objection to 'quota-hopping' (in which boats registered in one member state are bought by operators in other EU countries, which are thus able to gain part of the former member state's fishing quotas), quotas were set for 1997. These fixed catch reductions at 30% for species most at risk, and at 20% for other overfished species. Moreover, the Council in 1998 agreed a ban on fishing using drift nets, which would come into effect in January 2002. However, the issues of equal access, capacity and overfishing persisted and remained as politically sensitive as ever.

It was not until 1994 that agreement was reached between the EU fisheries ministers on a revision of the CFP, allowing Spain and Portugal to be integrated into the CFP by 1 January 1996. A compromise accord was reached on Spanish access to waters around Ireland and South-West Great Britain (the 'Irish Box'); this was strongly opposed by Irish and British fishermen.

In 1999 the Council adopted a new regulation on fisheries that outlined its objectives for the period from 2000 until 2006. It aimed to encourage fishermen to catch only what could be sold; to strengthen the industry organizations and make them more competitive; to protect employment; and to provide greater information for consumers on what they were buying. According to the Commission's 2001 **Green Paper**, much more needed to be done to relieve the depressed state of fisheries in the EU, and the Commission recommended urgent change to the CFP (which had to be revised by 2003). Some degree of reform was vital to tackle the problem of overfishing, the difficulties of policing 'blue Europe', and the impact of eastern **enlargement** and in particular the absorption of the Polish fishing fleet into EU waters.

In December 2002 the EU fisheries ministers met in **Brussels** to decide on the much-needed reform of the CFP. Agreement was reached at the end of a five-day consideration of the Commission's proposals on CFP reform. Ministers agreed on three major issues: the need to reform the CFP; the adoption of urgent recovery measures for some cod stocks that were in imminent danger of collapse; and the establishment of TACs and quotas for 2003, including substantial reductions for a number of threatened stocks. In general, the objectives of the CFP were reviewed to focus more on the sustainable exploitation of living aquatic resources—based on sound scientific advice and on the precautionary approach to fisheries management—on the one hand, and on sustainable aquaculture on the other.

According to the Commission, the decisions taken in December 2002 would make fisheries management more effective and better able to ensure the long-term viability of the fisheries sector through sustainable exploitation of resources. The Council accepted the necessity of a more long-term approach to fisheries management, involving the setting of multi-annual recovery plans for stocks outside safe biological limits and of multi-annual management plans for other stocks. It also endorsed a simpler system for limiting the fishing capacity of the EU fleet in order to reach a better match with available resources. To this end, it was to replace the former system of Multi-annual Guidance Programmes (MAGPs), generally regarded as ineffective, with a new system which was designed to give more responsibility to the member states to achieve a better balance between the fishing capacity of their fleets and the available resources.

The plans were not welcomed by many EU fishermen, for example in areas of the United Kingdom such as Scotland and Northern Ireland where widespread disenchantment was expressed about the future for the fishing communities in these regions. To compensate for the continuing decline of the EU fishing fleet, the EU has instigated a series of socio-economic measures. These include the provision of aid from member states to fishermen and vessel owners who have temporarily to stop their fishing activity. Aid is also being increased to support the retraining of fishermen to help them convert to professional activities outside the fisheries sector, while allowing them to continue fishing on a part-time basis.

The new measures entered into force on 1 January 2003. They replaced the basic rules governing the CFP since 1993 and substantially amended the Regulation on structural assistance in the fisheries sector through the FIFG. A new Regulation establishing an emergency fund to encourage the decommissioning of vessels (the so-called 'Scrapping Fund') was also adopted.

The problem of overfishing endured throughout 2003. In view of the high risk of collapse of a number of cod stocks and the difficulty of controlling compliance with low catch limits, scientists from the International Council for the Exploration for the Sea (ICES) and the Scientific, Technical, Economic Committee on Fisheries (STECF) recommended in 2003 a moratorium on the fisheries concerned. Aware of the potential economic and social impact of such measures on fishing communities, the Commission proposed, rather than a moratorium, substantially reduced fishing possibilities for a number of stocks (primarily cod) as well as improved measures to ensure their proper implementation. Accordingly, the TAC reductions were less severe than had been initially proposed. For example, the TACs for Celtic Sea cod stocks and stocks associated with recovery stocks in this area were reduced by 15% (instead of by 47% as initially proposed) for cod in the Celtic Sea, west of Ireland and the English Channel, by 15% (instead of 55.5%) for whiting and by 15% (instead of 33%) for sole. The Council's request that Commission proposals be presented for incorporation within existing recovery plans for stocks newly identified as being below safe biological limits also permitted less stringent measures in 2004. For example, the TAC for plaice in the North Sea was reduced by 17% instead of by 41% as initially proposed.

The Council also decided in December 2003 to retain and extend the scope of the interim measures restricting fishing effort adopted by the Council in December 2002 to protect certain cod stocks. These measures, which had been applied in the Skagerrak, the Kattegat, the North Sea and west of Scotland since 1 February 2003, would now also include the eastern Channel and the Irish Sea. The aim is to limit the number of days that vessels spend in the areas concerned fishing for endangered stocks, in order to prevent overshooting of quotas. Reinforced inspection and control measures have also been adopted in this context. These measures became applicable from 1 February 2004 and were to remain in force until the Council agreed alternative measures to replace them.

As a corollary to the CFP, the EC signed reciprocal agreements with other European and Atlantic states that permit some limited access to one another's zones and markets. Nevertheless, in early 1995 Spanish vessels fishing in the North Atlantic were the subject of an acrimonious dispute between Canada and Spain, and the EC played a significant role in subsequent negotiations. In 1996, following the publication of a report warning that herring stocks were in danger of being completely eradicated, the EU and Norway agreed an emergency measure to reduce by 50% catches in the North Sea and the waters around Denmark. Further afield, agreements have been signed with some African and Indian Ocean countries which allow EU vessels access to their waters in return for the provision of technical and financial aid.

In late December 2005 the Fisheries Council agreed its latest annual fishing TACs. With regard to cod, fishing possibilities were reduced by 15%, as proposed by the Commission. Conservation was very much at the heart of the Commission's thinking. The effects of these more modest reductions agreed by the Council were to be complemented by a further reduction in the number of days that fishermen could stay at sea, and this would also apply to the fleets for which cod is a by-catch but which are responsible for 60% of cod catches. It was hoped that these measures would enable a recovery of cod stocks.

The December 2005 deal also saw reductions in the fishing possibilities for other species. These reductions were as usual smaller than the Commission's proposals, but the general trend of recent times was again reinforced as the overall TACs were lower in 2006 than in 2005. Ministers agreed to further reductions in catches for herring and whiting and a 13% cut in haddock fishing.

More positively, ministers were able to agree to a 30% increase in North Sea prawn quotas, a 5% rise in Irish Sea monkfish and a 3% increase in the catch level for hake in most fishing grounds.

The cuts have rarely been received warmly by British fishing communities, which have been ready to dispute the accuracy of the scientific findings on fish stocks. They also vent their frustrations about whether other member states actually enforce the Council's decisions. This is a very significant challenge for the member state governments and their fishing industries, as failure to enforce fisheries measures works against the interests of fishermen because it leads to overfishing, depleted fish stocks, smaller catches and shrinking incomes.

Poland is the main fishing nation among the 10 EU member states that acceded in 2004. The Polish fishing fleet comprises approximately 1,280 vessels and their average age is some 26 years. This particular fishing fleet is involved with three main types of fishing: coastal fleet, cutter fleet and high-seas fleet. The small fishing vessels operate in the territorial waters and in the Vistula and Szczecin lagoons and are after cod, herring and flatfish. The cutter fleet operates in the Baltic Sea and to a lesser extent in the North-east Atlantic, and is fishing mainly for cod, herring and salmon. The Polish high-seas fleet traverses the North Atlantic in search of shrimp, Antarctic krill and poutassou.

The Council agreed in December 2007 to reduce cod quotas further, by between 9% and 18%, and to reduce the number of days that can be spent at sea by fishermen. The deal was a compromise and a smaller reduction in quotas than the Commission had wanted (25%). Ministers also agreed to make quota cuts for other fish, such as blue whiting, herring and plaice. The deal again may have satisfied the member states, but it pleased few others. Environmentalists were highly critical of the agreement, as were fishermen's associations. Around 200 environmental activists had used barriers and concrete blocks to seal off the entrance to the Council building to express their anger at overfishing in European waters.

The issue of the CFP and its quota system was one of the priority areas identified by **Nicolas Sarkozy** for the French presidency of the EU in the second half of 2008. The fishing quotas agreed in December 2007 were widely condemned by the French fishing industry, as cuts of 44% and 56% were imposed on French fishermen in terms of their herring and whiting catches, respectively. France, like all EU fishing states, had seen a reduction in the number of boats (to 5,345, representing a decline of 40% since 1992).

The issue of fishing has proved a particularly sensitive one for **Croatia** in its efforts to join the EU. There have been a number of spats between the Commission and the Croatian Government over the latter's attempt to protect a certain part of the Adriatic. The Polish Government has also expressed its concerns over the EU's cod fishing quotas, and there have been numerous stand-offs between Poland and the Commission, and Poland took the issue before the **European Court of First Instance**.

Confronted with growing opposition from both the fishing industry and the wider public, the Council opted to initiate measures in May 2009 towards radically overhauling the way in which the CFP operates. The Commission published a Green Paper that sought views on how to reform the CFP, and it provided the findings in its April 2010 synthesis report. The moves towards a new approach to fishing were endorsed by all 27 member states and were greeted enthusiastically by the industry in general. In May 2011 the Commissioner responsible for Maritime Affairs and Fisheries, **Maria Damanaki**, of Greece, stated that the Commission was committed to delivering a thorough reorganization of the way the CFP was run. The Commission published its draft proposals for the reform of the CFP in July 2011. The proposals provided for returning fish stocks to sustainable levels by 2015, using an ecosystem approach and one that was based on hard scientific advice. The proposals also aimed to provide consumers with a stable, secure and healthy food supply while ending the dependence on subsidies and creating new employment opportunities in coastal areas; to eliminate 'discards' (unwanted fish or other marine organisms that are dumped overboard, having been caught unintentionally); and to provide for the establishment of clear targets and timetables to prevent overfishing. The Commission intended the new framework for fisheries policy to enter into force by 1 January 2013, following the approval of the reform package by the European Parliament and the Council. Debates on the package of proposals are ongoing within both institutions. In December 2011 the Commission also proposed a new fund—the European Maritime and Fisheries Fund (EMFF) for the period 2014–20. This new fund, which would replace the EFF, was primarily designed to deliver the ambitious goals of the proposed CFP reforms, but it was also aimed at ensuring that fishermen accepted the need for sustainable fishing and providing fishing communities with greater opportunities to diversify into other economic areas and secure more jobs. The EMFF is currently under consideration by the Council.

The **COMMON FOREIGN AND SECURITY POLICY** (CFSP) was one of the three **pillars** that form the European Union (EU) created by the **Treaty on European Union** (TEU). The **intergovernmental conference** of 1990 that prepared drafts on political union for the **Maastricht summit** had as one of its briefs the task of considering collective action by the member states in the post-**Cold War** era. In part, this came from a desire that the European Communities (EC) should develop an international role more commensurate with their economic standing. It was felt that **European political co-operation** (EPC) was no longer adequate, a view underlined by the different national positions in relation to the Gulf War in 1991. The CFSP became the successor to EPC. Not being part of the EC, the CFSP was not subject to normal EC **decision-making** procedures: direction was given by the **European Council**, not the **European Commission**. With the Treaty of Amsterdam, the Secretary-General of the Council acted also as the **High Representative for the Common Foreign and Security Policy**, and in this capacity assisted the presidency of the EU and was responsible for policy planning and monitoring international developments. The actions of the CFSP were also not subject to scrutiny by the **Court of Justice**. With the entry into force of the **Treaty of Lisbon**, some aspects of the CFSP changed. However, despite abandonment of the EU's pillar structure, the CFSP remains essentially intergovernmental in character.

The objectives of the CFSP are to safeguard the common values, interests and security of the EU, to preserve peace and strengthen international security, and to promote international co-operation, democracy, the rule of law and respect for **human rights**. While the European Council is free to define how the CFSP is to be implemented, the TEU defines the member states' duty, first to pursue a practice of 'systematic co-operation' through information, consultation and policy co-ordination, and second to adopt 'common positions' and 'joint action' when dealing with CFSP matters. The CFSP also includes 'the eventual framing of a common defence policy, which might in time lead to a common defence'. Originally, it was accepted that, until such a position could be reached, the **Western European Union** (WEU) would act for the EU where defence implications arose, and those EU states not members of the WEU were invited to join the organization, at least as observers. Since then, the EU itself has taken a more prominent role in military matters, as seen in the development of a **European security and defence policy** (ESDP) and the creation of a **European rapid reaction force**. This has not been without its problems, given concerns over the impact that such developments might have on the role of the **North Atlantic Treaty Organization** (NATO) and consequently on the effectiveness of that body. Moreover, conflicts in the former **Yugoslavia** illustrated the extreme difficulty of achieving a co-ordinated policy among the member states, even when there was a predisposition to work together.

That there were difficulties in implementing a CFSP was recognized in the **Treaty of Amsterdam**, which encouraged the adoption of **common strategies**, facilitated decision-making through the introduction of **constructive abstention** and encouraged closer co-operation with the WEU. Thereafter, the **Treaty of Nice** downplayed relations with the WEU and removed the requirement for all the member states to co-operate on CFSP matters, through the introduction of a modified definition of **enhanced co-operation**. This was followed in 2003 by the adoption of a **European security strategy**. Various reforms were subsequently agreed as part of the **Treaty establishing a Constitution for Europe**. These included the creation of a **Union Minister for Foreign Affairs** and a **President of the European Council**, the establishment of a **European External Action Service**, greater use of **qualified majority voting** and permanent structured co-operation in defence matters. The non-**ratification** of the Treaty establishing a Constitution for Europe threatened these, although most were subsequently carried forward into the **Treaty of Lisbon**. Moreover, work began as early as 2005 on the creation of a **European External Action Service**.

This, alongside the development of the ESDP, emphasizes the commitment that exists among the member states to ensure that the CFSP continues to develop. Despite differences over, for example, Iraq in 2003–06, and concerns that **enlargement** in 2004 would lead to a more Atlanticist outlook within the EU and a greater preference for developing security through NATO, the CFSP has widespread support. It has also enjoyed a number of relative successes in recent years, notably in promoting stability in the **Western Balkans**. This is not to say that its future is without organizational and procedural challenges.

COMMON MARKET is a popular alternative name for the **European Economic Community** and, later, for the European Communities (EC) and the European Union (EU). It summarizes the primary economic objectives of the **Treaty of Rome**, a goal that originally was to be achieved by 1970. While in the 1960s it was a relatively neutral term, it later acquired some political connotations, often being used in preference to the term European Communities by those who reject any notion of political integration, insisting that the common market should be the only ambition of the EC.

The **COMMON SECURITY AND DEFENCE POLICY** (CSDP), which was established as the European Security and Defence Policy (ESDP), is a relatively recent development, emerging from the **common foreign and security policy** (CFSP) and European Union (EU) efforts to assume a greater role in military and defence matters since the late 1990s. It thus represents progress towards establishing a **common defence policy** and ultimately a **common defence** for the EU. As part of the ESDP, the EU assumed greater responsibility for the so-called **Petersberg tasks**—humanitarian and rescue operations, peace-keeping activities and combat-force tasks in crisis management, including peace-making—and established a **European rapid reaction force** of 60,000 persons, as well as **battlegroups**, to carry out the full range of them at short notice. In addition, new institutional structures have been put in place, notably the **European Union Military Committee** and the European Union Military Staff. These provide military expertise and support to the ESDP, including the conduct of EU-led military crisis management operations. Closer links have also been developed with the **North Atlantic Treaty Organization** (NATO), but the conflict in Iraq in early 2003 clearly laid bare the differences and disagreements among the members of both the EU and NATO on security issues. In an attempt to give greater strategic direction to the ESDP, the **High Representative for the Common Foreign and Security Policy**, **Javier Solana**, subsequently devised a **European security strategy** for the EU. This was formally adopted by the **European Council** in December 2003. Further initiatives designed to promote the development of the ESDP were agreed as part of the **Treaty establishing a Constitution for Europe** and subsequently included in the **Treaty of Lisbon**. These include **permanent structured co-operation**, further development of the **European**

Defence Agency, and the introduction of a mutual assistance clause in the event of a member state being the victim of armed aggression on its territory. The Treaty of Lisbon also renamed the ESDP as the Common Security and Defence Policy (CSDP).

COMMON STRATEGIES are an instrument for implementing the **common foreign and security policy** (CFSP), which were introduced by the 1997 **Treaty of Amsterdam**. Article 21 of the **Treaty on European Union** sets down the principles and general guidelines for the CFSP. These are decided by the **European Council**. The same body also determines whether to introduce common strategies in areas where the member states share important interests in common. A common strategy defines aims, objectives and timetables involved and, more importantly, outlines the means to be made available by the European Union and the member states in order to realize them. Common strategies are then implemented by the Council, through the adoption of joint actions and common positions and the recommendation of common strategies to the European Council.

The **COMMONWEALTH OF INDEPENDENT STATES** (CIS) is a loose association of most of the former constituent republics of the **USSR**. It was established in December 1991 and in September 1993 agreed a framework that would serve as the basis of an economic union. The CIS was the focus of much attention from the European Union in terms of political co-operation and economic aid and agreements.

COMMUNICATIONS POLICY: See **European Communications Policy**

COMMUNISTS AND ALLIES is the title of one of the original transnational **party groups** in the **European Parliament** (EP). It consisted of members of national Communist parties and independents elected on a Communist list, and was formed in 1973. It was always dominated by the French and Italian parties but, because these two major national components were invariably deeply divided over both domestic political strategies and those at a European level, the group was one of the least cohesive in the EP. After the 1989 **direct elections** the group formally divided into two separate factions, the Group for the European Unitarian Left and **Left Unity** (LU). While the former still exists as the **Confederal Group of the European United Left/ Nordic Green Left**, having 35 **Members of the European Parliament** (MEPs) after the 2009 EP elections, LU has disbanded.

COMMUNITARIZATION is a term used to describe the transfer of competences to the European Communities **pillar** of the European Union.

COMMUNITY ASSISTANCE FOR RECONSTRUCTION, DEVEL-OPMENT AND STABILIZATION: See **CARDS**

COMMUNITY METHOD was a term often used to describe policy-making procedures undertaken through the institutions of the European Communities, as opposed to those carried out through intergovernmental structures and mechanisms.

The **COMMUNITY PATENT CONVENTION** (CPC) is an initiative aimed at overcoming some of the problems experienced by European companies in registering **patents** and **trademarks**. A general European Patent Convention was signed in 1973. It was designed to eliminate, for companies, the costly procedure of applying for patent protection separately in each country, through the introduction of a single application for European patent protection. A European Patent Office was set up in Munich, Germany. The original Convention was not a European Communities (EC) instrument, since the member states could not agree on a common policy, and some did not join the scheme. The major problem was that, while it introduced a common registration procedure, where patent infringements occurred, the plaintiff had to pursue separate litigation in each country where the infringements were alleged to have taken place. In 1989 the **European Commission** proposed a new Community Patent Regulation that sought to remedy this problem by formulating a single EC patent and grievances procedure that complied with the requirements of the **internal market**. Although the regulation never came into force, efforts to establish a European Union (EU) Patent continued, albeit falteringly. The languages in which applications would be made became a major obstacle to agreement. Eventually, in 2011 agreement was reached by 25 EU member states to use **enhanced co-operation** to establish an EU Patent applicable among them. Italy and Spain objected to the exclusive use of English, French and German for applications and opposed the move.

The **COMMUNITY PLANT VARIETY OFFICE**, established in 1995 and located in Angers, **France**, is a decentralized European Union (EU) agency which implements and applies an EU scheme to allow intellectual property rights to be granted for plant varieties. These rights are valid throughout the EU.

COMMUNITY PREFERENCE is a term that refers to the situation within the **common agricultural policy** when the price of domestic agricultural products falls below that of imported products.

COMMUNITY SUPPORT FRAMEWORKS: See **Structural Funds**

The **COMPANY LAW STATUTE** has long been a contentious issue among European Union (EU) member states. The original **European Commission** proposal dates back to 1975 and was an attempt to facilitate the establishment of new multinational companies across the European Communities (EC). The proposal encountered immediate opposition, largely as a result of its focus on workers' rights, and was promptly dropped. A second proposal in 1989, which suggested that companies might choose to adopt a company statute in return for certain tax incentives, proved equally contentious. All issues relating to the rights and interests of the labour force can only be decided upon by unanimity in the **Council of the European Union**. These proposals were particularly unacceptable to the German Government, which insisted that a European company law statute must contain a requirement for workers' representatives to sit on supervisory boards and to be consulted on all aspects of workforce-related decision-making, in keeping with the German national model.

However, pressure for a European company law statute intensified following the European Council's Nice declaration in favour of harmonizing company law across the EU. Nevertheless, the Council still needed to address concerns among the member states and some doubts expressed by the **European Parliament**. The latter was anxious to ensure that **legislation** in the area of workers' rights should be subject to the **co-decision procedure** and continued to press the case for greater protection of workers' rights within any European company statute.

Finally, however, after some 30 years of debate, on 8 October 2001 the Council Regulation (EC) No. 2157/2001 on the Statute for a European Company (or Societas Europaea, SE) was adopted. Member states had to adopt the laws, **regulations** and administrative provisions necessary to comply with the Directive by 8 October 2004 (the date on which the European Company Statute, or ECS, Regulation, which is directly applicable in the member states, came into force), or ensure by then that management and labour introduced the required provisions by agreement.

The ECS Regulation gives companies the option of forming a European Company (SE), which can operate on a Europe-wide basis and be governed by Community law directly applicable in all member states (rather than national law). The Directive lays down the employee involvement provisions to apply to SEs, providing for negotiations between management and employees' representatives in each SE on the arrangements to apply, with a set of back-up statutory 'standard rules' where no agreement is reached. Involvement constitutes the information and consultation of employees and, in some cases, board-level participation. The adoption of the ECS was without doubt a highly significant development in both EU company law and social policy.

COMPETENCE is a term that describes the authority of the European Communities to undertake specific activities. The authority is usually based upon an **Article** of one of the **Founding Treaties**.

COMPETITION POLICY is crucial to the creation of a successful **internal market**. It would have been counter-productive to dismantle trade barriers between the member states if private industry had been free and able to engage in cartel-like restrictions on competition and undermine the advantages of opening up the markets in the first place. Moreover, from an economic viewpoint, the force of competition is to be welcomed as it unleashes dynamic effects that can be transformed into greater efficiencies, innovation and, ultimately, lower prices for the consumer. In short, competition policy describes the objective of striking a balance between the imposition, by **legislation**, of necessary restrictions upon unbridled economic competition, and the elimination of harmful restrictive practices that prevent a coherent integration of markets. As such, it formed an essential part of both the **Treaty of Paris** and the **Treaty of Rome**. The original competition rules were contained in Articles 85–94, but these were renumbered under the **Treaty of Amsterdam** in 1999 to run from Article 81 to Article 90. The **Treaty of Lisbon** renumbered the articles again, and they now run from 101 to 110 of the **Treaty on the Functioning of the European Union**.

The European Union (EU) competition rules extend over five substantial policy areas. The first of these addresses the endemic cartels and restrictive practices (such as price-fixing and market-sharing agreements). Cartel policy has emerged as the core activity in terms of staff, time and resources and is the most developed aspect of policy. The malignant threat posed by cartels to both the business environment and the consumer was recognized under Article 101, which prohibits all agreements 'which may affect trade between member states and which have as their object, the prevention, restriction or distortion of competition within the common market'. Framed in very general terms, it is designed to catch and prohibit (paragraph 2) all agreements that restrict the spirit of free competition. Some types of anti-competitive agreement are entitled to exemptions if they improve the production or distribution of goods, promote technical and economic progress or ensure that consumers reap considerable benefits. The second policy area centres on merger control and the Commission's power to prohibit mergers. **Merger policy** (originally omitted in the Treaty of Rome) was added as a belated weapon to the Commission's arsenal in 1990 after the member states bowed to the wishes of the Commission and demands from the business community for a level playing field and a single point of entry for assessing EU mergers. In effect, this regulation bestowed a Community dimension on the Commission's responsibility for all mergers that exceeded specified thresholds. The Commission's handling of mergers has drawn almost universal praise from industry as the European competition regulator has been able to process merger notifications speedily.

The third and fourth key aspects of EU competition policy focus, respectively, on monopolies that are abusing their dominant position in the market place (under Article 102) and on efforts to inject greater competition into the public utility sectors such as telecommunications and energy (under Article 106).

All these four areas bring the Commission into direct dealings with the business world, but uniquely the fifth area, which centres on the granting of state subsidies (under Articles 8108–9110), involves direct contact with member state governments and has proven the most contentious aspect of the EU competition brief. State aid (see **subsidies**) has featured as an aspect of government–industry relations to varying degrees across Western Europe since 1945. It has often been justified as an essential aspect of government-driven industrial policy and has been designed to secure employment, particularly in peripheral and economically depressed regions, to respond to issues of national prestige (e.g. Air France and Olympic Airways), or to create European champions (e.g. Bull, to compete directly with US and other international companies).

The **European Commission** (and particularly the **Directorate-General**— DG—for Competition) is the body entrusted with the task of ensuring that the member states and companies conform to the provisions of the treaty. In this policy field the Commission operates as an autonomous and quasi-judicial policy-making institution, largely free from interference from either the **Council of Ministers** or the **European Parliamen**t in day-to-day decision-making. The member states simply delegated responsibility for all competition issues to the Commission, and competition policy became one of the few exclusive competences (see **Treaty of Lisbon**) of European governance.

The Commission's decisions on competition policy are subject to review only by the European courts. While the Commission's powers were first established in 1962 (under Regulation 17), before the mid-1980s, competition policy was a relatively low priority. Since then, as a result of a shift in economic philosophy (towards neo-liberalism), the accumulation of case law and the involvement of a succession of dynamic and forceful personalities (including Peter Sutherland, **Leon Brittan**, Karel van Miert, **Mario Monti**, **Neelie Kroes**, **Joaquín Almunia** and, currently, **Alexander Italianer**), there has been enormous growth in the role and prominence of competition policy. This policy area represents one of the best examples of supranational regulation. The competition regime in relation to Articles 101 and 102 was 'modernized' through the adoption of Regulation 1/2003, which replaced the original procedural 'bible' encapsulated by Regulation 17.

The Commission has the authority to act, either on its own initiative, or upon receipt of complaints from member states, companies or individuals, without reference to the **Council of the European Union**, concerning possible infringements of EC rules. Its powers to investigate alleged breaches of competition policy are very wide. In the first stage of investigation, its inspectors are entitled to visit companies without prior warning, to see any documents they wish, and to retain photographic evidence. The national authorities are contacted in advance and assist in such 'dawn raids'. The Commission is also allowed, under Regulation 1/2003, to conduct home searches. The second stage of the process is a series of hearings with the company concerned and other competitors. On the basis of the evidence and depositions, the Commission then issues its verdict. If it finds against the company, it has the right to demand a change of policy, impose a fine or combine both courses of action. The level of fines can be substantial in order to deter anti-competitive practices. In the last 10 years or so there has been a noticeable trend to impose very large fines. This reflects the Commission's growing determination to tackle anti-competitive activities. Cartels have become the principal focus of anti-trust regulators worldwide, and the 17 highest fines imposed on cartels have all occurred since late 2001. For example, in November 2001 a group of vitamins producers, including European firms Roche and BAST, were fined a then record €855m. for operating an illegal price cartel between 1990 and 1998. The highest ever fine in the history of the Commission's war against cartel arrangements (under Article 101) was levied on a group of suppliers of car glass (for use in windscreens and wing mirrors) in November 2008. The overall fine exceeded €1,300m. The Commission imposed its highest fine under Article 102 (€1,000m.) in May 2009, on Intel for abusing its dominant position in the computer market. Companies that have been found guilty by the Commission of infringing the EU competition rules have the right of appeal to the **Court of First Instance** and then to the **Court of Justice**. The decision of the latter is final, in appeals against either the verdict or the size of the financial penalty. The Commission usually investigates several hundred cases of alleged infringements each year. Through the multitude of appeals against Commission decisions that have come before them, the European Courts have built up a substantial body of case-law.

In short, competition policy rules apply to both private and publicly owned companies, and to nationalized industries. Companies that are negotiating or contemplating an agreement that may not satisfy the treaty provisions are obliged to inform the European Commission of their intentions. In addition, companies have the right to apply to the Commission for either a 'negative clearance', which recognizes that there is no threat to competition policy, or an 'exemption', which may be granted if the company or companies can demonstrate that, competition rules notwithstanding, a restrictive agreement should nevertheless be permitted on the grounds that it will provide substantial public benefits. With the **internal market** programme, which did not specifically deal with competition policy, the Commission also devoted considerably more attention to **public procurement**, and between 1990 and 1992 a series of **directives** on **public utilities** demanded that public contracts be put out to open tendering.

The European Commission may use its discretion to grant exemptions on the grounds mentioned above, or where the effect on free competition would be minimal. In particular, it has sought to balance a strict application of competition policy with its concern for the viability of small companies. Because it has wished to encourage co-operation between small companies, the Commission has outlined several categories of agreement that it may be prepared to exempt from a general ban: small-scale agreements in cases where turnover is less than €200m. and the market share less than 5%; agreements in various areas such as research and development and the exchange of information; and those that are essentially franchising or sub-contractual. The Commission is also prepared to be flexible where companies are confronted with adverse economic conditions and a sustained decline in demand. In such circumstances, companies may be permitted to collaborate in co-ordinating an orderly reduction in the resulting over-capacity.

The European Commission also monitors government activity on a regular basis. This has been a more difficult task, because of the tendency of governments to shield their own companies from competition through a variety of techniques and mechanisms, which may or may not amount to state aid. The Commission is, however, willing to accept exceptions to the general ban on state subsidies that might distort competition. Member states wishing to provide aid to companies are expected to inform the Commission of their intentions. If the Commission rejects the plan, and if the latter goes ahead, it has the authority to demand the repayment of unauthorized subsidies, and even to impose fines on recalcitrant member states. Categories of state aid that have been exempted from the general rules include grants to areas afflicted by a natural disaster and aid to economically depressed regions that is designed to assist the development of new forms of economic activity. The Commission has also issued guidelines governing state aid to industries severely affected by recession, but has insisted that such aid must have a specific purpose and fixed duration, and be regarded as totally exceptional. In the past, shipbuilding, steel, synthetic fibres and textiles have benefited from these guidelines. Disputes between the EC and the member states about state aid may, in the last resort, be resolved by the Court of Justice. Competition policy does not necessarily apply to goods imported into the EU, where several bilateral or international agreements exist, and where some products have been affected by voluntary export restraints.

The workload of the DG for Competition has been immense. Concerns have been expressed about inadequate staffing, lengthy time delays in investigating cases under Articles 101 and 102, opaque and unpredictable decision-making and a tendency for some cases to be politicized (especially with regard to merger control). In response, the DG for Competition has been trying to address some of these issues. Most importantly, its plans for 'modernization' were published in 1999 and led to the Council's adoption of Regulation 1/2003, which brought in a series of internal measures. It decentralized antitrust enforcement by allowing the national competition authorities to deal with cases under EC competition law; it established the International Competition Network to foster greater interaction and the construction of a competition culture among all 27 EU national competition authorities and the Commission; it allowed for tougher powers of inquiry for the DG for Competition (e.g. home raids); and it abolished the notification system. The Commission hoped that these reforms would enable it to concentrate its limited resources on the more problematic cases. Some concerns were expressed, principally among lawyers, as to whether or not this process of decentralization would operate efficiently, but the Council approved the proposal (Council Regulation No. 1/2003), and it entered into force in May 2004. Many observers believed that this regulation would indeed prove a very effective move on the part of the Commission, as it would enhance its role and allow it to determine which cases it intended to investigate and which to pass to the member state competition authorities.

1 May 2004 was therefore a momentous date in the history of EC competition policy, as it marked the entry into force of a revised merger control regulation (Regulation 139/2004) and the arrival of the 10 **candidate countries**. All the candidate countries were required to have adopted national competition laws that reflected the principles of the *acquis communautaire* before accession negotiations could be concluded successfully. The EC merger policy was revamped both to provide greater transparency and efficiency and to respond to growing criticism of administrative procedures and case analysis, and was introduced with a number of other simultaneous internal Commission reforms. Together, both regulations enhance the 'federal' characteristics of competition governance. The process of reform continues, and the Commission is proposing to reform Article 102; it is also expected to accelerate its campaign against monopolistic utilities and the politicians who defend such activities. Its principal target will be those companies that control both the supply and distribution of energy. The DG for Competition suggested in late 2005 that firms and individuals who have been the victims of deliberate anti-competitive practices should be able to seek financial damages through the courts.

In recent years the European Commission has devoted considerable effort to creating an International Competition Network (ICN). This network was established in October 2001 as, essentially, an informal forum in which competition authorities from around the world exchange views and discuss the issue and function of competition policy and its enforcement. It is an almost purely virtual network (although it also holds regular seminars), but it is slowly emerging as a credible forum that is seeking to encourage information exchange and spread best practices. Progress has been more pronounced in respect of merger investigations than in cartel cases.

Competition policy in the EU has undergone a huge degree of modernization over the last decade. The introduction and development of a 'leniency programme' has been judged a huge success in detecting cartels. For the immediate future it will be interesting to observe how the credit crunch and economic recession will affect the goals of competition policy and how far member state governments will insist on taking account of other non-competition criteria (especially state aid). It will also be interesting to consider whether the EU should move towards the introduction of criminal sanctions for those engaging in anti-competitive activities, as is the case in the **USA**. This would introduce the possibility of prison sentences being imposed on individuals (as in **Ireland** and the **United Kingdom**). Although any such step would represent arguably the greatest deterrent, it would also prove a highly sensitive issue for some member state governments.

COMPETITIVENESS was the focus of the **European Commission's White Paper** on Growth, Competitiveness and Employment. This paper, dating from 1994, presented guidelines for pursuing a policy of global competitiveness. The policy comprised four objectives: provision for assistance to those European firms seeking to adapt to the new globalized economy; the ability for firms to exploit the competitive advantages associated with the rapid move to a knowledge-based economy; the ability to foster and promote sustainable industrial development; and the need to reduce the time differential between the pace of change in supply and the corresponding adjustments in demand. The White Paper's recommendations informed negotiations on the new title on employment introduced by the 1997 **Treaty of Amsterdam**. Competitiveness has emerged as a highly salient theme in both the Commission and the **Council**. Its significance is illustrated in the **Lisbon agenda** and in a new heading of priorities in the annual **budget**. Indeed, €13,500m. was allocated to competitiveness initiatives under the 2011 budget.

COMPULSORY EXPENDITURE is related to the **budgetary decision-making procedure** of the European Union (EU). Prior to the **Treaty of Lisbon**, during the negotiations surrounding the annual budgetary process, a distinction was made between compulsory and **non-compulsory expenditure**. This mattered because the distinction determined the ability of the **European Parliament** (EP) to influence outcomes. The EP had the last word in relation to non-compulsory expenditure, while the **Council of the European Union** had the last word in relation to compulsory expenditure. The distinction between the two types of expenditure led to ongoing tension between the Council and the EP. According to the old Article 272 (prior to the Treaty of Lisbon amendments), compulsory expenditure referred to spending on those policies arising directly out of the **founding treaties** and their amendments. The major item of cost has traditionally been the **common agricultural policy** (CAP). In reviewing the annual draft budget submitted to it by the Council of the European Union, the EP had been allowed to modify only the proposals on non-compulsory expenditure. It should be noted that, in a major shift of policy, the **Treaty of Lisbon** introduced significant changes regarding the financial and budgetary procedures of the EU. It shortened the annual budgetary policy-making procedure, confirmed existing practices of working within the multi-annual financial framework (MFF) and abolished the distinction between compulsory and non-compulsory expenditure, and provided for practically full parity between the EP and the Council over EU expenditure items. This enabled, for example, the EP to be involved fully in discussions and decisions over the running of the CAP.

The **CONCILIATION COMMITTEE** is composed of 27 members of the **Council of the European Union**, or their representatives, and an equal number of representatives of the **European Parliament** (EP). The rules are laid down in Article 294 of the **Treaty on the Functioning of the European Union**. It meets as part of the **co-decision procedure** when the EP fails to adopt the common position of the Council. The **European Commission** participates in the Committee's proceedings, initiating proposals to overcome any impasse between the Council and the EP's representatives. Indeed, the most meaningful negotiations occur in the so-called trialogue between all three institutions. The aim of the Conciliation Committee is to approve a joint text that is acceptable to all sides and may subsequently be adopted by the Council and by a plenary session of the EP.

CONDITIONALITY is widely used in the context of European Union (EU) external relations and **enlargement**, with the EU making closer ties conditional on non-member states meeting certain political if not economic conditions. The conditionality underpinning enlargement is based on **applicant countries** meeting the so-called **Copenhagen criteria** adopted in 1993. Once a country is a member of the EU, conditionality is still relevant. Since the **Treaty of Amsterdam**, member states that do not respect principles of liberty, democracy, respect for **human rights** and fundamental freedoms and the rule of law may have certain of their rights under the **European treaties** suspended.

CONECCS: See **Interest Groups**; **Lobbying**

The **CONFEDERAL GROUP OF THE EUROPEAN UNITED LEFT/ NORDIC GREEN LEFT** (GUE/NGL) **party groups** in the **European Parliament** (EP). Prior to the 1994 elections it was known as the Group for the European Unitarian Left (GUE) and was one of the two Communist groups that emerged in 1989 following a division of the original **Communists and Allies** group. Originally dominated by the Italian Communists, GUE had a more Eurocommunist profile than the former French-dominated **Left Unity** group. The group changed its name again in early 1995 when it was joined by **Members of the European Parliament** (MEPs) from Denmark, Finland and Sweden. The two largest national delegations represented within the GUE/ NGL group in the 2009–14 Parliament came from Germany and the Czech Republic. The fortunes of the group, which is still very much opposed to neo-liberalism, have remained rather stagnant in recent years. At the 2004 EP elections the GUE/NGL group secured 41 members (as opposed to the 44 members that sat in Parliament in 2002). At the 2009 EP elections this group returned 35 MEPs from 13 member states and 17 political parties. Two of its members come from the United Kingdom and were drawn from Sinn Fein (in Northern Ireland) and Plaid Cymru (in Wales). The parliamentary group supports the construction of a new vision of European co-operation and is particularly keen to tackle the **democratic deficit** and promote ecology. The group also campaigns for better job and educational opportunities and places considerable emphasis on social solidarity, securing peace and pursuing sustainable economic development.

CONFERENCE ON SECURITY AND CO-OPERATION IN EUROPE (CSCE): See **Organization for Security and Co-operation in Europe**

CONFERENCES OF THE PARLIAMENTS: See **Assizes**

CONGRESS OF EUROPE was the name of the first post-war European gathering, held in The Hague in May 1948. It was organized by the **International Committee of the Movements for European Unity** and was attended by several hundred delegates from 16 countries, as well as by observers from the **USA** and Canada. Most political groupings, except those at the extremes, were represented, and many leading political figures attended. The major absentee was a strong delegation from the British Labour Party, in power at the time in the United Kingdom, which had dismissed the Congress as a body of 'unrepresentative interests'. The Congress sought the establishment of a European assembly, a charter of **human rights** and a European court. It demanded that the European states 'transfer and merge some portion of their sovereign rights so as to secure common political and economic action for the integration and proper development of their common resources'. Few practical measures were adopted, but it did agree to the formation of a **European Movement**. The latter, responding to a request from **Paul–Henri Spaak**, the Prime Minister of Belgium, produced a memorandum that contained the first draft for what would become the **Council of Europe**.

CONSENT PROCEDURE: See **Assent Procedure**

CONSTITUTION: The European Union (EU) has no formal constitution, although the **European treaties** are regarded as providing the constitutional framework of the EU, and the **Court of Justice** has referred to the **Treaty of Rome** as being the 'Constitutional Charter' of the European Communities. However, the issue of whether the EU should have a constitution was placed on the agenda of the **European Convention** launched in February 2002. This produced a **draft Treaty establishing a Constitution for Europe** which subsequently formed the focus of negotiations in an **intergovernmental conference** convened in October 2003. This produced the **Treaty establishing a Constitution for Europe**. Although this was formally abandoned as a text, much of its content found its way into the **Treaty of Lisbon**, leading to claims that this was the 'EU Constitution' in all but name.

CONSTITUTIONAL TREATY is the term often used to describe the outcome of the **intergovernmental conference** launched in October 2003. (See: **Treaty establishing a Constitution for Europe**.)

CONSTITUTIVE TREATIES: See **Founding Treaties**

CONSTRUCTIVE ABSTENTION is employed during consideration of matters of **common foreign and security policy** and allows decisions requiring unanimity within the **Council of the European Union** to be taken without the express support of all member states. Abstentions do not count as votes in opposition to a proposal.

The **CONSULTATION PROCEDURE** is the oldest and simplest of all decision-making procedures in the European Communities: the **Council of the European Union** has only to consult the **European Parliament** when adopting **legislation** proposed by the **European Commission**. Although the consultation procedure is still used for legislation adopted as part of the **common agricultural policy**, for example, most decisions within the European Union are now adopted under the **co-decision procedure**. (See also **Co-operation procedure**; **Assent procedure**.)

The **CONSULTATIVE COMMITTEE OF THE EUROPEAN COAL AND STEEL COMMUNITY** was established in 1951 as a part of the now defunct **European Coal and Steel Community** (ECSC). It was charged with advising the High Authority, the executive of the ECSC, on all aspects of the operation of the ECSC and of the national **coal** and **steel** industries. The Committee assumed a similar role in relation to the **European Commission** following the merger of the executives of the European Communities in 1967. Composed of representatives of producers, employees and consumers, it had a purely advisory and consultative role, with no decision-making authority.

The **CONSULTATIVE COUNCIL OF SOCIAL AND REGIONAL AUTHORITIES** was an advisory body attached to the **European Commission**, and was consulted on issues of regional development. Its role was taken over by the **Committee of the Regions**.

The **CONSUMER COMMITTEE**: See **European Consumer Consultative Group**

CONSUMER CONSULTATIVE COUNCIL: See **European Consumer Consultative Group**

CONSUMER POLICY was not mentioned in the **Treaty of Rome**. Although consumer interests and the **European Parliament** pressed for a consumer policy for several years, action was not taken until the Paris summit of the heads of government in 1972. Agreement was reached on the establishment within the **European Commission** of a section, later upgraded to a **Directorate-General** (DG), DG-XI, for consumer and environmental protection, a Consumer Consultative Committee (later the Consumer Consultative Council, or CCC, then the **Consumer Committee**, and now known as the **European Consumer Consultative Group**, or ECCG) and a Consumer Policy Service (which later became DG-XXIV, for consumer policy and health protection). In April 1975 the Council of Ministers (see **Council of the European Union**) launched a consumer information and protection programme which established five fundamental consumer rights: safeguards against risks to **health and safety;** economic justice; redress for damages; consultation; and information and education. These rights were to be the basis of specific measures of consumer protection. Although consumer policy was strengthened in 1983, when the national ministers responsible for consumer affairs began to meet regularly within the Council of Ministers, the bulk of consumer protection **legislation** was not adopted until after the launch of the Third Consumer Programme of 1986. The action was part of the effort to prepare for the **internal market**, and the **Single European Act** incorporated consumer policy within the treaty framework. A firm legal basis for consumer policy was created via the **Treaty on European Union**.

More recently, the Commission adopted a Consumer Policy Strategy (2007–13) in March 2007. The strategy was the product of a prolonged consultation exercise between the Commission and numerous consumer organizations (including the European Consumers' Organization) from 2004 to 2006. In terms of priorities, the Commission aimed to increase consumer confidence in the internal market (by establishing a uniform regulatory environment); to strengthen the individual consumer's position and rights in the marketplace; and to seek to ensure that consumers' concerns were incorporated into all European Union policies. The Consumer Policy Strategy was to be succeeded by a new European Consumer Agenda (drawn up and agreed in 2012), which would build directly on the former. Essentially, the agenda aimed to maximize consumer participation and trust in the marketplace. It contained four main objectives: reinforcing consumer safety; enhancing knowledge; stepping up enforcement and securing redress; and aligning consumers.

CONTINENTAL CAN is the name of a large US multinational company manufacturing metal containers that had achieved a dominant position (see **dominant firm abuse**) in the West German market through its acquisition of a domestic competitor. When this was followed by the further acquisition of a major Dutch manufacturer, in 1972 the **European Commission** took the company to the **Court of Justice** under the **competition policy** rules relating to abuse of dominant position. Although the following year the Court ruled against the Commission's argument that Continental Can had created and abused a dominant position, the verdict was significant because it recognized that the Commission had the ability to examine mergers of companies from different member states.

CONVENTION ON THE FUTURE OF EUROPE: See **European Convention**

CONVERGENCE is a term used to describe the objective of encouraging the economies of the member states to develop in the same way, especially with regard to inflation, deficits and interest rates. It emerged during the arguments in the 1980s for an **internal market**, and later was applied to the declared objective of **economic and monetary union** by 1999. In a wider context, it has also been used to explain why a number of other policy areas, such as **competition policy**, have been aligned at both the national and European Union levels.

CONVERGENCE CRITERIA for progression to stage three of **economic and monetary union** (EMU) were established by the **Treaty on European Union**. The four criteria were: an avoidance of excessive government deficits (i.e. an annual deficit of no more than 3% of gross domestic product—GDP, and no more than 60% of GDP for stock of government debt); a rate of inflation no more than 1.5 percentage points above the average of that of the three best-performing member states; exchange rate stability within the **European Monetary System** over the two previous years, without devaluation; and long-term interest rates to be within two percentage points of the average in the three member states with the lowest inflation rates in the European Union. However, economic difficulties were such that few states met the convergence criteria. Consequently, a less strict interpretation of the criteria was applied, and in 1998 it was declared that, of those member states wishing to participate in EMU, only Greece had failed to meet the convergence criteria.

CO-OPERATION refers more specifically to intergovernmental co-operation, a process of collaboration by the member states, with the intention of securing agreement on objectives and strategies without the involvement of supranational institutions. It is the opposite of the **community method**.

CO-OPERATION AGREEMENTS are similar to (but less comprehensive than) **association agreements**, which aim to promote intensive economic co-operation. Co-operation agreements have been concluded since the mid-1970s by the European Communities with many countries outside Europe, as well as

101

being, before 1991, the favoured form of relationship with Eastern European countries. After 1989 many Central and Eastern European countries preferred to seek **Europe agreements**, the new form of association agreement being offered to them. Successor states to the **USSR** were offered **partnership and co-operation agreements**.

The **CO-OPERATION PROCEDURE** was introduced by the **Single European Act** in 1987 as a means of enhancing the role of the **European Parliament** in EC decision-making. With the subsequent emergence of and increased recourse to the **co-decision procedure**, its use was soon limited to certain decisions in the area of **economic and monetary union**. It was eventually abandoned entirely with the **Treaty of Lisbon**.

COPA: See **Committee of Professional Agricultural Organizations in the European Union**

The **COPENHAGEN CRITERIA**, sometimes referred to as the **accession criteria**, are the conditions that countries of **Central and Eastern Europe** must meet if they are to be admitted to the European Union (EU). They were adopted at the **Copenhagen summit** of the **European Council** in June 1993 and require those countries seeking to join the EU to possess stable institutions which guarantee democracy; to respect the rule of law and human and minority rights; to possess a functioning market economy able to cope with competitive pressure and market forces; and to be capable of meeting the obligations of membership (i.e. adherence to the *acquis communautaire* as well as the *finalité politique* of the EU).

Two **COPENHAGEN SUMMITS** of the **European Council** met specifically to discuss the eastward **enlargement** of the European Union (EU). The first met in 1993 and established the **Copenhagen criteria** for EU membership, while the second, convened in December 2002, formally approved the accession of the first 10 **candidate countries** to the EU. The states were: Cyprus, the Czech Republic, Estonia, Hungary, Latvia, Lithuania, Malta, Poland, Slovakia and Slovenia. Following the successful outcome of the second Copenhagen summit, the **Treaty of Accession** was signed, and the 10 states joined the EU on 1 May 2004.

COR: See **Committee of the Regions**

CORDIS stands for Community Research and Development Information Service. It provides a database and summary information on all current research projects within the European Union.

CORE EUROPE refers to the notion that a group of states within the European Union would opt to forge closer economic, political and military links between themselves, if some of the other states showed a degree of reluctance to pursue the policy agenda of a core group. The concept of core Europe is usually understood to mean **France**, **Germany** and the **Benelux** states, that is, all the original members of the **European Coal and Steel Community** except Italy.

COREPER: See **Committee of Permanent Representatives**

CO-RESPONSIBILITY LEVIES were introduced in 1986 and, along with the later **stabilizers**, were seen as a means of attempting to halt the open-ended **subsidies** on production and the huge surpluses that the guaranteed price support system had imposed upon the **common agricultural policy**. The levies were set to come into operation whenever predetermined production quantities for a product were exceeded, making them, in effect, a tax on excess output. Many people argued that the levies had been set at too low a level to be properly effective.

COREU (Correspondance Européenne) is a secure communications system that connects all the foreign ministries of the European Union (EU) member states. The objective of this link is to improve and foster co-operation in the development of the EU's **common foreign and security policy**.

CORPORATION TAX is a tax levied on company profits. To generalize, the member states each operate one of three different systems of calculation and application. The question of the **harmonization** of corporation tax has been discussed by the European Communities since 1963, but agreement has been difficult to achieve.

UWE CORSEPIUS (1960–) was selected in 2009 as the next Secretary-General of the **Council of the European Union** and assumed the post in June 2011 (replacing Pierre de Boissieu). Corsepius was born in Berlin, Germany, and studied economics at the University of Erlangen-Nuremberg in Bavaria. He received his doctorate at the Kiel Institute for the World Economy (Institut für Weltwirtschaft) before briefly joining the German Ministry of Economy and Labour as a civil servant. He became an official within the German Federal Chancellery in 1994 and worked under a succession of German Chancellors (**Helmut Kohl**, **Gerhard Schröder** and **Angela Merkel**) prior to assuming his current post.

COSAC is the acronym for Conférence des Organes Spécialisés dans les Affaires Communautaires, the gathering, every six months, of **Members of the European Parliament** and members of the European Union affairs committees of **national parliaments**.

COSI is the acronym for the Standing Committee on Operational Cooperation on Internal Security, created by the **Council** under the terms of the **Treaty of Lisbon** to facilitate co-operation on internal security within the European Union (EU). The rationale for this committee stems from Article 71 of the **TFEU**. COSI is expected to co-ordinate activities relating to e.g. policy and customs co-operation, external border protection and judicial co-operation in criminal matters. It is also expected that COSI will be responsible for informing the Council, the **European Parliament** and national parliaments about its activities. COSI is mandated to help the Council in accordance with the so-called 'Solidarity Clause' contained within Article 222 of the TFEU, which pledges the EU to use all the tools at its disposal to assist a member state that becomes the target of a terrorist attack or suffers a disaster, whether natural or manmade. Responsibility for preparing legislative acts pertaining to any of the above issues remains with **COREPER** rather than COSI.

COST, the acronym used to refer to European Co-operation in the Field of Scientific and Technical Research, is a concept rather than an institution or programme. It is a framework for the preparation and implementation of European projects relating to applied scientific research. It was established in 1970 with a membership of 19 countries, which increased to 25 countries in 1994, including all the member states of the European Union. By 2007 it had 35 members. The COST Secretariat is attached to the **Council of the European Union** and the technical management of projects has been handled by the **European Commission**. Each project, however, has been individually negotiated by those states that wish to participate in it. Several collaborative projects have been pursued in 10 areas: information technology, **telecommunications**, transport, oceanography, metallurgy and materials science, meteorology, agriculture, food technology, environmental protection and medical research and health. (See also **EUREKA**.)

COSTA V ENEL the name of an important case in which the **Court of Justice**, in 1964, established the primacy of European Community law and confirmed that it could not be overruled.

The **COTONOU AGREEMENT** was signed in June 2000 by the European Union (EU) and 77 **ACP** (African, Caribbean and Pacific) **States** and superseded the fourth **Lomé Convention** (1990–2000). It provided longer-term (20-year) support for the EU-ACP relationship, which was to be developed on the basis of five interdependent pillars: comprehensive political dialogue; the enhanced participation of civil society in partnership affairs; a strengthened focus on poverty reduction; a new framework for economic and trade co-operation; and a reform of financial co-operation. The new Agreement therefore placed greater emphasis on establishing and maintaining good governance in the **ACP States**. It also envisaged the establishment of an EU-ACP free trade area by 2020, and committed €13,500m. in aid for the first five years of the Agreement. These funds were directed at poverty reduction and at encouraging non-state sectors to participate in the development process. The new Agreement was also notable for its insistence that respect for **human rights**, democratic principles and the rule of law should form the core criteria for aid policy decisions. From a practical perspective, the Agreement can be revisited every five years, as can the aid **protocols**, which are bound to a similar timetable. Progress is reviewed on an annual basis. Negotiations to revise the Cotonou Agreement were initiated in May 2004 and concluded in February 2005. The political dimension of the Agreement was broadly strengthened and a reference to co-operation in counter-terrorism and the prevention of the proliferation of weapons of mass destruction was included. The revised Cotonou Agreement was signed on 24 June 2005. The second revised Cotonou Agreement was formally signed in Ouagadougou, Burkina Faso, in June 2010, and entered into effect, on a provisional basis, on 1 November. This revised Agreement placed an emphasis on the importance of regional integration among ACP states (fostering co-operation, peace and security, and promoting growth) and on the relevance of the **African Union** as a partner in EU-ACP relations. It also sought to promote conflict resolution and, for the first time, recognized the global challenge of climate change and the need for the ACP states to address some of the concerns surrounding this pressing issue. The revised Agreement also took into account other urgent problems and realities for the ACP states (including HIV/AIDS and food security). From its perspective, the EU displayed a strong interest in developing contacts and relations with a broad range of actors in the ACP states—national and local parliaments, civil society and the private sector.

The **COUNCIL FOR MUTUAL ECONOMIC ASSISTANCE** (CMEA), also known as Comecon, was established in 1949 by the **USSR** and subsequently developed into an organ for economic co-operation and co-ordination in the Communist bloc. At first, the European Communities (EC) expressed little interest in an arrangement with the CMEA. Any agreement would have been difficult because of the non-convertibility of CMEA currencies and its operation of a centralized planning and production system, whereby trade was based on an exchange or barter system rather than money transfers. These problems were compounded by Soviet hostility towards the EC. Talks between the EC and the CMEA began only in 1976. They had not produced any results by 1980, when discussions were broken off as a result of the Soviet invasion of Afghanistan. They were not resumed until 1986, after Mikhail Gorbachev's accession to power in the USSR, and a mutual recognition agreement was signed in June 1988. Among other things, it permitted the establishment of diplomatic relations between the EC and individual Eastern European countries: several, including the USSR, established diplomatic posts in **Brussels** with accreditation to the EC. Prior to the 1988 agreement, the EC had signed only limited sectoral agreements with Eastern European countries. The German Democratic Republic (GDR—East Germany) had been in a different position since the 1972 **Ostpolitik** agreement with the Federal Republic of Germany (FRG—West Germany), which had given its products access to the EC.

The relationship with the CMEA was confused and disrupted by the events of 1989, which removed the Communist parties from power or forced them to share it. In October 1990 the former GDR automatically became part of the EC when it was subsumed into the FRG by German reunification. At a CMEA meeting in 1990 the new governments of the other Eastern European states expressed strong dissatisfaction with the past performance of the CMEA and its current condition: several declared an interest in EC membership in the medium term. In 1991 it was agreed to replace the CMEA by a two-year interim organization based upon market economy principles, to be called the Organization for International Economic Co-operation. However, with the disintegration of the USSR at the end of 1991, all semblance of continuing collaboration ceased, and the CMEA effectively disappeared.

The **COUNCIL OF THE BARS AND LAW SOCIETIES OF EUROPE** (CCBE) is the officially recognized representative organization for the legal profession in the European Union and the **European Economic Area**.

The **COUNCIL OF EUROPE**, which should not be confused with either the **Council of the European Union** or the **European Council**, was formed in 1949 as Western Europe's first post-war political organization. Its Statute was signed as the Treaty of Westminster by 10 states, and permanent offices were provided for the organization in Strasbourg, France. The Council has established other offices with specific functions and responsibilities in cities across Europe. For example, the Europe Development Bank is located in Paris and the Centre for Modern Languages is situated in Graz in Austria. In addition the Council has placed heavy emphasis on youth and operates a European Youth Centre from Budapest. As an organization the Council of Europe is well resourced and maintains offices in Paris and in other European capital cities. The Council's declared objective was to achieve 'a greater unity between its members for the purpose of safeguarding and realizing the ideals and principles which are their common heritage and facilitating their economic and social progress'. These objectives were to be secured through 'discussions of questions of common concern and by agreements and common action in economic, social, scientific, legal and administrative matters and in the maintenance and further realization of **human rights** and fundamental freedoms'. Its membership grew until, by the 1980s, it incorporated all the non-Communist states of Europe.

The Council consists of two main bodies: a Committee of Ministers and an Assembly. With each state having one vote and a veto, the Committee of Ministers is essentially an intergovernmental conference of foreign ministers from all 47 member states, meeting twice yearly. Chairmanships of the Committee of Ministers are held for six months and the recent and upcoming running order has the **United Kingdom** (November 2011–May 2012), **Albania** (May–November 2012), Andorra (November 2012–May 2013), Armenia (May–November 2013) and **Austria** (November 2013–May 2014) take up their positions. Since 1952, the practice of deputies (usually diplomats) representing the ministers has been normal for all but the most symbolic meetings. In relaying decisions to the member states, the Committee is allowed only to make recommendations. States are not obliged to accept decisions of the Council of Europe.

Similarly, the Assembly, renamed the Parliamentary Assembly (PACE) in 1974, is essentially a discussion chamber, with hardly any substantive powers (and it should not be confused with the **European Parliament**). It comprises national parliamentarians from all 47 member states, who elect a President for a three-year term (which is renewable). The Assembly appoints members as *rapporteurs*, with the mandate to prepare parliamentary reports on specific subjects which cover a multitude of areas and most recently, rendition flights, the abolition of the death penalty in Europe and, of course, regular reports on the human rights situation across Europe. Ever since its first session in 1949, the majority of the delegates, who are appointed by their national parliaments, have been strong supporters of European integration. The fact that it has shared a common home in Strasbourg with the **European Parliament** has helped this commitment. However, the Assembly can only put recommendations forward to the Committee of Ministers, which can, and often does, ignore or reject them.

The Council of Europe has produced about 200 conventions and agreements, most of which have been accepted by almost all the member states. Its greatest achievement, perhaps, was to secure agreement on a **European Convention on Human Rights** in 1950, with a concomitant **European Commission of Human Rights** and a **European Court of Human Rights**, both of which operate under the aegis of the Council. Much of the Council of Europe's success has been in the less politically contentious cultural field. It sponsored, for example, the European Cultural Convention in 1954 and a European Social Charter in 1961. In 1960 it was handed the social and cultural responsibilities that the **Western European Union** had been granted by the **Treaty of Brussels**.

In the 1950s it also sought to achieve some form of policy co-ordination in agriculture, civil aviation and transport. However, by itself the Council could not advance European integration much beyond such symbolic actions as seating the Assembly delegates in alphabetical order rather than by nationality. The United Kingdom and the Scandinavian states were firmly opposed to it becoming anything more than an intergovernmental deliberative body. After the early 1950s it was overtaken by the developments that led to the establishment of the European Communities (EC). Although its major historical significance was that it was the first European organization of a political nature, its later importance was twofold. It was the European organization with the broadest membership, albeit limited to democracies, a claim that was later challenged by the formation of the **Conference on Security and Co-operation in Europe**. Also, because of its broad membership, it remained important as a forum where a wide range of ideas and views could be expressed, and as a central clearing-house for co-operation and co-ordination, receiving and discussing annual reports from a wide range of European and other international organizations and agencies, including the EC. The ending of the **Cold War** offered the Council an opportunity of expanding its membership, and in the early 1990s most of the Central and Eastern European countries and the western republics of the former **USSR** (for example **Russia**) either joined the Council or at least applied for membership. Today, the Council has 47 members.

Relations between the Council of Europe and the European Union (EU) are drawing ever closer. It is expected (under the **Treaty of Lisbon**) that the EU will join the European Convention on Human Rights in the near future as all 47 governments are keen to ensure consistent human rights protection across Europe and, above all, to avoid any inconsistency in the developing case-law between the EU Courts and the European Court of Human Rights.

COUNCIL OF MINISTERS: See **Council of the European Union**

The **COUNCIL OF THE EUROPEAN UNION** is frequently referred to as the Council of Ministers, and prior to 1993 its full official title was the Council of Ministers of the European Communities. It should not be confused with either the **Council of Europe** or the **European Council**, although it is closely related to the latter. The Council of the European Union shares executive responsibility in the European Union (EU) with the **European Commission**. Whereas the Commission represents and defends general European and EC interests, the Council essentially represents the interests of the individual member states. It began life with the **Treaty of Rome**, as the main decision-making institution, although, in later treaties, it has become a co-legislator with the **European Parliament** in most policy areas. The membership of the Council consists of ministerial representatives of the member states. Its meetings are serviced by officials from its own secretariat, the existence of which was formally acknowledged only in the **Treaty on European Union** (TEU), and they may also be attended by one or more Commissioners, depending on the topics listed on its agenda for the day. The Council's headquarters are in the **Justus Lipsius** building in **Brussels**, but on three occasions each year (in April, June and October) the Council meets in Luxembourg. This is a legacy of the merger of the executives of the EC in 1967: the executive High Authority of the **European Coal and Steel Community** had been based in Luxembourg.

Council meetings are normally held in private, although there have been some sessions where elements of the proceedings have been televised. Moreover, spokespersons for each of the member governments hold extensive and detailed press briefings after each Council session.

The Council of the European Union has no fixed membership other than permitting one representative from each member state. In purely legal terms there is only one Council, but its actual composition changes depending on the policy area in question. There are, in effect, a range of different Council formats (currently 10), some of which can even meet simultaneously in parallel sessions. Some meet more often than others, and this reflects the greater salience of some policy areas. The composition of each Council is determined by a particular policy agenda: if, for example, the topic to be discussed is agriculture, the Council consists of the national ministers with responsibility for agriculture; if the agenda is to deal with **consumer policy**, it will be the national ministers responsible for consumer affairs who are in attendance, and so on. When the EU **budget** is to be discussed, the national finance ministers form the Council. The four most important formats of the Council, which meet monthly, are those dealing with General Affairs (covering a range of policy issues, such as negotiations on EU enlargement, and budgetary and administrative issues), Foreign Affairs, Economic and Financial Affairs, and Agriculture and Fisheries. The other formats cover: co-operation in the fields of Justice and Home Affairs; Employment, Social Policy, Health and Consumer Affairs; Competitiveness; Transport, Telecommunications and Energy; Environment; and finally, Education, Youth, Culture and Sport.

The Council of the European Union is a core legislative element of the EU. While the **right of initiative** for most **legislation** lies with the European Commission, it is only the Council that, after some involvement of the European Parliament (EP) and consultation with one or more **advisory committees** and agencies, is empowered to adopt proposals and so legislate for the EU. Other responsibilities include the obligation, in conjunction with the EP, to adopt the EU budget, and the power of appointment to other EU institutions, including the Commission.

To aid it in its tasks, the Council has its own secretariat in Brussels. Central to this are the delegations or **Permanent Representations** that each member state maintains in Brussels. The **Committee of Permanent Representatives** (COREPER) has the task of ensuring that issues awaiting a decision by the Council have been thoroughly discussed and analysed by Council staff. When COREPER reaches agreement on proposals, these are normally adopted by the Council without discussion. On all other issues the Council reaches its decision by voting. The way in which the Council votes on issues is defined by the **Treaty of Rome** and its amendments. Depending upon the issue under discussion, a proposal may be adopted by **majority voting**, by **qualified majority voting**, or unanimously. The incidence and importance of decision-making by simple majority is negligible, and it is used only for a few minor questions, usually of a procedural nature.

The Treaty of Rome anticipated that, after an initial transitional period, qualified majority voting would become more usual, with **unanimity** restricted to a few issues of major importance. This plan was disrupted by the **empty chair crisis** of 1965 and the **Luxembourg Compromise** of 1966. The use of qualified majorities remained limited, with the Council preferring not to jeopardize unanimity by pushing issues to a vote. This made for slow progress. Almost all the reviews of EC practices conducted after the mid-1970s commented adversely on the slowness of decision-making, and recommended a greater use of majority voting; this was finally introduced by the **Single European Act**. The creation of the EU and its potentially extensive **enlargement** in the early years of the 21st century forced further re-examination of the decision-making process. In fact the TEU, the **Treaty of Amsterdam**, the **Treaty of Nice** and the **Treaty of Lisbon** all extended the use of qualified majority voting to new areas of policy. The Treaty of Lisbon also provided for the eventual switch to a form of **double majority voting**.

The task of directing the Council in its various functions falls to its President. Member states hold the **Council presidency** in rotation, the position shifting from state to state every six months. The member state currently holding the presidency is responsible during those six months for organizing the business of the Council, in conjunction with the secretariat. With the Treaty of Lisbon, the situation has changed somewhat (see below). While each member state holding the presidency will hope to advance its own priority issues, by convention, the President is expected to be a neutral arbiter, securing, by compromise and bargaining, Council agreement on as many issues as possible.

As a result of measures introduced by the Treaty of Amsterdam, the Council plays a more active role in **employment** affairs by encouraging member states to exchange information and best practice in this field. Its role in protecting **citizens' rights** was also expanded, a new **Article** permitting the Council to take action, by unanimity, in cases of discrimination. However, the Treaty of Amsterdam also increased the powers of the EP at the expense of the Council, by strengthening the **co-decision procedure**, granting the EP full co-legislative powers in a number of policy areas. The areas in which the Council can take decisions using qualified majority voting have been extended by the Treaty of Amsterdam, the Treaty of Nice and the **Treaty of Lisbon**, although unanimity is still required in core areas such as taxation and in constitutional matters. Attempts to speed up the EU's reaction in times of international crisis have also been introduced as part of reforms to the **common foreign and security policy** (CFSP). In situations in which member states have common foreign policy interests, the Council of the European Union is to decide by consensus the principles and strategies to be employed in joint actions. If agreement cannot be reached by the Council of the European Union, the final decision on EU foreign policy actions is to be taken by the European Council. For member states not opposed to proposed actions but not prepared to participate directly, there is the '**constructive abstention**' option. The **Treaty of Lisbon** has sought to enable the EU to speak with a single voice on foreign policy issues through the enhanced role of the **High Representative of the Union for Foreign Affairs and Security Policy** (currently **Catherine Ashton**). According to the Treaty of Lisbon the new High Representative combines three different functions: she is the Council's representative on foreign policy issues, she is President of the Foreign Affairs Council, and she serves as a Vice-President of the Commission. In terms of fulfilling her duties, she is supported by a policy-planning and early warning unit and by a new **European External Action Service**. Reflecting developments within the CFSP, a **European Union Military Committee** has also been established within the Council.

The **COUNCIL PRESIDENCY** rotates in a predetermined sequence (until 1995 it was arranged alphabetically) among the members of the European Union (EU). Each member state holds the presidency for a period of six months and can influence the focus of its presidency and attempt to steer policy agendas accordingly. However, it is extremely difficult to carry through specific **legislation** in this short period. Moreover, there are concerns that this mode of organization will not be productive in an enlarged EU. Hence, the **Treaty establishing a Constitution for Europe** envisaged three changes: team pre-sidencies comprising three member states and lasting 18 months; a **President of the European Council** in office for two and a half years; and a **Union Minister for Foreign Affairs** chairing Council meetings dealing with foreign affairs. These changes have since been carried forward into the **Treaty of Lisbon**, although the term of Union Minister for Foreign Affairs has been dropped in favour of **High Representative of the Union for Foreign Affairs and Security Policy**. The Council presidency rotated as follows in recent years: Spain and Belgium in 2010, Hungary and Poland in 2011, and Denmark and Cyprus in 2012. Ireland will hold the presidency in January–June 2013, Lithuania in July–December 2013, Greece in January–June 2014 and Italy in July–December 2014.

The **COUNCIL SECRETARIAT** (officially entitled the General Secretariat of the Council of the European Union) is a professional civil service that forms part of the **Eurocracy** residing in Brussels. The Council Secretariat is con-siderably smaller than the **European Commission** and currently comprises approximately 3,200 people. The purpose of the Council Secretariat is essen-tially to draft the six-month legislative programme for each **Council pre-sidency**, providing legal service, briefing government ministers on salient EU issues and preparing the agenda for Council meetings and drafting Council meetings minutes. In terms of structure, the Council Secretariat mirrors the Commission in so far as it is divided into Directorates-General, although along very different lines. The Council Secretariat comprises seven Directorates-General, together with a legal service and a private office for the Secretary-General. The Directorates-General handle issues such as personnel and administration, agriculture, the internal market, external economic relations, the press and communication, economic and social affairs, justice and home affairs and the environment and consumer protection. The legal service exists to represent the Council before the **courts**. The **Treaty of Amsterdam** provided for the Council Secretary-General becoming **High Representative for the Common Foreign and Security Policy** and a Deputy Secretary-General assuming responsibility for the Secretariat. This development meant that the role of the Secretary-General changed from civil servant to high-ranking politician. The **Treaty of Lisbon** has reversed this situation. The current Secretary-General of the Council Secretariat is **Uwe Corsepius**. It should be noted that the respective Secretariats of the **Western European Union** and the **Schengen Agreement** have been merged into the Council Secretariat. As a result of recent changes, it is expected that the Council Secretariat will for the first time become an active participant in the design of policy formulation, especially in the realm of the **common foreign and security policy** and the **Common Security and Defence Policy**. Many people are engaged on foreign policy issues within the Secretariat's Directorates, and the Secretariat also hosts the European Union Military Staff. Since January 2007, the Council Secretariat has functioned with its own independent Operations Centre.

COUNCIL TRADE POLICY COMMITTEE, as the Article 133 Committee (formerly the Article 113 Committee) became known under the **Treaty of Lisbon**, consists of representatives of European Union member states. It assists the **European Commission** in trade negotiations with non-member states and within the **World Trade Organization**.

The **COURT OF AUDITORS** (ECA) is a body established in 1977, under the 1975 Treaty of Brussels, replacing an earlier and more limited Audit Board, which was responsible for examining the accounts of **revenue** and **expenditure** for the European Communities (EC). Its powers were limited, and in 1977 it was replaced by a more authoritative Court of Auditors that scrutinizes the accounts of EC institutions and agencies in order to verify that they possess satisfactory financial management, with all revenue having been legally received and all expenditure properly accounted for. The Court publishes an annual report detailing its findings. It may, either on its own initiative or at the request of another EC institution, prepare other, more specific reports. The Court has in the past drawn attention to the existence of wasteful expenditure in several policy areas, and on a few occasions has found evidence of financial mismanagement. Its role has been important in forcing the EC to improve their procedures and introduce a more effective financial regimen, but there is widespread agreement that much more needs to be done. The **Treaty on European Union** elevated the Court to the status of a European Union institution, with the consequent implications of legality and **decision-making** authority. Its status was further enhanced by the **Treaty of Amsterdam**, which aimed to ensure better financial management of EC money by introducing measures to curtail fraud by extending the ECA's auditing powers to the then second and third **pillars**, and by giving it an additional right to refer cases to the **Court of Justice**. The ECA provides and audits all of the Community's revenue and expenditure. It examines accounts and produces a sound annual financial management plan. It also provides the **European Parliament** and the **Council of the European Union** with a statement of assurance.

The membership of the Court consists of one individual from each member state, and the ECA has a total staff of around 800. Prior to the **European Council** summit in Nice in December 2000 the Commission put forward the suggestion of capping the membership of the Court rather than allowing it to expand with each new accession. This view did not prevail at Nice where agreement was reached by the member states to maintain the current practice of requiring the Court of Auditors to consist of one member from each member state. It was generally assumed that having a national member would facilitate co-operation with the national audit offices. Appointments to the Court are made by the **Council of the European Union** for renewable six-year terms and, since Nice, by **qualified majority voting** on the basis of a list drawn up in accordance with proposals made by each member state. In practice, however, the Council simply endorses the candidates put forward by the member states. In making the appointments, the Council must normally select individuals who belong to, or have had experience of, the external audit departments of their own national administration. Exceptionally, individuals with other special qualifications may also be eligible for appointment. The Court elects its President from among its own members, for a renewable term of three years. The Court is based in Luxembourg.

COURT OF FIRST INSTANCE: See General Court

The **COURT OF JUSTICE**, based in Luxembourg, was, until the establishment of the **Court of First Instance**, the only court of the former European Communities (EC). The Court of Justice is charged with ensuring that the operation of the European Union (EU) concurs with the provisions of the **founding treaties** and their amendments. It has no hierarchical links with the courts of the different legal systems of the member states, and has no jurisdiction over the application and interpretation of purely national laws by the national courts, except insofar as those laws conflict with EU law, which takes precedence over them. Within its area of competence the Court is supreme: there is no appeal against its rulings.

The **pillar structure** that was introduced under the **Treaty on European Union** (TEU) has been abolished under the **Treaty of Lisbon**. Under the Treaty of Lisbon the entire court system of the EU is now known as the Court of Justice of the European Union, and it comprises three courts: the **Court of Justice**, the **General Court** and the **Civil Service Tribunal**. The Court of Justice is concerned primarily with EU law. Although the pillar structure has been abolished, the **common foreign and security policy** (CFSP) remains subject to special rules and specific procedures and, thus, the Court's rule-making powers in this area are curtailed.

The Court is composed of one judge from each member state, so that all of the EU's national legal systems are represented. Even after the EU's **enlargement** to 27 member states in January 2007, there was still to be one judge per member state. For the sake of efficiency, however, the Court may sit as a 'Grand Chamber' of just 13 judges instead of always having to meet in a plenary session attended by all the judges. There are also eight **Advocates-General**. These have similar privileges to judges, but act more as consultants and advisers than as referees. Members of the Court have to be individuals 'whose independence is beyond doubt and who possess the qualifications required for appointment to the highest judicial offices in their respective countries or who are jurisconsults of recognized competence'. While it is the member governments who formally submit nominations to the Court, appointment is made by the **Council of Ministers** (see **Council of the European Union**). Judges and Advocates General are appointed for renewable six-year terms of office, with one-half of the Court being renewed every three years. The President of the Court is elected by the judges from among their own members for a renewable three-year term.

The Court meets both in plenary sessions and in smaller subdivisions called Chambers. The latter enable the Court to carry a larger case-load at any one time. Important cases, including virtually all those brought by an EC institution or by a member state, are heard in plenary session, where eight judges constitute a quorum. Other cases are referred to a Chamber, of which there are six. Any Chamber is free to request that a case currently before it should be transferred to the full Court when it considers that the case merits the fullest possible hearing.

In its various guises, the Court hears three different types of case: opinions, referrals and disputes. The least contentious are opinions, which refer to opinions given by the Court on international agreements to which the EU is party. Referrals describe preliminary rulings by the Court on cases brought before it from national court systems. When a point of EU law is raised in a case before a national court, the point at issue is referred to the Court of Justice for a preliminary ruling, because EU law takes precedence over national law. The national court must take this into account in hearing the case before it. Referrals have been an important way in which the Court has been able to ensure that EU law is applied uniformly across all the member states. Under the **Treaty of Lisbon** the preliminary ruling procedure has been extended to acts of EU bodies, offices or agencies. It also introduces a provision that requires the Court of Justice to act with the minimum of delay when dealing with preliminary rulings. The Court of Justice can also review acts of the **European Council**. Most cases involve disputes, and the Court is largely reactive. There are four main types of dispute: those between the EU and member states; between member states; between EU institutions; and between individuals or corporate bodies (including EC employees) and the EU. Any of these categories can initiate Court proceedings. In the case of an individual, he or she must be able to demonstrate a direct personal interest in the case and its outcome. Under the terms of the TEU, disputes between individuals and the EU were made the responsibility of the Court of First Instance, which now has jurisdiction in this fourth area of disputes.

When the Court first receives a written complaint, it has to establish whether the charge falls within its remit and within the time limits stipulated by the treaties. If it decides in the affirmative, the written charge is sent to the defendant, who has one month in which to make a rebuttal. The plaintiff is then granted an additional month in which a response may be made to the defendant's statement. Finally, the defendant has a further month in which to prepare an additional response. Once this process is completed, the case, if not settled out of court, moves to the stage of a formal hearing. The responsibility for a case belongs to a judge rapporteur, who is appointed by the President of the Court. The judge rapporteur, after studying all the documents, sends a preliminary report to the Court, which must then decide whether to hold a preliminary inquiry, which could involve a request for further documentation and/or the need for the two sides in the case to give oral testimony before the Court. It is at this point that the Court decides whether to hear the case in plenary session or to refer it to one of the Chambers. A date for the public hearing is set by the President of the Court. The conduct of the public hearing follows normal legal convention: plaintiff and defendant present their arguments and call witnesses; cross-questioning is done by the judges and the Advocate-General appointed to the case. The Advocate-General acts as a public prosecutor of the kind found in many European legal systems. The Court does not give its verdict immediately upon the conclusion of the public hearing. A further hearing is held some weeks later at which the Advocate-General reviews the oral and written evidence and proposes a verdict. The opinion of the Advocate-General is not final, but in the majority of cases it is a good indication of the likely decision of the Court. If, during their consideration of the evidence, the judges feel they need more information or explanation, they may extend the hearing. Finally, the Court delivers its verdict at a public hearing. Unanimity is not required, and judgments are reached by majority vote. Normally, the case will be heard by an uneven number of judges: where this is not the case and there is no majority, a decision is reached by eliminating the vote of the most junior judge. Judgments are nevertheless collective, to emphasize the independence of the Court from both other EC institutions and national governments. Voting is secret, and the voting record of any individual judge is not known.

The average length of time between the lodging of a complaint and final judgment has been around 23 months. This tardiness has led to considerable complaints about the Court, but the delays are due not only to the lengthy procedure that must be followed, but also to the increasing volume of cases that the Court has had to hear. Even though about one-third of the submissions do not result in a judgment, they have contributed to the Court's burden. While a large number of cases involving EC employees, as well as certain other categories of cases, were transferred in 1989 to a new Court of First Instance, this has had only a marginal effect upon reducing the time taken to reach a judgment. It was hoped that reforms introduced by the **Treaty of Nice**, which included the creation of **Grand Chambers** and **Judicial Panels**, would help reduce the backlog of cases. At the end of 2011, the Court had a total of 849 cases pending. In all, 688 new cases were lodged in 2011, and 638 were successfully dealt with.

Apart from EU employees, the largest number of cases have related to agriculture and the **common agricultural policy**, followed by those concerning the **customs union**, **freedom of movement**, **competition policy** and **workers' rights**. The majority of actions have been brought by individuals and companies, mostly protesting against EC **regulations**, although a significant number have been directed against member states. The **European Commission** has been the most vigorous plaintiff, as well as being the most common defendant. Cases brought by one EC institution against another have been comparatively rare, but the Council of Ministers and the **European Parliament** (EP) have, on occasions, brought each other before the Court. The TEU increased the ability of the EP to bring cases before the Court. Member states have initiated actions less frequently. They have often, however, been the subject of actions brought by the Commission, when the latter alleged failure to carry out their obligations. The country most involved in legal action has been Italy, most notably as a defendant, owing mainly to its tardiness in implementing EU **legislation**, but also as the state that has initiated the most actions. The TEU remedied a previous deficiency by giving the Court powers of enforcement (usually fines) against member states that do not conform to its judgments.

In many ways, the Court has become the most important EC institution, playing a vital role in consolidating and harmonizing the EU. In the cases brought before it both by the Commission and by individuals, it has made a significant contribution towards ensuring that member states and their governments acknowledge the superiority of EU law and honour their EU obligations.

BRIAN COWEN (1960–) became the 12th Prime Minister of the Irish Republic on 7 May 2008 when he succeeded his former colleague and leader, Bertie Ahern, who had opted to step down from office. At the outset he was generally considered to be one of the most gifted and able of contemporary Irish parliamentarians. However, Cowen's time in office proved particularly challenging. His first year in office was troubled from the outset following the decision of the Irish electorate to reject the **Treaty of Lisbon** on 12 June. After much anguish about how to proceed with the Lisbon issue, Cowen finally opted to hold a second referendum in late 2009 following concessions from his European counterparts vis-à-vis guarantees for Ireland on abortion and neutrality. As the economic situation deteriorated in the wake of the international credit crisis, the Irish economy came under increasing strain. Cowen's popularity with the electorate declined severely in the wake of a series of austere budgets designed to alleviate Ireland's huge deficit, and the intervention of the IMF. This decline in support culminated in Cowen's resignation as party leader on 22 January 2011, and his decision not to contest his parliamentary seat at the upcoming elections. However, he continued to serve as Irish Prime Minister until a general election on 25 February 2011, when his party secured its worst results since the 1920s, thus losing power. He was replaced as Prime Minister by **Enda Kenny**.

CPC: See **Community Patent Convention**

CREEPING COMPETENCE is a phrase that has been used, mainly by critics of further integration, to refer to the extension of the role and powers of the supranational institutions at the expense of the member states, usually through a more expansive interpretation of the treaties and their amendments.

CREST: See **Scientific and Technical Research Committee**

CROATIA, a country of 4.5m. people, emerged as an independent European state following its secession from the **Yugoslav** federation in 1991. This successful move to independence was due in large amount to Germany's unilateral decision to recognize the new state, even though Croatia's action aroused Belgrade's animosity and led to a short and bitter war with the Serbian minority in Croatia from 1991 to 1994, which included the bombardment of the historic city of Dubrovnik. Initially, Croatia was beset by severe problems, which were epitomized by economic stagnation and a high rate of unemployment (which had soared to 20% by 2000) and by the stubbornness and style of authoritarian nationalism created under the President, Franjo Tudjman, who died in 1999. In 2000 the new Government was determined to bring Croatia into the European mainstream, and signalled its intention to reform the economy and to apply for membership of the European Union (EU). In October 2001 it signed a **stabilization and association agreement** with the EU, which subsequently entered into force on 1 February 2005. By early 2003 it had made sufficient economic and political progress to apply formally for EU membership, becoming the second former Yugoslav republic, after Slovenia, to do so. In June 2004, following a positive *avis* from the **European Commission**, the **European Council** conferred candidate country status on Croatia and announced that **accession negotiations** would be opened in 2005. Croatia's failure to co-operate fully with the International Criminal Tribunal for the Former Yugoslavia (ICTY) or to hand over General Ante Gotovina, who had been accused of ordering the killing of more than 100 ethnic Serbs and expelling 150,000 in 1995, meant that the planned opening of negotiations in early 2005 was postponed. Only following confirmation from the ICTY chief prosecutor, Carla del Ponte, that

Croatia was now fully co-operating with the ICTY did the EU's member states agree to open negotiations in early October 2005. The decision was somewhat controversial and was widely seen as part of a deal that allowed Austria to abandon its opposition to the opening of accession negotiations with **Turkey**.

With Gotovina finally captured and handed over to the ICTY in December 2005, the EU opened substantive negotiations. It also adopted a revised **accession partnership** and allocated Croatia €140m. pre-accession financial assistance for the year. A further €141m. was allocated for 2007 under the **instrument for pre-accession assistance**. Although this facilitated preparations for accession, the Commission's 2007 progress report identified a number of areas where further reform was needed. It nevertheless noted progress in negotiations. Indeed, by the end of February 2010, 30 out of 35 negotiating chapters had been opened and 17 closed. Progress could have been quicker had Slovenia not vetoed negotiations for much of 2009 over a bilateral dispute concerning territorial waters. On 30 June 2011 the EU confirmed that Croatia had complied with the requirements of the final outstanding negotiating chapters of the *acquis communautaire*, thereby allowing the country's accession to the Union, which was expected to take effect on 1 July 2013 (more than two years later than the Croatian Government had originally hoped). The Croatian Government officially signed the EU **Treaty of Accession** on 9 December 2011. Croatia's membership of the EU was submitted for approval at a national referendum on 22 January 2012, when it was endorsed by some 66.3% of votes cast (with a participation rate of only about 44%). Croatia joined the **North Atlantic Treaty Organization** on 1 April 2009.

CROCODILE GROUP is the name of an action group founded in July 1980 by **Altiero Spinelli** and other **Members of the European Parliament** (MEPs) who wished to persuade the new, directly elected **European Parliament** (EP) to develop a plan for a radical reform of the European Communities and a grand strategy for an all-embracing European union. The name derived from the restaurant in Strasbourg where the Group first met. The Group met at frequent intervals to plan strategy and formulate proposals, and circulated newsletters (*Crocodile letters*) to all MEPs. Its key argument was that the EP had a duty to consider constitutional reforms and to compile a draft that would be transmitted to the proper constitutional authorities in the member states for **ratification**. By 1981, it had won the support of a substantial number of MEPs, and the EP voted to establish an Institutional Committee to deliberate on the topic. This process resulted in the **draft Treaty establishing the European Union**.

CRONOS: See **New Cronos**

CSCE: See **Organization for Security and Co-operation in Europe**

CSDP: See **Common Security and Defence Policy**

CSF (Community Support Frameworks): See **Structural Funds**

CULTURAL POLICY has been a relatively undeveloped European Communities (EC) policy sector. The EC have supported the initiatives of the **Council of Europe**, which has always been active in seeking to protect and develop the European cultural heritage. It was the rapid advance of technological developments in the 1980s that pushed the EC into greater activity, and the **European Commission** began to define the outlines of a cultural policy. Most of its efforts have been concentrated upon film and television (see **media policy**). It has also focused upon free trade in cultural goods, improving the working conditions and prospects of artists, encouraging a wider audience for cultural activities, and preserving the architectural heritage of the European Union (EU). It has emphasized the **freedom of movement** of both artists and their products throughout the EU, although it is agreed that 'national art treasures' should be excluded from these general provisions. Such treasures, however, have to be strictly defined. The EC have attempted to seek greater **harmonization** in various areas, including national copyright laws, public subsidies, resale rights and royalties. Several activities have been sponsored: the EU Youth and Baroque Orchestras; the translation of contemporary literature, especially from the minority languages of the EU; a European Film Festival (held in a different city each year); and the European Theatre in Milan and Paris. The most widely known initiative, perhaps, is the designation each year, beginning with Athens in 1985, of a different city as European City of Culture, where the EC sponsor several events. The most contentious policy has been that contained in the 1991 **TV Without Frontiers** Directive, which attempts to protect EU television producers against non-European programmes. Since 1982 grants, as well as loans from the **European Investment Bank**, have been advanced for architectural preservation and restoration, and have benefited more than 30 sites that are deemed to be of significance for the EU as a whole or that are located in poorer and undeveloped regions of the EU. A more concerted effort linking these activities was launched in a four-year Action Programme in 1988, and in 1991 the **Treaty on European Union** made specific references to cultural policy. A **Culture 2000** framework programme was proposed in 1998 to cover the period 2000–04. This was to operate in three main areas: **legislation** favourable to culture, the cultural dimension of existing policies, and culture and external relations. It superseded the **Kaleidoscope, Ariane** and **Raphael** programmes. It was expected that further initiatives would depend upon finance, and would probably continue to be opposed by many who feared that an emphasis upon a 'common cultural heritage' would lead to transnational cultural conformity and damage national and regional cultural diversity. In January 2005 the Commission adopted Decision 2005/56/EC setting up a new **Education, Audiovisual and**

Culture Executive Agency (EACEA). This Agency, which began operations in January 2006, took over responsibility for the management of certain parts of the EU's programmes in the education, culture and audiovisual fields.

A new **CULTURE 2007–13** framework was established for the period from 2007 to 2013, taking over from the previous Culture 2000 programme and extending it, with a budget of €408m. The programme operates in three main areas: **legislation** favourable to culture, the cultural dimension of existing policies, and culture and external relations. Its main aim is to promote a 'common cultural area' inclusive of cultural diversity and common cultural heritage, with a view to encouraging the emergence of European citizenship.

CUSTOMS 2013 is a customs co-operation programme. It runs from 1 January 2008 until 31 December 2013, with a budget of €324m. It succeeded Customs 2007, which ran from 2003 until the end of 2007.

CUSTOMS DUTIES are those taxes levied by states at their border upon imports into their territory. The **Treaty of Rome** committed the member states to 'the elimination, as between member states, of customs duties and of quantitative restrictions on the import and export of goods, and of all other measures having equivalent effect'. The removal of internal duties and restrictions, and the imposition of a **common external tariff** (CET), constitute a **customs union**. Customs duties on goods imported from outside the European Union (EU) are collected by the member states in accordance with the CET, but they are regarded as part of EC **own resources** and are a source of **revenue** for the EU **budget**.

CUSTOMS UNION is the name of an economic structure whereby a group of states agree to belong to a single tariff area, where there are no **customs duties** on goods circulating within the union, but where there is a **common external tariff** (CET) levied on all imports into the union. The **Treaty of Rome** created a precise timetable for the establishment of a customs union, which was largely completed by July 1968. New members of the European Communities (EC) were granted a short transitional period of adjustment in which to comply with the full requirements of a customs union. The CET was introduced in the 1960s, but its level was determined by the terms of the several accords with the now superseded GATT (**General Agreement on Tariffs and Trade**), to which the European Union member states individually and collectively were party. It was generally accepted that a customs union would not be sufficient to bring about the original EC goal of a **common market**, but it was not until the late 1980s that the EC began to consider seriously the problem of non-customs obstacles to the establishment of a common **internal market**.

Certain non-member states—for example, **Turkey**—signed agreements with the EC whereby they were incorporated into the customs union.

CYPRUS became a member of the European Union (EU) on 1 May 2004. Prior to this, it concluded an **association agreement** with the European Community (EC) in 1972. The intention was that the agreement would prepare the way for a full **customs union** between Cyprus and the EC. Developments proved to be much slower than originally anticipated, and were complicated by the de facto partition of the island after the invasion of northern Cyprus by **Turkey** in 1974. The EC refused to deal with the administration of the Turkish-controlled sector of the island. In 1987 Cyprus concluded a customs union agreement with the EC, which included arrangements concerning agriculture. The customs union was to come into force in stages over a 10-year period. In 1990, however, Cyprus applied for full membership of the EC. Given the wish of Turkey also to become a member, this created a dilemma for the EC. The **European Commission** published its *avis* in 1993, and indicated that, if partition was not ended, the EC would consider negotiating only with the Greek Cypriot Government. Following this *avis*, in 1995 the **European Council** decided that negotiations with Cyprus would begin six months after the end of the **intergovernmental conference** which was held in 1996–97. Formal negotiations began in March 1998 and were concluded in December 2002. Although some member states still had reservations about admitting a divided island into the EU, the signing of the **Treaty of Accession** in April 2003 committed the EU to admitting Cyprus irrespective of the political situation on the island. Nevertheless, the prospect of membership did lead to improved relations between the two parts of the island, notably in 2003 when travel restrictions were substantially eased. Subsequently, and despite the breakdown of earlier UN-brokered talks, frantic efforts were made during the months leading up to membership on 1 May 2004 to secure agreement on the reunification of the island so that it could join the EU as a single political entity. Although an agreement was reached, it failed to gain the approval of Greek Cypriots in a referendum in April 2004. As a result, only the southern half of the island became part of the EU the following month.

Cyprus ratified the **Treaty establishing a Constitution for Europe** in June 2005, but efforts, including those originating from the **United Nations**, to end the division of the island have stalled. At elections in 2006 a majority of Greek Cypriot voters backed the ruling coalition's opposition to reunification, which angered Turkey. Relations between Cyprus and Turkey remained strained. The Turkish Government stated in June 2006 that it was not prepared to open its ports and airports to Cyprus so long as the Turkish Cypriots in the north of the island remained isolated. In response, Cyprus vowed to block the EU's ongoing talks with Turkey until the ports and airports were opened. In practice the blockage was not total. It nevertheless showed how much influence a small state could wield within the EU. Frustration within the EU with

Cyprus' attempts to block negotiations with Turkey did not prevent agreement being reached in 2007 on Cyprus joining the **eurozone** and adopting the **euro** from 1 January 2008. Demetris Christofias won the presidential election in 2008 and pledged to recommence negotiations regarding reunification of the island. Although contact was quickly re-established with the then leader of Northern Cyprus, Mehmet Ali Talat, progress was very slow and the election of the pro-Turkey nationalist party in Northern Cyprus in April 2009 was expected to undermine further developments in the negotiations.

The **CZECH REPUBLIC** signed a **Europe agreement** with the European Community (EC) in 1993, whereby the EC accepted in principle the possibility of membership. This accord superseded the earlier Europe agreement signed between the EC and the former Czech and Slovak Federative Republic (Czechoslovakia) in 1991. The first agreement had become obsolete in January 1993 with the creation of two separate states, the Czech Republic and Slovakia. There existed a strong body of opinion that the Czech Republic's application could not be considered until the European Union (EU) had been consolidated, and the **European Free Trade Association** states admitted. In 1997 the Czech Republic's 1996 application to join the EU was considered favourably, and **accession negotiations** began in March 1998. The country was deemed to have completed the necessary economic and institutional reforms. The application was considered by the **European Commission** to be integral to its **Agenda 2000** 'for a stronger and wider Europe' initiative, although it noted that investment would be needed to transpose EC rules on agriculture, the environment and energy, and that administrative reforms would be required to 'provide the country with the structures it needs for effective application and enforcement of the full body of Community law.' Although the Czech Republic had long been considered among the best placed of the **candidate countries** to join the EU, this did not prevent the Commission from criticizing its preparations for membership. However, the Czech Republic completed accession negotiations with the EU in December 2002. Following its signing in April 2003, the **Accession Treaty** was approved in a national referendum held in mid-June 2003. With participation by the electorate of 55.2%, 77.3% of voters favoured membership. The Czech Republic joined the EU on 1 May 2004. Domestic political infighting contrived to mar the build-up to the occasion, with the prospective Czech member of the European Commission resigning within a week of being nominated. Relations between the Czech Government and the EU have on occasions been somewhat tense given the Eurosceptic views of the Czech President, Vaclav Klaus. Klaus trained as an economist prior to entering politics and served as Minister of Finance of Czechoslovakia in 1989–92 and as Prime Minister in 1993–97, and has been President since 2003.

The Government planned to hold a referendum on the **Treaty establishing a Constitution for Europe** in early 2006, but this was 'postponed' following the rejection of the treaty in both France and the Netherlands in May/June 2005. A Czech general election at the beginning of June 2006 proved indecisive and resulted in a hung parliament and political deadlock. The opposition centre-right Civic Democratic Party (ODS) won the largest number of seats (81 out of 200) and was asked by the Czech President to initiate talks towards the creation of a coalition government. In contrast the Social Democrats won 74 seats. The ODS is highly Eurosceptic and is pursuing closer ties with **David Cameron** and the British Conservative Party. The Czech Republic became part of the EU's **Schengen Area** in December 2007 and assumed the presidency of the **Council of the European Union** in January 2009. At the outset, Prague was keen to develop closer EU–US relations and also to establish ever better links with the countries of the Western Balkans. The Czech presidency, however, was viewed as lukewarm at best and did not get off to a very good start when President Klaus refused to allow the EU flag to be flown from government buildings. Klaus was elected as President by the Czech parliament in 2003 and was narrowly re-elected in 2007. Although the role of the Czech President is largely ceremonial, Klaus has consistently displayed his Eurosceptic tendencies. More seriously, the Czech presidency of the Council of the European Union was not aided by the fall of the national Government (under the pro-European Mirel Topolanek) after a vote of no confidence in March 2009. Jan Fischer emerged after lengthy discussions between the coalition partners as a caretaker Prime Minister in April 2009 and steered the country through the EU presidency and to elections in 2010, in which the centre-right made most gains. A new ODS-led Government was subsequently formed under Petr Nečas.

The **Treaty of Lisbon** was ratified easily by both houses of parliament, but the process of final **ratification** required presidential assent. Klaus had long expressed his opposition to the Treaty of Lisbon and resisted giving his approval for as long as possible, but he eventually signed once the Irish Government had successfully carried out its second referendum on the treaty, after the German courts had not found it to be in conflict with the German Constitution, and after the Polish President had signed it. The Czech Republic was the last EU member state to ratify the Treaty of Lisbon, in November 2009. A more recent example of Czech Euroscepticism and the Czech authorities' strong resistence to any moves that deepen EU integration was provided by the Czech Government's refusal to sign the **Treaty on Stability, Co-ordination and Governance in the Economic and Monetary Union** in March 2012.

D

JOHN DALLI (1948–) is one of the 27 European Commissioners in the Barroso II Commission (2010–14), wherein he has responsibility for health and consumer policy. Dalli is one of the most senior Maltese politicians of his generation. He entered the Maltese House of Representatives in 1987 and subsequently served in a number of governments, as Minister of Economic Affairs (1990–92) and as Minister of Finance (1992–96 and 1998–2004). He served briefly as Minister of Foreign Affairs (in 2004) but resigned after three months, citing personal reasons. He was appointed Minister for Social Policy in 2008 and was successfully nominated to the Barroso Commission in late 2009.

MARIA DAMANAKI (1952–) is one of the 27 European Commissioners of the Barroso II Commission (2010–14), where she has responsibility for Maritime Affairs and Fisheries. She was born in Crete and went on to study chemical engineering at the Technical University of Athens where she became politically active in her opposition to the dictatorship in Greece between 1969 and 1974. She had been a member of the Communist Youth of Greece, but became primarily known as a member of the radical left-leaning party, Synaspismos. She was first elected to the Greek parliament in 1977 at the age of 25 as a member of Synaspismos and became the first woman to be elected to the position of Vice-President of the parliament (1986–90). Furthermore, she became the first female to become President of a Greek political party, in 1989. Although she lost her seat in 1993 when Synaspismos polled badly, she was re-elected to parliament in 2000 and took a special interest in education and culture. Her political journey led her to resign from Synaspismos in 2003 and to join PASOK (the Greek Socialist Party). She was appointed chair of the Select Committee on Foreign Affairs and Defence in 2009 and was then nominated by the PASOK-led Government as their representative on the Barroso II Commission in 2009.

DANGEROUS SUBSTANCES were the subject of several European Communities (EC) **directives** regulating the classification, use, labelling and marketing of many products deemed to be potentially dangerous. These directives covered, *inter alia*, asbestos, glues, paints, pesticides and solvents. The production and distribution of **pharmaceuticals** were also controlled by EC directives. Nuclear-related matters have been handled by the **European Atomic Energy Community** (EAEC) and the **Joint Research Centre**. In

1981 the EC adopted a scheme for the rapid exchange of information between the appropriate national authorities about accidents and risks to **health and safety** that arise from the use of potentially dangerous products, and a system of monitoring accidents caused by consumer goods was subsequently introduced. (See also **Consumer policy**.)

DAPHNE was a programme, originally launched in 1997 but extended under Daphne II to cover the years 2000–04, that supported projects by non-governmental organizations to combat violence against women, young people and children, especially in the areas of trafficking in women and the sexual exploitation of children. Daphne III runs from 2007 until 2013, with a budget of €116.9m.

DAVIGNON REPORT is the name usually given to a document that was a product of the **Hague summit** of December 1969, when the heads of government agreed to return to the theme of political integration. The summit charged the foreign ministers with the responsibility of studying 'the best way of achieving progress in the matter of political unification, within the context of **enlargement**'. Mindful perhaps of the arguments that this had caused in the past, the leaders did not try to be specific as to which route such political progress might follow. The foreign ministers opted for a compromise solution in order to achieve agreement. The conclusions were presented in a report compiled by Etienne Davignon (1932–), political director in the Ministry of Foreign Affairs of Belgium. The Davignon Report of 1970 accepted that political integration should ideally begin in a policy sphere where the member states, both current and projected, already possessed an identifiable common interest, and recommended that it should be in the co-ordination of foreign policy 'that the first concrete efforts should be made to show the world that Europe has a political vocation'. The Report included several specific recommendations: a regular consultation process of meetings of the foreign ministers, backed by a support group, a Political Committee, formed by the political directors of the national foreign ministries; ongoing liaison between European Communities (EC) ambassadors in foreign capitals; and the issuing, by the EC states, of common instructions on certain matters to their ambassadors abroad. The Report was widely welcomed, and its main recommendations were put into effect more or less immediately. The first ministerial meeting under the new regime was held in Munich, Germany, in November 1970, and the EC made their first joint policy declaration, on the Middle East, the following May. The process was judged a success, and a second Davignon Report in 1973 recommended its continuation. This second report stressed the non-binding aspects of political co-operation: its aims were 'to ensure a better mutual understanding of the major problems of international politics through regular information and consultation; to promote the **harmonization** of views and the co-ordination of positions; to attempt to achieve a common approach to specific cases'. The

Davignon Reports were the basis of what came to be known as **European political co-operation**.

DE: See **Group of the European People's Party (Christian Democrats) and European Democrats**

ALCIDE DE GASPERI (1881–1954) was the first and longest serving Prime Minister (1946–53) of Italy after 1945. A member of the dominant Christian Democrat Party (DC), he had been a member of the imperial Habsburg Parliament in Vienna before 1914. His opposition to Benito Mussolini led to a four-year prison term, followed by his effective exile in the Vatican. A skilled politician, he maintained successful control of his unwieldy party, and pursued an active pro-Western foreign policy. He was a committed supporter of all initiatives for European integration and was a close confidant of **Konrad Adenauer** and **Robert Schuman**. He believed not only that integration was intrinsically valuable, but also that it would benefit Italy in aiding the country's economic development as well as strengthening its democratic system against potential challenges from the strong political extremes. His efforts on behalf of the European integration project led to his election as President of the Common Assembly of the **European Coal and Steel Community** in 1954, just months before his death. In general terms, he set the tone of Italy's attitude towards European integration: until 1954 he was perhaps the most consistent supporter of the concept in the European Communities.

CHARLES DE GAULLE (1890–1970) became the first President of the French Fifth Republic in 1959, serving until 1969. His foreign policy was directed towards the restoration of French influence in international affairs, the reassertion of national sovereignty, rapprochement with the Federal Republic of Germany, less reliance on and 'subservience' to the **USA**, and French leadership of the European Communities (EC). De Gaulle was not averse to economic integration, as long as it served French interests and did not limit French independence of action. For the same reasons, he was hostile to the political implications of the **Treaty of Rome**, preferring a looser intergovernmental structure of independent states. His political plans for the EC were the basis of the 1961 **Fouchet Plan**, which was rejected by the other member states. The 1963 **Treaty of Friendship** (Elysée Treaty) was a truncated version of the Plan, but provided the basis of the Franco-German axis that came to dominate much of future EC activity. Two further actions stand out in terms of their impact upon the EC. In 1963 and again in 1967, against the wishes of the other member states, he vetoed the application of the United Kingdom to join the EC, fearing that it would lead to undue British and US influence in Europe, and thus the dilution of French influence. The other episode was the **empty chair crisis** of 1965, which resulted in a reassertion of French national power within the EC

that reflected de Gaulle's hostility towards **supranationalism** and was perso-
nalized in his clashes with the first **European Commission** President, **Walter
Hallstein**. While de Gaulle effectively won both disputes, the United Kingdom
did eventually join the EC in 1973, and the drive towards integration was
renewed in the 1980s. His vision of what the EC should be like politically
was partially reflected in the emergence of the **European Council** under one
of his successors, **Valéry Giscard d'Estaing**. De Gaulle resigned in 1969 and
died the following year.

KAREL DE GUCHT (1954–) is one of the 27 European Commissioners in
the Barroso II Commission (2010–14), within which he holds responsibility for
trade policy. De Gucht is a Belgian national and is a senior figure from the
Flanders region of the country, where he is a member of the Flemish Liberals
and Democrats (VLD) party. He served as a member of the **European
Parliament** (EP) in the second half of the 1990s before he entered first the
Flanders parliament in 1999, and then the federal parliament in 2003. Although
he was elected to the EP in 2004 he did not take up his seat and instead became
the Belgian Minister of Foreign Affairs (until July 2009). During this time he
often found himself in the headlines over personal statements about his political
opponents both at home and abroad. He was appointed Commissioner of the
European Union in July 2009 and took responsibility for Development and
Humanitarian Aid issues when the incumbent (Louis Michel) opted to
become a **Member of the European Parliament**. De Gucht was successfully
renominated, to the Barroso II Commission, in 2009.

DECISION-MAKING in the European Union is often considered complex,
malleable and incomprehensible. In a 1995 report the **European Commission**
itself identified 29 different decision-making procedures. The key to understanding the decision-making processes lies within the **founding treaties** and
subsequent **regulations**. The decisions can be classified loosely into different
category headings: constitutional decisions (concern the **European Council**);
legislative decisions (concern the Commission, the **Council of the European
Union** and the **European Parliament** (EP) and are subject to either **consultation,
co-decision** or **consent procedures**); **trade** policy decisions (Council and
Commission); **competition policy** decisions (Commission and courts); **common
foreign and security policy** (concerns primarily the member states, as did
justice and home affairs issues falling under the former pillar III); and finally,
decisions relating to the **budget** (which fall to the EP and the Council). Recent
treaty changes have sought to simplify procedures and create more effective and
efficient decision-making. The **Treaty of Lisbon** created a new **double
majority voting** system in the Council and made co-decision, which is now
rebranded as the '**ordinary legislative procedure**', the default decision-making
procedure.

DECISIONS are one of three different types of **legal instrument** that the **European Commission** and the **Council of the European Union** are empowered to issue. Decisions by either the Commission or the Council are binding upon the member states; they may be addressed to named individuals or enterprises. Decisions can be made by the European Union executives on the basis of the direct authority they possess under the terms of the **Treaty of Rome** and its amendments, or on the basis of earlier **regulations** or **directives**. Decisions made under the **Treaty of Paris** are slightly different: they are binding in their entirety and are thus closer to EC regulations. (See also **Law**; **Opinions**; **Recommendations**; **Resolutions**.)

A **DECLARATION**, as far as the **European treaties** are concerned, is a political statement issued by one or more member states or the **intergovernmental conference** clarifying provisions of a treaty or outcomes of the negotiations. Of lesser status than a **protocol**, it has limited judicial force; its main purpose is to express the intention of the signatories. Declarations are also often issued following meetings of the **European Council**. The deliberations are usually produced in the form of 'conclusions of the presidency' and supplemented by declarations containing more detailed information on certain points of substance.

DECT: See **Digital European Cordless Telecommunications**

A **DEEP AND COMPREHENSIVE FREE TRADE AREA** (DCFTA) is the goal of negotiations between the European Union (EU) and various countries involved in the European Neighbourhood Policy, notably **Ukraine** and **Moldova**. A DCFTA differs from a **free trade area** in that it involves not only the removal of tariff barriers and quotas, but also the adoption by the EU's partner of EU laws and standards.

DEEPENING refers to the process of European integration. From its early incarnation as a **customs union** and through its steady evolution to a **common market** and now the **eurozone**, the European Union (EU) has aspired to 'ever closer union' among the peoples of Europe. Since the **Treaty of Paris** the EU's competence, policy remit and powers have steadily increased. The debate on deepening usually occurs alongside that of widening (**enlargement**) and there is a generally held view that the 2004 and 2007 enlargements to 27 member states, coupled with the prospect of further enlargement, must be accompanied by further deepening, or the EU will become a weaker entity, as it will be increasingly difficult to reach agreement on key **decisions**. Such thinking was part of the rationale behind the **Laeken Declaration** on the Future of the European Union, the establishment of the **European Convention** and the convening of a further **intergovernmental conference** in

2003, which led to the adoption of the **Treaty establishing a Constitution for Europe** in June 2004 and the subsequent adoption of its replacement, the **Treaty of Lisbon**.

DEFENCE: See **Common Defence Policy**; **Common Security and Defence Policy**.

DEFICIENCY PAYMENTS are a means of ensuring producers a fair price for their products and labour when the costs of the latter are higher than the prices for produce obtainable on the free market. When market prices are too low to cover the costs of production, compensation is given to the producer in the form of **subsidies**. Deficiency payments have been employed in the **common agricultural policy** as an integral part of the price guarantee system.

JACQUES DELORS (1925–), a former financier and French government minister, was appointed President of the **European Commission** in 1985 and remained in office, serving a record three terms, until early 1995. He insisted that the schedule set down for the implementation of the single **internal market** by 1992 be maintained. He was equally insistent that the European Communities (EC) and the member states should think beyond economic integration and 1992, towards working for closer political integration. His commitment and efforts made him the most active President since **Walter Hallstein**, and probably the most powerful in the EC's history. In pursuit of his goals, he was prominent in the drafting of the **Charter of Fundamental Social Rights of Workers** (the Social Charter), which he argued had to be adopted as an essential contribution to the internal market. He was also the main author of the Commission proposals (**Delors I**) of 1987 on budgetary reform, which were designed to place the EC **budget** on a sound basis until at least 1992. He chaired the committee, composed mainly of the central bankers of the member states, mandated by the **European Council** in 1988 to consider how the EC might achieve **economic and monetary union** (EMU): the result was the **Delors Plan**. All three initiatives were, for Delors, to be an integral part of a radical restructuring of the EC by the 1991 **Maastricht summit**. It was a restructuring in which, he argued, the Commission must be given greater decision-making powers to become a 'real executive', answerable to, and counterbalanced by, 'the democratic institutions of the future Federation' (primarily an enhanced **European Parliament**). The Maastricht summit and the subsequent **Treaty on European Union** did not quite live up to Delors' expectations in terms of the social dimension, institutional reform or the **opt-outs** conceded to Denmark and the United Kingdom. The turmoil in the money markets during 1992 and 1993 further adversely affected his hopes for EMU. Nevertheless, the policies followed by the EC in the 1990s were due in large measure to Delors' efforts.

DELORS I is a name that was given to a set of ambitious budgetary measures put forward in February 1987 by the **European Commission**, as a response to the continued difficulties in funding European Communities (EC) operations (see **budget**). The collection of reforms was intended to enable the EC to realize the aim of implementing an **internal market** by the end of 1992. It outlined four objectives: an increase in EC **revenue**; firmer budgetary discipline; reforms and stricter control of the **common agricultural policy** in order to release more funds for other initiatives, especially in the field of **research and technological development policy**; and increased resources for the **structural funds** and the policy of **cohesion**. The proposed measures proved controversial among the 12 member states. Three meetings of the **European Council** were necessary before agreement on the reforms could be reached at a special European Council meeting in Brussels in February 1988 under the German presidency. The 1988 deal established the first of the multi-annual **financial perspectives**, which ran from 1988 to 1992, and saw an effective doubling of the money devoted to the structural funds for Greece, Ireland, Portugal and Spain. With the agreement secure, the Commission felt able to turn its attention to the issue of **economic and monetary union**.

DELORS II is the popular name of a set of budgetary measures proposed by the **European Commission** in February 1992. It sought a one-third increase in European Communities (EC) **revenue** in order to cover the additional costs imposed by the **Treaty on European Union**, in particular those incurred by the objectives of **cohesion**, improving the **competitiveness** of EC industry, and greater foreign policy obligations, while still maintaining budgetary discipline and reflecting the ability and willingness of member states to pay. The proposals' progress was hindered by the difficulties surrounding **ratification** of the treaty, and final agreement upon a revised version was not reached until late 1992 at the meeting of the **European Council** in Edinburgh, United Kingdom, in December.

The **DELORS PLAN** is the popular name of a report on **economic and monetary union** (EMU) published in April 1989. The official title is the Report of the Committee for the Study of Economic and Monetary Union. The report was the work of a committee appointed by the **European Council**. Mainly composed of the central bank governors, it was chaired by **Jacques Delors** and outlined a sequence of three stages, with full EMU to be achieved by the end of the 20th century. The first stage involved consolidating the achievement of free movement of capital, and closer monetary and macro-economic co-operation between the member states and their central banks. The second stage comprised a new system of European central banks, before the **implementation** of full EMU. The European Council, despite British objections, agreed in December 1989 that an **intergovernmental conference** would consider the treaty changes necessary for implementation of the Plan. The conclusions were presented at the **Maastricht summit**, and the relevant provisions in the **Treaty on European Union** on EMU largely followed the structure of the Delors Plan.

DEMANDEUR is the French term often used to refer to a state requesting something (e.g. increased **structural fund** receipts) from the European Union.

DEMOCRATIC DEFICIT is a term that has frequently been applied to procedures and structures relating to the European Union (EU) over the past two decades or so. It refers to the belief that there is a lack of proper democratic and parliamentary supervision and **accountability** in European Community (EC)/EU decision-making procedures. The lack has occurred because of the diminution of national **sovereignty** and the relative inability of national legislatures, owing to legal restraints and pressure of time, to monitor both the **European Commission** and the **Council of the European Union**, and because the **European Parliament** (EP) had insufficient authority to fill the gap.

As European integration has progressed, the question of democratic legitimacy has become increasingly sensitive. The more recent treaties (Maastricht, Amsterdam, Nice and Lisbon) have triggered the inclusion of the principle of democratic legitimacy within the institutional system by reinforcing the powers of Parliament with regard to the appointment and control of the Commission and successively extending the scope of the **co-decision procedure**.

The **Treaty of Amsterdam**, for example, sought to address this problem by expanding the areas in which the EP participates under the co-decision procedure. Members of member state **national parliaments** may also be able to play a greater role in EC decision-making, since the treaty includes a **protocol** stipulating that, in the area of **justice and home affairs**, there must be a six-week interval between the tabling of a legislative proposal and its appearance on the Council's agenda. This should permit national members of parliament to participate more directly in EC **decisions**. The Conference of European Affairs Committees of national parliaments of the member states is also encouraged to provide its views on **subsidiarity**, justice and security, and fundamental rights and freedoms. In addition, the EC institutions have been opened to public scrutiny, with easier access to the documents of the European Commission, and to the voting results of the Council of the European Union, where decisions have legal effect. Institutional design and inter-institutional relationships formed a core rationale behind the **Treaty of Nice**, which was agreed in December 2000 and came into force on 1 February 2003. It re-examined such issues as the use of **qualified majority voting** in the Council, allocation of seats in the EP and the extension of the co-decision procedure in an effort to inject greater **accountability** and **transparency** in the **decision-making** processes. More innovative measures for reducing the democratic deficit were contained in the **Treaty of Lisbon**. Indeed, measures to enhance democratic equality and improve both representative and participatory democracy include stronger powers for the EP through the extension of co-decision to almost all policy areas (especially agriculture and the budget), a stronger role for national parliaments in scrutinizing EU **legislation** (and provision for a 'yellow card' in respect of Commission proposals), the creation of a President for the European Council, the opening up of Council meetings to the public and the possibility of a citizens' petition. How far such issues can really reduce notions of a democratic deficit is debatable, and some have urged increased direct participation of the electorate, for example, in the election of the Commission President.

DENMARK is a constitutional monarchy, currently under Queen Margrethe II. Denmark has had a particularly difficult relationship with the European Communities (EC) over the past two decades, as its citizens have twice (in 1992 and 2000) voted against participation in further stages of European integration, namely **ratification** of the **Treaty on European Union** (TEU) and adoption of the single European currency (**euro**). This reflects a tradition of rather marked Euroscepticism encouraged by a history of notable maritime achievement and long-standing trading links with the **USA**. Originally Denmark declined in the 1940s and 1950s to participate in any integrative venture that went beyond intergovernmental co-operation. In 1960 it became a founder member of the **European Free Trade Association**. However, it reversed its position as a consequence of the British decision to apply for EC membership, and submitted its own application in 1961, and a re-application in 1967. Denmark was not willing, primarily on economic grounds, to join the EC without the United Kingdom, although it was informed that it was not affected by the veto on British membership. Discussions on accession were resumed in 1970, and the Enabling Act ratifying the **Accession Treaty** was passed by the Danish Folketing (parliament) in September 1972. Because the parliamentary majority was slightly less than the five-sixths' majority constitutionally required to approve any delegation of national sovereignty, a referendum had to be held. In October 1972 the referendum resulted in a vote of 63.3% in favour of EC entry. Denmark formally acceded to the EC on 1 January 1973.

One of the wealthiest member states, Denmark has been a net beneficiary of the **common agricultural policy** and has benefited from the **internal market**. It has strongly supported a more comprehensive and rigorous **environmental policy** and **workers' rights**, but has had doubts about full monetary union and, to an even greater extent, about a **common defence policy**. Along with the United Kingdom, Denmark has been the least enthusiastic member on the issue of closer political integration. Its policy within and towards the EC has been generally based upon a strict constructionist interpretation of the

founding treaties and their amendments. Because the country has been governed by relatively weak minority coalition governments since the 1970s, the Danish Folketing has acquired a decisive voice in European affairs. The Folketing rejected the **Single European Act** (SEA), and the Prime Minister had to attempt to bypass the opposition by calling a referendum, before which he made it clear that Denmark's continuing membership of the EC was at stake. Even so, in the referendum he managed to gain only a small majority (56.2%) in favour of ratifying the SEA. Denmark's doubts returned in the aftermath of the **Maastricht summit**. While the Government endorsed the TEU, **ratification** was rejected by a small majority in a referendum held in 1992, a result which threw the EC into disarray. The result was significant because it was the first of several popular expressions of discontent within the EC over the pace of integration, indicating that there were limits to how far governments could proceed without paying attention to their electorates. More specifically, crisis meetings had to be held to maintain the momentum of integration and resolve the Danish problem. At the **Edinburgh summit** of 1992, the **European Council** dealt with virtually all of the Danish concerns. Denmark was granted a number of exemptions, or **opt-outs**, from provisions of the TEU. The new conditions were subsequently approved by a small majority in a further referendum in 1993. In 1998 a referendum narrowly endorsed the **Treaty of Amsterdam**, which contains **protocols** relating to Denmark and its decision to opt out of certain provisions of the treaty. Denmark has also opted to remain outside moves towards a single currency and **economic and monetary union**, and again decided against participating in the first wave of euro membership in September 2000. Denmark was scheduled to hold a referendum on the **Treaty establishing a Constitution for Europe** in 2005, but postponed the poll in June of that year following the rejection of the treaty in both France and the Netherlands. The Danish Government decided not to hold a referendum on the **Treaty of Lisbon**, and the Folketing ratified the treaty in 2008. The current Prime Minister is the Social Democrat Helle Thorning Schmidt, who became Denmark's first female Prime Minister, following a general election in September 2011.

DEP is the acronym for a European Depository Library, where holdings of European Union documents are less complete than those in a **European Documentation Centre** (EDC). A DEP is intended primarily for use by the general public.

DEREGULATION has a specific meaning within the European Union. It refers not just to the ending of unnecessary rules inhibiting the working of the economy or to the reduction of government interference, but also more directly to all those measures intended to remove restrictions to **trade** as part of the implementation of the **internal market**.

DEROGATION is a term that refers to a decision by the European Communities (EC)/EU to exempt one or more member states from the provisions of a **directive**; it may apply to the whole or part of a directive or **regulation**. Member states that feel that their situation constitutes special circumstances may apply to the **European Commission** for a derogation, subject to agreement by the **European Council**. In principle, derogations are meant to be temporary, to permit a member state time in which to adapt itself to EC requirements more gradually. For example, Greece, Ireland, Luxembourg, Spain and Portugal all received five-year derogations from the planned start of a single market in **telecommunications** (the liberalization of voice telephony and network operation that began in 1998). In practice, derogations sometimes continue indefinitely. Derogations are most widely granted to new member states for periods of five or 10 years under the terms of the relevant **accession treaty**.

DÉTENTE is a term first used in the mid–1950s to describe a lessening of the tensions between East and West during the **Cold War**. The term is a highly subjective one: while the hostility of the late 1940s and early 1950s may not have been repeated, the two sides never ceased entirely their competition and rivalry. The importance of détente for European integration lies less in its questionable reality than in the perception by Europe of a lessening of international tension. This perception allowed Western Europe to rely less heavily upon the **USA** and perhaps permitted the member states of the European Communities (EC) to concentrate more upon their own plans and development. The changes in **Central and Eastern Europe** after 1989 may have, in a way, created a new sense of détente, but they also persuaded many that the EC should develop their own **common foreign and security policy**.

DEVELOPMENT AID comes from the **budget** of the European Union (EU), the **European Development Fund** (EDF), and the **European Investment Bank** (EIB) and falls into several different categories. Firstly, there is the aid provided to the **African, Caribbean and Pacific** (ACP) **States** (79 countries) under the terms of the **Cotonou Agreement** and previously the **Lomé Conventions**. The EU have also concluded agreements with a number of countries in **Asia** and **South and Central America**, which incorporate provisions for development aid. Similar help has been given to the **Maghreb states** and to the **Mashreq states**, as well as to Israel, under **protocols** in the agreements signed between these countries and the EU. A further element of aid is food and emergency provision forwarded to countries requesting EU assistance in coping with severe food shortages or the aftermath of natural disasters. This form of assistance has mainly been given to African and Asian countries, but in July 1989 the EC agriculture ministers agreed to provide food aid to Poland as part of what became known as operation **Phare**. In 1992 the **European Commission** created the **European Community Humanitarian Office** to help provide emergency relief to the former **Yugoslavia**. The amount of development aid provided by the EU has been substantial as a proportion of gross national product (GNP). The EU is currently the world's largest donor of humanitarian aid. Collectively, the **ACP States** have consumed the largest amount of aid, although, because of their number, the funds have been distributed rather thinly among them. The largest element of aid to ACP States consists of grants from the EDF and low-interest loans from the EIB, together comprising just over two-thirds of EU assistance in this area. EC development aid policy has not been entirely disinterested. Food aid has been a means of reducing EC surpluses, while the aid programmes have benefited EU companies and enterprises, which have won most of the contracts awarded under the programmes. For 2008–13 some €22,700m. was made available for EDF-backed projects that seek to reform education, modernize health and transport systems, support debt relief and balance of payments difficulties and further institutional development.

DEVELOPMENT POLICY in the European Union (EU) seeks to reduce and ultimately to eradicate poverty in the developing countries and to promote sustainable development, peace and security as well as a stable and democratic political environment in the EU's partner countries. This particular theme has grown in importance as a priority for the **European Commission** and has been developed considerably since 2000.

The central EU institution in this policy area remains the Commission, and specifically (until recently) the **Directorate-General** (DG) for Development. DG Development was charged with the role of initiating and formulating the EU's development co-operation policy for all developing countries as defined in Title XX of the **Treaty establishing the European Community**, and with co-ordinating relations with the sub-Saharan **African, Caribbean and Pacific** (ACP) **States** and the **Overseas Countries and Territories** (OCTs). The **Cotonou Agreement** provides the framework for a 20-year partnership for **development aid** to the 79 ACP countries, funded mainly by the **European Development Fund**. DG Development was also assisted by specified budget lines in terms of the EU **budget**; it prepared strategies for co-operation with ACP countries and OCTs, and also monitored their **implementation**.

In fulfilling its role, DG Development worked in close collaboration and interaction with other services of the European Commission, in particular the EuropeAid Co-operation Office, the **European Community Humanitarian Office** (ECHO), and the Directorates-General for External Relations, Trade, Economic and Financial Affairs, Fisheries, Agriculture, Environment, Transport, Energy and Justice and Home Affairs. It was committed to strong co-ordination and complementarity between the Commission, the EU member states and organizations such as the World Bank, regional development banks, the **OECD** and the **United Nations** system. DG Development worked in partnership with government, civil society, and the economic and social spheres, including the private sector in ACP countries and other developing countries.

The European Commission published its European Consensus on Development in 2005. This document identified a number of shared values, goals and commitments that the EU and its member states are tasked with implementing. These come under the headings of reducing poverty, promoting development based on Europe's democratic values (i.e. human rights, democracy, rule of law, good governance and social justice) and assisting the countries of the developing world in designing their own national strategies. The Commission is also keen to deliver more, but better focused, EU aid. EU aid already accounts for over 50% of all development aid worldwide (some €53,800m. in 2010) of which more than one-half goes to Africa.

In October 2011 the Commission presented its 'Agenda for Change', which aims to produce a more strategic EU approach to reducing poverty. EU assistance is to be focused on two main themes: first, human rights, democracy and good governance, and, second, inclusive and sustainable growth for human development. Importantly, a new Directorate-General had been created in January 2011 to deal with these themes. The new DG Development and Cooperation—EuropeAid (an amalgamation of DG Development and DG EuropeAid) is now responsible for designing EU development policies and delivering aid through a number of programmes across the globe. It was hoped that having one DG would provide greater coherence to EU development strategy by providing a single contact point and speaking with one voice. The remit of the new DG is considerable and includes promoting good governance, human and economic development, fighting hunger and preserving natural resources.

DG: See **Directorates-General**

DIANE: See **Direct Information Access Network for Europe**

DIFFERENTIATED INTEGRATION: See **À La Carte Europe**

DIPLOMATIC REPRESENTATION abroad was not initially formally maintained by the European Union (EU), although the **European Commission** had External Delegations in most countries and to international organizations. Collaboration between ambassadors of the EU states was developed as part of **European political co-operation**, and member states began to agree to share embassies and missions. The EU also had its own non-diplomatic representation in several international economic forums, such as the **World Trade Organization** (formerly the **General Agreement on Tariffs and Trade**). Many states have diplomatic representatives accredited to the EU, giving the latter a partial diplomatic status. These are often the countries' ambassadors to Belgium. (See also **Permanent mission**; **Permanent representation**.) With the entry into force of the **Treaty of Lisbon**, the EU's external representation was increased with the creation of a **European External Action Service**.

DIRECT EFFECT, together with primacy, is one of the fundamental legal principles underpinning European Communities (EC) **law**. Essentially, by interpreting the **Treaty of Rome** as having established individual rights that had to be protected at member state level, the **Court of Justice** established the doctrine of direct effect. As a result a mechanism was created for individuals and institutions to challenge the compatibility of national law with EC law. Thenceforth the Court of Justice could be invoked in national policy debates and, more importantly, any national laws that were deemed to run contrary to EC law had to be set aside.

DIRECT ELECTIONS to the **European Parliament** (EP) were provided for by the **Treaty of Rome**. The Council of Ministers (see **Council of the European Union**) declined for some time to initiate the legislation for direct elections, despite considerable agitation by the EP, which even threatened to take the Council to the **Court of Justice** for failing to honour its treaty obligations. The first direct elections were eventually held in June 1979, and since then they have been held regularly at five-year intervals. Despite a widespread belief that there should be electoral **harmonization** across the member states, it has proved impossible to reach an agreement on either a single day for the election or a common electoral system, although all now use varying systems of proportional representation. The elections are spread over several days because states insist on holding them on the day traditionally used for national elections (Sunday in most countries, Thursday in the others). Counting of votes does not begin until polls have closed in all member states. Each member state has also been free to decide upon its own electoral system: this is usually the same as, or is based upon, that used for the election of the national legislature. The United Kingdom initially retained its traditional single member, simple majority constituency system, also known as the first-past-the-post system, except in Northern Ireland, where since 1979 three seats have always been determined by the single transferable vote (STV) method of proportional representation. (Constituencies in the United Kingdom, essentially amalgamations of those for national elections, are determined by the national Boundary Commission.) The British Government, however, introduced a method of proportional representation, using a regional party list system, for the first time in the European elections held in June 1999. All the other member states employ proportional representation and, with the exception of Ireland, which uses the STV method, they all employ a party list system. The lists of candidates submitted by the competing political parties are national lists in most countries, including Austria, where direct elections to the EP were held for the first time in late 1996.

However, in Belgium, Germany, Italy and Spain—as well as Finland, where the first elections were held in 1996—regional party lists are employed, so that the region becomes, in effect, a kind of constituency. (See also **Party groups**.) Those of June 2004 were the first European elections to involve the new member states from **Central and Eastern Europe** and the Mediterranean. The overall rate of voter participation across the European Union was 45%. The most recent, seventh elections to the EP took place in June 2009, when the rate of participation by the electorate fell again, to just under 43%.

DIRECT INFORMATION ACCESS NETWORK FOR EUROPE (DIANE), also known as Euronet DIANE, was one of the first European information networks of its kind. It was a **European Commission** initiative to encourage developments in **telecommunications**. Based upon electronic packet switching, it was established in 1980 as a collaborative effort between the European Communities (EC) and the postal and telephone authorities of the member states. It enabled users to utilize the resources of some 750 databanks and databases in the EC by means of a computer and telephone. The control and management centre for the network was established in London, with further regional nodes in other parts of the European Union.

DIRECTIVES are one of three different types of **legal instrument** that the **European Commission** and the **Council of the European Union** are empowered to issue for the adoption of **legislation**. A directive is the most common form of European Union legislation. Directives are binding upon all member states, but take the form of general instructions on the goal to be achieved, while leaving the way in which it will be attained to the discretion of each member state. The conditions of a directive are normally met by the member states introducing national legislation in conformity with EU stipulations. (See also **Decisions**; **Law**; **Opinions**; **Recommendations**; **Regulations**; **Resolutions**.)

DIRECTORATES-GENERAL (DGs) are the principal bureaucratic 'ministries' or departments of the **European Commission**, to which they are responsible. The General Secretariat of the **Council of the European Union** and the Secretariat-General of the **European Parliament** also have DGs, but these are fewer in number, have fewer powers and are generally less well known. The duty of the DGs of the European Commission is to carry out, or to ensure that the member states carry out, European Union (EU) policy, and to administer allocations from the **budget** to different policy areas and the **structural funds**. They are, in turn, divided into Directorates and Units. Each DG is expected to serve and advise the Commission through the Commissioner or Commissioners who hold the portfolios for its areas of responsibility. Appointment of staff to the DGs is by competition and merit, although the allocation of posts has to ensure a fair distribution between nationals of the member states. In addition, as far as possible, it is usual for the Director-General in charge of a given DG and any relevant Commissioners not to be of the same nationality.

The European Commission is currently divided into some 33 DGs, 11 Service departments and numerous decentralized agencies and bodies. The number of DGs has altered over the years as new ones have been created and others have been merged. Until the late 1990s they were usually identified by number (e.g. DG IV), but, since reorganization in 2000, they are now identified by their policy area (e.g. DG for Competition). The titles of the DGs are susceptible to tweaks and changes, but at mid-2012 they were named as follows: Agriculture and Rural Development (AGRI); Budget (BUDG); Climate Action (CLIMA); Communication (COMM); Communications Networks, Content and Technology (CNECT); Competition (COMP); Development and Cooperation—EuropeAid (DEVCO); Economic and Financial Affairs (ECFIN); Education and Culture (EAC); Employment, Social Affairs and Inclusion (EMPL); Energy (ENER); Enlargement (ELARG); Enterprise and Industry (ENTR); Environment (ENV); Eurostat (ESTAT); Health and Consumers (SANCO); Home Affairs (HOME); Humanitarian Aid (ECHO); Human Resources and Security (HR); Informatics (DIGIT); Internal Market and Services (MARKT); Interpretation (SCIC); Joint Research Centre (JRC); Justice (JUST); Maritime Affairs and Fisheries (MARE); Mobility and Transport (MOVE); Regional Policy (REGIO); Research and Innovation (RTD); Secretariat-General (SG); Service for Foreign Policy Instruments (FPI); Taxation and Customs Union (TAXUD); Trade (TRADE); and Translation (DGT). Given the uneven degree of EC development in different policy areas, DGs have been far from equal in size. Groups of Directors-General meet at intervals to discuss the linkages and overlaps between their areas of responsibility, of which there are many. These have led to 'turf wars' within the College of Commissioners. In particular, the DG responsible for the **budget** attempts to keep an overview of EC **expenditure**—and hence that of all the other DGs—though with less success and authority than national finance ministries.

The DGs are complemented by European Commission Service departments and agencies which carry out specialized functions. These include the **Legal Service**, the Internal Audit Service, the European **Anti-Fraud Office** (OLAF), the Bureau of European Policy Advisers, the **European Atomic Energy Community** (Euratom) Supply Agency and the **Publications Office of the European Union**. A few other agencies of the Commission are based in centres throughout the EU.

DISCRIMINATION can refer to the application of restrictive **trade** practices by one member state at the expense of goods and companies from other member states. Equally, it has long been used within the European Communities (EC) to refer to inequitable treatment between individuals based on nationality and, with regard to pay, sex. The **Treaty of Amsterdam** demanded that the EC to take measures to combat discrimination on the basis of racial or ethnic origin, religion or belief, disability, age or sexual orientation.

The **DOHA ROUND** is the latest round in a series of ongoing trade negotiations that commenced in the late 1940s. These rounds were designed to work towards a system of more liberalized trade rules and, in more recent times, ones that were fairer to developing countries. This latest trade round was agreed after arduous negotiations during 9–13 November 2001 in Qatar. It resulted in some far-reaching decisions on the future development of the **World Trade Organization** (WTO); these included the launch of a new round of trade negotiations—the Doha Development Agenda (DDA)—comprising both further trade liberalization and new rule-making, underpinned by commitments substantially to strengthen assistance to developing countries. It also sought to assist developing countries to implement the existing WTO agreements. In addition, the meeting approved the long-awaited waiver from WTO rules of the **Cotonou Agreement** between the European Union (EU) and **African, Caribbean and Pacific States**.

Each trade round is not a new set of rules, principles or procedures for global trade, but rather a catch-all term for the painstaking discussions that aim to result in such rules. The last successful attempt, the **Uruguay Round**, ran from 1986 to 1993, before the WTO itself was formed in 1995. Attempts to set up a Seattle Round floundered under the weight of international protests and economic tension in 1999. The initial deal in Doha merely helps to set the agenda for a new set of trade talks, which commenced in 2002. The fact that 142 countries were able to clinch a trade deal in Doha was greeted as a triumph by governments and commentators around the world. The result was a clear success, given that the gulfs separating various trade blocs were alarmingly wide. However, Doha is a preliminary to a deal, rather than a deal in itself. The main issues dealt with at Doha included the liberalization of agricultural trade; the opening up of the financial services market; the general reduction of tariff barriers; rules on subsidies for steel and textiles; a boost to the dispute settlement system; new 'greener' rules for trade; the labelling of and copyright protection for drinks; and the relaxation of control of drug manufacturing. It quickly became evident that reaching a deal was going to be extremely difficult.

In September 2003, in Cancún, Mexico, a summit took place that sought to make progress on agreement on the Doha Round, and concentrated on four main areas: agriculture, industrial goods, trade in services, and a new customs code. However, these talks failed; a new alliance of developing nations emerged that refused to sign a proposed agreement which they felt favoured the richer WTO members. A deal was finally reached, however, in Geneva, Switzerland, in August 2004. This deal opened the way for full negotiations to start. Many analysts felt that it was vital that any new deal be agreed before 2007, when what is known as 'fast-track legislation' expired in the **USA**. Without fast-track, which limited the power of the US Congress to alter trade deals negotiated by Washington, there was little prospect that the USA would adopt a new pact.

However, the next WTO ministerial meeting in Hong Kong in December 2005 broke up without any agreements being reached. The WTO operates through consensus, and the entire experience of the Doha Round illustrated how difficult it was to attain. The Doha Round was characterized by the more active participation (than in earlier Rounds) of the developing countries, but their involvement further complicated negotiations. Agriculture proved to be the substantial point of contention. Discussions on agriculture had centred on three main aspects—market access, levels of domestic support and export competition policies—but clear division between the players prevented any chance of a deal. It should be noted that the EU had agreed in 2005 to eradicate all agricultural export **subsidies** by 2013. The group of seven WTO members—the EU member states, **the USA**, India, Brazil, China, **Japan** and Australia—met again in London in March 2006 to see if they could further advance the talks, but these were suspended in July. The most problematic point of the discussions centred on the support that the richer nations give to their farmers. Other issues included the USA's unwillingness to reduce its domestic subsidies to agriculture, concerns about the openness of the EU agricultural markets and a reticence from emerging economies such as Brazil and India to allow better access to their own markets. Within the EU, France remained one of the most vocal opponents of plans to reduce tariffs. Further unsuccessful rounds of negotiations took place in Potsdam, Germany, in 2007, and in Geneva, Switzerland, in 2008. At 2012 the impasse prevailed and the future of the Doha Round appeared uncertain. Some argue that the collapse of the Doha Round and multilateral negotiations might reinforce the growing trend towards regionalism.

DOMINANT FIRM ABUSE is dealt with under Article 102 of the **Treaty on the Functioning of the European Union** on **competition policy** and refers to companies that enjoy a hegemonic market position for particular products. It is not monopolies in themselves that are problematic or the focus of attention, but rather those holding a monopoly that use it to try to undermine competition by attempting to eject competitors from the market through the imposition of unfair pricing regimes or by deliberately imposing restrictions on the distributors of their own goods. Article 102 has been more severely limited in operation than the more widely used Article 101, which targets **cartels**, but the **European Commission** has upheld the tenets of the treaty, and its charges, when cases have proceeded to such an advanced stage, have usually been supported by the **Court of Justice** (but see **Continental Can**) and the **Court of First Instance**. Perhaps the most famous case of alleged abuse was the Commission's charge against the US-owned International Business Machines Corporation (IBM), alleging that it had infringed the treaty, firstly by withholding information on new products, and secondly by packaging several of its products together, which obliged a customer to purchase a whole package even when only one item was required. The argument lasted for four years until IBM eventually agreed, in 1984, to modify its practices voluntarily.

Firms that are found to have infringed Article 102 are subject to financial levies. Recent activity under Article 102 has seen condemnation heaped on Unilever (for tying its customers to selling certain brands of ice cream in Ireland); on British Airways (BA) (for granting extra commission to those travel agents who sold BA tickets in preference to Virgin tickets); and on the organizers of the 1998 football World Cup in France, where French citizens were given preferential treatment with regard to the sale of tickets for the final stages of the competition. In June 2005 the Commission imposed a fine of €60m. on the pharmaceutical giant AstraZeneca on the grounds that the company had attempted to prevent the manufacturers of low-cost drugs from launching a cheaper version of a particular (stomach ulcer) medicine. AstraZeneca immediately denied such allegations and planned to challenge the Commission's decision through the European Courts. Meanwhile in 2004 the Commission ruled that US software company Microsoft Corporation had violated European Union competition rules by abusing its near monopoly in the PC operating system. The case against Microsoft has not only been one of the most high-profile examples of Article 102 in operation, but also one of the most contentious, as Microsoft was highly critical of DG Competition's analysis. In July 2006 Microsoft was given a €280.5m. fine by the European Commission for failing to comply with its earlier anti-competition ruling. Microsoft appealed to the European Courts, but in September 2007 the judges backed the Commission's earlier decision against the company. The situation intensified further when Microsoft was handed a €899m. fine (later reduced to €860m.) for not abiding by the Commission's 2004 decision. The latest battle in the ongoing war between DG Competition and Microsoft opened up on another front when the Commission announced its intention in January 2009 to investigate a new case involving Microsoft's bundling package. In response, Microsoft announced that it would not bundle Internet Explorer with the version of Windows 7 to be sold in Europe. The Commission imposed its highest fine (of €1,060m.) for dominance abuse against Intel in May 2009 and was considering how to improve and modernize the workings of Article 102.

DOOGE COMMITTEE, also known as the Committee on Institutions, is the name of an ad hoc group of 'personal representatives' of the heads of government, which the **European Council** agreed to establish at its **Fontainebleau summit** in June 1984. The task of the group was to examine the possibility of institutional reform of the European Communities (EC) in the light of the **draft Treaty establishing the European Union** issued by the **European Parliament** (EP). Chaired by James Dooge of **Ireland**, the Committee was intended to conduct a preliminary exploration of the positions of the heads of government in order to determine the extent to which there existed common ground for further integration. The Dooge report drew closely on the

Genscher–Colombo Plan and the EP's draft Treaty. It issued a preliminary report in December 1984, and its final report was presented for discussion at the **Milan summit** of the Council in June 1985. The Committee stated that its overall aim was to turn the EC into a 'true political entity with the power to take decisions in the name of all citizens by a democratic process'. It outlined the following themes of institutional reform: strengthening both the **European Commission** and the EP—the former to be made more independent and streamlined, with only one Commissioner per country, the latter to be given joint decision-making authority with the Council of Ministers (see **Council of the European Union**); simplifying decision-making in the Council of Ministers by restricting the requirement of unanimity to proposals for new areas of EC action and to applications for EC membership; and allotting a strategic role to the European Council, which, meeting twice instead of three times a year, should concern itself with diplomatic and external affairs, and not the daily routine of the EC.

There were several disagreements over the report at the Milan summit, with the non-founding member states all expressing reservations about some sections of the report. In general, however, its major recommendations were not rejected outright. The Committee had also suggested that a special **inter-governmental conference** be established to consider its ideas and construct a reform package from all the reports and initiatives delivered over the previous few years. This proposal was also accepted at the Milan summit, although Denmark, Greece and the United Kingdom voted against it. The inter-governmental conference prepared the way for the **Single European Act**.

DOUBLE MAJORITY VOTING is a system of voting that, under the **Treaty of Lisbon**, will replace **qualified majority voting** (QMV) in the **Council of the European Union** from 1 November 2014. Originally envisaged in the **Treaty establishing a Constitution for Europe**, the double majority voting system allows decisions to be taken provided they have the support of 55% of member states representing 65% of the population of the European Union (EU). The measure being adopted also has to command the support of at least 15 member states. In certain areas of **justice and home affairs**, the **common foreign and security policy** and economic and monetary policy, where the Council does not act on the basis of a proposal from the Commission, a measure requires the support of 72% of member states representing 65% of the EU's population. A blocking minority needs to include at least four member states. Thanks to the uncompromising position adopted by Poland in the 2007 **inter-governmental conference**, until 31 March 2017 member states will be able to request that a decision be adopted using the existing QMV system. At Poland's insistence, a modified version of the **Ioannina Compromise** will also be available during this period and after. It is anticipated that the double majority voting system will facilitate decision-making and make the process easier to understand.

The **DRAFT TREATY ESTABLISHING A CONSTITUTION FOR EUROPE** was drawn up by the **European Convention** under the chairmanship of **Valéry Giscard d'Estaing**. It brought together the existing **Treaty on European Union** and the **Treaty of Rome** to create a 'constitution' for the European Union (EU). In addition, the draft contained a variety of policy and institutional innovations and reforms. All this was brought together via four parts. The first, *inter alia*, set out the objectives of the EU, established EU **citizens' rights**, defined the EU's **competences**, presented the EU's **institutions**, determined how the EU should exercise its competences, established mechanisms for **enhanced co-operation**, outlined the EU's **budget**, and determined the mechanisms for accession. The second part incorporated the **Charter of Fundamental Rights**. The third part then outlined in much greater detail the policies (e.g. **economic and monetary union**, **social policy**) and functioning (e.g. **decision-making**) of the EU. The fourth part contained 'general and final provisions' and was followed by a number of **protocols** and **declarations**.

Following its adoption on the basis of 'consensus' by the European Convention in June and July 2003, the draft Treaty establishing a Constitution for Europe was submitted to the **European Council**, which welcomed it as 'a good basis' for starting negotiations on a '**Constitutional Treaty**'. These negotiations began with the launch of an **intergovernmental conference** (IGC) in October 2003, which was scheduled to complete its work prior to the **enlargement** of the EU on 1 May 2004. Although broad agreement existed on adopting the structure of the European Convention's draft Treaty as the basis for the 'Constitutional Treaty', some of its provisions proved unacceptable to certain member states, as was evident at the Brussels European Council in 2003 when Spain and Poland rejected replacement of the existing system of **qualified majority voting** in the Council with a system based on dual majority of member states and population. This meant that the timetable for the IGC was somewhat disrupted, with negotiations continuing until June 2004 when agreement on the **Treaty establishing a Constitution for Europe** was finally reached.

DRAFT TREATY ESTABLISHING THE EUROPEAN UNION is the name of a document prepared by the **European Parliament** (EP) under the direction of **Altiero Spinelli**. An EP Institutional Committee began drafting the document in 1981. The Draft Treaty originated in the work of the **Crocodile Group** (a group of **Members of the European Parliament**— MEPs—who first met in the *Crocodile* restaurant in Strasbourg) and sought to revive the European project. Spinelli believed that following the first **direct elections** to the EP in 1979 the MEPs were now in a position (in terms of legitimacy) to re-examine the original three treaties establishing the European Communities (EC) in the 1950s. Moreover, it was generally felt that a new treaty was needed to reorder the European institutions and to expand the policy remit. This document proposed greater powers for the **European Commission** and EP, and a severe reduction of the member states' right of veto on proposed policies. The Commission, which would supervise the implementation of the new treaty establishing a European union, would become the sole EC executive, accountable to the EP and a weakened Council of Ministers (see **Council of the European Union**). The EP would have an independent revenue-raising responsibility and share budgetary powers with the downgraded Council, which was to be only a legislative body, renamed the Council of the Union. The EP approved the Draft Treaty in February 1984, but no action was taken on it directly by either the Council of Ministers or the **European Council**, owing to the sensitivity of many of its suggestions. However, several of its ideas were taken up by the **Dooge Committee** on institutional reform, and subsequently influenced the new integration initiatives of the late 1980s and 1990s.

MARIO DRAGHI (1947–) is an Italian banker, who was appointed Governor of the central bank of Italy in January 2006, and succeeded **Jean–Claude Trichet** as the third President of the European Central Bank (ECB) in November 2011. It remained to be seen whether Draghi's appointment would lead to substantive changes in the focus of the ECB, amid the uncertainties of the ongoing European sovereign debt crisis. None the less, in early September 2012 Draghi announced that the governing council of the ECB had approved a new plan for the introduction of outright monetary transactions (OMT). The OMT would allow the ECB to purchase, in unlimited quantities, the short-term bonds of member countries of the euro area seeking financial assistance from the EU's emergency funding mechanisms, and thereby protect the long-term future of the euro; Germany remained strongly opposed to the proposals.

DRIVING LICENCES were the subject of a **directive** adopted by the Council of Ministers (see **Council of the European Union**) in 1980. The directive required the introduction of a European Communities (EC) driving licence. The first stage of the process began in 1983 with reciprocal recognition by the member states of each other's licences. Since 1983 licences have been issued with common requirements and common specifications, and from January 1986 driving licences in all EC states had to conform to a common model. The format adopted also satisfies the requirements of the 1968 Vienna International Road Traffic Convention, making it valid in other countries that signed the Convention.

DUAL MANDATE refers to those politicians who were members both of the **European Parliament** (EP) and of a **national parliament**. Before **direct elections** to the EP were introduced in 1979 the double mandate was the norm, as **Members of the European Parliament** (MEPs) were selected from within the ranks of their own national parliaments. From 1979, however, double mandates became less common, as parties tended to discourage, and in some cases refuse to allow, their members to sit in both the EP and their national parliament simultaneously. However, many still existed. Indeed, it was also possible to speak of a triple mandate as some individuals sat in the EP, their national parliament and a regional assembly. The major concern surrounding double (and triple) mandates centred on the degree to which such members could adequately master their individual briefs and represent the electorate at both (or all three) levels. This situation caused general dissatisfaction. A proposal by European Union member state governments to abolish dual membership of the EP and **national parliaments** was approved by MEPs in 2003 (399 votes in favour of this motion, 111 against with 25 abstentions). The proposal formed part of a number of changes to the 1976 Act on the election of members of the EP. The abolition of the dual mandate took effect at the 2004 elections to the EP, although the United Kingdom negotiated an exemption until the June 2009 EP elections.

The **DUBLIN CONVENTION ON ASYLUM** is a document outlining common formal arrangements relating to asylum throughout the European Union. It was a response to worries that the **internal market** and the **freedom of movement** it entailed would attract large numbers of economic asylum-seekers, especially from Eastern Europe. The Convention was signed by member states in June 1990 (with the exception of Denmark, which signed a year later), but the slowness of the **ratification** process in many member states delayed its introduction. It stipulates that when an individual has been refused asylum in one member state, he or she may not seek asylum in any other signatory state. Even this, however, was deemed to be insufficient after the disintegration of the Socialist Federal Republic of **Yugoslavia**, and in June 1991 the states agreed to establish a Quick Reaction Consultation Centre.

DUBLIN FOUNDATION: See **European Foundation for the Improvement of Living and Working Conditions**

DUMPING is the selling of produce at greatly reduced, below-cost prices, and such practices by any member state within the European Union (EU) are banned. The **European Commission** has the authority to permit the affected member states to take appropriate protective measures if the offending country does not heed its recommendations and warnings. One difficulty is that national perceptions of what constitutes dumping can vary, because of different rates and costs of production, and on occasion this has led to disputes between member states. The Commission can also act by imposing anti-dumping duties where it believes that other countries are engaged in dumping within the EU. By contrast, the policy of disposing of surplus agricultural produce (accumulated under the intervention element of the **common agricultural policy**) at greatly reduced prices abroad has often been claimed by other countries with a major agricultural export industry to constitute a dumping practice.

DUNKIRK TREATY: See **Treaty of Dunkirk**

E

eEUROPE: See **Information Society**

E-NUMBERS are pan-European code numbers identifying a range of food additives. Their use is demanded by various **directives**.

EACEA (Education, Audiovisual and Culture Executive Agency): See **MEDIA 2007**

EAEC: See **European Atomic Energy Community**

EAGGF: See **European Agricultural Guidance and Guarantee Fund**

EAP: See **Eastern Partnership**

EAP: See **Environmental Action Programme**

EASA (European Aviation Safety Agency): See **Air Transport Policy**

EAST GERMANY: See **Germany**

The **EASTERN PARTNERSHIP** (EaP) between the European Union (EU) and its eastern neighbours—**Armenia, Azerbaijan, Belarus, Georgia, Moldova** and **Ukraine**—was launched at a dedicated summit in Prague in May 2009 as part of EU efforts to respond to the wish of most of these countries for closer ties. The EaP is part of the **European neighbourhood policy** (ENP) and is aimed at strengthening relations through increased bilateral co-operation, new **association agreements**, **deep and comprehensive free trade area**s, visa facilitation and liberalization, and co-operation on energy security matters, notably security of supply to the EU. Multilateral co-operation is also envisaged, with heads of government and state expected to meet every two years. Although in 2011 the **European Commission**, as part of its review of the

ENP, advocated an increased emphasis on regional partnerships within the ENP, the postponement of, and poor attendance by EU leaders at, EaP summits has led the EU's eastern neighbours to question the EU's commitment to the 'partnership'.

EBN: See **European Business and Innovation Centre Network**

EBRD: See **European Bank for Reconstruction and Development**

EBU: See **European Broadcasting Union**

EC: See **European Communities**; **European Community**, but note that, in a streamlining and simplification exercise under the **Treaty of Lisbon**, this term has been replaced by the term **European Union**.

ECA: See **Court of Auditors**

ECB: See **European Central Bank**

ECCG: See **Consumer Committee**

ECCP: See **European Climate Change Programme**

ECDIN: See **Environmental Chemicals Data Information Network**

ECE: See **Economic Commission for Europe**

ECHO: See **European Community Humanitarian Office**

ECISS: See **European Committee for Iron and Steel Standards**

ECLAS is the **European Commission**'s automated library system. It is accessible online at ec.europa.eu/eclas/F.

ECOLABEL has been designed as a means of promoting products with a reduced environmental impact and of providing consumers with accurate information about the product. Regulation No. 1980/2000 replaced the earlier 1992 regulation on a European Communities Ecolabel award scheme. Certain categories are excluded from the new Regulation's scope, including foodstuffs, beverages and pharmaceutical products.

The **ECO-MANAGEMENT AND AUDIT SCHEME** (EMAS) of the European Communities (EC) is a 1993 initiative to promote responsible environmental management in industry. (An existing regulation—No. 1836/93—was replaced by Regulation No. 761/2001.) Participation in the scheme is voluntary. The objective of EMAS is to promote continuous improvement in the environmental achievements of all European organizations, while providing the public and interested parties with any relevant information.

ECOFIN: See **Economic and Financial Affairs Council of Ministers**

ECOIN is the acronym of the European core inventory of chemicals.

The **ECONOMIC AND FINANCIAL AFFAIRS COUNCIL OF MINISTERS** (Ecofin) is one of the most important formats of the **Council of the European Union** (alongside the **General Council, the Foreign Affairs Council** and the Special Council for Agriculture) through which specific policy areas are addressed. Ecofin is the name given to the regular meetings of the economic and finance ministers of the member states, which are held, on average, once a month. The ministers, who also meet in the **Economic and Financial Committee**, discuss both broad and more detailed issues of economic management. Issues pertaining to **economic and monetary union** are discussed by the informal **Eurogroup** (EURO-17) group of finance ministers of the participating member states.

ECONOMIC AND FINANCIAL COMMITTEE is the name of an institution created by the **Treaty on European Union** as part of the development of **economic and monetary union** (EMU). It was first instituted at the start of the third and final stage of EMU on 1 January 1999, as a replacement for the **Monetary Committee**, although it was not charged with reviewing the monetary situation in the European Communities. The committee comprises senior individuals from member state finance ministries and representatives from the **European Central Bank**. The Treaty charged it with monitoring the economic situation in the European Union and reporting to and advising the **European Commission** and the **Council of the European Union**. Despite its largely advisory function, the Committee is highly influential, given its policy remit over EMU.

ECONOMIC AND FINANCIAL POLICY is mentioned in the **Treaty of Rome**, which obligates the member states to co-operate with each other in planning their economic policies. Since the establishment of the European Communities (EC), the member states have broadly followed similar economic policies, but this has owed less to co-ordination of effort and more to common reactions to worldwide problems and trends in the international economy. The **European Commission** has issued annual economic reports, which have included recommendations, but its advice and suggestions have not been binding upon the member states. Broad questions of economic policy have been discussed by the **European Council** and have been a concern of what is now the **Economic and Financial Affairs Council of Ministers**. Further co-operation was achieved through the regular meetings of the consultative **Committee of the Governors of the Central Banks**. These consultation exercises together constituted a reasonable level of co-operation, but they fell short of the level of co-ordination anticipated by the Treaty of Rome. Only in two areas have the EC been able to wield a significant influence upon economic policy. The first is the raising of loans on behalf of member states through a variety of instruments: the **European Investment Bank**, the **European Coal and Steel Community**, the **European Atomic Energy Community** and the New Community Instrument. The other, prior to **economic and monetary union** (EMU), was the ability to limit exchange-rate fluctuations through the **exchange-rate mechanism** of the **European Monetary System**. More generally, however, EC authority and the EC **budget** have been too limited to have any kind of decisive impact upon macroeconomic policy analogous to that wielded by national governments. These deficiencies explain the interest in EMU. The details and timetable for EMU set down by the **Treaty on European Union** were intended to provide the EC with a common economic and financial policy by 1999. Eleven member states were ready to participate as planned by this date, but the reality of four member states (Greece, Denmark, Sweden and the United Kingdom) not taking part in EMU imposed some limitations on that objective. Greece entered EMU in 2001, but the decision for the other three states was to be determined by **referenda**. Two have already taken place: in Denmark and Sweden. In both instances the respective electorates voted against participation, leaving only the United Kingdom still to hold a referendum.

ECONOMIC AND MONETARY UNION (EMU) was on the European Communities (EC) agenda from 1969, when the **Six** agreed to the principle at the **Hague summit** and set 1980 as the completion date for full EMU. The **Werner Report** of 1970 established a timetable for the programme. The plans for EMU were effectively destroyed by the severe decline and general turmoil in the international economic climate of the 1970s. The member states became more introspective in their economic policies, and the idea of EMU by the end of the decade was abandoned. All that survived was the **European Monetary Co-operation Fund**. The **European Monetary System**, launched in 1979, was not a replacement for EMU, though it did constitute a step in that direction. The next step towards EMU was precipitated by the plans for a single market that comprised the substance of the **Single European Act**. Although this treaty did not describe EMU as an immediate objective it did refer to the idea in the preamble to the treaty, which **Jacques Delors** pushed forward and presented to the Hanover meeting of the **European Council** in June 1988. Despite the objections of the United Kingdom, the European Council agreed to establish a committee to examine the idea and benefits of realizing EMU; Delors was asked to chair this committee.

EMU was revived formally in June 1989, when the European Council accepted the proposals of the **Delors Plan**, which envisaged a three-stage movement towards the goal, with the first stage, the involvement of all member states in the **exchange-rate mechanism** (ERM), to begin in July 1990. In Rome in October 1990, the Council endorsed January 1994 as the beginning of the second stage of a more intensive economic and monetary co-ordination in anticipation of the creation of a **European Central Bank** (ECB) and single currency. An **intergovernmental conference** of EC finance ministers began in December 1990. Its deliberations were synchronous with those on closer political integration, and EMU became therefore a major theme of the **Maastricht summit** and the consequent **Treaty on European Union**. The Treaty provisions relating to EMU broadly followed the outline of the Delors Plan, confirming January 1994 as the date for commencement of closer co-ordination, and preparing for the establishment of a **European Monetary Institute**, which would assume some responsibility from the **Council of the European Union** for monitoring how national policies and budget deficits were conforming to guidelines. The final stage of EMU was set for January 1999. It would entail a **European System of Central Banks** along with the ECB, with the **European Currency Unit** (ecu) becoming the single currency of the European Union (EU) (however, it was decided in 1995 that the new single currency would be the **euro**, which would replace the ecu on a one-for-one basis).

Participation in the third stage would depend upon individual member states meeting the following **convergence criteria**: a high degree of price stability measured by an inflation rate no higher than 1.5% above the average of that of the three best performing member states; a budget deficit no greater than 3% of gross domestic product (GDP) and a governmental debt no greater than 60% of GDP; staying within the permissible fluctuation limits of the ERM for at least two years without any realignment or devaluation; and interest rates no more than 2% higher than the three best-performing member states in terms of price stability. However, it was agreed that EMU would begin in 1999 regardless of how many states had met the criteria. The schedule and deadlines were immediately questioned, not least because Denmark and the United Kingdom were later given exemptions, or **opt-outs**, from the final stage. There was also considerable popular opposition in Germany to a single currency. Economic and monetary conditions in the 1990s threatened the achievement of EMU. Turmoil and speculation on the money markets in 1992 and 1993 put the ERM under extreme pressure, revealing that the EMU plans and the ERM took little account of the real strength of national currencies.

The United Kingdom and Italy were forced to leave the ERM, and many other countries' currencies were devalued. The ERM survived only by extending the permissible fluctuation limits to such an extent that what resulted was almost a system of floating currencies. Equally important was the recession in Western Europe. The economic difficulties were such that by 1994 very few states met the convergence criteria. However, a much less strict interpretation of the criteria was eventually applied, and in 1998 it was declared that, of those member states that wished to be part of EMU, only Greece had failed to meet the criteria. Denmark, Sweden and the United Kingdom had already decided not to join in the venture, which was launched in January 1999, after the inauguration of the ECB and the launch of the euro. Greece joined the initial 11 member states in 2001, leaving only Denmark, Sweden and the United Kingdom outside the eurozone; their entry would depend on the outcome of a referendum that would be held in each state if and when their governments decided they were ready to join. The Danish people rejected membership of the euro in a referendum in September 2000. Full EMU for participating states occurred in 2002, when national notes and coins were replaced by the euro. Ireland was the first EU member state successfully to replace its former national currency, in early February 2002. In a referendum in Sweden in September 2003 a majority of voters opted to reject membership of the **eurozone**, while in the United Kingdom there is little likelihood of a referendum in the foreseeable future. As regards the states that joined the EU on 1 May 2004, it was considered unlikely that any would adopt the euro until at least two years after accession. Slovenia's application was successful and the country became the 13th to adopt the euro, on 1 January 2007. Malta and Cyprus both adopted the euro on 1 January 2008. Slovakia joined the eurozone on 1 January 2009, and Estonia became the eurozone's 17th member, adopting the euro on 1 January 2011.

The 10th anniversary of the launch of EMU in 2009 was an occasion for modest self-congratulation on the part of the EU. The euro had been introduced, the ECB had established its credibility as a force for monetary stability, and EMU was attracting new members. However, the concurrent economic and financial crisis laid bare a number of important structural weaknesses, notably the absence of EU-level tools for effective economic governance, and the presence in the eurozone of some member states running excessive deficits. It must be remembered that the euro has constituted only a monetary union and not an economic union. The euro had functioned well in the boom years but worsening economic circumstances came to test the stability and durability of the euro in 2010. Greece became the focal point. As the economic situation in Greece deteriorated in early 2010 the Greek Government introduced an austerity programme which was greeted with public opposition. The German Government sought to maintain the stability of the euro by co-ordinating substantial loans to Greece, but did not dispel the doubts of its critics about the longer-term prospects for the euro and particularly the future of certain states within the **eurozone**. Ensuing problems in **Ireland**, **Portugal** and **Spain** by early 2013 only intensified the criticism of the euro and both its suitability and desirability for all current participant states.

ECONOMIC AND SOCIAL COMMITTEE: See **European Economic and Social Committee**

The **ECONOMIC COMMISSION FOR EUROPE** (ECE) is a regional agency of the **United Nations** established in 1947. Until the formation of the **Conference on Security and Co-operation in Europe**, it was the only European body that allowed the states of both Eastern and Western Europe an opportunity to meet on a regular basis. It concerned itself primarily with the exchange of information and development of ideas in non-contentious areas, especially relating to environmental problems.

ECONOMIC PARTNERSHIP AGREEMENTS (EPAs) have been con-cluded by the European Union (EU) with a number of **African, Caribbean and Pacific** (ACP) countries following the **World Trade Organization**'s (WTO) ruling that the 2000 **Cotonou Agreement** contravened its rules. The bilateral agreements, the first of which were concluded in 2007, provide for the liberalization of trade and are designed to support regional integration among ACP countries and foster their 'smooth and gradual integration … into the world economy, particularly by helping create larger ACP regional markets, thereby contributing to sustainable development and poverty reduction'. EPAs are expected to be extended to cover service sector liberalization and rules governing foreign direct investment. Critics of EPAs claim that the require-ment for reciprocal trade liberalization damages the economic development of the ACP countries and that, in its haste to conclude the agreements by the WTO deadline of 31 January 2007, the EU did little to ensure that they promote regional integration.

ECOSOC: See **European Economic and Social Committee**

ECSAS: See **European Community Studies Associations**

ECSC: See **European Coal and Steel Community**

ECTS stands for the European Communities course credit transfer system, established as part of the European Community action scheme for the mobility of university students (**Erasmus**).

ECU is the acronym commonly used to refer to the European Currency Unit. The ecu was introduced in 1979 as a central element of the **European Monetary System** (EMS), namely a common artificial currency unit supporting the **exchange-rate mechanism** (ERM) of the EMS. It replaced the **European Unit of Account** (EUA). While not all the member states participated in the ERM, all subscribed to the ecu. Its value was based upon a weighted basket of currencies. Each currency received a different 'weight' in the basket, with the allocation of weights being subject to regular review. The weights (in percentages) for each national currency were frozen as follows in November 1993 under the terms of the **Treaty on European Union** (TEU): Germany 32.0; France 20.4; the United Kingdom 11.2; the Netherlands 10.0; Italy 8.5; Belgium 8.2; Spain 4.5; Denmark 2.7; Ireland 1.1; Portugal 0.7; Greece 0.5; Luxembourg 0.3. (The currencies of Austria, Finland and Sweden were not represented in the ecu basket.) The US dollar was used as a reference point. The specified amounts of the national currencies were converted into dollars, and added together to give the value of the ecu, which could then be translated back into national currencies and used for transactions. The central rate of the ecu was used to calculate bilateral central rates for each pair of European Union (EU) currencies. The ecu was supported by the **European Monetary Co-operation Fund** (EMCF), a reserve fund into which the countries participating in the basket had to place 20% of both their gold and dollar reserves. It established itself as an accepted currency in international money markets, widely used in international Eurobond issues, as well as in commercial transactions, loans, bank deposits and cheques. Internally, it became a book-keeping device, fully replacing the EUA for all European Communities transactions and calculations in 1981. It was also originally conceived to evolve into the single currency of the EU once full **economic and monetary union** (EMU) was established. This was confirmed by the TEU, which set completion of the third and final stage of EMU for 1997–99, at which point the ecu would replace the national currencies throughout the participating member states. However, at the **European Council** meeting in Dublin in 1995, it was decided that the ecu would be replaced by the **euro** on 1 January 1999, on a one-for-one basis. The euro became the new currency unit within the newly established **eurozone**, and replaced the national currencies of those 11 member states participating in EMU at that stage.

ED: See **European Democratic Group**

EDA: See **European Defence Agency**

EDC: See **European Defence Community**

EDCS: See **European Documentation Centres**

EDD: See **Group for a Europe of Democracies and Diversities**

EDF: See **European Development Fund**

The **EDINBURGH SUMMIT** of the **European Council** in 1992 took place in the aftermath of the Danish electorate's rejection of the **Treaty on European Union** and saw the European Council agree on a number of exemptions, or **opt-outs**, for **Denmark** as well as issuing a statement that sought to clarify the principle of **subsidiarity** and emphasize the European Union's commitment to **transparency** and greater **openness**.

The **EDUCATION, AUDIOVISUAL AND CULTURE EXECUTIVE AGENCY** (EACEA) was established in January 2006. It is based in Brussels and seeks to co-ordinate and implement more than 15 existing EU-funded programmes in the areas of education and training, citizenship and youth policy, as well as schemes that focus on audiovisual and cultural themes. Although it possesses its own legal identity, the EACEA reports directly to the **European Commission** and specifically three of its Directorates-General— Education and Culture, Communication and Development and Cooperation— EuropeAid. The EACEA manages the following programmes: **Lifelong learning**, **Erasmus Mundus**, **Tempus**, Bilateral Cooperation, Intra-ACP Academic Mobility Scheme, Culture, Media, Europe for Citizens and Youth in Action. In practice, the Commission maintains responsibility for the running of the programmes and their evaluation, while the EACEA takes control when it comes to drawing up proposals and selecting projects, and is involved in the constant monitoring of existing projects. The EACEA is particularly charged with managing funding opportunities and networks in the fields of education and training.

EDUCATION INFORMATION NETWORK IN THE EUROPEAN COMMUNITY: See **EURYDICE**

EDUCATION, VOCATIONAL TRAINING AND YOUTH POLICY was originally largely excluded from the **Treaty of Rome**, other than in a reference to the reciprocal recognition by the member states of diplomas, professional qualifications and vocational training. The European Communities long accepted that national traditions and practices in education are both important and too complex or sensitive to be easily standardized. Initiatives to foster member state co-operation on educational matters only began to materialize in the 1970s in a series of non-binding **resolutions**. The **Single European Act** emphasized the need for a European dimension in this area. This manifested itself in a 1988 resolution urging all member states to integrate the European dimension into the school curriculum. Education was first recognized as a policy competence when Articles 149 and 150 were inserted into the Treaty of Rome by the **Treaty on European Union**. These— now Articles 165–166 of the **Treaty on the Functioning of the European Union**—spoke of 'the development of quality education by encouraging co-operation … with a view to developing the European dimension in education' and envisaged, for example, the teaching of member state **languages** in other European Union (EU) states, plans to encourage greater mobility of students and teachers, and efforts to develop educational exchanges and establish distance-learning programmes.

The **Treaty of Amsterdam** altered nothing substantial, but did determine that measures relating to education and vocational training were to be adopted under **co-decision procedures**. Progress in these areas has been limited. Even a 1989 **directive** requiring all member states to recognize diplomas and degrees of three years' study has proved problematic. Education policy continues to confine itself to stressing the need for closer collaboration and mutual under-standing, and continues to take the form of **recommendations** to member states, rather than binding **legislation**. States have been urged to improve training opportunities for, and the cultural integration of, migrant workers; to co-operate in higher education; and to improve the quality and extent of the teaching of EU languages. The few **directives** that have been issued relate to **freedom of movement** in jobs and professions. Three main education and vocational training programmes were introduced in 1985: **Socrates**, to encou-rage student mobility; **Leonardo** (da Vinci), to promote access to vocational training and lifelong learning, training exchanges and cross-border projects, and to foster innovation and entrepreneurship, improve the quality of training and make it easier to obtain and use vocational training and skills in other European countries; and **Youth for Europe**, which aimed to facilitate the mobility of young people from disadvantaged backgrounds. In addition, the **Tempus** programme, launched in 1990, encouraged exchanges in higher education between the EU and the states of **Central and Eastern Europe**. The Tempus programme was extended in 2004 to enable students from around the world (the so-called Tempus Mundus) to study in the EU. These programmes were open to people of all ages because lifelong learning and building a Europe of knowledge know no age barriers. In addition, under the Socrates programme, more than 10,000 schools benefited each year from **Lingua**, to promote the learning of languages, particularly lesser-used languages, and **Minerva**, to apply new technologies in education.

The oldest and probably the best known sub-programme established under the Socrates umbrella is **Erasmus**. It devotes more than €100m. annually to grants for students and teachers to spend time at higher education establish-ments in other European countries. Some 4,000 institutions in 33 countries are currently involved in the programme. By 2007 more than 2.2m. students had studied in another country, thanks to Erasmus. From 2007 Erasmus and Leonardo were incorporated into the new **Lifelong Learning Programme 2007–13**, which replaced the Socrates and eLearning programmes (which expired at the end of 2006). (See also **European Centre for the Development of Vocational Training; European schools; European University Institute**.) Other sub-programmes within the Lifelong Learning Programme include **Grundtvig**, for adult learners and their teachers, to develop European teaching materials and networks and short teaching exchanges, the **Jean Monnet** Programme, which supports institutions and actions in favour of European integration, and **Comenius**, for schools and their teachers. The Lifelong Learning Programme remains the flagship policy in the education field and offers opportunities for a wide range of educational programmes for people from early childhood until old age. It was to provide €7,000m. in funding over its duration.

The Commission's activities in education and training are designed to improve the quality of learning systems across the EU and to provide greater opportunities for people. The Commission co-operates with member state authorities to improve policies and exchange best practices and continues to fund a range of education-based programmes. Co-operation between the Commission and the national authorities in the education and training arena intensified following the European Council's adoption of the **Lisbon agenda** in 2000. Indeed, as part of this strategy the Commission launched its 'Education and Training 2010' programme in 2002. This programme led to a number of initiatives to support lifelong learning and included the European Qualifications Framework (EQF), which is essentially a framework of main competences that every EU citizen should possess in today's knowledge society.

The Education and Training 2010 programme also supported the **Bologna Process** and greater co-operation and coherence in the provision of university education and the creation of a European Higher Education Area. Even more importantly, the European Institute of Innovation and Technology (EIT) was established in an effort to foster greater cross-European research and education. It is seen as a European counterpart to the world famous Massachusetts Institute of Technology (MIT).

In 2009 a new strategic framework, 'Education and Training 2020', was drawn up to build on the work of its predecessor `Education and Training 2010'.

EEA: See **European Economic Area**

EEA: See **European Environment Agency**

EEAS: See **European External Action Service**

EEC: See **European Economic Community**

EEIG: See **European Economic Interest Grouping**

EESC: See **European Economic and Social Committee**

EFA: See **European Free Alliance**

EFDA: See **European Fusion Development Agreement**

EFDO: See **European Film Distribution Office**

EFSF: See **European Financial Stability Facility**

EFSM: See **European Financial Stabilization Mechanism**

EFTA: See **European Free Trade Association**

The **EHIC** or European health insurance card replaced the E111 form from January 2006, and entitles its holders to reduced-cost, or sometimes free, medical treatment should it become necessary when they are staying in another EU member state, a member of the European Economic Area (EEA—**Iceland**, **Liechtenstein** and **Norway**) or **Switzerland**. The EHIC is normally valid for three to five years. The card provides access to state-provided medical treatment only, and specifically does not cover those who are intent on travelling to one of the states listed above solely for the purpose of receiving medical treatment.

EIB: See **European Investment Bank**

EIC: See **Euro Info Centres**

EIF: See **European Investment Fund**

EINECS: See **European Inventory of Existing Chemical Substances**

EIS: See **Schengen Information System**

EJN: See **European Judicial Network in Criminal Matters**

ELDR: See **Group of the European Liberal Democrats**

ELECTIONS: See **Direct Elections**

ELECTRICITY has been considered by the European Communities (EC) in the context of its overall **energy policy**. The first programme concerning electricity was drawn up by the Council of Ministers (see **Council of the European Union**) in 1974, and updated in 1980 and 1986. The 1986 review defined objectives for the period up to 1995. It urged continuation of the policy of reducing the reliance of electricity generation on petroleum, which was to constitute less than 15% of total electricity generation by 1995. It further suggested that by 1995 40% of electricity generation should be nuclear-based, rising to 50% by 2000. Owing to subsequent concerns about the safety and costs of nuclear energy, these projections have become less realistic.

Electricity policy forms a core element of the EC's pursuit of an **internal market** for energy. In the case of electricity, its objective is to ensure the free movement of electricity while improving security of supply and the competitiveness of this particular sector. In 1997 a **directive** (96/92/EC) concerning common rules for the internal market in electricity came into force. The **European Commission** has subsequently monitored this sector, and in its second report on the state of liberalization in the energy markets, published in May 1999, accepted that substantial progress was being made in relation to the restructuring of this sector across all member states. It reported that progress had exceeded the original minimum market opening prescribed in the original directive, and that 60% of the electricity market had been liberalized. The Lisbon **European Council** meeting in March 2000 urged a more rapid opening up of the European Union (EU) energy market. In March 2001 the Commission adopted a set of measures to liberalize the electricity market fully by 2005. These included a communication on the completion of the internal market, a draft directive amending existing directives and introducing common rules for the electricity market, and a draft regulation on conditions of access to cross-border trade in electricity. These initiatives reflect the Commission's zeal to create a genuine internal market that is subject to fair competition and guarantees the rights of the consumer. These moves were complemented by a series of measures to strengthen economic and social cohesion, which includes, for example, the establishment of trans-European energy networks across the continent. These have been in existence for the last decade or so and have helped to connect both halves of Europe. Indeed, the CENTREL electricity grid (which covers Poland, the Czech Republic, Slovakia and Hungary) has been connected to the main European grid since 1995. The EU is currently developing a much broader policy and establishing other close energy links with countries such as **Russia**, the People's Republic of China and the Balkan states.

ÉLYSÉE TREATY: See **Treaty of Friendship**

EMA: See **European Medicines Agency**

EMAS: See **Eco-management and Audit Scheme**

EMCDDA: See **European Monitoring Centre for Drugs and Drug Addiction**

EMCF: See **European Monetary Co-operation Fund**

EMEA: See **Euro-Mediterranean Economic Area**

EMEP is the acronym of a co-operative programme set up in 1986 to monitor and evaluate the transmission of air pollutants over long distances.

EMFTA: See **Euro-Mediterranean Free Trade Area**

EMI: See **European Monetary Institute**

EMP: See **Euro-Mediterranean Partnership**

EMPLOYMENT is the focus of a **title** inserted into the **Treaty of Rome** (Articles 125–130—now Articles 145–150 of the **Treaty on the Functioning of the European Union**) by the **Treaty of Amsterdam**. The promotion of employment ranks as one of the European Union's objectives and as a matter of common concern. Member states are encouraged to co-ordinate their employment strategies in moves to combat high unemployment, although there are no plans for a common employment policy. Under the terms of the Treaty, the **European Council** is to conduct an annual review of the state of employment, and the **Council of the European Union** must play a more active role in employment affairs by encouraging the exchange of information in this field between member states. This objective was reinforced at the Luxembourg jobs summit, an extraordinary European Council meeting convened in November 1997, where it was decided to develop a **European Employment Strategy** built on thematic priorities and described in employment guidelines adopted by the **Essen summit** meeting of the European Council. Every year these guidelines have to be translated by member states into national action plans for employment, which are later assessed by the Council of the European Union and the **European Commission** prior to the publication of a joint employment report. An **Employment Committee** was established to oversee the co-ordination of the employment strategies of the member states.

The European Commission has its own specific **Directorate-General** (DG) for Employment, Social Affairs and Inclusion that seeks to stimulate more and better jobs, secure better working conditions and promote social inclusion and non-discrimination and equality between men and women. The Commissioner responsible for employment, social affairs and inclusion is **László Andor**. This DG works closely with national authorities, social partners and other relevant actors, and addresses the challenges that confront the working environment, such as the impact of the credit crunch and an ageing population.

The **EMPLOYMENT COMMITTEE**, established under the **Treaty of Amsterdam**, replaced the Employment and Labour Market Committee set up in 1996. It comprises two representatives from each European Union member state and two representatives from the **European Commission**. The Committee is charged with monitoring member state employment and labour market policies, and promotes their co-ordination and delivers opinions on them. (See also **Standing Committee on Employment**.)

EMPTY CHAIR CRISIS refers to the period of seven months after June 1965, when **France** boycotted meetings of the Council of Ministers (see **Council of the European Union**) and the **Committee of Permanent Representatives** (COREPER), although it continued to send junior representatives to some sessions in order for minor routine business to be carried out. This French ploy effectively paralysed the European Communities (EC). The French protest was over the EC timetable for the increased use of **qualified majority voting** in the Council of Ministers after January 1966, and over a collection of proposals from the **European Commission**. These included the finalization of the financial regulations for the **common agricultural policy** (of which France was in favour), as well as more powers for the **European Parliament**—especially in relation to the **budget**—and an independent source of **revenue** for the Commission (both of which proposals France opposed). The crisis was resolved by a compromise, which was largely to France's advantage and **Charles de Gaulle**'s satisfaction. The most important element of the resolution was the **Luxembourg Compromise**, which, although maintaining the principle of majority voting, extended to member states the right to use a veto in the Council of Ministers if they believed that their national interests were being compromised. This agreement among the **Six** undermined the prestige of the Commission and impaired the EC's political development for nearly 20 years, until the **Single European Act**. (See also **Walter Hallstein**.)

EMS: See **European Monetary System**

EMSA: See **European Maritime Safety Agency**

EMU: See **Economic and Monetary Union**

ENERGY POLICY has been a rather problematic area for the European Communities (EC), as it touches on sensitive national concerns. It should be remembered that two of the initial Communities (**ECSC** and **Euratom**) dealt with energy. A first attempt at trying to co-ordinate member states' energy policy (to secure fair competition, low process and freedom of choice for the consumer) occurred in a **protocol** on Energy in 1964, but progress was very limited. A further, unsuccessful effort was made in 1968. The difficulties were revealed by the different national responses to the petroleum crisis of 1973. In 1974 a **European Commission** energy programme was accepted by the Council of Ministers (see **Council of the European Union**) and it has since served as the basis for discussions on energy policy. It was revised in 1980, and again in 1986. The original priority was to reduce EC dependence on petroleum, especially on supplies from politically volatile regions. Within 10 years, petroleum imports had been reduced by one-half owing to savings achieved through increased efficiency, the successful exploitation of North Sea petroleum, and a diversification of energy sources.

The 1986 revision of energy policy set priority targets until 1995. As far as the supply and use of energy were concerned, it urged that petroleum imports be held at a level below one-third of total EC energy consumption, with greater reliance upon **coal** and nuclear energy, the latter to supply 40% of EC needs by 1995. All developments were to take place within the context of greater efficiency, and a further improvement in energy saving of at least 20% was to be secured by 1995. More financial assistance was to be made available for the exploration of alternative energy sources such as solar, wave and wind energy, in the hope that these would provide up to 5% of EC needs by 2000. The programme also set several further objectives. It recommended more internal trade in natural gas and **electricity** (accepting that little more could be done for trade in petroleum and coal), and urgeda common pricing system across all energy sectors. It confirmed the importance of maintaining a contingency supply of fuel reserves equal to 30 days' consumption at power stations (and 90 days' consumption in the case of petroleum stocks), and of increased flexibility and co-operation between the member states. It suggested that the EC should seek to use more effectively their position as a major energy consumer to negotiate agreements with energy suppliers. Finally, it emphasized the need for a major and coherent research and development programme, and for energy policy to be consistent with environmental protection.

The programme was an ambitious one, and doubts were soon raised as to whether all of its objectives could be met. There were potential conflicts between energy needs and environmental protection, and a growing objection to nuclear power. In the 1990s there were three major aspects to energy policy. First, as a consequence of the **internal market**, there was a new emphasis upon a single energy market. This would entail liberalization of gas and electricity markets by removing the dominance of state monopolies by 2000. The European Commission issued several **directives**: on price transparency, the transit of energy, and the development of energy infrastructures. The EC also took the lead in the establishment in 1991 of a **European Energy Charter** linking Western with Eastern Europe. Later, in 1996, the Commission would establish as part of its **Mediterranean policy** a Euro-Mediterranean Energy Forum to assist in the development of co-operation projects. Finally, the Commission linked the development of energy more closely with **environment policy**. The major symbol of this commitment was the proposal for a **carbon tax**.

Much of the proposed energy programme was contentious, since the energy requirements of the European Union (EU) were likely to continue to grow. Given its potential importance, it is surprising that only limited reference was made to energy in the **Treaty on European Union** (TEU): it referred only to the existence of EC powers in the area of energy and the need for the development of European energy infrastructures. Moreover, although it was agreed that the possibility of incorporating energy into the treaty basis of the EU would be reviewed by an **intergovernmental conference** at the end of 1996 considering possible revisions of the Treaty, the **Treaty of Amsterdam** went no further than the TEU. In 1995 the European Commission published a **White Paper** on energy policy, prioritizing security of supply and improved **competitiveness** of European businesses, and emphasizing environmental constraints. Following this, in 1997 the Commission proposed a framework programme for the energy sector, which, following approval by the Council of the European Union in December 1998, covered the period 1998–2002. The objective of this programme was to guarantee the coherence and efficiency of EC energy policy by bringing together all ongoing energy actions and programmes across all EC policies. EC energy policy does not seek to replace member states' initiatives, nor other EC initiatives, but aims to reinforce cohesion between these different actions. Objectives for this five-year period included: the strengthening of international co-operation; the promotion of renewable energy sources; the encouragement of an efficient use of energy sources; an improvement of safety in the use of nuclear energy; and increased industrial co-operation with **Russia**. The Commission was charged with reviewing the **implementation** of this framework on an annual basis. In November 2000 the Commission launched a **Green Paper** on the security of energy supply. This aimed to ensure a supply of energy to consumers at reasonable prices while maintaining the competitiveness of the sector and respecting both the environment and sustainable development. It resulted in the **Intelligent Energy—Europe** initiative.

Technology is expected to play an important role in using energy more rationally. Money was allocated for energy research in the EU's Sixth Framework Programme for Research and Technological Development (2002–06). In addition, the EU planned to spend €200m. from its *Intelligent Energy for Europe* programme between 2003 and 2006 to support research into energy saving, energy efficiency, renewable energies and the energy-related aspects of transport. The focus was to be on research programmes that help strengthen security of supply, fight climate change and make industry more competitive. Much has changed in the energy sector in the course of the last two decades. The Lisbon summit meeting of the **European Council** in March 2000 urged the creation of a genuine single market for energy, and in March 2001 the Commission responded by adopting a series of measures to open up the gas and **electricity** markets completely by the end of 2005. In the past, national gas and electricity markets were separate 'islands' within the EU, where supply and distribution were in the hands of monopolies. Now, consumers not only have the right to choose their supplier, but they also have a right to gas and electricity supply at reasonable prices. Some states have gone further than others, and for several years there was a notable reduction in prices in the United Kingdom and Sweden in particular. Problems still persist as a result of limited progress in cross-border trade and differing stages of implementation across member states. Further progress needs to be made, particularly with regard to the pricing of cross-border trade and the rules for the allocation and management of scarce resources. To facilitate further developments the Commission established two new consultative bodies: the Electricity Regulatory Forum of Florence and the Gas Regulatory Forum of Madrid. In September 2002 the Commission, increasingly aware of the EU's heavy reliance and dependence on external supplies of petroleum and gas, adopted two directive proposals that were designed to maintain the security of EU energy sources at affordable prices. In March 2003 the Commission raised the issue of energy sources again in a communication to the Council and the **European Parliament** on the consequences of the war in Iraq. Concern was particularly expressed over the impact of the war on the price of petroleum, which had been steadily rising in the months leading up to the outbreak of war.

By mid-2004 all businesses were free to choose their own suppliers of gas and electricity, and consumers followed suit by mid-2007. For their part, all suppliers have guarantees under single energy market rules that they can have access to the distribution grid and pipeline networks of other EU countries and that they will pay a fair price for access. Consideration of energy policy has always provoked controversy at the EU level. Nevertheless, the dependence of many EU states on foreign-owned energy sources is undeniable. The dangers of such dependency were apparent when Russia threatened to suspend all gas supplies to **Ukraine** in January 2006 and thereby disrupt gas supplies to Western Europe via Ukraine.

The European Commission published its Green Paper on a Secure, Competitive and Sustainable Energy Policy for Europe in March 2006. The paper sought to secure sufficient energy supplies and to lay the base for a number of issues, including: a policy on gas storage; a single European electricity grid; the need for a new infrastructure; the construction of new terminals for gas from the Caspian Sea and North Africa; a broad debate on the future of nuclear power; and more open energy markets. The Commission's initiatives to liberalize the electricity and gas markets since the early 1990s have met with mixed results, and certain member state governments have sought to resist proposed mergers in the energy sector. Cases of economic protectionism found illustration in early 2006 when Gaz de France attempted to merge with fellow French supplier Suez, in spite of an Italian offer from Enel to acquire the same company. The French Government strongly favoured a merger between purely French companies in an area that it deems to be vital to national security. Spain also expressed its unease and opposition regarding cross-border mergers in any energy sector. **Barroso** and his Commission are strong advocates for the creation of large cross-border energy companies that can compete in the single market. The scene is set for battle between these conflicting positions, but logic suggests that some form of common energy policy is required to tackle Europe's deficiencies and to encourage investment in new forms of energy. The Commissioner in charge of energy policy in the Barroso II Commission is **Günther Oettinger**.

Energy is rapidly climbing the EU's priority agenda. The Commission has published a number of Green Papers in an attempt to initiate greater debate. It also produced a number of legislative proposals in this area in September 2007. The issues of most concern are as follows: the security of supply, especially Europe's dependence on supplies from Russia; the need to lower consumption; ways to find and promote renewable sources of energy; environmental implications; and, of course, the need to create an effective, competitive and efficient energy market. The EU really has little room for manoeuvre; it has insufficient energy resources, hence the emphasis on renewable energy. The **Twenty-Five** relied on imports for 50.5% of their energy needs. The figures relating to oil and gas requirements were higher, at 80.2% and 54.5% respectively. According to Commission statistics, the former USSR supplied 36.4% of EU oil imports in 2005, followed by **Norway** (16.4%), Saudi Arabia (11.1%), Libya (9.2%) and Iran (6.3%). The situation was similar that year with regard to the supply of natural gas, where Russia provided 36.7%, Norway 24.5%, Algeria 19.2% and Nigeria 3.7%.

The European Council recognized the rather grim realities of the situation when it settled on an action plan for energy policy in March 2007. This programme ran from 2007 and sought to improve energy efficiency and save up to 20% of energy consumption by 2020. It simultaneously wanted to increase the amount of renewable energy and raise the share of biofuels. Energy (and especially energy security) remains a crucial and highly sensitive issue. In November 2010 the Commission adopted the communication 'Energy 2020: a strategy for competitive, sustainable and secure energy'. This strategy seeks to define the energy challenges for Europe over the next decade and how best to meet these challenges. This communication was followed by the first ever special European Council summit on energy, which took place in February 2011. Agreement was reached on a number of strategic energy-related areas. In particular, the summit concluded that work should be undertaken to develop a transparent, rule-governed relationship with Russia. The summit also made clear its intention to promote investment in renewable energy, and sustainable low-carbon technologies; to accelerate the full liberalization of energy markets, in order to bring them into accordance with EU law; to improve adherence to the 2020 20% energy-efficiency target (which aimed to reduce the use of greenhouse gases by 20%, to increase the proportion of renewable energy used to 20%, and to improve overall energy efficiency by 20% by 2020); and to investigate the potential extraction and use of unconventional fossil fuel sources, such as shale gas and oil shale, favoured, in particular, by Poland.

ENERGY TAX: See **Carbon Tax**

ENGRENAGE is a term that comes from a French expression meaning 'getting caught up in the gears'. It relates closely to the '**Monnet method**' of integration, whereby individuals, governments, interest groups and European Communities/ EU institutions, having embarked on a particular course of action, find themselves compelled to take additional measures that deepen European integration.

ENHANCED CO-OPERATION was substantially overhauled at the **intergovernmental conference** convened in Nice in December 2000, specifically by listing in a single provision the 10 conditions necessary to establish enhanced co-operation. Although the essential characteristics of this instrument (whereby enhanced co-operation should only be taken as a measure of last resort) were not changed significantly, there were some notable alterations. For example, the minimum number of member states required to establish enhanced co-operation was designated as eight, rather than a majority, thus facilitating use of enhanced co-operation on the **enlargement** of the European Union (EU).

In pillar I (the European Communities) and in pillar III (**police and judicial co-operation in criminal matters**) the possibility of opposing enhanced co-operation (by employing a veto) was removed. With regard to pillar II on the **common foreign and security policy** (CFSP), the deliberations in Nice made it possible to establish enhanced co-operation for the implementation of joint action or a common position; this does not apply to matters of defence. Authorization for enhanced co-operation rests with the **Council of the European Union**, and the Council will decide by **qualified majority voting** (QMV). Member states are still entitled to ask the Council to adopt a decision by unanimity if they are convinced that an issue is of particular importance. When enhanced co-operation concerns an area determined by the **co-decision procedure**, the consent of the **European Parliament** is required. With the **ratification** of the **Treaty of Lisbon** there have been a number of significant changes concerning enhanced co-operation (that were originally contained in the **Treaty establishing a Constitution for Europe**). First, the minimum number of states needed for enhanced co-operation has changed, from eight to one-third of the total membership. Second, the launching of enhanced co-operation no longer requires unanimity, but QMV. The exception here is in relation to the CFSP, where unanimity is still necessary. And third, in those policy areas where the Council acts by unanimity, member states participating in enhanced co-operation are now able to use QMV and to introduce co-decision when adopting measures other than those that have either military or defence implications. Finally, the Treaty of Lisbon, like the Treaty establishing a Constitution for Europe before it, provided for a further form of enhanced co-operation—**permanent structured co-operation**—under the Common Security and Defence Policy.

Enhanced co-operation has proven exceptionally difficult to establish. Member states supportive of a particular measure have generally been unwilling to isolate member states that are opposed. However, two enhanced co-operation measures have been launched in recent years. These relate to cross-border divorce (2010) and the adoption of an **EU Patent** (2011).

ENLARGEMENT is a general term used to describe the process of admission of new states into the European Union (EU). The procedures for enlargement are contained in Article 49 of the **Treaty on European Union**. All applicants for membership must possess a democratic form of government, respect the principles on which the EU is based (i.e. liberty, democracy, respect for **human rights** and fundamental freedoms, and the rule of law), and be prepared to accept not only the provisions of the **European treaties**, but also the *acquis communautaire*, the accumulated **legislation** of the EU. Because of the last-mentioned requirement and the desire of both member states and applicants to protect their own interests as much as possible, negotiations tend to be complex and protracted. The **European Commission** undertakes an analysis of each country's application, focusing on both the economic situation and the political stability of each state. Thereafter the Commission presents its *avis* to the **Council of the European Union**, where a decision on the applicant will be made. If negotiations are successful and an **Accession Treaty** is signed, this must be ratified by the **national parliaments** of the acceding states, by all the member states and, since the **Single European Act**, also by the **European Parliament** (EP).

The first round of enlargement involved applications in 1961–62, and again in 1967, from Denmark, Ireland, **Norway** and the United Kingdom. On each occasion, the British application was vetoed by France, and the other three applicants chose not to pursue the matter further without the United Kingdom. The applications were renewed in 1970, leading to the signing of Treaties of Accession in 1972. As a result of a national referendum, Norway declined to join. The other three states became full members of the EC on 1 January 1973. The second and third rounds involved Greece, Portugal and Spain, all of which applied for membership after establishing a democratic form of government in the mid-1970s. Greece formally became a member on 1 January 1981, followed by Portugal and Spain on 1 January 1986.

The EC decision to create an **internal market** was a matter of concern to the **European Free Trade Association** (EFTA) states, most of which between 1989 and 1992 eventually submitted formal applications for membership. Negotiations with Austria, Finland, Norway and Sweden were concluded in 1994, with membership offered subject to **ratification**. Following another national referendum, Norway again declined membership, but the other three states joined the EU on 1 January 1995.

After the collapse of Communism in Eastern Europe in 1989, most of the newly democratized states indicated an interest in seeking membership in the medium term. The EC's response was that this would be limited in the first instance to members of the **Visegrad Group**, namely Hungary, Poland and the former Czechoslovakia (see the Czech Republic and Slovakia). Other applicant states have been **Turkey** in 1987, and Cyprus and Malta in 1990. These applications initially met with considerable resistance within the EU even though the countries had all signed **association agreements**. However, in 1996 the **European Council** decided that **accession negotiations** with Cyprus would begin six months after the conclusion of the 1996 **inter-governmental conference**.

By this time the EU had also received applications for membership from the 10 Central and Eastern European countries with which **Europe agreements** had already been signed: Hungary, Poland, Romania, Slovakia, Latvia, Estonia, Lithuania, Bulgaria, the Czech Republic and Slovenia. This block of applications constituted the largest enlargement of the EU to date and also the most difficult, given the economic challenges facing the countries of **Central and Eastern Europe**. As a result, the EU progressed with the applications cautiously. In 1997, as part of **Agenda 2000**, the European Commission, using the **accession criteria** established in 1993 at the **Copenhagen summit**, assessed each country's ability to fulfil membership obligations, and recommended that accession negotiations begin with Hungary, Poland, Estonia, the Czech Republic and Slovenia. Negotiations with these five countries (plus Cyprus) began in March 1998. Meanwhile, the other applicants were included in an 'inclusive and evolutive' accession process, and would have to wait until late 1999 before they, along with Malta—which had renewed its application for membership in 1998—were recommended for negotiations. Following the recommendation, the European Council, meeting in Helsinki in December 1999, decided to open negotiations in 2000. Moreover, it conferred on all the applicant states, including Turkey, the status of **candidate country**.

The completion of accession negotiations currently requires the closure of 35 chapters, most of which deal with particular areas of the *acquis communautaire* (e.g. **competition policy**, the **common agricultural policy**, **tele-communications** policy, and **energy policy**). In the case of 10 candidate countries—Cyprus, the Czech Republic, Estonia, Hungary, Latvia, Lithuania, Malta, Poland, Slovakia and Slovenia—the then 31 chapters were finally closed in December 2002. This paved the way for the EU to enlarge to 25 member states on 1 May 2004. As a consequence, the EU underwent its greatest enlargement to become a union covering another third of the European continent and comprising nearly 500m. people.

Prior to the 2004 enlargement, each of the candidate countries, as well as the member states, had to ratify the **Accession Treaty** signed on 16 April 2003. Nine candidate countries—the exception being Cyprus—successfully held **referenda** on EU membership between March and September 2003. At the same time, negotiations with Bulgaria and Romania continued, with the EU committing itself to realizing the two countries' goal of membership in 2007. This it did, although consideration was given to delaying accession by one year owing to concerns over judicial reform and corruption. Turkey, meanwhile, continues to present a more problematic case, and the Commission is working with the Turkish authorities to ensure that the country is able to meet the **Copenhagen criteria**. To this end, the EU has provided Turkey with increased financial assistance, and opened negotiations in October 2005. The prospects for Turkish accession look decidedly gloomy, especially after President **Jacques Chirac** of France decreed in early 2005 that the French people would be able, through a referendum, to permit or prevent Turkish membership. The issue of Turkey featured as a strong element in the debate leading up to the French referendum on the **Treaty establishing a Constitution for Europe** in May 2005.

Enlargement is not a straightforward process, since it has budgetary implications and threatens to result in institutional paralysis unless there is institutional reform. This is why since the mid-1990s the EU has been seeking to reform its most significant areas of expenditure—the **common agricultural policy** (CAP) and the **structural funds**—as well as its **institutions**. Progress on the former was made at the Berlin summit meeting of the European Council in March 1999 when a new **financial perspective** for 2000–06, and reforms to the CAP and structural funds, were agreed. Prior to the 2004 enlargement the EU provided pre-accession assistance to the candidate countries. This included €1,500m. annually under the **Phare** programme; €1,000m. annually under the **instrument for structural policies for pre-accession**; and €540m. annually under the Special Accession Programme for Agriculture and Regional Development (**Sapard**). Less progress was initially made on institutional reform. Measures introduced by the **Treaty of Amsterdam** prepared the EU only marginally for future enlargement, by avoiding any significant changes to the institutions so as to enable them to cope with the extra demands that would be placed on them. However, the following reforms were introduced as a result: a limit was placed on the size of the EP; the European Commission was to undergo a review process; the **co-decision procedure** was simplified; and agreement was reached on greater use of **qualified majority voting** in the Council of the European Union, to ensure that decision-making was not slowed down unduly. In **protocol**s attached to the **Treaty of Amsterdam** references were made to the fact that each member state would have only one

Commissioner after enlargement: the larger member states were previously entitled to have two Commissioners each. The Treaty also promised that a further review of the institutions was to take place if the EU grew to more than 20 member states. In other words, the key decisions on institutional reform were postponed.

The whole array of institutional issues relating to enlargement was tackled more fully by the **Treaty of Nice**, agreed by the Governments of the 15 existing member states in December 2000. This reformed the Commission, the **Court of Justice** and the **Court of First Instance**; extended qualified majority voting; re-allocated votes in the Council of the European Union; and agreed the distribution of votes and seats in an enlarged EU of 27 members. Yet concerns that the reforms were insufficient to ensure that a substantially enlarged EU could function smoothly persisted. The result was the **European Convention**'s reform proposals contained in the **draft Treaty establishing a Constitution for Europe**. Many of these survived the intergovernmental conference launched in October 2003 and appeared in the Treaty establishing a Constitution for Europe. They also appeared in the replacement **Treaty of Lisbon**.

With Bulgaria and Romania joining the EU on 1 January 2007, the fifth enlargement was completed. However, it will not be the last enlargement round. Enlargement is an ongoing process. A range of countries aspire to EU membership. **Croatia** submitted its application to join in February 2003 and was followed in 2004 by the **former Yugoslav republic of Macedonia**, by **Montenegro** in 2008 and by **Albania, Iceland** and **Serbia** in 2009. In June 2004 the European Council announced that accession negotiations with Croatia would begin in 2005, and they eventually commenced in October. Negotiations were closed in June 2011, and Croatia was expected to accede to full membership of the EU on 1 July 2013. Iceland opened negotiations in July 2010; Montenegro followed in June 2012. Meanwhile, membership bids from other countries in Western Europe cannot be ruled out. Norway may apply again, and **Switzerland** may reactivate its 1992 application. **Moldova** and **Ukraine** have also expressed great interest in future EU membership. So, too, have other countries from the **Western Balkans**.

However, how big is too big? Increasingly concerns are being expressed that the EU does not have sufficient '**integration capacity**' to admit more states, although the entry into force of the Treaty of Lisbon has assuaged immediate concerns over admitting a small number. The EU seems intent on continuing with enlargement. It is certainly supporting, through the **stabilization and association process**, the **European partnerships**, the **accession partnerships** and the **instrument for pre-accession assistance**, the efforts of countries wishing to join. However, popular support within the EU for further enlargement is far from universal. The Turkish accession bid is controversial, and constantly requires some very skilful diplomacy. Accession negotiations have been opened, but progress has been slower than anticipated. The eventual outcome of Iceland's membership bid is also uncertain, since domestic opinion polls rarely reveal majority support for EU membership. The prospects for the accession of other countries from the Western Balkans will depend very much on their own domestic reform efforts, especially with regard to the establishment of rule of law and the eradication of corruption.

ENTERPRISE POLICY aims to ensure that the European Union (EU) helps to stimulate a climate in which enterprise, industry and innovation flourish. Enterprise is crucial to the EU's economic growth and the EU hopes to foster and encourage innovative business practices that will create jobs and promote growth. Enterprise policy was designed at European Communities (EC) level to meet the requirements of the entire business community (whether large or small businesses) and its environment. Article 157 of the **Treaty of Rome** (now Article 173 of the **Treaty on the Functioning of the European Union**) provides the legal basis for enterprise policy. Historically, work on enterprise policy has consisted of three key areas: **small and medium-sized enterprises** (SMEs), innovation and **competitiveness**, and making the most of opportunities and benefits arising from the single market. The level of EC interest in all three aspects was evident from the number of action programmes and **Green** and **White Papers** dedicated to these matters over the last two decades.

Support for SMEs dates back to 1983 and the adoption of the first EC action programme to assist their development. The business community currently places considerable emphasis on the notion of promoting innovation. In 1995 the **European Commission** produced a Green Paper on this subject, and this led in 1996 to the first action programme for innovation in Europe. This identified several objectives, including the need to promote an innovation culture; to create a good business environment; and to foster more effective links between research, innovation and business.

Enterprise policy has also been facilitated by the Commission's promotion of competitiveness, an initiative that was most apparent in its 1993 *White Paper on Growth, Competitiveness and Employment*. In January 2000 a new **Directorate-General** (DG) for Enterprise policy was created, with a range of responsibilities combining some of those previously held by the DG for Industry with the innovation activities that had previously been dealt with by the Information Society DG. In March 2000, at a meeting of the **European Council** in Lisbon, the 15 member states confirmed the promotion of enterprise policy to be a new strategic objective for the EU, a measure which it is hoped will transform the EU into one of the most competitive and dynamic knowledge-based economies in the world, capable of sustained economic growth and higher levels of **employment**.

In April 2000 the Commission produced a communication on the challenges ahead for enterprise policy, which envisaged an 'Enterprise Europe' by 2005. This was accompanied by a proposal for a multi-annual programme to consider how enterprise policy can meet the challenges of **globalization** and the new knowledge-driven world economy. In December 2000 a new multi-annual programme on enterprise and entrepreneurship was adopted, focusing specifically on the role of SMEs (which provide the largest number of jobs across the EU) and built on the earlier EC action programmes. The current aims of the Commission's enterprise policy are: to develop an entrepreneurial spirit; to promote an innovative business environment which makes good use of research and technology and fosters competition; to get more from the **internal market** by tackling some of the remaining barriers to trade, and facilitate trade in transport; to provide for greater co-ordination and sharing of experiences among the EU member states (to include benchmarking and sharing best practice); and lastly, to stimulate new business models in the 'e-economy' through the promotion of new information and communication technologies.

The collection and dissemination of examples of innovative practice are crucial for the success of 'Enterprise Europe'. To facilitate information exchanges and examples of best practice, the Commission aims, through its new Business Environment Simplification Task Force (BEST) procedure, to highlight the results and experiences of businesses engaged in innovation through seminars, conferences, peer reviews and studies. Enterprise policy is financed by various sources. Although the principal source is the multi-annual programme on enterprise and entrepreneurship, grants for training programmes, protecting the environment and fostering co-operation, for example, can be obtained from the **European Investment Bank** and the **structural funds**.

The first **ENVIRONMENTAL ACTION PROGRAMME** (EAP) of the European Communities (EC) was introduced in 1973. The sixth EAP was proposed by the **European Commission** in January 2001, and adopted by the European Parliament and the European Council in July 2002. The programme covered the period 2002–12 and was an integral element of EC **environmental policy**. The sixth EAP expired on 30 June 2012 and a seventh EAP was to be announced.

The **ENVIRONMENTAL CHEMICALS DATA INFORMATION NETWORK** (ECDIN) is a database that also contains the **European inventory of existing commercial chemical substances** (EINECS).

ENVIRONMENTAL POLICY was not specifically mentioned or provided for in the **Treaty of Rome**. The **Single European Act** gave the European Communities (EC) competence, and this was extended into a policy remit by the **Treaty on European Union** (TEU). The objectives are those that the EC has pursued for some time. The aim of EC environmental policy is to preserve, protect and improve the quality of the environment and to protect people's health. The TEU added another dimension: the promotion of measures for dealing with global environmental problems. The concept of sustainable development was enshrined in the **Treaty of Amsterdam** as one of the EC's objectives. Moreover, environmental protection requirements were given greater emphasis in other EC policies, and especially in relation to the single market. Significantly, the treaty also simplified decision-making by allowing **co-decision procedure** to replace **co-operation procedure** where the latter had applied to certain parts of environmental policy-making. European Union (EU) environmental policy is one of those areas that resonate strongly with the average European citizen. The June 2007 **Eurobarometer** report displayed agreement among the public for the EU to be active in tackling global warming (88%) and reducing greenhouse gases (89%).

EC activity in the area of environment policy first commenced in the early 1970s, when specific environmental problems were incorporated into a series of five-year programmes for dealing with generalized issues of environmental enhancement and protection. The main policy principles were defined in the first **Environmental Action Programme** (EAP): the polluter must pay the costs of repair to the environment; prevention of environmental damage is preferable to remedial measures; and all EC initiatives in all policy areas must take their likely effect upon the environment into account. The TEU further stressed the precautionary principle and the need for environment policy to take into account the regional economic diversity of the EU.

Environmental policy has become increasingly significant for the EU. More than 300 **directives** or **regulations** on the environment had been adopted by the mid-1990s. Since then there has been a noticeable decline in the number of regulations and directives, reflecting the sensitivity and controversy surrounding environmental policy or, more accurately, the costs of implementing tougher environmental regimes that impact either on central and local government or on the business community. Nevertheless, activity has concentrated on six broad problem areas: **water**; **atmospheric pollution**; **noise**; chemical products; waste disposal; and the preservation and restoration of natural habitats and the conservation of wildlife. Several directives deal with the pollution of all forms of water and with relevant quality standards, and the EC have participated in international conventions dealing with the reduction of pollution in international waterways and rivers. Other directives cover the discharge of pollutants into the atmosphere from industrial plants, and exhaust emissions from motor vehicles. Maximum noise levels have been established for a range of machinery and household equipment. Chemical products have been subject to regulation since 1967. Control of chemicals became more urgent after the Seveso incident in Italy in 1976, leading to a range of further directives on their manufacture and usage, and on safety precautions. A **European Inventory of Existing Chemical Substances** (EINECS) was established in 1986. The EC committed themselves to reducing chlorofluorocarbons (CFCs) by 85% by 2000, and in 1993 the **European Commission** proposed the elimination of hydrochlorofluorocarbons by 2014. To protect natural habitats and conserve wildlife, a number of directives relate to the preservation of species and to scientific experiments on animals. Funds have been provided for the preservation of natural habitats, and the EC have signed several international conventions on the conservation of wildlife. EC **legislation** also covers the dangers posed by radiation. Following the accident at the Chernobyl nuclear power station in the former **USSR** in 1986, maximum levels of radiation contamination in foodstuffs were set.

As part of the EC's efforts to promote awareness of environmental issues and encourage companies to do likewise, an **eco-management and audit scheme** (EMAS) was set up in 1995. Participation is voluntary and involves industrial companies undergoing an independent audit of their environmental performance. In the area of transport, harmful emissions from road vehicles were to be reduced by 60%–70% by 2010, and measures were agreed to lower the allowable limits for certain chemical substances in petrol and diesel fuel by 2000. Leaded petrol was to be phased out, for most vehicles, by 2000. There has also been legislation concerning the protection of groundwater resources, waste disposal in landfill sites, genetically engineered foods, and trade in endangered species. In 1997 the European Commission agreed to provide funding for 188 environmental projects.

The fourth EAP (1987–92) increased EC activity, conferring stronger powers on the European Commission, including the right to take member states to the **Court of Justice** for non-compliance with environmental legislation. As part of the task of raising public awareness, 1987 was designated as the European Year of the Environment (EYE), and the Network for Environmental Technology Transfer (NETT) was established to aid the realization of its activities. The pursuance of these objectives was potentially strengthened by the 1990 decision to set up a **European Environment Agency** (EEA) and a special environment fund, **LIFE**. The EC also agreed, in principle, to introduce a **carbon tax**. The importance of these measures and programmes was reiterated in the fifth EAP (1993–2000), which also stressed that EC activity must be more anticipatory, less devoted to problem-solving, focusing more on the causes of environmental problems as part of a commitment to 'sustainable development'. The programme listed several initiatives that should be pursued, including better resource management by industry, the curbing of consumer demand for products that generate pollution, the development of more environmentally friendly agriculture and a more effective management of mass tourism. The sixth EAP (2002–12) was guided by the fifth programme, and defined the priorities and aims of EC environmental policy to 2012. This programme sought to alert 'business, consumers, policy planners and citizens' to the issues confronting the environment. In particular, it wanted to improve the implementation of existing legislation, integrate environmental concern into other policy areas, work more closely with the market and try to get citizens to change their behaviour and approach to the environment. Four areas were given particular emphasis: climate change, nature and bio-diversity, environment and health, management of natural resources and waste. It also identified explicitly the measures needed to implement successfully the EU's sustainable development strategy, which had been given much wider prominence following the adoption of the EU Sustainable Development Strategy in 2001.

In December 2003 the European Commission adopted its first ever Environmental Policy Review. This review should be placed within the context of the 2000 Lisbon strategy which was supplemented by a third economic **pillar** after the adoption of the EU Sustainable Development Strategy at the Gothenburg **European Council summit** in 2001. The primary objective of this review was to examine the most pressing threats to the environment and to report on developments since 2001 in both EU and national environmental policies. Essentially, this report maintained that more needed to be done to improve the state of the environment and it recommended, in order to ensure a credible policy of sustainable development, that the following three steps must be taken: the integration of environmental concerns into other policy areas; the implementation of existing environmental legislation; and the provision of more information on environmental themes. The challenge confronting the EU and its member states is to ensure, on the one hand, the development of balanced policies that are designed to stimulate growth and investment, and, on the other, the protection of the environment and human health for future generations.

The environment remains an increasingly fundamental aspect of EU activities. An initiative launched in January 2004, deriving from the priorities of the sixth EAP, envisaged a 'Thematic Strategy on the Urban Environment'. This communication from the Commission seeks to identify the problems and challenges experienced by urban areas. Environmental problems are a global concern, and in the last two decades there have been high-profile conferences at the international level (Rio de Janeiro, 1992; Kyoto, 1997; and The Hague, 2000) to address the issues of ozone depletion and global warming. The **Fifteen** (EU15), at the time of the **ratification** of the Kyoto **Protocol**, agreed to reduce their emissions to 8% below the base year's level (usually 1990) by 2012. Progress towards tackling the necessary reduction in dangerous emissions was begun in earnest. According to the Commission, the **Twenty-Five** (EU25) succeeded in bringing about a 7.3% reduction in emissions between 1990 and 2004. There is still a long way to go and, interestingly, US emissions rose by 15.8% for the same reporting period.

The Kyoto Protocol finally entered into force in early 2005. By September 2011, 191 countries had signed and ratified the protocol, although certain emerging economies, such as China and India, were exempt (at least for now) from the obligations to reduce emissions. In December 2011 Canada formally withdrew from the Protocol. The **USA** remains the only major country that has not agreed to the terms of Kyoto. However, it should be noted that some US federal states, such as California, are moving towards the adoption of Kyoto's emission standards. This international dimension has enabled the EU to establish a global presence in the field of environmental policy, a position that has led it into dispute with the USA. More positively, the German **European Council** presidency in the first half of 2007 laid particular emphasis on the need to tackle climate change, and it was agreed by the EU25 to cut emissions by 20% from 1990 levels by 2020. More recently, the Council (environment ministers) agreed to impose emissions quotas on airlines (which are estimated to account for 3% of carbon emissions) in an effort to confront climate change. Under this agreement, the EU would set the limits, but the decision encountered severe opposition from the USA, where it is feared that any such change might spell disaster and financial ruin for some carriers.

Progress was made on the international front, as in 2007 the **G-8** committed themselves to agreeing a successor to Kyoto by the end of 2012. In December 2007, delegates at a UN conference in Bali finally agreed (after much controversy) on a new deal to tackle climate change. The final text was rather vague and did not quantify the actual percentage cuts, but it explicitly acknowledged the need for them. It is important to stress that the USA agreed to participate, despite some reservations, along with both Canada and Japan. All three states vociferously opposed and rejected EU demands for cuts of 25%–40% by 2020. Nevertheless, this so-called 'Bali Roadmap' provides evidence of greater international recognition of the problem and a determination to do something.

In recent years the EU has been instrumental in pushing the climate change agenda forward and some member states have been keen to initiate substantive cuts in emissions. In a landmark move, **José Manuel Barroso** announced ambitious plans in January 2008 to make Europe the first economy for the low-carbon age. The Commission seeks to take the global lead and reduce greenhouse gas emissions by 20% by 2020, and possibly even 30% if progress can be made on securing an international deal. The plan has been received enthusiastically by environmentalists. In order to work, the Commission's proposals necessitate the extension of the Emissions Trading Scheme (ETS) to include more economic sectors. Where certain sectors are not covered by the ETS scheme (as is the case with the agriculture, building and transport sectors) the Commission proposed the setting of national targets. These targets will vary from member state to member state and will fall hardest on the EU15, with the newest member states being allowed more flexibility and even being permitted to raise their emissions temporarily. Discussions on all aspects of the proposed plan have proved contentious because, although few member state governments deny the overall aims, many find the targets difficult to reach.

A special UN-sponsored conference on climate change took place in Copenhagen, Denmark, in December 2009. The Copenhagen Summit was attended by 119 world leaders and attracted considerable media attention. However, divisions were apparent among the delegates at Copenhagen. There was disagreement and resistance on the depth of such cuts from many countries in the developing world and from other key states such as Brazil, China and South Africa. The different visions became evident at the summit, and at one point the entire summit looked in real danger of collapsing; however, a last-minute push enabled some agreement. Although a deal was reached to cut emissions and to raise finance to assist developing countries to reduce emissions, many commentators argued that the summit had produced limited results, and for some it constituted a failure, especially as the agreement was not legally binding. Other states (for instance, China) were happy with the outcome.

More positively, former leaders such as **Gordon Brown** and **Nicolas Sarkozy** described the outcome of the summit as representing progress in the right direction, and the agreement was to be reviewed in 2015.

EP: See **European Parliament**

EPAs: See **Economic Partnership Agreements**

EPC: See **European Political Co-operation**

EPU: See **European Payments Union**

EQUAL PAY policy was laid down in Article 141 of the **Treaty of Rome**. It now appears in Article 157 of the **Treaty on the Functioning of the European Union**. While it refers specifically to gender discrimination, obliging the member states to 'ensure and subsequently maintain the application of the principle that men and women should receive equal pay for equal work', the Article has been taken to refer to equality in general. A series of **directives** between 1975 and 1986 extended the meaning of equal pay for equal work, as well as enabling those who consider themselves to be discriminated against to take their case, without fear of dismissal or reprisal, to a national tribunal. Where there is a difference of opinion over the meaning of European Communities **law**, the question may be referred to the **Court of Justice**, the rulings of which are binding on all national bodies.

ERASMUS stands for European Community Action Scheme for the Mobility of University Students, a programme established in 1987 with the purpose of encouraging students to spend an integral part of their studies at a university in another country of the European Communities (EC). This programme of student mobility was widened to include **European Free Trade Association** (EFTA) countries in 1991 and countries from **Central and Eastern Europe** as well as Cyprus in 1998. The periods of study abroad are recognized by the students' home universities by means of a course credit transfer scheme. The original goal was that some 10% of the EC student population would be participants in the scheme by 1992. Despite the problems created by linguistic diversity and different national systems of higher education, Erasmus proved a huge success. Its popularity increased the costs of the programme at a time when EC expenditure came under closer scrutiny, leading to pressure for the target figure to be reduced to 5% of the student population. Erasmus encompasses more than just student mobility, and contains chapters on: teacher exchanges; joint preparation of courses, where at least three establishments from different countries pool their resources to create a programme of study, a module, a curriculum or a Master's programme; intensive programmes (such as summer schools); and thematic networks on a subject area or a specific platform for analysis and discussion of a European theme. The Thematic Network in Public Administration (based at Leiden University), for example, is an initiative whereby academics meet on an annual basis to discuss the Europeanization of public administration and to seek co-operation and teaching links across Europe. Erasmus became part of the **Socrates** programme in 1995. In 2007 the new **Lifelong Learning Programme** 2007–13 replaced the existing Socrates, Leonardo da Vinci, and eLearning programmes, which expired at the end of 2006. Erasmus is one of the six sub-programmes supported under the Lifelong Learning Programme.

ERASMUS MUNDUS has been designed as a co-operation and mobility programme in the field of higher education. It aims to promote the European Union as a centre of excellence in learning around the world. It supports European top-quality Masters Courses and Doctorates and enhances the visibility and attractiveness of European higher education in third countries. It also provides EU-funded scholarships for third country nationals participating in these Masters Courses and Doctorates, as well as scholarships for EU nationals studying in third countries.

ERDF: See **European Regional Development Fund**

ERM: See **Exchange-rate Mechanism**

ERTA **JUDGMENT**: See *AETR* **Judgment**

ESA: See **European Space Agency**

ESA: See **European System of Integrated Economic Accounts**

ESC: See **European Economic and Social Committee**

ESCB: See **European System of Central Banks**

ESF: See **European Social Fund**

ESM: See **European Stability Mechanism**

ESPRIT: See **European Strategic Programme for Research and Development in Information Technology**

ESRO: See **European Space Research Organization**

ESTI is the European Solar Test Installation at Ispra, the **Joint Research Centre** (JRC) establishment in Italy.

ESTONIA joined the European Union (EU) on 1 May 2004. It is one of the smallest member states, with a population of some 1.3m. Following the collapse of the **USSR** in the early 1990s, the Baltic states of Estonia, Latvia and Lithuania immediately began to develop closer links with Western Europe and particularly the EU. The EU responded by providing technical (see **Phare**) and financial assistance to Estonia. Relations with Estonia progressed swiftly from a **free trade agreement** to a **Europe agreement**, and then to preparations for eventual EU membership. Estonia applied for membership in November 1995 and participated in the first phase of **accession negotiations**, which began in March 1998. Negotiations were completed in December 2002, the outcome being approved by popular referendum nine months later. With a rate of participation by the electorate of just over 64%, two-thirds (66.8%) of voters voted in favour of accession. Estonia opted to approve the **Treaty establishing a Constitution for Europe** through the normal parliamentary process rather than holding a referendum, and the Government was determined to press on with **ratification**, even after events in France and the Netherlands. Estonia duly became the 15th country in the EU to complete the parliamentary stage of ratifying the draft European Constitution in May 2006. The text was approved by 73 votes in favour, with one vote against in the 101-seat parliament. Estonia became part of the EU's **Schengen Area** in December 2007. The Commission approved Estonia's application to join the **euro** after it judged that the country easily fulfilled the target criteria, and Estonia became a member of the eurozone from 1 January 2011.

ETF: See **European Training Foundation**

ETSI is the European Telecommunications Standards Institute, set up in 1987 to harmonize European technological specifications and standards in the field of **telecommunications**. ETSI aims to harmonize standards in the European Union through the development of mandatory norms known as 'common technical regulations'. The Institute is based at the Sophia Antipolis technology park near Nice, France. In 2010 ETSI's budget was more than €22m.

ETUC: See **European Trade Union Confederation**

EU: See **European Union**

EUA: See **European Unit of Account**

EUDOR superseded ABEL, which was a database comprising the contents of the 'L' series of the Official Journal of the European Communities (OJ), and enabled users to order legal texts, documents and publications directly from the **Publications Office of the European Union**. EUDOR, which is available in English, French and nine other European Union languages, is an electronic archive system accessible via the internet, and is updated daily, allowing greater **transparency** of, and accessibility to, European law.

EUI: See **European University Institute**

EUMC: See **European Monitoring Centre on Racism and Xenophobia**

EUMETSAT is the acronym of the European Organization for the Exploitation of Meteorological Satellites, a body that was established in 1986. Twenty-six of the European Union (EU) member states belong to EUMETSAT, which does not have formal links with the EU. EUMETSAT formalized the co-operation between the national meteorological institutions, which began with the launch of the first European meteorological satellite in 1977, and took over the operational programme agreed upon in 1981. Funded by the national authorities, EUMETSAT works in conjunction with the **European Space Agency** (ESA).

EU PATENT: See **Community Patent Convention**

EURAM: See **BRITE-EURAM**

EURATEX is the European Apparel and Textile Organisation and represents the European textile and clothing industry on matters of common interest. Its main objective is to promote the interests of its members while taking into account the institutional framework of the European Union (EU) and its international obligations. It resulted from the merger of various textile and clothing organizations, including the Co-ordinating Committee for the Textile Industries in the EEC (Comitextil) in 1994. The EU is the world's second largest exporter of textiles and third largest for clothing, and the industry employs some 2.4m. people across Europe. Euratex is based in Brussels, close to the principal EU institutions and seeks to engage with the **Commission**, the **Council** and the **European Parliament** in all matters relating to the textiles industry.

EURATOM: See **European Atomic Energy Community**

EUREKA is the acronym of the European Research Co-ordination Agency, a body established in 1985 in **Brussels**. It originated in an initiative by President **François Mitterrand** of France to establish a programme of non-military **research and technological development** that would keep the European Communities (EC) at the forefront in these fields. EUREKA was intended to be responsible for a European Programme for High Technology Research and Development agreed to by several European countries, including non-EC states. EUREKA is more a sponsor of projects than a programme, and in that sense it overlaps with the activities of the European Co-operation in the field of Scientific and Technical Research (**COST**) programme. It has launched well over 100 separate transnational collaborative projects in a diverse number of fields, including factory automation, ceramic turbines, computers, lasers and robotics. It raises most of its funding from private sources or on the capital markets, since the EC and the member states of the European Union make only relatively small contributions to its budget.

EURES was established in 1994 as the successor to **SEDOC**. SEDOC was the acronym of the European System for the International Clearing of Vacancies and Applications for Employment, an agency established by the **European Commission** to operate a scheme that would permit member states to exchange information on job opportunities for migrant workers. In 1980 the Council of Ministers (see **Council of the European Union**) adopted a **resolution** on the co-ordination of national employment policies. SEDOC's activities were extended to become a kind of job placement service for the European Communities (EC) as part of the objective of balancing the supply and demand for labour throughout the EC. It was complemented by the Electronic Loan Insurance Scheme for Employment (ELISE), to which it was linked. EURES operates as a network to liaise between the public employment services of the member states along with those of two other countries and the European Commission in order to exchange data relating to **employment**. The network generally lists 5,000–10,000 employment vacancies daily in 31 European states, holds a databank of over 930,000 curricula vitae and has some 28,500 companies registered. All information is available online.

EURISTOTE is an online directory of university theses and studies on the theme of European integration.

EUR-LEX is a European Union (EU) database containing the contents of the *Official Journal of the European Union* (OJ) 'L' and 'C' series. It was to be extended to include all **legislation** in force, along with the treaties, proposals for legislation, and recent judgments of the **Court of Justice**. EUR-Lex is available online (in 23 official languages of the EU), and is updated daily.

The **EURO** (€) was adopted in 1995 as the name of the common currency of the European Union (EU), and was to replace the **European Currency Unit** on a one-for-one basis at the start of **economic and monetary union** (EMU). By 1998, however, only 11 member states (the Euro-11) had agreed to proceed with EMU and adopt the euro on 1 January 1999. (Greece did not meet the **convergence criteria** at that time, although it joined in 2001, while Denmark, Sweden and the United Kingdom decided not to join.) On 1 January 1999 the conversion rates of the national currencies of the participating member states against the euro were fixed, and a single monetary policy implemented by the new **European Central Bank** (ECB) and the **European System of Central Banks** (ESCB).

The movement towards EMU and a single currency in the EU was slow. However, pressure from business and financial sectors within the EU forced governments to co-operate and to harmonize their approach to introducing a common currency. Belgium was the first member state to announce that its government departments would change to the euro. In all participant member states there was a transition period between 1999 and 2002 (by which time euro banknotes and coins were to have been introduced), during which national budgets were drawn up in national currencies, but payments by government departments were made in euros. From 1999 businesses were able to make social security contributions and pay taxes in euros. They were also able to establish capital in euros. Moreover, in participating member states, with the exception of Germany, tax returns were accepted in euros, and in most participating states people were also able to pay their taxes, including income tax, in euros. Financial markets were also to use the euro.

The three member states remaining outside the euro area were to continue to work towards EMU. In 1998 Denmark retained the position it held during the **Treaty on European Union** (TEU) debate in 1992, remaining firmly opposed to the idea and the practice of the single currency. Despite broad support from government and business circles, the people of Denmark voted against Danish adoption of the euro by a narrow margin in 2000. Sweden held a referendum in September 2003, as a result of which it, too, elected not to join the euro area. The British Government, although realizing that British business would participate in the euro area to an extent, remained cautious about full participation and, combined with considerable public opposition to the euro, postponed indefinitely any plans for a referendum on the issue. Slovenia adopted the euro in January 2007, followed by Cyprus and Malta in January 2008. Following a positive recommendation from the European Commission, Slovakia joined the **eurozone** in January 2009. Estonia adopted the euro in January 2011, bringing the number of EU member states using the euro to 17. The euro is also the sole currency in a number of small non-EU states, such as Andorra, Kosovo, Monaco, Montenegro, San Marino and Vatican City.

The euro entered its most turbulent phase in early 2010 when the financial difficulties and levels of debt in some states led several eurozone counties (most notably Greece, Ireland, Portugal and Spain) to introduce severe austerity programmes, which in turn led speculators to gamble on the stability of the euro and to test the determination of other eurozone states (most notably Germany) to come to the defence of these states. Among the emergency measures adopted were the **European Financial Stabilization Mechanism** and a **European Financial Stability Facility**. Subsequently plans were agreed for a more substantial **European Stability Mechanism**. For the first time in the euro's short history serious doubts were raised about the durability of the euro in the context of a lack of a genuine economic policy across the EU and demands for some countries to be decoupled from the eurozone, notably Greece. Subsequent bailouts awarded to both Ireland and Portugal, and more specifically the crisis surrounding Greece's state finances, amid growing fears throughout 2011 and 2012 about the country's ability to avoid default on its mounting debts, underlined the major challenges confronting the eurozone in maintaining a single currency for the 17 participating member states.

EURO-AIM is the European Organization for an Audiovisual Independent Market. It is part of the MEDIA programme (see **Media policy**), and its purpose is to offer independent producers in Europe a support and advice service for the marketing and sale of their products. EURO-AIM is based in **Brussels**.

The **EURO-ATLANTIC PARTNERSHIP COUNCIL** (EAPC) is the forum in which members of the **North Atlantic Treaty Organization** (NATO) meet on a regular basis with representatives of its 27 partner countries to discuss political and security-related issues and develop co-operation in a wide range of areas. It replaced the **North Atlantic Co-operation Council** in 1997.

EUROBAROMETER is the name of a series of public opinion polls carried out and published on a biannual basis throughout all the member states of the European Union (EU) since 1973. The operation is the responsibility of **Eurostat**. A diverse range of topics are covered by the questionnaires used for polling purposes. These include questions on knowledge of the EU institutions, questions on the availability of information on the EU and questions on a range of EU policies. As well as providing profiles of the European population, the Eurobarometers are used by the **European Commission** and its agencies for planning purposes.

EUROCODES are common codes for the European construction industry, which are intended to standardize and replace the different national specifications for materials, skills and personnel.

EURO COOP: See **Consumer Committee**

EUROCORPS is the name given to an integrated transnational military unit formally inaugurated in November 1992, following agreement at the 59th Franco-German summit in La Rochelle, France, in May 1992. Its origins lay in a joint Franco-German brigade formed in 1987. Its supporters have argued that it could become the nucleus of a European army at the centre of a reconstructed **Western European Union** (WEU), and therefore a central element of security in the European Union (EU). In July 1993 Belgium indicated that it would join the Eurocorps. Spain agreed to contribute troops to the force in December 1993 and Luxembourg joined in May 1996. Based in Strasbourg, the Eurocorps became operational in November 1995. From May 1995 it was complemented by two new WEU bodies: Euroforce (based in Florence, Italy) and Euromarforce (a maritime force serving the Mediterranean), constituted by France, Italy, Portugal and Spain. Since Eurocorps' establishment, the EU has gradually taken over many of the roles of the WEU as part of the development of a **European security and defence policy** (ESDP). Hence, in June 1999, at the Cologne meeting of the **European Council**, it was announced that Eurocorps would be put at the disposal of the EU for crisis response operations. It was subsequently decided that Eurocorps would become part of the **European Rapid Reaction Force**, a process that began in June 2001.

EUROCRAT is a colloquial term used to describe a bureaucrat or administrator employed by the European Union.

EURODICAUTOM was a Commission database, which was created in 1975 and contained multilingual terms for use by translators. In 2007 Eurodicautom was incorporated into **Inter-Active Terminology for Europe** (IATE).

EUROFER: See **European Confederation of Iron and Steel Industries**

The **EUROGROUP** is the informal council of economic and finance ministers of the 17 member states participating in **economic and monetary union**. It held its first meeting in Luxembourg in June 1998. The group, sometimes also referred to as euro-X or Euro-12 group (before the addition of Slovenia, Cyprus, Malta, Slovakia and Estonia), was to be a forum for policy co-ordination rather than **decision-making**, which would continue under the aegis of what is now the **Economic and Financial Affairs Council of Ministers**, the monthly meetings of the finance ministers of the 27 full member states of the European Union.

EUROIZATION refers to the process whereby non-participants in **economic and monetary union** link their national currencies to the **euro** (€). Examples include **Montenegro** and **Bosnia and Herzegovina**.

EUROJUST is a European Union body charged with promoting co-operation among authorities in the member states dealing with the investigation and prosecution of serious cross-border and organized crimes. Established in 2002, it comprises a representative from each of the member states. (See also **police and judicial co-operation in criminal matters**.)

EUROKOM was set up as a teleconference and e-mail facility that would contain details of organizations and enterprises seeking partners in other member states for participation in projects of the **European strategic programme for research and development in information technology** (Esprit) and the European Research Co-ordination Agency (**EUREKA**).

EUROLAND, generally referred to as the **eurozone**, is an informal way of referring to those European Union member states (numbering 17 in 2012: Austria, Belgium, Cyprus, Estonia, Finland, France, Germany, Greece, Ireland, Italy, Luxembourg, Malta, the Netherlands, Portugal, Slovakia, Slovenia and Spain) participating in full **economic and monetary union**, having replaced their national currencies with the **euro**.

The **EURO-MEDITERRANEAN ECONOMIC AREA** (EMEA) now generally referred to as the Euro-Mediterranean Free Trade Area, is the medium-term goal of the **Euro-Mediterranean partnership**. Based on the idea of the **European Economic Area**, this is a key element of the European Union's **Mediterranean policy**.

EURO-MEDITERRANEAN FREE TRADE AREA: See **Euro-Mediterranean Economic Area**

The **EURO-MEDITERRANEAN PARTNERSHIP** (EUROMED) lies at the heart of the **Mediterranean policy** of the European Union (EU). Often referred to as the **Barcelona Process**, EUROMED was launched in 1995 and today involves the 27 member states of the EU and 16 non-member states in the Mediterranean region: Albania, Algeria, **Bosnia and Herzegovina**, **Croatia**, Egypt, Israel, Jordan, Lebanon, Mauritania, Monaco, **Montenegro**,

Morocco, the Palestinian Authority (now Palestinian Autonomous Areas), Syria, Tunisia and **Turkey**. The three main components of the partnership are: political and security partnership; economic and financial partnership; and partnership in social, cultural and human affairs. Agreements have been concluded in a range of specific policy areas such as energy, the environment, media and migration. They are supported through finance from the **MEDA** programme. EUROMED was effectively relaunched in 2008 with the establishment of a **Union for the Mediterranean**.

EURONET DIANE: See **Direct Information Access Network for Europe**

EURONORMS or ENs, were originally standards produced by the **European Coal and Steel Community** covering the quality, dimensions, tolerances and methods of testing of steel, as well as providing a glossary of terms. The term was later also used for more general European standards set by **CEN** and **Cenelec**.

EUR-OP: See **Publications Office of the European Union**

EUROPA is the name of the main **European Commission** internet information site (europa.eu), which provides information on the institutions and activities of the European Union.

EUROPE 2020: The **European Commission** launched its Europe 2020 Strategy in March 2010. The 10-year strategy is designed to help steer the European Union (EU) economy through and out of the current economic crisis, encouraging growth and fostering innovation. It seeks to achieve more sustainable growth and a low-carbon economy. It sets a number of specific targets, with aims that include seeing 75% of the population (people aged between 20 and 64 years) in work, getting 3% of EU gross domestic product (GDP) put into research and development, and removing 20m. more people from the risk of poverty. To this end, the strategy envisages a series of initiatives that include a new agenda for skills and jobs, the pursuit of a digital agenda (i.e. access to the internet for all), greater student and young professional mobility across Europe, and an EU platform against poverty. The Commission's strategy was approved by the **European Council** in March 2010.

EUROPE AGREEMENTS are types of **association agreement** and were concluded by the European Communities with countries in **Central and Eastern Europe** (CEE) subsequent to the latter's democratization after 1989. The first such agreements were signed in December 1991, and by mid-1995 agreements existed with nine countries (Bulgaria, the Czech Republic, Estonia, Hungary, Latvia, Lithuania, Poland, Romania and Slovakia). A further agreement was signed with Slovenia in June 1996, which came into effect in early 1999. Each agreement provided for free trade in industrial goods, political dialogue, wide-ranging co-operation and legislative **harmonization**. Bilateral institutions were also established to manage the association created. After concluding Europe agreements, each of the CEE countries went on to apply for membership of the European Union (EU). All except Bulgaria and Romania joined the EU on 1 May 2004; those two countries joined on 1 January 2007. When devising stabilization and association agreements for the countries of the **Western Balkans**, the **European Commission** drew heavily on the structure and content of the Europe agreements.

EUROPE BY SATELLITE (EBS) is the TV news agency of the European Union (EU). It provides EU-related information for professionals working in television and radio and for other European institutions. EbS transmits via satellite a 'free to air' signal. It can be received in the EU, as well as the Mediterranean region and **Central and Eastern Europe**. For the rest of the world (**Asia**, Africa, Latin America, southern regions of the **USA** and north Australia), EbS provides an hour-long selection from its daily transmissions in collaboration with Canal France International (CFI). EbS is also available via the internet. The Commission wants to make much more of this resource, and sees it as a valuable tool in its communications strategy.

EUROPE DAY refers to 9 May 1950, the day when **Robert Schuman**, the French Foreign Minister, presented **Jean Monnet**'s proposal for the creation of a new European institution that became the **European Coal and Steel Community**. This date marks the birth of what is now known as the European Union (EU), and 9 May is 'celebrated' across the EU as Europe Day. The day is marked at EU level by activities and festivities that are aimed to enhance the relationship between the EU and its citizens. However, it is fair to say that the date goes largely unnoticed by most people, the media and politicians in the **United Kingdom**.

The **EUROPE DIRECT INFORMATION NETWORK** was launched in May 2005 to provide a new means for the European Union (EU) to communicate with ordinary citizens. The information centres provide, among other things, brochures on how the EU works and takes **decisions** and also about EC laws, institutions and policies. The network is open to all member states and it has a presence, comprising a total of some 480 information centres, in every country in the EU. It also has 400 documentation centres at European universities and research centres.

EUROPE OF DEMOCRACIES AND DIVERSITIES was a group comprising a number of anti-European Union parties in the **European**

Parliament. Formally known as the Europe of Nations group after the 1994 elections, it regrouped and renamed itself the Europe of Democracies and Diversities Group after the 1999 elections. Some 16 **Members of the European Parliament** belonged to the group. In 2004 this group remodelled itself once again and formed the **Independence and Democracy Group** (ID).

THE EUROPE OF FREEDOM AND DEMOCRACY GROUP (EFD) is one of the latest **party groups**, as at July 2009, to be formed within the **European Parliament** (EP). The EFD effectively replaced the **Independence and Democracy Group**, which collapsed when it failed to return enough **Members of the European Parliament** (MEPs) at the 2009 elections to be allowed to form a party group within the EP. Under existing EP rules, 25 MEPs are required from at least seven member states to form a party group. Membership of the EFD was a little fluid at the outset, but by March 2012 the group comprised 34 MEPs. It is dominated in terms of numbers by the UK Independence Party (UKIP)'s 10 MEPs. The Co-Chairmen of the EFD are Nigel Farage (from UKIP) and Francesco Speroni (from Italy's Lega Nord). Other members include nine MEPs from Lega Nord, one from the Dansk Folkeparti, one from the Dutch Staatkundig Gereformeerde Partij, one from the True Finns, two each from Greece and Lithuania and one each from France and Slovakia. The new group contains many colourful personalities and seems to be adopting a more nationalist approach towards politics and is set on placing stronger emphasis on anti-immigration as a core policy tenet of its activities than did its predecessor group. According to its political platform, the EFD is committed to the principles of democracy, freedom and co-operation among nation states and welcomes co-operation among sovereign states, but opposes any further European integration and argues that any new treaty should be subject to approval by referendum across the entire European Union.

EUROPE OF THE REGIONS is a phrase that came into common usage in the late 1980s. It was used by those who wished local and regional authorities, many of which already maintained liaison offices in **Brussels**, to have a greater input into the European Communities. Its importance was recognized by the establishment of the **Committee of the Regions** under the **Treaty on European Union**.

The **EUROPEAN AGENCY FOR RECONSTRUCTION** (EAR) was established in February 2000 and based in Thessaloniki, Greece. It was responsible for management of the main European Union (EU) assistance programmes in **Montenegro**, **Serbia** and the **former Yugoslav republic of Macedonia** (FYRM). The EAR evolved from a previous commitment made by the **European Council** to assume an active role in helping the reconstruction and recovery of the **Kosovo** region, but this was extended in late 2000 to cover the whole of the Federal Republic of **Yugoslavia**. In December 2001 the agency also acquired management responsibility for the FYRM. During its existence (2000–08) the agency oversaw the disbursement of almost €3,000m. in assistance. This was used to conduct immediate physical and economic reconstruction (repair of infrastructure and public utilities); to lay the foundations for the development of a market-orientated economy; and to support the establishment of democracy, respect for **human rights** and the rule of law (e.g. freedom of press and judiciary).

The **EUROPEAN AGENCY FOR SAFETY AND HEALTH AT WORK** (EU-OSHA) is a decentralized European Union agency, established in 1996 to promote the exchange of information and co-operation on measures dealing with health and safety at work. It is located in Bilbao, Spain. EU-OSHA played a central role in the EU's strategy for health and safety at work 2007–12, and aims to reduce the number of work-related injuries and to work with governments, employers and workers to promote a risk-prevention culture, to collect and analyse new scientific statistics on risks at work, to share information and disseminate examples of good practice. One of the current concerns being promoted by EU-OSHA centres on the dangers of smoking in the workplace. EU-OSHA strongly supports smoke-free workplaces and the Commission accelerated its campaign in 2011 to draw attention to the dangers of both active and passive smoking.

The **EUROPEAN AGRICULTURE FUND FOR RURAL DEVELOP-MENT** (EAFRD): See the **European Agriculture Guarantee Fund** (EAGF)

The **EUROPEAN AGRICULTURAL GUARANTEE FUND** (EAGF), together with the **European Agriculture Fund for Rural Development** (EAFRD), replaced the **European Agricultural Guidance and Guarantee Fund** (EAGFF) on 1 January 2007.

The **EUROPEAN AGRICULTURAL GUIDANCE AND GUARANTEE FUND** (EAGGF): See the **European Agricultural Guarantee Fund** (EAGF)

The **EUROPEAN ANTHEM** adopted by both the European Union in 1986 and the **Council of Europe** in 1972 for use on ceremonial occasions, consists of the words of Schiller's *Ode to Joy* as set to music in the final movement of Beethoven's Ninth Symphony. The **Treaty establishing a Constitution for Europe** was due to give it formal status, but the idea was abandoned during the negotiations that led to the **Treaty of Lisbon**.

EUROPEAN ARMAMENTS, RESEARCH AND MILITARY CAPABILITIES AGENCY: See **European Defence Agency**

The **EUROPEAN ARREST WARRANT** (EAW) allows a person to be transferred from one member state to another without the judiciary having to go through a formal extradition procedure, where a person is wanted for criminal prosecution or for a custodial sentence. The Council Framework decision on a European Arrest Warrant was agreed on 13 June 2002 and came into force in January 2004.

The **EUROPEAN ATOMIC ENERGY COMMUNITY** (EAEC) is also known by its acronym Euratom. One of several sectoral organizations conceived by **Jean Monnet**, the EAEC was established in 1957 at the same time as the **European Economic Community**. With the entry into force of the **Treaty of Lisbon**, it is the only remaining 'community'. When established, it was regarded by many supporters of integration as potentially the more significant initiative. The aims of the EAEC are defined as promoting research and disseminating technical information; establishing uniform safety standards; facilitating investment and the establishment of the necessary basic installations for the development of nuclear energy; ensuring a regular and equitable supply of ores and nuclear fuels; preventing the improper use of fissile materials; exercising the right of ownership over fissile materials (mainly uranium and plutonium); developing wide commercial outlets; and working for progress in the peaceful uses of nuclear energy. The EAEC has experienced many problems, being from the outset somewhat overshadowed by other developments in the European Communities (EC). Technical problems, costs and worries about nuclear safety have hindered its work, and the EAEC has found it difficult to control and direct national developments.

However, EC **energy policy** has placed considerable emphasis on nuclear energy. In seeking to facilitate nuclear research, the **European Commission** has the right to insist that national programmes are co-ordinated in order to avoid unnecessary duplication of effort. It also undertakes regular reviews of nuclear research and indicates areas of possible future research. It was under the aegis of the EAEC that the **Joint Research Centres** and the **Joint European Torus** were established. Beyond research, the EAEC may also help states to acquire nuclear ores and materials: supply policy is administered through the EAEC Supply Agency. While bound by the obligations of professional secrecy, the Commission is entitled to receive details of all relevant patents sought or obtained in the member states. In certain circumstances, it may seek licences to use them through a compulsory purchase order, although this would probably be impossible to implement without the consent of the member state concerned. There have also been several initiatives on **health and safety** standards for workers in the industry. The Commission may also demand the imposition of extra precautions where particularly dangerous experiments are being conducted, especially if these may affect other member states. The task of the routine monitoring of nuclear installations is, however, the responsibility of the member states.

From its inception the EAEC was considered the least significant of the three founding communities, and its identity and sense of autonomy essentially disappeared following its merger with the EC executives in 1967 (see **Merger Treaty**). Concerns about the safety of nuclear installations and doubts about their economic viability may well have been expected to reduce the significance of nuclear energy and the role of the EAEC, but nuclear energy is resurfacing, for example in the United Kingdom, as, for some, the only credible means to meet energy needs.

EUROPEAN AVIATION SAFETY AGENCY (EASA): See **Air Transport Policy**

The **EUROPEAN BANK FOR RECONSTRUCTION AND DEVELOPMENT** (EBRD) was established as a body, the purpose of which was initially to provide aid for countries in **Central and Eastern Europe** that had adopted a democratic form of government and had managed the transition towards stable market economies. A proposal from the French President, **François Mitterrand**, for the creation of such a body to assist these regions was accepted in December 1989 by the **European Council** in Strasbourg, which also agreed to the participation of other Western countries (something that had not been part of the original French proposal). The EBRD was sited in London and its first President was Jacques Attali, a close associate of Mitterrand. The bank began operations in March 1991, with a membership of European and other countries belonging to the International Monetary Fund (IMF), as well as the **European Communities** (EC, now the European Union, EU) and the **European Investment Bank** (EIB). The EC took a 51% stake in the enterprise, which set out to help eligible countries with market transition, privatization programmes, direct investment and environmental rehabilitation. In 1992 participation was extended to the successor states of the **USSR**. It was affected by scandal in 1993 when it was disclosed that it had spent more on furnishing its headquarters in London and on expense accounts than it had advanced in loans. In addition, there was a strong view that its establishment had been primarily a political gesture, since it could not provide anything not already available from the IMF and the International Bank for Reconstruction and Development (IBRD—World Bank). The scandal toppled Attali, who was replaced by Jacques de Larosière (1993–98), and it was under the latter's tenure that the EBRD secured international credibility and began to see returns from its investments in Central and Eastern Europe. The EBRD has a subscribed capital totalling some €20,000m. and a triple-A credit rating. The EBRD has played a significant role in the redevelopment of 27 countries, mostly the former Soviet states and countries of Central and Eastern Europe.

Today the EBRD provides financing for banks, industries and businesses. As well as boosting economic transformation, the EBRD has promoted political change, with loans conditional on guarantees that countries apply the principles of multi-party democracy and are openly pluralist. By 2012 63 countries (as well as the EU and the EIB) had placed capital subscriptions with the EBRD and the ERBD was working in 29 countries in Europe and Central Asia. Jean Lemierre took office as the fourth President of the EBRD on 3 July 2000, and was reappointed for a second four-year term of office in 2004. He was replaced in 2008 by Thomas Mirow, who was, in turn, replaced by Suma Chakrabarti in 2012. In 2006 the EBRD signalled that from 2010 it intended to shift funding away from the countries of the Baltic region and Central Europe and instead towards Armenia, Kazakhstan, **Russia**, **Ukraine** and Uzbekistan.

The **EUROPEAN BROADCASTING UNION** (EBU) is an international federation of broadcasting organizations formed in 1950 and based in Geneva, **Switzerland**. It has 74 active members, including all the member states of the European Union. The EBU has encouraged collaboration and development within European broadcasting, especially in terms of increasing the European content of programming, but it has no authority over national broadcasting networks. It has collaborated with the **European Commission** on several initiatives. Its most recognizable broadcast in the United Kingdom, outside the sporting arena, remains the annual Eurovision Song Contest.

The **EUROPEAN BUSINESS AND INNOVATION CENTRE NETWORK** (EBN) is a **European Commission** initiative to encourage **small and medium-sized enterprises** (SMEs), and to ensure that they are able to benefit from European Union **competition policy** and the **internal market**. It is essentially an advisory body that disseminates information on innovations and ideas to companies. (See also **European Venture Capital Association**; **SME Task Force**; and **Business and Innovation Centres**.)

The **EUROPEAN CAPITAL OF CULTURE**, which was known as the European City of Culture until 1999, is one of the best-known examples of the fledgling cultural policy of the European Communities (EC). The programme dates from 1985 and was temporarily included under the EC's **Kaleidoscope** programme for general cultural events; it is now funded as part of the EC **cultural policy**. It has subsequently become one of most keenly sought-after titles among cities across Europe. Cities were formerly chosen by member states and are given a subsidy by the **European Commission**. A new procedure was adopted in 2005 for selecting the capitals for the period 2005–19, in order to enable the new member states to participate. Recent and imminent Capitals of Culture include Turku, Finland, and Tallinn, Estonia (2011), Guimarães, Portugal, and Maribor, Slovenia (2012), Marseilles, France, and

Košice, Slovakia (2013) and Umeå, Sweden, Riga, Latvia, and Sarajevo, Bosnia and Herzegovina (2014).

The **EUROPEAN CENTRAL BANK** (ECB) has long been held to be essential to **economic and monetary union** (EMU) as a body with powers to issue the European single currency (the **euro**) and control monetary policy for the 17 members of the eurozone. At its core the ECB is tasked with managing the euro and safeguarding price stability. Its origins lie in the **Treaty on European Union**, which confirmed that the ECB would come into operation at the beginning of the third stage of EMU, between 1997 and 1999. The ECB was preceded by a **European Monetary Institute** (EMI). In 1993 it was agreed that the ECB would be located in Frankfurt am Main, Germany, and it was formally established in June 1998. The first President, appointed for a period of eight years, was Wim Duisenberg. He was replaced in July 2003 by **Jean-Claude Trichet**, formerly Governor of the Banque de France, who was, in turn, succeeded by **Mario Draghi**, the erstwhile Governor of the Bank of Italy, in November 2011.

Prior to the launching of stage three of EMU in January 1999, the ECB's capital was just under €4,000m. The national central banks of the member states are the only subscribers to and holders of the ECB's capital. The percentage shares of the national central banks of the member states in the ECB's capital were initially set by the ECB Governing Council in June 1998 (based on the member states' respective shares in the gross domestic product and population of the European Communities). They were subsequently revised, with effect from 1 January 2004, and were revised again following the 2004 and 2007 **enlargements** of the (EU). At 1 January 2011 they were as follows: Austria 1.9417; Belgium 2.4256; Bulgaria 0.8686; Cyprus 0.1369; Czech Republic 1.4472; Denmark 1.4835; Estonia 0.1790; Finland 1.2539; France 14.3875; Germany 18.9373; Greece 1.8168; Hungary 1.3856; Ireland 1.1107; Italy 12.4966; Latvia 0.2837; Lithuania 0.4256; Luxembourg 0.1747; Malta 0.0632; Netherlands 3.9882; Poland 4.8954; Portugal 1.7504; Romania 2.4645; Slovakia 0.6934; Slovenia 0.3288; Spain 7.5498; Sweden 2.2582; and the United Kingdom 14.5172.

The Governing Council of the ECB is the main **decision-making** body of the Eurosystem. It comprises 23 individuals; all the members of the Executive Board of the ECB as well as the governors and/or presidents of all the national central banks (NCBs) where the euro has been adopted. The Governing Council takes the most important and strategically significant decisions for the Eurosystem. When taking decisions on monetary policy and on other tasks of the Eurosystem, the members of the Governing Council are expected to act with mind to the overall economy in a fully independent capacity.

The Governing Council currently meets twice a month, usually on the first and third Thursday. Interest rate decisions are normally discussed at the first meeting of the month only. The President of the EU Council/**Eurogroup** and a member of the **European Commission** are entitled to attend these meetings but they do not have a vote. Votes are taken by simple majority and where a tie occurs, the President has the casting vote. Although the proceedings of the meetings are confidential, the Governing Council makes the outcome of its deliberations public, primarily those about setting the key interest rates. The number of staff of the ECB amounts to around 1,607 (in 2010) and it is truly European. It is worth noting that its members come from all 27 countries of the EU. In the early days, the EMI and the ECB recruited many staff from the national central banks of the EU member states, but nowadays the ECB also attracts staff members from other sectors. Under the terms of the **Treaty of Lisbon** (Article 13) the ECB was upgraded to the status of an EU institution. A new purpose-built headquarters is being constructed for the ECB in Frankfurt and is expected to be ready by 2014.

The **EUROPEAN CENTRE FOR THE DEVELOPMENT OF VOCATIONAL TRAINING** (Cedefop) is a service agency of the **European Commission**, established in 1975. Originally located in Berlin, Cedefop relocated to Thessaloniki, Greece, in 1995. It is charged with the task of encouraging the development of vocational and in-service training for adults, and of standardizing national qualifications. It assists the Commission in the preparation of European Union training programmes. Much of its recent work has focused upon the **employment** problems of women, especially those who wish to return to work after a long absence. Its work is directed by a council consisting of representatives from the national governments, employers, trade unions and the Commission. Cedefop is closely involved with the **European Training Foundation**, with **Eurostat** and with the **Lifelong Learning Programme**.

EUROPEAN CITY OF CULTURE: See **European Capital of Culture**

The **EUROPEAN CLIMATE CHANGE PROGRAMME** (ECCP) is a European Communities initiative launched in June 2000. Its main purpose is to identify and develop all the necessary elements of a European Union strategy to implement the Kyoto Protocol to the **United Nations** Framework Convention on Climate Change, the purpose of which was to reduce 'greenhouse' gas emissions to 8% below 1990 levels by 2008–12.

The **EUROPEAN COAL AND STEEL COMMUNITY** (ECSC) was the body that emerged from the **Schuman Plan**. It was established by the **Treaty of Paris** of 18 April 1951, which was effective from 23 July 1952 until 23 July 2002 when the ECSC was disbanded. One of the greatest difficulties during the negotiations between France and West Germany centred on the scope and content of the **competition policy** provisions and specifically French demands for further German decartelization, but agreement was finally reached. Formed by the **Six** European states (Belgium, France, the Federal Republic of Germany, Italy, Luxembourg and the Netherlands) that later went on to create the **European Economic Community** (EEC) and the **European Atomic Energy Community** (EAEC or Euratom), the ECSC had as its general objective the fostering of 'economic expansion, growth of employment and a rising standard of living' in the member states through the development of a common market in **coal** and **steel**. The common market would commence after a transitional period of five years.

The ECSC's historic importance lies in the fact that it was the first European organization to embrace supranationalism. This was represented by the executive High Authority, which was complemented as an executive by a Council of Ministers. Its indirectly elected Assembly, though possessing only advisory powers, was the first European assembly with a legally guaranteed basis. The other institutions of the ECSC were a **Court of Justice** as a final arbiter of the Treaty of Paris, and a Consultative Committee of representatives of national interest groups. This institutional framework was the model used later for the EEC.

The ECSC enjoyed some success in the 1950s, presiding over a large expansion in output, although this was due as much to world economic conditions as to the ECSC. However, it failed to cope satisfactorily with a major crisis in the coal industry in 1959 and to overcome the many barriers to the establishment of a common market. Moreover, it did not by itself make much progress towards political integration. One of its major problems was that it was difficult to achieve co-ordination and integration in only one economic sector; it was difficult, if not impossible, to isolate coal and steel from the national economies in general. This was a major reason for the switch by the Six from **sectoral integration** to the broader EEC.

With the establishment of the EEC and Euratom, the ECSC lost all its independent institutions except for its two executive bodies. In 1967 these were merged with those of the other two European Communities (EC). The ECSC continued, however, to have a semi-independent existence, with its own source of **revenue**, derived from a direct levy upon coal and steel producers, and its own **budget** out of which it financed development and restructuring plans for the industries. It also set prices and supervised production levels in the coal and steel industries. Much of its activity had to be devoted to helping remedy the severe social and economic consequences of the reduction in the workforces of both industries through early retirement schemes, retraining and redeployment, especially in those regions where these industries had traditionally dominated the local economy. The **European Commission** inherited the powers of the old High Authority over the coal and steel industries, powers which were much more substantial than in most policy areas of the EC, and used them to the extent of seeking the declaration of a state of **manifest crisis**, which gave the Commission even greater powers of direction and punishment. A state of manifest crisis was declared in the steel industry between 1980 and 1988.

The **EUROPEAN COMMISSION**, officially known as the Commission of the European Union (after the **Treaty of Lisbon**), was established as one of the two executive institutions of the European Communities (EC). As opposed to the then Council of Ministers (see **Council of the European Union**), which represents the member states, the Commission has been regarded as both the European, or supranational, and the administrative arm of the European Union (EU) executive. The term refers to the collectivity of first, the College of Commissioners (currently 27 in number, including the executive head of this institution), and second, the administrative apparatus that serves them. The Commission employs a workforce of some 23,800 people. These are mainly based in Brussels, but some are in Luxembourg, in EU offices in member states, or in delegations to non-member countries. Others, primarily engaged in scientific projects, are located in centres throughout the EU.

Under the treaty base, the Commission was charged with bringing policy proposals forward and it holds the monopoly on policy initiation. It is also charged with operating as the 'guardian of the treaties'. In terms of supervision, the Commission was given a general responsibility to ensure that other EU institutions and the member states fulfilled those tasks and provisions assigned to them under the **founding treaties**. It had a duty to ensure that **decisions** taken by the Council and, increasingly the norm after 2009, by the Council and the **European Parliament** under the **co-decision procedure**, are carried out, or adhered to, by the member states. Most EU legislation is implemented, not at the EU level, but at the national level, and the Commission has a duty to see that legislation is implemented correctly and on time. If implementation does not occur, the Commission is empowered to bring the recalcitrant states before the judges of the Court of Justice, where fines can be levied against the states in question. In addition to these general areas of constitutional obligation, the Commission came to enjoy further and significant autonomous authority in the operation of the **common agricultural policy** (CAP) and **competition policy**. A further area of autonomy lay, after the 1967 **Merger Treaty**, in its inheritance of the substantial decision-making powers of the previous High Authority of the **European Coal and Steel Community**, which gave it the right to act without regard to the Council of Ministers.

These 'constitutional' powers do not give a complete picture of the overall role acquired by the European Commission since 1957. The extent of its activities, along with its unelected nature, has made it the most controversial of the EU institutions. While its original activism under the leadership of **Walter Hallstein** was obstructed by President **Charles de Gaulle** of France in the **empty chair crisis**, events internal and external to the EU after the early 1980s contributed to a new dynamism on the part of the Commission, especially under the first half of the presidency of **Jacques Delors** (1985–95). The **Treaty on European Union** (TEU) made few constitutional changes to the Commission's role. Some of those changes recognized an extension of its competence, while others perhaps indicated a reduction in its independence (see below) as the powers of the EP were extended and the **European**

Council became more of an agenda setter. Moreover, the **Treaty of Amsterdam** stipulated that the President of the Commission must be formally approved by the **European Parliament** (EP). The Treaty also enhanced the authority of the President as the Commission prepared to review its organization and procedures prior to **enlargement**.

The Commission is also responsible for the financial management of the EU. It prepares the preliminary draft annual **budget** that must be submitted to both the Council of the European Union and the EP for approval and adoption. It is further responsible for the administration of the budget and the allocation of money from the budget to the **structural funds**, other programmes and salaries. The TEU imposed more stringent controls and **accountability** on the Commission. A further responsibility is the representation of the EU abroad. It is the Commission that negotiates international agreements on behalf of the EU, and that maintains and staffs EU offices in other countries. Finally, because of its multifarious roles, the Commission has one further task. It has become widely regarded as the body that deals with the problems and issues that other EU institutions cannot or will not tackle. An activist Commission can seek to utilize this role to maintain the momentum of integration as has occurred in the past, for example, in relation to both the **single market** and the **single currency** initiatives.

The 27 Commissioners meet formally, as the College of Commissioners, once a week to discuss an agenda that has been prepared in advance. Additional and sometimes more informal meetings can be held to discuss general questions of European development, or more specific problems. If a majority of Commissioners are present, a meeting is considered to be quorate and decisions are taken by a simple majority. Once the Commission has taken a decision, however, its members are expected to abide by the principle of collective responsibility.

Each member state is entitled to put forward one candidate as its prospective Commissioner. The Commissioners are nominated by the national governments but, since the **Treaty of Nice**, only after intensive consultation with the Commission President, who is chosen first and who will determine the policy portfolio for each Commissioner. Formally governments submit nominations for approval by the Council of the European Union, but in practice each Commissioner-designate has to appear before the EP to answer questions about his or her aims and objectives over the next five years, which allows the MEPs to grill future Commissioners. The EP must take a vote to approve all 27 Commissioners. As the EP gets ever stronger, strong opposition within the EP in respect of the competence of some individuals is increasingly sufficient to compel a Commissioner-designate to stand aside.

On assuming office, each Commissioner has to take an oath of loyalty to the EU, swearing that he or she will serve EU interests exclusively, and will not seek or take instructions from any national government or other body. Commissioners are appointed for a five-year term, which is renewable. The fact that about one-half are not reappointed for a further term suggests that

Commissioners who act more independently than their governments might wish do not receive a further nomination. Most Commissioners have previously been national politicians, and normally belong to the party, or one of the parties, making up the government that submits their nomination. A few have previously been university academics, bureaucrats, industrialists or trade union leaders. There is no means of dismissal other than by a collective vote of censure in the EP. Since 1995 terms of office for Commissioners have begun after the election of the EP and coincided with the duration of the Parliament. Since 2004 each member state has been entitled to nominate just one Commissioner. In other words, France, Germany, Italy, Spain and the United Kingdom each lost a Commissioner. The **Barroso** Commission initially contained 25 Commissioners when it took up office in November 2004, two weeks later than planned after the mini-crisis of the Buttiglione affair. Membership has grown to 27 following the successful accession of both Bulgaria and Romania in January 2007.

Before the TEU, the President of the European Commission was appointed by the Council of Ministers for a two-year term, but in practice this was automatically extended to four years, with **Walter Hallstein** and **Jacques Delors** serving even longer. Former Presidents of the Commission and the years of their appointment are as follows: Walter Hallstein 1958; Jean Rey 1967; Franco Maria Malfatti 1970; Sicco Mansholt (see **Mansholt Plan**) 1972; François-Xavier Ortoli 1973; **Roy Jenkins** 1977; **Gaston Thorn** 1981; Jacques Delors 1985; **Jacques Santer** 1995; **Romano Prodi** 1999. José Manuel Barroso was appointed President by the **European Council** in 2004 and again in 2009, and this appointment was subsequently approved by the EP.

While the President has rather less authority over Commission members than does a national prime minister over ministers in a government, the view of the President as just one of several Commissioners increasingly belied the true role of the office, which was enhanced and clarified by the more recent treaties. The TEU ensured that the EP must be consulted on nominations for the presidency, which are made by the Council of the European Union, and the Council's choice then requires **ratification** by the EP, along with the other proposed members of the Commission. Under the terms of the TEU, the President now has the formal right to be consulted on the selection of other Commissioners. This enhanced presidential authority reflects the established practice of the President attending **European Council** meetings, representing the EU at international meetings and reporting on proposals and progress to the EP. However, under the terms of the TEU, the President does not have the power to dismiss other Commissioners from office, and has only a limited influence upon the distribution of portfolios, which is ultimately a collegiate decision. Some portfolios are more important than others, and larger member states tend to believe they have a prior claim to these. Equally, each newly appointed Commissioner, because of personal interest or because a policy area is important for his or her own country, will have a personal preference. Before the TEU, six of the Commissioners were also appointed as Vice-Presidents: these offices, however, had little political significance.

Each Commissioner has a portfolio, which usually consists of several areas of policy responsibility, and which may not correspond exactly to the fields of activity of the **Directorates-General** (DGs) and the special services that together constitute the administrative arm of the EU. While the relevant sections of the bureaucracy report directly to the appropriate Commissioners, the latter have adopted the French practice of employing **Cabinets**, a group of personally appointed advisers and aides answerable solely to their Commissioner, providing him or her with assistance and liaising with other Commissioners and the various parts of the administration.

The Treaty of Amsterdam increased the Commission's role in formulating international agreements on services and intellectual property rights, to be exercised at the discretion of the Council. The Treaty also stipulated that a further review of the Commission had to be undertaken.

The Commission can be dismissed en bloc through a vote of censure by the EP. In January 1999 the EP's Socialist group (see **Group of the Party of European Socialists**) presented a censure motion, in order to ensure the Commission's **accountability** in the face of allegations of fraud, financial mismanagement and nepotism. Although a compromise deal ensured that the motion was defeated, concessions won by the EP during the dispute were widely felt to mark a significant reduction in the extent of the Commission's perceived autonomy. This was reinforced two months later, when an independent report into the allegations found considerable evidence of incompetence and corruption and, while detailing charges against several Commissioners, also judged the Commission to be collectively responsible for a 'dysfunctional' political environment, marked by a culture of evasion and an absence of leadership. On 16 March 1999, for the first time in its history, the Commission resigned en masse. The Commissioners retained their positions and exercised limited duties until a new Commission was appointed. The EP ratified the appointment of Romano Prodi as President of the Commission, and of the new Commissioners, in late 1999. The EP also exerted its power in late 2004 when it successfully threatened to block the incoming Barroso Commission unless Commissioner-designate Rocco Buttiglione was replaced.

The Commission under Prodi, whose term ran until the latter part of 2004, launched a programme of wide-ranging reforms and two important **White Papers**. The first of these, on governance, proposed to modernize the institutional machinery of the Commission, and the second to increase **transparency**, efficiency and interaction with outside interests (the public, **non-governmental organizations** and the private sector). The Barroso Commission launched a more ambitious five-year programme which was first presented to the EP in January 2005. It sought to unleash Europe's potential and placed its emphasis on policies that would bring economic growth and secure and create more jobs. The proposals were not unproblematic and Barroso was swift to pre-empt left-wing critics by arguing that such 'liberal' policies were essential in order to narrow social disparities and protect the environment. Other priorities included: the need for investment in research and development; greater consideration of how to tackle problems such as climate change; and the sustainable management of natural resources, as well as initiatives to bring the states of the **Western Balkans** closer to EU membership.

The Treaty of Nice made a further significant alteration to rules pertaining to the **nomination procedure** for the Commission. Under its terms, the nomination of the President is a matter for the European Council acting by **qualified majority**, rather than unanimity. This appointment still has to be approved by the EP. Once a President is selected, he or she then liaises with the Council to adopt a list of other Commissioners who in turn require endorsement from both the Council and the EP. Moreover, the Treaty of Nice increased the Commission President's powers to allow him or her to decide on how the Commission is structured internally; to enable him or her to allocate portfolios, and if necessary to reassign policy portfolios; and to enable him or her to demand the resignation of an individual Commissioner.

The **Treaty of Lisbon** has ushered in further reforms. The original plan of cutting the size of the College of Commissioners initially to 18 after 2014 (and introducing an equal rotation among the member states) was dropped in the discussions following Ireland's rejection of the Treaty of Lisbon in June 2008. The European Council agreed to retain one Commissioner per member state in an attempt to encourage Irish voters to endorse the treaty at a second time of asking, which they duly did in October 2009.

The **EUROPEAN COMMISSION OF HUMAN RIGHTS** is a body established in 1953 which operates under the aegis of the **Council of Europe** in **Strasbourg**. Although it has no formal connection with the European Union, the latter accepts the principles that govern the operation of the Commission and acknowledges its role in the field of **human rights**, including the right to investigate alleged infringements of the **European Convention on Human Rights** by and within the member states. These can be brought before the **European Court of Human Rights**.

EUROPEAN COMMITTEE FOR ELECTROTECHNICAL STAN-DARDIZATION: See **CENELEC**

The **EUROPEAN COMMITTEE FOR IRON AND STEEL STAN-DARDS** (ECISS) is a body established in 1986 that replaced an Iron and Steel Nomenclature and Co-ordinating Committee. Its purpose was to replace national iron and steel standards with common European standards.

EUROPEAN COMMITTEE FOR STANDARDIZATION: See **CEN**

The **EUROPEAN COMMITTEE TO COMBAT DRUGS** (CELAD) is a group within the **TREVI** framework established in December 1989. The idea originated with French President François Mitterrand, who wanted to tackle the growing drugs problem in Europe. It was intended to follow up work carried out since 1971 by the so-called Pompidou Group of the **Council of Europe** on the promotion of collaborative measures within the European Communities (EC) and between the EC and other states and international organizations on drugs-related problems and issues, especially the illegal traffic in drugs, the monitoring of drugs that have a potential for being misused, and the prevention of the laundering of money gained from drugs-trafficking. The Pompidou initiative had been purely intergovernmental, and outside the EC framework. Mitterrand's idea envisaged a specific EC angle, greater political co-ordination among the member states and a role for the Commission. Mitterrand's proposal led to the creation of the ad hoc European Committee to Combat Drugs group (CELAD) as a first step in this direction. Agreement on the Treaty on European Union (1991) provided the first references to drugs in the European Union (EU) treaty base and led to the creation of the **European Monitoring Centre for Drugs and Drug Addiction** (EMCDDA) in 1994.

A **White Paper** on a **EUROPEAN COMMUNICATIONS POLICY** was published in early February 2006. This policy was presented by the **Commission** as a new approach to explaining what the EU does, and was an attempt to try and close the recognized gap in interest between EU citizens and EU policymakers. The **Barroso** Commission made communication one of its strategic priorities in 2005, and the White Paper set out 50 practical steps which the Commission could take to improve communication and thereby enhance democracy and legitimacy within the EU. The White Paper comprised five key parts, identified under the following headings: Putting Communication at the Service of Citizens; Taking Work Forward; Working with the Media and New Technologies; Understanding European Public Opinion; and Doing the Job Together. In short, the document sought both to inform and to consult the public about EU policies.

EUROPEAN COMMUNITIES (EC) is a term that described the unified body that resulted from the merger in 1967 of the administrative networks of the **European Economic Community** (EEC), the **European Coal and Steel Community** (ECSC) and the **European Atomic Energy Community** (EAEC or Euratom). The term was also formerly used to describe collectively the signatories of the three Communities' **founding treaties** and their territories. The singular of the term (European Community) was widely used as an alternative for both meanings.

The main institutions of the EC were the **European Commission**, the **Council of the European Union** (known as the Council of Ministers until November 1993), the **European Parliament** and the **Court of Justice**.

Under the **Treaty on European Union** (TEU), signed in 1992, the EC institutions became one of the then three **pillars** of the broader European Union (EU). Although European Union was subsequently the preferred term for the collective member states, it nevertheless remained correct to refer to the relevant institutions as the EC and to the law made by the Court of Justice as EC law.

Following the first **enlargement** beyond the original **Six** member states, the EC expanded progressively until, by January 2007, the EU had **Twenty-Seven** member states. The **Treaty of Lisbon** replaced all references to the European Communities in favour of the term European Union. The EC as such ceased to exist, although Euratom continued to operate as the last remaining 'community'.

EUROPEAN COMMUNITY (EC) was the often-used singular of the term **European Communities**. Following **ratification** of the **Treaty on European Union** (TEU), it also became the official title of the **European Economic Community** (EEC). The **Treaty of Lisbon** replaced all references to the EC in favour of the term **European Union**. With the Treaty of Lisbon's entry into force, the EC ceased to exist.

EUROPEAN COMMUNITY ACTION SCHEME FOR THE MOBILITY OF UNIVERSITY STUDENTS: See **ERASMUS**

EUROPEAN COMMUNITY OF CONSUMER CO-OPERATIVES: See **Consumer Committee**

The **EUROPEAN COMMUNITY HUMANITARIAN OFFICE** (ECHO) is a division of the **European Commission**. This office, established in 1992, is based in **Brussels** and aims to provide emergency **humanitarian assistance** and food aid to many parts of the world, including the countries of the former **Yugoslavia**, the **African, Caribbean and Pacific** (ACP) **States**, the Near and Middle East, the **Commonwealth of Independent States** and the Far East. ECHO aims to meet the immediate needs of victims of mostly man-made disasters worldwide, in such areas as assisting displaced persons, and health, sanitary and mine-clearance programmes. In 2010 ECHO granted €1,115m. in humanitarian aid, which funded aid projects providing assistance to around 151m. people in more than 80 countries worldwide.

EUROPEAN COMMUNITY LAW: See **Court of First Instance**; **Court of Justice**; **Law**

EUROPEAN COMMUNITY STUDIES ASSOCIATIONS (ECSAs) are nationally based academic organizations (from some 52 countries and with a membership of around 9,000) that support research on all aspects of the European integration process. The activities of the European associations are co-ordinated through ECSA-Europe, an umbrella organization largely funded by the **European Commission**. ECSA-Europe seeks to promote teaching and university research on European integration; to develop co-operation among its members; to encourage and manage transnational programmes of research and technical assistance; to foster networks of academic co-operation; and to disseminate information on university activities, especially through use of the internet. The representative organization in the United Kingdom is the University Association for Contemporary European Studies (UACES). The representative organization in the **USA** is the European Union Studies Association (EUSA).

EUROPEAN COMMUNITY TRADE MARKS OFFICE: See **Office for Harmonization in the Internal Market**

EUROPEAN COMPANY STATUTE: See **Company Law Statute**

The **EUROPEAN CONFEDERATION OF IRON AND STEEL INDUSTRIES** (Eurofer) brings together all the steel companies and national steel federations from across Europe to promote the interests of stainless steel. The steel industry still represents a sizeable sector for the European economy and employs about 360,000 people across the European Union (EU). It has an annual revenue of some €190,000m. Eurofer was created in 1976 and is based in Brussels. The initiative was taken by the **European Commission**, which hoped that such a body would be able to deal more decisively with a continuing crisis caused by decreasing demand for steel, poor productivity, an under-utilization of capacity, and the reluctance of national governments to accept mass redundancies. Eurofer was meant to work for a rationalization of the industry, assisted by the Commission, through reductions in output, to bring productivity and capacity more in line with demand. It had some limited success, but its voluntary nature could not persuade national governments always to follow its guidelines, nor could it prevent individual companies from taking unilateral action to protect themselves. Today, Eurofer continues to promote co-operation amongst national federations and companies in all matters concerning the development of the European steel industry. It organizes conferences and seeks to influence EU developments. It also represents the common interests of its members vis-à-vis third parties, notably the EU institutions and other international organizations.

The **EUROPEAN CONSERVATIVES AND REFORMISTS GROUP** (ECR) was established as a political group within the **European Parliament** (EP) on 22 June 2009. The group owes its origins primarily to the British Conservative Party under **David Cameron**, who carried out his earlier promise to withdraw his **Members of the European Parliament** (MEPs) from what he considered the more 'Eurofederalist' stance of the **European People's Party** (EPP). The ECR currently comprises 52 MEPs from nine European Union (EU) member states and forms the fifth largest force within the current EP. Twenty-five of its members come from the British Conservative Party, and they sit alongside nine members from the Czech Civic Democratic Party, six Polish MEPs from the Party of Law and Justice, three Polish MEPs from Poland Comes First and representatives from a number of smaller parties across the EU (from Belgium, Latvia, Lithuania, the Netherlands and the United Kingdom), who have one MEP each. There are, in addition, four independent MEPs in the group. The ECR believes that the creation of a non-federalist centre/centre-right group in the EP enhances European democracy. The ECR claims to be making its presence felt within the EP, where it is represented on all the major committees, is actively engaging with issues, and was supportive of **Barroso**'s bid for a second term as Commission President.

EUROPEAN CONSTITUTION: See **Treaty Establishing a Constitution for Europe**

The **EUROPEAN CONSUMER CONSULTATIVE GROUP** (ECCG) was established, as the Consumer Committee, in 1995 as a successor to the Consumers' Consultative Council (CCC), a body that had been established as the Consumer Consultative Committee in 1973. The CCC had been active in forwarding opinions and proposals for action to the Commission. However, by 1995 it had 48 members, which meant that it found it difficult to co-ordinate the views of its disparate membership. It was therefore replaced by a Consumer Committee, appointed by the **European Commission**, and consisting of 20 members. The Consumer Committee was rebranded the European Consumer Consultative Group (ECCG) in October 2003 and is the Commission's preferred forum for engaging with consumer organizations. It meets in Brussels four times per year. Membership is made up of one member from each of the European Consumers' Organization (BEUC), the European Association for the Co-ordination of Consumer Representation in Standardisation (ANEC), the Confederation of Family Organizations in the European Union (COFACE), the European Community of Consumer Co-operatives (Euro Coop), the European Trade Union Confederation (ETUC) and the Institut européen interrégional de la consommation (IEIC—a grouping of regional bodies concerned with consumer affairs), together with two observers from Iceland and Norway, and representatives from member states. Meetings are chaired by a senior official from the **Directorate-General** (DG) in charge of consumer policy. The ECCG, while only an advisory body, is consulted by the Commission on proposed initiatives that may have a bearing on consumer interests.

EUROPEAN CONSUMERS' ORGANIZATION (BEUC): See **European Consumer Consultative Group**

The **EUROPEAN CONVENTION**, formally the **Convention on the Future of Europe**, and not to be confused with the **European Convention on Human Rights**, was launched on 28 February 2002 under the chairmanship of the former French President **Valéry Giscard d'Estaing**. It brought together representatives of the heads of governments and of the parliaments of the member states and the **candidate countries**, and representatives from the **European Commission** and the **European Parliament**, as well as a number of observers. In total there were 207 participants (including alternates) whose task was to debate the issues raised by the **Laeken Declaration** and formulate an agenda for the **intergovernmental conference** (IGC) that began work in October 2003.

The Convention was modelled on that which successfully drafted the **Charter of Fundamental Rights** in 2000, and was a response to growing concerns about popular perceptions of the remoteness of IGCs. Supporters of the Convention believed that it was more likely than an IGC to reach decisions on the future of the European Union (EU) that would accurately reflect the concerns and wishes of EU citizens. While this may have been a key assumption behind the launching of the Convention, the deliberations of the 207 participants failed to generate much popular interest. The same was generally true of the Convention's output, the **draft Treaty establishing a Constitution for Europe**, which was adopted 'by consensus' in June and July 2003 and forwarded to the **European Council**.

The **EUROPEAN CONVENTION ON HUMAN RIGHTS**, the full title of which is the European Convention for the Protection of Human Rights and Fundamental Freedoms, is a document sponsored in 1950 by the **Council of Europe**. It represents an unprecedented system of international protection for **human rights** and enables individuals to apply to the courts for the enforcement of their rights. It came into operation in 1953. All the member states of the European Union (EU) are signatories of the Convention and, in accepting it, the EU has also accepted the role and predominance in this area of both the associated **European Commission of Human Rights** and the **European Court of Human Rights**. The EU is not a signatory to the Convention, although concerns about its democratic credentials and the meaning of citizens' rights led to some pressure to accede. The EU's response was to draw up its own **Charter of Fundamental Rights**, which was proclaimed in 2000. Moreover, the **Treaty of Lisbon**, like the abandoned **Treaty establishing a Constitution for Europe**, contains a provision committing the EU to accede to the Convention.

EUROPEAN CO-OPERATION IN THE FIELD OF SCIENTIFIC AND TECHNICAL RESEARCH: See **COST**

EUROPEAN COUNCIL is the name used to describe meetings of the heads of state or government of European Union (EU) member states, their foreign ministers, and senior officials of the **European Commission**. It should not be confused with the **Council of Europe**, which is an entirely unrelated body, nor should it be identified too closely with the **Council of the European Union**. The **Treaty of Rome** made no provision for the existence of the European Council, and this created some lack of clarity about its constitutional position in, and relationship to, the European Communities (EC). The Treaty had stipulated the Council of Ministers (see Council of the European Union) as the only executive body in the EC representing the national governments. No provision was made for meetings of the heads of state or government, and the latter at first seemingly paid little attention to EC affairs, meeting on only three occasions during the first decade. The problems of the 1960s and the **Luxembourg Compromise** suggested that if the member states were serious about membership of the EC, then the heads of government, who ultimately controlled the Council of Ministers, should become more directly involved, particularly in order to give a strategic purpose to the EC on a range of issues where the normal institutional framework could not proceed without the consent of the national governments.

Four ad hoc **summit meetings** were held between 1969 and 1974. At the fourth, in Paris, the government leaders accepted 'the need for an overall approach to the internal problems in achieving European unity and the external problems facing Europe'; they agreed to a proposal from President **Valéry Giscard d'Estaing** of France that they should meet on a regular basis under the rubric of the European Council. The meetings would take place three times a year (amended in December 1985 to twice yearly) 'to ensure progress and overall consistency in the activities of the Communities and in the work on political co-operation'. The presidency of the Council would rotate between the member states, changing every six months, with the meetings being held in the capital of the country currently occupying the presidency, and the third meeting each year (until 1985) being held in **Brussels**. Further extraordinary sessions could be arranged, should circumstances demand it. The first meeting was held in Dublin in March 1975.

The principle of rotation emphasizes that all member states are equal. Despite the heavy workload that the presidency involves, it is particularly important for the smaller states since it offers them the opportunity to become a centre of European, and even world, diplomacy once every few years. All states treat the presidency seriously, and most have attempted to use their presidency to promote numerous potentially important initiatives. **Enlargement** of the EU since 2004, however, prompted consideration of moving away from existing practice and establishing a **President of the European Council** who would hold office for two and a half years.

Before the **ratification** of the **Single European Act** (SEA), the European Council had no legal recognition within the EC. This suited the interests of the member states, since the more informal atmosphere gave them freedom to discuss broad questions of politics and policy without the pressure of having to come to a decision. The European Council became the only EC institution where such broad-ranging discussions could occur. Each meeting normally lasts for two days. Their informality is indicated by the fact that most meetings are not attended by large numbers of national officials and advisers. Only the foreign ministers accompany their leaders. The only other participants are the President of the European Commission, one of the Vice-Presidents and, since 1983, the Secretary-General. The European Council gatherings also provide an opportunity for informal discussion of more sensitive topics outside the scheduled plenary sessions.

The European Council has become central to the EU. Its emergence confirmed that nothing could be achieved unless the member states were in agreement, and virtually all the major advances since the mid-1980s have occurred because of European Council agreement on their desirability. However, its presence has sometimes hindered effective decision-making at lower EU levels. Because ultimate authority rests with the government leaders, they have often been expected to resolve relatively minor issues, which other agencies were competent, but either unwilling or unable, to deal with.

The position of the European Council within the EC was acknowledged and regularized by the SEA. It is another version of the Council of the European Union, albeit the most senior. When policy decisions are taken by the European Council that conform to the constitutional requirements of the **founding treaties**, they have the force of EU **legislation**. More generally, European Council agreements are framed as general principles or a broad consensus on future action, which are then passed on to the European Commission and the Council of the European Union for further research, discussion and possible adoption. The **Treaty on European Union** (TEU) strengthened the role of the European Council further. It was directly responsible for the two new **pillars** of the EU: the **common foreign and security policy** (CFSP) and **justice and home affairs** (JHA). It is also the body to which changes in **economic and monetary union** (EMU) are reported and which puts forward further guidelines for EMU. The European Council's decisions have normally been taken on the basis of **unanimity**, although on a few occasions a vote has been employed to overcome the resistance of one or two member states. In 2002, new rules governing the organization and proceedings of the European Council were adopted to ensure its effective functioning in the new EU of **Twenty-Seven**. These effectively limit the duration of the meetings to two days, enhance the preparatory role of the **General Affairs and External Relations Council**, limit the size of each meeting and, as with formations of the Council of the European Union, strengthen the role of the presidency as chair.

Further change has also been introduced as a consequence of a declaration annexed to the **Treaty of Nice**. This stipulated that, as from 2002, one European Council meeting per presidency would be held in Brussels, and went on to declare that once the EU comprised 18 member states, all European Councils would be held in Brussels. In practice, formal meetings of the European Council have all been held in Brussels since the Italian presidency in the second half of 2003. The **Treaty establishing a Constitution for Europe** provided for the election by **qualified majority** of a **President of the European Council** to give greater coherence and direction to EU initiatives. This post was scheduled to last for a period of two-and-a-half years with the possibility of one further term. The same post and job description was written into the **Treaty of Lisbon**. Under this latest treaty, which came into force in December 2009, the European Council became a fully fledged EU institution in its own right. It did not gain any new powers, but became headed by the newly created **European Council President**, currently **Herman Van Rompuy**.

EUROPEAN COUNCIL PRESIDENT: see **President of the European Council**

The **EUROPEAN COURT OF HUMAN RIGHTS**, which is based in Strasbourg, operates under the aegis of the **Council of Europe**. It hears cases concerning individuals and practices in those states that are party to the **European Convention on Human Rights**. Cases may be brought by individuals or by the **European Commission of Human Rights**. All the member states of the European Union (EU) have ratified the Convention, and the EU has accepted the jurisdiction of this court in the sphere of **human rights**.

EUROPEAN COURT OF JUSTICE: See **Court of Justice**

EUROPEAN CURRENCY UNIT: See **Ecu**

The **EUROPEAN DEFENCE AGENCY** (EDA) was established in July 2004 to support member states' efforts to improve European defence capabilities in the field of crisis management and to sustain the **European security and defence policy**. Its key functions relate to defence capabilities development; armaments co-operation; the European defence technological and industrial base and defence equipment market; and research and technology.

The **EUROPEAN DEFENCE COMMUNITY** (EDC) was an initiative based on the 1950 Pleven Plan (named after a former French premier, René

Pleven). It was established by a treaty signed in Paris, in May 1952, by representatives of the **Six** states that had formed the **European Coal and Steel Community** (ECSC). Attempts to persuade other European countries, especially the United Kingdom, to join the venture failed. The origins of the EDC lay in the evaluation by the **USA**, as a result of the Korean War, of its global commitments, and in US demands for greater European support for the **North Atlantic Treaty Organization** (NATO), either by increased expenditure or through the rearmament of the Federal Republic of Germany (FRG—West Germany). However, no state was willing to consider increased expenditure, and none, apart from the FRG, really desired West German rearmament. The EDC was a device to permit rearmament without a separate and independent West German military contingent under national command. It also served a European purpose, being viewed as a further sectoral advance towards integration, with an institutional framework modelled upon that of the ECSC. Unlike the ECSC, however, it was not to be a partnership of equals: more restrictions would be placed upon the FRG.

The proposal provoked a great deal of opposition throughout the Six, but especially in France. No French government, fearing defeat, dared for some time to submit the treaty to a parliamentary vote. The French legislature finally defeated it on a technicality in August 1954, and the EDC project was abandoned. West German rearmament nevertheless took place on a national basis within NATO, supervised, at least implicitly, by the newly created but virtually non-existent **Western European Union** (WEU). At the same time, the collapse of the EDC was widely regarded as a major setback for European integration. (See also **European Political Community**.)

EUROPEAN DEMOCRATIC ALLIANCE: See **Group of the European Democratic Alliance**

The **EUROPEAN DEMOCRATS** (DE) sit with the Group of the European People's Party in the **European Parliament**. (See **Group of the European People's Party (Christian Democrats) and European Democrats**.)

EUROPEAN DEPOSITORY LIBRARIES: See **DEP**

The **EUROPEAN DEVELOPMENT FUND** (EDF) was established under the terms of the First **Yaoundé Convention** of 1963, and was retained in the subsequent **Lomé Convention** between the European Communities (EC) and the **African, Caribbean and Pacific** (ACP) **States**. It was set up to provide grants to the ACP States for development programmes, focusing after 1984 on rural and agricultural projects, and on broad integrated development programmes. As the member states were signatories of the 1963 Convention in their own right, and as they are eager to control spending in this area, the EDF is not included in the development section of the European Union **budget**, much to the dissatisfaction of many in the **European Parliament**. Under the **Cotonou Agreement**, the EDF was allocated €13,500m. for 2000–07. The 10th EDF, for 2008–13, was allocated €22,682m., of which €21,966m. was for the ACP countries. (See also **Development Aid**.)

EUROPEAN DOCUMENTATION CENTRES (EDCs) are information centres that contain European Union (EU) documentation. Their function is to stimulate the development of European studies in academic institutions and to provide an information service on the EU to the public. They are usually based in university libraries, and can also be found in non-EU countries. (See also **Europe Direct Information Network**.)

The **EUROPEAN ECONOMIC AND SOCIAL COMMITTEE** (EESC), which was also known by the alternative acronyms of ESC and ECOSOC, is not to be confused with the **United Nations** Economic and Social Council, which also uses the abbreviation ECOSOC. It was one of the main European Communities (EC) bodies set up by the **Treaty of Rome**. It was established as a non-political body that enables those active in economic and social fields to voice opinions on EC policy formulation. It has a purely advisory function, but the **European Commission** and the **Council of the European Union** are mandated to consult it on a wide range of issues before they can arrive at a **decision**. The **Single European Act** and the **Treaty on European Union** extended the areas on which it had to be consulted (to environmental and regional issues). In practice, both the Council and the Commission have consulted the EESC on a number of other non-mandatory topics, though they do not always heed its advice. The **Treaty of Amsterdam** also allows for the EESC to be consulted by the **European Parliament**. The **Treaty of Lisbon** reinforced the position of the EESC in the overall EU architecture as a bridge between civil society and the European Union (EU) institutions. It gave the EESC the right to be consulted by the Commission on a new range of policy areas, such as sport, research and energy. The treaty also strengthens the EESC's consultative role vis-á-vis the European Parliament. Staffan Nilsson was elected as President of the EESC for a 30-month term in 2010.

Its membership, which is drawn from national interest groups throughout the member states, increased from 222 to 317 with **enlargement** on 1 May 2004, and to 344 after the arrival of Bulgaria and Romania on 1 January 2007. The members are appointed for a four-year period, which is renewable. In the enlarged body, Germany, France, Italy and the United Kingdom each have 24 members; Spain and Poland 21 each; Romania has 15; Belgium, Bulgaria, the Czech Republic, Greece, Hungary, the Netherlands, Portugal, Austria and Sweden have 12 each; Denmark, Finland, Ireland, Lithuania and Slovakia 9 each; Estonia, Latvia and Slovenia 7 each, Cyprus and Luxembourg 6 each, and Malta 5. Each national delegation consists of three separate categories: workers, employers and a miscellany of other groups such as farmers, consumers and the self-employed. Members are nominated by national governments, normally after consultation with the major national interest groups, and appointed by the Council of the European Union. The Committee elects its own chairman for a period of two years, and it is conventional for the chairmanship to rotate between the three categories of membership. Participation in the EESC is a part-time commitment, and appointees are expected to be granted time off from their employment to attend meetings. Much of its work is done in specialized working groups, which correspond to the major policy concerns of the EU. The groups provide draft opinions for approval in a plenary session of the Committee. The EESC can be divided into six main areas of interest and activity. These relate to agriculture, rural development and the environment; **economic and monetary union** and economic and social cohesion; **employment**, social affairs and **citizenship**; external relations; the **single market**, production and consumption; and finally, transport, energy, infrastructure and the information society. The EESC has often been divided between left and right, between workers and employers, on many social and economic questions. How effective it has been in directly influencing proposed EU **legislation** is debatable. Its relevance has often been sidelined by both the Commission and the Council, as the former prefers to deal directly with sectoral organizations.

Critics would argue that the impact of the EESC has been rather limited. It can be seen as representing an attempt at fostering a type of corporatist interest intermediation that suited the 1950s environment. More than 50 years later its influence has waned to a large degree, as many of the groups it seeks to represent have established more direct means to influence policy formulation. Nevertheless, it still has an important role in the formal EU policymaking process. Both the Commission and the Council are obliged to consult the EESC in certain cases. Later treaties from the **Single European Act** onwards have extended the range of issues that must be referred to the Committee, in particular new policy areas such as regional and **environmental policy**. The EESC can also adopt its own opinions. On average the EESC delivers 170 advisory documents and opinions a year (of which about 15% are issued on its own initiative). All opinions are forwarded to the EU's main decision-making institutions and are published in the *Official Journal of the European Union*.

The **EUROPEAN ECONOMIC AREA** (EEA) is a trading area agreed upon in 1991 by the European Communities (EC) and members of the **European Free Trade Association** (EFTA). It was a consequence of fears by the EFTA countries that the development of the **internal market** might negatively affect their own economies. In 1989 they agreed upon a joint approach to the EC, using the phrase European Economic Space to describe the kind of structured partnership they wanted. Negotiations began in June 1990, and were completed by November 1991, largely upon EC terms, with an agreement on participation in the internal market. **Ratification** was delayed because of a query by the **Court of Justice** (ECJ) about the constitutional compatibility with the **founding treaties** of the proposed arbitration procedures. This led to the EFTA states having to create their own EFTA court and greater powers being placed in the hands of the ECJ. A referendum in **Switzerland** in 1992 rejected involvement in the EEA, and it came into existence without Swiss participation in January 1994. Although **Liechtenstein** had voted to join the EEA in a referendum held one week after the Swiss vote, the nature of its **customs union** with Switzerland made participation in the EEA problematic. When a number of necessary modifications had been made to the customs union, Liechtenstein voted again to join the EEA, in a second referendum held in April 1995. By this time, the EEA had lost three of its EFTA members, Austria, Finland and Sweden having joined the **European Union** (EU) on 1 January 1995. Indeed, from a positive perspective the EEA helped pave the way for their accession. However, the departure of these countries from EFTA turned the EEA into a rather more minor economic arrangement than the one originally envisaged. Despite expectations to the contrary, the EEA has survived and continues to expand its scope. It has therefore provided an adequate basis for relations between the EU and three of the most economically developed European non-EU states (**Iceland**, Liechtenstein and **Norway**). However, after the financial crisis of 2008–09 Iceland initiated the process of seeking EU membership.

EUROPEAN ECONOMIC COMMUNITY (EEC) was the official title of the organization established by the **Treaty of Rome** in 1958. The administrative network of the EEC was formally merged with that of the **European Coal and Steel Community** (ECSC) and the **European Atomic Energy Community** (EAEC or Euratom) in July 1967, after which the three bodies were collectively known as the European Communities or European Community (EC), although the abbreviation EEC remained in common usage, somewhat erroneously, to describe the Communities collectively. It also often carried a political connotation, being used by people who wished to emphasize that the EC should remain an economic organization without any implications of political union. The **Treaty on European Union** (TEU) confirmed that the EEC would in future be referred to as the European Community, and the founding Treaty of Rome was amended accordingly. The Treaty of Lisbon replaced the term European Community with the term **European Union**.

The **EUROPEAN ECONOMIC INTEREST GROUPING** (EEIG) is an arrangement established to enable European companies to collaborate more effectively on possible joint projects and enterprises. These EEIGs are not companies, but vehicles to allow individual companies to work together. They are legal entities in their own right and there are specific rules pertaining to their creation. The EEIG falls under the European Union's (EU) single market strategy and is designed to create more competitive consortia. One example of an EEIG is **Airbus**. Another is the creation of the Franco-German television channel *Arte*. An EEIG provides a legal structure for companies of different member states to link their activities while retaining economic and legal independence. By 2012 several thousand EEIGs had been established in a variety of areas. The Regie initiative promotes EEIGs.

EUROPEAN ECONOMIC SPACE: See **European Economic Area**

EUROPEAN EMPLOYMENT STRATEGY: Each year, the **European Council** agrees on a series of guidelines setting out common priorities and individual objectives for member states' **employment** policies. The overall aims include creating jobs, improving job quality, making it easier for people to balance the demands of work and personal life, promoting active ageing and ensuring that race, gender or disabilities do not limit opportunities for employment in the formal economy.

Each EU government produces its own annual action plan describing how it is putting the guidelines into practice. Progress is measured against some 100 indicators, ranging from basic economic figures (e.g. gross domestic product—GDP—growth and unemployment levels) to the availability of career breaks and childcare.

EUROPEAN ENERGY CHARTER is the name of a document inspired by the European Communities (EC) and signed at The Hague in December 1991 by 38 countries. Its purpose was to make European energy supplies more secure by linking the natural resources of Eastern Europe with the West through a grid of supply lines. In return, Eastern Europe would receive investment from Western countries, and the EC proposed to extend the **Organization for the Promotion of Energy Technology** (OPET) scheme for the international transfer of energy-efficient and environmentally friendly technologies to Eastern Europe and the **Commonwealth of Independent States** (CIS). A further objective was to strengthen the Eastern democracies by easing their balance of payments problems, and to offer the Russian Federation an alternative to membership of the petroleum producers' **cartel**, the Organization of Petroleum Exporting Countries (OPEC). The wider aim of the Charter was the creation of a legally binding document, the Energy Charter Treaty. This Treaty aimed to enhance East-West industrial co-operation through a number of legal guarantees concerning investments, transit and trade. In December 1994 all signatories of the 1991 agreement, with the exception of Canada and the **USA**, signed the Energy Charter Treaty and the Energy Charter Protocol. There are 52 signatories (51 states plus the European Union) throughout Europe, including Russia, while 24 other countries (including the USA, Canada and **Japan**) and 10 international organizations are observers.

The **EUROPEAN ENVIRONMENT AGENCY** (EEA) was established in May 1990 by the European Communities (EC) to collect and disseminate detailed information on environmental questions and problems, including air quality, water quality, state of the soil, land use, waste management, noise emissions and coastal erosion. Membership of this body is open also to non-European Union (EU) states. Its inauguration was blocked by France because of its dispute with the EC over the future permanent location of the **European Parliament** and controversy over the siting of other European agencies. In November 1993, however, it was agreed that the EEA would be located in Copenhagen. The agency was the first EU body to have members from the 13 **candidate** states. After EU **enlargements** in May 2004 and January 2007, membership totalled 32 countries, comprising the EU of **Twenty-Seven** plus **Iceland, Liechtenstein, Norway, Switzerland** and **Turkey**.

The **EUROPEAN EXTERNAL ACTION SERVICE** (EEAS) was established following the entry into force of the **Treaty of Lisbon**. The EEAS can be viewed as an embryonic European Union (EU) Ministry of Foreign Affairs, which seeks to work in close co-operation with the diplomatic services of the EU member states. It assists the **High Representative of the Union for the Common Foreign and Security Policy**, Baroness **Catherine Ashton**, and is staffed by a mix of officials from the **European Commission**, the **Council Secretariat** and seconded diplomats from the member states.

The **EUROPEAN FEDERALIST MOVEMENT** has been the main proponent of the federalist ideal for Europe since the 1950s. **Altiero Spinelli**, who largely inspired it, led the movement until 1962. It had little impact upon European developments, although, thanks to Spinelli, some of its ideas can be found in the **draft Treaty establishing the European Union**.

The **EUROPEAN FIGHTER AIRCRAFT PROGRAMME** was the first major joint European armaments project, although it was not a European Union project. It consisted of an agreement in 1985 by the arms procurement directors of Germany, Italy, Spain and the United Kingdom to work collectively towards the development of a replacement for aircraft that would be obsolete by the mid-1990s. The first aircraft were scheduled to be in service by 1997, but rising costs, technical problems, and the lower priority given to defence after the ending of the **Cold War** created doubts about the programme's viability and necessity. After 1992 the programme was scaled down in size and renamed the Eurofighter—Typhoon 2000 project. The first orders were placed in 1998. The project has proved very successful for the European aerospace industry and is, to date, Europe's largest military collaborative programme. The Eurofighter Typhoon is regarded by many as one of the world's most advanced fighter aircrafts. Over 550 aircraft have been built and sold (to Austria, Germany, Italy, Saudi Arabia, Spain and the United Kingdom).

The **EUROPEAN FILM DISTRIBUTION OFFICE** (EFDO) was established under the MEDIA programme (see **media policy**) to sponsor and help to market European-produced films. The Office is based in Lisbon.

The **EUROPEAN FINANCIAL STABILISATION MECHANISM** (EFSM) is an emergency funding mechanism that allows the **European Commission** to raise funds from financial markets to assist, via loan or credit guarantee, any European Union (EU) member state experiencing or approaching serious financial difficulties. In raising funds, the European Commission uses the EU budget as collateral. The value of the EFSM is €60,000m.

The **EUROPEAN FINANCIAL STABILITY FACILITY** (EFSF) provides emergency financial assistance to member states of the eurozone encountering financial difficulties. Agreed by eurozone member states in May 2010, it issued loans worth €3,600m. to Ireland in February 2011 and €3,700m. to Portugal in June 2011. EFSF loans were originally supported by eurozone member states (€440,000m.), the **European Financial Stabilisation Mechanism** (€60,000m.) and the **International Monetary Fund** (€250,000m.). It is planned that the EFSF, which is a temporary facility, will be replaced by a permanent **European Stability Mechanism** in 2013. In the interim, as the eurozone crisis worsened, the scope of the EFSF's activities was widened and in October 2011 its participants' guarantee commitments were increased from €440,000m. to €780,000m. The Chief Executive Officer of the EFSF is Klaus Regling, who took office on 1 July 2010.

The **EUROPEAN FISHERIES FUND** (EFF) replaced the **Financial Instrument for Fisheries Guidance** (FIFG) on 1 January 2007. The new scheme runs for the duration of the current financial perspective to 2013 and has a budget of some €4,300m. The fund has many echoes of its predecessor. Full details of the fund are laid down in Commission Regulation (EC) No. 498/2007. The EFF targets five priority areas: the adaptation of the European Union (EU) fishing fleet; aquaculture, inland fishing, and processing and marketing of the products of fishing and aquaculture; measures of collective benefit; sustainable development of fisheries areas; and technical assistance to facilitate the delivery of aid. Basically, the fund seeks to secure a sustainable fishing and aquaculture industry. The fund has been designed to assist the industry as it adapts its fleet to make it more competitive, and also to encourage measures to protect and enhance the environment. As before, the fund seeks also to help the fisheries communities most affected by the changes by assisting them to diversify where possible. The fund exists to facilitate and support the major objectives of the **common fisheries policy** (CFP). This includes in particular the sustainable exploitation of fisheries resources and achieving a stable balance between these resources and the capacity of the EU fishing fleet, as well as strengthening the competitiveness and viability of operators in the sector and fostering the sustainable development of fisheries areas.

The new fund is intended to be easier to manage and has been designed to integrate fisheries policy more closely with other policies in the fields of the environment and employment. Much is the same as in the old FIFG but there are a number of new and innovative measures to take account of the changing needs of the sector. The most striking examples are the measures to encourage selective fishing methods and the emphasis on the sustainable development of fisheries areas. **Implementation** of the fund has been considerably simplified. Whereas FIFG support for fisheries was divided among different programmes in a member state, there is now a single EFF programme for each member state. This should enable member states to concentrate support, maximize the efficiency of measures and establish a national strategic plan for the entire fisheries sector. The EFF is to be replaced by a European Maritime and Fisheries Fund from January 2014.

A **EUROPEAN FLAG** was adopted by the European Communities (EC) in 1986. Its design is a crown of 12 five-pointed stars set against an azure background. It is the same flag as that used by the **Council of Europe** since 1955; hence it was merely coincidental that the number of stars on the flag corresponded to the membership of the EC from 1986 to 1994. The stars were placed in a circle to represent the union of the European states. The flag is flown over the European Union (EU) headquarters in **Brussels**, and is otherwise used at national and international meetings and ceremonies where the EU is represented.

The **EUROPEAN FOOD SAFETY AGENCY** (EFSA) was established in Parma, Italy, in 2002 following various food safety scares in the 1990s, notably BSE (see **Bovine Spongiform Encephalopathy**). Its purpose is to provide independent scientific advice on all matters linked to food and feed safety, including animal health and welfare, and plant protection. It also provides scientific advice on nutrition in relation to EU **legislation**. EFSA's budget for 2010 was €73m. (See also **Foodstuffs**.)

EUROPEAN FOUNDATION FOR THE IMPROVEMENT OF LIVING AND WORKING CONDITIONS (EUROFOUND) is the name of a **European Commission** agency established in 1975 and now based in Dublin. It holds a broad mandate to provide information, advice and expertise—on the living and working environment of employees, industrial relations and managing change in Europe—for principal actors in the field of European

Union (EU) social policy. Four themes were identified in Eurofound's work programme for 2009–12. These centred on: globalization; demographic change; technological change; and climate change. Given the worsening economic situation following the onset of the global recession in 2008, Eurofound is particularly keen to place emphasis on measures to help create jobs and boost competitiveness, initiatives to help the young, and moves to reduce poverty and social exclusion. Eurofound appreciates that public sector reform will be a major issue to be dealt with over the next decade. The Foundation is staffed by representatives of the Commission, the member states and employers' and employees' organizations.

The **EUROPEAN FREE ALLIANCE** (EFA/ALE) forms part of the **Group of the Greens/European Free Alliance** in the **European Parliament**. It is made up of representatives of 'stateless nations'.

The **EUROPEAN FREE TRADE ASSOCIATION** (EFTA) was established by the **Stockholm Convention** of 4 January 1960. It consisted of seven states—Austria, Denmark, **Norway**, Portugal, Sweden, **Switzerland** and the United Kingdom—which were unwilling or, for various reasons, unable to accept the supranational and **common market** principles of the **Treaty of Rome** and the **European Economic Community** (EEC). EFTA's objectives were limited to securing a gradual elimination of **tariffs** on trade in most industrial goods between its members. It did not have an agricultural policy or any kind of **common external tariff** (CET), and its institutional structure was to be limited to a Council of Ministers which would meet only two or three times a year, although a council of heads of national delegations was to meet every two weeks. It brought together a very disparate group of countries which seemed to be agreed on only two things. Firstly, they agreed on a rejection of the sequence of events postulated by the Treaty of Rome, apart from the establishment of a free trade area. Secondly, they believed that some form of unity would place them in an advantageous position vis-à-vis the EEC compared with the position they would be in if each country separately attempted to negotiate some accommodation with it.

Within its limited terms of reference, EFTA worked quite well, establishing its free trade area fairly quickly. After the late 1960s, it collaborated quite closely with the European Communities (EC). When Denmark and the United Kingdom joined the EC in 1973, they left EFTA. The remaining EFTA states, which now also included **Iceland** and **Liechtenstein**, with Finland as an associate, negotiated a series of **free trade agreements** with the EC, which came into force in 1973. With some variations from country to country, these agreements provided for the gradual introduction of free trade in industrial goods (but not in agriculture). The relationship was the province of a joint EC–EFTA executive committee meeting twice yearly. While the EFTA states avoided the obligations of full EC membership, the disadvantage was that they were not party to EC **decisions**, many of which had an important effect upon their own economies. The arrangement, however, worked quite well, and by the 1980s EFTA had moved very close to the EC in its economic practices.

In the late 1980s, the EFTA states felt obliged to review their situation in the light of the **Single European Act** and the EC decision to establish an **internal market**. In 1989 the creation of a broad European Economic Space was proposed, which, after protracted negotiations, came into being, albeit without Switzerland's participation, as the **European Economic Area** (EEA) in 1994. However, the EFTA states began to conclude that even EEA membership would leave them at a disadvantage and thus Austria, Finland, Norway and Sweden all applied for membership of the EC. In January 1995 Austria, Sweden and Finland joined the European Union (EU), Norway having withdrawn its application following a referendum result that rejected EU membership. EFTA was left as a rump (comprising Iceland, Liechtenstein, Norway and Switzerland), the viability of which was in considerable doubt. The Association has nevertheless survived. Iceland's possible future membership of the EU would weaken EFTA further.

The **EUROPEAN FUSION DEVELOPMENT AGREEMENT** (EFDA) was created in 1999 and took over the operations of the **Joint European Torus**, one of the world's largest fusion experiments, in 2000. The Agreement has long aimed to promote collaboration in the field of nuclear fusion research by member states of the European Union (EU), **Switzerland** and certain **candidate countries** of **Central and Eastern Europe** (the Czech Republic, Hungary and Romania). The former two countries joined the EU in May 2004, and Romania in January 2007. Given that fusion energy is both a long term and highly costly undertaking, research collaboration is essential and the EU has been pursuing a strongly co-ordinated strategy in this area since 1958 (under **EURATOM**). EFDA also manages the **ITER** nuclear research project. Two support units are based in Garching, Germany, and Culham, United Kingdom; these units integrate research carried out in various centres into the European Fusion Programme. In 2008 a revised EFDA came into force and had two main objectives: to prepare for the operation and exploitation of ITER and to broaden further the knowledge base for overall fusion development, especially in relation to the proposed DEMO (the first electricity-producing experimental fusion power plant, which was planned to be built upon the expected success of the ITER experimental nuclear fusion reactor).

The **EUROPEAN GROUP ON ETHICS IN SCIENCE AND NEW TECHNOLOGIES** (EGE) was established in 1998 to advise the **European Commission** on ethical aspects of science and technology. An independent and multidisciplinary group, the EGE has provided opinions on a range of issues, including: human embryo research, doping in sport, human stem cell research, clinical research in developing countries and genetic testing in the workplace.

EUROPEAN INFORMATION SYSTEM: See **Schengen Information System**

The **EUROPEAN INVENTORY OF EXISTING CHEMICAL SUBSTANCES** (EINECS) is a programme set up by the **European Commission** in 1986 as a response to widespread alarm about the hazards to both individuals and the environment of many chemical products. The inventory, which forms part of the **Environmental Chemicals Data Information Network**, is intended to record all commercially available chemical products. The Commission uses it to evaluate and control their application, and in the formulation of **consumer policy**, **environmental policy** and **health and safety** policy.

The **EUROPEAN INVESTMENT BANK** (EIB) was set up by the **Treaty of Rome** as a separate and autonomous institution within the European Communities. Based in Luxembourg, the EIB was designed to be a bank for the financing of capital investment that would benefit the process of European Union (EU) integration. In sum, the EIB finances viable capital projects and borrows on the world's financial markets to finance its projects. The EIB has evolved since 1958 in both importance and stature and today is the world's largest bank of its kind, with subscribed capital of €232,000m. in 2012. The member states are the basic members of the Bank, collectively subscribing to its capital. The EIB has a number of regional offices throughout Europe, as well as in other parts of the world (including Egypt, Morocco, South Africa, Turkey and Tunisia).

The ultimate decision-making body of the EIB is the Board of Governors, normally consisting of the finance ministers of the member states. The Board of Governors normally meets only once a year. Supervision of the daily operations of the Bank is performed by a part-time Board of Directors, composed of nominees from the member states and from the **European Commission**. The management of operations is the responsibility of a Management Committee composed of the Bank's President and eight Vice-Presidents, nominated by the Board of Directors and appointed by the Board of Governors for renewable six-year terms. Werner Hoyer was appointed as the seventh President of the EIB on 1 January 2012.

In addition to its subscription capital, the EIB raises funds on the international capital markets, where it enjoys the highest possible credit rating. Its bonds are regularly rated 'AAA' by the leading rating agencies. As it works on a non-profit basis the EIB can pass on to projects the excellent conditions obtained as an AAA borrower. The EIB has three general aims: to assist less developed regions, to help to modernize the economy of the EU, and to support projects that are of interest to more than one member state. It provides fixed-rate loans, usually for periods of between five and 12 years (but up to 20 years for infrastructural projects), and occasionally also guarantees loans and credit.

National governments, regional authorities and companies may all apply for EIB loans or guarantees. The EIB never provides all the funding for a project. It considers only large-scale projects, and normally advances up to 50% of the projected costs. The balance has to be met by loans from other sources, the applicant's own resources or state assistance. Some 5% of EIB activity is devoted to external aid programmes, mainly benefiting the **African, Caribbean and Pacific** (ACP) **States** under the terms of the **Lomé Convention**. Under the terms of Lomé's successor, the **Cotonou Agreement**, €3,900m. was channelled to projects in ACP States between 2002 and 2006. The Bank publishes an annual report of its operations, with details of the projects it has funded. With a level of lending approaching that of the International Bank for Reconstruction and Development (IBRD—World Bank), it arguably constitutes the most successful of the funds available from the EU. After 1994 it administered a **European Investment Fund** (EIF) which was intended to promote economic growth and reduce unemployment through the provision of financial aid for major infrastructural projects, and for capital investments by smaller companies.

The responsibilities of the EIB were extended in June 1998 to include the Amsterdam Special Action programme, which allows the EIB to lend money for health and education projects and to provide risk capital for small and medium-sized companies, particularly in new high-technology areas. In recent years the EIB has tended to move its focus from long-term infrastructure projects towards supporting initiatives that increase employment and facilitate research and development across the EU. In 2008–09 the EIB increased its lending activities in the light of the financial crisis. Particular emphasis in recent years has been placed on supporting **small and medium-sized enterprises** (SMEs), environmental sustainability, the development of **Trans-European Networks** (TENs) and **cohesion** and convergence. In 2011 the EIB approved some €61,000m. in loans, mainly to the EU and the **European Free Trade Association** (EFTA). Its lending mandates are based on EU external co-operation arrangements and can be classified under the headings of Pre-accession States; European Neighbourhood States, Development (ACPs and South Africa) and Economic Co-operation (Asia and Latin America).

EUROPEAN INVESTMENT FUND (EIF) is the name of a body proposed by the **European Council** in 1992, as part of a collection of measures designed to combat the economic depression prevalent in the early 1990s, with the objective of providing additional aid for transnational infrastructural projects. The Fund was established in 1994 by the **European Investment Bank** (EIB), the European Communities (represented by the **European Commission**) and a group of 76 banks and financial institutions from throughout the European Union (EU). Its main task was to provide financial institutions with infrastructure and **small and medium-sized enterprise** (SME) guarantees. The EIB subscribed 40% of the EIF's **ecu** 2,000m. capital. The Fund assists SMEs and provides guarantees for the long-term financing of European infrastructure projects, in particular **Trans-European Networks** (TENs). The EIF became operational in 1995 and commenced its involvement in venture capital in 1997, as part of the **European Commission**'s 'Growth and Employment' initiative. In June 2000 the EIF's statutes were restructured and its shareholding structure was modified (with the EIB becoming the majority shareholder) so as to endorse the role of the EIF as the exclusive vehicle for venture capital of the EIB. The EIF is active in the member states of the EU as well as in countries that have applied to become members and in those where the accession process is under way. The EIF is also active in the four **EFTA** states.

The **EUROPEAN JUDICIAL NETWORK IN CIVIL AND COMMERCIAL MATTERS** was established in 2001 as part of the European Union's activities in the area of **justice and home affairs** following the **Tampere summit** of the **European Council**. The network consists of representatives of the member states' judicial and administrative authorities and meets several times each year to exchange information and experience and promote co-operation in the areas of civil and commercial law.

The **EUROPEAN JUDICIAL NETWORK IN CRIMINAL MATTERS** (EJN) was established in 1998 and plays a major role in the European Union's efforts to promote **police and judicial co-operation in criminal matters**. It brings together experts from the member states dealing with criminal matters and has a Secretariat in The Hague linked to that of **Eurojust**.

The **EUROPEAN MARITIME SAFETY AGENCY** (EMSA) was created in 2002 to promote an improved maritime safety system within the European Union. The Agency moved to Lisbon, from **Brussels**, in 2006. Its main goals are to reduce the risk of maritime accidents, marine pollution from ships and the loss of human lives at sea.

The **EUROPEAN MEDICINES AGENCY** (EMA) was established as a decentralized agency of the European Communities by the **Council of the European Union**. Located in London, the United Kingdom, it began operations in early 1995 as the European Agency for the Evaluation of Medicinal Products (it was renamed as above in 2004). It is responsible for the licensing of all human and veterinary medicinal products in the European Union (EU), and for monitoring their efficacy. Once a **pharmaceuticals** company has obtained a licence, it may sell its products anywhere in the EU, in an arrangement that has brought to an end member states' former protective practices in the interests of their own companies. However, national regulatory bodies continue to operate and provide an alternative means for approving new drugs in the EU.

EUROPEAN MONETARY AGREEMENT: See **European Payments Union**

The **EUROPEAN MONETARY CO-OPERATION FUND** (EMCF) was established in 1973. By the end of that decade it was the only survivor of plans made in the early 1970s for **economic and monetary union** (EMU). In 1979 it was incorporated into the **European Monetary System** (EMS), where it was the reserve fund that supported the European Currency Unit (**ecu**). Member states participating in the basket of currencies that determined the value of the ecu were required to deposit 20% of both their gold and dollar reserves with the Fund. The EMCF was used to regulate the interventions made on the exchange markets by the central banks of the member states to support the **exchange-rate mechanism** of the EMS, and it kept account of short-term borrowings used to support currencies. Its most important credit facility was its Very Short-Term Financing Facility (VSTF), which permitted borrowing by the central banks, with the proviso that credit must be settled within 45 days. It was superseded by the **European Monetary Institute** in January 1994, at the beginning of stage two of EMU.

The **EUROPEAN MONETARY INSTITUTE** (EMI) was established under the **Treaty on European Union** (TEU) and superseded the **European Monetary Co-operation Fund**. Its operations began with the commencement of stage two of **economic and monetary union** (EMU) and were completed shortly before stage three was launched on 1 January 1999. The EMI's role was to facilitate closer co-operation between the central banks of the member states, co-ordinate monetary policies, monitor the **European Monetary System** and eventually advise the **European Council** as to whether the conditions for stage three of EMU had been met. Located in Frankfurt am Main, Germany, it was the forerunner of the **European Central Bank** (ECB), which effectively replaced it in 1998.

The **EUROPEAN MONETARY SYSTEM** (EMS) constituted the second attempt by the European Communities (EC) to secure some form of monetary co-operation after the failure of the plans of 1970 for **economic and monetary union** (EMU). The EMS, established in 1979, was a more limited and practical attempt to secure, in the first instance, a zone of monetary stability in Western Europe. The core of the EMS was the **exchange-rate mechanism** (ERM), which linked the currencies of the participating member states and limited the amount by which each currency was permitted to fluctuate against its counterparts. If a currency went beyond these limits, the central banks, with the help of the **European Monetary Co-operation Fund**, intervened in the exchange markets, selling or buying as the case might be, to maintain the currency within the agreed limits. A central rate was calculated for each currency on the basis of the central rate of the European Currency Unit (**ecu**), a notional EC currency that existed alongside the national currencies. Special arrangements existed to provide help for countries that experienced short-term difficulties. Where a currency persistently had difficulty in staying within its agreed limits, the EMS made provision for its realignment.

The EMS had some considerable success in the 1980s. It was widely credited with contributing to the decline in inflation levels and to the increasing economic **convergence** of the member states. While the EMS was not a replacement for EMU, as it was unable to impose economic policy restraints upon the states, by the late 1980s it was widely felt that conditions were more appropriate for the EC to move on to full EMU. One weakness was that not all the member states were members of the ERM. The plans for EMU contained in the **Treaty on European Union** (TEU) were disrupted during the currency crises of 1992–93, with the United Kingdom and Italy leaving the ERM, which itself greatly extended the permissible limits of currency fluctuation. While these events may have delayed the EMU programme, they did not seriously affect the existence of the EMS, which remained essentially an instrument of co-operation in monetary policy until the formal establishment of EMU.

EUROPEAN MONITORING CENTRE FOR DRUGS AND DRUG ADDICTION (EMCDDA) is the name of an agency that resulted from the growing recognition by European leaders of the dangers of drugs and drug addiction. The **Treaty on European Union** provided the first references in the European Union treaty base to drugs. The EMCDDA was established in 1994 and subsequently secured greater European co-operation in this area under **CELAD**. The Centre itself opened in September 1995 and is located in Lisbon, Portugal.

The **EUROPEAN MONITORING CENTRE ON RACISM AND XENOPHOBIA** (EUMC) was established by the European Union (EU) in 1997 to study and review the extent and development of racism, xenophobia and anti-Semitism in Europe, and to report its findings to the EU. EUMC works with the **Council of Europe**, the **United Nations** and other international organizations. It established a European Racism and Xenophobia Information Network (RAXEN), which collects statistics on racist incidents and passes them to EUMC. EUMC then uses the materials gathered to construct a European database for conducting research and disseminating information on racism and how to combat it. EUMC has set up a series of 'Round Table' discussions on racism and has launched some of its own research initiatives.

EUROPEAN MOVEMENT is the name of an influential pressure group working for integration in the late 1940s and early 1950s. It was founded at the **Congress of Europe** of 1948. It was the Movement that drew up the first draft of what was to become the **Council of Europe**. While its influence faded after the early 1950s, it remained active in supporting schemes for further political integration. With a membership that covers most European countries, it has come to act more as an umbrella organization, disseminating information to all groups, associations and institutions with an interest in European affairs, and liaising between them.

EUROPEAN NATO refers superficially to all members of the **North Atlantic Treaty Organization** (NATO) except the **USA** and Canada. It more precisely refers to the original European NATO membership of 1949, including France, despite the latter's partial membership of NATO, and with the addition of Germany. It is a descriptive expression rather than a specific subgroup within NATO, and has often been used in the context of the need to strengthen the European pillar of NATO.

The **EUROPEAN NEIGHBOURHOOD POLICY** (ENP) is the European Union's (EU) initiative to place relations with neighbouring regions (i.e. Eastern Europe, the Middle East and the Southern Mediterranean, but not **South-Eastern Europe** or **Russia**), on a new footing following **enlargement** in 2004 and 2007. It aims to 'reduce poverty and create an area of shared prosperity and values based on deeper economic integration, intensified political and cultural relations, enhanced cross-border co-operation and shared responsibility for conflict prevention between the EU and its neighbours ... [and to] anchor the EU's offer of concrete benefits and preferential relations within a differentiated framework which responds to progress made by the partner countries in political and economic reform'. To this end, ENP Action Plans have been drawn up. These contain an agenda of political and economic reforms with short- and medium-term priorities. Plans have so far been agreed with Armenia, Azerbaijan, Egypt, Georgia, Israel, Jordan, Lebanon, **Moldova**, **Morocco**, the Palestinian Authority, Tunisia and **Ukraine**. The ENP is designed to cover increased trade relations, involvement in the EU's **internal market**, and co-operation on justice and home affairs, energy, transport, information society, environment and research and innovation, and social policy. 'Enhanced Agreements' are also envisaged and will involve more political dialogue, a free trade area and strengthened co-operation in these areas. Negotiations on a first Enhanced Agreement were opened with Ukraine in March 2007. Negotiations with Moldova, initially expected to commence in late 2008, were delayed until 2009. Financial assistance worth almost €11,200m. has been allocated through a European Neighbourhood and Partnership Instrument (ENPI) for the period 2007–13. EU membership, however, is not envisaged as part of either the

Action Plans or the ENP more generally. This is despite the membership aspirations of some ENP participants, notably Ukraine and Moldova.

The ENP has been heavily criticised by the EU's neighbours and others for lacking 'added value' compared with their existing relations and for being an essentially EU-imposed policy. Recognition of such criticisms has come in the efforts of the **European Commission** to enhance the EU's offer. In 2006 it published a set of proposals entitled *Strengthening the European Neighbourhood Policy*. A year later it was reporting progress in developing the ENP, noting financial allocations under a Governance Facility, the establishment of a Neighbourhood Investment Facility worth €700m. in 2007–13, the launching of a regional dimension for the eastern neighbours through a new EU *Black Sea Synergy* initiative, and the opening up of EU programmes and agencies to ENP partners. That said, it added that 'a great deal remains to be done'. However, the emphasis was placed as much if not more on the ENP partner countries where, the Commission observed, 'the need for political, social and economic reform is huge'. For observers of the ENP this was a familiar message. Successive country and progress reports have pointed out the shortcomings, in the EU's eyes, in the ENP partner countries and have been quite prescriptive about what should be done. The EU appears nevertheless to be responding to some of the criticisms. Efforts are being made to ensure greater differentiation between partners by allowing those more advanced in terms of political and economic reform and capacity to benefit from closer, upgraded relations, possibly through 'tailor-made' **deep and comprehensive free trade area**s, improved mobility arrangements, enhanced political dialogue and greater participation in EU programmes. The EU also envisages playing a greater role in conflict resolution.

For some member states, the EU has to offer more. In 2008 Sweden and Portugal proposed an **Eastern partnership** for the eastern European states which included an offer of 'more profound integration'. This followed proposals for a **Union for the Mediterranean** from the French President, **Nicolas Sarkozy**. The Eastern partnership was eventually launched in May 2009. In 2010–11 the Commission undertook a routine review of the functioning of the ENP. This coincided with the so-called 'Arab Spring' (revolutionary demonstrations and protests throughout several Middle Eastern and North African countries) in 2011, and the final report proposed a 'new response to a changing neighbourhood', comprising, *inter alia*, greater support for political reforms, enhanced EU involvement in solving protracted crises, increased support for economic and social development, visa facilitation measures, strengthened trade ties and more effective regional partnerships within the ENP. The Commission also proposed increasing financial assistance by €1,200m. during 2011–13 and recommended adapting funding to individual countries' needs. At the same time it advocated greater use of conditionality. Co-operation, improved market access and financial assistance would only be provided if political and economic reform programmes were implemented.

EUROPEAN ORGANIZATION FOR NUCLEAR RESEARCH: See CERN

EUROPEAN ORGANIZATION FOR THE EXPLOITATION OF METEOROLOGICAL SATELLITES: See **EUMETSAT**

The **EUROPEAN PARLIAMENT** (EP) originated in the Strasbourg-based advisory Assembly of the **European Coal and Steel Community** (ECSC). With the establishment of the **European Economic Community** (EEC) and the **European Atomic Energy Community** (EAEC or Euratom) in 1958, one Parliamentary Assembly was created to serve all three Communities, with a membership of 142. The composition of the EP has changed repeatedly to reflect the waves of **enlargement**. Membership, for example, had increased to 626 by January 1995, to 732 by June 2004 and after January 2007 increased further to 785 (to incorporate the accession of Bulgaria and Romania and serve a European Union—EU—population of some 492m.). The number of seats was altered again for the June 2009 EP elections, when candidates from across the 27 member states contested 736 places. With the entry into force of the **Treaty of Lisbon**, the number was temporarily increased to 754 for the period to 2014. The Treaty of Lisbon provides for 751 MEPs thereafter.

Members were initially appointed by the **national parliaments** from among their own members, although the **Treaty of Rome** had called for the introduction of **direct elections**. The first direct elections to the EP took place in 1979. The powers of the Parliament were defined as the supervision of both the **European Commission** and the Council of Ministers (see **Council of the European Union**), and participation in the legislative and **budget** processes. Essentially, however, it was allotted a secondary position in the institutional framework, being more of an advisory and consultative body than a genuine decision-making body. Unlike national parliaments, the EP does not have the right to raise taxes, does not bring forward legislation, and does not provide the government of the EU, although it has become an extremely important aspect of the entire EU system of governance.

From the outset, the Assembly (as it was then called), which was firmly in favour of rapid moves towards political union, was dissatisfied with its second-ary role, campaigning constantly for greater influence and authority. In 1962 it took the symbolic step of calling itself the European Parliament: although this was accepted by the European Commission (but not by the Council of Ministers), the EP was given a legal basis only in the **Single European Act** (SEA) of 1987. The EP also asserted a right to meet whenever it wished, circumventing the Treaty of Rome's provisions for an annual session by simply dividing the latter into several segments of time, spanning the whole calendar year. Some slight increases in powers were granted by the 1970 **Treaty of Luxembourg**, with a further modest rise in budgetary influence in 1975, when the EP was given the right to reject the budget in its entirety with effect from

1977. The SEA, the **Treaty on European Union** (TEU), the **Treaty of Amsterdam** and the **Treaty of Nice** extended the EP's competences further by introducing the **co-operation procedure** and **assent procedure** under the SEA and introducing the **co-decision procedure** under the TEU (extending the latter under both the Amsterdam and Nice Treaties). Even so, the EP remains the weakest of the EC central institutions.

The EP is not yet a true legitimating body for the EU. Although it has to approve **Accession Treaties** and **association agreements**, it plays no active role in their negotiations, and has only a minor role in any constitutional revision of the EU treaties. However, the EP is the single major EU institution that has been gradually gaining power in terms of its involvement with EU decision-making (e.g. through co-decision) with every successive treaty change.

The EP's representative character has also been criticized. Since 1979 the EP has been elected at five-yearly intervals. In 2009 the seventh parliament was elected. There is no standard electoral system across all the member states, though all states now use some form of proportional representation. The EP elections are generally deemed in the British context to represent second-order elections (with a reduced turn-out and on a par with local and regional elections). The electorates tend to use the elections to express a verdict on their national governments and domestic problems: there has never been a true European election fought on exactly the same day by a series of European political parties running on a common manifesto. Furthermore, electorates tend to have only a vague perception of the EP, often seeing it as secondary to their own national legislatures. The fact that EP plenary sessions have often been attended by less than one-half of its members has not helped its cause, though this is now changing.

The TEU strengthened the EP's right of scrutiny and supervision. The EP was given a formal right to establish committees of inquiry, to appoint an **Ombudsman** from among its members to investigate complaints of maladministration in EC institutions, and to be consulted on the nomination of a new President of the European Commission and to ratify the choice of President and members of the Commission. Furthermore, in accordance with the Treaty of Amsterdam, the EP must formally approve the appointment of the President of the Commission. These powers are in addition to its right to put both oral and written questions to the Commission, a right it has taken seriously. Members of the Commission and its bureaucracy also attend meetings of the various EP committees. The EP has the right to submit questions to the Council of the European Union, which responds through ministers of the member state currently holding the Council presidency, who attend EP plenary sessions to deliver the Council's replies. Since 1981 the head of government currently occupying the presidency of the **Council of the European Union** attends the EP after each European Council **summit meeting** to report on its proceedings. The EP's most severe power—to censure and thus collectively dismiss the Commission—requires a two-thirds' majority of the votes cast, which must also be a majority of the total EP membership; there is no power to dismiss an individual Commissioner. A censure motion was initiated in January 1999, following allegations of financial and other irregularities against the European Commission, and although a compromise deal ensured that the motion was defeated, the concessions won by the EP during that dispute were felt to represent an important shift in the balance of power from Commission to Parliament.

The role of the EP was further enhanced by the TEU's introduction of a co-decision procedure which builds upon the co-operation procedure introduced by the SEA. While these decision-making procedures make the legislative process highly complex, they broadly follow five phases. The Commission first presents a proposal to both the Council of the European Union and the EP. The EP is entitled to give an opinion that must be considered by the Council. A suitably revised version approved by **qualified majority voting** is returned to the EP and, if the EP rejects the common position proposed by the Council, the issue is referred to a **Conciliation Committee** which may result in approval, rejection or further amendment. Amendments can lead to a repetition of the evaluation process by the Council and EP. The new procedure gives the EP a decision-making role and a potential power of veto. The procedure applies only to those **Articles** of the treaty that specifically refer to its use. The co-operation procedure introduced by the SEA applies to other policy areas, mostly in the area of **economic and monetary union**: under the co-operation procedure, where the Council rejects an EP opinion, it must give a reasoned common position that will become law unless the EP proposes amendments. The Council can override such amendments only by a unanimous vote.

The Treaty of Amsterdam simplified the decision-making process, while extending the EP's powers. Co-decision between the Council and the EP was extended into a wider range of policy areas, and the EP may be consulted in decisions taken by unanimity in Council. International agreements, treaty decisions and the accession of new member states all require the consent of the EP. The Treaty also calls for the EP to establish a formal code of conduct by which to regulate its members. On **ratification**, the Treaty of Nice was to introduce a new distribution of seats in the EP. With the exception of Germany and Luxembourg, the arrangements envisaged a reduction in the number of seats allocated to the **fifteen** member states at that time. This was deemed necessary for an enlarged EU with up to 27 members.

The most recent elections to the EP took place in June 2009 and heralded electoral success for the forces of the centre-right. These elections may have been the largest in the EU's history and the best example of transnational democracy in action, but the turn-out was disappointing. Only just over 43% of the total eligible electorate in the EU turned out to cast their vote—the lowest ever turn-out in EP elections. This was the sixth time in succession that the turn-out had fallen since the first EP elections in 1979. (The comparative turn-out figure for 2004 was 45%.) Within the overall decline in turn-out, there were wide discrepancies at the national level. Luxembourg topped the poll turn-out chart with 90.8%, almost equalled by Belgium, with 90.4%.

There were good showings in Malta (78.8%) and Italy (65.0%). Denmark and Ireland had turn-outs of 59.5% and 58.6%, respectively. More ominously for pro-integrationists, the turn-out in France fell again, to 40.6% (2004: 42.8%), while turn-out in Germany stayed fairly stable at just over 43%. The rate of participation by the electorate was generally very low in the newest EU member states. For example, it was 21.0% in Lithuania (down from 48.4% in 2004), 27.7% in Romania, 28.3% (2004: 28.4%) in Slovenia and 28.2% (2004: 28.3%) in the Czech Republic. A slight improvement in turn-out figures was recorded in Poland, with 24.5% (2004: 20.9%), while in Estonia turn-out rose to 43.9%, from just 26.8% in 2004. There was a modest upturn in Slovakia but, none the less, fewer than one in five of the electorate turned out to vote (2009: 19.6%; 2004: 17.0%). Turn-out in the United Kingdom declined from 38.5% in 2004 to 34.7%. (The lowest level for the United Kingdom was 24% in 1999.) It is widely believed that an expenses scandal concerning members of parliament had a negative impact on the United Kingdom's main political parties and improved the prospects and fortunes of the more minor parties. That said, the Conservative Party topped the British poll and captured nearly 29% of the vote. It was followed by the Eurosceptic **United Kingdom Independence Party** (UKIP), which picked up 13 British seats and secured over 17% of the vote. The Labour Party was beaten into third place. One of the most striking results of the British elections in 2009 was the election for the very first time of two members from the far-right **British National Party**. Indeed, there was electoral support in the 2009 elections for a number of far-right parties right across the EU.

Most of the newly elected **Members of the European Parliament** (MEPs) have opted to belong to one of the **party groups** within the EP. The remainder are unattached to any group. Labour's MEPs, for example, sit with the Progressive Alliance of Socialists and Democrats in Europe (formerly the **Party of European Socialists**—PSE), and the Liberal Democrats sit with the **Alliance of Liberals and Democrats for Europe** (ALDE). Conservative MEPs sit with the newly created **European Conservatives and Reformists Group**. The UKIP MEPs belonged to the short-lived **Identity, Tradition and Sovereignty Group**, which was established following the accession of Bulgaria (18 MEPs) and Romania (35 MEPs) on 1 January 2007. As of July 2009, the UKIP members sit in the newly formed **Europe of Freedom and Democracy Group** (EFD). Specific rules and statutes specify the exact conditions that are required for the creation of new party groups.

The EP has substantial budgetary powers, where it again shares authority with the Council of the European Union. It must approve the budget: if it fails to do so, EU **expenditure** is frozen at the previous year's level, with only one-12th of the budgetary expenditure approved for the previous year being available each month until the issue is resolved. The EP's freedom of action is substantially greater on **non-compulsory expenditure**. However, while it can block a budget, it cannot substitute one of its own.

The EP was to be provided with further powers under the proposed **Treaty establishing a Constitution for Europe**. Essentially, this would have extended the use of co-decision and, significantly, given the EP greater say over both the final settlement of the **budget** and the **common agricultural policy**. These changes, along with others contained in the abandoned Treaty establishing a Constitution for Europe, were built into the **Treaty of Lisbon**. This latest treaty, which came into force in December 2009, enhances the EP's powers in relation to the budget by removing the distinction between compulsory and non-compulsory expenditure.

The EP normally meets for one week each month (except in August), with further meetings in March and October when agricultural prices and the budget are considered. Most of its work is done in its 20 specialized committees, which correspond to different policy areas and European Commission agencies. Committee memberships are determined by the **party groups** in proportion to the number of seats they occupy in the EP. MEPs sit not by nationality, but in transnational party groups, which have official recognition and receive administrative expenses. MEPs who choose not to belong to a party group are each entitled to serve on one committee. Each committee appoints a *rapporteur*, who draws up the programme for discussion and prepares drafts for resolution by the committee, which are then presented to the full EP. The MEPs elect a president who serves for a two-and-a-half year term. The EP President for 2012–14 is **Martin Schulz**.

In all its functions the effectiveness of the EP is diminished by two structural conditions. The first is the fact that it conducts its business in 23 officially recognized **languages**, with all the costs and consequences of translating its oral and written business. The second condition is that its operations are dispersed across three member states. Plenary sessions continue to be held mainly in Strasbourg. Most committees meet in **Brussels** in order to be close to the executive centre of the EU; after 1994 some plenary sessions were also held there. By contrast, much of the supporting secretariat is located in Luxembourg, and must move to Brussels or Strasbourg, along with the necessary documentation and paraphernalia, for EP sessions. France and Luxembourg have resisted the EP's efforts to relocate all its operations to Brussels, and in 1992 and 1997 it was confirmed that the present, unsatisfactory arrangements would remain until the member states could unanimously agree upon a change.

EUROPEAN PARTNERSHIPS were launched in 2003 and first adopted in 2004 by the European Union (EU) for the countries of the **Western Balkans**. They are similar to **accession partnerships** in that they identify short- and medium-term priorities that the countries need to address in order to integrate with the EU. It is envisaged that the successful fulfilment of the priorities will equip the countries with the institutional and legislative framework and administrative capacity required for a functioning democracy and market economy. It should also assist their progress towards EU membership.

A **EUROPEAN PASSPORT** was first proposed in 1974. In 1981 the member states agreed upon the size and layout of a common format burgundy-coloured passport that would be marked 'European Community'. It was due to be introduced in January 1985. While only three member states met the deadline, all began to comply over the next few years. European passports were marked 'European Union' from 1995.

EUROPEAN PASSPORT: See **Community Patent Convention**

The **EUROPEAN PAYMENTS UNION** (EPU) was established in 1950 under the auspices of the **Organisation for European Economic Co-operation** (OEEC). It was intended to tackle the problem of reciprocal credits and facilitate multilateral trade once the **Marshall Plan** had come to an end. The EPU proved to be highly successful, and in 1959 was replaced by a broader European Monetary Agreement, which fulfilled the same purpose. It contributed to the ability of the **Six** to co-operate economically in the 1950s, and it was used by the **European Economic Community** (EEC) during the latter's first year of operation.

EUROPEAN PEOPLE'S PARTY AND EUROPEAN DEMOCRATS: See **Group of the European People's Party (Christian Democrats) and European Democrats**

EUROPEAN POLICE OFFICE: See **Europol**

EUROPEAN POLITICAL COMMUNITY was the name of a concept that arose out of the attempts to establish the **European Defence Community** (EDC) in the early 1950s; it was based on the view that a common defence structure ideally required a correspondingly unified foreign policy. It involved only the **Six** countries that had established the **European Coal and Steel Community** (ECSC) and had committed themselves to the EDC. The unratified EDC treaty required its proposed Common Assembly to study ways of establishing federal institutions. The ECSC Assembly was transformed into an ad hoc EDC Assembly to consider a more wide-ranging political co-operation than could be provided by the ECSC and EDC. The Assembly began its work in September 1952 and reported six months later in favour of a European Political Community that would go beyond **sectoral integration** and form the basis of a comprehensive political federation to which the ECSC and EDC would be subordinated. A draft treaty, with a proposed institutional structure based upon the ECSC model, was drawn up in March 1953. However, the EDC treaty had still not been ratified by any state when the Political Community treaty was published. Despite the significant implications of the proposed European Political Community, it was the subject of very little debate; its fate was totally dependent upon the EDC. The important arguments of the time concerned the EDC treaty, the **ratification** or rejection of which would determine the fate of the European Political Community. The refusal of France to ratify the EDC treaty in August 1954 effectively meant the abandonment of the draft Political Community treaty.

EUROPEAN POLITICAL CO-OPERATION (EPC), also known by the acronym POCO, was more of a concept than a structure. It was a term used to describe co-operation in foreign policy and foreign affairs by the member states of the European Communities (EC). Its origins lay in the **Davignon Report** of 1970, and its objectives were to ensure a better mutual understanding of international problems and issues among the member states through a regular process of consultation and exchange of information, to work towards a **harmonization** of views and a co-ordination of foreign policy positions, and, where appropriate, to attempt to establish a common EC position. The first ministerial meeting under EPC took place in 1970 and the first joint statement, on the **Middle East**, was issued in May 1971.

EPC was not based on the **founding treaties**, and its development occurred outside the institutional framework of the EC. It developed as an essentially intergovernmental operation involving close and continuing liaison between the national foreign ministries, with an ongoing consultation process involving ambassadors from the EC states to foreign countries and the **United Nations** (UN), and the issuing of common instructions by the foreign ministries to their diplomatic representatives abroad. Three major types of initiative emerged from EPC. The first was the practice for the EC, wherever possible, to have a single representation and single position in international meetings: the EC position was normally presented by the country occupying the presidency of the Council of Ministers (see **Council of the European Union**). In particular, great efforts were made to ensure that the member states agreed upon a common position on issues in the UN General Assembly. The second element of EPC involved the adoption of common policy statements and initiatives by the **European Council**, occasionally leading to action towards developing a common policy position. Finally, the most specific outcome of EPC was agreement to impose common economic **sanctions** on named countries.

The **Single European Act** regularized the position of EPC within the EC framework, committing the member states to 'endeavour jointly to formulate and implement a European foreign policy'. It also provided EPC with a small secretariat in **Brussels**, and made it responsible for the political and economic aspects of a security policy. Despite its intergovernmental character and the non-binding nature of its agreements, EPC proved to be a successful operation, although one that was far from constituting a European foreign policy. It was the changing nature of world politics after 1989, as much as the desire for further integration, which led the EC to reconsider EPC. With the **Treaty on**

European Union (TEU), EPC was replaced by the **common foreign and security policy** (CFSP).

The **EUROPEAN PRIVATE EQUITY AND VENTURE CAPITAL ASSOCIATION** (EVCA) was formed in 1983 and is intended to promote the discussion and study of the management and investment of venture capital. Supported by the **European Commission**, EVCA has as its broader aim to develop a European capital market. It has been particularly concerned with the development of small and medium-sized companies. Projects developed under EVCA have received a maximum of 30% funding from the European Union (EU), and are required, ideally, to complement other EC policies and programmes. (See also **European Business and Innovation Centre Network**.)

EUROPEAN PROGRAMME FOR HIGH TECHNOLOGY RESEARCH AND DEVELOPMENT: See **EUREKA**

A **EUROPEAN PUBLIC PROSECUTOR'S OFFICE** was envisaged in the **Treaty establishing a Constitution for Europe** and is provided for in under Article 86 in the **Treaty of Lisbon**. Provided the member states unanimously agree on its establishment, the office will be responsible for 'investigating, prosecuting and bringing to judgment ... the perpetrators of, and accomplices in, offences against the Union's financial interests'. Its powers can be extended, by unanimity, to include 'serious crime having a cross-border dimension'. The European Public Prosecutor's Office is expected to work closely with Europol, and may eventually move towards tackling cross-border crime.

The **EUROPEAN RAPID REACTION FORCE** (ERRF) was formed in 1999–2003 to support the European Union's (EU) efforts to move beyond a **common foreign and security policy** and establish a **European security and defence policy**. Technically, the ERRF is not a standing force. Instead, it is based on commitments from the member states to ensure that the EU has at its disposal an ERRF of 60,000 troops that can be mobilized at 60 days' notice (the Helsinki Headline Goal). Currently, there is a resource of 100,000 persons and approximately 400 combat aircraft and 100 vessels on which the EU can draw. The ERRF has been deployed to date in **the former Yugoslav republic of Macedonia** (Operation Concordia) and the Democratic Republic of Congo (Operation Artemis). Subsequent to the development of the ERRF, the concept of **battlegroups** was adopted and developed.

EUROPEAN RECOVERY PROGRAMME: See **Marshall Plan**

The **EUROPEAN REGIONAL DEVELOPMENT FUND** (ERDF) is one of the four **structural funds**. It was established in 1975 and is the central element of efforts by the European Union (EU) to develop an effective **regional policy**. It is run by a Regional Fund Committee, structured along the lines of the **Management Committees** of the **common agricultural policy** (CAP), and a Regional Policy Committee consisting of two representatives from each member state and the **European Commission**, with a chairperson elected from among the government representatives, and with a secretariat provided by the Commission.

The bulk of ERDF **expenditure** is devoted to specific projects for regional infrastructural developments proposed by the member states, including grants to enterprises as well as for public works. While only national governments may bid for support from the Fund, these projects often originate from regional and local authorities, other public bodies, or private companies. Financial assistance from the ERDF is mainly focused on: supporting **small and medium-sized enterprises** (SMEs); promoting productive investment; and improving infrastructure and further local development. One of its prime aims is to create **employment** by fostering competitive and sustainable development.

The ERDF is also used to support EU programmes proposed by the Commission as being of particular importance, often to two or more regions, and it may also be used to support national programmes deemed to possess a value for the EU as a whole. Each member state must submit a list of the programmes and projects for which it is seeking support. National programmes and some major individual projects are evaluated by the Regional Policy Committee. Decisions on smaller projects may be taken by the Regional Fund Committee. To be considered by the ERDF, national programmes must receive Commission endorsement. They must be located in those regions that the member state has designated as being eligible for support under its own regional aid schemes; they must be consistent with EU objectives; and they must appear to be economically worthwhile. The ERDF operates under the principle of **additionality**, providing a maximum of 50% of the costs, with the member state having to fund the remainder.

Originally, ERDF resources did not go exclusively to the poorest regions of the European Communities (EC). Each member state was allocated a percentage quota of the Fund, against which it could bid for support. This provided aid for the weakest regions in each country, no matter how healthy they might be in the context of the EC as a whole. The quota system was a constant source of contention among the member states. A limited non-quota element (totalling only 5%), to be utilized by the European Commission for its own programmes, was added in 1979, and in 1985 quotas were abandoned in favour of a percentile range of the ERDF budget being allocated to each member state; the range indicates the maximum and minimum levels of support a state can receive, provided that an appropriate number of eligible programmes submitted receive endorsement.

In 1987 the Commission introduced a five-year budgetary package to cover all EC expenditure. As part of this the Commission proposed the reform of, and increased resources for, the structural funds in the period from 1988 to 1992. This so-called proposal, which became known as **Delors I**, was supported at a special **European Council** summit in **Brussels** in 1988. The issue had proved to be problematic, as the British Prime Minister, **Margaret Thatcher**, had strong reservations over aspects of regional funding and preferred to let market liberalization erode regional disparities within member states. However, the German Chancellor, **Helmut Kohl**, sympathized with the four poorest EC states (Ireland, Greece, Portugal and Spain) and wished to compensate them financially. Under the agreement reached, EC structural spending rose from 15% to 31% of total spending. **Jacques Delors**, then President of the Commission, described the European Council's decision as a 'second Marshall Plan'. The 1988 reform radically revised structural policy by introducing a number of new principles, Additionality, Partnership, Programming and Concentration, and identified five priority objective areas (development of lagging regions under objective 1; conversion of regions facing industrial decline under objective 2; combating long-term unemployment under objective 3; combating youth unemployment under objective 4; and development of rural areas under objective 5).

In 1992 the Commission proposed an ambitious new five-year budgetary package (**Delors II**) to the European Council. At the Edinburgh summit in December the European Council agreed to double EC assistance to the least prosperous regions. The decision again reflected pressure from the four poorest states and the willingness of Germany (albeit now more reluctant post unification in 1990) largely to finance it. When Austria, Finland and Sweden joined the EU in 1995 a new objective was created to help low population density regions (objective 6). By 1999 **structural and cohesion funds** made up more than one-third of the EU **budget**. Spending had risen from **ecu** 18,000m. in 1992 to ecu 31,000m. by 1999.

The multi-annual programme for 2000–06 was determined at the European Council summit in Berlin in March 1999. This followed the Commission's action plan, **Agenda 2000**, which aimed to provide the EU with a new financial framework in preparation for **enlargement**. Under this framework, the funds available for spending on structural assistance were to decrease. Spending on such assistance was still to account for about one-third of the EU's total budget for this period, some €195,000m. (at 1999 prices). In 2003 spending on the EU's structural operations (including the **Cohesion Fund**) accounted for 34.3% of the EU budget (€33,164m.). Financial assistance was concentrated, moreover, on the most needy areas and to this end the number of objective areas was reduced from seven to three and redefined. The bulk of the funds available was designated for the new objective 1 areas (i.e. towards the development and structural adjustment of the least-developed regions), the poorest EU areas, which consisted mainly of eastern regions of Germany, and Greece, Italy, Spain and Portugal. In 2003, for example, €21,577m. was directed to these areas. In contrast, €3,652m. was spent on objective 2 regions (to support the economic and social conversion of areas facing structural difficulties) and €3,719m. on the new objective 3 areas (supporting the adaptation and modernization of policies and systems of education, training and employment).

Negotiations for the new multi-annual programme (2007–13) commenced in early 2004 and agreement was reached at the end of 2005. The total amount of money allocated to the structural and cohesion funds for this period is (at 2007 prices) €347,410m. The ERDF constitutes the largest part of the EU's structural and cohesion funds (at €201,000m.). The operations and aims of the structural and cohesion policy for the current financing period have been altered. Instead of the objective 1, 2 and 3 areas, the new policy focuses its attention on three themes. These are **convergence**, regional **competitiveness** and **employment**, and territorial co-operation. The vast majority of the monies available are focused on the first aim of convergence. Some €283,000m. is directed here and is met by the ERDF, the **ESF** and the **Cohesion Fund**. In the United Kingdom, the North-East region is to receive some £255m. from the ERDF in the period up to 2013.

EUROPEAN RESEARCH CO-ORDINATION AGENCY: See **EUREKA**

EUROPEAN RIGHT (DR) was the name of one of the cross-national **party groups** in the **European Parliament** (EP) until 1994. It was formed after the 1984 **direct elections** by extreme right-wing and neo-Fascist groups. Because of the political attitudes of its members, the DR was the most isolated group in the EP, with no other group willing to be associated with it: indeed, in 1984 other party groups strove to avoid having to be seated beside it. Its share of the vote dwindled over the last decade or so to such an extent that it was represented neither in the 1999–2004 parliament nor in the sixth one (2004–09). However, the prospects for the **far right** in the EP changed after the 2009 elections, when a number of far-right individuals were returned as **Members of the European Parliament** (MEPs). These included, for example, members of the **British National Party** and the Dutch Freedom Party, and it was generally expected that these and their like-minded peers from across the EU would combine to form a new group. This occurred with the creation of a new Alliance of European National Movements, which included members from the French Front National and the Hungarian Jobbik party. Although this alliance cannot be recognized as a political group within the EP, as it does not meet the necessary numbers (25) and has insufficient transnational membership (members must come from at least seven EU member states), it may still be entitled to some funding as a pan-European bloc. This new alliance rejects all attempts to create a European superstate, calls for strong pro-family policies and seeks to fight against the destructive effects of globalization.

The **EUROPEAN ROUND TABLE OF INDUSTRIALISTS** (ERT) is an influential **Brussels**-based organization that seeks to promote the interests of business in the strategic thinking of the European Union (EU) and in particular the **European Commission**. It was established in 1983 and comprises about 50 chief executives of the largest firms across the EU. These include representatives, for example, from the United Kingdom (AstraZeneca, British American Tobacco and BT), from Germany (Siemens, Volkswagen and Bayer), from France (Suez, Renault and Total) and from Italy (Pirelli and Fiat). ERT members strongly endorse the benefits of European economic integration and the role of business within it. Notably, they believe that a dynamic, wealth-producing industrial sector benefits society as a whole. Membership is personal and not corporate, but it is by invitation only. The ERT is funded by multi-national firms and maintains some 10 personnel in Brussels. In terms of sectoral areas, the ERT has taken a particular interest in information technology and lifelong learning skills. It was highly influential in the development of plans to complete the **internal market** and to promote **Trans-European Networks**. (See also **interest groups**.) The ERT strongly encourages the promotion of the **Lisbon agenda**, but also recognizes that European industry cannot flourish unless it is competitive with other businesses around the world. The prevailing economic and social policy framework is, the ERT argues, crucially important and must be flexible enough to adapt to changes in global conditions. ERT constantly demands policies that provide flexibility and enable European companies to build and improve their competitive strengths. The current Chairman of ERT is Leif Johansson (of the Swedish telecommunications company Ericsson), who was appointed in 2009.

EUROPEAN SCHOOLS have been established by the **European Commission** in several countries. They are intended primarily for the children of European Union (EU) employees, in particular those working in a member state other than their own. Subject to the availability of space, they are open to other pupils. The schools (of which there were 15 in 2012) try to provide a European education by offering an international syllabus in which tuition is given in several EU **languages**. The syllabus leads to the European Baccalaureate, a recognized system of academic attainment that allows for entry to universities. The headteachers are appointed by an intergovernmental committee on which the Commission is also represented. Each national government appoints a proportion of the other teaching staff.

EUROPEAN SECURITY AND DEFENCE IDENTITY (ESDI) is often used to describe the goal of increased co-operation within the **North Atlantic Treaty Organization** (NATO) between its European members, particularly after 1994. Such co-operation was designed to complement the development of the **common foreign and security policy** of the European Union. More recently, efforts to develop a **European security and defence policy** have promoted the ESDI.

The **EUROPEAN SECURITY AND DEFENCE POLICY** (ESDP): See **Common Security and Defence Policy** (CSDP)

A **EUROPEAN SECURITY STRATEGY** entitled 'A Secure Europe in a Better World' and devised by the European Union (EU)'s **High Representative for the Common Foreign and Security Policy, Javier Solana**, was adopted by the **European Council** in December 2003. The strategy is to guide the **common foreign and security policy** and the **European security and defence policy**. It consists of three main objectives: addressing threats posed by terrorism, nuclear proliferation and regional conflicts; building security in the EU's neighbourhood; and establishing an international order based on effective multilateralism. It commits the EU to greater activity in realizing these objectives, an enhancement of capabilities, greater coherence, and increased co-operation with other parties (e.g. the **USA** and **Russia**). A first five-year report adopted in December 2008 sought to reinforce the strategy. It noted in particular the increased complexity of the security challenges facing the EU and called on the EU to be more effective in addressing them.

EUROPEAN SOCIAL CHARTER: See **Charter of Fundamental Social Rights of Workers**

The **EUROPEAN SOCIAL FUND** (ESF) was established as required by the **Treaty of Rome** in order for the European Communities (EC) to develop 'employment opportunities for workers', to raise their standard of living, and to make 'the employment of workers easier', especially by 'increasing their geographical and occupational mobility within the Community'. From its inception in 1960, therefore, the ESF has been concerned with the specific field of **employment** and training rather than with broad issues of general social welfare. During the 1960s the Fund's operations were limited, being confined mainly to the retraining of workers made redundant by structural economic change. With the dramatic increase in unemployment after 1973, the role of the Fund was redefined and enhanced in terms of retraining, redeployment and the provision of vocational training for young people. Persisting high levels of unemployment, and budgetary restrictions, obliged the ESF to narrow its priorities, and it refocused its activities on retraining and the development of employment skills among young people, with particular attention paid to the long-term unemployed and women. In 1988 it was agreed that 75% of ESF resources would be spent on projects for people under 25 years of age. These funds included substantial amounts spent on the (now-defunct) Programme for the Vocational Training of Young People and their Preparation for Adult and

Working Life (PETRA) and EUROFORM initiatives. In addition, the ESF was obliged to focus more intensively on the most economically disadvantaged regions of the EC.

In 1999 a new **regulation** was adopted by the **Council of the European Union** and the **European Parliament**, laying down general provisions on, and the three new objectives for, the **structural funds**. On the social front, the regulation provides for action in five general areas. These include: the development of active labour market policies to combat unemployment; the promotion of **equal opportunities** for all in terms of access to the market and particularly for those at risk from social exclusion; the promotion of vocational training; the promotion of a skilled, well-trained and flexible workforce; and specific measures to improve access to the labour market, especially for women. These objectives are in line with the EU strategy and guidelines on employment.

ESF resources are available for both large- and small-scale projects proposed or accepted by a member state. It operates under the principle of **additionality**, normally providing only 50% of the projected costs of a scheme, the balance having to be met by the member state. In poor regions that have been given absolute priority status, the ESF contribution is permitted to rise to 75%. A small proportion (some 5%) of ESF expenditure is reserved for other more general purposes or special operations defined by the **European Commission**, which typically involve contributions from several EU sources combined into an integrated programme. The ESF is managed by a Social Fund Committee, and consumes some 8%–10% of the EU **budget**. The European Social Fund spent €60,000m. between 2000 and 2006. Special attention was paid to funding for areas of the EU with particularly high levels of unemployment or low average incomes. Around €3,000m. was reserved during this period for the **EQUAL** programme. The ESF remains focused on promoting employment, combating discrimination and supporting social inclusion. Funds are directed towards initiatives that develop human resources, secure better integration in the workplace and ensure equality between the sexes. The ESF has also been seeking to ensure that Europe's companies are better equipped to meet the new global challenges. For the period 2007–13 some €75,000m. was directed to the ESF. The Commission is placing an emphasis on increasing the adaptability of workers, enterprises and entrepreneurs. Lifelong learning, for example, is deemed to be an integral aspect of this drive. The ESF is considered a core element of the **Europe 2020** strategy.

The **EUROPEAN SPACE AGENCY** (ESA) was established in 1975. It represents a consortium of countries that produce the **Ariane** rocket used to send commercial satellites into space. Its origins lie with the inadequacies of the first collaborative European organization for space research, the **European Space Research Organization** (ESRO), and its re-evaluation by a European Space Conference. Negotiations between 1971 and 1973 produced an agreement to establish ESA as a replacement for ESRO. ESA's 19 member states are

Austria, Belgium, the Czech Republic, Denmark, Finland, France, Germany, Greece, Ireland, Italy, Luxembourg, the Netherlands, **Norway**, Portugal, Romania, Spain, Sweden, **Switzerland** and the United Kingdom. Canada is an associated member and participates in certain ESA projects. ESA is an independent European agency that employs more than 2,000 people and has its headquarters in Paris as well as a number of other centres such as ESTEC. ESTEC, the European Space Research and Technology Centre, is the design hub for most ESA spacecraft and technology development, and is situated in Noordwijk, the Netherlands. ESA is governed by a Council, which comprises members from each of the ESA member states. ESA does not form part of the European Union (EU). There are, however, close ties between the two bodies and they are linked by a common aim: to strengthen Europe and benefit its citizens.

ESA is funded by its member countries, and its objective is 'to provide and to promote, for exclusively peaceful purposes, co-operation among European states in space research and technology and their space applications, with a view to their being used for scientific purposes and for operational space applications'. ESA has been active in satellite development, and in 1984 adopted the long-term 'Horizon 2000' programme to work towards manned European space flight. The 'Horizon 2000 Plus' extension programme, covering the years 2005–16, was initiated in 1994 for the inclusion of projects using new technologies and for participation in future international space activities. A further programme, 'Cosmic Vision 2015–25, was announced in 2005. ESA's budget for 2012 amounted to €4,020m. (See also **EUMETSAT**.)

ESA's ties with the EU have developed considerably in recent years because of the increasing role of space in strengthening Europe's political and economic role. The necessity of ensuring Europe's guaranteed access to space is becoming ever more apparent as satellites are used to improve communications and navigation, monitor the environment, strengthen technology and increase scientific knowledge. To this end ESA has also set up a liaison office in Brussels to facilitate relations between the two organizations. Recent joint initiatives include Galileo, a European global navigation satellite system, and the Global Monitoring for Environment and Security suite of services, known as GMES. A forthcoming initiative concerns satellite-based measures to overcome the digital divide within Europe.

In January 2003 the then European Research Commissioner, Philippe Busquin, introduced a **Green Paper** on European Space Policy, prepared in co-operation with ESA. The Green Paper examined Europe's strengths and weaknesses in the space sector and sought to launch a debate on Europe's space policy and to increase awareness of the strategic importance of space and space policy for Europe and its citizens. In November 2003 the ESA Council adopted the Framework Agreement, previously endorsed by the EU Council of Ministers in October. Its origins date from an ESA Ministerial Council meeting in November 2001 that gave clear directions on the Agency's evolution and policy, and called for a Framework Agreement to formalize co-operation between ESA and the EU.

This Agreement marks a milestone in ESA/EU relations. It recognizes that both parties have specific complementary strengths, and commits them to working together. The Agreement has two main aims: firstly, the establishment of a common basis and appropriate practical arrangements for efficient and mutually beneficial co-operation between ESA and the EU; and secondly, the progressive development of a European space policy to link the demand for services and applications in support of EU policies with the supply, through ESA, of the space systems and infrastructure needed to meet that demand.

As a result the EU adopted this action plan for implementing an enlarged European space policy in November 2003. Drafted by the EU and ESA, the **White Paper** includes proposals for joint ESA–EU space activities and takes the Framework Agreement as its basis for implementation.

The **EUROPEAN SPACE RESEARCH ORGANIZATION** (ESRO) was a multi-purpose organization established in 1961 with the participation of several European countries. It was intended both to carry out scientific research and to design and develop European satellites built on a collaborative basis by its members. During its existence, it was beset with disputes between scientists, and arguments over both projects and costs between the participating countries. It became the core of the **European Space Agency** established in 1975.

The **EUROPEAN STABILITY MECHANISM** (ESM) will, when imple-mented, be a permanent crisis mechanism designed to safeguard the financial stability of the euro area. It is based on the **European Financial Stability Facility** (EFSF), which it will replace once the **Treaty establishing the European Stability Mechanism** enters into force. At August 2012 14 of the 17 members of the euro area had ratified the Treaty. Of the three remaining members, Italy and Germany must ratify the Treaty in order for the ESM to be established. The ESM is expected to have authorized capital of €700,000m.

EUROPEAN STANDARDS COMMITTEE: See **CEN**

The **EUROPEAN STRATEGIC PROGRAMME FOR RESEARCH AND DEVELOPMENT IN INFORMATION TECHNOLOGY** (Esprit) was a European Communities (EC) initiative established in 1984. In order to foster and increase co-operation by the member states in science and technology **research and technological development**, the EC sponsored a pilot scheme involving 38 separate contracts that entailed co-operation between companies from at least two member states. On the basis of this experience, Esprit was launched as a five-year programme to develop EC resources in information technology to full-systems capability based on semiconductor technology. A series of projects were conducted under the auspices of Esprit in a number of technology areas. The overall programme was defined by a specially commissioned Task Force for Information Technology and Telecommunications, which in 1987 was fully absorbed within the **European Commission**. EC funding, which extended to a maximum level of only 50% of the projected research and development costs, was available only for applications that included companies, universities or research institutes from at least two member states. The programme was deemed to be a success in terms of the number of projects funded, the number of participants involved and the practical applications resulting from them, and it was agreed in 1994 to extend Esprit for a further five-year term. The extension was given funds triple those available for the first programme, and the new schedule called for a concentration of effort in applied technologies, information technology processing systems and microelectronics. As part of a new framework programme in 1998, Esprit was subsumed into the **Information Society Technologies** (IST) programme.

EUROPEAN SYSTEM FOR THE INTERNATIONAL CLEARING OF VACANCIES AND APPLICATIONS FOR EMPLOYMENT: See EURES

The **EUROPEAN SYSTEM OF CENTRAL BANKS** (ESCB) came into existence in 1998 once the date for the third and final stage of **economic and monetary union** (EMU) had been set. It coexists with the **European Central Bank** (ECB), having the responsibility of maintaining price stability, defining and implementing a common monetary policy, and supervising the foreign reserves and foreign exchange operations of the member states. It consists of the national central banks of the 27 European Union member states, along with the ECB, although those member states not participating in EMU are unable to take part in **decision-making** in this area.

The **EUROPEAN SYSTEM OF INTEGRATED ECONOMIC ACCOUNTS** (ESA) was established to assist in the development of a European information system in connection with the **internal market**. This was to be compatible with the System of National Accounts (SNA), which was to be used to monitor the development of **economic and monetary union** (EMU).

EUROPEAN TELECOMMUNICATIONS SATELLITE ORGANIZATION: See EUTELSAT

The **EUROPEAN TRADE UNION CONFEDERATION** (ETUC) was created in 1973 and gave itself the task of promoting and defending the interests of working people throughout the European Union (EU). The ETUC has become the major overarching organization for member states' national trade unions, and for union federations outside the EU. In 2012 ETUC comprised 85 national trade union confederations from 36 countries in Europe, and 10 federations representing European industry, resulting in a total membership of some 60m. people. Other trade union structures such as Eurocadres (the Council of European Professional and Managerial Staff) and EFREP/FERPA (European Federation of Retired and Elderly Persons) operate under the auspices of the ETUC. In addition, ETUC co-ordinates the activities of the 44 Inter-regional Trade Union Councils (ITUCs), which organize trade union co-operation at cross-border level. Based in **Brussels**, the ETUC is represented on several EU committees and organizations, and is generally recognized as a body with a legitimate interest in EU affairs. ETUC is recognized by the EU, by the **Council of Europe** and by the **European Free Trade Association** as the only representative cross-sectoral trade union organization at European level.

ETUC exists to represent workers in Europe. It strives to promote the 'European Social Model', which ETUC believes should embody a society combining sustainable economic growth with ever-improving living and working standards, full employment, social protection, equal opportunities and social inclusion. ETUC campaigns constantly for the EU to have a strong social dimension. It has developed close relations with the **European Parliament**, has membership of a number of advisory bodies, consults other social partners and takes part in discussions on the **Lisbon agenda**. ETUC has been particularly active in supporting EU initiatives on **workers' rights**, notably the **Charter of Fundamental Social Rights of Workers**, but less active in seeking to promote industrial development. Under the **Treaty on European Union** (TEU, as amended by the **Treaty of Amsterdam**) ETUC is recognized as one of the three 'social partners', alongside industry associations such as BUSINESS EUROPE (formerly the **Union of Industrial and Employers' Confederations of Europe**, or UNICE), with which the **European Commission** negotiates draft social and economic legislation. In 2004 ETUC was particularly vocal on a number of issues. For example, it strongly condemned calls for a longer working week, urged the Dutch presidency of the **Council of the EU** to push for a greater social agenda and supported the **Treaty establishing a Constitution for Europe** as a starting point for progress towards greater social values in the EU. ETUC has played a key role in helping to formulate principal parts of EC/EU legislation, for example the European Works Councils Directive of 1994 and the Information and Consultation Directive of 2002. More recently it has also been active in organizing a number of high-profile demonstrations or Action Days to coincide with **summit meetings** or to protest about the impact of policies that threaten to undermine the 'European Social Model'.

The **EUROPEAN TRAINING FOUNDATION** (ETF) was established by the Council of Ministers (see **Council of the European Union**) in 1990. In

November 1993 it was agreed that the Foundation was to be located in Turin, Italy. The ETF is open also to states outside the European Union (EU). Its aims are to develop vocational training and retraining, and to channel aid to training projects, particularly those concerning Eastern Europe, and especially the **candidate countries**. It has also been made responsible for co-ordinating EU higher education programmes in the **Phare** states of **Central and Eastern Europe**. (See also **European Centre for the Development of Vocational Training**; **TEMPUS**.)

EUROPEAN TREATIES is a term used to refer to the combination of **founding treaties** (see **Treaty of Paris**; **Treaty of Rome**), **accession treaties** and amending treaties (e.g. the **Single European Act**, **Treaty on European Union**, **Treaty of Amsterdam** and **Treaty of Nice**), which make up the treaty base of the European Union (EU). The latest addition is the **Treaty of Lisbon**, which entered into force on 1 December 2009 and which also renamed the **Treaty establishing the European Community**—one of the Treaties of Rome—as the **Treaty on the Functioning of the European Union**.

EUROPEAN UNION (EU) is the name of the body established in 1993 by the **Treaty on European Union** (TEU), although its exact status was not fully and clearly defined by the treaty. It had a notional structure consisting of three **pillars**. At the centre was pillar I, which comprised the European Communities (EC). This was complemented by two pillars of intergovernmental co-operation: **common foreign and security policy** (pillar II) and **justice and home affairs** (pillar III). This pillar structure enhanced the powers of the **European Council**, whose role encompassed all the components of the EU. The supranational institutions, meanwhile, concerned themselves mainly with matters covered by pillar I. Hence, the **European Commission** had only a limited role in pillars II and III. The same was also true of the **Court of Justice** and the **European Parliament**. While the EU is a political entity that seeks to improve and deepen the relationships between the member states, and claims to have its own **citizenship**, it nevertheless accepts the principle of **subsidiarity** and recognizes national identity. In addition, it is not described by the TEU as a fixed structure, but as a 'new stage in the process of creating an ever closer union'. Further timetables and targets were therefore established, most of which were reviewed by an **intergovernmental conference** (IGC) in 1996. This produced the **Treaty of Amsterdam** which reformed elements of each of the EU's three pillars, notably pillar III, various activities of which were 'communitarized' (i.e. moved to the first supranational pillar) and whose title was consequently changed to **police and judicial co-operation in criminal matters**. Further reforms were introduced via the **Treaty of Nice** in 2003. The future shape of the EU was a key focus of debates within the **European Convention** in 2002–03 and the subsequent IGC launched in October 2003. The resulting **Treaty establishing a Constitution for Europe** never entered into force, however. Its replacement, the **Treaty of Lisbon**, which came into force on 1 December 2009, further reformed the EU, removed all references to the EC in favour of the EU and formally abandoned the pillar structure.

EUROPEAN UNION LAW is a generic term to describe all the law produced by the European Union (EU). Prior to the **Treaty of Lisbon** and the abolition of the EU's 'community' **pillar**, there was, according to some, a need to distinguish between, on the one hand, the law of the supranational European Communities (EC) and the *acquis communautaire*—EC law—and, on the other, the law that was created under the EU's two intergovernmental pillars covering the **common foreign and security policy** and **police and judicial co-operation in criminal matters**.

The **EUROPEAN UNION MILITARY COMMITTEE** (EUMC) was created in 2000 as part of the development of the European Union's **European security and defence policy**. The EUMC is composed of the Chiefs of Defence of the member states, who are represented on a regular basis by their permanent military representatives in Brussels. The EUMC gives military advice to the **Political and Security Committee** and to the **High Representative of the Union for Foreign Affairs and Security Policy**. It also oversees the European Union Military Staff.

EUROPEAN UNION OF FEDERALISTS is the name of an organization established in 1946 to harness and combine, on a transnational basis, the energy and ideas of the several groups and organizations that had emerged in 1945 to advocate a federal European state. While supporting the **Congress of Europe**, it was effectively superseded after 1948 by the **European Movement**. By 1950, both federalism and the Union itself had fallen out of favour. Riven by internal disputes, it disintegrated in 1956.

The **EUROPEAN UNION SATELLITE CENTRE** was established in 2001. Situated in Torrejón in Spain, it is an agency of the Council of Ministers (see **Council of the European Union**) responsible for producing satellite imagery to aid decision-making in the field of the **common foreign and security policy**, notably where crisis monitoring and conflict prevention are concerned.

The **EUROPEAN UNIT OF ACCOUNT** (EUA) was the book-keeping device introduced by the European Communities (EC) for recording the relative value of payments into and from EC accounts. In 1981 it was replaced by the **ecu**, which, in turn, was replaced by the **euro** in 1999.

EUROPEAN UNITARIAN LEFT: See **Confederal Group of the European United Left/Nordic Green Left**

The **EUROPEAN UNIVERSITY INSTITUTE** (EUI) was founded in 1976 as part of the European Communities (EC) policy of encouraging co-operation in higher education. Based in Florence, Italy, the EUI is an establishment for research and training in postgraduate education, offering doctoral programmes in economics, history and civilization, law and political and social sciences. Entry for students is competitive. Those accepted on the programmes are funded by their national governments and are expected to have some competence in more than one **language** of the European Union (EU). Staff appointments, made on the basis of open competition, are funded by the EU and are for fixed terms of between three and seven years. The EUI is the depository for the historical archives of the EU institutions.

The **EUROPEAN VOLUNTARY SERVICE** (EVS) programme enables young people between the ages of 18 and 25 to participate in voluntary work within other member states of the European Union. The programme, which was piloted in 1996, proved to be so successful that the **European Parliament** and the **European Council** supported a proposal to grant the EVS a budget of **ecu** 47.5m. for 1998–99. The programme subsequently proposed to encourage short-term projects, as well as exchange visits, involving multinational groups and third countries. EVS forms part of the **Youth in Action Programme** for 2007 to 2013, which has a total budget of €885m.

EUROPEAN YOUTH FORUM is the name of a body established in the mid-1970s as a contribution to the European Communities' educational objective of achieving a better mutual understanding in higher education between the member states. It was set up to advise and aid the **European Commission** on policy issues that concern young people. Its membership consists of the leaders of the national student and youth organizations. The Forum's impact has been limited, not least because, by its very nature, there is a lack of continuity in its membership. (See also **Youth for Europe**.)

EUROPEANIZATION (or arguably, and more accurately, EUization) is a popular theme of current academic research and is used most often to describe and assess the impact that the European Union (EU) exerts on both member states and non-member states, notably in terms of domestic legislation, policy priorities and administrative structures. Discussions of Europeanization can be measured by looking at the EU's impact on public policies, politics and the public. It affects much more than just member state governments, and can be applied to a whole range of non-governmental actors who have likewise adjusted their activities and responses to EU structures and activities. The term remains a very fashionable one in contemporary academic literature, but it is often a disputed concept.

EUROPOL (European Police Office) is the European Law Enforcement Agency, an agency that was established in The Hague under the terms of the **Treaty on European Union**. Its objective is to support national police activities in the member states more effectively, as an integral element of **justice and home affairs**, especially in combating drugs-trafficking, fraud and terrorism. The Convention establishing the agency was signed in June 1995, but Europol only became fully operational on 1 July 1999 (although the **Europol Drugs Unit** was already in operation by this time). Starting in January 2002, its mandate was extended to include all serious forms of international crime. From 2010 was Europol extended to cover all 27 EU member states, but it also worked in conjunction with other countries, from **Albania** and Australia to **Russia** and **Turkey**, to tackle effectively cross-border and international crime. The directorate of Europol is appointed by the **Council of the European Union** and the Director (since 2009) is a British national, Rob Wainwright.

The **EUROPOL DRUGS UNIT** operated from 1995 until 1999 before being absorbed into **Europol**.

EUROSCEPTICS is a term used to describe those people who opposed the **Treaty on European Union** and attempts by the European Communities (EC) to introduce further integration. Their preference is for intergovernmental and free trade co-operation only. Although opposition to the activities and aims of the European Union (EU) can be traced back to the very early days of EC membership in many states, Euroscepticism emerged as a particular feature of British politics in the late 1980s, especially under the final years of **Margaret Thatcher**'s premiership. Subsequently, opposition within Conservative ranks to the Maastricht Treaty (see **Treaty on European Union**) bedevilled the **John Major** Governments and continued to cast increasing shadows over the second and third **Tony Blair** administrations. In early 2013 the Government led by David Cameron expressed a desire to renegotiate its relationship with the EU. The rising tide of Euroscepticism has not been confined to the United Kingdom: there is evidence of similar tendencies emerging in many of the current EU states. Indeed, within the EP itself these more critical voices have been represented by both the **Independence and Democracy Group** and the short-lived **Identity, Tradition and Sovereignty Group**, and they are echoed within the parties of the left as well. Euroscepticism (both soft and harder versions) remains a vibrant force in the current EP after the 2009 elections, and indeed 16 of the United Kingdom's 72 **Members of the European Parliament** (MEPs) (from the **British National Party**—BNP, Sinn Fein and UKIP) hold fairly negative views on the benefits of EU membership. The newly established **European Conservatives and Reformists Group** was expected to add to the Eurosceptic voice.

EUROSTAT is the abbreviated and popularized form of the Statistical Office of the European Union. It is one of the special services under the jurisdiction of the **European Commission**, and is responsible for the collection and publication of statistics covering the whole range of the economic and social affairs of the European Union. While the information is intended in the first instance for use by the Commission and its administration, its document-ation is publicly available, both in book form and in databases such as **New Cronos**.

The **EUROZONE**, also called the euro area and sometimes more informally referred to as '**Euroland**', consists of those member states that are full partici-pants in **economic and monetary union** and have adopted the **euro**.

EURYDICE is the commonly used name for the Education Information Network in the European Union (EU). It was established in 1980 and was one of the European Communities' first essays into both **information technology** and the development of collaboration in **education policy**. The networked information service is based upon databanks of educational statistics, and is available for use by the **European Commission** and national education officials. At 2012 the Eurydice network consisted of 38 national units based in all 34 countries participating in the EU's **Lifelong Learning Programme** (EU member states, **EFTA** countries, **Croatia**, **Serbia** and **Turkey**). It is co-ordinated and managed by the EU Education, Audiovisual and Culture Executive Agency in Brussels, which drafts its studies and provides a range of online resources.

EUTELSAT is the acronym of the European Telecommunications Satellite Organization, an intergovernmental organization that was established in 1977. The aim of Eutelsat was to foster collaboration in the development of a European communications satellite system, and in the co-ordination and implementation of requirements relating to satellites being developed by the **European Space Agency**. It was designed to operate a satellite-based system telecommunications infrastructure for Europe. Eutelsat launched its first satellite in 1983 and has since become the world's third largest satellite operator. Although created to meet the needs of Western Europe's demand for satellite communications, Eutelsat's interests now extend across all Europe, into Africa and the Middle East, as well as large parts of Asia and the Americas. Eutelsat has no direct links with the European Union (EU), although all the EU member states are represented. In the wider context of telecommunications liberalization, Eutelsat was restruc-tured in 2001 as a private company incorporated under French law and now it markets its services through a network of partners who include leading tele-communications operators and service providers.

EVCA: See **European Private Equity and Venture Capital Association**

EVS: See **European Voluntary Service**

The **EXCHANGE-RATE MECHANISM** (ERM), along with the **ecu**, was one of the core components of the **European Monetary System** (EMS) established in 1979. It was the central instrument by which the EMS sought to stabilize and limit currency fluctuations. Under the ERM, a currency received a central exchange rate against the ecu, the value of which was derived from a basket of currencies. From these central rates, a grid of cross-parities was constructed, within which bilateral central rates were calculated for each pair of currencies participating in the ERM. For each currency there was a permissible range of fluctuation around these central rates, as well as a divergence indicator (a threshold point that indicated that the margins of permissible fluctuation were in danger of being breached). The permissible range was set at ±2.25%, with a broader range of ±6.0% for some currencies. The divergence indicator was 75% of this range. Normally, a currency would have reached the divergence threshold before it hit its bilateral limit, but because each currency had a differ-ent weighting in the ecu basket, this was not always the case. When the limit for a currency was breached or its divergence indicator triggered, the central banks of the affected states intervened in the exchange markets to keep the currency within the prescribed limits. The banks were supported by the **European Monetary Co-operation Fund** (EMCF), which supplied short-term credit facilities, but the national authorities could also have been required to take appropriate domestic measures to correct the situation, such as changing interest rates or adopting an incomes policy. Where it proved persistently difficult to hold a currency within its permissible range, mechanisms were available for realigning its central rate. There were 12 exchange rate realignments between 1979 and 1989.

The ERM was credited with contributing to the much lower levels of currency fluctuation in the 1980s, and to the increasing economic **convergence** of the member states. Its weakness was that not all the member states were part of it. Greece stayed outside the ERM until 1998; Spain joined the wider band in 1989, as did the United Kingdom in 1990 and Portugal in 1992. The 1989 **Delors Plan** saw the ERM as an integral element of **economic and monetary union** (EMU). It called for all member states to join the ERM as an essential condition for the first of three stages of progress towards full EMU. Partly because of the incorporation of the ERM into the EMU timetable, and partly because of the interpretation of the ERM's previous success, it became a more rigid mechanism after 1990, the scope for adjustments—at least without causing a crisis in the system—being greatly reduced. A more rigid system, however, tended to discount the substantial variations in national economic performance and currency strengths as perceived by the international money markets. The Danish referendum result rejecting the **Treaty on European Union** in 1992 was a catalyst for great anxiety and uncertainties in the exchange markets, compounded by the dominance within the ERM of Germany, which, confronted with the escalating costs of reunification, was pursuing a strong domestic anti-inflation policy. The consequent high German interest rates forced other ERM members to pursue similar policies, leading to severe economic problems in several countries. In September 1992 a wave of speculation was unleashed against ERM currencies. Despite massive central bank intervention, there were several involuntary devaluations, and Italy and the United Kingdom withdrew from the ERM. Further speculative pressure in August 1993, especially against the French franc, resulted after much acrimony in an extension of the broad range of permissible fluctuation to such a degree that, with only Germany and the Netherlands agreeing to stay within the narrow band, the ERM effectively ceased to be a regulatory mechanism. These episodes cast severe doubts on the viability of the timetable for EMU. Austria joined the ERM in January 1995 and a further realignment of exchange rates took place in March 1995, when the Spanish peseta was devalued by 7% and the Portuguese escudo by 3.5% in relation to other currencies. Finland joined the ERM in October 1996, and Italy rejoined in November of that year. Greece entered the ERM in March 1998.

The need for the ERM, in its original form, ended when the final stage of EMU started on 1 January 1999 (with 11 of the member states taking part—Denmark, Greece, Sweden and the United Kingdom did not participate, although Greece subsequently met the **convergence criteria** and took part in EMU from 2001) and when the **euro** was introduced as a single currency. However, the ERM was to continue, as ERM II, from 1 January 1999, to regulate the relationship between the euro and the currencies of member states remaining outside EMU, although some of the non-participating member states indicated they would not take part in ERM II. European Union countries that have not adopted the euro are expected to participate for at least two years in the ERM II before joining the euro area. A currency in ERM II is allowed to float within a range of ±15% with respect to a central rate against the euro. In 2012 there were three members of ERM II—Denmark, Lithuania and Latvia. Former members of the ERM II that have since joined the eurozone are Greece, Slovenia, Cyprus, Estonia, Malta and Slovakia.

EXCHANGE RATES: See **Bretton Woods**; **Exchange-rate Mechanism**; **European Monetary System**; **Snake**

EXCISE DUTIES: See **Competition Policy**; **Harmonization**; **Internal Market**; **White Paper**

EXCLUSIVE AGREEMENTS between companies have been banned under the European Union's **competition policy**. The ban covers exclusive purchasing agreements on a wide variety of products, several kinds of exclusive distribution agreements, including **market-sharing and price-fixing agreements**, and the use of **patents** and **trademarks**.

EXPENDITURE relates to the **budget** of the European Union (EU). The budget itself is made up from the EU's **own resources**, and is expected to fund both the policies pursued by the EU, and administrative running costs. The budget in 2012 was divided into separate headings and most of the funds were directed towards the two principal areas of sustainable growth (**competitiveness** and **cohesion**) and towards natural resources (including agricultural expenditure, rural development and fisheries). There are also three further budget categories, namely: citizenship, freedom, security and justice; the EU as a global player; and administration. The **Court of Auditors** is responsible for ensuring that all EU expenditure has occurred in a legal manner.

The draft **EXTERNAL FRONTIERS CONVENTION** proposed determining controls on the crossing of the European Union's (EU) external borders by nationals of non-member states, thereby facilitating the implementation of common EU policies on **visas** and **immigration**. The draft was eventually abandoned because of Spain's desire for Gibraltar to be excluded from the Convention. (See also **Schengen Agreement**.)

EXTERNAL RELATIONS is a collective term which describes the formal bilateral and multilateral trading agreements made by the European Union (EU) with third countries, for example: **association agreements**, **co-operation agreements**, **Europe agreements**, **partnership and co-operation agreements** and the **Cotonou Agreement**. It also refers to attempts by the member states to develop, outside the institutional structures of the EU, a common set of foreign policies through **European political co-operation** and the **common foreign and security policy**.

F

The ***FACTORTAME* JUDGMENT** of 1990 (*R v Secretary of State for Transport, ex parte Factortame Ltd*) was an important verdict by the **Court of Justice**, confirming that national legislation in conflict with European Communities law must be suspended. More specifically, the Court ruled that a member state cannot be liable unless it can be established that the state has severely and deliberately disregarded EC **law**. In order to determine this the following criteria have to be considered: the clarity and precision of the **directive**; the level of discretion left to the member state to implement the directive; whether damages were intentional and whether the failure to implement EU law can be explained by other extenuating circumstances.

FAIR stands for Fisheries, Agriculture and agro-Industrial Research programme. Established in 1994, this programme replaced all previous agricultural research programmes: AIR, CAMAR, ÉCLAIR, FAR and FLAIR. The objectives of FAIR were: 'To contribute to the improvement of the competitiveness of European agro-industry and primary production by the development of new technologies compatible with sustainable growth and taking account of consumer needs; to improve the quality of agricultural, forestry and fish products in general and food products in particular; to contribute to the **implementation** of the Community's agriculture, rural development, fisheries, environment and **internal market** policies; to contribute to a better match between the production and utilization of biological primary materials.' It was subsumed into the **quality of life and management of living resources programme** in 1999.

The **FAR RIGHT** resurfaced as an element within the current seventh **European Parliament** (EP) (2009–14) following a series of electoral gains across the European Union (EU), but especially in Hungary, Italy, the Netherlands and the United Kingdom. Such parties had generally campaigned on a range of issues, advocating explicitly anti-immigrant and anti-Islamic policies, maintaining ardent opposition to Turkish accession and stressing uncompromising nationalist positions which included the withdrawal of their respective countries from the EU. Among these parties, the Italian Northern League practically doubled its vote (to 10.2%), and in Hungary the Jobbik Party's anti-gypsy and anti-immigration platform secured three seats. In the Netherlands the increasingly anti-Islamic Freedom Party won four seats. In the United Kingdom the

British National Party (BNP) won its first ever (two) seats in the EP. The immediate challenge facing these parties was whether they could muster enough support within the EP to be able to form a distinct parliamentary group. Inter-party rivalries and tensions mean that this goal will prove difficult to achieve.

The BNP has attempted to foster a closer working relationship among elements of the far right through the creation of a new Alliance of European National Movements. However, this body cannot be recognized as a formal political group within the EP as it does not meet the necessary numbers (25 MEPs) and has insufficient transnational membership (members must come from at least seven EU member states). Nevertheless, in February 2012 the alliance was awarded some €260,000 in funding as a pan-European bloc. This new alliance rejects all attempts to create a European superstate, calls for strong, pro-family policies and seeks to fight against the destructive effects of globalization.

The **FAROE ISLANDS** have internal autonomy under Danish sovereignty (see **Denmark**). The parliament of the Islands opposed entry into the European Communities (EC). After extensive negotiations, mainly over fishing rights, an agreement was reached in January 1972. The Islands were granted special status, with the option of applying for full membership by the end of 1975. The Islands, however, have continued to reject membership, and participate only in free trade arrangements with the European Union (EU). Thus, common EU policies do not apply to the Faroe Islands.

FEDERAL REPUBLIC OF GERMANY: See **Germany**

The **FEDERAL REPUBLIC OF YUGOSLAVIA** (FRY): See **Serbia**; **Montenegro**

FEDERALISM is a system of government where different levels of authority (usually national and regional) exercise responsibility for particular areas, and maintain their own institutions, and whose specific powers are constitutionally guaranteed. The term has been used loosely and confusingly in the context of the European Union (EU) to describe the result of both centralization and decentralization. **Eurosceptics** have used the term to criticize what they see as an undue concentration of power at the supranational level of the EU institutions, while others see federalism as the way of preventing such a concentration. In discussions of the **European Council**, it has been used vaguely to refer both to the acquisition of more authority by the supranational institutions and to decentralization, with respect not only to the member states, but also beyond them to the regions. However, by themselves, concepts such as the **Europe of the Regions** or **subsidiarity** do not fully represent a proper federal structure.

FEOGA: See **European Agricultural Guidance and Guarantee Fund**

FIFTEEN, or Europe of the Fifteen, is a term sometimes used to describe the membership of the European Union after January 1995, when Austria, Finland and Sweden joined the existing **Twelve** member states.

FIFTH DIRECTIVE is the name of the first of several major **European Commission** initiatives relating to the structure of industrial companies and the protection of **workers' rights**. The Directive was proposed in 1972, and its target was those limited companies in the European Communities with a payroll of more than 500 workers. The Directive established conditions for the structure of such companies which, modelled to some extent on the experience of the Federal Republic of Germany (West Germany), would entail obligatory worker representation on supervisory boards. It faced powerful opposition from employers' organizations and some member states, and failed to gain the necessary unanimous approval in the Council of Ministers (see **Council of the European Union**). The idea of worker representation was eventually incorporated into the **Charter of Fundamental Social Rights of Workers** (the Social Charter) and the Social Chapter.

FINALITÉ POLITIQUE is a term used to describe the possible end goals and structure of the European Union. Beyond the references to an 'ever closer union' in the **Treaty of Rome** and the **Treaty on European Union**, there is nothing specific written in the treaties regarding this *finalité politique*, although discussions on a **constitution**, particularly in the context of the **Laeken Declaration**, have led to increased pressure to define it. For many, however, the current situation where the *finalité politique* is left undefined is attractive, since it allows for greater flexibility within the process of European **integration**.

THE FINANCIAL INSTRUMENT FOR FISHERIES GUIDANCE (FIFG) was established in 1992, and was the main instrument whereby the European Union (EU) afforded aid to the fisheries sector under the **common fisheries policy** (CFP). It ran until December 2006. It aimed to support the CFP and, in pursuance of that objective, it sought to help to achieve lasting balance between fish stocks and fishing; to strengthen the **competitiveness** of operating structures and develop economically viable firms in the sector; to improve supplies and enhance the commercial value of fishery and aquaculture products; and to help revitalize areas dependent on fisheries and aquaculture. It advocated a restructuring of the industry and encouraged a reduction in fishing in EU waters, the decommissioning of vessels, establishment of joint ventures with foreign investors, and increasing competitiveness and assistance for the aquaculture industry, while also promoting economic and social cohesion. National and regional authorities were obliged to contribute to projects, although increased funding was available for poorer regions of the EU. **Decision-making** concerning the FIFG could be broken down into two stages. In the first, a member state submitted a draft programme to the Commission for structural interventions in the fisheries sector: this set out the strategy and priorities for assistance, as well as a request for funding, in the form of a coherent package of multi-annual measures. Thereafter, the Commission negotiated the programme on the basis of this draft with the member state and, having reached an agreement with the member state, approved it. The competitiveness of the EU fishing fleet remains a crucial factor, and the FIFG provided support for building and modernizing vessels. FIFG support was also available for the aquaculture sector and for the creation of protected coastal areas. Port facilities, processing, marketing and promotional operations were also eligible for funding. In addition, the private sector, through the producers' organizations, could apply for funding for various measures relating to the management of the resource and/or fishing effort. Finally, financial contributions to redundancy payments and pensions for fishermen retiring early were also made. (See also **PESCA**.) Programmed **expenditure** under the FIFG for 2000–06 amounted to €3,746m. Over this specific period the EU contribution accounted to 75% of the planned total cost of infrastructure in less-developed regions (objective 1) and 50% in other regions. Where the aid went to enterprises, the EU contributions were limited to 35% and 15%, respectively. The FIFG was replaced by the **European Fisheries Fund** (EFF) in January 2007, which aimed to heighten the competitivess of the sector and its longer term viability. This programme runs until the end of 2013 and has a budget of some €4,304m.; it is to be succeeded by a new European Maritime and Fisheries Fund (EMFF) from 2014. The EMFF has been designed to achieve the above-mentioned objectives of the CFP and is structured around four broad pillars: Smart, Green Fisheries; Smart, Green Aquaculture; Sustainable Development of Fisheries Areas; and an Integrated Maritime Policy. This last pillar is the most innovative and centres on marine spatial planning and integrated coastal zone management.

FINANCIAL PERSPECTIVES are the multi-annual **budget** programmes of the European Union (EU). The first, often referred to as the **Delors I** package, covered the period 1988–92 and was adopted in 1987 in an attempt to limit the annual wrangling over the budget between what is now the **Council of the European Union** and the **European Parliament** (EP) and provide a firmer foundation for medium-term policy planning. The second financial perspective, the so-called **Delors II** package, covered the years 1993–99. A further perspective was agreed at the Berlin summit of the **European Council** in March 1999 and was designed to finance **enlargement**. It was to cover the period until 2006. Each financial perspective is accompanied by an **inter-institutional agreement**, an understanding between the **European Commission**, the Council of the European Union and the EP, by which they commit themselves in advance to observing agreed limits on the main budgetary priorities and establish a framework for EU **expenditure** in the form of the financial perspective over a particular time period. In other words, the financial perspective shows the maximum amount and the composition of foreseeable EU expenditure. The main categories of EU expenditure are divided into headings; each of these headings carries an amount of commitment appropriations for each year. The headings are agriculture; structural actions; internal policies; external actions; administration; reserves; compensations; and pre-accession aid. Negotiations among the member state governments for the new financial perspective running from 2007 to 2013 proved contentious, but a deal was finally reached in December 2005. The next perspective will run from 2014–20.

FINANCIAL POLICY: See **Economic and Financial Policy**

FINLAND has emerged as the most pro-European Union (EU) member state within Scandinavia and, unlike both Denmark and Sweden, signed up as one of the initial members of the **euro**. This identity with the EU and the wider Europe reflects Finland's somewhat troubled history, when its geographical position between both **Russia** and Sweden has often curtailed the independence of this smaller state. In the immediate post-war period, for example, Finland was restricted in its relationships with other Western European countries by the Finno-Soviet Pact of Friendship, Co-operation and Mutual Assistance, which had been signed with the **USSR** in 1948. This in effect forced Finland to pursue a foreign policy based on neutrality, making its government wary of participation in any organization that the USSR might interpret as violating the terms of the treaty. Hence for a number of years Finland played a minimal role in Western European developments. In the early 1960s it did not approach the European Communities (EC), as did the other Nordic states, for some form of association. Moreover, it became only an associate member of the **European Free Trade Association** (EFTA). However, it later joined the EFTA states in seeking some form of closer co-operation with the EC. The signing of a **free trade agreement** was delayed until 1973, again because of arguments over whether it violated Finland's neutrality, and doubts about its acceptability to the USSR. The Agreement came into force in January 1974 with an accelerated rate of tariff reductions, in order to synchronize the date for implementation with that for the other EFTA states. Finland became a full member of EFTA in 1986 and in the more relaxed atmosphere of the late 1980s and the collapse of the Iron Curtain felt able to join the other EFTA states in negotiations with the EC over a **European Economic Area**. In 1992, after much discussion, it formally submitted an application to join the EC. Negotiations were completed by 1994 and endorsed by a popular referendum, allowing Finland to join the EU on 1 January 1995. Finland still remains the only Nordic EU member to have adopted the euro as its national currency.

The **FISCAL COMPACT TREATY**, formally the **Treaty on Stability, Co-ordination and Governance in the Economic and Monetary Union**, was signed by 25 of the European Union (EU) member states on 2 March 2012. The Czech Republic and the United Kingdom are not signatories. The Treaty is designed to ensure improved financial discipline within the EU and especially within the eurozone. To this end, it stipulates that the signatory states introduce in primary law by 1 January 2014 a so-called 'debt brake' requiring national budgets to be in balance (i.e. with a deficit equivalent to less than 3% of gross domestic product—GDP) or in surplus, and for the annual structural deficit to be no greater than 0.5% or 1.0% of GDP (depending on a country's debt-to-GDP ratio). A breach of the agreed ceiling could result in a fine from the **Court of Justice**. The Treaty also reinforces commitments to improved economic and fiscal governance contained in existing agreements and legislation, notably the revised **Stability and Growth Pact** and the so-called 'six pack' of legislative measures designed to enforce budgetary discipline through, for example, increased budgetary surveillance. The Fiscal Compact Treaty also provides for two 'summits' per year of heads of government and state from the member countries of the euro area; non-euro area signatories will be permitted to attend at least one of these summits. The Treaty is not formally part of EU law, but an intergovernmental document. It is scheduled to enter into force on 1 January 2013, if it has been ratified by at least 12 member countries of the euro area. Only member states that complete ratification of the Treaty will be eligible for access to financial assistance from the **European Stability Mechanism**.

JOSCHKA FISCHER (1948–) served as Federal Minister of Foreign Affairs and Vice-Chancellor of the Federal Republic of Germany from 1998 until 2005. He became Germany's first 'green' foreign minister following the general election victory of the Social Democratic Party and its decision to enter into a coalition government with Die Grünen, the Greens. Fischer was elected as one of the first members of the Green Party in the Bundestag in 1983 and emerged as one of Germany's most popular and trusted politicians. Early in 2001, however, his career faced a crisis over his activities as a militant left-wing activist in the 1970s. He apologized for this and retained his portfolio following the re-election of the Red–Green coalition Government in 2002. A committed supporter of the European Union, Fischer was instrumental in promoting discussion of further political integration and a European **constitution**. He was also noted for overseeing the deployment of German forces, albeit under the umbrella of the **North Atlantic Treaty Organization**, during the **Kosovo** conflict in 1999.

FISHERIES: See **Common Fisheries Policy**; **North Atlantic Fisheries Organization**

FLANKING MEASURES is a term used in the European Union to describe measures or actions that are intended to support the implementation and objectives of a specific common policy or programme, but are not integral to it. The term is most often used in the context of the **internal market**. Among the most prominent flanking measures are those concerning **economic and monetary union**, **competition policy**, **social policy** and **environmental policy**.

FLEXIBILITY is a term used to describe the effects of different approaches to **integration**, such as **multi-speed Europe**, **à la carte Europe** and **two-speed Europe**. It is also used to describe the effects of the mechanisms for **enhanced co-operation** introduced by the **Treaty of Amsterdam**.

The **FONTAINEBLEAU SUMMIT** of the **European Council**, held in France in June 1984, was one of the most decisive in the history of **summit meetings**. It dealt conclusively with several major issues that had hindered the development of the European Communities (EC) for a number of years. Agreement was reached on the United Kingdom's budgetary position and on raising the limit of **value-added tax** contributions to the EC **budget** to avoid threatened insolvency; limits were placed upon **common agricultural policy** spending, and the way was opened for the entry into the EC of Portugal and Spain. By resolving such issues and authorizing the establishment of a **Committee for a People's Europe** and the **Dooge Committee**, the summit contributed to the EC's later progress towards further integration.

FOOD AID: See **Development Aid**

FOODSTUFFS are the subject of several European Union **directives** intended to protect the **health and safety** of consumers and strengthen **consumer policy**. The directives govern the manufacturing, labelling and marketing of foodstuffs. Their provisions include: the publication of listings of permitted substances and additives along with the requisite purity standards; regulations governing the production of a range of foodstuffs; the fixing of maximum permitted levels for pesticide residues in fruit, vegetable and oil products; and regulations specifying that a list of ingredients and their quantities, as well as a 'best before' date, must be included on the labelling of foodstuffs. In addition, a general ban has been placed upon the use of animal growth promoters containing substances that might generate adverse hormonal or other side effects. The **European Parliament** in 2002 proposed stricter labelling regulations for foodstuffs containing genetically modified ingredients. Following a proposal in the **European Commission**'s 2000 **White Paper** on food safety, a **European Food Safety Agency** was created.

FOREIGN POLICY: See **Common Foreign and Security Policy**; **European Political Co-operation**

FORESTRY has been the subject of several European Communities initiatives designed to combine the economic development of the industry with measures for environmental protection and conservation. The initiatives were brought together in the Forestry Sectoral Research and Technology (FOREST) action programme of 1990. This was later absorbed into AIR in 1991, and then into **FAIR**, which was subsequently subsumed into the **quality of life and management of living resources programme**. In 1999 the **Council of the European Union** adopted a **resolution** on a Forestry Strategy for the European Union (EU). The EU also dedicates approximately €120m. a year to forest conservation and management projects in less developed countries.

FORTRESS EUROPE is a term popularized in the 1980s and early 1990s that summarizes the concerns expressed by politicians and economists in several countries about some of the possible consequences of the **internal market**. It refers to fears that while the European Union would have free trade within its borders, it might adopt a more protectionist attitude towards imports from the rest of the world. These concerns have been expressed most strongly by the **USA**, which believes that in some respects the European Communities have always been unduly protectionist. The term has also been used in the context of the growing stringency of border controls and **immigration policies** in the member states, as the prospect of internal **freedom of movement** becomes increasingly real.

FORZA EUROPA GROUP (FE) was a **party group** in the **European Parliament** in 1994–95. It consisted of Italian **members of the European Parliament** from the national centre-right party Forza Italia; it was the only group formed exclusively from members of a single national party. In mid-1995 FE merged with the **Group of the European Democratic Alliance** (RDE) to form the **Union for Europe of the Nations Group** (UPE/UEN).

FOUCHET PLAN is the name commonly given to the outcome of a proposal by President **Charles de Gaulle** of France in 1961 that the **Six** members of the **European Economic Community** (EEC) should explore ways of achieving a 'Union of States'. A committee, headed by Christian Fouchet of France, considered the matter and produced a draft treaty in November 1961. A modified second version was produced the following year. The components of the Plan included a council of heads of government or of foreign ministers where decisions would be taken only by unanimous agreement, a permanent intergovernmental secretariat and four permanent intergovernmental committees to take responsibility for the policy fields of foreign affairs, defence, commerce and cultural affairs. The scheme was opposed by most of the other five states, especially the Netherlands. The Plan represented a considerable shift in direction from that envisaged by the **Treaty of Rome**, and in addition the smaller states wished first to settle the question of **enlargement**, particularly the possible entry into the EEC of the United Kingdom. With France unable to generate support among its partners, the Plan was abandoned in 1963. A truncated version survived in the form of the 1963 **Treaty of Friendship** between France and the Federal Republic of Germany (West Germany).

FOUNDING TREATIES is a phrase, like 'constitutive treaties', that refers to the four documents that established the European Communities and the European Union: the **Treaty of Paris** of 1951 establishing the **European Coal and Steel Community** (ECSC), the two treaties of 1957 (see **Treaty of Rome**) establishing the **European Atomic Energy Community** (EAEC or Euratom) and the **European Economic Community** (EEC), and the **Treaty on European Union** (TEU) of 1992. The founding treaties have all been amended by, among others, the **Single European Act**, the TEU, the **Treaty of Amsterdam** and the **Treaty of Nice**. The founding treaties and the amending treaties are increasingly referred to as the **European treaties**. If it had been ratified, the **Treaty establishing a Constitution for Europe** would have replaced the Treaty of Rome and the TEU. Its replacement, the **Treaty of Lisbon**, amended the founding treaties and renamed the **Treaty establishing the European Community** the **Treaty on the Functioning of the European Union**.

FRANCE has been one of the most prominent supporters of European integration since 1948. It provided a location for the **Council of Europe** in 1949. The **European Coal and Steel Community** was initially conceived by **Jean Monnet** and was realized by **Robert Schuman**. France was a founder member of the European Communities (EC), and its involvement in their development has been such that French governments have taken an almost proprietorial interest in the EC. Their actions have had important consequences for the EC, even if not always to their benefit. The policies of President **Charles de Gaulle** (1959–69), for example, profoundly altered the nature of the EC and delayed its **enlargement**. His successor, Georges Pompidou (1969–74), opened the way to enlargement in return for obtaining the kind of **common agricultural policy** (CAP) that France wanted. President **Valéry Giscard d'Estaing** (1974–81) proposed the **European Council** and co-sponsored the **European Monetary System**. The tradition was maintained by **François Mitterrand** (1981–95), who campaigned strongly for further intensive integration, and by **Jacques Chirac** (1995–2007). In 2000 the French presidency of the European Council was responsible for bringing about the conclusion, albeit unsatisfactory, of the 2000 **intergovernmental conference** and the adoption of the **Treaty of Nice**.

France has benefited economically from the EC, above all from the CAP. Just as the EC provided the Federal Republic of Germany (FRG—West Germany) with an outlet for its export-orientated industry, so it gave France a bigger market for its large and variegated agriculture, although by the 1980s some French products faced severe competition from cheaper Mediterranean produce. On the whole, the French attitude towards the EC has been highly utilitarian, and governments have always been prepared to emphasize national interests should this seem advisable for domestic political and economic reasons. Nevertheless, its political influence within the EC has been greater than that of any other member state. To some extent, this was due to its close relationship with the FRG. The EC served one basic purpose of French foreign policy: to influence, even perhaps control, the FRG. That reason decreased in importance after German reunification. In particular, the currency crises of 1992–93 indicated that the two countries had different economic concerns. In the 1990s there emerged a stronger anti-integration mood, as exemplified by the 1992 referendum on the **Treaty on European Union**. This was held by President Mitterrand to emphasize France's European commitment, but he narrowly escaped a humiliating defeat, because government policy, intended to enable the country to meet the criteria for participation in **economic and monetary union**, contributed to high levels of unemployment. His successor, Jacques Chirac, proved less fortunate when in May 2005 the French people (with a rate of participation of 70%) rejected (by 55% to 45%) the **Treaty establishing a Constitution for Europe**. When Chirac had opted to call a referendum, support for the treaty was relatively high, and it was expected that the treaty would find easy endorsement. However, in retrospect, it is clear that support for the 'no' campaign rose steadily from January 2005, and the final outcome owed much to a variety of concerns over issues such as the 2004 enlargement, the next wave of enlargement, a British economic blueprint being imposed on the European Union, and some dissatisfaction with Chirac's decade-long rule. Chirac was succeeded by **Nicolas Sarkozy** in May 2007. Sarkozy initially emerged as one of the most dynamic and flamboyant of the incumbent European leaders and as someone who was determined to reform and revive France's economic model, but he raised some concerns in his first six months of office over comments on both **competition policy** and the future of the **common fisheries policy**. France successfully completed ratification of the **Treaty of Lisbon** without holding a referendum. This decision did not excite much public reaction, and Sarkozy went on to score major electoral success at the EP 2009 elections when his party's share of the vote increased by 15%. It was also noticeable that relations with Germany on European affairs and strategies reverted to the cordiality of the **Schmidt/Giscard d'Estaing** and **Kohl/Mitterrand** periods. However, Sarkozy's bid for a second term as French President failed and he was replaced by **François Hollande** in May 2012. The election of this new, Socialist head of state may result in a period of more fraught meetings with Germany over the issue of the ailing euro and the requisite austerity policies.

FRANCO-GERMAN MIXED BRIGADE: See **Eurocorps**

FRANCO-GERMAN TREATY OF FRIENDSHIP: See **Treaty of Friendship**

The *FRANCOVICH* JUDGMENT is the common name of a case (*Francovich et al.* v *Italy*) heard by the **Court of Justice** in 1992. The Italian Government was accused of not implementing European Communities (EC) rules. Specifically, it had failed to implement Directive 80/987/EEC, which seeks to protect employees in cases of insolvency, despite several reminders from the Commission. A worker named Francovich duly opted to initiate legal proceedings against the Italian Government for his lost pension rights when his company became insolvent. In finding against Italy, the Court established the principle that individuals could appeal against the non-implementation of European Union law by member states on the grounds that their individual rights had been infringed. It also confirmed that member states found guilty could be deemed liable and fined.

FRAUD rose to prominence on the political agenda of the European Communities (EC) in the 1990s. In particular there were growing concerns about the amount of the EC **budget** that was being lost through fraud, concerns that were often reinforced by the annual reports of the **Court of Auditors** and criticisms coming from the **European Parliament**. On top of these came the allegations of corruption that led to the downfall of the **European Commission** under President **Jacques Santer** in 1999. Early concerns led to the creation in 1994 of an **Advisory Committee for the Co-ordination of Fraud Prevention**, which was followed in 1999 by the establishment of a European **Anti-Fraud Office** (OLAF) within the Commission. Beyond combating fraud within the institutions and policies of the European Union, much attention has also been focused since the early 1990s on the need to counter cross-border fraud. Hence, combating fraud features as one of the activities to be pursued as part of policy on **justice and home affairs**. Concerns about fraud have also been instrumental in moves to create a **European Public Prosecutor's Office**.

FREE TRADE AGREEMENTS are signed by the European Union with European countries that, at the time of signing, have traditionally not been applicants for membership. They provide for a phased introduction of industrial free trade. Notable signatories have been members of the **European Free Trade Association** and the Baltic States (see Estonia, Latvia and Lithuania). So-called 'deep free trade areas' are envisaged as part of the **European neighbourhood policy**.

FREEDOM OF MOVEMENT lies at the heart of the objectives outlined in the **Treaty of Rome**, which required the abolition of barriers to the 'freedom of movement for persons, services and capital'. Frontier formalities and checks, different indirect tax rates, government appointive, contractual and procurement policies, and the national basis of many professional qualifications all effectively hindered the establishment of free movement. While some slight progress was taken towards removing the barriers, a significant impetus was not achieved until the decision to establish the **internal market** was made. The principle was reconfirmed and formally applied to goods by the **Treaty on European Union**, but the objective had still not been fully realized by the late 1990s. The **Treaty of Amsterdam** attempted to make improvements in this field by setting a timetable of five years within which an area of freedom, justice and security should be established. Common rules on **immigration**, **asylum** and **visa policy** were intended to promote greater freedom of movement between the member states. International crime was to be dealt with through improved co-operation between national police forces and customs authorities. Moreover, the **Schengen Agreement** was incorporated into the Treaties.

FRONTEX is a European Union (EU) agency based in Warsaw, Poland. It was created in 2005 to co-ordinate co-operation between EU member states on border security issues. Its tasks include risk analysis, co-ordination of operational co-operation in the field of external border management and assistance in the training of national border guards, research relevant for the control and surveillance of external borders, technical and operational assistance at external borders, and support for member states in organizing joint return operations. It also pursues co-operation with non-member states to improve border security. Its budget in 2011 was an estimated €86.4m.

Štefan Füle (1962–) is one of the Commissioners in the Barroso II Commission (2010–14). He comes from the Czech Republic and has responsibility in the current Commission for **Enlargement** and the **European neighbourhood policy**. Prior to joining the Commission he served as the Czech Minister for European Affairs and previously had been the Czech ambassador to both **Lithuania** and the **United Kingdom**.

FUNCTIONALISM is an early theory of integration on which **neofunctionalism** draws. It holds that the creation of international agencies is the consequence of a shared need among states for technocratic management of policy.

FYRM: See **former Yugoslav republic of Macedonia**

G

G-7: See **G-8**

G-8, or the Group of Eight, is an exclusive club comprising the world's seven most industrialized states along with **Russia**. Originally known as G-7, this was officially the title of meetings between the finance ministers of Canada, France, Germany, Italy, **Japan**, the United Kingdom and the **USA**, a practice that was established in Tokyo in May 1986. The term was also used more generally to describe the summit meetings of the heads of government of the same seven countries, which began at Rambouillet, France, in 1975 (although Canada did not become involved in the G-7 process until some months after the initial meeting). Leaders of the **USSR** and, later, Russia were invited to attend the summits after 1991. Russia demanded equal representation and became a full member in 2002, thereby making the group G-8. Originally intended to discuss common economic problems, after 1989 the summit agendas became increasingly political in tone and have sought to tackle some of the thorniest issues such as trade with the Third World, global poverty and environmental issues. The meetings of the world's richest countries have, over the years, become the target for protesters, as in Rostock, Germany in June 2007. The European Union is represented by the President of the **European Commission** and by the President of the **European Council**.

GATT: See **General Agreement on Tariffs and Trade**

GENERAL AFFAIRS AND EXTERNAL RELATIONS COUNCIL was the name of the body usually regarded as the most senior manifestation of the **Council of the European Union** and its central co-ordinating body. Known prior to 2002 as the General Affairs Council, it was the regular meeting of the national foreign ministers at which broad issues of foreign policy were discussed. Often, the foreign ministers were also called upon to consider a range of other questions. These may have concerned particularly difficult political problems, those that arose out of a conflict of interests between different departmental or policy area meetings of the Council, or those that could not easily be assigned to a particular departmental competence. In forming the Council, the foreign

265

ministers were also widely regarded as the personal representatives of the heads of government, keeping the latter briefed on the views of other member states. To streamline issues and to recognize the growing volume of work arising from foreign policy concerns, this Council was divided into two separate Council formats in 2009, namely the General Council and the Foreign Affairs Council.

The **GENERAL AGREEMENT ON TARIFFS AND TRADE** (GATT) was a convention signed in 1947 by 23 countries (although the number of contracting parties subsequently increased to several times that number), and maintained as a specialized agency of the **United Nations**. Its intention was to secure a pattern of free trade in the post-war world. GATT's objectives were to work towards an orderly framework for international trade, through the elimination of unilateral actions by states and the gradual reduction of tariff barriers. The organization was based upon the principle of non-discrimination: trade advantages offered by one country to another had to be extended to all. There were, however, many exceptions to the principle of non-discrimination. The **Treaty of Rome** specified that the European Communities (EC) should represent the member states and their interests in external trade affairs and negotiations. Accordingly, the **European Commission** represented the member states in all GATT rounds of negotiations after the **Kennedy Round** of the 1960s. While GATT was generally successful, the later negotiations were highly contentious as the agenda extended from manufactured products to cover, for example, agriculture, copyright and services. The **Uruguay Round** of negotiations of 1986–94 was dominated by arguments between the EC and the **USA**, which had been highly critical of what it perceived as EC protectionism in a variety of areas, particularly in relation to the **common agricultural policy** (CAP). France's objections to lowering protection for its farmers caused considerable tension and the US Government threatened to walk away from the entire Round unless the CAP was tackled. This position found sympathy among some EC member states, including the United Kingdom. The Blair House Agreement of November 1992 between the EC and the USA greatly limited financial assistance to EC farmers and antagonized France. The French Government threatened to boycott the discussions until France secured concessions at a special EC **summit meeting** in December 1992. Negotiations on a successor to GATT were completed in 1993, and on 1 January 1995 the **World Trade Organization** was established.

GENERAL COURT: Formerly known as the **Court of First Instance**, and after the **Lisbon Treaty** known as the General Court, it is an innovation of the late 1980s. Under the **Treaty of Rome** the **Court of Justice** was made responsible for cases brought against the European Communities (EC) by their employees. These cases involved such issues as recruitment, promotion, salaries and disciplinary measures. They were, to a large degree, responsible for the increasing volume of work with which the Court had to cope, accounting for almost one-half of the cases heard. In order to reduce the Court's burden, by removing from its competence minor cases, including those involving EC staff that could easily be handled by a lower court, the **Single European Act** created the Court of First Instance (CFI). Composed of one judge from each member state, but chosen by common accord, the new Court began to operate in September 1989. Its role and status were further enhanced by the **Treaty on European Union** in 1991, but only after the **Treaty of Nice** was it instituted as a genuine court of first instance. Prior to this, it was competent primarily for cases relating to **competition policy** and the **European Coal and Steel Community**. Many other cases went directly to the Court of Justice, bypassing the CFI. Currently the General Court deals with a range of cases covering, *inter alia*, actions for annulment of European Union (EU) legislation and actions for failure to act by an EU institution. In all cases, appeals against its decisions can be directed to the Court of Justice on grounds of its lack of jurisdiction over a case or its misinterpretation of precedents. In 2009 the CFI (as it was known until 30 November 1999) completed 555 cases, while 1,191 cases remained pending. Under the **Treaty of Lisbon** the Court of First Instance was rebranded as the General Court. The treaty also introduced the term 'Court of Justice of the European Union' to describe the entire court system of the EU, comprising the **Court of Justice**, the General Court and the **Civil Service Tribunal**.

The **GENERAL SECRETARIAT OF THE COUNCIL OF THE EUROPEAN UNION**: See **Council Secretariat**

GENERALIZED SYSTEM OF PREFERENCES (GSP) is a term that refers to preferential treatment granted by the European Union to some exports from countries not otherwise associated with them in a formal agreement. GSPs were first proposed in 1968 by the **United Nations** Conference on Trade and Development (UNCTAD), and the European Communities introduced their own scheme in 1971. It applies only to some developing countries, and is of limited value as, in practice, these countries are preferred to only a very small number of industrialized states, and the GSP applies to only some of their products.

HANS-DIETRICH GENSCHER (1927–) was a long-serving Minister of Foreign Affairs (1974–92) of the Federal Republic of Germany (West Germany) and a strong supporter of European integration. He was the principal architect of the **Genscher–Colombo Plan**, on which he subsequently collaborated with the Italian Minister of Foreign Affairs, Emilio Colombo, arguing that implementation of the Plan was necessary to revive the integrationist objectives of the European Communities. Genscher, alongside the German Chancellor, **Helmut Kohl**, was quick to seize the opportunity presented by the collapse of communist rule in **Central and Eastern Europe** to pave the way for German reunification in 1990.

GENSCHER–COLOMBO PLAN is the name given to an initiative for political union sponsored by **Hans-Dietrich Genscher** and Emilio Colombo. Presented in the form of a Draft European Act and draft declaration on economic integration, it argued for more common policies, especially in foreign affairs; for greater cultural and legal co-operation; that the **European Council** should report annually to the **European Parliament** (EP), with the latter being able to submit proposals on all aspects of European union to the Council; and that the use of **qualified majority voting** in the Council of Ministers (see **Council of the European Union**) should be significantly increased. It further recommended the establishment of a mechanism whereby the member states could rapidly convene meetings of the European Communities (EC) institutions in response to crises. At the heart of the Plan was a belief that the role of the EC institutions should be made more explicit, especially that of the European Council. Various member states, including the Federal Republic of Germany (FRG—West Germany), objected to several of the proposals. In London in November 1981, the European Council invited the member states' foreign ministers and the **European Commission** to consider and report on the Plan. When it was eventually discussed by the European Council at Stuttgart, FRG, in June 1983, no action was taken other than the signing of a **Solemn Declaration on European Union**. The major supporter of the Genscher–Colombo Plan was the EP, and many of its ideas found their way into the EP's own **Draft Treaty on European Union**.

MÁIRE GEOGHEGAN-QUINN (1950–) is one of the 27 Commissioners of the **Barroso** II Commission (2010–14), in which she has responsibility for Research, Innovation and Science. She is a career politician and was first elected to the Irish parliament in 1975 as a member of Fianna Fáil. In 1979 she became the first female to hold cabinet office in the history of the Irish state and went on to hold other positions in government. These included being, briefly, Minister for Education in 1982, Minister for European Affairs from 1987 to 1991, Minister for Tourism in 1992 and Minister for Justice in 1993. She had announced her decision to stand to lead the party in 1997, but opted to withdraw (for family reasons) in favour of Bertie Ahern and temporarily left the political stage in the late 1990s. However, she was appointed to the **European Court of Auditors** in 2000, was re-appointed in 2006, and is now the first woman from Ireland to hold the post of European Commissioner.

KRISTALINA GEORGIEVA (1953–) is one of the 27 Commissioners of the **Barroso** II Commission (2010–14), in which she has responsibility for international co-operation, humanitarian aid and crisis response. She is a

Bulgarian national, who holds a doctorate in economics from the University of National and World Economy in Sofia, Bulgaria. Following postgraduate reseach, she held a range of academic and consulting positions in Bulgaria and the USA and lectured in various universities around the world. In 1993 she launched her career at the World Bank, where she rose through the ranks to become Director in the Environment Department and then Vice-President and Corporate Secretary. She is affiliated to the **European People's Party**.

GERMANY was occupied after its military defeat in 1945 by the four victors: France, the **USSR**, the United Kingdom and the **USA**. Each of these states administered a part of Germany. The original intention was to demilitarize, de-Nazify and re-educate the German people before returning the reins of power to a German government. The onset of the **Cold War** between the USSR and the USA led to the division of Europe and the division of Germany in 1949. From then until October 1990, two separate countries, the Federal Republic of Germany (FRG—West Germany) and the German Democratic Republic (GDR—East Germany), existed in Germany. The FRG was a founder member of the European Communities (EC), and one of the most Europe-orientated of the member states, although there was not necessarily a strong correlation between this commitment and West German influence within the EC. On the whole, German influence in the EC has been monetary and economic rather than political. It was the largest and richest member state, with the strongest economy and manufacturing system, and after 1979 its currency dominated the **European Monetary System**. Its lesser political influence was, in part, the result of its historical legacy. In the 1950s, West German commitment to European integration was seen by **Konrad Adenauer** not only as a means of access to important markets for its export-orientated economy, but also as a central element of his strategy to link the FRG firmly in a Western alliance, rehabilitating it in the eyes of its neighbours and allaying fears of a possible future resurgence of German militarism. Adenauer also saw European integration as being based upon a Franco-German rapprochement, even if this meant that the FRG would, because of post-war realities, be the junior partner. The rapprochement was formally acknowledged in the 1963 **Treaty of Friendship**.

It was not until the 1970s that the FRG began to seek to exert a political influence in the EC more commensurate with its economic strength. Its support was more tempered by an evaluation of the consequences of EC policies for West German national interests. Between 1974 and 1982 Chancellor **Helmut Schmidt** was particularly concerned, in a period of general economic downturn, about the cost of EC initiatives. His successor, the longest serving post-war German Chancellor, **Helmut Kohl** (1982–98), was a more unreserved supporter of further integration, and active in the initiatives of the 1980s—the single market (see **internal market**), **economic and monetary union** (EMU) and moves towards deeper political integration—which culminated in the **Treaty on European Union**.

The GDR had been given access to the EC for its products as a result of the **Ostpolitik** treaties, and upon German reunification automatically became part of the EC. The reunited Germany was subsequently the largest unit in the EC by an even greater margin, and Kohl increased the pressure for political union. His reasoning was much the same as that of Adenauer: the reduction of German sovereignty within a political Europe would also reduce fears abroad of German power and limit the effect of potential German nationalism. Nevertheless, there was resistance in Germany to Kohl's commitment to European union, especially over the replacement of the German mark by a single European currency. However, the coalition governments under **Gerhard Schröder** (1998–2002; 2002–05) maintained Germany's pro-European Union (EU) stance and saw German entry into EMU in January 1999. Today Germany remains strongly in favour of the EU, but its Government is prepared to raise its concerns with the EU more often than it has in the past, as, for example, over its contributions to the EU **budget**, which it believes are too high. Both houses of the German parliament convincingly endorsed the **Treaty establishing a Constitution for Europe** in May 2005. In the Bundestag (lower house) some 569 votes were cast in favour of the treaty with only 23 against. In the latter part of 2005 **Angela Merkel** was elected the first female German Chancellor; she headed a grand coalition Government between the Christian Democrats (CDU) and the Social Democrats (SPD). Merkel is largely credited with being responsible for both securing agreement on the budgetary settlement for the period 2007–13 and doing most of the groundwork prior to agreement in the **European Council** on the **Treaty of Lisbon**. Merkel has emerged as one of Europe's most substantial political personalities and successfully ran for re-election as Chancellor in the latter part of 2009. On this occasion the CDU, as it had hoped, was able to remove the 'problematic constraints' of the grand coalition with the SPD by disbanding it and entered instead into a coalition with the smaller Free Democratic Party. Merkel was also centrally involved in the appointment of her fellow Christian Democrat, the Belgian **Herman Van Rompuy**, as the first **President of the European Council** under the terms of the Treaty of Lisbon. In addition, Merkel was at the forefront of plans financially to address the perilous state of the Greek economy in 2010–12 as a means of stabilizing the **euro**. Merkel's efforts at safeguarding the stability of the eurozone and the future of the euro led directly to her key role in the drawing up of the 2012 **Fiscal Compact Treaty** (**Treaty on Stability, Co-ordination and Governance in the Economic and Monetary Union**).

VALÉRY GISCARD D'ESTAING (1926–) has a long and distinguished record in French and European politics. He was elected to the French National Assembly at the age of 29 and rapidly emerged as a leading figure, serving as finance minister and, ultimately, as the President of France between 1974 and 1981. He was one of the most influential figures within the European Communities (EC) in the 1970s. He established a close relationship with **Helmut**

Schmidt of Germany, with whom he sought to utilize and develop the EC as an instrument of pragmatic political co-operation and economic integration in which the **European Commission**, which he disliked, would have a more subordinate role. He was largely responsible for the formalization of what had become the reality of the EC: the involvement of heads of state and of government in the operation and development of the EC as a countermeasure to the setting of goals that were unrealistic and overly ambitious. It was he who in 1974 argued for the institutionalization of **summit meetings** in the form of a **Council of the European Union**. While he supported the creation of the **European Monetary System**, he opposed the entry of Spain for fear of its challenges to French agriculture. His more pragmatic approach may have brought short-term gains to the EC, but it could be said to have contributed to the accumulation of more long-term issues with which the European Council had to struggle in the 1980s.

After his defeat by **François Mitterrand** in the presidential election of 1981, Giscard went on to serve as a **Member of the European Parliament** in the 1980s. His intimate knowledge of the workings of the European Union (EU) was clearly an instrumental factor in his appointment as President of the **European Convention** set up in February 2002 following the **Laeken Declaration** in December 2001. A more important factor was the support he had from **Jacques Chirac**, the French President and a former protégé and Prime Minister of France under Giscard in the 1970s. Giscard chaired the 207-member Convention and after more than 16 months of deliberation formally presented a **Draft Treaty establishing a Constitution for Europe** to the Italian presidency of the European Council in July 2003. The text served as the basis for the negotiations of the **intergovernmental conference** that began in October 2003 and resulted in the **Treaty establishing a Constitution for Europe**. Its rejection by the French people in the May 2005 referendum was a clear disappointment to Giscard, who subsequently campaigned in favour of the Constitutional Treaty's rejuvenation. At the same time he spoke passionately against the admission of **Turkey** into the EU, calling it 'the end of Europe'.

GLOBAL MEDITERRANEAN POLICY: See **Mediterranean Policy**

GLOBALIZATION is one of the major challenges facing the European Union (EU). The phenomenon refers to a process of economic integration on a global level. The main characteristics and driving forces behind globalization are: the liberalization of international trade (through the **World Trade Organization—** WTO) and capital movements; developing technological progress and the advance of the information society; and the process of **deregulation**. All taken together they stimulate international trade by removing barriers and promoting new forms of technology. Many EU policy areas have a global dimension, such as trade policy, **competition policy**, **environmental policy** and the

common foreign and security policy. Some regard globalization with alarm and question how democratic, accountable and legitimate are some of these new forums such as the WTO, and who is taking decisions on the public's behalf. Recent years have seen the emergence of a well co-ordinated anti-capitalist protest movement at gatherings of the WTO and, on occasions, at meetings of the **European Council**.

GOLDEN TRIANGLE is a phrase that has often been used to describe what is commonly perceived to be the economic centre and motivating force of the European Union, an area bounded by Paris, the German Ruhr area and Milan (Italy).

The **GONZALEZ GROUP** is a reflection group established in December 2008 with the goal of identifying how best the European Union (EU) can 'more effectively anticipate and meet challenges in the longer term horizon of 2020 to 2030'. Chaired by **Felipe González Márquez**, the group submitted its report to the European Council on 8 May 2010 during the **euro** crisis. The report—*Project Europe 2030*—urged courageous leadership to address a range of challenges that the EU would face over the next 20 years to 2030. The challenges covered financial governance, social rights, education, research, migration and demographic change, foreign and security policy, and the engagement of EU citizens with the 'European project'.

FELIPE GONZÁLEZ MÁRQUEZ (1942–) became Prime Minister of Spain in 1982. He committed himself fully to membership of the European Communities (EC) as a means of regenerating the weak Spanish economy, and fervently supported moves to intensify European integration, while demanding and ensuring that Spain would continue to be a major beneficiary of EC funding. Conversely, his commitment to **economic and monetary union** imposed severe strains upon Spain. However, he was re-elected in 1993 after winning the Basque and Catalan national votes, and remained Prime Minster until his election defeat in 1996.

The **GOVERNANCE WHITE PAPER** was launched in mid-2001 and sought to open up a debate on the nature and workings of European govern-ance, and essentially contains a set of recommendations on how to enhance and open up democracy in the European Union (EU). The Paper considers how it might be possible to inject the EU institutions with greater legitimacy among the citizens of the EU. Two points should be made about it. Firstly, the timing (late July) was unfortunate and restricted its impact in the media. Secondly, there was a degree of confusion as to the meaning of the term 'governance' across the member states (the word does not exist in some languages). Together these ensured less attention in the media for what amounts to the beginnings of a serious and far-reaching debate. On assuming the presidency of the **European Commission**, **Romano Prodi** had placed considerable emphasis on the concept of governance and identified new forms of European governance as one of his four strategic priorities. Definitions of governance vary widely, but the European Commission adopted its own distinctive definition of the term governance, which it equated to the rules, processes and practices that affect how powers are exercised at the European level. It identified five principles of good governance, namely openness, participation, accountability, effectiveness and coherence. These five principles were supposed to reinforce those of **subsidiarity** and **proportionality**. The White Paper was followed by a public consultation that ended in March 2002 and the Commission pledged to report back with its conclusions by the end of that calendar year. Its findings would be used to provide a firm basis for further inter-institutional co-operation on reforming European governance within the constraints imposed by the existing **founding treaties**.

The Governance White Paper is inevitably interwoven with and forms part of the ongoing 'future of Europe' debate, and it was expected that both would inform and pave the way for further institutional changes at the **intergovernmental conference** (IGC) scheduled for 2004. The Commission, bound by the **Laeken Declaration**, was actively involved with the **European Convention** preceding the IGC and used this White Paper as its reference point.

GRAND CHAMBERS are an innovation of the **Treaty of Nice**. They are composed of the President of the **Court of Justice** and eight other judges.

GREECE is a parliamentary republic and was one of the first countries to approach the **European Economic Community** (EEC) for some form of association in the late 1950s. An **association agreement** was signed in July 1961, coming into effect in November 1962. A **customs union** was to be introduced gradually over a period of 10 years, but, in order to aid the development of Greek industry, a transitional period of 22 years was to apply to most Greek industrial goods. The EEC also agreed to provide loans to Greece during the first five years of the Agreement. The association was soon, however, frozen following the military coup of April 1967 in Greece, its provisions not being reactivated until the restoration of a civilian democratic regime in July 1974. Six months later, the new Greek Government notified the European Communities (EC) that it wished to apply for full membership, with similar transitional arrangements to those that had been part of the first **enlargement** process. The association agreement was restored in December 1974, and a formal application to join the EC submitted in June 1975. Negotiations took four years, and the **Accession Treaty** was signed in Athens in May 1979, with **ratification** occurring the following month. Greece became the 10th member of the EC in January 1981.

After its electoral victory in October 1981, a new left-wing Government criticized the terms of membership accepted by its conservative predecessor for creating and exacerbating economic problems in Greece, and demanded a special status that, based upon a renegotiation of the terms, would take account of what was claimed to be the very different nature of the Greek economy. In 1983 the **European Council** recognized Greece's 'special problems', and negotiations culminated in several concessions to Greece and the adoption in 1985 of the **Integrated Mediterranean Programmes** (IMPs). Greece had earlier indicated that its acceptance of the entry of Portugal and Spain was conditional upon a satisfactory resolution of its complaints.

As one of the poorest members of the European Union (EU), Greece has been a major beneficiary of EU programmes and has been keen to see their expenditure increased. More or less the whole country has priority status for the **structural funds**, and it is a major recipient of the **cohesion policy**, in the form of the **Cohesion Fund**. Under left-wing governments in particular, Greece's attitude towards the EU, especially in terms of foreign policy, has been more openly influenced by national interest than that of most member states, and this has occasionally caused some irritation among its partners. This national interest often emerges over relations with **Turkey** and Cyprus. Overall, however, any assessment of Greek membership should be a positive one. The tensions of the early years of Greek membership were replaced (until recently at least) by a much more pro-EU stance of a younger and less ideo-logical leadership. The country adapted well to EU membership. The Greek people consistently proved to be some of the most integrationist within the EU; the economy grew and there was consistent political stability. Greece joined the **exchange-rate mechanism** (ERM) in March 1998. However, Greece's inability to meet the criteria for **economic and monetary union** (EMU) was not in doubt, and in 1998 it was the only member state wishing to participate in EMU that was excluded from doing so. This did not dilute Greek determination to join, and the country, after meeting the criteria for joining, acceded to EMU in 2001. Greece successfully ratified the **Treaty establishing a Constitution for Europe** in April 2005. The document was backed by 268 votes in the 300-member parliament. Only 17 lawmakers voted against, while another 15 abstained. The New Democracy Party, led by Kostas Karamanlis, took over the reins of government from the Panhellenic Socialist Movement (PASOK) following a convincing win in elections in early March 2004. However, the party was returned to power after a much narrower result in September 2007. The Greek parliament endorsed the **Treaty of Lisbon**. The Greek Conservative Government fared badly at the EP 2009 elections, while the polls brought renewed success for both the Socialist and Communist parties. The Greek results ran very much against the general trend of the EP elections, which saw rising support for the centre-right. This national trend was confirmed when PASOK (under the leadership of George Papandreou) won the national elections in October 2009 and brought the five-year Conservative administration to an end. The new Government soon found itself confronting a severe economic crisis and was compelled to introduce austerity programmes to tackle the huge level of government debt. In so doing, it triggered social unrest and impacted on the stability of the **euro**. The Greek Government was offered a three-year financial rescue package by the EU and the IMF (totalling some €110,000m.) to assist it in its efforts at restoring confidence abroad and support at home. The sense of crisis was such, however, that many analysts were convinced that Greece would eventually default on its debt and come under increasing pressure to leave the eurozone. The economic situation deteriorated further in 2011 as political tensions and anger intensified as unemployment soared. The EU, the **European Central Bank** and the IMF offered Greece a second bailout loan, worth €130,000m., in October on the condition that the country implemented further austerity measures and agreed to a restructuring of its debt. Papandreou resigned as Prime Minister in November to make way for a new national unity government. The second bailout was ratified by all parties in February 2012 and was activated the following month. After an indecisive general election in May failed to lead to the formation of a new government, fresh elections were scheduled for 17 June. At the polls the conservative New Democracy party, led by Antonis Samaras, won a narrow majority of seats and entered into a coalition government with PASOK and the Democratic Left. Samaras' party were pro-euro and fully supported the bailout programme. However, Greek politics have undergone a major change as the 2012 elections heralded the rise of a new political force, the Coalition of the Radical Left (SYRIZA). SYRIZA had been a marginal actor in 2007 when it had secured only 5% of the vote, but, under the leadership of the charismatic Alexis Tsipras, had emerged as the second largest party in Greece in June 2012 (with just under 27% of the vote). SYRIZA is opposed to the austerity programme and rejected a request to join a coalition government.

GREEN CURRENCIES were introduced into the **common agricultural policy** at the end of the 1960s, as a way of preserving the common price structure that had been established after 1962 for most agricultural products. The ability to maintain the common price structure depended upon the continuation of fixed exchange rates. By the end of the 1960s the **Bretton Woods** system of fixed exchange rates was becoming more difficult to sustain, and several currencies had been revalued. The European Communities decided to retain the common agricultural prices at their original level: these prices, expressed in the currencies of each of the member states, were the green currencies. They were artificial price figures that bore no relationship to the actual market prices of agricultural products. In effect, each agricultural product had two prices: its real value and one expressed in green currencies. To adjust the common price structure and the green currencies to the real world, the difference between the two values was covered by **Monetary Compensatory Amounts** (MCAs). The **European Commission** tried for some time to end the system of green currencies, and in 1984 agreement was reached on phasing out MCAs by 1989. In the event, they did not disappear until 1993.

GREEN GROUP: See **Group of the Greens/European Free Alliance**

A **GREEN PAPER** is a Commission document that is intended to stimulate public debate and launch a process of consultation at European level on a particular topic. The Commission produces some 10 Green Papers every year. These consultations may then lead to a **White Paper** (e.g. **Governance White Paper**), which translates the conclusions of the debate into practical proposals for European Union action.

GREENLAND, a Danish colony since 1721, was incorporated into Denmark in 1953. It became part of the European Communities (EC) in 1973, even though in the 1972 Danish referendum some 70% of Greenland's electorate opposed membership. In 1978 Denmark accepted home rule for Greenland, and the enabling legislation included a provision for Greenland to withdraw from the EC if it wished. A narrow majority in favour of **withdrawal** was recorded in a 1982 referendum on the issue and Denmark, still responsible for Greenland's foreign affairs, requested that the **European Commission** revise the treaties to permit withdrawal and the inclusion of Greenland among the **Overseas Countries and Territories** (OCTs). Agreement on the final terms was reached in February 1985, with OCT status being conceded to the island. Greenland remains the only territory to have left the EC.

The **GROUP FOR A EUROPE OF DEMOCRACIES AND DIVERSITIES** (EDD) was a former **party group** in the **European Parliament** (EP). Its members favoured 'a stable and democratic Europe of Nation States' and were not in favour of further European integration and centralization. In 2002 the group had 18 members in the EP, from four countries (Denmark, France, the Netherlands and the United Kingdom). The group represented a varying Eurosceptic voice in the EP and re-formed as the **Independence and Democracy Group** in June 2004. This group, which included the United Kingdom Independence Party (UKIP), was deeply Eurosceptic, rejected the **Treaty of Lisbon** and all moves to a federal superstate, and many members openly called for their own country's withdrawal from the European Union (EU). The group was led by Nigel Farage from UKIP, but, with only 21 members (13 of them from UKIP), it fell short of the 25 **Members of the European Parliament** (MEPs) needed to maintain a political group within the EP after the 2009 elections. The ethos and views of the EDD were quickly reborn within the **Europe of Freedom and Democracy Group**.

GROUP OF EIGHT: See **G-8**

GROUP OF SEVEN: See **G-8**

The **GROUP OF THE ALLIANCE OF LIBERALS AND DEMO-CRATS FOR EUROPE** (ALDE) was formed on 14 July 2004 following the 2004 **European Parliament** (EP) elections. This new group (which arose essentially from the **Group of the European Liberal Democrats**) in 2007 had 104 **Members of the European Parliament** (MEPs), who were drawn from 22 of the member states. It was led by Graham Watson (a United Kingdom MEP). This group constitutes the third largest grouping in the EP and plays a leading role in parliamentary activities. It is one of the most vocal groups in favour of European Union (EU) integration and seeks European solutions to many common challenges and problems. It is a firm supporter of the European single market and has been an advocate of neo-liberalism and greater competition. Its interests have been presented in a 10-point programme that espouses, amongst other things, the need for the EU to: bridge the gap between its economic and political dimensions and be able to speak with one voice on the international stage; secure greater democratization of its functioning; demand the protection of all minorities; aspire to a common economic policy; and aim to make itself the world leader in environmental protection and ensure that **globalization** works for everyone. After the 2009 elections the number of ALDE MEPs declined to 84 (from 19 member states), which in part reflected the reduction in size of the EP from 785 to 736 MEPs. The current President of ALDE is Guy Verhofstadt, a former Prime Minister of Belgium; he is assisted by seven Vice-Presidents.

The **GROUP OF THE EUROPEAN DEMOCRATIC ALLIANCE** (RDE) was a former **party group** in the **European Parliament**. It was established in 1973 (as the Progressive Democratic Group), largely as an arrangement of convenience, by the French Gaullist party (known as the Union des Démocrates (UDR) until 1976, as the Rassemblement pour la République (RPR) from then until 2002, and as the Union pour un Mouvement Populaire (UMP) since then) and the nationalist Irish party, Fianna Fáil, neither of which regarded any of the other available party groups as a natural home. While there were strains within the RDE, a common position was found in several policy areas, including agricultural, regional and social policy. In mid-1995 the RDE merged with **Forza Europa** to form what would become the **Union for Europe of the Nations Group**.

The **GROUP OF THE EUROPEAN LIBERAL DEMOCRATS** (ELDR) was one of the oldest **party groups** in the **European Parliament** (EP). In 2002 it was the third largest group in the EP, containing 53 **Members of the**

European Parliament (MEPs), although the Group was considerably smaller than the **Group of the Party of European Socialists** (PSE) and the **Group of the European People's Party** (EPP). The ELDR historically played a pivotal role between these two larger forces. Generally centrist in orientation, it experienced strains between its left- and right-wing elements, which reduced its cohesion and effectiveness. The arrival of the Nordic centre parties in the ELDR increased group heterogeneity. Throughout its existence the ELDR remained fully committed to deeper European Union integration. Following the 2004 European elections, the ELDR was replaced by the **Group of the Alliance of Liberals and Democrats for Europe** (ALDE). (See also **Group of the European People's Party (Christian Democrats) and European Democrats**.)

The **GROUP OF THE EUROPEAN PEOPLE'S PARTY (CHRISTIAN DEMOCRATS)** (EPP) is the new name adopted by the **Group of the European People's Party (Christian Democrats) and European Democrats** after the 2009 elections to the European Parliament. The current Chairman of the group is Joseph Daul.

The **GROUP OF THE EUROPEAN PEOPLE'S PARTY (CHRISTIAN DEMOCRATS) AND EUROPEAN DEMOCRATS** (EPP–ED) united Christian Democrat, Conservative and other mainstream centre and centre-right political forces from across the 27-member European Union until the 2009 elections to the European Parliament. The current group, renamed the **Group of the European People's Party (Christian Democrats)** (EPP) after the British Conservative Party and other European Democrat parties left to form the **European Conservatives and Reformists Group**, has its origins in the Group of the European People's Party (EPP), which was one of the first transnational **party groups** to emerge in the **European Parliament** (EP). Christian Democrats had dominated the assembly from 1951 through to 1975 and, in anticipation of the introduction of **direct elections**, in 1976 they formed the EPP, self-consciously constituting a party rather than a federation of national groups. The EPP was strongly committed to European integration, desiring more powers to be given to the supranational institutions, and favoured a federalist structure for Europe. While broadly Christian Democrat and moderate centre-right in orientation, it contained both progressive and conservative strands, which were not always exactly consistent with national delegations. From 1979 it was generally one of the two largest party groups in the EP, and in 1992 it also absorbed the **European Democratic Group** (ED). Following the 1999 elections, it became the largest group, with 233 **Members of the European Parliament** (MEPs). The results of the 2004 EP elections guaranteed the EPP–ED its relative majority with some 268 seats (out of 732), although by April 2006 this had fallen to 264. Following the accession of Bulgaria and Romania in January 2007, membership increased again, to 278.

This group remained the largest parliamentary group, and was the only one with deputies from all 27 member states of the Union. Given its size, it was arguably in the best position to influence the EP's political agenda. Its strength was reflected in the fact that, from 1999, the EPP–ED Group was on the winning side of more votes than any other group in the EP's monthly plenary sessions. The size of this party also ensured that EPP–ED group members held a range of key positions within the Parliament. For example, in the sixth parliament (2004–09), its members held the chairmanships of nine of the EP's 22 committees or subcommittees, seven of its 14 vice-presidencies and three of its five quaestorships. Within the parliamentary committees, EPP–ED group members were well placed to secure the right to author the EP's position on key pieces of draft legislation and other major reports. Moreover, the Group secured more of these rapporteurships, on more important subjects, than any other group. Although the Conservative Party's 25 MEPs left the EPP group as intended in June 2009, the EPP remained by far the largest group within the EP after the 2009 elections, with 265 members.

GROUP OF THE EUROPEAN UNITARIAN LEFT: See **Confederal Group of the European United Left/Nordic Green Left**

The **GROUP OF THE GREENS/EUROPEAN FREE ALLIANCE** in the **European Parliament** (EP) was formed in July 1999, and is made up of two main groups—Greens and environmentalists on the one hand, and representatives of 'stateless nations' (i.e. Wales, Scotland and the Basque region) or regions on the other. This group first emerged after the 1984 **direct elections** when nine representatives of national Green parties were elected to the EP. Under EP rules, however, this was an insufficient number to be recognized as a separate party group, and consequently the Green representatives joined with a heterogeneous collection of other **Members of the European Parliament** (**MEPs**) to form the **Rainbow Group**. The Green Group did not become a separate **party group** until 1989, following a significant increase in membership. It has continued to evolve. The Group of the Greens/European Free Alliance in the EP is the product of the political will of two separate and progressive European political families to co-operate in order to strengthen their mutual political interests in the EP. The group has since established itself as one of the main voices within the Parliament. It has been an increasingly cohesive force and has focused its energies on environmental protection, the decentralization of power and gender equality. It is generally well disposed towards the European integration process. Following the June 2004 elections, it had 42 MEPs from 13 member states (a marginal decrease from 45 MEPs following the 1999 elections). The MEPs came from Austria, Belgium, Denmark, Finland, France, Germany, Italy, Latvia, Luxembourg, the Netherlands, Spain, Sweden and the United Kingdom. The group became the fourth largest force in the EP. The Group's Bureau (or executive) is made up of eight members. Unlike all the other groups in the EP, the Greens/EFA have a co-presidency, i.e. two co-Presidents, always one male and one female. In 2012 the co-Presidents were Rebecca Harms and Daniel Cohn-Bendit. The first vice-presidency is held by the President of the European Free Alliance. The group polled particularly well at the 2009 EP elections and increased its membership to 55 MEPs (from some 17 member states).

The **GROUP OF THE PROGRESSIVE ALLIANCE OF SOCIALISTS AND DEMOCRATS IN THE EUROPEAN PARLIAMENT** (S&D) is the new name adopted by the former **Group of the Party of European Socialists** after the 2009 elections to the European Parliament.

The **GROUP OF THE PARTY OF EUROPEAN SOCIALISTS** (PSE) was one of the **party groups** in the **European Parliament** (EP) before it was succeeded in 2009 by the Group of the Progressive Alliance of Socialists and Democrats in the European Parliament (S&D). Between 1973 and the late 1990s it was consistently the largest group in the EP. Despite the common political background of its representatives, the group has often been divided by major ideological and policy issues. While it has permitted free votes in debates, it made great efforts to develop a common position on as many issues as possible, by means of pre-committee caucuses and working parties. The party group brings together the social democratic and socialist parties across the European Union (EU). The largest national groups within the PSE/S&D have traditionally come from the Social Democratic Party in Germany, the French and Spanish Socialist Parties and the Labour Party in the United Kingdom. The S&D supports deeper integration, particularly in the environmental and social fields. It campaigns on environmental issues, calls for social justice and decent minimum wages and supports the **Treaty of Lisbon**. In terms of representation, the PSE became the second major party group following the 1999 EP elections when it secured 181 **Members of the European Parliament** (MEPs). Despite an increase in representation (to 200) within the Parliament following the 2004 elections, reaching 218 after the accession of Bulgaria and Romania on 1 January 2007, it remained the second major force after the **European People's Party and European Democrats** (EPP–ED). This position did not alter after the 2009 EP elections when the vote for the centre-left declined in many EU member states and led to the return of 183 MEPs representing the group (under its new name of the Progressive Alliance of Socialists and Democrats in the European Parliament). The group's members are drawn from all of the 27 member states.

The Socialist Group is a major force and its input to, and support of, the legislative work of the EP is indispensable. Under the leadership of the Group President, Hannes Swoboda, the group works to enhance perspectives for European society and to implement changes. Its activities are co-ordinated by the Bureau, which comprises the Group President, the seven Vice-Presidents and the Treasurer. They are supported by National Delegation members along with the staff and secretariat.

GROUPS IN THE EUROPEAN PARLIAMENT: See Party Groups

The **GRUNDTVIG** programme is designed to promote and encourage adult education. The Commission's action in this area is aimed at enhancing the European dimension of lifelong learning, and from 2007 Grundtvig was incorporated into the new **Lifelong Learning Programme 2007–13**. It supports a wide range of activities designed to promote innovation and the improved availability, accessibility and quality of educational provision for adults, by means of European co-operation.

GSP: See **Generalized System of Preferences**

GUARANTEE THRESHOLDS were introduced in 1986 as a means of limiting the open-ended nature of production **subsidies** in the **common agricultural policy** that had been a consequence of the guaranteed price system. With the imposition of guarantee thresholds on agricultural products, an upper limit has been placed upon automatic financial support, with no subsidies given for production that exceeds the thresholds.

GUE/NGL: See **Confederal Group of the European United Left/Nordic Green Left**

GUIDE PRICES are prices offered to farmers for beef and veal under the **common agricultural policy**. They are the same as target prices. Guide prices also apply under the **common fisheries policy**.

The **FIRST GULF WAR** occurred in early 1991 when a **USA**-led coalition of states attacked Iraq. The origins of this international crisis date to August 1990, when Saddam Hussain, the Iraqi President, launched an invasion of Kuwait. At this point in the development of the European Union (EU), plans were being laid in the **intergovernmental conferences** that resulted in the **Treaty on European Union** (TEU). The Gulf War was significant as it focused the attention of member states on the issue of whether the EU should have some form of political role and even a military role. This would have been a major step in EU integration. The **European Defence Community** project of the early 1950s had proved just how controversial this area was, and little had changed some 40 years later. The Gulf War and the conflicts in **Yugoslavia** in the early 1990s could not persuade the governments of the member states to allow the EU a substantial military role. However, the TEU began the process, albeit tentatively. Throughout the 1990s doubts still lingered, principally in the USA, regarding Iraq's military capabilities and intentions and these were fuelled by Saddam Hussain's efforts to block several UN-backed searches for weapons of mass destruction (WMDs). Frustrated and angered by Iraq's defiance, the US Government under George W. Bush, with the diplomatic and military support of the Governments of the United Kingdom, Spain and Poland, finally launched a second Gulf War in March 2003. On this occasion, Saddam Hussain's regime was overthrown with relative ease, but to the detriment of the United Kingdom's relations with both France and Germany, which strongly opposed the war.

GYMNICH MEETINGS is a term that refers to specialist ministerial meetings that are held in conjunction with the **summit meetings** of the **European Council**. They are designed to be informal and private sessions without any detailed agenda, in order to permit ministers to consider longer-term issues and problems without being pressurized to reach a decision. The name derives from Schloss Gymnich in Germany where the first such gathering was held.

H

HAGUE CONGRESS: See **Congress of Europe**

The **HAGUE SUMMIT** of December 1969 was only the third summit meeting of the **Six** since the **Treaty of Rome**, and the first since the French vetoes on British membership of the European Communities (EC) and the **empty chair crisis**. The newly elected French President, Georges Pompidou, took the initiative in calling for a summit meeting that would address directly the several problems and issues facing the Six. The summit opened the way to the **enlargement** of the EC; it established guidelines for the consolidation and development of common policies; and it reaffirmed political union as the ultimate objective of the EC. More specifically, it endorsed proposals for the financing of the **common agricultural policy**, for extending the budgetary powers of the **European Parliament**, for full **economic and monetary union** to be reached by 1980, and for the development of closer political co-ordination. It heralded the new style of **decision-making** focusing on strategic leadership from heads of government and state (later institutionalized through the **European Council**), which would characterize the EC after 1970.

JOHANNES HAHN (1957–) is one of the 27 European Commissioners in the **Barroso** II Commission (2010–14), within which he has responsibility for **regional policy**. Hahn was born in Vienna and studied law and then philosophy at the city's university. He is a member of the Austrian People's Party (ÖVP) and, prior to becoming a European Commissioner (since January 2007), he was the Minister for Science and Research in the Austrian Government.

WALTER HALLSTEIN (1901–82) was the first President of the **European Commission**, serving from 1958 to 1967. He had led the West German delegation to the conference that discussed the **Schuman Plan** in 1950, and had attended the meeting in **Messina** in June 1955 that agreed to establish a **common market**. He believed strongly in economic and political integration, enjoyed considerable personal prestige throughout the **Six**, but especially in France, and in 1958 began to make the Commission the motivating force of the European Communities (EC). His vigorous leadership contributed to the rapid development of the EC in their first years of operation. Hallstein saw the

Commission as the nucleus of a future European government and on one occasion said that he could be regarded as a kind of European Prime Minister. He held a large part of the responsibility for some of the proposals rejected by President **Charles de Gaulle**, which led to the **empty chair crisis** of 1965. Hallstein interpreted the resolution of the crisis through the **Luxembourg Compromise** as effectively reducing the primary role of the Commission as the initiator of policy and the core of the EC. With his chances of re-election as President doubtful in 1967, he chose instead to resign.

HARD CORE: See **Core Europe**

The **HARD ECU** was conceived by the British Government in 1990 as an alternative to the **Delors Plan**, which proposed a single currency and a **European Central Bank** as the integral elements of **economic and monetary union**. The alternative proposal was for a strong European Currency Unit (**ecu**)—the hard ecu—that could not be devalued and would exist alongside the national currencies within a framework administered by a European Monetary Fund. It failed to generate support from other governments.

HARMONIZATION is a term used to describe the process whereby national policies and standards are brought more closely in line with one another. To many, it is synonymous with **approximation**, although legally speaking it involves a greater degree of integration. The harmonization and approximation of **legislation** are central to the **internal market** programme. Legislative harmonization and approximation with the *acquis communautaire* also feature as an obligation placed on non-member states in their relations with the European Union.

HEADS OF GOVERNMENT: See **European Council; Summit Meetings**

HEALTH AND SAFETY, particularly with regard to the provision of satisfactory conditions for workers at their place of employment, have been a long-standing concern of the European Union (EU), as was reconfirmed in the **Treaty on European Union**. General policy initiation in the area of health and safety is the responsibility of two **European Commission** agencies, the Advisory Committee on Safety, Hygiene and Health Protection at Work and the **European Foundation for the Improvement of Living and Working Conditions**. A more specific occupational remit rests with the Mines Safety and Health Commission. Health and safety also figure prominently in EU **consumer policy** and **environmental policy**. As a result of the **Single European Act**, **directives** and **regulations** on health and safety required only a **qualified majority vote** in the **Council of the European Union**.

Hence supporters of several initiatives, notably the **Working Time Directive** and many deriving from the Social Chapter (see **Charter of Fundamental Social Rights of Workers**), attempted to have the Council consider them under the rubric of health and safety, before the **Treaty of Amsterdam** incorporated the **protocol** based on the Social Chapter into the **Treaty of Rome** and extended the use of qualified majority voting to this area.

The **HEALTH POLICY** competences of the European Union (EU) are limited to the promotion of public health. They do not concern the organization of health-care provision. Hence, the efforts of the EU have been restricted to co-ordinating and enhancing national policies on health awareness and health protection. This has led to campaigns on AIDS, cancer and drug dependence. In October 2007 the **European Commission** presented a **White Paper** entitled *Together for Health: A Strategic Approach for the EU 2008–13*. The titles of the four main principles of the new health strategy were: A Strategy Based on Shared Health Values, Health is the Greatest Wealth, Health in All Policies and Strengthening the EU's Voice in Global Health. The three main objectives specified in the document were: fostering good health in an ageing Europe, protecting citizens from health threats, and supporting dynamic health systems and new technologies. The strategy was to be implemented in tandem with member states, regions and stakeholders, through a number of financial and organisational instruments created by the Commission.

EDWARD HEATH (1916–2005) was the leader of the United Kingdom's delegation to the negotiations over British entry to the European Communities (EC), held in 1961–63. As Conservative Prime Minister after June 1970, he was responsible for the renewal of discussions on British entry that were made possible by the decision of the 1969 **Hague summit** on **enlargement**. Heath had always been a committed supporter of European unity, the necessity of which had been the theme of his first speech in the House of Commons. Despite a growing popular rejection of the EC, he successfully ensured the support of the majority of his own party for membership. His major concerns in the negotiations were to secure a satisfactory transitional period of adjustment, and the adoption by the EC of a **regional policy** that would benefit the weaker British economy. His defeat in the first 1974 general election led to a Labour Party Government that was much more sceptical about, and badly divided over, membership of the EC, which contributed to the United Kingdom's isolated position in the EC, and possibly to a reduction of its potential influence in the organization.

CONNIE HEDEGAARD (1960–) is one of the 27 European Commissioners in the Barroso II Commission (2010–14), within which she has responsibility for climate action. Hedegaard was successfully nominated by the Danish

Government. Her recent background has equipped her for her current post. After studying literature and history at university, Hedegaard entered the Danish parliament in 1984 as a member of the Danish Conservative Party, but left in 1990 to pursue a career in journalism, before returning to parliament in 2004 and entering government, first as Minister for the Environment (2004–07) and Minister for Nordic Co-operation (2005–07), and then as Minister for Climate and Energy (2007–09).

HELSINKI FINAL ACT: See **Organization for Security and Co-operation in Europe**

HELSINKI GROUP: See **Accession Negotiations**

HIGH AUTHORITY: See **European Coal and Steel Community**

The **HIGH REPRESENTATIVE FOR THE COMMON FOREIGN AND SECURITY POLICY** was a post created under the terms of the **Treaty of Amsterdam** to provide a higher profile for the European Union's (EU) **common foreign and security policy** (CFSP). The **Secretary-General of the Council of the European Union** acted as the High Representative and, drawing on the French acronym for the CFSP, was often referred to as Monsieur or Madame PESC. The High Representative, along with the European Commissioner responsible for external relations and the representative of the **Council presidency**, constituted the EU's **Troika**, which represented the EU internationally. The first High Representative was **Javier Solana**. He was expected to become the first **Union Minister for Foreign Affairs**, once the **Treaty establishing a Constitution for Europe** was ratified. However, non-**ratification** of the treaty meant that the post was never created. Instead, the **Treaty of Lisbon** provided for the upgrading and cumbersome renaming of the post as **High Representative of the Union for Foreign Affairs and Security Policy**.

The **HIGH REPRESENTATIVE OF THE UNION FOR FOREIGN AFFAIRS AND SECURITY POLICY** is the new title for the **High Representative for the Common Foreign and Security Policy**, under the **Treaty of Lisbon**. The renaming of the post is accompanied by new powers. The first post-holder is Baroness **Catherine Ashton**, who was appointed by the **European Council** in late 2009 and took up her post in December. She chairs meetings of the Council of Ministers (see **Council of the European Union**) dealing with foreign affairs. She is also a Vice-President of the **European Commission**. The main responsibilities of the High Representative are to conduct and develop the **common foreign and security policy** (CFSP) and the **European security and defence policy**, with assistance in fulfilling these tasks from a **European External Action Service**. The creation of this 'double-hatted' post is designed to provide greater coherence and prominence to the role of the European Union (EU) in international affairs, although there is some concern over whether the High Representative's role in representing the EU will conflict with that of the **President of the European Council**, who is also responsible for the external representation of the EU on issues concerning the CFSP.

FRANÇOIS HOLLANDE (1954–) was elected as the new President of France on 6 May 2012, defeating the incumbent **Nicolas Sarkozy**. He became the second Socialist President of the Fifth French Republic (1958–) after **François Mitterrand** (1981–95). Hollande was born in Normandy but moved to Paris with his family at the age of 13 years. He graduated from the École Nationale d'Administration in 1980 and immediately entered the world of politics, working his way through various stages from advisor, to political candidate and eventually to elected politician. In March 2011 Hollande declared his candidacy to seek the nomination of the Parti Socialiste (PS) to contest the presidency. Following the withdrawal of the frontrunner Dominique Strauss-Kahn from the race to be selected as the Socialist presidential candidate (following his arrest in New York, USA, in May on charges of sexual assault), Hollande was selected as the presidential candidate of the PS at the party's primary election in October. In the first round of the presidential election, which was held on 22 April 2012, Hollande narrowly defeated Sarkozy, with 28.63% of the vote. At the second round of elections held on 6 May Hollande defeated Sarkozy, winning 51.64% of the votes, compared with Sarkozy's 48.36%. It is expected that, as President, Hollande will be keen to intensify France's working relationship with **Germany** (although differences may surface over the issue of austerity programmes and the **euro**). He supports the establishment of a European rating agency and wants to reassess the possibility of combining the positions of President of the **European Council** and President of the **European Commission**.

WERNER HOYER (1951–) assumed his current post as the seventh President of the **European Investment Bank** in January 2012. Hoyer was born in Wuppertal, Germany, and read economics at the University of Cologne. Following his attainment of a doctorate, he commenced his professional career as a senior research assistant/lecturer at the University of Cologne, specializing in international economics before being elected to the (West) German parliament in 1987 as a member of the Free Democratic Party (which he had joined in 1972). Hoyer served in **Helmut Kohl's** fifth and final administration as the Minister for State at the Foreign Office (1994–98) and held the same position in **Angela Merkel's** second administration during 2009–11.

HUMAN RIGHTS have become an increasingly important issue in debates over the role and future of the European Union (EU) since reference to respect for fundamental rights was included in the **Treaty on European Union** (TEU) in 1993 and later expanded by the **Treaty of Amsterdam**, which declared the EU to be founded on respect for human rights and fundamental freedoms. The rights themselves are not explicitly listed anywhere in the EU's treaty base. Instead, reference is made to the **European Convention on Human Rights** (formally the Convention for the Protection of Human Rights and Fundamental Freedoms) adopted by the **Council of Europe** in 1950, and to the constitutional traditions of the member states. This did not prevent the drawing up in 2000 of a **Charter of Fundamental Rights** of the EU. Nor has it prevented the EU in its external relations from making respect for human rights a precondition for closer ties and, indeed, membership. The EU has not, however, signed the European Convention on Human Rights, the **European Court of Justice** ruling in 1996 that it did not have the competence to do so.

That human rights enjoy an increasingly higher profile in the EU is underlined by the fact that a member state's suspected breach of them may be investigated. Ultimately its voting rights, as well as other rights deriving from the TEU and **Treaty of Rome**, may be suspended where a serious and persistent breach is confirmed.

HUMANITARIAN ASSISTANCE is an area in which the European Union is active as part of the **common foreign and security policy**. To this end it funds a **European Community Humanitarian Office**. Formal recognition of its involvement in humanitarian assistance work appeared in the **Treaty establishing a Constitution for Europe** and is now contained in the **Treaty of Lisbon**.

HUNGARY indicated, soon after the fall of the Communist regime in 1989, that it wished for a closer relationship with and eventual membership of the European Communities (EC) once it had adapted its economy to market conditions. A **Europe agreement** was signed in 1991, and the EC accepted in principle the possibility of membership, although not for a number of years. Hungary submitted a formal application for membership in March 1994. In **Agenda 2000** it was recognized as one of the best-placed applicants for membership and was invited to open **accession negotiations** in March 1998. These were concluded in December 2002 and in the following April almost 84% of those participating in a referendum opted for accession to the European Union (EU). The Hungarian Government welcomed the result and duly signed the **Accession Treaty** on 16 April 2003. The vote was not regarded, however, as an emphatic endorsement of EU membership: only 46% of the electorate actually participated in the referendum. Following its entry into the EU on 1 May 2004, Hungary became the second country to ratify the **Treaty establishing a Constitution for Europe**, with a parliamentary vote (304 votes to 9) in December 2004. It was the first member state to ratify the **Treaty of Lisbon** in December 2007, the same month that the country became part of the EU's **Schengen Area**.

I

ICELAND played little part in European developments during the first two decades following the Second World War. It joined the **European Free Trade Association** (EFTA) only in March 1970. The following November it began talks with the European Communities (EC) along with the other non-applicant EFTA states, and formal negotiations began the following year. These were hindered by Iceland's unilateral decision in 1972 to expand its territorial fishing limits to 50 nautical miles (93 kilometres). Although a **free trade agreement** was ratified in February 1973, the EC insisted that a satisfactory settlement of the fishing dispute had to be reached before Iceland would be allowed to obtain the full benefits of the Agreement, and an acceptable compromise was not reached until July 1976. After this, there were no significant qualitative changes in the relationship with the EC until the late 1980s, when discussions, followed by negotiations, on the **European Economic Area** (EEA) began. This arrangement satisfied Iceland's desire for access to the **internal market**. Hence, unlike most of its EFTA partners, Iceland did not apply for EC membership. Successive Icelandic governments remained rather sceptical on the subject of European Union (EU) entry. This attitude did not, however, prevent relations with the EU from developing further. Iceland, along with **Norway**, negotiated participation in the **Schengen Agreement** and regularly associated itself with EU positions adopted as part of the **common foreign and security policy**. The economic and financial turmoil unleashed in late 2008 had a heavy impact on Iceland, were banks had severely overstretched themselves on capital and bond markets. The crisis and ensuing credit crunch shook the economic and political infrastructure of Iceland to its core, toppled the Government and led Iceland to consider for the first time the possibility of EU membership. A new centre-left (Social Democrats and Greens) coalition Government, formed after elections in April 2009, was determined to bring the issue before parliament for debate. In July, after intense debate, the Icelandic parliament voted in favour (33 votes to 28, with two abstentions) of initiating the process for EU membership. The application was submitted later that month. The application was generally welcomed within the EU, although it was clear that accession was not a foregone conclusion. The period prior to the Commission's generally positive *avis* in February 2010 was overshadowed by a dispute with the United Kingdom and the Netherlands over the level of compensation that Iceland should pay British and Dutch investors in the collapsed Icesave bank. Iceland opened **accession negotiations** in July 2010, but these proved to be far more protracted than had been assumed despite Iceland's already close integration with the EU through the EEA. Negotiations over fishing and the **common fisheries policy** were expected to be particularly problematic. Added to this, popular support in Iceland for membership began to decline following the application, raising the question of whether any successfully negotiated **accession treaty** would be passed in a referendum. Negotiations continued, however, although by mid-2012—the Icelandic Government's original target date for accession—only 10 of the 35 negotiating chapters had been closed.

IDEA is an electronic directory of European Union (EU) institutions, the Inter-institutional Directory of the EU, accessible via the internet and in book form.

The **IDENTITY, TRADITION AND SOVEREIGNTY GROUP (ITS)** party group emerged in the sixth **European Parliament** (2004–09). It was established in January 2007 and had 23 members, thereby just surpassing the minimum requirement (of 20) for an EP political group. It largely owed its creation to the arrival of a number of Bulgarian (one) and Romanian (six) **Members of the European Parliament** (MEPs) after accession on 1 January 2007. The ITS was a rather loose-knit group which belonged to the right of the party spectrum and included such personalities as Jean Marie le Pen, toge-ther with five other members of the French Front National, and Alessandra Mussolini. The group highlighted a number of core values including: the recognition of national interests, sovereignties, identities and differences; a commitment to Christian values, heritage, culture and the traditions of Eur-opean civilization; a commitment to the traditional family as the natural unit within society; and strident opposition to a unitary and bureaucratic European superstate. It also espoused strong views on immigration and objected to Turkish accession to the European Union (EU). The ITS represented another Eurosceptic voice in the EP. This group was always volatile and had been created through political opportunity. It disintegrated in November 2007 after Alessandra Mussolini was deemed to have made disparaging remarks about Romanians and work ethics, whereupon the members from the Greater Romania Party withdrew from the ITS. This reduction in membership caused the disqualification of the ITS from its short-lived recognition as an official EP party group.

IEPG: See **Independent European Programme Group**

IFOP is the acronym (from *Instrument financier d'orientation de la pêche*) of a financial guidance instrument for fisheries that was established in 1994 and ran until 2006. It was intended to take over the financing of adaptation and mod-ernization of fisheries structures within the ambit of the **structural funds**.

IGC: See **Intergovernmental Conference**

IMMIGRATION POLICY was a low priority for the European Communities (EC) until the 1980s, and member states were free to pursue their own policies. A more structured approach began to emerge after the creation of **TREVI** (Terrorisme, Radicalisme, Extrémisme, Violence Internationale), and an ad hoc **Group on Immigration** was established in 1986 to work for greater co-operation on improving controls at the external borders of the EC and on the granting of visas. Although the political changes in **Central and Eastern Europe** after 1989 contributed to greater immigration pressure, the member states were reluctant to relinquish total control of immigration policy to the EC. Under the **Treaty on European Union**, only visas became a **competence** of the EC, immigration being incorporated into the then intergovernmental **pillar** of **justice and home affairs**. Closer co-operation in immigration policies was also a feature of the **Treaty of Amsterdam**, which conferred powers on the European Union (EU) in areas of migration and asylum. The **European Commission** believes that the ideal approach to the issue of immigration is an open procedure for co-ordination that will lead to the identification of common objectives that will, in turn, create pressure for a European response. To this end the Commission undertakes to co-ordinate national policies, to exchange best practices, to monitor the impact of EU policy and to organize regular consultations with third countries.

At the 1999 Tampere **European Council**, the member states set out the four key areas for the development of a common policy on asylum and immigration. These were: a solid partnership with the countries of origin; the establishment of a common European asylum system; fair treatment of third-country nationals; and a more efficient management of migration flows. In 2000 and 2001 the European Commission proposed several new measures that would facilitate the development of a common policy on asylum and migration. For example, the Commission proposed a directive on family reunification and another on the status of third-country nationals who have been long-term residents. In addition, the **Council of the European Union** adopted **directives** on the mutual recognition of decisions on the expulsion of third-country nationals and on harmonizing financial penalties imposed on carriers transporting into the EU third-country nationals lacking the documents necessary for admission. To assist the member states in their examination of immigration, the Council established the Centre for Information, Discussion and Exchange on the Crossing of Frontiers and Immigration (CIREFI) in 1992. This collected information on a range of issues including: legal immigration; illegal immigration; the entry of aliens through facilitator networks; and the use of falsified documents. As well as providing advice, it also encouraged the exchange of information. CIREFI reported to the Council on an annual basis. In December 2009 the **Committee of Permanent Representatives** decided to abolish CIREFI and to transfer its activities to **FRONTEX** and the Working Party on Frontiers. Since May 1999 an early warning system for the transmission of information on illegal immigration has been operational. In June 2002 immigration policy was discussed at a **summit meeting** held in Seville, Spain. (See also **Schengen Agreement**.) The availability of comparable statistics is of crucial importance for the effective monitoring of the immigration policy. At present, **Eurostat** compiles migration data in its work on demography. However, the data collected do not give reasons for migration or its duration. The Commission has suggested that statistics on legal entry and stay be compiled on a monthly basis. By the beginning of 2004 the issue of immigration had emerged again as a major theme in the domestic arenas of practically all the member states. Much of the media interest in the subject was directly linked to the implications of **enlargement** of the EU in May 2004 and was somewhat sensationalist. Given public attitudes and the recent successes of extreme right-wing political movements in parts of Europe, most member states, with the notable exception of Ireland and the United Kingdom, decided to impose restrictions on the free movement of people from **Central and Eastern Europe**. The 2004 Hague programme reiterated the Tampere objectives. Immigration policy in the EU has further developed as member states have sought to secure greater intra-European co-operation on the issue of a common **asylum** and immigration policy that affects them all.

IMP: See **Integrated Mediterranean Programmes**

IMPLEMENTATION is a crucial aspect of the process of European integration. As the European Union (EU) has evolved, so the body of laws and commitments aimed at establishing a genuine **internal market** has expanded. These laws have to be adhered to at national level, such as, for example, **environmental policy** and **competition policy**, if the project is to operate effectively and efficiently. However, this is not unproblematic, as member states may seek to delay or resist implementation for a variety of reasons, ranging from a dislike of a particular piece of **legislation** to a lack of sufficient technical expertise to apply EU rules. Implementation centres on the following three broad areas: transposition of EU law into national law; the application of EU law by the relevant national authorities; and the enforcement of EU law, including penalties for non-compliance. The **European Commission** has general responsibility for all implementation issues but, given its limited resources, it relies heavily on other specialized agencies (e.g. the **European Medicines Agency**) or on complaints from the wider public to inform it of cases of non-implementation. In order both to embarrass non-compliant member states and accelerate implementation relating to the completion of the single market, the **Directorate-General** responsible for the internal market initiated an internal market scoreboard to reveal the degree of implementation in each of the member states. This sort of **transparency** seems to work, but continues to reveal the existence of numerous infringements. Many questions remain over the ability of the **candidate countries** to implement the full *acquis communautaire* on joining the EU. Derogations or transitional periods are likely to be granted. Overall, the Commission does very little in the way of direct implementation and is much more concerned with indirect implementation, i.e. ensuring that the member states carefully transpose EU laws into national laws. One of its few areas of direct implementation is **competition policy**.

The **INDEPENDENCE AND DEMOCRACY GROUP** (ID) is a former **party group**. It was established in July 2004 following the 2004 **European Parliament** (EP) elections. It incorporated European Union (EU) critics, **Eurosceptics** and Eurorealists. It emerged following the rebranding of the former **Group for a Europe of Diversities and Democracies** (EDD) within the EP. The new group was numerically considerably stronger than the EDD, and in the 2004–09 parliament initially had 37 deputies (from nine member states) as opposed to 17 (from four) in the 1999–2004 parliament. In 2006, however, the delegation from Italy (Lega Nord) left the group, reducing the number of deputies to 24. The largest political party within the group was the United Kingdom Independence Party (UKIP), with 10 members, while other representatives were drawn from the Czech Republic (one), Denmark (one), France (three), Greece (one), Ireland (one), the Netherlands (two), Poland (three) and Sweden (two). The group was co-chaired by Jens-Peter Bonde, a Danish **Member of the European Parliament** (MEP), and Nigel Farage, a British MEP, and was essentially a marriage of convenience between two factions that had combined to fight and prevent the **ratification** of the **Treaty establishing a Constitution for Europe**. However, they had differing perspectives on the process of European integration. One, a more moderate wing, sought greater **transparency** in terms of EU decision-making and certainly did not advocate leaving the EU, while the second sought nothing less than **withdrawal** from the EU. National groups, such as the June Movement in Denmark and the French Mouvement pour la France, represented elements of the former position, while UKIP was the best example and the largest force in the latter group. Although at the 2009 elections UKIP secured 13 seats, the ID 'family' fell short of winning enough support and sufficient MEPs to obtain group status within the existing EP. The 13 members from UKIP now sit in the newly formed **Europe of Freedom and Democracy Group** (EFD).

INDUSTRIAL POLICY was not developed by the European Communities (EC) in any comprehensive or integrated form, although the **European Commission** launched a discussion paper dealing with a general EC industrial policy in November 1990. This new emphasis represented nothing less than a complete transformation in Commission thinking as it moved away markedly from espousing direct intervention in the economy to seeking to boost European industrial **competitiveness**. The change was later reflected in the restructuring of the Commission in 2000 that saw the former **Directorate-General** (DG) III (Industry) being rebranded as DG Enterprise. Indeed, industrial policy has likewise been rebranded as **enterprise policy**. (However, the current Directorate-General is now entitled the DG for Enterprise and Industry.) The **Treaty on European Union** in 1993 provided industry with its own specific **article** in the **Treaty of Rome** (Article 157, now Article 173 of the **Treaty on the Functioning of the European Union**). This requires the member states to secure the conditions necessary for the competitiveness of European Union (EU) industry. The EU is empowered to take special measures to boost industry, but only so long as these measures do not interfere with or distort competition. In 1995 the Commission presented an action programme that contained four major priority areas to strengthen industrial competitiveness. These were: solidifying the **internal market**; encouraging **research and technological development**; promoting the **information society**; and promoting industrial co-operation. Collectively, however, EU enterprise policy, research and development policy, **regional policy**, **social policy**, **competition policy**, **workers' rights**, **energy policy**, **transport policy** and **environmental policy** can be said to constitute an industrial policy. The basic concern has been to increase the efficiency and competitiveness of any industry within a free-market ethos. Apart from policies aimed at specifically targeted industries such as **coal** and **steel**, further general objectives have been industrial development in the poorer regions of the EU, a restructuring of traditional, declining industries (including retraining for those workers needing to be redeployed), and the encouragement of transnational collaboration in new technology-orientated industries.

While modern and often successful, European business and industry cannot afford to rest on their laurels. It is a constant challenge to remain competitive and keep up with technology. Meeting the challenge successfully is essential for sustainable growth and for greater prosperity and, consequently, EU enterprise policy seeks to play its part by fostering innovation, entrepreneurship and competitiveness in manufacturing and services. Innovation and entrepreneurship have emerged as central tenets of enterprise policy. The **European Commission** is the focal point for ensuring that innovation policy is coherent and cohesive across the EU, for benchmarking performance, for disseminating best practice, and for highlighting lessons to be learned from any failure of the market economy that might justify state intervention.

The EU's 23m. **small and medium-sized enterprises** (SMEs) are already the backbone of EU industry (representing around 99% of all EU enterprises), and are the main focus of proactive enterprise policies based on applying the principle 'think small first'. To this end, specific programmes have been devised to ensure that SMEs participate in EU-funded research and innovation projects. The rules on state aid (see **subsidies**) and other forms of funding are more generous for SMEs than for large firms. Entrepreneurs, and SMEs in particular, can obtain help in finding partners through the Innovation Relay Centre network in more than 30 countries. This network is part-funded by the Commission.

Through its Entrepreneurship Action Plan, which was published in 2004, the Commission is promoting a more entrepreneurial mindset, encouraging more people to set up businesses, helping those businesses grow and become more competitive, improving the flow of finance and creating a more SME-friendly regulatory and administrative environment. Indeed, the EU granted some €90m. annually from 2001 to 2005 for SME-orientated projects in the EU and three **candidate countries**, **Bulgaria**, **Romania** and **Turkey**. Money was provided, for example, to facilitate the participation of European SMEs in a knowledge-based, internationalized economy and to give business easier access to networks such as the **Euro Info Centres** in more than 40 countries. In June 2008 the Small Business Act for Europe was adopted by the European Commission which, for the first time, put in place a comprehensive SME policy framework for the EU and its member states. In addition, in November 2011 the Commission presented a new approach to ensure that the EU responded better to the requirements of small businesses. Thenceforth, the Commission would attempt wherever possible to exempt micro-enterprises from EU legislation or introduce special regimes so as to minimize the regulatory onus on them.

Enterprise policy is co-ordinated closely with other policies, in particular the single market (see **internal market**), research and innovation and information society policy. Conversely, when the EU is formulating policy on trade, education and training, or the environment, the business impacts are taken into account.

The **INFORMATION SOCIETY** has been gradually emerging in Europe as a result of advances in technology and communication (see **information technology**). One of the European Union's (EU) current priorities is to ensure that businesses, governments and citizens play an active role in shaping and participating in the global knowledge- and information-based economy. To achieve this, the **European Commission** actively wishes to stimulate research into the development and deployment of new information and communication technologies. It also wishes to set up and maintain a framework of regulation and standards that is designed to generate competition. In an attempt to encourage and promote a coherent information society within the EU, there have been a number of research and development programmes in fields of information technology and telematics since 1984. Programmes within the different fields are considered essential to the economic growth and **competitiveness** of the EU, and to the creation of new jobs and markets. In 1994 the European Commission Vice-President, Martin Bangemann, issued a report recommending that an Action Plan would be necessary to ensure that Europe played its part in the global information society. Maintaining and improving international competitiveness is also an important element of the information society programmes, one of the earliest of which was the **European strategic programme for research and development in information technology** (Esprit). By the end of the 1990s the latest technological developments (such as the internet and the emerging knowledge-based economy) required a fresh impetus, which culminated in the 1999 Commission communication on 'eEurope—An information society for all'. This was accepted by the **Council**

of the European Union in 2000, and the Council in turn asked the Commission to elaborate an eEurope Action Plan. This was adopted at the 2000 Feira summit of the **European Council**. The Commission's eEurope 2002 Action Plan identified a series of targets, which included securing a cheaper, faster and more secure internet; greater investment in people and skills; and finding ways to stimulate the use of the internet. The eEurope 2005 Action Plan was launched at the 2002 Seville summit of the European Council. In 2006 the Commission published the i2010 eGovernment Action Plan as part of the EU's i2010 strategy (launched in 2005), which aimed to stimulate the development of the digital economy in Europe. In order to foster an open and competitive internal market for the information society and the media, the primary objective of i2010 was to establish a Single European Information Space offering affordable and secure high-bandwidth communications, and rich and diverse content and digital services. Furthermore, the strategy would encourage greater funding of research and innovation programmes.

The importance of the information society cannot be overestimated as it has had a significant effect on certain areas of EU public policy and, for example, has accelerated the liberalization of the **telecommunications** sector. The EU's policy for the information society comprises the following four pillars: telecommunications policy; support to bring about technological development in information and communication technologies; creating the necessary conditions to ensure competitiveness exists; and to promote **Trans-European Networks** in transport, telecommunications and energy.

The **INFORMATION SOCIETY TECHNOLOGIES** (IST) programme was set up in 1998 as part of the European Communities **information technology** initiatives, and superseded various separate programmes, including the **European strategic programme for research and development in information technology** (Esprit), in order to create a single integrated programme in this area. Four main topic areas were: systems and services for the citizen; new methods of work and electronic commerce; multimedia content and tools; and essential technologies and infrastructures. The IST programme was subsequently restyled the Information and Communication Technologies (ICT) programme, which was allocated funding of €9,100m. for 2007–13.

INFORMATION TECHNOLOGY became a major European Communities (EC) theme in the 1980s. Concerned that Europe might fall behind its major competitors in the rapidly expanding and changing field of information technology, partly because the high costs involved might deter investment and development by private companies, and partly because the protected national public sector markets in electronics might lead to duplication of effort, the EC have been particularly keen to encourage transnational collaboration. A way forward was suggested by the successive programmes of FAST (Forecasting and Assessment in the Field of Science and Technology), as a result of which several collaborative **research and technological development** projects were developed: SPRINT (the Strategic Programme for Innovation and Technology Transfer); the **European strategic programme for research and development in information technology** (Esprit); and **RACE** (Research and Development in Advanced Communications Technologies in Europe). More specific programmes have been established to develop information technology in such diverse areas as banking and financial services (Development of Integrated Monetary Electronics—DIME), road traffic flow and control (Dedicated Road Infrastructure for Vehicle Safety in Europe—DRIVE), teaching using computers (Developing European Learning through Technological Advance—DELTA), and medicine (Advanced Informatics in Medicine—AIM). The EC also established information technology programmes to assist in their own operations, including: Co-operation in Automation of Data and Documentation for Imports/Exports and Agriculture (CADDIA); Customs Handling of Import and Export Freight (CHIEF); and Inter-institutional Integrated Services Information System (INSIS). The European Union (EU) institutions have several associated information networks. There are also databases, such as **New Cronos**, which contain EU statistics.

INFRINGEMENT PROCEDURES relate specifically to the **implementation** of European Union (EU) laws. The **Treaty of Rome** charged the **European Commission** with the responsibility of ensuring that all laws and rules are applied. In its guise as guardian of the treaties, the Commission can initiate infringement proceedings under Article 226 (now Article 258 of the **Treaty on the Functioning of the European Union**) against a member state for failure to do so. Most of the infringement issues relate to the free movement of goods, free movement of people and free movement of capital as well as to decisions relating to public procurement and financial services. The Commission becomes aware of infringement by various means, as anyone residing in the EU or outside can lodge a complaint with the Commission against a member state on any issue that is deemed to be inconsistent with EU law. The Commission then decides whether to take the issue any further. If it does, the Commission in the first instance may wish to bring the infringement to an end after presenting a letter of formal notice to the member state government concerned. Approximately 1,000 such letters are generated each year. This reasoned opinion alerts the member state concerned to the details of the infringement and asks the country to comply with EU law. If the state in question declines to end the infringement or ignores the letter, the Commission can then take the case to the **Court of Justice**. The **Treaty on European Union** gave the Courts the authority to levy fines against states infringing EU law. The Commission is also empowered under Regulation 1/2003 (an updated version of Regulation 17/62) to take action against a private company or a series of private companies for infringing the **competition policy** rules. In the last decade or so this has led to the imposition of ever more substantial fines on the companies concerned.

INLAND WATERWAYS form an essential part of the transport network of much of the European Union, especially for raw materials and industrial products. In 1976 the member states agreed to recognize, on a reciprocal basis, each other's decisions on the navigability and control of inland waterways. The type and technical specifications of commercial craft permitted to use the waterways have been subject to European Communities **regulations** since 1982, and the **European Commission** has continued to work towards broader international co-operation throughout the whole of Europe.

INNER CORE is an expression used to refer to a group of member states that may wish to pursue deeper integration at a much quicker pace than would find agreement among all member states, where **unanimity** is required. The concept is an old one and can be traced back to discussions on differentiated integration that have surfaced since the founding of the European Communities. (See also **enhanced co-operation**; **flexibility**; **variable geometry**.)

INSTITUTIONS in the context of the European Union (EU) are the central decision-making bodies of the organization. They possess a special status in EU treaties and practice. The **Treaty of Lisbon** identifies seven main EU institutions. These are the **Council of the European Union**, the **European Central Bank**, **the European Council**, the **European Commission**, the **European Parliament**, the European **Court of Justice** and the European **Court of Auditors**.

The **INSTRUMENT FOR PRE-ACCESSION ASSISTANCE** (IPA) was launched at the beginning of 2007 and replaced earlier pre-accession financial support programmes such as **Phare**, **Sapard**, **ISPA** and **CARDS**. It is aimed at providing pre-accession assistance in five areas—transition assistance and institution building, cross-border co-operation, regional development, human resource development and rural development—and is available to countries of the **Western Balkans**, **Turkey** and **Iceland**.

The **INSTRUMENT FOR STABILITY** (IfS) replaced the **Rapid Reaction Mechanism** in 2007. Since the launch of the IfS, the **European Commission** has considerably intensified its work in the area of conflict prevention, crisis management and peace building. To date, the instrument has financed a large number of crisis response projects worldwide. An innovative part of the IfS is the Peace-building Partnership, which was created to deepen the dialogue between civil society and the institutions of the European Union (EU). The IfS also enables the EU to help build long-term international, regional and national capacity to address pervasive transregional and global threats. The IfS had a budget of €2,000m. to cover the period 2007–13.

The **INSTRUMENT FOR STRUCTURAL POLICIES FOR PRE-ACCESSION** (ISPA) was a European Communities initiative to strengthen the infrastructure of the **candidate countries** of **Central and Eastern Europe** in order to prepare them for membership of the European Union (EU). The ISPA operated in the area of transport and the environment. It was agreed by the Council of the European Union in June 1999 and stemmed directly from the **Commission**'s **Agenda 2000** communication. The programme was scheduled to run from 2000 to 2006 and had an annual budget of €1,040m. for its duration. Financial assistance was granted to environmental projects that enabled the recipients to meet existing EU environmental standards and to initiatives in the transport sector that fostered **Trans-European Networks**. Between 2000 and the end of 2006 the Commission allocated some €1,040m. each year to ISPA projects. On accession to the EU a country automatically lost its entitlement to support under the ISPA. Since 1 January 2007, the ISPA has been replaced by the **instrument for pre-accession assistance**.

INSURANCE was identified by the **European Commission** in its 1985 **White Paper** on the **internal market** as one of the professional services that should be open to **freedom of movement** throughout the European Communities. While considerable liberalization has occurred, several national obstacles still hinder the emergence of a common insurance market.

INTAS is an independent international association that was originally established in 1993 to promote co-operation between scientists in Western Europe and those in the newly independent states of the former **USSR**. In 2007 its membership comprised the 27 member states of the enlarged European Union, plus **Iceland**, Israel, **Norway**, **Switzerland** and **Turkey**.

The **INTEGRATED MEDITERRANEAN PROGRAMMES** (IMPs) were a collection of European Communities (EC) aid initiatives established in 1985. The programmes were a response to the demand by Greece in 1981 for a renegotiation of its terms of entry to the EC, on the grounds that the structure and level of development of its economy differed markedly from those of the other member states and merited special treatment. Using the resources of the **structural funds**, the **European Investment Bank** (EIB) and the New Community Instrument, funding was to be made available over a period of seven years for combined programmes designed to develop and modernize the socio-economic structure of those Mediterranean regions of the EC largely dependent on agricultural production. The member states in receipt of IMPs were also expected to contribute towards the financing of approved projects. The work started by IMPs continued within the **MEDA** programme.

INTEGRATION CAPACITY is, alongside the **accession criteria**, one of the criteria governing the **enlargement** of the European Union (EU). It relates to the institutional, financial and political ability of the EU to take in new members. Although as a term it only gained prominence following the EU's 2004 enlargement, questions about the EU's capacity to enlarge have always been present on the EU's agenda as part of the so-called '**widening** versus **deepening**' debate.

INTEGRATION THEORY refers to explanations, primarily produced by political scientists, to explain the logic and factors behind the European integration process. There now exists a huge and ever-expanding literature on European integration, but there is no single meta-theory that explains the entire process. Instead there is a wide diversity of opinion that essentially divides into two major approaches, namely **intergovernmentalism** and **supranationalism**. The first derives from the study of international relations and regards the member states as the key figures in determining the shape and pace of integration. In contrast, the second approach prefers to extol the role of the supranational institutions and other interested parties (such as the business community) in pushing for and demanding deeper integration. In reality both approaches can help to explain different stages and indeed levels of the decision-making processes. Whereas major 'constitutional changes' are certainly determined by the member states in the **intergovernmental conferences** and involve a process of stating preferences and a considerable degree of bargaining, the day-to-day decisions in policy areas are left to the European Union (EU) institutions, while much of the policy formulation allows considerable scope for interest groups to express their views and have them incorporated into policy development. Alongside these 'classic' theories, there have emerged in recent years a number of mid-range theories or approaches to EU integration and public policy studies that come under the headings of, for example, policy network analysis, multi-level governance and constructivism.

INTELLIGENT ENERGY—EUROPE (IEE) is a support programme for non-technological actions in the field of energy (i.e. energy efficiency and renewable energy sources). It is intended to support the European Union's policies on energy as well as sustainable development. IEE had funding of some €730m. to cover the period 2007–13.

INTER-ACTIVE TERMINOLOGY FOR EUROPE (IATE) is the inter-institutional terminology database of the European Union (EU). The project was launched in 1999 and became operational throughout the EU in 2004. IATE incorporated all of the existing terminology databases of the EU's translation services into one inter-institutional database containing approximately 1.4m. multilingual entries.

INTEREST GROUPS seek to influence the European Union (EU) public policy process by forging close relations with the principal institutional actors, primarily the **European Commission** and, increasingly, the **European Parliament** (EP) since the **Treaty on European Union** and the arrival of the **co-decision procedure**; and also, to a lesser extent, the **Court of Justice**. The **Council of the European Union** cannot be lobbied directly and thus interest groups focus their attention on their national capitals. However, interest groups form a vital part of policy development, although their significance varies from group to group and from policy area to policy area. Some, such as the **European Round Table of Industrialists**, are clearly influential and have easy access to the institutions. Interest groups were a feature of European Communities (EC) business activity from the very outset. Given the EC's original economic activities, the first groups to establish themselves in **Brussels** were representatives from the business community (**BUSINESS EUROPE**, formerly the **Union of Industrial and Employers' Confederations of Europe**, or UNICE) and the agricultural community (**Committee of Agricultural Professional Organizations in the European Union**—COPA). By the end of the 1970s trade unions and other new movements such as environmentalists had established a presence. Their influence was initially limited until the **Single European Act** and later treaties transformed **decision-making** by enhancing the power of the EP and sought to establish a genuine **internal market** requiring EC-wide rules. By the late 1980s there was a noticeable expansion in the formation of interest groups. The emphasis on regions (see **Committee of the Regions**; **Europe of the Regions**) in the late 1980s and the 1990s added another dimension and led to the establishment of many offices representing sub-national authorities. In 2012 it was estimated that there were some 2,600 interest groups had a permanent office in Brussels, employing around 15,000 people. The Commission has set up a database, CONECCS (Consultation, the European Commission and Civil Society), of around 1,000 organizations working at EU level, covering approximately 100 branches of activity. (See also **lobbying**.)

An **INTERGOVERNMENTAL CONFERENCE** (IGC) is the set of negotiations between the governments of the member states launched with a view to amending the **founding treaties**. The IGC provides a forum through which the European Communities (EC), or more specifically the **European Council**, has chosen to explore in detail new organizational and other infrastructural initiatives. They have become key events in the integration project and are used to seek agreement on **resolutions** approved in principle by the Council, and to plan their details. There have been seven major IGCs in the history of the European Union (EU) and five of these have occurred since the **Single European Act** was negotiated in the mid-1980s. The most important were the two conferences that began in 1990 to discuss **economic and monetary union** and **political union**, which formed the basis of the **Treaty on European**

Union. Two further conferences on the future political integration of the EU were held in 1996 and 2000, and the measures suggested at these IGCs were formalized respectively in 1997 in the **Treaty of Amsterdam** and in 2000 in the **Treaty of Nice**. Following the December 2001 Laeken summit, a new means for discussing and debating the future structure and powers of the EU— the **European Convention**—was launched. This allowed the views of a much wider range of interested parties to be brought together in preparation for the IGC that began its work in October 2003. This produced the **Treaty establishing a Constitution for Europe**. The most recent IGC was launched in July 2007 and produced the **Treaty of Lisbon**. The IGC is notable for, among other things, the exceptionally detailed mandate for its work agreed by the European Council.

INTERGOVERNMENTALISM relates primarily to one approach of academic discourse on European **integration theory**. It assumes the supremacy of national governments in the integration process and in treaty design, and downplays the role of the supranational institutions, the **European Commission**, the **European Parliament** and the **Court of Justice**, and other actors (e.g. the business community).

INTERIM AGREEMENTS are often concluded by the European Union (EU) to implement the trade provisions of international agreements that contain a mixture of EU and member state competences, such as **partnership and co-operation agreements** and **Europe agreements**, pending the **ratification** of such agreements.

INTER-INSTITUTIONAL AGREEMENTS are agreements made between the **Council of the European Union**, the **European Commission** and the **European Parliament** in order to run the European Union more efficiently. They currently involve a range of legal, organizational and budgetary arrangements, and there are some 30 in existence. The most widely known are the Inter-Institutional Agreements on the **budget** in 1988, 1993 and 1999, which determined levels of **expenditure** on multi-annual spending programmes.

An **INTERNAL MARKET** achieved by 'progressively approximating the economic policies of member states' was an immediate general objective of the **Treaty of Rome**. The Treaty set down a specific timetable for the achievement of the **common market**. It was to be reached in a series of stages, and completed within 12 to 15 years. Although the **Six** successfully abolished quota restrictions and **tariffs** on internal trade, the broader objective was not attained within the stipulated time limit. It was not until the 1980s that the **European Communities** (EC) began to consider with greater urgency the need to tackle the numerous non-tariff barriers (so-called physical, technical and fiscal barriers) that restricted the **freedom of movement** of people, goods, services and capital. There was concern that the EC were not enjoying the economic advantage over their main trading rivals that their large population should provide. **European Commission** initiatives on economic liberalization were accumulating in the Council of Ministers (see **Council of the European Union**), where the effective requirement of unanimous agreement was seen as a major obstacle to any rapid progress. **Jacques Delors**, the incoming President of the Commission, had recognized the potential of pushing for a genuine internal market as a means not only of increasing trade and prosperity among the **Ten**, but also of relaunching the European integration project. In a tour of member state capital cities in the latter half of 1984 he found a general consensus in favour of the creation of an internal market, which he then presented to the **European Council** in Brussels in March 1985.

The Council accepted the principle of establishing a single market within a specified deadline, and instructed the European Commission to draw up a detailed programme, according to which the internal market would be completed by December 1992. The Commission responded with a **White Paper** prepared by Francis Cockfield, which listed some 300 actions (subsequently reduced to 282), with a timetable for each that would need to be taken. Three months after its Brussels meeting, the European Council set in motion the developments that resulted in the **Single European Act**. This made the process of **harmonization** less subject to delay by amending the provisions relating to voting in the Council of Ministers. By 1992, most of the measures included in the White Paper had been adopted (although many still required **implementation** at national level). The effort to complete the internal market helped to revive the European project. It also persuaded the **European Free Trade Association** (EFTA) countries to seek a closer relationship with the European Union (EU), and possibly even membership. Furthermore, it led directly to renewed pressure for both **economic and monetary union** and closer political integration, and so indirectly to the **Treaty on European Union**. The **Treaty of Amsterdam** also introduced measures to improve freedom of movement within the EU, which could have an impact on the internal market. Other measures that had to be agreed at European level included greater combating of state aids (see **subsidies**), more market liberalization (especially in the energy sector), a more concerted **research and technological development** strategy, greater assistance for small and medium-sized businesses, better **Trans-European Networks**, greater labour mobility and, most controversially of all, fiscal harmonization. The **Treaty of Lisbon** deleted all references to the internal market, preferring the term '**single market**'.

INTERNATIONAL COMMITTEE OF THE MOVEMENTS FOR EUROPEAN UNITY was the name of an umbrella organization founded in

December 1947 to co-ordinate and act as a link between the several bodies and the 1948 **Congress of Europe**.

The **INTERNATIONAL RUHR AUTHORITY** (IRA) was an agency established in April 1949 to supervise coal and steel production in the Ruhr region of Germany. It was intended to ensure that the Ruhr's resources in the new Federal Republic of Germany (FRG—West Germany) would not be used for aggressive purposes. As an alternative to keeping the FRG under military control, France had seen the IRA as a means of maintaining influence over German policy. The IRA was abandoned in 1950 as being unworkable. Its failure was one factor that made France look favourably upon the **Schuman Plan** as an alternative means of influencing German **coal** and **steel** production.

INTERNATIONAL SPACE STATION: See **Columbus**

INTERREG is the name of a **structural funds** initiative, which was launched in 1989 with the aim of assisting border areas of the European Union (EU) to overcome problems of development caused by their relative isolation either within a national economy or within the EU as a whole. It is financed solely through the **European Regional Development Fund**. Interreg II was introduced in 1994 to encourage transnational spatial planning. Interreg III was to cover the period 2000–06, and was given a budget of €4,875m. This phase of Interreg was designed to strengthen economic and social cohesion throughout the EU. It aimed to do this through the promotion of balanced development of the Continent through cross-border, transnational and inter-regional co-operation. It placed particular emphasis on integrating remote regions and those that share external borders with **candidate countries** of **Central and Eastern Europe**. Interreg IV is the latest incarnation and covers the programming period 2007–13. Some €7,800m. has been allocated to this programme, which can be distilled into three main areas of activity. These are cross-border co-operation, transnational co-operation (with 13 specific geographical programmes) and interregional co-operation (with no specific geographical boundaries for participation). The predominant theme of this latest phase is to strengthen and deepen cross-border co-operation, especially with regard to encouraging entrepreneurship and the development of **small and medium-sized enterprises** (SMEs), supporting links between rural and urban areas, promoting collaboration in health, culture and education, and sharing infra-structures (for example, in terms of waste management, energy systems and tourism). Since its inception, Interreg funding has always been available, for example, in Northern Ireland, but, whereas previous Interreg programmes operated on a Northern Ireland/Ireland cross-border basis, the new Interreg IV programme has redrawn the operational borders to include Western Scotland for the first time.

INTERVENTION AGENCY is the name of the body that, under the **common agricultural policy**, intervenes to purchase produce when market prices fall below previously agreed **intervention prices**.

INTERVENTION PRICE is the lynchpin of the **common agricultural policy**. It is a price support mechanism which ensures that if a product cannot be sold at an agreed price for that year then it goes into 'intervention' and is purchased and stored by the European Union. The cost is borne by the **budget**. In other words, intervention prices are fixed prices for farm commodities and are the minimum prices that producers are guaranteed for their commodities. When market prices fall below this level, produce is purchased by an **Intervention Agency** at the guaranteed price.

INVESTITURE is a term that refers to the process of conferring authority on the **European Commission** to act as a governmental body for the European Union. Because the membership of the Commission is now approved by both the **Council of the European Union** and the **European Parliament**, the term 'double investiture' is used. (See **nomination procedure**.)

The **INVESTMENT SECURITIES DIRECTIVE** of 1989, introduced in 1993, is a **directive** designed to permit a company authorized in one **member state** to offer its services throughout the European Union without the need to acquire further authorization. It also set standards for solvency and the protection of investors.

INWARD INVESTMENT refers to the establishment of operations within the European Union (EU) by non-EU companies. The potential of the large EU market, the **common external tariff** and, more recently, the **internal market** and the **European Economic Area** have encouraged multinational companies to invest within the EU. On the whole, inward investment has been welcomed despite concerns that it might encourage over-capacity or weaken indigenous industries. To ensure that plants owned by external investors do not simply assemble components produced outside the EU, the EU has ruled that 60% of the manufactured product of such operations, measured by ex-factory prices, must be locally made.

The **IOANNINA COMPROMISE** takes its name from an informal meeting of foreign ministers in Ioannina, Greece, in March 1994, where political agreement was reached on the operation of **qualified majority voting** (QMV) rules to be applied within the **Council of the European Union** after the 1995 **enlargement** of the European Union (EU). With enlargement, the number of votes under QMV required to block a proposal—the 'blocking minority'—was set to increase from 23 to 26. The United Kingdom and Spain objected strongly and argued that the blocking minority should remain at 23. The agreed compromise stated that if members of the Council representing a total of between 23 and 25 votes indicated their desire to oppose the adoption of a decision by a qualified majority, the Council would do all in its powers to reach a satisfactory conclusion that could be adopted by at least 65 votes. The compromise was essentially a device for the British Government to preserve its dignity, and the compromise in effect has had little practical impact on EU **decision-making**. A declaration annexed to the **Treaty of Amsterdam** extended the compromise until enlargement in 2004. With the new QMV rules agreed in the **Treaty of Nice**, it was anticipated that the Ioannina Compromise would be consigned to history. However, a new variant has been adopted with the entry into force of the **Treaty of Lisbon**. It owes its existence to the insistence of Poland during the 2007 **intergovernmental conference** that it be compensated for the replacement of the—for Poland, very favourable—QMV provisions that had been introduced by the Treaty of Nice with the Treaty of Lisbon's less favourable **double majority** voting system.

IPA: See **Instrument for Pre-accession Assistance**

The second **IRAQ WAR**, which commenced in March 2003, clearly revealed the sensitivities and difficulties within the European Union (EU) regarding efforts to create a **common foreign and security policy**. EU member states were deeply divided on the US invasion of Iraq and (leaving aside the four neutral countries—Austria, Finland, Ireland and Sweden) can be grouped into two camps. The first group supported the US attempt to remove President Saddam Hussein from power and included, among others, Italy, Poland, Spain, the United Kingdom and a number of the newest member states in **Central and Eastern Europe**. In contrast, the Governments of both France and Germany resolutely criticized the US move and led Donald Rumsfeld, the US Secretary of State for Defense, to talk of 'new' and 'old' Europe. Although the Saddam regime was swiftly defeated by superior fire power, all subsequent efforts to restore civil order and bring democracy to Iraq have been much harder to achieve. Sovereignty was transferred to an interim Government in June 2004, and six months later Iraqis voted in their country's first multi-party elections in 50 years. Saddam Hussein was caught and put on trial in 2005 for crimes against humanity. He was found guilty and was executed by hanging in December 2006. The security situation did not improve. On the ground, the US-led coalition forces faced almost daily armed rebellions and guerrilla-style attacks. They lost over 4,000 personnel in the process. Insurgents continually targeted civilians, Iraqi security forces and international agencies. Above all, suicide bombers became a regular reality and led to many thousands of civilian fatalities, and the dangers of the country spilling into full-scale civil war were not diminished. At the end of 2007 the United Kingdom handed over security of Basra province to Iraqi forces and effectively marked the end of nearly five years of British control of southern Iraq. During 2008–09 the violence abated as the security situation improved and there was notable progress in the 'Iraqization' of the governance of the country. The remaining US-led coalition forces ceased combat operations in 2010 and the final 50,000 US troops, who had stayed on in Iraq in an advisory capacity, had all withdrawn by the end of 2011.

IRELAND did not become involved in most immediate post-war European developments (**ECSC**, **EDC**, **EEC** and **Euratom**), in part because of its neutral status, which itself in some ways reflected a very nationalistic and inward-looking focus in the late 1940s and 1950s. It also did not participate in the development of multilateral trading agreements, and became associated with the **European Free Trade Association** only in December 1965 through signing a free trade area agreement with the United Kingdom. Its application to join the European Communities (EC) was closely related with that of the United Kingdom, because of the strong economic links between the two countries. Its application was submitted several days before the original British application, but **De Gaulle**'s opposition to the latter ensured that the other membership applications, from Dublin, Copenhagen and Oslo, ultimately failed. All four states were subsequently accepted to join the EC in January 1973, but **Norway** opted not to do so following the narrow rejection of membership in a **referendum**. Ireland has generally been a supporter of more economic and political integration, and the Irish electorate endorsed the **Single European Act**, the **Treaty on European Union** and the **Treaty of Amsterdam** in referenda. Ireland has also been the greatest single net beneficiary of the **common agricultural policy** and the **structural funds**, which have significantly helped to boost the Irish economy. The economic success of Ireland ensured that the country easily met the economic criteria to join **economic and monetary union**, and also meant that Ireland lost objective 1 status in relation to structural funds after 2006 (see **European Regional Development Fund**).

Interestingly, in the 1990s Ireland had one of the worst records among the member states on the implementation of EC **directives**. However, **Eurobarometer** frequently reveals that Ireland remains one of the most pro-European Union (EU) member states, despite the much-publicized rejection of the **Treaty of Nice** in a referendum in June 2001. This result shocked the Irish political system, but the outcome owed more to the low turn-out of voters (some 34%) and the inability of the major Irish political parties to campaign seriously on the issue than to any sudden change in opinion of the Irish public towards the EU. In a second referendum on the Nice Treaty, held in October 2002, the majority (some 62.9%) of those who participated supported the treaty, and thus paved the way for the **enlargement** of the EU. Nevertheless, the turn-out for the referendum was still regarded as problematic, since only 48.5% of the electorate opted to vote.

Ireland's economic turnaround transformed the country into an attractive destination for immigrants, especially from Poland and the Baltic States. Ireland was the only EU member state to hold a referendum on the **Treaty of Lisbon**. The outcome of the vote on 12 June 2008 was a victory for the treaty's opponents: 53.4% voted 'no' and 46.6% 'yes'. Given the relatively high turn-out (53%), an early post-vote assumption was that there could be no second referendum as there had been with the Treaty of Nice. However, the result was greeted with disappointment by the Government. The Irish vote initially threatened to force the formal abandonment of the Treaty of Lisbon, which, in turn, could potentially have marginalized Ireland politically within the EU. After much deliberation on why the result had been a 'no', the former Irish Government under **Brian Cowen** finally agreed to hold a second referendum in the latter part of 2009, once it had secured some 'guarantees' from the European Council—most notably on retaining an Irish Commissioner and safeguarding neutrality—and thereby addressing 'no' voters' concerns. The onset of economic recession seemed to have refocused peoples' minds, and opinion polls from early 2009 displayed a turnaround in views and indicated a 'yes' vote. Despite growing public dissatisfaction with the Irish Government and its junior coalition partner, the Green Party, which led to heavy defeats for both parties at the local and EP elections in June 2009, two-thirds of voters (67.1%) endorsed the Treaty of Lisbon in a second referendum which was held in October 2009. The Cowen Government was ultimately held responsible by the electorate for the economic difficulties that befell Ireland after 2008, and it was voted out of office in 25 February 2011 as Fianna Fáil experienced its worst election results since the founding of the Irish state. A coalition Government, comprising Fine Gael and the Labour Party, was appointed under the premiership of the leader of Fine Gael, **Enda Kenny**. On assuming power, Kenny stated that one of his top priorities was to renegotiate the terms of the €85,000m. bailout that had been agreed between the Irish Government and the **European Central Bank** and the IMF in November 2010. This aspiration proved rather optimistic and **Angela Merkel** and **Herman Van Rompuy** expressed certain reservations about any such move. Kenny participated in discussions with his peers over the terms of the **Fiscal Compact Treaty** in the latter half of 2011 and signed the agreement in March 2012. It was decided to call a referendum on this treaty and on the Government's approach towards resolving the ongoing financial crisis. On 31 May 60.3% of those who participated in the referendum (around 50% of the electorate) voted in favour of the Government ratifying the Fiscal Compact Treaty. Ireland was the sole EU member state to call a referendum on the treaty.

ISDN stands for Integrated Services Digital Network. In 1989 the European Communities (EC) launched an initiative to raise the international competitiveness of the EC **telecommunications** industries through the provision of a range of compatible and harmonized services.

ISIS is the acronym for the Information Society Initiatives in Standardization programme introduced in 1995 to support the development of standards in information society domains.

The **ISOGLUCOSE CASE** relates to a 1980 ruling by the **Court of Justice**. This case represented one of the Court's landmark decisions in the development of the European Union. The case centred on a complaint brought to the Court by the **European Parliament** (EP) with specific reference to the **consultation procedure**. Although this procedure recognized the Council of Ministers (see **Council of the European Union**) as the sole decision-maker, the **founding treaties** implied that the Council could only make legislative **decisions** once it had received the EP's opinion. In this particular instance, the Council had proceeded without waiting for the EP's response, which in this case went against the Council's decision. In Isoglucose, the Court upheld the EP's right to be consulted, and this marginally strengthened the EP's political position within the European Communities. Although following the case the EP still had few powers, this decision enabled the EP to delay the Council in its decision-making.

ISPA: See **Instrument for Structural Policies for Pre-accession**

IST: See **Information Society Technologies**

ISTC is the acronym for the International Science and Technology Centre, which was established in 1994 in order to encourage scientists and engineers previously involved with weapons and warfare research in the former **USSR** to co-operate and to collaborate for peaceful purposes with their counterparts in the **USA**, **Japan** and the European Union.

ITALY was one of the founder members of the European Communities (EC) and generally has been a supporter of the principle of economic and political integration. Since 1957 it has favoured **supranationalism**, arguing for reforms that would strengthen the **European Commission** and the **European Parliament**. In 1986 it initially refused to sign the **Single European Act** as a protest against the inadequate nature of its proposed reforms. While the richer, more industrialized northern regions of the country benefited substantially from EC membership, the poorer south has remained relatively impoverished, despite the infusion of substantial EC funding. On the other hand, Italy has been the subject of the greatest number of complaints against a member state (some one-third of the total) brought before the **Court of Justice**. The major reason has not been a reluctance to comply with EC **legislation**, but the cumbersome nature of the Italian parliament, which makes approval of any legislation a lengthy process. Most of the charges have related to Italy's failure to apply **directives** within the specified deadlines. Popular antipathy in Italy to the old political élites and parties, which were the subject of numerous national corruption charges after 1990, led to a new style of government that was more critical of the EC, the European Union (EU) and their objectives. In addition, speculative pressure in 1992 forced Italy to leave the **exchange–rate mechanism** (ERM). The country re-entered the ERM in November 1996, and Italy was one of the 11 member states to embrace **economic and monetary union** in January 1999. Critics questioned the degree to which Italy had actually met the **convergence criteria**, but there can be no doubting that the decision to join was politically motivated, and one that aroused a considerable degree of sensitivity in Rome.

The return of **Silvio Berlusconi** as Prime Minister in 2001 added an extra degree of controversy to the EU–Italian relationship as Berlusconi's style of leadership (for example, during the much criticized Italian presidency of the EU in the second half of 2003) and political gaffes angered other heads of government. Yet, there can be little doubt that talks in February 2004 and the emergence of a putative *directoire*, comprising France, Germany and the United Kingdom, to lead the EU aroused Italian sensitivities. Whether Berlusconi's dismissal of such meetings as a 'big mess' served Italy's interest in promoting itself as an equal player remained open to question. Italy became the first of the founding states of the EU to ratify the **Treaty establishing a Constitution for Europe** by parliamentary vote in April 2005. Berlusconi's premiership came to an end in May 2006 after his narrow defeat at the hands of his old adversary, **Romano Prodi**, in national elections. Following his victory, Prodi immediately signalled his intention to pull Italian troops out of Iraq. His tenure as Prime Minister, however, in the tradition of Italian post-war politics, was short-lived. He encountered difficulties, for example, over his foreign policy aspirations (especially the decision to allow the extension of a US military base) and some of his ministers were accused of corruption. He lost a vote of confidence in the Senate on 24 January 2008 and immediately tendered his resignation as Prime Minister. Nevertheless, he remained in office for almost four months for routine business until early elections were held, and a new right-of-centre Government under Silvio Berlusconi was formed in April 2008. The Berlusconi Government's popularity with the electorate continued and it secured fairly impressive results in the 2009 EP elections, where it outscored the centre-left forces and captured 42% of the vote. It repeated its success in the regional elections of April 2010, but experienced a decline in support in a series of regional and local elections in 2011. Following the loss of his party's parliamentary majority and the continuing decline in the country's financial situation, Berlusconi stood down as Prime Minister in November 2011. He was replaced by **Mario Monti**, a renowned economist and former EU commissioner, who appointed a cabinet of technocrats tasked with tackling the worsening economic crisis.

ITER stands for the International Thermonuclear Experimental Reactor (although this full title is no longer used), an international co-operation project comprising the member states of the **European Atomic Energy Community** (EAEC or Euratom), plus **Japan**, the **USA**, India, the People's Republic of China, the Republic of Korea and Russia. Completion of the nuclear fusion reactor, which is being built in Cadarache, France, is scheduled for 2019. (See also **European Fusion Development Agreement**; **Joint European Torus**.)

ITS: See The **Identity, Tradition and Sovereignty Group**

J

JAPAN has been regarded by the European Union (EU) as a major economic competitor, and perhaps also as an example to the EU, especially in terms of new technological industries. Much of EU **research and technological development policy** has been determined by the perceived need to compensate for the advantage that Japan is believed to hold. More generally, trade relations between the EU and Japan have been fraught with problems. The main reason is the large trade deficit that the EU has incurred with Japan. In 1993–2004, Japanese exports to the EU increased by almost 40% from €50,100m. to €73,500m., while EU exports to Japan rose from €28,800m. to €43,100m. In 2010 Japan accounted for 3.2% of the exports of the **Twenty-Seven** (EU27) and 4.3% of EU27 imports, and was the EU27's sixth most important trading partner. In addition, Japanese exports are concentrated in a few important consumer fields, such as cars, electronics and computers. Japan has traditionally been slow to ease the entry of imports to its domestic market by relaxing or removing a range of non-tariff barriers. On the other hand, the **European Commission** has regulated the entry of several Japanese products and has passed several anti-**dumping** measures. In addition, member states have imposed a number of restrictions on Japanese imports: the best known, perhaps, have been the so-called voluntary agreements limiting the volume of imports of Japanese cars. However, many Japanese companies have invested in the EU. Although the focus of EU meetings with Japanese ministers and officials has in the past been on the persistence of the trade imbalance, recent years have seen a shift in emphasis to requests for deregulation and structural reforms in Japan. In addition to the long-established bilateral negotiations and contacts on economic issues, a political dialogue between the EU and Japan also exists. This, dating back to a 1991 declaration, has gradually been developed through an annual summit meeting between the European Commission President, the European Council presidency and the Japanese Prime Minister. In 2001 a joint EU-Japan action plan entitled 'Shaping our Common Future' was adopted. The 20th annual summit took place in Brussels in May 2011. The 21st summit, which was scheduled to take place in Tokyo in mid-2012, was postponed owing to the reported reluctance of several key EU member states to negotiate a far-reaching free trade agreement with Japan.

ROY JENKINS (1920–2003), or as he became, Baron Jenkins of Hillhead, was President of the **European Commission** from 1977 to 1981. At the time of his appointment a senior political figure in the Labour Party in the United Kingdom, he had always been strongly in favour of that country joining the European Communities (EC): in 1971 he led a party minority in the House of Commons which voted in favour of the terms of entry to the EC, thus defying the three-line whip (a mandatory voting instruction) imposed by his party leadership. Jenkins' appointment as President raised hopes for a renewed momentum in EC developments after the presidency of François-Xavier Ortoli. These expectations were largely unfulfilled. A British President did not end continuing British scepticism about the EC and complaints about its budgetary contribution, but Jenkins did develop the concept of the **European Monetary System** and successfully fought for the right of the Commission President to attend the meetings of the Group of Seven (see **G-8**). The first achievement helped to reopen the debate on **economic and monetary union**, while the second increased the prestige and visibility of the Commission.

JEREMIE (JOINT EUROPEAN RESOURCES FOR MICRO TO MEDIUM ENTERPRISES) is an initiative from the **European Commission**, the **European Investment Bank** and **the European Investment Fund** to enable European Union (EU) member states and regions to use part of their **structural funds** to obtain a set of financial instruments that are specifically designed to support micro and small and medium-sized enterprises (SMEs). The initiative is designed to contribute to growth and employment in line with the revised **Lisbon agenda**. The European Commission's Communication *Cohesion Policy in Support of Growth and Jobs, Community Strategic Guidelines 2007–2013* laid heavy emphasis on the importance of improving access to finance for the development of SMEs, and especially the need to enhance support on competitive terms for start-ups and micro-enterprises, through technical assistance and grants, as well as non-grant instruments such as loans, equity, venture capital and guarantees.

JET: See **Joint European Torus**

JHA: See **Justice and Home Affairs**

JICS: See **Joint Interpreting and Conference Service**

JOINT ACTIONS are among the measures that can be adopted by the **Council of the European Union** under **common foreign and security policy** (CFSP). They commit the member states and are normally adopted unanimously. However, joint actions may in certain circumstances be adopted by a **qualified majority vote**. In all cases, the objectives of a joint action, its

scope, the means to be made available to the European Union, and the conditions governing implementation, must be laid down.

JOINT EUROPEAN TORUS (JET) was one of the principal operations of
the nuclear policy of the European Communities. Established in 1978, based at
Culham in the United Kingdom, and built and funded by the **European
Commission**, JET was the central institute for all West European research
into nuclear fusion. Some non-member states also participated in the project
(**Japan**, the **USA** and countries of the former **USSR**). JET was one of only
four such centres in the world, and its objective was to develop nuclear fusion
as a safer, cleaner, more efficient and economic source of energy than a nuclear
fission reactor. It maintained links with similar institutes in other parts of the
world. In 2000 the **European Fusion Development Agreement** took over
JET's operations. (See also **ITER**.)

JOINT INTERPRETING AND CONFERENCE SERVICE (JICS) is a
language service established by the European Union (EU) as an agency of the
European Commission in 1985. In addition to providing appropriate support
to EU institutions, one of its objectives is to assist in the training of conference
interpreters.

The **JOINT RESEARCH CENTRE** (JRC) is an organization established
under the **European Atomic Energy Community** (EAEC or Euratom).
Directed by the **European Commission**, but relying for much of its funding
on individual contracts, it is, in fact, a collection of seven institutes based in
Geel (Belgium), Karlsruhe (Germany), Ispra (Italy), Petten (Netherlands) and
Seville (Spain). While nuclear research and development remain major concerns
of the institutes, their research efforts have diversified to incorporate safety
standards and measurements, systems engineering, safety technology, **information
technology**, electronics, environmental protection, food and drug analysis, and
space applications. An Institute for Health and Consumer Protection was
established in Ispra in 1998 as part of the restructuring of the JRC.

JRC: See **Joint Research Centre**

JUDGES: See **Court of First Instance**; **Court of Justice**

JUDICIAL PANELS may be established by the **Council of the European
Union** to exercise judicial competence in specific areas. The **Treaty of Nice**
introduced provisions for the panels in an attempt to speed up legal proceedings. Explicit reference was made to establishing a judicial panel for cases
brought by European Union personnel.

JUSTICE AND HOME AFFAIRS (JHA) was the title given to the then intergovernmental third **pillar** of the European Union (EU) when it was established by the **Treaty on European Union** in 1993. The origins of the pillar can be found in the co-operation on anti-terrorism measures and external border security being undertaken by the member states under the umbrella of **TREVI** (Terrorisme, Radicalisme, Extrémisme, Violence Internationale). Faced with increasing problems in the late 1980s and early 1990s in these and other areas such as asylum, immigration, drugs trafficking and fraud, many of the member states were persuaded that something more formal and structured than TREVI was desirable. A further factor was the difficulties faced by the countries that had signed the **Schengen Agreement** in their efforts to agree on a **harmonization** of policies. While the provisions for JHA often simply gave a more formal recognition to already well-established co-operative procedures, the socio-economic environment in the mid-1990s and difficulties in the operation of the pillar pushed the member states towards consideration of a less intergovernmental approach to JHA co-operation. On the other hand, several member states were not prepared to consider incorporating JHA fully into the EU institutional structure, and this resistance inevitably placed limits upon its scope for action. The **Treaty of Amsterdam** transformed JHA by transferring a number of areas under the third pillar to the **Treaty of Rome**, and hence to the first, supranational, pillar of the EU as part of its aim of creating an **area of freedom, security and justice**. At the same time, pillar III was renamed **police and judicial co-operation in criminal matters** to reflect more precisely the areas of activity left for intergovernmental co-operation. (See also **Tampere summit**.) These residual issues were collapsed into the supranational activities of the EU with the coming into force of the **Treaty of Lisbon** and the abandonment of the pillar structure.

JUSTICIABLE means that, under the terms of the **European treaties**, a matter under dispute can be submitted to the **Court of Justice** or the **Court of First Instance** for resolution.

The **JUSTUS LIPSIUS** building in **Brussels** is the home of the **Council of the European Union** and the **European Council**. It is situated opposite the **Berlaymont** building, which is the home of the **European Commission**. Justus Lipsius (1547–1606) was a humanist and classical scholar.

K

KALEIDOSCOPE is the name of an initiative introduced in 1996 under the European Communities' cultural policy. The programme was intended to promote contemporary artistic creativity, encourage the training and mobility of young artists in all cultural areas, and support innovative cultural events with a European dimension, as well as seeking to encourage greater public awareness of Europe's cultural heritage. Although most of the activities that the programme financed were rather small-scale and amounted individually to a maximum of ecu 50,000, there were a number of larger projects such as the European Community Youth Orchestra and the **European Capital of Culture**. In 2000 the **Culture 2000** framework programme, which ran until 2004, replaced the previous activities of Kaleidoscope and aimed to implement a new approach to cultural action. (See also **Raphael**.)

KALININGRAD, formerly known as Königsberg, was part of German East Prussia until this territory was annexed by the **USSR** in 1946. The territory offered the USSR direct access to the Baltic Sea and was one of the most militarized places in Europe during the **Cold War**. However, the dissolution of the USSR in the early 1990s transformed the Kaliningrad region into what was effectively a Russian exclave that was cut off geographically from **Russia** by Lithuania, Latvia and Belarus, and whose economic situation has been desperate for much of the time since. In 1992 it was declared a 'free economic zone' in the hope of attracting foreign investment. The **enlargement** of the European Union (EU) and the **North Atlantic Treaty Organization** (NATO) to include Poland and Lithuania have heightened fears that the exclave could become completely isolated. Hence, the Russian Government has been keen to ensure land access to Kaliningrad. Its initial proposal of a closed land corridor was rejected by Lithuania and the EU during **accession negotiations**. Instead, agreement was reached in 2002 on introducing special transit arrangements for Russian citizens from 1 July 2003. Sensitive to the economic situation of the enclave, the EU established Kaliningrad as a priority area in the 2002–03 **Technical Assistance to the Commonwealth of Independent States** programme. This followed earlier financial assistance aimed at tackling severe environmental problems in the region, and was followed by funding worth €50m. for the period 2004–06. This was aimed at improving, *inter alia*, border crossings, local economic development, administrative capacity building, and the environmental situation in the territory.

SIIM KALLAS (1948–) is one of the Vice-Presidents of the second **Barroso** Commission of the European Union (2010–14). He comes from Estonia and is one of the few members of the College who is now serving a second term as Commissioner. During Barroso's first Commission (2004–09) Kallas was in charge of the Commission's portfolio for administrative affairs, audit and anti-fraud. He is currently responsible for the transport portfolio. Before coming to work within the Commission, Kallas had served as the Estonian Minister of Foreign Affairs (1995–96), was Estonian Prime Minister for nine months in 2002–03, and was leader of the free market, liberal Estonian Reform Party.

KENNEDY ROUND, named after President John F. Kennedy of the **USA**, was the name given to the sixth series of negotiations (1964–67) on tariff reductions held by the **General Agreement on Tariffs and Trade** (GATT). It was the first series of GATT talks where the **European Commission** was the sole representative of the European Communities (EC), according to the terms of the **Treaty of Rome**, which stipulated that the EC were to represent the member states in issues of external trade. As a result of the discussions, the EC **common external tariff** was reduced, on average, by some 35%.

ENDA KENNY (1951–) succeeded **Brian Cowen** as Prime Minister of **Ireland** in March 2011. Kenny has an established pedigree in politics and has served as a member of the Irish parliament since 1975. He was elected as the leader of Fine Gael in 2002 following the resignation of **John Bruton**. Kenny led his party to the largest success in its history at the February 2011 Irish elections. The party benefited from the severe unpopularity of the Cowen administration and this helped Kenny's party to capture 76 seats to become the largest party in the Irish parliament. Kenny negotiated an agreement with the Irish Labour party to form a coalition Government.

NEIL KINNOCK (1942–) became one of the British members of the **European Commission** in 1995 and assumed responsibility for transport. Prior to this appointment he had limited experience within the European Union, and his move to **Brussels** surprised many. He had spent his political career in Westminster, where he served as leader of the Labour Party from 1983 until 1992, when he resigned after Labour's election defeat, and was largely respon-sible for undertaking the full-scale review of the party that led to the emergence of 'New Labour' in the 1990s, which preceded **Tony Blair**'s election victory in 1997. Kinnock was one of the few members of the **Jacques Santer** Commis-sion (1995–99) to return to Brussels, becoming a senior figure in the **Romano Prodi** Commission. With his accession to the post of Vice-President for

317

Administrative Reform in 1999, he took responsibility for overhauling the structure and internal machinery of the Commission. He stepped down from the Commission when his term of office ended in November 2004 and now sits in the British House of Lords.

The **KIRCHBERG DECLARATION** dates from May 1994, when it was issued by the leaders of the **Western European Union** (WEU). Essentially it established categories of WEU membership. The four categories listed are: full members, which are members of both the **North Atlantic Treaty Organization** (NATO) and the European Union (EU), such as the United Kingdom; associate members, which are members only of NATO and not the EU; associate partners, which are members of neither NATO nor the EU; and finally, observers, such as Ireland, which are members of the EU but not of NATO.

HELMUT KOHL (1930–) became Chancellor of the Federal Republic of Germany (West Germany) in 1982, and was elected Chancellor of the reunified Germany in 1990, remaining Chancellor until his defeat at the September 1998 federal elections. A long-term advocate of **supranationalism**, he supported the moves towards integration in the 1980s that culminated in the **Single European Act**, while still seeking to defend German interests in the European Communities (EC). His commitment led to Germany's willingness to see the doubling of the **structural funds** in 1988 and the creation of the **Cohesion Fund** in 1993 to facilitate the reduction of economic disparities in the four poorest European Union (EU) member states (Greece, Ireland, Portugal and Spain). Wishing for a stronger **European Commission** and **European Parliament**, he called for European political union on several occasions, establishing a close alliance with President **François Mitterrand** of France in April 1990, and with the then Commission President, **Jacques Delors**. Following the collapse of the Communist regime in the German Democratic Republic (East Germany) in 1989 and German reunification in October 1990, Kohl's role in the EC increased. Reunification, in his view, gave a greater urgency to European union, for only through unification could concerns be allayed in other countries about a potentially more powerful Germany. Ultimately, the **Treaty on European Union** (TEU) did not entirely meet all his objectives, and there was opposition in Germany to some of its provisions (and specifically to **economic and monetary union**—EMU). After the TEU, Kohl continued to take a lead in pressing the EU to move swiftly to full EMU. In the mid-1990s he was a committed supporter of **enlargement** and sought greater European co-operation in the fields of **justice and home affairs**. He leaves a substantial legacy and will undoubtedly be identified as one of the most influential figures in the history of EU integration. Following his defeat in 1998 the prospects of Kohl becoming an international elder statesman seemed almost assured until he became embroiled in a political scandal on financial irregularities over party funding that had occurred during his term as party leader of the Christian Democrats. This scandal tarnished his political reputation, but he has gradually been rehabilitated as arguably one of the most significant post-war figures of European and German politics.

KOSOVO was formerly an autonomous region within **Serbia** and, before that, **Yugoslavia**. Following a three-year conflict in 1996–99 between Serbian and Yugoslav forces and the guerrilla Kosovo Liberation Army, the **North Atlantic Treaty Organization** (NATO) launched air strikes against Yugoslav forces in the region in an attempt to force a political settlement to the conflict. The Yugoslav and Serbian leaderships eventually accepted the presence of a NATO-led peacekeeping force—KFOR—in Kosovo. Over the next nine years, Kosovo was administered by the **United Nations** (UN), and pressure for independence grew within the province, culminating in a declaration of independence on 17 February 2008. This was strongly opposed by **Serbia** and by **Russia**. Within the European Union (EU), opinion on recognizing the newly independent state was divided, although most member states moved quickly to recognition. The EU also assumed responsibility from the UN for the administration and security of Kosovo, deploying a mission of some 1,800 international administrators, lawyers, judges and police (subsequently increased to 2,000) under the European Union Rule of Law Mission in Kosovo (EULEX Kosovo, which also employs local personnel) in an attempt to ensure the functioning of the new state. Kosovo is gradually being integrated with the EU as part of both the **Stabilization and Association Process** and the EU's more general approach to the **Western Balkans**. However, the process is complicated by the fact that five EU member states—Croatia, Greece, Romania, Slovakia and Spain—have so far refused to recognize Kosovo's independence and continue to consider it a breakaway province of Serbia. In June 2012 the Council of the European Union announced that the mandate of EULEX Kosovo had been extended for another two years until June 2014. A budget of €111m. was allocated for the first of these two additional years.

NEELIE KROES (1941–) gained responsibility for the digital agenda and became one of the Vice-Presidents in the Barroso II Commission (2010–14). This is her second term as a Commissioner: she was in charge of competition policy in 2004–09. She is one of the new Commission's free marketeers and is a member of the Dutch Liberal Party. Since the mid-1980s Kroes has emerged as one of the most powerful and well-known businesswomen in the Netherlands. She served several terms as Dutch minister responsible for transport in the 1980s. As Competition Commissioner, she placed considerable emphasis on tackling state aid (see **subsidies**) and **cartels**. She is one of the Barroso Commission's most high-profile personalities.

L

The **LAEKEN DECLARATION** on the Future of the European Union was adopted by the **European Council** at its summit in Laeken, Belgium, on 15 December 2001. The Declaration followed a similar Declaration on the Future of the Union adopted a year earlier at the same time as the **Treaty of Nice** and was significant for the issues it raised for consideration by the **European Convention**, which was launched in late February 2002. The Laeken Declaration begins by identifying the two key challenges facing Europe: the need to bring the European Union (EU) closer to its citizens; and defining the role for the EU in a fast-changing globalized world. It then proceeds to raise more than 50 questions and issues for the Convention to address. These include a better division and definition of the EU's competences; **simplification** of treaties and legislative measures; the need for more democracy, **transparency** and efficiency; and steps towards a **constitution** for the EU.

CHRISTINE LAGARDE (1956–) was appointed as the new Managing Director of the International Monetary Fund (IMF), replacing Dominique Strauss-Kahn, in July 2011. Lagarde was born in Paris and studied law at university in the French capital before taking a Master's degree in English and political science at the Institute of Political Studies in Aix-en-Provence. After graduation she was admitted into the French legal profession. She started working for a major US law company (Baker & McKenzie) in 1981, where she specialised in antitrust and labour law. She rose rapidly through the firm and became a partner in 1987, the head of its European division in 1995 and its first female chairman in 1999. She left Baker & McKenzie in 2005 to become Minister of Foreign Trade in the French Government of the centre-right Union pour un Mouvement Populaire. Under the presidency of **Nicolas Sarkozy** Lagarde served as Minister of Agriculture (for a month) and then Minister of the Economy, Finance and Industry.

The **LAMFALUSSY PROCEDURE** refers to a novel approach to the process of European **legislation** and regulation. It originated in February 2001, when a 'Group of Wise Men' headed by Baron Alexandre Lamfalussy presented a Report on the Regulation of European Securities Markets to the **Council of the European Union**. The report provided a clear and coherent argument calling for a change in European legislative and regulatory structures. Essentially, the authors of the report identified the economic benefits of further financial market integration in Europe, highlighted the key factors slowing down that integration process and arrived at the conclusion that the then existing regulatory system was unable to cope with the accelerating pace of market change. To overcome and reduce the deficiencies, the Group agreed upon what has become known as the Lamfalussy procedure. It is a four-level approach to law-making, based partially on procedures existing (but not widely used before in the area of financial markets) in the European Union (EU) constitutional framework, and partially on experience in member states, but it is also partially new and innovative. According to the Lamfalussy proposals, financial markets legislation and regulation should usefully involve the following four levels: framework principles to be decided by normal EU legislative procedures, i.e. in co-decision between Council and Parliament (EP—see **European Parliament**) upon a proposal by the Commission (see **European Commission**); **implementation** legislation by the Commission upon proposal by the newly established Council of European Securities Regulators (CESR) in consultation with member states through an EU Securities Committee; intense co-operation and networking between securities regulators in the CESR to ensure consistent and equivalent transposition of level I and II legislation; and strengthened enforcement, basically through Commission action, but with co-operation from member states, regulators, and the private sector. In the area of securities markets legislation, the Lamfalussy procedure was applied for the first time for the new Directives on Market Abuse and on Prospectuses. The first impressions were mixed; it appeared that not all of the parties involved may have fully understood (or fully appreciated) the mechanics as intended by the 'Wise Men'. Proposals have been made to extend the application of the Lamfalussy process beyond securities markets into other financial areas (notably banking, insurance and investment funds).

LANGUAGES are both an indication of the diversity of the European Union (EU) and a barrier to effective integration. Prior to **enlargement** in 2004, the EU had 11 official languages: Danish, Dutch, English, Finnish, French, German, Greek, Italian, Portuguese, Spanish and Swedish. With 10 countries joining, a further nine languages became official languages of the EU: Czech, Estonian, Hungarian, Latvian, Lithuanian, Maltese, Polish, Slovak and Slovenian. The total was thus raised to 20. In May 2005 the Irish language was officially recognized as a working language by the EU. Irish thus became the 21st language to be given such recognition by the EU. Prior to this development Irish had been recognized as a treaty language only. From January 2007 Bulgarian and Romanian also became official working languages, bringing the overall total to 23. Any one official language may be used in EU meetings; all official documents from all EU institutions need to be translated into all languages; and simultaneous interpreting between all languages is provided for most EU meetings (e.g. of the **European Council**, the **Council of the European Union**, the **Court of Justice** and the **European Parliament**).

The cost of translation is considerable, there being more than 400 different translation combinations, but arguably necessary if the EU's citizens are to be able to understand the **decisions** and laws that affect them. Within the **European Commission**, costs are reduced since the administration conducts most of its daily business in English and French. Other institutions have yet to follow suit to the same extent although many committees do conduct their business in either English or French. (See also **Lingua**.)

LATIN AMERICA: See **South and Central America**

LATVIA regained its independence from the then **USSR** in 1991. Soon thereafter it began negotiations with the European Communities (EC) on a **free trade agreement**, which was concluded in 1994. However, by the time the subsequently negotiated **Europe agreement** was signed in 1995, attention was focusing on an application for membership of the European Union (EU), which was duly submitted on 27 October 1995. Although the **European Commission**'s *avis* in 1997 was supportive of Latvia's desire to join the EU, it did not recommend **accession negotiations**, primarily because of concerns over the insufficient progress made with economic reform. Instead, Latvia had to wait for the Helsinki **summit meeting** of the **European Council** in December 1999 before being invited to negotiate membership. Despite coming late to accession negotiations, Latvia was among the **candidate countries** that concluded negotiations at the **Copenhagen summit** in December 2002. The Latvian electorate subsequently endorsed the terms of accession in a referendum in September 2003. In a turn-out of 72.5%, more than 67% voted in favour of EU membership. Latvia joined the EU in May 2004 and a year later approved (by parliamentary vote) the **Treaty establishing a Constitution for Europe**. The country became part of the EU's **Schengen Area** in December 2007. The Latvian Parliament approved the **Treaty of Lisbon** in early 2008.

LAW in the context of the European Communities (EC) is ultimately based upon the **Treaty of Rome**, according to which EC law takes precedence over national law. EC law derives from two sources. The first is **legislation** initiated and applied by the **European Commission** and adopted by the **Council of the European Union**. The second is the body of case-law arising from rulings given by the **European Court of Justice** and the **Court of First Instance** in interpreting the provisions of the treaties and EC legislation. Since the establishment of the European Union (EU) and prior to the abandonment of the EC with the **Treaty of Lisbon**'s entry into force, some sources also refer to **European Union Law**. This arguably differs from EC law in that it derives from the EU's two intergovernmental **pillars**. (See also **soft laws**.)

LDR: See **Group of the European Liberal Democrats**

LEADER is the acronym of a **structural funds** initiative, launched in 1991, to preserve the diversification of rural socio-economic structures within the European Union through the establishment of networks of rural development groups using new communications technologies, and the promotion of rural tourism. It continued as Leader II in 1994 before being replaced by Leader+ in 2000 (which ran until 2006). The rural development programme of 2007–13 was based on the policies implemented as part of the Leader initiative.

LEFT UNITY (LU), also known by the French title Coalition des Gauches (CG), was a transnational **party group** in the **European Parliament** between 1989 and 1994. It was formed as a result of the division of the original **Communists and Allies** group into two factions. LU, dominated by French Communists, was the more ideological and Marxist-Leninist of the two Communist groups.

The **LEGAL INSTRUMENTS** of the European Union include **directives**, **regulations** and **decisions**. The **Treaty establishing a Constitution for Europe** envisaged their replacement with a new range of instruments: European Laws and European Framework Laws, European Regulations and European Decisions. This was one of the few substantive elements of the treaty not carried forward into the **Treaty of Lisbon**.

LEGAL PERSONALITY is a concept that means that a body has the right under international law to take autonomous actions rather than relying upon governments to act on its behalf. The **Treaty of Rome** conferred legal personality upon the European Community (EC). This meant that the EC could act in law as an independent party, enter into legally binding agreements, and be subject to constitutional legal proceedings. The legal personality of the EC was distinct from that of the member states. By contrast, the **Treaty on European Union** did not explicitly confer legal personality on the European Union (EU). The fact that agreements could be and were concluded in the name of the EU strengthened the argument that the EU did in practice have legal personality. Had it entered into force, the **Treaty establishing a Constitution for Europe** would have resolved the situation by conferring legal personality on the EU. Legal personality for the EU has since been established with the entry into force of the **Treaty of Lisbon**.

The **LEGAL SERVICE** is a service of the **European Commission**. Its major task is to prepare and evaluate, from a legal perspective, European Union (EU) **legislation**; it also represents the Commission in all court cases. The Legal

Service has to ensure that all legislation, before being printed in the *Official Journal of the European Union*, has the same precise legal meaning in all EU **languages**. The **Council of the European Union** also has a Legal Service which advises the **Council Secretariat** and the **Council Presidency**.

LEGISLATION is enacted by complex procedures in the European Union (EU). The **Council of the European Union** and the **European Parliament** (EP) or the **European Commission** are empowered to issue three different kinds of legislation: **regulations**, **directives** and **decisions**. The **Court of Justice** institutes a fourth source of legislation: rulings given by the Court on the cases that come before it constitute a body of case-law which affects the interpretation and **implementation** of European Communities (EC) and national **law**. In addition there is so-called '**soft law**'.

The EU equivalent of national legislation is the combination of regulations and directives. The first stage of both lies with the Commission, which has the **right of initiative**. If adopted by the Council, the Commission's proposal becomes either a regulation or a directive. The distinction between the two is important. Regulations are more rigorous, the highest form of legislation. They are fairly detailed instructions, applicable throughout the EU, and directly binding upon all member states. Directives are also binding, but take the form of general instructions on the goal to be achieved, while leaving the way in which it will be attained to the discretion of each member state. The conditions of a directive are normally met by the member states introducing national legislation in conformity with EU stipulations.

Decisions by either the Commission or the Council are also binding upon the member states; they may be addressed to named individuals or enterprises. Decisions can be made by either of the EU executives on the basis of the direct authority they possess under the terms of the **Treaty of Rome** and its amendments, or on the basis of earlier regulations or directives. (Decisions made according to the provisions of the **Treaty of Paris** were slightly different: they were binding in their entirety upon member states and were thus more similar to regulations.)

Under the Treaty of Rome and its amendments, the Commission and the Council can also issue **recommendations**, which, like **opinions**, and in contrast to the pronouncements described above, do not constitute instructions but merely express an EU preference that member states are free to ignore. (However, recommendations made under the Treaty of Paris were binding as to the final result, but not the means to achieve it, rather like EU directives.)

Whereas originally, decisions to adopt EC legislation involved either the Commission or the Council, the EP now has a significant role to play. In 1987 the **Single European Act** introduced the **co-operation procedure**, which allowed the EP to table amendments to and reject proposed legislation. It also made **ratification** of **association agreements** and **accession treaties** conditional on the assent of the EP (see **assent procedure**). This was followed in

1993 by the introduction via the **Treaty on European Union** (TEU) of the **co-decision procedure**, along with a requirement that certain legislative proposals be adopted jointly by the Council and the EP. Since the TEU, the **Treaty of Amsterdam**, the **Treaty of Nice** and the **Treaty of Lisbon** have all extended use of the **ordinary legislative procedure** (formerly co-decision) and the **consent** (formerly assent) **procedure**, thus further enhancing the EP's role in the legislative process.

The **LEGITIMACY** of the European Communities (EC) prior to the early 1990s was hardly challenged thanks to the permissive consensus that surrounded the European integration project. Since then, and in particular since the establishment of the European Union (EU), the legitimacy of the EC and the EU has been increasingly challenged. This has been evident in the criticisms coming not just from politicians, but also from the citizens of the EU, as evidenced by the **ratification crises** surrounding the **Treaty on European Union** and the **Treaty of Nice**, and the low and falling turn-out of voters in **European Parliament** elections. Major concerns focus on the perceived inability of the EU to deliver benefits to the people and to solve problems; lack of popular identification with and support for the EU; the alleged intrusiveness of the EU as it increasingly touches on areas traditionally viewed as being the preserve of national governments; and concern over the direction in which the integration project is heading. The question of how to remedy the declining legitimacy of the EU, as well as associated problems concerning the EU's **democratic deficit**, informed many of the issues on the agenda of the **European Convention** launched in February 2002.

LENIENCY NOTICES were first introduced by the Commission in 1996 in relation to its handling of **competition policy**. The Directorate-General for Competition revised its leniency procedures in 2002 and again in 2006. In an attempt to uncover **cartel** activity, the Commission devised its leniency initiative as a means to persuade and entice cartel members to break rank and supply the Commission with full details of a particular cartel's operations and management. A firm that does so can be given full immunity from any fine that the Commission imposes on the cartel. Cartels are by nature often unstable, and such an inducement to turn 'whistle blower' can prove attractive and lead to more cartels being uncovered.

LEONARDO (full title: Leonardo da Vinci) was the name of a phased action programme on the implementation of a comprehensive European Communities **education, vocational training and youth policy** to absorb and replace all existing initiatives in the area of vocational training. The first phase of the programme started in 1995, superseding the vocational training programmes Eurotecnet, Comett and Force. In 1998 young people from Hungary, the Czech Republic, Romania and Cyprus were able to take part in vocational exchanges with European Union (EU) countries under the programme. To date, some 33 states have been involved in the programme, which aims to strengthen the skills and competences of people, and especially young people, through, *inter alia*, work-linked training and apprenticeships. Leonardo also seeks to improve the quality of, and access to, continuing vocational training and lifelong acquisition of skills and abilities with a view to developing adaptability, particularly to new technological changes. The emphasis of this programme is on lifelong learning; the use of new information and communication technologies (ICTs); the participation of **small and medium-sized enterprises** and craft industry; and support for the most vulnerable categories of people in the labour market, including the disabled. The second phase of the Leonardo programme ran from January 2000 to 31 December 2006. The central objective of the programme is to consolidate a European co-operation area for education and training. To this end, the programme actively supports the lifelong training policies conducted by the member states. Since its creation, the Leonardo programme has enabled around 860,000 people to travel abroad for training or work experience, or for professionals to gain new skills and develop vocational education and training tools, methods and systems. During the five-year period 2007–11 it provided €1,270m. in grants. From 2007 Leonardo was incorporated into the new **Lifelong Learning Programme** (2007–13).

LEVIES: See **Budget**; **Common Agricultural Policy**; **Own Resources**

JANUSZ LEWANDOWSKI (1951–) is one of the 27 European Commissioners in the Barroso II Commission (2010–14), within which he has responsibility for the budget and financial programming. Lewandowski was born in Lublin, Poland, studied economics at the University of Gdansk, before going on to lecture, work as an economics adviser to government, and also serve as a member of the Polish parliament. In 2004 he was elected to the **European Parliament** (where he was an observer from 2003 prior to Poland's accession to the European Union) and is affiliated to the **European People's Party** political group.

LIBERAL, DEMOCRAT AND REFORM GROUP: See **Group of the European Liberal Democrats**

LIBERAL INTERGOVERNMENTALISM is one of the most prominent approaches to understanding the major decisions in the history of the European Union. In contrast to **neo-functionalism**, it focuses on national preferences, interstate bargaining and institutional delegation. As a consequence it tends to downplay the significance of geostrategic factors, ideology and supranational institutions in **decision-making**.

LIBERALIZATION refers, in the context of the European Union, to the process of establishing the **internal market** by eliminating unnecessary obstacles and restraints to trade.

DAVID LIDINGTON (1956–) became a Minister of State at the British Foreign and Commonwealth Office, with special responsibility for Europe, in May 2010. Lidington studied history at Cambridge University and wrote his doctoral thesis on Elizabethan England. He has been a member of the British parliament for the Conservative Party since 1992. Prior to this he worked (from 1987 to 1992) as a special adviser to Douglas Hurd, a former British Foreign Secretary (1989–92). His appointment as Minister for Europe can be read as a softening of **David Cameron**'s approach to Europe and a recognition of the realities of the Conservative Party's coalition Government with the more European Union-friendly Liberal Democrats under **Nick Clegg**.

LIECHTENSTEIN is the fourth smallest country in Europe. It developed a customs union and common currency (the Swiss franc) with **Switzerland** in 1923, and therefore enjoyed a close relationship with the **European Free Trade Association** (EFTA) after that organization was formed in 1960, but only became a full member of EFTA in 1991. In December 1992 Liechtenstein voted in favour of the **European Economic Area** (EEA), one week after participation in the latter had been rejected by a Swiss referendum. The vote seemed to indicate that Liechtenstein saw the EEA as a way of preserving its prosperity and of becoming more politically independent of Switzerland. However, full membership of the EEA could not be realized until the 1923 agreement with Switzerland had been modified. When the necessary adjustments to the customs union had been completed, membership of the EEA was endorsed by 55.9% of the vote in a further referendum held on 9 April 1995. Liechtenstein signed the **Schengen Agreement** in February 2008 and became part of the **Schengen Area** in December 2011. Despite close ties with the European Union (EU), Liechtenstein has expressed scant interest in joining, not least because membership would most likely necessitate changes to its position as a tax haven, an issue that in recent years has resulted in tense relations with a number of EU member states, notably Germany.

LIFE is the name of the European Union's funding instrument for environmental and nature conservation projects. LIFE was agreed and commenced in 1992. To date, there have been three completed phases of the programme—LIFE I (1992–95), LIFE II (1996–99) and LIFE III (2000–06)—which saw some 3,104 projects being sponsored, contributing around €2,200m. to the protection of the environment. Its objectives have been to provide financial aid for environmental activities, to support the implementation of various aspects of **environmental policy**, and to aid the EU in meeting the obligations of international environmental agreements and conventions to which it is a signatory. It also provided aid for certain non-EU states (those bordering the Mediterranean and the Baltic Sea) that applied to join the EU in the late 1990s. LIFE was also charged with the supervision of various EU environment programmes. It replaced a number of earlier programmes, including MEDSPA, which operated in the Mediterranean region, and NORSPA, which operated in the North European maritime regions. The third phase of LIFE began in January 2000 with an initial budget of €640m., and was originally scheduled to end in December 2004. However, this programme was extended until the end of 2006 with the provision of an additional €317m. of funding. The new LIFE+ programme was agreed by the EU Environment Council meeting in Luxembourg in June 2006 and entered into force in 2007. LIFE+ runs from 2007–13 and has a budget of €2,143m. LIFE+ comprises three main themes. These are: LIFE+ Nature and Biodiversity (and the conservation of natural habitats); LIFE+ Environment Policy and Governance (to promote new innovative methods and techniques to aid EU environmental policy); and LIFE+ Information and Communication.

The **LIFELONG LEARNING PROGRAMME** (LLP) for 2007–13 came into force on 14 December 2006. This programme aspires to foster lifelong learning opportunities for all citizens of the European Union (EU) from childhood to old age. It seeks to help create an advanced knowledge society and greater social cohesion and promote greater interaction, co-operation and mobility among the education and training systems throughout the EU. The programme can be distilled into four specific educational sectors or pillars. These are primary and secondary school education (**Comenius**), higher education exchanges (**Erasmus**), vocational education and training (**Leonardo da Vinci**) and adult education (**Grundtvig**). The programme is complemented by a transversal programme focusing on policy co-operation, **languages**, information and communication technology, and dissemination and exploitation of results. It also has responsibility for the long-established and successful Jean Monnet Programme which promotes European integration in higher educational establishments. The LLP has a budget of some €6,970m. for 2007–13. The Commission has set targets for this period, and these include a drive under Grundtvig to support the mobility of 7,000 individuals per year by 2013, under Leonardo da Vinci to create an additional 80,000 placements per year, under Comenius to have some 3m. pupils involved in joint educational activities and under Erasmus to have some 3m. students involved in university exchange schemes. To this end, the Commission launched a general call for proposals in 2007 for applications to secure these objectives. In 2008 it issued a call for proposals relating to the Jean Monnet Programme and another on the Erasmus

University Charter. The LLP is managed in the United Kingdom by the British Council.

LINGUA is the name of an action programme on the promotion and development of the teaching of the 23 official **languages** (with the addition of Letzeburgisch) of the European Union (EU), and the exchange of foreign-language teachers between the member states. It was a continuation of the 1984 commitment to ensure that schoolchildren would acquire a working knowledge of two other European Communities (EC) languages by the time they reached the statutory school-leaving age. More generally, it was intended as a contribution to increasing the cultural cohesion of the EC through creating awareness of languages and the notion of 'Europe' among the general public. Lingua was opposed in the Council of Ministers (see **Council of the European Union**) by the United Kingdom in 1989, on the grounds that its objectives were not provided for by the EC treaties. In adopting Lingua by a **qualified majority**, the Council accepted that the United Kingdom would initially be excluded from the programme. In 1995 Lingua was incorporated into the **Socrates** and **Leonardo** programmes. Today the Lingua action centres on language learning and teaching and has three main aims. These are: to encourage and support linguistic diversity throughout theEU; to contribute to an improvement in the quality of language teaching and learning; and to foster and facilitate access to lifelong language learning opportunities. To achieve these, action and activities have been divided into two parts. *Lingua 1* seeks to raise citizens' awareness of the Union's multilingual wealth, encourage people to learn languages throughout their lifetime, and improve access to foreign language learning resources across Europe. *Lingua 2* seeks to ensure that a sufficiently wide range of language learning tools is available to language learners.

The **LISBON AGENDA** (or **2010 strategy**) was the product of a special **European Council** held in the city of Lisbon in March 2000. It was decided on that occasion to set the European Union (EU) a 10-year strategic goal of becoming 'the most competitive and dynamic knowledge-based economy in the world, capable of sustaining and encouraging economic growth with more and better jobs (some 20m. more jobs) and greater social cohesion'. To this end, the Council established a series of targets, which included raising the employment rate and increasing the number of women in employment. Various mechanisms were subsequently developed to enable these goals to be achieved in areas such as **employment**, innovation, enterprise, liberalization and the environment.

Progress was reviewed on an annual basis and, where necessary, updated. In retrospect, these targets were over-ambitious. They were agreed at a time of growing economic and business confidence. It was the height of the 'dot.com' boom and economic prospects looked rather good. By 2005 it was clear that the EU was far from being a beacon of economic growth. In fact growth rates in France, Germany and Italy had been disappointing. Instead of things getting better, in many European countries the economic outlook had actually deteriorated. In France and Germany, for example, unemployment was around 10%. Overall, the EU was struggling to compete with the **USA**, and European leaders were increasingly aware of the acute dangers and challenges to EU economic success that were presented by the rapidly growing competition from the Asian economies. The EU leaders realized that something had to be done to secure EU economic **competitiveness**, but also recognized some of the difficulties in trying to push for liberalization and greater economic reform. One of the clearest illustrations of such difficulties was revealed by the resistance to the EU's drive to open up the services market and, particularly, the fate of the **Bolkestein Directive** in 2005. The **European Commission** has argued that the opening up of this important sector would have created 600,000 new jobs and that the ensuing increase in output in the EU economy would have been in the region of €33,000m. The EU leaders agreed their determination to pursue the Lisbon objectives in early 2005, but scaled back their ambitious targets. In March 2010 the Commission launched the successor programme, **Europe 2020**.

LITHUANIA, like its Baltic neighbours, Estonia and Latvia, regained its independence from the **USSR** in 1991. It then proceeded to conclude a **free trade agreement** (1994) and a **Europe agreement** (1995) with the European Union (EU) before applying to join the EU in December 1995. In its *avis* on the application, the **European Commission** expressed concern about the economic preparedness of Lithuania for membership. Consequently, Lithuania was not included among the countries of **Central and Eastern Europe** invited to open **accession negotiations** in early 1998. It did, however, start negotiations two years later, following a positive regular report from the Commission in October 1999 and an invitation to negotiate from the Helsinki **European Council** in December 1999. Although a latecomer to negotiations, by mid-2002 Lithuania had completed negotiations on more than two-thirds of the 31 negotiating chapters. As anticipated, the remaining chapters were closed by the time of the **Copenhagen summit** of the **European Council** in December 2002. Lithuania therefore joined nine other **candidate countries** in signing the **Accession Treaty** in April 2003. In the following month, of the 63.4% of the electorate who participated in a referendum, 91.1% voted in favour of joining the EU. Lithuania joined the EU on 1 May 2004, and in November 2004 became the first EU member state successfully to ratify the **Treaty establishing a Constitution for Europe**. In March 2006 Lithuania applied to join the **eurozone**, seeking membership from 1 January 2007. In the event, this target proved just too ambitious, as the Lithuanian Government was unable to stabilize the country's inflation rate. Lithuania is not expected to join the euro area before 2014. The country did, however, become part of the EU's **Schengen Area** in December 2007.

LOBBYING of major institutions of the European Communities (EC) and the European Union (EU), such as the **European Commission** and the **European Parliament** (EP), has grown dramatically since the mid-1980s, primarily as a consequence of the increase in the amount of **legislation** emanating from the EC and EU. Lobbyists range from individual companies and single-issue pressure groups to trade associations and so-called Eurogroups such as the **European Round Table of Industrialists**. In addition, a range of regional interests are represented in **Brussels** seeking to gain influence over the decision-making process. The Commission has set up a database, CONECCS (Consultation, the European Commission and Civil Society), of around 1,000 organizations working at EU level and covering approximately 100 branches of activity. (See also **interest groups**.)

The **LOMÉ CONVENTION** is the title of a series of agreements named after the capital of Togo and, until the entry into force of the **Cotonou Agreement**, the Convention was the central element of the European Communities' (EC) relations with developing countries. It derived from a commitment in the original **Treaty of Rome** to develop a relationship between the original **Six** members of the **European Economic Community** (EEC) and their former colonies, in order to promote the interests of the latter and 'to lead them to the economic, social and cultural development to which they aspire'. The first agreements towards these ends were the **Yaoundé Convention** agreements of 1963 and 1969. The First Lomé Convention (Lomé I), signed in 1975, was an extension of the Yaoundé Conventions to involve the EC more formally in development activities in more countries. The recipient states, some of which already had agreements with the EC (e.g. the Arusha Agreements with Kenya, Tanzania and Uganda), were known as the **African, Caribbean and Pacific** (ACP) **States**. Three further Lomé Conventions were signed in 1979, 1984 and 1989. Some 70 ACP countries were party to Lomé IV, compared with 46 signatories of Lomé I.

There were two central themes to the Lomé Conventions. The first was the provision for duty-free access to the EC, on a non-reciprocal basis, for most ACP exports. There has always been discontent on the part of the ACP States over two major exceptions to the principle of free access: those agricultural products that would compete with European Union (EU) produce protected by the **common agricultural policy**; and textiles, which have been governed by the **multifibre arrangement**. However, exemptions have been made in the case of sugar, despite sugar beet over-production in the EU, according to which the EU buys an annual quota of ACP sugar at high EU prices. The second theme is **development aid** through grants from the **European Development Fund** (EDF) and low-interest loans from the **European Investment Bank**. Although funding has increased substantially since 1975, it has to be shared among a great number of eligible recipients. Lomé II introduced further assistance for ACP countries whose export earnings are heavily dependent on one or a few staple products, and which are consequently more exposed to market fluctuations, with the establishment of the System of Stabilization of Export Earnings (STABEX). More specialized assistance was subsequently provided through the System for Safeguarding and Developing Mineral Production (SYSMIN). Neither form of assistance survived the transition to the Cotonou Agreement. Under Lomé III, the EDF set agricultural and rural development as a first priority, with an emphasis on food crops as opposed to cash crops, small EC-based projects, and measures designed to combat drought and desertification. Lomé IV continued these broad emphases, but offered more money for shorter-term structural projects and increased the proportion of grants, as opposed to loans, made under STABEX.

The Lomé Conventions created a legal framework for bilateral co-operation, and a series of joint institutions were made responsible for supervising the operation of the Conventions and the **implementation** of their programmes: these were the ACP-EU Council of Ministers, a Committee of Ambassadors and a Joint Assembly of representatives from the **ACP States** and the **European Parliament**.

LU: See **Left Unity**

JOSEPH LUNS (1911–2002) of the Netherlands is perhaps best known as having been a vigorous and effective Secretary-General of the **North Atlantic Treaty Organization** (1971–84). Earlier, as Dutch foreign minister from 1956 to 1971, he had been the most forthright opponent of the proposals by President **Charles de Gaulle** of France for a form of political union in which decisions would be taken by unanimous agreement, and he played a major role in the rejection of the **Fouchet Plan**. He was a firm supporter of **enlargement**, and strongly criticized the French veto in 1963 of the British application for membership.

LUXEMBOURG participates with Belgium and the Netherlands in the **Benelux** Union and was a founder member of the European Communities (EC). Currently one of the smallest member states, and one that has always been exposed to external influences, it has perhaps had fewer reservations than most about diminution of national sovereignty and independence. Its governments have been strong supporters of initiatives for further integration, especially those relating to institutional reform, and several of its statesmen have figured prominently in the development of the EC. Several European institutions are based in Luxembourg rather than in **Brussels**: the **European Court of Justice** and the **Court of Auditors**, the **European Investment Bank** and part of the **European Commission**'s staff, as well as part of the **European Parliament**'s. Luxembourg was also the headquarters of the **European Coal and Steel Community** before 1967. Luxembourg has been one of the most pro-EU minded member states and was determined to go ahead as planned with its referendum on the **Treaty establishing a Constitution for Europe** in July 2005, even after the rejections in France and the Netherlands. A majority—56%—of Luxembourg's voters approved the constitution, and Prime Minister Jean-Claude Juncker, who had threatened to resign in the case of a 'no' vote, claimed the treaty had been resurrected by the vote. Luxembourg ratified the **Treaty of Lisbon** in May 2008.

The **LUXEMBOURG COMPROMISE** is the name of the agreement reached by the **Six** in January 1966 that resolved the **empty chair crisis** between France and the five other member states. It was essentially acquiescence to French demands regarding **supranationalism**, and it specifically dealt with the operation of the Council of Ministers (see **Council of the European Union**) and the permissible use of **qualified majority voting** (QMV). The essential sentence of the Compromise states: 'Where, in the case of decisions which may be taken by a majority vote on a proposal from the Commission, very important interests of one or more partners are at stake, the Members of the Council will endeavour, within a reasonable time, to reach solutions which can be adopted by all the Members of the Council while respecting their mutual interests and those of the Community'. The member states also noted that 'there is a divergence of views on what should be done in the event of a failure to reach complete agreement', but that 'this divergence does not prevent the Community's work being resumed in accordance with the normal procedure'. In essence, the Six agreed to accept the right of any member state to veto proposals before the Council of Ministers whenever it believed its own national interests might be adversely affected.

The Compromise decisively altered the direction of the European Communities (EC) and the balance of power within it. It reduced the importance of the **European Commission**, emphasized the centrality of the member governments and delayed the completion of the **common market**. Despite all the rhetoric and initiatives for closer integration, it set the tone for EC developments until the mid-1980s. This is despite the fact that, as a document outside the framework of the treaties, the Compromise possesses no legal force. In practice, the phrase 'very important interests' has had an unrestricted definition. It was not that the member states chose to exercise a **veto** under the terms of the Compromise. Rather, the Council of Ministers chose to rely more upon unanimous agreement or consensus, being generally unwilling to proceed with any issue to the point where a veto might be invoked. This was a major factor in the steady accumulation of European Commission initiatives and proposals awaiting consideration by the Council of Ministers.

The widespread feeling that the Compromise was nevertheless hindering European developments was one of the factors that persuaded the member states to include institutional reform in the **Single European Act** (SEA) of 1986. By reducing the number and kinds of issues requiring unanimous approval in the Council of Ministers, the SEA succeeded in limiting the potential impact of the Luxembourg Compromise in the future. However, neither the SEA nor the subsequent **Treaty on European Union** disposed of or regularized the Compromise. Nevertheless, owing in part to a change in the rules of procedure of the Council, scant use of the Compromise has been made since. Indeed, many authorities contend that it is now obsolete. However, the **Treaty of Amsterdam** introduced what has been referred to as a Luxembourg Compromise Mark II, where **decisions** are taken by QMV as part of the **common foreign and security policy**.

LUXEMBOURG GROUP: See **Accession Negotiations**

M

The **MAASTRICHT SUMMIT**, held in the town of that name in the Netherlands in December 1991, was one of the most decisive meetings of the **European Council**. It had been preceded by two **intergovernmental conferences** on political and monetary union. These provided the agenda of the **European Council**, which, after much and often acrimonious discussion, agreed upon a fundamental revision of the **Treaty of Rome** in the form of the **Treaty on European Union**.

MAASTRICHT TREATY: See **Treaty on European Union**

The **FORMER YUGOSLAV REPUBLIC OF MACEDONIA** (FYRM) was part of **Yugoslavia** from 1919 until its declaration of independence in 1991. The decision on the country's name drew a hostile response from Greece, which had a province of the same name, and the Greek Government feared that any international recognition of the new 'Macedonian' state might encourage a false claim to future territorial expansion. Greek opposition culminated in thwarting the European Union's (EU) recognition of Macedonia's independence from Yugoslavia until 1995, by which time the new state had become known as the FYRM. Once recognized, the FYRM concluded a **trade and co-operation agreement** with the EU in 1997. A **stabilization and association agreement** (SAA) followed in 2000, along with medium-term financial assistance via the former **CARDS** programme. While it was keen to join the EU, civil unrest in 2001 put paid to the FYRM's chances of joining the countries of **Central and Eastern Europe** in **accession negotiations**. The FYRM was nevertheless recognized as a **potential candidate state**. Successful **ratification** of its SAA in early 2004 was scheduled to be swiftly followed by the submission of an application for EU membership on 26 February 2004. The death in an air crash of the country's President, Boris Trajkovski, earlier on that day meant that the application was postponed to 22 March 2004. The **European Commission**'s response to the application came in November 2005 and was positive. The following month the European Council upgraded the status of the FYRM to **candidate country**, although no timetable was given for the opening of accession negotiations. The situation remained unchanged two years later when the Commission, in its progress report, noted that there was a general need in the FYRM to accelerate the domestic political and economic reform process, which had been undermined by political tensions in the country. The Commission did, however, propose the adoption of an **accession partnership** for the FYRM, thus upgrading relations from the **European partnership** of 2004 to a mechanism focused, symbolically, more squarely on accession. As of September 2012, accession negotiations had still not been opened. This was as much attributable to Greece's insistence that the name dispute between the Governments of Greece and FYRM be resolved as it was to the shortcomings in Macedonia's preparedness for accession negotiations.

HAROLD MACMILLAN (1894–1986), Conservative Prime Minister of the United Kingdom from 1957 to 1963, reversed the United Kingdom's post-war policy of non-involvement in any European venture that went beyond inter-governmental co-operation. In July 1961 he announced that the United Kingdom would seek membership of the European Communities (EC). Several factors influenced this reversal of policy: the unsatisfactory nature of the **European Free Trade Association** by comparison with the EC as an outlet for British trade; the diminishing influence of the United Kingdom in world politics; and the persistently poor performance of the British economy. While Macmillan accepted and cited the economic reasons why the United Kingdom should join the EC, he also believed that entry was politically necessary 'to preserve the power and strength of Britain in the world'. The British application was initially and unilaterally vetoed by France in January 1963.

RAY MACSHARRY (1938–) of Ireland served as Commissioner with responsibility for Agriculture and Rural Development from 1989 to 1993 and was largely responsible for the largest overhaul to that date (since Sicco Mansholt—see **Mansholt Plan**) of the **common agricultural policy** (CAP). MacSharry's efforts at reforming the CAP, which had become a huge drain on the European Communities' (EC) limited budgetary resources, need to be set against the wider global effort under the **Uruguay Round** of the **General Agreement on Tariffs and Trade** (GATT) to liberalize world trade and to reduce the levels of protection for the EC agricultural sector. This Round had seen the inclusion of agriculture for the first time, largely at the insistence of the **USA**. The 1991 MacSharry Plan sought to reconcile the goals of reducing agricultural surpluses and abolishing trade-distorting export **subsidies** while simultaneously trying to maintain high farm incomes. His plans to reduce farm income support aroused considerable anger in France and Ireland but had the backing of a majority of EC states, including the United Kingdom and the Netherlands. The Council of Ministers (see **Council of the European Union**) adopted MacSharry's proposals in 1992. In 2002 MacSharry was appointed the Irish representative to the **European Convention**.

The **MAGHREB STATES** of Algeria, **Morocco** and Tunisia signed a collective bilateral trade and aid agreement with the European Communities (EC) in 1976, covering financial, industrial and technical affairs. The agreement allowed duty-free access to the EC for most industrial products from these states and special concessions for some of their agricultural produce. An **association agreement** was signed between the European Union (EU) and Tunisia in 1995, with Morocco in 1996 and with Algeria in 2002. The states also have access to EU **development aid**, and a new financial arrangement was negotiated in 1991. Since then, their relations with the EU have developed within the context of the **Euro–Mediterranean partnership** and proposals to establish a **Euro–Mediterranean Economic Area**.

JOHN MAJOR (1943–) was Conservative Prime Minister of the United Kingdom from 1990 to 1997, succeeding **Margaret Thatcher**. He declared his intention early on to place Britain 'at the heart of Europe'. While certainly more favourably disposed towards European involvement than his predecessor, he faced determined opposition from some members of his own party. In order to balance the various interests within the party, he was forced to act cautiously during the **Maastricht summit** and secured **opt-outs** for the United Kingdom from **economic and monetary union** and the new **social policy** developments. These policies served only to reinforce perceptions that seemed to confirm the view of several other member states that the United Kingdom remained a half-hearted participant in the European Communities. Major's negotiating position was severely weakened when the Conservatives were left with a narrow majority in Parliament after the 1992 elections. As his majority of 16 Members of Parliament (MPs) shrank during the period from 1992 to 1997, the influence of a small group of Eurosceptic MPs grew and effectively restricted his movements with regard to the European Union.

MAJORITY VOTING is one of the ways in which **decisions** may be taken in the **Council of the European Union**. Simple majorities apply only to a limited number of minor issues, usually dealing with procedural matters. It is unlikely that the member states would accept it as the normal mode of **decision-making**. Member states do, however, accept the use of **Qualified Majority Voting**.

MALTA initially played little part in the European integration process. It gained independence from the United Kingdom in 1964, joined the **Council of Europe** in 1965, and in 1970 concluded an **association agreement** with the European Communities (EC). The agreement was regarded by the EC as another element of their **Mediterranean policy**, and constituted a progressive move towards a **customs union**. Owing to domestic politics, however, little came out of the relationship. In July 1990, Malta formally applied for EC membership, receiving a favourable *avis* in 1993, but in 1996 the incoming Labour Government decided to freeze the country's application. A change of government in 1998 led Malta to revive its application, and in February 1999 the **European Commission** recommended that **accession negotiations** should begin, alongside those taking place with certain countries of **Central and Eastern Europe** and with Cyprus. Of all the **candidate countries**, Malta was often judged to be the one applicant state that was most likely to reject membership, and the outcome proved a difficult one to predict to the very end, as the country seemed evenly split on the issue. On 8 March 2003 91% of the Maltese electorate participated in a referendum on membership of the European Union (EU). The final result showed that 53.6% of those who participated in the referendum supported accession, while 46.4% voted against. This vote was further endorsed a month later when the pro-EU Nationalist Party defeated the Labour Party in a general election. This paved the way for Malta to join the EU (as the smallest member state, with some 380,000 citizens) in May 2004. Malta's accession to the EU posed very few policy-related problems. In June 2006 it was agreed that Malta would join the **eurozone** and adopt the **euro**, which it did on 1 January 2008. The previous month it joined the EU's **Schengen Area**. Malta's parliament unanimously ratified the **Treaty of Lisbon** in January 2008. The Maltese Prime Minister Lawrence Gonzi argued that the treaty was in Malta's interests and would provide Malta with an extra, sixth seat in the European Parliament.

CECILIA MALMSTRÖM (1968–) is one of the 27 European Commissioners in the **Barroso** II Commission (2010–14), within which she has responsibility for home affairs. Malmström holds a doctorate in political science (from the University of Gothenburg, Sweden) and, prior to her current role, served as a **Member of the European Parliament** from 1999, sitting as a member of the **ALDE** group, before returning to serve in the Swedish Government as Minister for European Union Affairs from 2006–10.

MANAGEMENT COMMITTEES, set up in 1962, are part of the structure of the **common agricultural policy** (CAP). The remit of the CAP is so broad, with varying economic and climatic conditions affecting different products, that it has been divided according to product. Each commodity has its own Management Committee, composed of national government officials. The role of the Management Committees is to assist the **European Commission** in formulating regulations for the **implementation** of **decisions** made by the **Council of the European Union**, in order to achieve a uniform application of decisions that nevertheless takes account of different national circumstances. The Committees are also responsible for fixing levels of export refunds and import levies. Their opinions are not binding on the Commission but, if a Commission proposal is rejected by a Committee, the proposal must be presented to the Council for consideration.

PETER MANDELSON (1953–) was nominated as the United Kingdom's incoming European Commissioner in July 2004 and he took up his position in November 2004. He was born in London and graduated from St Catherine's College, Oxford, in 1976 with a degree in Philosophy, Politics and Economics. Mandelson first came to prominence as the Labour Party's director of communications from 1985 to 1990 and was seen as a leading figure in the party's attempt to modernize and reform. He became a Member of the British Parliament at the 1992 general election, representing the constituency of Hartlepool (1992–2004), and was highly instrumental in the campaign that brought the Labour Party back to power in 1997. As a close ally of **Tony Blair**, leader of the Labour Party and Prime Minister, he was appointed first to a junior ministerial post and then to the Cabinet in 1998 as Secretary of State for Trade and Industry (July–December 1998). His rapid rise proved temporary because, after allegations of financial misconduct, he resigned in December 1998. Unusually for a 'disgraced' minister, he received a second opportunity when he was appointed as Secretary of State for Northern Ireland in 2000. Once again, however, he became embroiled in a political scandal (over the granting of British passports) and was forced to resign in 2001, although he was later cleared of any wrongdoing. His posting to **Brussels** was greeted with surprise by many commentators, but he rapidly emerged as a highly competent member of **Barroso**'s team. Mandelson handled the high-profile portfolio with responsibility for trade policy and trade negotiations. He strongly pushed the case for economic reform and called for changes to the **common agricultural policy**. He has long been a committed European and sought hard to exert a strong pro-European influence on Tony Blair. His relations with **Gordon Brown** were generally very good until he supported Blair for the leadership of the Labour Party in 1994 when, for a while, they became much less cordial. Relations improved, however, and Mandelson was recalled by Brown in 2008 to serve in the United Kingdom Government before his tenure as European Commissioner had ended. Mandelson was ennobled with a peerage and was handed a key government department as Secretary of State for Business, Innovation and Skills. His role and centrality in the British Government, prior to the general election of May 2010, increased further following the dismal outcome of the **European Parliament** elections for the Labour Party, when Brown's position weakened and Mandelson became, additionally, First Secretary of State and Lord President of the Council.

MANSHOLT PLAN is the name of the document that was the origin of the **common agricultural policy** (CAP). Named after the Dutch statesman Sicco Mansholt, in its final version of 1968 it gave equal importance to price guarantees and to a restructuring and modernization of agriculture. Prior to this, the vast majority of agricultural expenditure was being directed towards price support rather than modernization schemes. The plan accepted that rationalization would incur heavy short-term costs, and proposed an extensive programme of compensation. In the longer term, it suggested that rationalization would produce a more cost-effective agriculture, so limiting the amount of **expenditure** required for price guarantees. The agricultural sector protested at the plans, and there were large demonstrations in **Brussels**. The CAP outline adopted by the European Communities (EC) in 1972 was a moderated version of the Mansholt Plan. It gave a greatly reduced emphasis to structural reform, an emphasis that disappeared almost completely when the policy began to operate. At the time, farming organizations almost everywhere in the EC rejected the plan, and Mansholt was much reviled by farmers.

A **MARKET ACCESS STRATEGY** was devised by the **European Commission** in 1996 as a means of promoting European Union (EU) exports. It aims to provide information for businesses regarding trade policy questions, to improve access for EU exporters to other markets and to increase the efficiency of EU **trade** policy.

MARKET-SHARING AGREEMENTS are banned by the **European Commission** on the grounds that they run contrary to the rules of European Union (EU) **competition policy**, and particularly to Article 81 of the **Treaty of Rome** (now Article 101 of the **Treaty on the Functioning of the European Union**), which targets restrictive agreements and **cartels**. Cartels remain an endemic feature of European business activity. The Commission, particularly since the early 1990s, has endeavoured to combat these agreements through the levying of fines on companies engaged in such practices.

The **MARSHALL PLAN** or the European Recovery Programme, named after US Secretary of State George Marshall (1880–1959), was an extensive programme of US aid to assist and stimulate economic reconstruction and recovery in Europe after the Second World War. It came into operation in 1948 and brought both economic and military stability and facilitated the reconstruction of Western Europe. The **USA** insisted that the allocation and operation of priorities had to be a European responsibility. The result was the formation of the **Organisation for European Economic Co-operation**. The Marshall Plan played an instrumental role in promoting European integration which indirectly can be said to have inspired the Schuman Declaration (see **Robert Schuman**; **Schuman Plan**). Reconciliation was an integral aspect of US foreign policy towards Western Europe, particularly given the onset of the **Cold War** in the late 1940s. By the time the Plan ended in 1952, some US $17,000m. had been given to Western Europe, to the latter's considerable financial and psychological benefit, as well as providing Western Europe with experience in intergovernmental co-operation.

MASHREQ STATES is a term used to describe Egypt, Jordan, Lebanon and Syria, with which the European Communities (EC) signed a collective bilateral trade and aid agreement in 1977. In addition to granting **development aid**, the agreement allowed the Mashreq states to export several manufactured products to the EC duty-free. A further collection of financial aid measures was negotiated in 1991. Since then, relations between the European Union and the Mashreq states have developed within the context of the **Euro-Mediterranean partnership** and a proposal to establish a **Euro-Mediterranean Economic Area**.

MCAS: See **Monetary Compensatory Amounts**

CHARLIE MCCREEVY (1949–) was nominated as the Irish representative to the **Barroso** Commission in 2004 to be the Commissioner with responsibility for the **internal market** and services. Prior to this he had served in Bertie Ahern's two administrations as the Irish Minister for Finance. He was widely credited with presiding over the European Union's best-performing economy and is a staunch free marketeer, although questions are increasingly being asked, given the tough economic climate in Ireland since 2008, about the direction of government policy and the state of Irish finances from the mid-1990s onwards. He slowly developed a recognizable profile and in particular condemned attempts by certain member states to protect their utility sectors from greater competition. He stepped down at the end of his term as Commissioner at the end of 2009 and was replaced in Barroso II by **Máire Geoghegan-Quinn**.

MEDA was the acronym for a Mediterranean Special programme (launched in 1996 and amended in 2000 as MEDA II) that aimed to introduce financial and technical measures in parallel with economic and social structural reforms in the **Euro-Mediterranean partnership**. It was modelled on the aid programmes **Phare** and **Technical Assistance to the Commonwealth of Independent States** (Tacis). The MEDA programme commenced in 1996 and replaced all the bilateral **protocols** between the European Union (EU) and the so-called MED-12 non-EU member Mediterranean states (Algeria, **Cyprus**, Egypt, Israel, Jordan, Lebanon, **Malta**, **Morocco**, the Palestinian Authority (now Palestinian Autonomous Areas), Syria, Tunisia and **Turkey**). MEDA was designed to support the economic transition in those Mediterranean non-EU member states and aimed for the establishment of a Euro-Mediterranean free trade area by promoting reforms that encouraged small and medium-sized businesses, opened up markets, and promoted private investment and industrial co-operation. It also supported the wider participation of civil society, the improvement of social and educational services, the upgrading of economic infrastructure and the protection of the environment, and placed emphasis on the strengthening of democracy and the rule of law. Both MEDA programmes encouraged regional co-operation. MEDA II was allocated some €5,350m. for 2000–06.

MEDIA 2007 is the fourth phase of the MEDIA Programme (Measures to Encourage the Development of the Audiovisual Production Industry—see **media policy**). The first phase of the programme, MEDIA I, covered the period 1991–95 and was succeeded in turn by MEDIA II (1996–2000) and **MEDIA Plus** (2001–06). The MEDIA Plus programme sought to aid and bolster the audiovisual industry by supporting the development, distribution and promotion of European audiovisual works (especially fiction in cinema and television, documentary making and the high-cost field of animation). The scheme also provided financial assistance and support for vocational training programmes to instruct audiovisual-industry professionals in business management, scriptwriting techniques and new technologies. In January 2005 the **European Commission** adopted Decision 2005/56/EC setting up a new **Education, Audiovisual and Culture Executive Agency** (EACEA). This Agency is responsible for the management of certain parts of the European Union's (EU) programmes in the education, culture and audiovisual fields and it officially took over the operational management of the MEDIA programme as of 1 January 2006. MEDIA 2007 (2007–13) replaced Media Plus and had an initial budget of €755m. This new generational programme aims to consolidate training with development and distribution and should receive an expanded budget of some €1,055m. Membership of the MEDIA 2007 programme comprises the 27 EU member states plus **Iceland**, **Liechtenstein**, **Norway** and **Switzerland**.

MEDIA POLICY, or at least that element which relates to film and television, represents the one area of **cultural policy** where the European Union (EU) has been noticeably active. While the **European Commission** aims to encourage co-operation within the EU, it has also been restrictive in seeking to control the effect on Europe of direct broadcasting by satellite and cable networks. The first draft **directive** in 1985 established a plan for the adoption by the member states of the television standards sponsored by the **European Broadcasting Union**, their immediate use in direct satellite broadcasting, and their gradual introduction into both cable and ground transmitter systems. This plan later encountered difficulties. A second and highly controversial directive, entitled *Television Without Frontiers*, came into force in 1991. It is designed to ensure increasing co-ordination in broadcasting, and requires the member states to ensure that a specified and substantial proportion of their national production and broadcast programmes is of European origin. Through the MEDIA (Measures for Encouraging the Development of the Audiovisual Production Industry) and SCRIPT (Support for Creative Independent Production Talent) programmes, the EU has also contributed to the financing, production and distribution of co-operative multilingual European broadcasting, and to the annual Geneva-Europe Prize for the best television scripts for fiction series. In addition, funding is provided for a media business school, a **European Film Distribution Office** and a European Group of Cinema and Audiovisual Financiers.

MEDICI stands for Multimedia for Education and Employment through Integrated Cultural Initiative, a programme established by the then **Directorates-General** X and XIII to encourage innovative use of multimedia technology for the promotion of Europe's cultural heritage, through partnerships between museums, cultural institutions and industry. Its secretariat is based in Milan, Italy.

MEDITERRANEAN POLICY, sometimes known as the Global Mediterranean Policy, is a term which is normally used to describe not a policy in the sense of a coherent integrated programme, but the varied collection of trade agreements that the European Union (EU) has signed with almost all the states that border the Mediterranean Sea, as well as various educational, economic and scientific initiatives that have the Mediterranean as their focus. A **European Commission** initiative of 1994 envisaged the creation of a **Euro-Mediterranean Economic Area**, which would include the **Maghreb** and **Mashreq** countries, Israel, the Palestinian Authority (now Palestinian Autonomous Areas) and **Turkey**. Despite the initial enthusiasm accompanying the 1995 **Barcelona Declaration** that launched the process and laid the seeds for **MEDA**, there remains a great degree of scepticism as to how effective the EU's policy towards these Mediterranean countries has been and will be in the future. The primary reason for this is that distrust of and suspicion towards the EU still prevail among these states and greater efforts will be needed to ensure increased co-operation from them. Moreover, the benefits of relations have been viewed as primarily favouring the EU. There is also little enthusiasm for the **European neighbourhood policy** launched in 2003. However, progress has been made in developing a Euro-Mediterranean Energy Partnership and a further enhancement of relations could come through the French-inspired 'Barcelona process: **Union for the Mediterranean**' initiative, which was launched in July 2008.

MEDITERRANEAN UNION: See **Union for the Mediterranean**

MEMBER STATES is a term that is used to refer to the 27 countries that currently comprise the European Union. These are Austria, Belgium, Bulgaria, Cyprus, the Czech Republic, Denmark, Estonia, Finland, France, Germany, Greece, Hungary, Ireland, Italy, Latvia, Lithuania, Luxembourg, Malta, the Netherlands, Poland, Portugal, Romania, Slovakia, Slovenia, Spain, Sweden and the United Kingdom.

MEMBERS OF THE EUROPEAN PARLIAMENT (MEPs) are elected for fixed five-year terms. The first direct elections occurred in 1979. In the **European Parliament** (EP), MEPs sit in transnational **party groups**, not by national party affiliations or in delegations, although a minority of MEPs prefers to sit as non-aligned independents. For a long time, MEPs were paid the same salary as the national parliamentary representatives in their own country, and there was therefore a substantial range in salary levels. This has now changed. All MEPs, however, have always received the same level of European Communities/Union resources, including allowances for research, secretarial assistance and travel. In the past many MEPs held a **dual mandate**, but could only draw on their salary and expenses as an MEP or as a member of their **national parliament**, but not as both. The dual mandate system has been phased out. Over the last decade or so the number of MEPs has altered to reflect EU enlargement waves (1999: 626; 2004: 732; 2007: 785; 2009: 736). Under the **Treaty of Lisbon** the number of MEPs from the **Twenty-Seven** has been settled finally at 751. As a transitional measure the number of MEPs in the current parliament (2009–14) has been increased to 754.

MEPS: See **Members of the European Parliament**

MERCATOR is the European Network of Language Diversity Centres, which is a European Union (EU)-funded project connecting multilingual communities across Europe, promoting knowledge sharing and facilitating the structured exchange of best practice and groundbreaking initiatives through its programme of activities. The project is mainly focused on dealing with regional or minority **languages** in multilingual regions, but also on immigrant languages and smaller state languages, with emphasis on language needs arising from migration and globalization. The network builds on the achievements of the European Network for Regional or Minority Languages and Education, which was established in 1987.

MERGER POLICY is a leading aspect of current European Union (EU) **competition policy**. It is, however, a belated weapon in the armoury of the **European Commission** as it was omitted completely from the **Treaty of Rome**. The concept of a European merger control regime was first proposed by the Commission as a draft **regulation** in 1973. Its aim was to give the Commission the ability to approve in advance any proposed transnational mergers, leaving the member states with the responsibility of policing mergers within their own territories. The Commission initiative and three subsequent efforts all failed to find any substantial favour within the Council of Ministers (see **Council of the European Union**). Finally, however, a renewed proposal in 1987 was submitted, was approved in 1989 and came into force in September 1990. The regulation owed much to the growing demands from the business community for an integrated policy with regard to merger rules at the European level, thus avoiding the existing confusions and discrepancies in approach to mergers across the EU. Their calls were also vindicated by the business restructuring that was occurring prior to 1992 and the **internal market** initiative. The regulation required that all proposed mergers of companies with an aggregate world turnover of €5,000m., where at least two of the companies involved had a turnover within the EU of more than €250m. (unless they each realized more than two-thirds of their European turnover in one member state), and where the merger was likely to affect EU **competition policy**, had to be submitted to the Commission for assessment and approval. As such, the regulation was designed to cover only the largest mergers, some 50 to 60 a year in the early years. Proposed mergers that fell below these levels, which constituted the majority of cases, remained the responsibility of the national authorities.

The number of proposed mergers notified to the Commission increased during the 1990s, so that by the end of that decade almost as many as five times the number were being processed than at its beginning. In 2001, for example, some 335 mergers were notified to the Commission. The reactions of member states to enforcing the regulation against their own industries was mixed, but the merger regulation was hailed as a substantial success for the speed with which cases were processed, although some critics pointed to potential weaknesses in terms of economic analysis. Most cases were dealt with within one month and the remainder within a further four months. By December 2002 the Commission had formally closed some 2,000 cases. Only about 100 of these had become subject to more detailed Phase Two four-month investigations. Outright prohibitions were very rare and represented less than 1% (18 at the end of 2002) of all notified transactions. A 2001 Green Paper heralded a revised examination of merger thresholds that led the Commission to adopt a far-reaching reform of merger policy in December 2002, leading in turn to a new merger regulation that was agreed by the Council (for Economic and Monetary Affairs) in January 2004. The new merger regulation came into force on 1 May 2004. Essentially, the new regulation formed part of a package of comprehensive reforms for improving what had already been hailed as a major success story. The new package of reforms built on 13 years of experience and included guidelines on the assessment of mergers between competing firms and the Commission. The Commission itself had already introduced a set of best practices on the conduct of merger investigations, including the appointment of a chief economist in merger cases, which were designed to streamline **decision-making** and to make it more transparent. These initiatives were designed to restore Commission credibility in merger cases, particularly after the **Court of First Instance** overturned for the first time in the history of EU merger policy three Commission prohibition orders in 2002, severely reprimanded the Commission for its methods and procedures, and stressed the need for greater economic analysis capable of standing up to scrutiny.

MERGER TREATY is the name often given to the treaty that formally integrated the executives of the **European Atomic Energy Community**, the **European Coal and Steel Community** and the **European Economic Community** (EEC). While technically there were still three **European Communities**, it became commonplace thereafter to refer to them collectively as the **European Community**. The Treaty created a single **European Commission** and a single Council of Ministers (see **Council of the European Union**), and was signed on 8 April 1965, coming into effect on 1 July 1967. The degree of personal animosity between **Charles de Gaulle** and **Walter Hallstein** ensured that the latter, who by this stage was the outgoing President of the EEC Commission, was not nominated for the position of President of a single Commission.

ANGELA MERKEL (1954–) made history on 22 November 2005 when she was elected by the Bundestag (parliament) as Germany's first ever female Chancellor. It should also be noted that her second claim to fame stems from the fact that she is the first citizen of the former German Democratic Republic (1949–90) to lead post-unification Germany (although she was actually born in Hamburg). In political terms, Merkel's rise has been nothing short of meteoric. She was initially spotted and nurtured as a protégée by **Helmut Kohl** in the early 1990s and thereafter made a rapid advance through the Christian Democratic Union (CDU) party's ranks before being chosen to contest the 2005 federal elections as the CDU's candidate for Chancellor. Opinion polls in early 2005 pointed to a decisive Merkel victory, but, in the event, **Gerhard Schröder**'s Social Democratic Party (SPD) staged a remarkable comeback. At the September 2005 elections Merkel's CDU/CSU (Christian Social Union) polled 35.2% of the vote, while the SPD obtained 34.2%. With these results, neither the incumbent SPD–Green coalition nor the CDU/CSU and its preferred coalition partner, the Free Democratic Party, was in a position to muster a majority in the Bundestag. Options for the parties were limited after such an inconclusive election and, after weeks of speculation and deliberation, Merkel led the CDU/CSU into a 'Grand Coalition' with the SPD. This arrangement supplied Merkel with the Chancellorship and the SPD with 8 out of 16 seats in the cabinet, and it was the second time (the first occurred in 1966–69) in post-war German history that the two largest parties had formed a coalition government. The product of such negotiations had its critics, and some predicted a short history. Yet, in the event, it worked admirably well.

Merkel has emerged as a high-profile individual and, in terms of foreign policy, has generally been given the credit for enabling the **Council of the European Union** to secure agreement on the European Union (EU) **budget** and the financing arrangements for the period 2007–13. Merkel's star was in the ascendant as the incumbent leaders of France and the United Kingdom fast approached the end of their terms in office. Merkel remains an advocate of closer European co-operation and used the German presidency of the Council in the first half of 2007 to advance a number of ambitious targets. The most important was her determination to revive the debate on the **Treaty establishing a Constitution for Europe** and the necessity of agreeing some form of charter on EU **decision-making** before the next **European Parliament** (EP) elections in June 2009. Merkel succeeded and presented the text of a draft mandate (which very much determined the content of the **Treaty of Lisbon**) at the concluding **European Council** summit under the German presidency in June 2007. Merkel also committed herself to making further progress on energy security and climate change, a global trade deal, a new partnership agreement with **Russia**, and greater peace efforts for the **Middle East**. She successfully sought much better relations with the **USA**. The situation on the domestic front proved to be more contentious, and the coalition Government entered stormier seas as it sought to cut public spending and raise income tax. Accordingly, tensions between the two grand coalition partners became more apparent. The 2009 EP elections, when Merkel's CDU/CSU party comfortably beat the Social Democrats into second place, served as a barometer for support for the Government in the run-up to the 2009 federal elections. Merkel successfully ran again as the CDU candidate for Chancellor in the federal elections of September 2009. The election results gave the CDU/CSU a strong victory over its former grand coalition partner, the SPD, which was easily pushed into second place. Nevertheless, the percentage of the votes for both the CDU/CSU and the SPD was down, at 33.4% and 27.2%, respectively, and Merkel's CDU/CSU received its lowest share of the vote since 1949. The arithmetic of the election results enabled Merkel to form a new coalition with the Free Democrats, which had captured over 14% of the votes cast, their largest share in the party's history. Merkel's second administration was immediately beset with clashes between the governing parties over policy priorities, which damaged the Chancellor's popularity and reputation at home at the beginning of 2010. However, in European affairs, Merkel has been much more successful, emerging as one of the established players. She was instrumental in the appointment of **Herman Van Rompuy** as the first **President of the European Council**. However, her positive standing was undermined by her reaction to the euro crisis from 2010, her most trenchant critics accusing her of a lack of decisiveness and of acting very much in Germany's, as opposed to the EU's, interests, accusations she has strongly denied. She was a principal architect of the **Fiscal Compact Treaty** (**Treaty on Stability, Co-ordination and Governance in the Economic and Monetary Union**), which was signed in March 2012.

The **MESSINA CONFERENCE** was the meeting of the foreign ministers of the **Six**, held in the Italian city of that name in June 1955. Its aim was to consider new initiatives in integration after the failure of the proposals for a **European Defence Community** and **European Political Community**. An invitation to participate officially was extended to the United Kingdom, but was not accepted. The ministers agreed to begin 'a fresh advance towards the building of Europe' and to create a market that was 'free from all customs duties and all quantitative restrictions'. They also proposed a pooling of information and work on the uses of nuclear energy. The meeting established an intergovernmental committee, headed by **Paul-Henri Spaak** of Belgium, which was to consider and elaborate upon the proposals before submitting its report. The conference was the first stage of the process that culminated in the two **Treaties of Rome**, which established the **European Economic Community** and the **European Atomic Energy Community**.

MFA: See **Multifibre Arrangement**

The **MIDDLE EAST** has, since the early 1970s, been a region that has attracted the attention of the European Communities/Union. It was, for example, the focus of early attempts to forge closer foreign policy co-ordination among member states through **European political co-operation**. Trade agreements have also been signed with countries in the region, many of which have since been replaced by new arrangements agreed as part of the European Union's efforts to promote a **Euro-Mediterranean partnership** that includes the Middle East.

The **MILAN SUMMIT** held in Italy in June 1985 proved to be one of the more decisive sessions of the **European Council**. The Council was to consider the report from the **Dooge Committee** on institutional reform of the European Communities (EC) and the report from the **Committee for a People's Europe**, both of which had been commissioned at the 1984 **Fontainebleau summit**, as well as the decision at the Council's previous session in **Brussels** to establish a detailed timetable for the completion of an **internal market**. It was perhaps the first summit to be dominated by discussions on a comprehensive overhaul of the EC as established primarily by the **Treaty of Rome** almost 30 years earlier. In a way that was quite unprecedented for the European Council, which hitherto had always proceeded according to the principle of **unanimity**, a vote was called for on the establishment of an **intergovernmental conference** to discuss institutional reform; only a simple majority was needed. Denmark, Greece and the United Kingdom opposed the proposal, but were outvoted by the other seven member states and subsequently agreed to participate in the conference, which led, some six months later, to the **Single European Act**. At the time, the Milan summit seemed more of a failure than a success as it had clearly revealed a degree of opposition from Denmark, Greece and the United Kingdom towards any deeper integration. In retrospect, it is now recognized as a watershed in the history of European integration and one that relaunched the European integration project.

MINERVA was an action of the former **Socrates** programme. Minerva aimed to promote and assess the use of information and communication technologies (ICT) in education, and especially in open and distance learning (ODL). Minerva Action had three main objectives: firstly, to promote understanding among teachers, learners, decision-makers and the public at large of the implications of the use of ICT in education, as well as the critical and responsible use of ICT for educational purposes; secondly, to ensure that pedagogical considerations were given proper weight in the development of ICT and multimedia-based educational products and services; and thirdly, to promote access to improved methods and educational resources as well as to results and best practices in this field. To these ends it aimed to create a dialogue at the European level in order to exchange ideas and approaches for the use of ICT. Through Minerva, the **European Commission** supported four major types of activity: firstly, projects to better understand and foster innovation; secondly, activities to design new teaching methods and resources; thirdly, activities intended to communicate and provide access to the results of projects in order to increase the publication of their findings; and lastly, projects intended to network and encourage the exchange of ideas. From 2007 Minerva was incorporated into the new **Lifelong Learning Programme** 2007–13.

MINORITY RIGHTS, unlike **human rights**, are not among the various rights that the member states of the European Union (EU) are expressly obliged to uphold under the **Treaty on European Union**. The EU does, however, insist in the **Copenhagen Criteria** for accession to the EU that respect for the rights of minorities is a prerequisite for membership.

FRANÇOIS MITTERRAND (1916–96), of the French Socialist Party, was President of France from 1981 until 1995. His policy towards the European Communities (EC) tended to emphasize closer political and economic integration to a greater extent than that of his predecessors, while still seeking to preserve and strengthen French interests and influence within the organization. His first major initiatives were taken during the French presidency of the **Council of the European Union** in the first half of 1984. In a major speech to the **European Parliament**, he called for a renewal of the EC on the basis of the **Solemn Declaration on European Union** signed by the **European Council** the previous year, for a revision of the **Treaty of Rome** that would give the EC greater powers in more areas, and for the adoption of many more common policies. These were all themes that he reiterated later in the 1980s, after he had played an instrumental role at the 1984 **Fontainebleau summit**, which resolved several important issues, such as the complaints of the United Kingdom with regard to the EC **budget**, which had been impeding EC progress. It was President Mitterrand who encouraged the development of the European Research Co-ordination Agency (**EUREKA**), and he was instrumental in the reactivation of **Western European Union**. A strong supporter of EC institutional reform, economic **harmonization** and further political integration, he established a close relationship with the German Chancellor, **Helmut Kohl**, and the Commission President, **Jacques Delors**. Their common interests provided much of the impetus for change that culminated in the **Treaty on European Union**. Mitterrand's place and reputation as one of post-war Europe's most prominent statesmen is assured. Through his strong commitment to a successful Franco-German partnership he helped further to stabilize relations between the two states and was able to develop the EC into a more dynamic system. While EC developments owed much to Mitterrand's efforts, the effect of the latter was not always positive. He continued to seek limitations on free trade in industry and agriculture to protect French interests, and his insistence on a strong French currency created high interest rates and unemployment problems in France.

MOLDOVA gained its independence from the **USSR** in 1991 and has since struggled with the political and economic challenges of the transition from Communist rule to democracy and a market economy. It also endured a civil war that left the country divided between Moldova proper and the separatist and pro-Russia Transnistria. Relations with the European Union (EU) have nevertheless developed, primarily on the basis of a **partnership and co-operation agreement** signed in 1995 and financial assistance under the former **Technical Assistance to the Commonwealth of Independent States** (Tacis) programme. Since then, Moldova has sought some form of **association agreement** with the EU and joined the **stability pact for South Eastern Europe** in 2001. The EU's response has been to include Moldova in its **European neighbourhood policy** and more recently its **Eastern partnership**. This resulted in an Action Plan designed to promote closer ties between the EU and Moldova. Evidence of the EU's increasing engagement with Moldova—now a country on the EU's border following Romania's accession in 2007—came with the appointment in 2005 of an EU Special Representative on Moldova whose role is to strengthen the EU's contribution to the resolution of the Transnistria issue. There is a notional domestic political consensus in Moldova on the country eventually becoming a member of the EU. From the EU's point of view, such a goal can only be seriously contemplated if considerable progress is made in implementing democratic and market-focused economic reforms. The need for the former was amply highlighted by the political crisis triggered by the elections in April 2009. Since then, the Government's reform efforts have been rewarded with progress in negotiations—launched in January 2010—on an **association agreement** similar to that under discussion with **Ukraine**. In December 2011 the EU agreed to instigate negotiations with Moldova on a **deep and comprehensive free trade area**, as an integral part of the association agreement talks, although the EU remains steadfast in not offering Moldova a clear perspective of membership.

MONETARY COMMITTEE was the name of a body of senior officials from the national finance ministries and the national central banks of member states that was established in 1958. It met monthly in **Brussels**, a chair being elected from its own membership for a period of two years. The Committee's objective was to advise the **European Commission** on monetary policy, performing, to some extent, some of the functions of COREPER (see **Committee of Permanent Representatives**) in the area of monetary affairs. Under the **Treaty on European Union**, it was given the task of co-ordinating the monetary policies of the member states during the first stage of **economic and monetary union** (EMU). It was dissolved during the third stage of EMU and replaced by an **Economic and Financial Committee**.

MONETARY COMPENSATORY AMOUNTS (MCAs) were introduced into the **common agricultural policy** (CAP) as a temporary measure to ease the problems created by the decision, following the collapse of the **Bretton Woods** system of fixed exchange rates, to retain the common agricultural prices at their original level of exchange. These prices would form the **green currencies**. In order to compensate farmers for loss of income caused by currency fluctuations, MCAs would constitute the difference between the common price structure and prices determined by existing exchange rates in both the internal and the external trade of the European Communities (EC). Originally, it was agreed that national governments would finance MCAs, but the EC took control of MCA financing for external trade in 1972 and for internal trade in the following year. MCAs were intended to last only until the EC established a definitive financial system for the CAP and introduced a coherent monetary policy. The failure of both of these objectives effectively meant that MCAs became permanent. While providing some form of short-term price stability in the context of floating currencies, MCAs introduced a high degree of complexity into the CAP, varying both between different products and, because of currency fluctuations, over time. At their nadir in 1973, some MCAs were liable to change almost from week to week, and they steadily grew as a proportion of agricultural **expenditure**. Greater currency stability in the 1980s persuaded the **European Commission** that MCAs hindered rather than helped the **common market**. In 1984 the Commission persuaded the member states to phase out MCAs by 1989, although it was eventually agreed that they would only be fully dismantled by the end of 1992.

MONETARY POLICY is fundamental to **economic and monetary union** (EMU). **Decision-making** in this area varies with regard to the topic in question: for the issue of coins by the member states the **co-operation procedure** applies, after consultation with the **European Central Bank** (ECB); for the formulation of exchange-rate policy guidelines, the **Council of the European Union** decides by **qualified majority voting** (QMV) following a recommendation from the ECB; for technical adjustments to the Statute of the

European System of Central Banks, the Council decides by QMV on a recommendation from the ECB after consulting the **European Commission** and obtaining the assessment of the **European Parliament** (EP); for the exchange rate of the **euro** against non-EMU currencies, the Council decides by **unanimity**, following a recommendation from the ECB or the Commission and after consulting the EP.

The **MONETARY POLICY COMMITTEE** is the name of an adjunct to the **Council of the European Union**. Along with the **Economic and Financial Affairs Council of Ministers** and the **Economic Policy Committee**, it is one of the bodies that provide a regular meeting place for representatives of the economic and finance ministers of the member states.

JEAN MONNET (1888–1979) probably contributed more than any other single individual to the post-war developments that established the building blocks that became the European Union (EU). Although he was pragmatic in his approach to integration, his contribution was in the form of ideas rather than as a practising politician. Monnet already had a distinguished diplomatic and business career when, in 1940, he contributed to the formulation of the plan for an Anglo-French Union subsequently advocated by **Winston Churchill**. After the Second World War, Monnet was appointed head of the French Planning Commission in charge of the Modernization Plan. His experiences there persuaded him that no European country could, by itself and using its own resources, plan an effective programme of economic growth, development and prosperity. While Monnet's ultimate objective was a European political union, he tended to be suspicious of ostentatious political gestures. He believed that a programme of integration had to be practical and long-term: effective political integration could only be built on an accretion of proven and accepted experiences of co-operation. For Monnet, the means of achieving progress was a gradual integration of discrete economic sectors that would, through a process of **spillover**, lead in time to full economic and political union.

Monnet was the original conceiver of the **Schuman Plan**, and was appointed as the first President of the High Authority of the **European Coal and Steel Community**. He was the originator of the Pleven Plan that produced the ill-fated **European Defence Community** (EDC). When the EDC collapsed, Monnet resigned from the High Authority to found the **Action Committee for a United States of Europe**. He successfully sponsored the creation of the **European Atomic Energy Community**, which, after the collapse of the EDC, he thought had more chance of success than the proposal for a **common market**.

Monnet's vision of a united Europe was not exclusive. While he believed that reconciliation between France and Germany was essential, it was a matter of regret to him that only six countries were willing to participate in experiments in integration. He continually urged the **Six** to encourage other states to join them; in particular, he believed that European integration would be incomplete without the involvement of the United Kingdom. Monnet's labours are commemorated in several ways by the EU, mainly through the funding of Monnet fellowships and other positions in the field of education.

MONNET METHOD is the term used to describe a strategy of integration based on **spillover** from one area of activity to another. It proved successful in the early years of European integration and again under **Jacques Delors** in the late 1980s and early 1990s. Since then, it has proved more difficult to implement.

MONTENEGRO emerged again as a sovereign and independent European nation state (after nearly 90 years) in May 2006 when it severed its union with **Serbia** following the outcome of a referendum in which some 55% of the population opted for independence. The vote heralded the end of the former Union of Serbia and Montenegro, which came into being in 2003 and which was itself the rump of the former **Yugoslavia** that had been created in 1919. The Government expressed at the outset its intention to join the **European Union** (EU), and Montenegro has made some progress in this direction since the split with Serbia. In January 2007 the EU adopted a **European partnership** for Montenegro and two months later it concluded negotiations on a **stabilization and association agreement**. This was then signed in September 2007 (and came into force in May 2010), as was a visa facilitation agreement. EU assistance under the new **instrument for pre-accession assistance** was set at €31.4m. for 2007. In November of that year the **European Commission** issued its second progress report on Montenegro, which was generally encouraging, although it did note a range of areas where progress was still needed in the country's preparations for closer integration with the EU. An Interim Agreement on free trade entered into force on 1 January 2008 and, more significantly, Montenegro applied for EU membership on 15 December 2008. After some delay the Commission was asked to prepare its *avis* on the application. This was published in November 2010. The Commission proposed the conferral of candidate status (which was officially granted on 17 December 2010). A year later it also recommended the opening of **accession negotiations**, which, following a decision of the European Council, were duly opened on 29 June 2012.

MARIO MONTI (1943–) was appointed one of the two members of the **European Commission** from Italy in 1995. His term was renewed in 1999. In his first term as Commissioner, Monti was responsible for the **internal market**, financial services and financial integration, customs and taxation; from 1999 he had responsibility for **competition policy**. An academic in the field of economics by profession, he was regarded as a highly capable individual who mastered his brief with ease. His record as competition commissioner was highly impressive and in that post he gaining renown for initiating a long and drawn-out anti-monopoly lawsuit against Microsoft. He had developed into one of the **Prodi** Commission's heavyweights, but his hopes of continuing within the new **Barroso** Commission were dashed when he failed to secure reappointment. His preferred successor was **Rocco Buttiglione**, who proved unacceptable to the **European Parliament**, and he was replaced by Franco Frattini. In November 2011 Monti replaced **Silvio Berlusconi** as Prime Minister of Italy and formed a government of technocrats who were to tackle the problems surrounding the ailing Italian economy.

MOROCCO, one of the **Maghreb states**, entered into a bilateral trade and aid agreement with the European Communities (EC) in 1976. A decade later, in 1987, it submitted a formal application for membership, but was informed by the EC that because Morocco is not a European state it was not eligible for membership. An **association agreement** was signed with the European Union (EU) in 1996 (which came into effect in March 2000), and the country is now part of the **Euro–Mediterranean partnership**. Morocco received around €205m. in EU financial aid, under the **European Neighbourhood Policy**, in 2009. The first EU-Morocco summit took place in March 2010.

MULTIFIBRE ARRANGEMENT (MFA), the full title of which is the Arrangement regarding International Trade in Textiles, was first negotiated within the **General Agreement on Tariffs and Trade** (GATT) in 1973. It was an agreement between Western industrial states and suppliers of low-cost textile goods from developing countries. The textile industries of the developed world had already been severely damaged by low-cost imports, and the MFA was established as a means of controlling imports in such a way that Western markets would be gradually opened to developing countries as an orderly contraction and restructuring of the Western textile industries was taking place. In practice, the MFA operated as a protectionist mechanism restricting the level of low-cost imports. In the renegotiations of the MFA in 1977, 1981 and 1986, Western governments successfully imposed stricter quotas on the developing countries. Textiles were therefore generally excluded from GATT and the European Communities' commitment to free trade. However, as a result of the **Uruguay Round** of GATT trade negotiations, the MFA was progressively eliminated over a 10-year period. The agreement finally expired on 1 January 2005. Immediately, exports from the People's Republic of China into the European Union (EU) soared and ultimately compelled the EU to bring in a quota system to protect some European manufacturers, especially in Greece and Portugal.

MULTI-SPEED EUROPE is a term that is used to describe the notion of differentiated integration, whereby common objectives are pursued by a group of member states that are both willing and able to advance them. The term assumes that the other member states, which may be temporarily unable or not willing to advance a given objective at that moment in time, will join the participating member states at a later date.

MUTUAL RECOGNITION, as a principle, is essential for the proper functioning of the **internal market**. It means that when a product is legally manufactured and marketed in one member state, it may be freely offered for sale in other member states, irrespective of whether it complies with the relevant national legislation in that country. The principle was established by the **Court of Justice** in 1979 in the *Cassis de Dijon* case.

N

NACC: See **North Atlantic Co-operation Council**

NAFO: See **North Atlantic Fisheries Organization**

The **NATIONAL ASSEMBLY FOR WALES EU OFFICE** was established in Brussels in 2000 and acts as a link for this region of the United Kingdom with the European Union (EU) and its institutions. The Office is staffed by Assembly officials and is directly accountable to the National Assembly of Wales. It is also part of the United Kingdom Permanent Representation (UKREP) family and works closely with officials from UKREP and alongside the Office of the Northern Ireland Executive in Brussels (ONIEB) and **Scotland Europa**. The office was set up as a consequence of devolving powers to Wales in 1999. The Assembly seeks to engage directly with the EU across a broad front and the Brussels Office has several functions. These include: providing intelligence and information for ministers and committees from the Welsh Assembly; taking a policy lead on EU horizontal issues and constitutional developments; providing specialist support and acting as a focal point for Assembly visitors and staff based in **Brussels**; acting as the public face of the Assembly in Brussels; and representing the Assembly on a range of Brussels-based working groups.

NATIONAL PARLIAMENTS have always played a role in the development of the European Communities (EC) and European Union (EU), not least in adopting the necessary implementing legislation for **directives**, undertaking the **ratification** of treaties and agreements, and scrutinizing the activities of the EU and national governments. To these ends, national parliaments have created specialized committees dealing with EU matters. These committees meet with a group of **Members of the European Parliament** every six months under the umbrella of **COSAC** (Conférence des Organes Spécialisés dans les Affaires Communautaires). Meetings of the Conference of Presidents and Speakers of Parliaments in the EU are also held every six months. Less regular are the so-called **assizes** (or Conferences of the Parliaments) that are supposed to meet to discuss major developments in the EU.

Despite such involvement in EU affairs, concerns have long been voiced that closer integration at the EU level is leading to a reduction in the powers and roles of national parliaments. Moreover, there have been persistent concerns about the **democratic deficit** within the EU. Various, often half-hearted, attempts have been made to remedy the situation. Hence, the **Treaty of Amsterdam** sought to improve the flow of information on EC/EU matters to national parliaments, particularly on matters concerning **Police and Judicial Co-operation in Criminal Matters**, and to encourage a greater input from COSAC on the legislative activities of the EC/EU. These did little, however, to assuage concerns. Consequently, one of the main issues highlighted in the Declaration on the Future of the Union, adopted at the Nice **European Council** meeting in December 2000, was the 'role of national parliaments in the European architecture'. This was developed in the **Laeken Declaration**, which called on the **European Convention** to look at what role national parliaments should play in the future, possibly as part of a new institution in which they would be represented alongside the **European Parliament** and the **Council of the European Union**. The hope was that an increased involvement of national parliaments might help improve the **legitimacy** of the EU and reduce the democratic deficit. The **Treaty of Lisbon**, which came into force on 1 December 2009, provides a more formal role for the national parliaments in the policymaking process and invites them to comment on and (if enough agree) to block certain policy proposals.

NATO: See **North Atlantic Treaty Organization**

NEGATIVE ASSENT is a phrase that has been used in the United Kingdom to describe the power of veto over **legislation** and the generally enhanced authority given to the **European Parliament** under the **Treaty on European Union** by the latter's implementation of the **co-decision procedure**, which created a joint **decision-making** mechanism.

NEO-FUNCTIONALISM embodies one of the classical theories of European integration. It was devised in the 1950s as an attempt to explain and account for the political integration process that emerged in its unique form in Western Europe in that decade. According to Ernst B. Haas regional integration was the process of how and why states cease to be wholly sovereign, how and why they voluntarily mingle, merge and mix with their neighbours so as to lose the factual attributes of sovereignty while acquiring new techniques for resolving conflict themselves. For neo-functionalists the available evidence as manifest in the **European Coal and Steel Community** (ECSC), the **European Economic Community** (EEC) and the **European Atomic Energy Community** (Euratom) treaties seemed to suggest that the nation state was becoming redundant as an authorative source of governance. In this European laboratory powers and sovereignty were being transferred from the nation states to a set of supranational institutions. Supranationality appeared to offer a new and definitive answer to resolving conflict through the pooling of sovereignty and the beginnings of a new Europe, but could a model explain what was happening in such advanced countries and what were the dynamics pushing the process onward? Haas devised such a model. It refers to the placing of emphasis on a process of economic and political co-operation in limited and specified areas, rather than a commitment to a grand design such as **federalism**. Central to neo-functionalism is the idea of **spillover**, whereby co-operation in one area creates demands for and leads to co-operation in another. The appropriateness of neo-functionalism in explaining the process of integration has been challenged by, *inter alia*, **liberal intergovernmentalism**.

NETD@YS EUROPE is an annual operation designed to illustrate how the new forms of electronic media and the expanding information society can help facilitate learning and research. The one-week operation commenced in 1997 and was initially focused on schools, but in recent years it has been extended to cover youth clubs, libraries, cinemas, museums and vocational training centres. This operation facilitates projects that are financed from a **European Commission** grant and involve partnerships between at least two European states.

The **NETHERLANDS** has been deeply involved in European integration ever since 1945. Its Government-in-exile during the Second World War agreed on the establishment of the **Benelux** Economic Union (renamed the Benelux Union in 2010) and the Netherlands was also a founder member of the European Communities (EC). Several of its statesmen have made major contributions to European co-operative efforts. In the 1960s the Netherlands was a strong supporter of **enlargement**: it opposed the **Fouchet Plan**, wanting the question of enlargement to be settled first, and supported closer links between the EC and the **European Free Trade Association**. It also, albeit unsuccessfully, urged a reactivation of **Western European Union**. With its efficient agriculture, the Netherlands was a strong advocate of the **common agricultural policy**, of which it has been a major beneficiary. It later stressed the need for a stronger **environmental policy**, and after 1989 emphasized the importance of developing closer political links with **Central and Eastern Europe**. It has persistently supported closer economic and political collaboration, favouring institutional reform and a substantially greater role for the **European Parliament** (EP). As the host of the **Maastricht summit**, which was to consider a constitutional reform of the EC, it was responsible for constructing the summit agenda. The Netherlands produced a draft that went beyond what most member states were prepared to accept, and it had to moderate its position, making the **Treaty on European Union** less comprehensive than it desired. It proved more successful in handling the end stages of the 1996 **intergovernmental conference**, which led to the **Treaty of Amsterdam**. The Dutch Government took a bold decision when it opted to hold a referendum on the **Treaty establishing a Constitution for Europe**.

Referenda are practically alien to Dutch political culture and it was assumed that the generally pro-European Union (EU) Dutch population would simply endorse the Government's position on the constitutional treaty. However, on 1 June 2005, three days after the French 'no' vote, some 62% voted against the treaty in the Netherlands, and so plunged the EU into a state of crisis. The Dutch Government decided not to hold a referendum on the **Treaty of Lisbon**. This treaty was ratified in the Dutch parliament in 2008. In a surprise result at the 2009 EP elections, the Dutch far-right Freedom Party (PVV) secured nearly 17% of the vote and finished in second place behind the ruling conservatives. The PVV openly campaigns against immigration, rejects the idea that **Turkey** should have **candidate country** status and is openly anti-Islamic.

The former Dutch Prime Minister Jan Peter Balkenende had earlier been strongly tipped as one of the possible contenders for the new post of **President of the European Council** that was created by the Treaty of Lisbon, but lost out to **Herman Van Rompuy**.

NEUTRALITY, in some form, characterizes the foreign policies of six of the member states comprising the European Union: Austria, Cyprus, Finland, Ireland, Malta, and Sweden. It means that in times of war the neutral states refrain from becoming engaged in the conflict and treat the belligerents equally. For most of the **Cold War**, this meant that Austria, Finland and Sweden felt unable to join the European Communities. Once they did apply for membership in 1989–92, concerns were raised about the impact that their membership and continued adherence to neutrality would have on plans for **common foreign and security policy** (CFSP). In practice, the neutral countries have not raised significant or insurmountable objections to the development of CFSP. The issue always surfaces as a controversial theme in the Irish **referenda** on European treaties.

NEW CRONOS is the name of the main statistical database of the European Union (EU), previously known as Cronos and covering every economic and social sector. It is compiled by **Eurostat**, the Statistical Office, and is divided into nine themes: general statistics; economy and finance; population and social conditions; industry, trade and services; agriculture and fisheries; external trade; transport; environment and energy; and science and technology. These themes are themselves subdivided into various domains of information. New Cronos comprises more than 100m. items of social and economic statistical data covering the EU member states, and, in some cases, the **USA**, **Japan** and other main economic partners, including countries, especially those of **Central and Eastern Europe**, that have applied for membership of the EU.

The **NEW TRANSATLANTIC AGENDA** (NTA) of 1995 represents an extension of the 1990 **Transatlantic Declaration** and provides a framework for European Union (EU)–US partnership and co-operation across a wide range of activities. The NTA contained four main priorities: to promote peace and stability, democracy and development throughout the world (e.g. joint co-operation over the former **Yugoslavia** and the **Middle East**); to respond effectively to global challenges (e.g. co-operation in fields such as public health); to promote economic relations and contribute to the growth of world trade; and to build closer links between Europe and the **USA**. The last two aims have led to a number of transatlantic dialogues being established in areas such as the environment, consumer protection and business issues. The NTA was accompanied by an EU-US Joint Action Plan that contained some 150 specific areas of action. The aims were diverse and ranged from promoting economic reform in **Ukraine** and combating AIDS to developing closer links between universities and colleges on both sides of the Atlantic. Since 1995 the EU and the USA have made considerable progress in many of these areas, from combating illicit drugs to educational training. In May 1997 both parties reached agreement on Customs Co-operation and Mutual Assistance in Customs Matters, and in 1998 they signed a Mutual Recognition Agreement, which covers particular goods such as pharmaceuticals and medical devices and telecommunications equipment. In 1998 a further development included the launch of the Transatlantic Economic Partnership, which sought to develop a regular dialogue on multilateral trade issues.

The NTA launched an era of unprecedented co-operation on a wide range of political, economic and civil society issues between the EU and the USA, although this has not by any means resolved all differences between the two economic powers over issues such as the environment, the structure of labour markets and economic protection of the US steel industry. The EU–US partnership is a highly strategic relationship. It represents an ongoing means for dialogue on a range of issues that have evolved into formal biannual EU-US summits between the Presidents of the **European Council** and the **European Commission** and the President of the USA.

In May 2002 leaders from both the EU and the USA met in Washington, DC, and agreed to establish a Positive Economic Agenda, which foresaw a highly developed scheme of bilateral co-operation in specific sectors, including financial markets, the insurance sector, organic farming, electronic tendering and electronic customs.

NGO: See **Non-governmental Organizations**

NICE TREATY: See **Treaty of Nice**

NINE is a popular term referring to the membership of the European Communities after the first **enlargement** of 1973. It is used to describe the collectivity of the nine member states between 1973 and 1981: the **Six** founder members, plus Denmark, Ireland and the United Kingdom.

ÉMILE NOEL (1922–96) was the first Secretary-General of the **European Commission**. Appointed to the position of Executive Secretary of the Commission of the **European Economic Community** (EEC) in 1958, from 1967 to 1987 he served as head of the **Secretariat-General** of the European Commission, the most senior administrator, and assistant to the Commissioners. He played a major role in the development of the European Union (EU) over three decades and, by leadership and example, contributed much to the ethos and consolidation of the EU administration.

NOISE is the subject of several European Union (EU) **directives** agreed as part of the EU's **environmental policy**. Maximum noise limits have been set for a wide range of commercial and domestic equipment. Manufacturers of many household appliances are required, moreover, to indicate the noise level on the packaging. Limits have also been set for decibel levels in the workplace.

NOMENCLATURE OF TERRITORIAL UNITS FOR STATISTICS (NUTS) describes a classification of regions in the European Union (EU) by the Statistical Office of the European Communities (**Eurostat**). The NUTS system has three levels: each level 1 unit is normally subdivided into a certain number of level 2 units, and level 2 units are composed of smaller level 3 units. NUTS units often correspond to national administrative divisions, but are sometimes ad hoc groupings of smaller national units for the purposes of EU regional statistics. Not all member states are subdivided at all three levels.

The **NOMINATION PROCEDURE** is used to nominate the **European Commission** and its President. Originally, nomination involved only the 'common accord' of the governments of the member states. Following the adoption of the **Treaty on European Union**, the **European Parliament** (EP) was involved more, and the procedure split into four stages: nomination of the Commission President; nomination of the remainder of the Commission; approval by the EP; and appointment by 'common accord' of the member states. The **Treaty of Amsterdam** further involved the EP, requiring its approval of the Commission President before the rest of the Commission was nominated. Under the terms of the **Treaty of Nice**, the **Council of the European Union** took over the responsibilities of the member states and makes **decisions** in this procedure by **qualified majority voting**.

NON-COMPULSORY EXPENDITURE referred to that part of the European Communities' (EC) **budget** (about 40%) that related to policies that were not directly provided for by the **Treaty of Rome** and its subsequent amendments. In practice, it included most EC **expenditure** except that on agriculture. After 1988 greater emphasis was placed upon 'privileged' non-compulsory expenditure, a phrase that refers to spending on long-term programmes. This development was criticized by the **European Parliament** (EP) for reducing its ability to influence the budget. The EP had greater influence over the non-compulsory part of the budget, and continually sought a redefinition and expansion of what that term covered. In practice, EP amendments to non-compulsory expenditure were not allowed to exceed an overall maximum figure previously set each year by the **Council of the European Union**. The criteria that determined the maximum level were the trend in gross national product (GNP), the average variation in the budgets of the member states, and the trend during the previous year in the cost of living. The **Treaty of Lisbon** ended the distinction between compulsory and non-compulsory expenditure as far as the EP was concerned and gave the **Members of the European Parliament** an equal voice with the Council on the entire European Union budget.

NON-GOVERNMENTAL ORGANIZATIONS (NGOs) is a term which, when used in the context of the European Union (EU), refers to those **interest groups**, or **lobbies**, that are involved with the EU and active in seeking to influence EU policy development, but have no formal connection with the EU. There are numerous ways of classifying interest groups, such as according to type and number and whether they operate as national groups or Euro-groups. The majority of these groups represent business interests (e.g. ERT, BUSINESSEUROPE/UNICE) alongside a smaller number of non-business or more diffuse interests (e.g. trade unions, consumers' and environmental associations). There are multiple points of access to the EU policy process, including the **European Commission**, the **European Parliament** (EP), the **Council of the European Union** and even the Courts. The EU system is very open to interest groups and, indeed, the European institutions consider interest group involvement to be essential in the development of legitimate and appropriate policies. The Commission has set up a database, CONECCS (Consultation, the European Commission and Civil Society), of around 1,000 NGOs working at EU level, covering approximately 100 branches of activity. Both the Commission and the EP have been seeking to regulate NGO activities in recent years in order to improve **transparency** and to establish minimum standards. (See also **lobbying**.)

NORDIC COUNCIL is the name of a body established in 1952 by the Nordic states as a loose association of intergovernmental co-operation. Despite its purely consultative character, the Nordic Council has achieved a high degree of co-operation and co-ordination in a wide range of policy fields. However, it failed, despite several initiatives, to secure an agreement on a

Nordic economic union. After 1970 the Council created a limited institutional structure, with a small secretariat. In their membership applications to the European Communities (EC), Denmark and **Norway** made their continued membership of the Council an essential element of their submissions, a condition that was accepted by the EC. Denmark remained a member of the Council after joining the EC in 1973. It saw its role as one of liaison between the two organizations. Membership of both organizations did not create any severe policy problems for Denmark, and the Council's continued existence is currently in little doubt, despite the accession of Finland and Sweden to the European Union.

NORM PRICE is the term usually used to describe the price guaranteed to tobacco producers under the **common agricultural policy**.

The **NORTH ATLANTIC CO-OPERATION COUNCIL** (NACC) was a body linking the **North Atlantic Treaty Organization** with the new democracies of **Central and Eastern Europe** and the **Commonwealth of Independent States**. It was established in 1991 as a framework for co-operation in defence and security to ensure stability throughout the continent of Europe. Its formation was criticized by some for duplicating and confusing the role of the Conference on Security and Co-operation in Europe, now the **Organization for Security and Co-operation in Europe**. The NACC was replaced by the **Euro-Atlantic Partnership Council** in 1997.

The **NORTH ATLANTIC FISHERIES ORGANIZATION** (NAFO) is a body that consists of all those states with a major fisheries interest in the North Atlantic. NAFO was established in 1979 as a successor to the International Commission of the Northwest Atlantic Fisheries (ICNAF, 1949–78). It deals with questions of fishing limits and zones, permissible quotas and catches, conservation of stocks and the types of equipment allowed. Given the existence of the **common fisheries policy**, the member states are represented in the organization by the **European Commission**.

The **NORTH ATLANTIC TREATY ORGANIZATION** (NATO) owes its existence to the Washington Treaty of 4 April 1949 that brought the **USA** and Canada together with 10 European countries (Belgium, Denmark, France, Iceland, Italy, Luxembourg, the Netherlands, Norway, Portugal and the United Kingdom) in a military arrangement for the collective defence of Western Europe. During the **Cold War** the membership of NATO was enlarged to include Greece and **Turkey** in 1952, the Federal Republic of Germany in 1955, and Spain in 1986. France, however, withdrew from the integrated military command structure in 1966, although in 1996 it resumed participation in some of the military organs of NATO. Since then, NATO has undergone three further rounds of enlargement. As a result, only six of the **Twenty-Seven** European Union (EU) member states—Austria, Cyprus, Finland, Ireland, Malta and Sweden—are not NATO members. France returned to the integrated military command structure in 2009.

NATO member states are committed to providing military forces according to their means; these forces are subject to the NATO chain of military command. An attack upon one state is regarded as an attack upon all, although the treaty does not specify how the affected member state will receive assistance from its partners, who are required to take only such action as they deem necessary. The organization was not meant to be an agent of integration, but NATO and the other new international organizations of the late 1940s made an important contribution to integration by bringing Western European countries together in a series of institutional frameworks that obliged them to co-operate and liaise with each other on an intensive and continuous basis. After the end of the Cold War, there was some doubt over the future of NATO.

After 1990 it sought to redefine its role as a political and security alliance in association with the Conference on Security and Co-operation in Europe (now the **Organization for Security and Co-operation in Europe**—OSCE), and in 1992 it brought the former Communist states of Eastern Europe into its consultative processes through the formation of the **North Atlantic Co-operation Council** (since 1997 replaced by the **Euro-Atlantic Partnership Council**—EAPC). In 1994 the **partnerships for peace** programme was established under the aegis of NATO. This is open to EAPC and OSCE states and aims to promote political and military co-operation throughout Europe. By December 1997, 27 countries from **Central and Eastern Europe** and the former **USSR** had joined the initiative. Moreover, in March 1999 three Central and Eastern European countries—the Czech Republic, Hungary and Poland—joined NATO proper. At their Prague summit in November 2002, NATO leaders agreed to extend membership invitations to up to seven more countries from the former Soviet bloc: Bulgaria, Estonia, Latvia, Lithuania, Romania, Slovakia and Slovenia. These countries joined NATO in 2004. Further invitations were issued in 2008 to **Croatia** and **Albania**, and both joined on 1 April 2009. The **former Yugoslav republic of Macedonia**, Georgia and **Ukraine** have also expressed a desire to join NATO.

In general, relations between NATO and the European Communities (EC) and EU have been close. NATO's protection permitted the EC to develop and consolidate themselves, while conversely the economic co-operation engendered by the EC contributed to a stronger Western Europe. Some states, especially France, wished to see **Western European Union** (WEU) reformed to become a European replacement for NATO. In establishing the **common foreign and security policy**, the **Treaty on European Union** re-emphasized the potential significance of WEU for the EU. The response of NATO was to build on regular joint NATO–WEU meetings and support the proposed improvement of WEU's operational capabilities. Fearful that such developments might undermine NATO, many member states insisted that NATO must remain the major European security organization. This has not, however, prevented the establishment of either the **Eurocorps** in 1992 or the **European Rapid Reaction Force**. Nor has it prevented the EU from developing a **European security and defence policy** and pursuing the goal of a common defence, flagged as part of the **common foreign and security policy** in the **Treaty on European Union** and most recently confirmed in the **Treaty of Lisbon**. Such developments have not always contributed to harmonious relations between the EU and NATO, despite their overlapping membership. However, despite misgivings in some NATO circles, more often than not voiced from within the **USA**, about the EU's aspirations regarding security and defence matters, the EU–NATO relationship has become closer over time. This is most evident in the Berlin-Plus Agreement of 2002, which provides for EU access to NATO assets and planning capabilities in the event of EU-led crisis management operations, and in the more institutionalized nature of dialogue. That there is scope for a closer relationship is evident in the call for a 'strategic partnership' from the then NATO Secretary-General, Jaap de Hoop Scheffer, in 2007. This and similar calls have not always been met with an enthusiastic response from the EU, which clearly has its own ambitions, as well as having some member states that are sceptical of NATO. However, **enlargement** to include the countries of Central and Eastern Europe in 2004 and 2007 certainly increased the ranks of pro-NATO member states within the EU.

NORWAY has been, in general, suspicious of close European relations that involve anything more than intergovernmental co-operation. It first applied to join the European Communities (EC) in 1962, doing so out of necessity more than enthusiasm for European integration. Indeed, there was considerable disquiet in the country over what membership might mean in terms of national sovereignty and the 'special problems' arising from the country's 'geographical location and economic structure', which the Government had said would need to be resolved by the negotiations. Hence, France's **veto** of the United Kingdom's application in 1963 and again in 1967 was not wholly unwelcome. Opposition to membership increased after the resumption of negotiations in 1970, and the deep feelings aroused had widespread repercussions throughout Norway. In September 1972 a narrow majority (53%) voted against membership in a consultative referendum. Preparations for accession were halted and replaced by discussions on a **free trade agreement**, which entered into force in 1973. Thereafter, EC membership disappeared from the Norwegian political agenda until 1988, when it re-emerged because of concerns over the possible effect of the **internal market**. Initially, the preference was for the **European Economic Area** (EEA), but Norway soon found itself following its neighbours in applying for EC membership in 1992. **Accession negotiations** were concluded in 1994, but once again membership was rejected in a referendum. Since then, Norway's relations have been based on full participation in the

EEA as well as involvement in the **Schengen Agreement**. Future membership of the European Union has not, however, been ruled out.

NOUVELLES ÉQUIPES INTERNATIONALES was the name of a transnational association of Christian Democrat political parties formed in 1947. In 1965 it changed its name to the European Union of Christian Democrats, and in 1976 its members from member states of the European Communities founded the European People's Party (see **Group of the European People's Party (Christian Democrats) and European Democrats**) as a transnational organization.

NOUVELLES FRONTIÈRES is the name of a French travel agency that challenged the price-fixing regulations of the French Civil Aviation Code in the **Court of Justice**. In April 1986 the Court ruled in favour of the company, declaring that air transport was not exempt from the **competition policy** of the European Communities, and that, under the **Treaty of Rome**, member states were not permitted to approve air fares that resulted from agreements between airlines. This was the first major challenge to the **cartel** arrangements on air fares pursued by both governments and airlines. The Court also pointed out that responsibility for determining whether an air-fare agreement transgresses the treaty rests with the **European Commission** and the national antitrust authorities. The ruling gave the Commission greater powers, although subsequent progress on air transport liberalization was slow.

NUCLEAR ENERGY: See **Energy Policy; European Atomic Energy Community; European Fusion Development Agreement; Joint European Torus**

NUTS: See **Nomenclature of Territorial Units for Statistics**

O

OCTS: See **Overseas Countries and Territories**

OECD: See **Organisation for Economic Co-operation and Development**

OEEC: See **Organisation for European Economic Co-operation**

GÜNTHER OETTINGER (1953–) was successfully nominated by the re-elected Merkel Government as the prospective German Commissioner in the **Barroso** II Commission (2010–14) in the latter part of 2009. Oettinger replaced the much-respected **Günther Verheugen**, and is responsible for the highly sensitive and important issue of energy (especially in terms of energy security). He may have been something of a surprise choice, but he has been active in German politics as a member of the Christian Democratic Union (CDU) for over 30 years. After reading law at the University of Tübingen and working in a legal firm he opted to focus his energies on a professional career in politics. He rapidly rose through the ranks. He became chairman of his local CDU branch in Ditzingen in 1977 and first entered the state (regional) parliament of Baden-Württemberg in 1984. He became Minister President of this state (Land) in 2004 following the resignation of his predecessor and he remained in the post (being successfully re-elected to head a coalition government with the Free Democrats in 2006) until he became a Commissioner.

The **OFFICE FOR HARMONIZATION IN THE INTERNAL MARKET** (OHIM) is a decentralized European Union agency responsible for the **harmonization** of intellectual property rights, **trademarks** and design rights across the member states. It was established in 1994, and is located in Alicante, Spain.

OFFICE FOR OFFICIAL PUBLICATIONS OF THE EUROPEAN COMMUNITIES (EUR-OP): See **Publications Office of the European Union**.

The **OFFICE OF THE NORTHERN IRELAND EXECUTIVE IN BRUSSELS** (ONIEB) was established in 2001 and is one of some 200 offices in **Brussels** that operate on behalf of regional and local authorities in the European Union (EU). The ONIEB was created, as part of the Belfast Agreement, as a means of enabling the newly devolved Northern Ireland executive to play a role in Europe. The functions of the ONIEB are essentially: to monitor the development by EU institutions of policies relevant to Northern Ireland; to provide up-to-date information to ministers and departments in Belfast; and to ensure that the interests of Northern Ireland are fully represented in policy developments by EU institutions. Moreover, the ONIEB seeks to raise the profile of Northern Ireland among European policymakers and to form inter-regional links with other regions in Europe. Technically the ONIEB forms part of the United Kingdom's Permanent Representation (UKREP) and works closely with it and both the **Scottish Executive** Office and the **National Assembly for Wales EU Office**.

The **OFFICIAL JOURNAL OF THE EUROPEAN UNION** (OJ) is one of the principal publications of the **Publications Office of the European Union**, covering all of the major European Union (EU) **institutions**. The journal was first published in 1952. It contains the details of all EU (and, earlier, EC) **legislation**. **Regulations** become law throughout the EU as soon as they are published in the *Journal*. It also carries details of EU initiatives, and advertisements of staff vacancies. The OJ has three parts: the 'L' Series contains EU legislation, the 'C' Series draft legislation, information and notices, while the 'S' Series is a supplement comprising notices and advertisements for public works, supplies, services and research contracts. Before the entry into force of the **Treaty of Nice**, the OJ was called the *Official Journal of the European Communities*. Since 1998 an electronic version of the OJ has been made available on **EUR-Lex** with every printed edition.

OHIM: See **Office for Harmonization in the Internal Market**

OJ: See *Official Journal of the European Union*

OLAF: See **Anti-fraud Office**

An **OMBUDSMAN**, a post created by the **Treaty on European Union**, is appointed by the **European Parliament** (EP) to deal with complaints of maladministration in European Union (EU) **institutions** (with the exception of the **Court of Justice** and the **Court of First Instance**) and initiatives. Upon the receipt of complaints from citizens, business and other interests working in the EU, the Ombudsman launches an inquiry to try to resolve any particular issue of concern. The first Ombudsman, who took office in September 1995, was Jacob Söderman of Finland; he remained in the post until

March 2003. His successor was Nikiforos Diamandouros, who, having served as the first ombudsman in his native Greece, was elected by the EP in January 2003. Diamandouros assumed the post on 1 April 2003 and was re-elected in 2005. In January 2010 Diamandouros was re-elected by a majority of the **Members of the European Parliament** to another five-year term (he beat the Belgian contender, Pierre-Yves Monnet, by 340 votes to 289). The Ombudsman submits an annual report on his or her activities to the EP. The 2009 report, for example, indicated that the inability of citizens to see certain documents remained by far the most common complaint from EU citizens.

OMC: See **Open Method of Co-ordination**

ONIEB: See **Office of the Northern Ireland Executive in Brussels**

ONP stands for Open Network Provision, an initiative dating back to 1989 intended to harmonize the national regulations of the member states regarding telecommunications services.

OPEN METHOD OF CO-ORDINATION (OMC) is associated with a relatively new policy method that essentially involves the comparison of national policies across the European Union (EU) and the dissemination of best practices in such areas as social policy and employment policy. This new instrument is expected to facilitate the exchange of ideas and experiences between the member states and is intended to foster policy and learning. It is hoped that, under this method, member states will agree to and apply non-binding EU guidelines to national and regional policies, while avoiding the necessity of enacting new EU **legislation**.

OPENNESS relates primarily to increasing calls from the 1990s onwards for the provision of greater information about European Union (EU) policy debates and the EU decision-making processes within the EU **institutions** and, in particular, the **Council of the European Union**. Openness is closely associated with the other concepts such as **transparency**, **legitimacy** and **accountability** that are familiar, recurrent themes of European **governance**. The EU institutions have promised greater openness in a serious effort both to reduce the criticisms of a '**democratic deficit**' and to enable the public to appreciate and understand much better the workings of the EU. The **Treaty of Amsterdam** included a chapter on transparency that gives 'any citizen…a right of access to **European Parliament**, Council and **European Commission** documents'. Despite these aspirations, access remains rather restricted, especially to the workings of the **Council of the European Union**. The launch of the **European Convention** in February 2002, following the meeting of the Laeken **European Council** of December 2001, must be recognized as a further means to draw the people of Europe closer to the EU, as are efforts to enable citizens to petition the EU institutions (under the **Treaty of Lisbon**) and also to have recourse to the European **Ombudsman**.

OPET: See **Organization for the Promotion of Energy Technology**

OPINIONS are one of two kinds of non-binding pronouncement that may be issued by the **Council of the European Union** and the **European Commission**. Like **recommendations** they do not constitute instructions, but merely express the preference of the European Union, and may be disregarded by the member states. (See also **Court of Justice**; **decisions**; **directives**; **law**; **legislation**; **regulations**; **resolutions**.)

OPTIMUM CURRENCY AREA is a term, attributed to the US economist Robert Mundell, which refers to a group of countries bound together by a system of fixed exchange rates. From 1970 such an area was an objective of the European Communities and was to be achieved through the establishment of **economic and monetary union**.

OPT-OUT is a term that came into common usage after the 1991 **Maastricht summit**. It refers to a decision to allow a member state the statutory right not to take part in any specific activity pursued by the European Union. Opt-outs are in fact exemptions from treaty provisions and have been granted to Denmark and the United Kingdom over **economic and monetary union**, and enabled the United Kingdom to remain outside the aspirations and all decisions pertaining to the Social Chapter of the **Treaty on European Union** (TEU) until the new Labour administration abandoned this opt-out in 1997. (See also **Charter of Fundamental Social Rights of Workers**.) Denmark also secured some political opt-outs from the defence elements of the **common foreign and security policy** following its initial rejection of the TEU in 1992. Denmark, the United Kingdom and Ireland were granted various opt-out and opt-in arrangements governing the **area of freedom, security and justice** and **Schengen**, which were both established by the **Treaty of Amsterdam**. These arrangements survived the **Treaty of Nice** and the **Treaty of Lisbon**, the latter updating those on the **area of freedom, security and justice** and **Schengen** and creating a new partial opt-out from the application of the **Charter of Fundamental Rights** for Poland and the United Kingdom.

The **ORDINARY LEGISLATIVE PROCEDURE** was the title given to the **co-decision procedure** by the **Treaty of Lisbon**. The new title reflected the procedure's new status as the default decision-making procedure for European Union policymaking outside the **common foreign and security policy**.

The **ORDINARY REVISION PROCEDURE** is the means by which the European Union's member states amend the **founding treaties**. Traditionally it has involved an **intergovernmental conference** and **ratification** of the new treaty by **national parliaments** and/or **referenda**. With the entry into force of the **Treaty of Lisbon**, a new element has been included: a convention. This will examine proposed amendments and adopt recommendations, and follow structurally the model of the **European Convention** of 2002–04 that produced the **Draft Treaty establishing a Constitution for Europe**. The Treaty of Lisbon also introduced a **simplified revision procedure**.

The **ORGANISATION FOR ECONOMIC CO-OPERATION AND DEVELOPMENT** (OECD) was established under US leadership in 1961 as a successor to the **Organisation for European Economic Co-operation**. The **USA** sought a collaborative body that might mitigate some of the feared adverse consequences of the division of Western Europe into the **European Economic Community** and the **European Free Trade Association**. The USA and Canada became full members of the new organization, and **Japan** joined in 1964. All the European Union member states belong to OECD, which is a forum for the advanced industrial democracies, concerned not only with the effectiveness of the domestic economies of its members, but also with the broader and long-term problems of the international economic system. OECD membership increased in size with a spate of accessions in the mid-1990s (including Mexico in 1994, the Czech Republic in 1995 and Hungary, Poland and the Republic of Korea in 1996) and in 2010 (when Chile, Estonia, Israel and Slovenia joined). Today OECD has 34 member countries and is based in Paris, France, where it maintains a substantial organization staffed by economic experts. It has often acted as a pioneer in developing economic concepts, for example on **competition policy** and labour markets, and its regular economic reports and surveys on the international and national economies are detailed and highly regarded. The recommendations of its reports are often implemented, although OECD cannot impose a policy upon any one state. OECD seeks to foster good governance in the public service and in corporate activity. It also provides a forum to assist policy-makers in adopting strategic orientations. OECD is currently headed by José Ángel Gurría Treviño, who took up the post of Secretary-General on 1 June 2006.

The **ORGANISATION FOR EUROPEAN ECONOMIC CO-OPERATION** (OEEC) was established in 1948 by 14 states, with the **USA** and Canada as associate members. It owed its existence to the fact that, in offering aid to Europe through the **Marshall Plan**, the USA had insisted that the European states must determine a method of allocating the aid in a way that was consistent with achieving the maximum economic effect throughout the Continent. The US offer was considered by a Committee for European Economic Co-operation, which consisted of representatives of the interested European countries. The Committee was then reconstructed as the OEEC. Decisions by the OEEC Council of Ministers were to be binding on all members, but in practice the Council operated only on the basis of unanimous agreement. The OEEC administered the Marshall Aid programme, but with a substantial number of specialized boards and expert groups it outlived the programme, and went on, in the 1950s, to work for the liberalization of trade and the full convertibility of currencies. The OEEC's objective was not economic integration, but economic co-operation, an area where it was the first European body to work effectively. It provided both a base and useful lessons for subsequent developments in integration. In 1961 the OEEC was transformed into the **Organisation for Economic Co-operation and Development**.

The **ORGANISATIONS FOR THE PROMOTION OF ENERGY TECHNOLOGY** (OPET) is a network of organizations already active in the promotion of relevant technology in various scientific and industrial areas. It was established, in conjunction with the Thermie programme, in 1996 in order to encourage the development of energy technology in Europe.

The **ORGANIZATION FOR SECURITY AND CO-OPERATION IN EUROPE** (OSCE) was originally known as the **Conference on Security and Co-operation in Europe** (CSCE), a series of European conferences on security, science and technology, economic, environmental and **human rights** issues. A meeting place for all European countries, the **USSR**, the **USA** and Canada, it first convened in Helsinki in July 1973. The conclusion of this first meeting was the Helsinki Final Act, which marked agreement in three main areas: economic co-operation, human rights and the exchange of information about military activities. Further meetings were held at regular intervals in Belgrade in 1977–78, Madrid in 1980–83, Vienna in 1986–89, Paris in 1990, Helsinki again in 1992, and Budapest in 1994, in addition to a number of more specialized sessions, primarily on arms control, disarmament and human rights. The CSCE quickly assumed considerable importance as the principal opportunity for dialogue between East and West during the **Cold War**. Nevertheless, its significance as a pan-European forum could even be said to have increased after the ending of the Cold War.

Under the terms according to which the CSCE was established, and also at the insistence of the USSR, the European Communities (EC) were not allowed to have a common representation of their own at the first Helsinki meeting. However, the EC member states collaborated closely with one another in one of the first successful applications of **European political co-operation**, and the Helsinki Final Act was signed by Aldo Moro of Italy (the holder of the presidency of the Council of Ministers—see **Council of the European Union**—at the time) 'for Italy, and in the name of the European Community'. At the 1990 Paris meeting, which concluded with the signing of the **Charter of Paris for a New Europe**, which endowed the CSCE with permanent institutions, the EC participated as a single entity, and not as separate states. In December 1994 the Budapest summit conference adopted the new name OSCE to indicate the organization's permanent nature and growing political role. The OSCE maintains a secretariat in Vienna, Austria, and has 56 member states (if the European Union countries are counted separately), including all the former republics of the USSR. The abrupt rise in membership from 35 in 1990 to 55 by 1997 reflects the disintegration of the USSR and **Yugoslavia** in the early 1990s. The Federal Republic of Yugoslavia (now divided between **Serbia** and **Montenegro**), which was suspended from the CSCE in 1992, was admitted to the OSCE in 2000.

OSCE: See **Organization for Security and Co-operation in Europe**

OSTPOLITIK refers to the reorientation of the foreign policy of the Federal Republic of **Germany** (FRG—West Germany) after 1969 under the new left-of-centre Chancellor, **Willy Brandt**, which led to a series of treaties concluded by the FRG with the **USSR**, the German Democratic Republic (GDR—East Germany), Poland, and Czechoslovakia, and a Four Power agreement on Berlin. This change in policy was denounced by the Christian Democrats and their allies in Germany and caused a degree of concern in the West about Bonn's rapprochement with Moscow. To counter this, however, Brandt reinforced his support for European integration and strongly backed British membership of the European Communities (EC). As a result of the agreement with East Germany, the latter's products gained access to the EC in such great numbers that East Germany was sometimes described as the silent member of the EC.

OUTER SEVEN was a phrase often used in the 1960s to describe the member states of the **European Free Trade Association**.

OUTERMOST REGIONS were formally acknowledged in the **Treaty on European Union** (TEU). There are eight such regions: four French overseas departments (Guadeloupe, French Guiana, Martinique and Réunion), one French overseas collectivity (Saint Martin), the Azores, Madeira and the Canary Islands. All, by nature of their size, remoteness and climate, are dependent economically on a small number of export products. All the outermost regions are relatively depressed and receive substantial financial assistance through the European Union **budget**. The outermost regions are subject to a declaration drawn up at the time of the TEU, which acknowledges their major structural problems, and the **Council of the European Union**, acting under the rules of **qualified majority voting**, can give these areas exemption from the application of the provisions of the common policies.

The **OVERSEAS COUNTRIES AND TERRITORIES** (OCTs) are colonies or former colonies constitutionally subject to European Union (EU) member states and are the subject of Articles 182–187 of the **Treaty of Rome** (now Articles 198–204 of the **Treaty on the Functioning of the European Union**). Mainly French possessions when the treaty was signed in 1957, they were either overseas adjuncts to the metropolitan country or, in practice, colonies. A special convention annexed to the treaty specified the details of the association. Products from OCTs would have access to the European Communities (EC) market on the same terms as those of the member states, with a gradual removal of customs duties over five years. An Overseas Development Fund was established to finance development projects. After 1963 OCTs were absorbed into the broader EC agreements of the **Yaoundé Convention**, the **Lomé Convention** and the **Cotonou Agreement**. However, in 2001 a new **association agreement** was adopted, which was to last until the end of 2013, and which provided a new co-operation framework for EU-OCT relations. There were 21 OCTs at mid-2012: 12 linked to the United Kingdom, six to France, two to the Netherlands and one to Denmark.

OWN RESOURCES is a term that refers to the possession by the European Union (EU) of financial resources that belong to it as of right and together form the **budget**. When the **European Economic Community** was established, its funding relied on the receipt of annual contributions from the member states. With the 1970 **Treaty of Luxembourg**, the member states agreed to move to a funding system of own resources, an independent source of income for the European Communities to spend as they wished within the limits of the obligations and decision-making criteria set down by the treaties. Own resources were to be phased in over a period of five years. The own resources of the EU collected for it by the member states consist of **customs duties** on imports from third countries, levies on agricultural imports and the sugar and isoglucose levies, a contribution from the member states based on each country's share of total gross national product (GNP) in the EU and a proportion of the **value-added tax** levied by the member states.

P

PADOA-SCHIOPPA REPORT is the name of a report commissioned by the **European Commission** and submitted in April 1987 by a committee headed by Tommaso Padoa-Schioppa (1940–2010), the Deputy Director-General of the Bank of Italy. The committee had been asked to evaluate the effect of the entry into the European Communities (EC) of Portugal and Spain, and of the commitment to an **internal market** upon the EC's economic system. The Report contained four major recommendations: the establishment of a common monetary policy; the promotion of cohesion; the completion on schedule of the internal market; and the development of a macroeconomic strategy. These steps, it argued, were necessary to promote economic development while preventing an aggravation of regional economic differences within the EC.

A **PARAGRAPH** is a sub-element of an **Article** in the **European treaties**. Paragraphs within an Article are usually numbered.

A **PART** is a main sub-division in the **Treaty of Rome** and its successor, the **Treaty on the Functioning of the European Union**. Parts may in turn be sub-divided into **Titles**. The **Treaty on European Union** does not contain Parts, but is divided instead into Titles.

PARTNERSHIP AND CO-OPERATION AGREEMENTS (PCAs) provide a framework for closer political, cultural and economic relations between the European Union (EU) and former republics of the **USSR**. In some cases, the agreements make reference to the possibility of eventual free trade with the EU. In all cases, emphasis is placed on the commitment of the contracting parties to **human rights** and democracy. PCAs have been concluded, initially for a 10-year period, with **Russia** (June 1994), **Ukraine** (June 1994), Tajikistan (October 1994) and **Moldova** (November 1994). Similar agreements were concluded with Belarus, Kazakhstan and Kyrgyzstan in 1995, with Georgia, Armenia and Azerbaijan in January 1996, with Uzbekistan in July 1996 and with Turkmenistan in 1998.

PARTNERSHIPS FOR PEACE (PfP) have been signed by more than 30 countries keen on developing their relationship with the **North Atlantic Treaty Organization** (NATO). They allow for joint defence planning, joint military exercises and permanent high-level contacts. For countries in **Central and Eastern Europe**, PfPs, coupled with Membership Action Plans, became a preparatory step towards membership of NATO. By April 2009 all 12 of these countries had become NATO members.

PARTY GROUPS are the basic organizational feature of the **European Parliament** (EP). While **Members of the European Parliament** (MEPs) normally belong to national political parties, in the EP they band together in transnational party groups. The criteria for what constitutes a party group were originally laid down by the EP in 1979. At that time, if a proposed group contained MEPs elected from at least five member states, then the minimum size required was 20 MEPs. The rules have changed as the European Union (EU) has enlarged, and currently party groups need to comprise at least 25 individuals from at least 13 member states. A Member may not belong to more than one political group. Party groups cannot in theory be established if the proposed membership consists of MEPs from only one member state. However, in the past, it has been possible for one-party groups to be created. The first example, following the 1994 EP elections, was the **Forza Europa Group**, which consisted exclusively of Italian MEPs. The President shall be notified in a statement when a political group is set up. This statement shall specify the name of the group, its members and its bureau. In each EP, a few MEPs have chosen to remain unaffiliated to any group, but, in general, groups are the basis of parliamentary procedure. They nominate and elect the President and Vice-President of the EP; all committee chairmanships and memberships are filled on a group basis (although some provision is made for the few independent MEPs), and seating in the EP is by party group. The groups also receive funding, in proportion to their size and the number of countries represented, to enable them to maintain a secretariat and their various activities. The **Court of Justice** has ruled that these funds cannot be used for electoral purposes.

An examination of the history of party groups in the EP reveals a considerable degree of fluidity and instability as groups (with the exception of the Socialists) have become subject to regular change as they form, disband, amalgamate, constitute and reconstitute themselves. Consequently, the EP party groups can be said to be weakly institutionalized. There are currently seven political groups in the recently elected seventh parliament (2009–14). These include: the **European People's Party** (EPP), with 271 members (at September 2012); the Progressive Alliance of Socialists and Democrats in Europe (formerly the **Party of European Socialists**—PSE), with 189 members; the **Alliance of Liberals and Democrats for Europe** (ALDE), with 86 members; the **Greens/European Free Alliance**, with 59 members; and the **European United Left/Nordic Green Left** (GUE/NGL), with 34 members. In addition, there are two new party groups: the **European Conservatives and Reformists** (ECR), with 52 members, and the **Europe of Freedom and Democracy** (EFD), with 34 members. Two former groups, **Independence and Democracy** (ID) and **Union for Europe of the Nations** (UEN), no longer exist following poor performances at the June 2009 EP elections, and any former members have joined either ECR or EFD. The remaining 29 MEPs are independents (the so-called *non-inscrits*).

The fluidity within the EP can be illustrated by examining the evolution and fate of some of the more recent and well-known groups such as: **Rainbow Group** (ARC); **Communists and Allies**; **Group for a Europe of Democracies and Diversities** (EDD); **Group of the European Democratic Alliance** (RDE); **Group of the European Liberal Democrats** (ELDR); the short-lived **Identity, Tradition and Sovereignty Group** (ITS, which lasted for 11 months in 2007); and **Left Unity** (LU).

The 2004 and 2007 **enlargements** of the EU, however, may still destabilize the party group structure even more with the arrival of a host of new parties and MEPs. The real test for the party groups—and one that has not been successfully tackled to date—is the challenge to command loyalty and respect from EU citizens and to foster the idea and benefits of EU integration. Overall voter turn-out at the 2004 and 2009 EP elections was lower than at preceding elections, at some 45% and 43%, respectively. The rate of participation in many of the countries of **Central and Eastern Europe** fell below 40%, as it did in the United Kingdom.

PARTY OF EUROPEAN SOCIALISTS: See **Group of the Party of European Socialists**

The **PASSERELLE CLAUSE** was originally found in Article 42 of the **Treaty on European Union** and allowed the **Council of the European Union**, acting unanimously, to transfer policy competences from the intergovernmental **pillar** III to the supranational European Community pillar of the European Union. Any transfer had first to be ratified by the member states. Since the abandonment of the pillar structure with the **Treaty of Lisbon**, the passerelle clause has been replaced by the **simplified revision procedure**.

PATENTS are not necessarily exempt from the **competition policy** of the European Union. The **European Commission** has the authority to decide whether a patent or trademark violates the rules of competition. The general principle of the non-exclusiveness of patents has been upheld by the **Court of Justice**. Conversely, the Commission has launched several initiatives to facilitate the registration and protection of patents. (See **Community Patent Convention**; **Office for Harmonization in the Internal Market**.)

CHRIS (CHRISTOPHER) PATTEN (1944–) of the United Kingdom was appointed to the **European Commission** in 1999 and served until 2004 in the **Prodi** Commission as Commissioner responsible for External Relations, Common Foreign and Security Policy, Delegations to Non-member Countries and the Common Service for External Relations. Prior to taking up his post in the Commission, Patten was Governor of Hong Kong in 1992–97, at the time of the handover of the colony to the People's Republic of China. Previously he had been a Conservative Member of Parliament and had held several ministerial positions in the United Kingdom. He was elected to the position of Chancellor of Oxford University in March 2003 and to the position of Chairman of the BBC (British Broadcasting Corporation) Trust in May 2011. As part of the search for a successor to **Romano Prodi**, the United Kingdom Government suggested Patten as a possible candidate for the presidency of the Commission in June 2004. President **Jacques Chirac** essentially vetoed this possibility when he argued that only individuals from member states fully participating in the **eurozone** should be considered.

PCAS: See **Partnership and Co-operation Agreements**

PEOPLE'S EUROPE: See **Citizenship**; **Committee for a People's Europe**

PERMANENT MISSION is the name given to the diplomatic representation of a non-member state to the European Union.

PERMANENT REPRESENTATION is the name given to the large delegation that each member state maintains in **Brussels**. It consists of both diplomats and administrative officials seconded from those national ministries whose work is affected by **decisions** of the European Union. Each delegation is headed by a Permanent Representative, who possesses senior ambassadorial status. Collectively, the Permanent Representatives meet at least weekly as the **Committee of Permanent Representatives** (COREPER).

PERMANENT STRUCTURED CO-OPERATION is a form of **enhanced co-operation** in the area of the **European security and defence policy**, originally envisaged in the **Treaty establishing a Constitution for Europe** and since provided for in the **Treaty of Lisbon**. It involves the pooling of military means and capabilities and measures to enhance the availability, interoperability, flexibility and deployability of the armed forces of participating member states.

The term **PERMISSIVE CONSENSUS** was coined by academics in the 1970s to describe the way in which European publics appeared to take for granted or readily accept the process of European integration. The permissive consensus has since been seriously challenged, as seen in: the rise of Euro-scepticism; the **ratification crises** surrounding the **Treaty on European Union**, the **Treaty of Nice** and, more recently, the **Treaty establishing a Constitution for Europe** and the **Treaty of Lisbon**; and the concerns expressed about the **legitimacy** of the European Union (EU). The way in which a gap now exists between the political and economic élite and the wider populations of the former **Fifteen** and now **Twenty-Seven** member states cannot be disputed and has also been clearly displayed in the findings of **Eurobarometer** from 1992 onwards and in the **referenda** on the **euro** in Denmark (2000) and Sweden (2003). These have led to repeated calls for greater 'civic participation' in the EU project.

PESCA was a European Union initiative that was created to address the problems of areas particularly dependent on fishing. (See **Common fisheries policy**.) PESCA existed (from 1994–99) as an addition to the **structural funds** and afforded these areas access to the structural funds for specific schemes aimed at lessening their dependence on fishing. **Agenda 2000** introduced new approaches in the fisheries sector, including bringing the structural problems of fisheries-dependent areas into the new Structural Funds Objective 2 and not renewing the PESCA initiative in 2000.

The **PETERSBERG TASKS** were originally set out in the Petersberg Declaration issued by foreign and defence ministers of the member states of the **Western European Union** (WEU) in June 1992. They cover humanitarian and rescue operations, peace-keeping activities and tasks for combat forces in crisis management, including peace-making. At the time, it was anticipated that the WEU would undertake these tasks. Since then, however, the emphasis has shifted to the European Union (EU), notably through the **Treaty of Amsterdam** and, more recently, the further development of the **common foreign and security policy** and the creation of a **European Rapid Reaction Force**. With the de facto transfer of many of the WEU's activities to the EU, the latter's responsibilities for, and commitment to, undertaking Petersberg tasks have increased.

PETITIONS may be referred to in the context of the right of citizens of the European Union (EU) to petition the **European Parliament** (EP) on any matter that falls within the EU's areas of authority, and that affects them directly. The right of petition was formalized by the **Treaty on European Union**, which empowered the EP to appoint an independent **Ombudsman** to receive and evaluate petitions and complaints. Where an allegation of maladministration is upheld by the Ombudsman, a report is submitted to both the institution concerned and the EP. The formalization of the right of petition was part of the attempt to develop a notion of EU **citizenship**.

PHARE, sometimes known as Operation **Phare**, is the name originally given to the Poland and Hungary Assistance for Economic Restructuring programme, a system for co-ordinating economic aid set up by the **Organisation for Economic Co-operation and Development**, and co-ordinated by the European Communities. Established in 1989, it was subsequently extended to include Albania, Bulgaria, the Czech Republic, Estonia, Latvia, Lithuania, Romania, Slovakia and Slovenia. In March 1997 the **European Commission** agreed to the extension of Phare in order to provide specific assistance to the **applicant countries** of **Central and Eastern Europe**, to help these countries implement the reforms required to fulfil the criteria for European Union membership. Assistance was to focus on building democratic institutions and administrations and financing investment (especially in the areas of the environment, transport, product quality, working conditions and major infrastructure projects). Among the new projects funded were **twinning**, the **instrument for structural policies for pre-accession** (ISPA) and **Sapard**. A Technical Assistance Information Exchange Office (TAIEX) was opened in 1996 as part of Phare operations. Overall annual funding available under Phare, Sapard and ISPA in the period 1999–2003 amounted to €2,645m. This compares with an annual figure for Phare during 1995–99 of €730m. Assistance programmes similar to Phare were established for the former **USSR** (see **Technical Assistance to the Commonwealth of Independent States**) and the **Western Balkans** (see **CARDS**). Since 1 January 2007, Phare has been replaced by the **instrument for pre-accession assistance**.

PHARMACEUTICALS have been a central concern of the **European Commission**. In pursuance of its **health and safety** policy, the Commission has been active in regulating pharmaceutical products, and a series of **directives** apply to their testing, patenting, production, marketing and labelling. Patenting in the use of brand names has also been held, in principle, to contravene **competition policy**, which has encouraged the growth of generic products that are often substantially cheaper than the branded product. In 1994 the European Agency for the Evaluation of Medicinal Products was established in London as a decentralized agency of the European Union responsible for overseeing the registration of human and veterinary medicinal products; the agency was renamed the **European Medicines Agency** in 2004.

ANDRIS PIEBALGS (1957–) is one of the 27 European Commissioners in the Barroso II Commission (2010–14), within which he has responsibility for development issues. He was successfully nominated again by the Latvian Government after having been responsible for the energy portfolio under Barroso's first Commission (2004–09). Piebalgs worked as a teacher, before entering the political arena in the 1990s following Latvia's independence from the former **USSR**. He served as his country's ambassador to Estonia (1995–97) and to the European Union (EU, 1997–2003) and was heavily involved in the negotiations prior to Latvian accession to the EU in 2004.

PILLAR is a term that was applied to the notional structure of the European Union (EU) prior to the **Treaty of Lisbon**, which came into force in December 2009. During this period the EU was held to consist of three pillars, the **European Council** being the only body capable of co-ordinating all three. The central pillar, the first pillar, was the European Communities (EC), where the **Community method** applied and the **European Commission**, **European Parliament** and the **Court of Justice** exercised their full powers. The two other pillars were **common foreign and security policy** (CFSP), pillar II, and **justice and home affairs** (JHA), pillar III. These were governed by principles of intergovernmental co-operation where the constitutional authority of the EC did not apply. The **Treaty of Amsterdam** amended the third pillar to the effect that it was now concerned with **police and judicial co-operation in criminal matters**. With the **Treaty of Lisbon**, the pillars were replaced by a more integrated structure, although the CFSP retains many of its intergovernmental characteristics.

POCO: See **European Political Co-operation**

HANS-GERT PÖTTERING (1945–) was elected President of the **European Parliament** (EP) in January 2007 and served for the second half of the sixth parliament's life-span until the EP elections in June 2009. He was born in Lower Saxony, Germany and studied law, politics and economics at the universities of Bonn and Geneva and at Columbia University (New York). He is a member of the Christian Democratic Union and a close colleague and ally of **Angela Merkel**. He is a strong advocate of European integration and pushed hard to see the revival of the **Treaty establishing a Constitution for Europe**. Pöttering belongs to the **European People's Party** (EPP) group in the EP and held its chairmanship from 1999 to 2007. It is worth noting that he is one of only six individuals within the current cohort of **Members of the European Parliament** who also sat in the first directly elected EP in 1979. Pöttering demonstrated a much more sympathetic approach to Washington than his predecessor, Josep Borrell. He was succeeded as President of the EP in July 2009 by **Jerzy Buzek**.

POLAND was an original beneficiary of the **Phare** programme when it was launched in 1989. Subsequently, the new democratic Government entered into negotiations for association with the European Communities, and a **Europe**

agreement was signed in December 1991. This was the first major step by Poland towards the ultimate objective of membership, and in April 1994 it submitted a formal application to join the European Union (EU). Three years later, the application received formal approval, although the **European Commission**'s report made clear that investment would be needed if the country was 'to comply with Community rules on agriculture, environment and transport', and that further administrative reform would be required for the application and enforcement of the *acquis communautaire*, **Accession negotiations** began in March 1998 and, despite some concerns within the EU about the capacity of the country to take on all the obligations of membership, were successfully concluded in December 2002. Six months later, in June 2003, 81.7% of those who participated in a national referendum (turn-out was 58.8%) voted in favour of EU membership. Poland therefore joined the EU on 1 May 2004 as its largest new member.

Concerns that Poland might prove to be among the most difficult of the new members to integrate were borne out at the **European Council** meeting in December 2003 when the Polish and Spanish Governments opposed changes to **qualified majority voting** rules, thereby preventing conclusion of the **intergovernmental conference** that had begun work three months earlier. This Polish/Spanish alliance came to an abrupt end with the election of a new Spanish Government in early 2004. The incoming socialist administration in Spain was more ready to reach agreement and effectively compelled the Polish Government to do likewise. All member states reached agreement on a treaty text in June 2004. Poland was one of a number of states that adopted a very tough bargaining stance towards the financing of the new budgetary package (covering the period 2007 to 2013), and was highly critical of the British rebate. Nevertheless, Poland readily accepted the deal struck in December 2005. The EU remains a contested issue within Polish politics. Poland possessed one of the most Eurosceptic governments in the run-up to agreement on the **Treaty of Lisbon**, and battled so hard to realize its own interests on issues such as voting rights and the place of Christianity within the treaty base that it often antagonized its fellow EU member states. However, the Eurosceptic Government of Jarosław Kaczyński was replaced in October 2007 by a new administration under Donald Tusk which sought to steer a more EU-friendly (albeit with degrees of soft Euroscepticism) and pro-German course. Poland became part of the EU's **Schengen Area** in December 2007. The Polish parliament endorsed the Treaty of Lisbon in April 2008, but the then Polish President, Lech Kaczyński, waited until he knew the outcome of the second vote on the treaty in Ireland before he signed off the **ratification** process in Poland in October 2009. The Polish government coalition parties performed well in the 2009 **European Parliament** elections and polled over 50% of the vote (with a turn-out of some 28%) and were subsequently expected to play an ever greater role within the **Group of the European People's Party**. Kaczyński's death in a plane crash in April 2010 precipitated a new presidential election over two rounds in June and July 2010, which was won by Bronisław Komorowski.

POLICE AND JUDICIAL CO-OPERATION IN CRIMINAL MATTERS was the name given to Title VI of the **Treaty on European Union** prior to the **Treaty of Lisbon**. Originally known as **justice and home affairs**, this third pillar of the European Union (EU) was renamed by the **Treaty of Amsterdam**. The objective of police and judicial co-operation in criminal matters is to prevent and combat: problems of racism and xenophobia; terrorism; trafficking in human beings and crimes against children; drugs-trafficking; weapons-trafficking; and corruption and fraud. Through **Europol**, the European Police Office, there is scope for closer co-operation between national police forces and customs and judicial authorities, co-operation in the latter area also being provided for through **Eurojust**. This co-operation may lead to closer **approximation** of rules on criminal matters in the member states. The Treaty of Lisbon transferred responsibility for such co-operation to the EU's supranational decision-making procedures.

POLICY in the context of the European Union (EU) refers to the collectivity of proposals, initiatives and **legislation** intended to achieve EU aims in specific fields of activity.

The **POLICY PLANNING AND EARLY WARNING UNIT** was set up as part of the reforms to the **common foreign and security policy** (CFSP) introduced by the **Treaty of Amsterdam** in 1999. Its main role is to monitor and analyse developments in areas relevant to the CFSP, provide assessments of and early warning reports on issues of concern to the European Union, and prepare papers on options for policies. The unit is staffed by personnel drawn from the member states, the **European Commission**, the General Secretariat of the **Council of the European Union**, and **Western European Union**.

The **POLITICAL AND SECURITY COMMITTEE** is the successor to the **Political Committee**. It was renamed and had its powers increased by the **Treaty of Nice**. Hence, acting under the responsibility of the **Council of the European Union**, the Committee exercises political control and strategic direction of crisis management operations undertaken by the European Union (EU). It may also be authorized to take specific implementing **decisions**. With the development of a more explicit defence dimension to the **common foreign and security policy**, the Committee has also provided support for the EU Military Staff, which is under the authority of the **European Union Military Committee**.

The **POLITICAL COMMITTEE** is the name of a body that had its origins in the committee of **Political Directors** originally charged with preparing the quarterly meetings of the member state foreign ministers under **European political co-operation**. It was formally established by the **Treaty on European Union** as part of the **common foreign and security policy** (CFSP). The tasks of the Political Committee, which was composed of the Political Directors, were to monitor the international situation in areas covered by the CFSP, and to advise and submit proposals to the **Council of the European Union** on foreign and security policy. In conjunction with the Council presidency, the Committee also had responsibility for implementing policies decided upon according to the CFSP structure. The **Treaty of Nice** enhanced the committee's powers and renamed it the **Political and Security Committee**.

POLITICAL CO-OPERATION: See **Common Foreign and Security Policy**; **European Political Co-operation**

POLITICAL DIRECTORS, each of whom is appointed by a member state as an aide to its foreign minister, are invariably senior diplomats. They formerly played an essential role in the operation of **European political co-operation**. Collectively, the Directors were responsible for the co-ordination and implementation of foreign policy initiatives, meeting monthly to review progress and urgent current issues. Under the **Single European Act**, the Directors were provided with their own secretariat in **Brussels**, and under the **Treaty on European Union**, they were formally constituted as a **Political Committee** with a major role in the **common foreign and security policy**. The **Treaty of Nice** enhanced the committee's powers and renamed it the **Political and Security Committee**. The responsibility for organizing the Directors belongs to the foreign ministry of the member state currently holding the presidency of the **Council of the European Union**, and therefore rotates between the Political Directors, changing every six months. The division of labour between the Directors and the **Committee of Permanent Representatives** is under constant review. The immediate subordinate of the Political Director, responsible for routine business, is known as the European Correspondent.

POLITICAL UNION: See **European Union**; **Maastricht Summit**; **Treaty on European Union**

PORTUGAL originally had no prospect of becoming a member of the European Communities (EC) as long as it remained under an authoritarian regime. In 1962, along with other members of the **European Free Trade Association**, Portugal approached the EC, but without specifying the form of association it desired. Negotiations had not begun when the British application for entry was vetoed by France, and Portugal's proposed schedule was abandoned. Discussions were not resumed until 1970, and a **free trade agreement** was signed in July 1972. After the 1974 revolution, the new Government expressed a desire for further co-operation with, and financial assistance from, the EC. A **protocol** to the free trade agreement, providing for financial aid, was signed in September 1976; further protocols were signed in 1979 and 1980. Portugal formally applied for full membership in March 1977. Progress on the negotiations was slow. Officially commencing in October 1978, they did not begin in earnest until 1980. While there were some problems between the two sides, the slowness of the negotiations was perhaps due more to the simultaneous negotiations with Spain, about whose application there were more substantive concerns among some member states. However, the two applications tended to be treated in conjunction with each other. The negotiations were concluded in March 1985, and Portugal joined the EC in January 1986. One of the poorest states in the European Union (EU), it has benefited substantially from the **structural funds**, the **Cohesion Fund** and other aid programmes. Portugal has generally been well disposed towards the EU, but in more recent times difficulties have arisen. In June 2005 the Portuguese Government was requested to cut its budget deficit to fall in line with EU rules on the **stability and growth pact**. Portugal's economy had certainly been in trouble, running into recession in 2003 and recording only 1% growth the following year. Unemployment reached an eight-year high (some 7.5%) in 2005. The Portuguese presidency of the **Council of the European Union** in the second half of 2007 culminated with the signing of the **Treaty of Lisbon** which has since re-shaped the EU institutions and their decision-making capabilities. The Portuguese Government decided not to hold a referendum on the treaty, and the Portuguese parliament ratified it with a strong majority in April 2008. The slump in Portugal's economy following the onset of the global financial crisis in 2008 led the Government to seek a bailout (of €78,000m.) from the EU and the IMF in April 2011—which was approved the following month—and to introduce a more stringent austerity programme in an attempt to bring the country's finances back under control. This move proved unpopular,especially given the drastic rise in the number of unemployed (which by April 2012 had almost reached 15%). Following the defeat in the legislature of further government austerity proposals, Prime Minister José Sócrates resigned in March 2011 and an early general election was scheduled for June. The Social Democrats, under Passos Coelho, triumphed in these polls, but remained committed to the austerity programme and participated in the negotiations leading to the signing of the **Fiscal Compact Treaty** (**Treaty on Stability, Co-ordination and Governance in the Economic and Monetary Union**) in March 2012.

POTENTIAL CANDIDATE STATE, as opposed to **candidate state**, was the status assigned to the countries of the **Western Balkans** by the Feira summit of the **European Council** in June 2000. The term has since been confirmed in the preambles to the **stabilization and association agreements**. It is to be assumed that a potential candidate state becomes a candidate state once it is admitted to the accession process.

JANEZ POTOČNIK (1958–) is one of the 27 European Commissioners in the **Barroso** II Commission (2010–14), within which he has responsibility for the environment portfolio. He is a Slovenian national and a university economist (he has a PhD in Economics from the University of Ljubljana). This is his second term as a Commissioner, as he served as the Commissioner for Science and Research in Barroso's first Commission (2004–09).

PPE: See **Group of the European People's Party (Christian Democrats) and European Democrats**

A **PRE-ACCESSION STRATEGY** to help prepare countries from **Central and Eastern Europe** for membership of the European Union was launched in 1994 by the **Essen summit** of the **European Council**. The idea was to build on the existing relationship based on the **Europe agreements** by intensifying co-operation and by outlining more precisely the steps necessary for meeting the obligations of membership, notably concerning adoption of the *acquis communautaire*. In 1998 the strategy was enhanced by the launch of **accession negotiations** and the conclusion of **accession partnerships**.

PREAMBLE refers to the opening recitals of a treaty. In the case of the European Union (EU), the preambles to the **founding treaties** outline the aims and purposes of the EU. Preambles have often been referred to by the **Court of Justice** in defining EU **law**.

PREFERENTIAL TRADE AGREEMENTS signed by the European Union (EU) with other countries are intended to lead, within a reasonable period of time, to the establishment of either a free trade area or a **customs union**. This is a requirement that the **General Agreement on Tariffs and Trade** demanded of all preferential trade agreements. Those signed by the EU form part of the **common commercial policy** and fall into several categories: **trade and co-operation agreements**; **association agreements** (see also **Europe agreements** and **stabilization and association agreements**); the several individual and collective agreements signed with states bordering the Mediterranean; the **Cotonou Agreement** (see also the **Lomé Convention**); and **partnership and co-operation agreements**. In the overwhelming majority of cases, the agreements are not restricted to purely economic matters.

The **PRELIMINARY RULING** procedure is a key element of the legal system of the European Union (EU). Under the procedure, a national court may refer a question about the meaning of an EU law to the **Court of Justice**. Once the Court issues its decision, it is applied to the relevant case by the national court.

PRESIDENCY: See **Council Presidency**

A **PRESIDENT OF THE EUROPEAN COUNCIL**, to be elected by the other members of the **European Council** for a term of two and a half years, was one of the institutional innovations originally contained in the **Treaty establishing a Constitution for Europe** and carried forward in the **Treaty of Lisbon**. The incumbent has five key tasks: chairing the European Council and driving forward its work; ensuring proper preparation for meetings and continuity in co-operation with the **European Commission** President; facilitating cohesion and consensus within the European Council; reporting to the **European Parliament** after each European Council meeting; and ensuring the external representation of the European Union on issues concerning the **common foreign and security policy**. The first person to occupy the position was **Herman Van Rompuy**, who assumed his post on 1 December 2009.

PRICE-FIXING AGREEMENTS have been declared illegal by the **European Commission** on the grounds that they are contrary to the **competition policy** of the European Communities. The precedent was set in 1969 when the Commission successfully prosecuted the dyestuffs **cartel** that controlled some 80% of the European market at that time. Yet, price-fixing agreements remain an established fact of contemporary business activity across the European Union (EU). In recent years the European Commission has intensified its efforts to deter companies from engaging in such anti-competitive price-fixing arrangements. This resolve has seen a significant increase in the size of the fines imposed on companies that have deliberately sought to fix prices, as well as the adoption of **leniency notices**. In December 2002 the member states agreed to radical reforms (under regulation 1/2003) of the EU's anti-trust rules which are designed to make it easier for the Commission to act against price fixers (see **competition policy, cartels**). The new regime came into force in May 2004. Cartel busting was identified by **Neelie Kroes**, the Competition Commissioner in the first **Barroso** Commission, as a particular focus of her term of office. Two of the highest ever fines in the history of the Commission's war against cartel arrangements were levied on a group of lift manufacturers in March 2007 and a number of glass manufacturers in November 2008. The overall fines totalled €992.3m. and €1,318m., respectively. Price-fixing agreements remain a focus for the Commission.

The **PRIMACY OF EUROPEAN COMMUNITY LAW** is a doctrine established by the **European Court of Justice** in 1964. The case that provided this landmark decision was *Costa v Enel* and, when this decision is taken together with the doctrine of **direct effect**, it signifies nothing less than a complete metamorphosis of the nature and scope of EC law. These two doctrines transform the EC into a powerful means to advance the **supranational** idea and to challenge existing national law. A first formal reference to primacy was contained in a declaration adopted with the **Treaty of Lisbon**.

The **PRIVILEGES AND IMMUNITIES** of the European Communities (EC) were laid down in a **protocol** of the 1965 **Merger Treaty**. It defines the privileges and immunities of all those who are members of, or who work for, EC **institutions**. It further establishes the rights of the Communities themselves within the territory of the member states.

ROMANO PRODI (1939–), Prime Minister of Italy from 1996 to 1998, and again from 2006 to 2008, has been one of the most successful incumbents of that office. He was nominated as President of the **European Commission** following the resignation of **Jacques Santer** and his college of Commissioners in March 1999 over allegations of favouritism and failure to crack down on corruption. Once his appointment had been ratified by the **European Parliament**, Prodi's term of office began in September 1999. Charged with rebuilding the credibility of the Commission, he set about introducing a radical infrastructural reform. Prodi was also keen to re-establish the agenda-setting role of the Commission within the European Union. For many, his leadership proved to be weak, however. He stepped down as President in November 2004. Although he ruled out returning to domestic politics in Italy once his term as Commission President expired, the continued presence in Italian politics of his bitter rival, **Silvio Berlusconi**, caused many on the left to encourage Prodi to lead them in the April 2006 legislative elections. Prodi did not disappoint, although his victory at the polls was particularly slender. Prodi's time in office was limited. Although he became the first President of the newly established and left-leaning Democratic Party in October 2007, his tenure in office as Prime Minister was upset by a number of scandals and disagreements on policy within government circles, which ultimately led to a vote of no confidence in his administration in the Italian Senate in January 2008. Prodi duly tendered his resignation to the Italian President but remained as head of a 'caretaker' Government until new elections were arranged and took place in April 2008. By this stage Prodi had decided not to stand as the leader of the Democratic Party again and watched the party and its allies lose the elections to his long-time rival Berlusconi.

PRODUCTION QUOTAS can be imposed by the **European Commission** on the **coal** and **steel** industries. Under the powers it inherited from the High Authority of the **European Coal and Steel Community**, the Commission has the authority, if a state of **manifest crisis** is adopted, to impose quotas on individual companies. Severe production quotas were imposed upon steel companies in 1980, and were not abolished until June 1988. In the late 1980s, production quotas were also introduced into the **common agricultural policy**.

PROJECT EUROPE 2030: See **Gonzalez Group**

PROPORTIONALITY, like **subsidiarity**, is a principle invoked to contain the accumulation of powers by the European Union (EU). In line with the principle of proportionality, the EU should not be taking any action that goes beyond the minimum necessary to achieve its objectives as laid down in the **European treaties**. Hence, proportionality is concerned with the scale and effect of any EU action.

A **PROTOCOL** is an additional element of a treaty. It either provides details of the implementation of treaty requirements or is too lengthy for inclusion in the treaty itself. However, protocols are equal in status to the main body of a treaty.

PROVISIONS is a term generally used in the context of the European Union to describe the contents of the **European treaties**.

The **PRÜM CONVENTION**, also known as the Treaty of Prüm or Schengen III, was signed in May 2005 by Austria, Belgium, France, Germany, Luxembourg, the Netherlands and Spain. It facilitates, for the purpose of combating terrorism, cross-border crime and illegal migration, the sharing between signatories of personal data (e.g. DNA, fingerprints). It builds on existing co-operation under the **Schengen Agreement** and on **police and judicial co-operation in criminal matters**.

PSE: See **Group of the Party of European Socialists**

PUBLIC HEALTH: See **Health Policy**

PUBLIC PROCUREMENT, although referred to in the **Treaty of Rome**, has only recently become a major objective of European Union (EU) **competition policy**. Since 1990, a series of **directives** have required all public contracts above a specific cost threshold to be open to competitive tender throughout the member states. The threshold varies according to the product or service involved, but is otherwise the same throughout the EU.

PUBLIC SERVICES do not enjoy the privileged status within the European Union (EU) that some member states would like to see. Certainly their status often appears ambiguous. In principle, except where exemptions are approved, EU rules on **state aid** apply as much to public services as they do to commercial enterprises. That said, Article 16 of the **Treaty of Rome**, as introduced by the **Treaty of Amsterdam** (and now Article 14 of the **Treaty on the Functioning of the European Union**), draws particular attention to the role of 'services of general economic interest' and calls on the EU and the member states to 'take care that such services operate on the basis of principles and conditions which enable them to fulfil their missions'. The Treaty of Lisbon introduced a dedicated **protocol** on the subject.

The **PUBLICATIONS OFFICE OF THE EUROPEAN UNION**, which was formerly called the Office for Official Publications of the European Communities (EUR-OP), is based in Luxembourg. It is an agency of the **European Commission**, but provides services to, and is managed by, all European Union (EU) **institutions**. It is responsible for the publication and dissemination of EU publications, including official reports and pamphlets. These are available directly from the EU Bookshop and are also lodged in several educational institutions throughout the EU, which have been recognized as depositories for EU publications and are known as **European Documentation Centres**. The office also offers a number of online services giving free access to information on EU law (**EUR-Lex**), EU publications (EU Bookshop), public procurement (Tenders Electronic Daily—TED—the online format of the Supplement to the **Official Journal of the European Union**), and EU research and development (**CORDIS**).

Q

QMV: See **Qualified Majority Voting**

The **QUAD** comprises meetings between officials from the European Union, the **USA**, **Japan** and Canada, where multilateral trade issues are discussed. (See also **G-8**.)

QUAESTORS are five individuals elected from the ranks of the **Members of the European Parliament** (MEPs). They sit in an advisory capacity in the Bureau of the **European Parliament** and are responsible for financial and administrative matters affecting MEPs.

QUALIFIED MAJORITY VOTING (QMV) is one of the ways in which the **Council of the European Union** arrives at a decision on issues and proposals put before it. The vote is qualified in two ways. Firstly, a qualified majority must be substantially in excess of 50%: traditionally, it has been more than two-thirds. Secondly, it is qualified in that it is based on a weighted voting system, where each member state has an indivisible block of votes at its disposal, the size of which is based roughly on the size of its population.

The **Treaty of Rome** envisaged that QMV would apply to most proposals after 1965. The achievement of this objective was prevented by the **empty chair crisis** and the **Luxembourg Compromise**. The possibilities for a greater use of QMV did not increase until the **Single European Act**. With the adoption of the **Treaty on European Union** and further **enlargement** of the European Union (EU), there was renewed pressure for an increase in the size of the minority that would be needed to obstruct a proposal, in the hope that this reform would speed up the process of integration. From January 1995, when the **General Affairs and External Relations Council** agreed on amendments to voting procedures in the Council which took into account the accession of three new member states, the total number of votes was 87, weighted as follows: France, Germany, Italy and the United Kingdom had 10 votes each; Spain, eight votes; Belgium, Greece, the Netherlands and Portugal, five votes each; Austria and Sweden, four votes each; Denmark, Finland and Ireland, three votes each; and Luxembourg, two votes. A qualified majority was constituted by 62 votes, and thus 26 votes were sufficient for a blocking minority. However, as a result of pressure from Spain and the United Kingdom, the so-called **Ioannina compromise** of March 1994 meant that 23–25 opposing votes ensured the continued discussion of proposed **legislation** by the Council for a 'reasonable' period until a consensus was obtained.

QMV was extended by the **Treaty of Amsterdam** into a number of areas previously subject to unanimous decision. The **European Parliament** was also to have the right of co-decision in these areas (see **co-decision procedure**). As the EU expanded, the use of qualified majority voting in a wider range of **decisions** was expected to minimize 'policy drag'. Under the terms of the **Treaty of Nice**, a further range of areas, mostly minor in nature and relating to appointments to various EU institutions (such as the **Court of Auditors**), became subject to QMV. By 2002 most areas under pillar I were determined by QMV, although there were some notable exceptions, including decisions in the area of **economic and monetary union**.

With EU enlargement imminent there was general acceptance in the Council in the late 1990s that the voting procedures would have to be altered. Agreement would not be easy, given political sensitivities. Not surprisingly therefore, the issue was postponed at the Amsterdam **summit meeting** and agreement was finally reached, after a great deal of acrimony, at the Nice summit in December 2000. The **Treaty of Nice** had two major impacts. First, it complicated decision-making by requiring a triple majority for a decision to be adopted by QMV. This comprises: firstly, a qualified majority of the weighted votes; secondly, a majority of the member states (which was already implicit under the existing regime); and, lastly, a demographic majority of at least 62% of the EU's total population. In effect, this new formula ensures that numbers and percentages have become more important in determining voting in the Council. It also increases the leverage of the larger EU states.

Second, the Treaty of Nice reformulated the votes for an EU of **Fifteen** and agreed the anticipated vote allocations for the **candidate countries** in an EU of **Twenty–Five**. These were subsequently confirmed in the **Accession Treaty**. Hence, from 1 November 2004, the total number of votes in the Council was 321, weighted as follows: France, Germany, Italy and the United Kingdom had 29 votes each; Spain and Poland, 27 votes; the Netherlands, 13; Belgium, the Czech Republic, Greece, Hungary and Portugal, 12 votes each; Austria and Sweden, 10 votes each; Denmark, Finland, Ireland, Lithuania and Slovakia, seven votes each; Cyprus, Estonia, Latvia, Luxembourg and Slovenia, four votes each; and Malta, three votes. A qualified majority could now be attained with 232 votes. With the accession of Romania and Bulgaria in January 2007, there was a further recalculation, and the new states were allocated 14 and 10 votes, respectively. From 1 November 2014, in accordance with the terms of the **Treaty of Lisbon**, the existing QMV system was to be replaced by a **double majority voting** system.

The **QUALITY OF LIFE AND MANAGEMENT OF LIVING RESOURCES PROGRAMME** superseded existing programmes covering agricultural research (i.e. **FAIR**), biomedicine and health (Biomed) and bio-technology (**Biotech**) in 1998. The programme, which ran until 2002 and had a budget of €2,413m., supported research carried out by industry or educational establishments in member states and non-member states in all areas of the life sciences, including infectious diseases, nutrition, environment and health, sustainable agriculture, ageing, public health and neurosciences.

QUANTITATIVE RESTRICTIONS: See **Quota Restrictions**

QUOTA RESTRICTIONS on internal trade in the European Communities (EC) were abolished by the **Six** by 1968. Later entrants to the EC were allowed a transitional period of between four and six years in which to complete the process of abolition. In external trade, quota restrictions have been removed by many of the international agreements that the European Union has signed with other countries. They still exist, however, in certain areas such as agriculture and textiles, and for specified manufactured goods from some countries. For example, under the **common agricultural policy**, milk quotas were introduced in 1984 as a means of stabilizing milk production.

R

RACE (Research and Development in Advanced Communications Technologies in Europe) was a major **European Commission** initiative launched in 1987 and aimed at ensuring that the European Communities remained in the forefront of developments in the **telecommunications** sector and continued to be competitive. It complemented the **European strategic programme for research and development in information technology** (Esprit) and other more specific **information technology** projects; it was replaced in 1994 by **ACTS**.

RAILWAYS have not been a prominent element of European Union (EU) **transport policy**. While accepting that state **subsidies** are in conflict with **competition policy**, the EU has agreed to the public service function of railways, and policy has been designed to make the railways more competitive with other forms of transport. Infrastructure development has been at the centre of EU involvement in the railways, particularly within the context of efforts to develop **Trans-European Networks**.

RAINBOW GROUP (ARC) was one of the **party groups** in the **European Parliament** until 1994. It was formed after the 1984 **direct elections** as a disparate alliance between various small and mainly regionalist-nationalist parties and Green parties that, on account of their numerical weakness, were unable to create their own groups. It had little hierarchical organization and no coherent policy position, deficiencies that did not disappear in 1989, when the Greens left to form their own Green Group (see **Group of the Greens/European Free Alliance**).

MARIANO RAJOY (1955–) was appointed Prime Minister of Spain on 21 December 2011. Rajoy was born in Santiago de Compostela in Galicia. He studied law at the University of Santiago de Compostela and after graduating joined the Spanish civil service. His political career commenced in 1981 when he was elected as a deputy in the Galician parliament as a member of the centre-right Alianza Popular (AP, renamed the Partido Popular—PP—in 1989). Rahoy entered the national political arena in 1996 following his election to the Spanish parliament. As a protégé of **José María Aznar**, he rose rapidly in the ranks of the PP and was appointed Minister of Public Administration in the first

Aznar Government. He became First Deputy Prime Minister in 2000 and Minister of Home Affairs the following year. In 2004 Aznar stepped down as Prime Minister and proposed Rajoy as his possible successor. The PP lost the 2004 elections and Rajoy became leader of the opposition. Rajoy continued to lead the party after its further defeat at the polls in 2008, but finally became Prime Minister in November 2011 when the PP won a convincing victory in an early general election.

RAPHAEL was a cultural programme that supported natural heritage activities, including co-operation between European Union museums, training for cultural heritage professionals, and the study, preservation and enhancement of European heritage. It was introduced in 1997 for three years (with a budget of €30m.), after which it was subsumed into the **Culture 2000** framework programme. (See also **Kaleidoscope**.)

The **RAPID REACTION MECHANISM** (RRM) was created in February 2001 to ensure the swift deployment of civilian experts to crisis areas while negotiations on the structure and composition of a **European rapid reaction force** continued. The RRM was granted funds of €25m. for 2002; by 2005 the budget had risen to €30m. While the RRM was a very flexible instrument, the Council Regulation establishing it imposed a number of legal constraints, notably: the maximum duration of any RRM project was six months; the RRM could not finance **humanitarian assistance**; and it could only finance an operation where other European Union instruments were unable to respond within the timeframe necessary. The RRM was replaced by the **Instrument for Stability** in 2007.

RAPPORTEUR is the title given to the **Member of the European Parliament** (MEP) responsible for drafting and presenting a report to a committee and to the plenary session of the **European Parliament**.

RATIFICATION refers to the process of approval of a treaty (e.g. one of the **European treaties**, or an **Accession Treaty**, or an external relations agreement) by the member states according to the rules and procedures established by their own constitutions. In certain member states (i.e. Denmark, Ireland) this has often involved a referendum. Treaties and agreements requiring ratification cannot come into force unless ratified by all the member states. In the case of an **accession treaty** or an **association agreement**, ratification also involves the **European Parliament** giving its approval via the **consent procedure**.

RATIFICATION CRISES is the term given to the political crises that have followed the popular rejection of a Treaty. The first ratification crisis came after the Danish 'no' to the **Treaty on European Union** (TEU) in June 1992, a crisis that intensified when the French people only narrowly gave their support to the TEU in a referendum three months later. The Danish 'no' was later overturned by popular endorsement of the TEU in a further referendum in May 1993. A second ratification crisis occurred following the rejection by Irish voters of the **Treaty of Nice** in June 2001. The response was to hold a second referendum in the latter half of 2002, when the original result was overturned by a vote in favour of the treaty. A third crisis, and the most major to date, occurred when the **Treaty establishing a Constitution for Europe** was rejected by French and Dutch voters in the first half of 2005. This led to the formal abandonment of the treaty. Much of its content was subsequently included in the **Treaty of Lisbon**. This treaty, in turn, was the focus of a fourth ratification crisis following a clear-cut 'no' in the Irish referendum in June 2008. This crisis involved various challenges and delays in three other states, Germany, Poland and the Czech Republic. All member states ultimately ratified the treaty, and it came into force on 1 December 2009.

RDE: See **Group of the European Democratic Alliance**

RECHAR was the acronym of a major initiative of the **European Coal and Steel Community** (ECSC), introduced in 1989 for the reconversion and redevelopment of coal-mining areas. The objectives were to provide occupational training for redundant workers, and economic diversification in areas severely affected by the contraction of the coal industry. RECHAR II funded projects from 1994 to 1999.

RECITE stands for Regions and Cities in Europe, a 1991 initiative launched as part of the objective of establishing greater social and economic cohesion in the territory of the European Communities. Its purpose was to encourage and provide support for co-operative networks of joint economic projects undertaken by regions and cities throughout the member states. The original programme ran until 1995 before being replaced by RECITE II, which lasted until 2001.

RECOMMENDATIONS are one of two kinds of non-binding pronouncement that may be issued by the **Council of the European Union** and the **European Commission**. Like **opinions**, they do not constitute instructions, but merely express the preference of the European Union (EU), and may be disregarded by the member states. Recommendations made according to the provisions of the **Treaty of Paris** were slightly different, however: they were binding upon member states as to the final result, but not the means of achieving it, and were thus more similar to EU **directives**. (See also **legislation**.)

VIVIANE REDING (1951–) is one of the Vice-Presidents of the second **Barroso** Commission of the European Union (2010–14). She is the longest-serving Commissioner, and comes from the Grand Duchy of Luxembourg. In her new post she assumed responsibility for justice, fundamental rights and citizenship. Reding has developed a rich and detailed knowledge of European Union affairs. Prior to becoming a European Commissioner in 1999 (first under the **Prodi** Commission) and then being reappointed to serve in the first Barroso Commission, she was a member of the European Parliament from 1989 and, in the 10 years prior to this, was a member of the Luxembourg parliament. Her profession prior to entering politics was journalism.

REDISTRIBUTIVE POLICIES are those policies of the European Union (EU) that primarily involve the redistribution of resources from the richer to the less developed areas of the EU as part of the process of promoting economic and social cohesion. Such policies are generally financed from the **structural funds**. Also included under the broad heading of redistributive policies are those policies that involve financial support being given to particular areas of production, for example, agriculture (via the **common agricultural policy**) and fisheries (via the **common fisheries policy**).

The **REFERENCE PRICE** is a key price in the **common agricultural policy**. It is the average price calculated from the market prices for fruit and vegetables in each member state. If the price of foodstuffs imported into the European Union is lower than the reference price, the imports incur a levy to raise their price to the same level.

REFERENDA on European Union (EU) issues play an increasingly important role in the European integration process. Countries joining the EU have tended to submit the terms of accession to their people for approval, while some member states have sought popular support, often in line with a constitutional requirement, for various of the more recent **European treaties** such as the **Treaty on European Union** (TEU) and the **Treaty of Nice**. In the case of referenda on accession to the EU, the outcome of a referendum has always been respected. The Norwegian Government, for example, has been forced twice to abandon plans to join the European Communities and the EU following a 'no' vote. By contrast, where a member state's electorate has rejected the TEU or the Treaty of Nice and therefore brought about a **ratification crisis**, a second referendum has so far been held. Nine of the 10 **candidate countries** that joined in May 2004 held a referendum on EU membership. In each case the outcome was positive.

Following the adoption of the **Treaty establishing a Constitution for Europe** in 2004 the EU geared itself up for what amounted to the most important series of referenda. A total of 10 member states (the Czech Republic,

Denmark, France, Ireland, Luxembourg, the Netherlands, Poland, Portugal, Spain and the United Kingdom) had pledged to hold a referendum on **ratification** of the new treaty, and it was generally assumed, on the basis of early opinion polls, that the treaty would be endorsed by the public where and when it was put to a referendum. However, events took a rather different course. The first of the referenda took place in Spain in February 2005, with the treaty being approved, but the rejections of the treaty in France and the Netherlands (two of the founding member states of the EU) in the late spring of 2005 sent out shockwaves that resonated throughout the entire EU. The approval of the treaty in Luxembourg in July 2005 was welcome, but it could not conceal the immediate difficulties confronting European leaders. The French and Dutch results killed off the treaty altogether as all member states needed to endorse the Constitution, whether by referendum or by parliament or by both, in order for it to come into effect. The United Kingdom simply postponed its planned referendum for the time being after the French and Dutch votes. It was left to the **European Council** to consider how to proceed as the Treaty establishing a Constitution for Europe had held some very valuable alterations to existing decision-making instruments. After much internal debate, it was decided to scale back the contents of the rejected treaty and to produce an amending treaty to incorporate many of the key elements. A new text that bore considerable resemblance to the Treaty establishing a Constitution for Europe was agreed and the **Treaty of Lisbon** was signed in December 2007. Only Ireland was scheduled to hold a referendum on the text, although there was considerable pressure on **Gordon Brown** to do the same in the United Kingdom. Victory for the 'no' campaign in Ireland in June 2008 led to the latest in a succession of **ratification crises** for the EU. In the United Kingdom the Conservative Party continued to call for a referendum on the Treaty of Lisbon (even though the treaty had been approved by both Houses of Parliament) until the 'yes' vote in the second Irish referendum on the Treaty of Lisbon in October 2009.

On taking office in 2010, the Conservative-Liberal Democrat coalition Government in the United Kingdom introduced in Parliament an 'EU Bill' designed to subject future amending treaties and other major decisions affecting the United Kingdom's position within the EU (e.g. joining the euro) to a referendum; this bill became law in July 2011. The move followed an amendment to the French Constitution to establish the referendum as the default means by which France would, once **Croatia** had joined the EU, ratify each future **accession treaty**.

REFERRALS: See **Court of Justice**

A **REFLECTION GROUP** has been established on two occasions to consider reforms to the European Union (EU). A first group consisted of representatives of the ministers of foreign affairs of the member states and of the

European Parliament and **European Commission**. It was responsible for preparing the agenda of the 1996 **intergovernmental conference** (IGC), which resulted in the **Treaty of Amsterdam**. A more recent group, the **Gonzalez Group**, was established in December 2008 with the goal of identifying how best the EU could 'more effectively anticipate and meet challenges in the longer term horizon of 2020 to 2030'. It presented its report, called *Project Europe 2030*, to the European Council in May 2010.

A **REFORM TREATY** was the planned outcome of the **intergovernmental conference** (IGC) called by the **European Council** in June 2007. Having concluded negotiations, the **member states** dropped the 'Reform Treaty' title and instead decided to name the new treaty the **Treaty of Lisbon**.

REFUGEE POLICY forms part of the European Union's **asylum policy** and is a relatively new area of competence of the European Union. Explicit reference to refugees in the **founding treaties** came with the **Treaty of Amsterdam** and the goal of creating an **area of freedom**, **security and justice**. This placed emphasis on adopting measures to ease the sharing of the burden of incoming refugees, and on proceeding in accordance with the 1951 Geneva Convention and the 1967 **protocol** concerning refugees, as well as on consulting with the United Nations High Commissioner for Refugees.

REGIO is one of the European Union (EU) statistical domains of the **New Cronos** database, which deals with EU socio-economic statistics at regional (**nomenclature of territorial units for statistics**—NUTS) level.

REGIONAL FUND COMMITTEE: See **European Regional Development Fund**

REGIONAL POLICY was not specifically covered by the **Treaty of Rome**, although the **Preamble** refers to the need to reduce 'the differences existing between the various regions and the backwardness of the less favoured regions', while a special **protocol** stated that the Italian *Mezzogiorno* (the southern half of the country) was a European responsibility. Pressure for a regional policy grew in the late 1960s and early 1970s, firstly because of increasing pessimism about the rate of economic growth, and secondly because of **enlargement**, with the United Kingdom and Ireland joining Italy in insisting upon a regional policy. Although formally established in 1973, it did not acquire a high profile as a European Communities (EC) activity until the enlargements of the 1980s.

The **European Commission** has the responsibility of developing policy relating to the regions. The targets of European Union (EU) regional policy are twofold: underdeveloped rural areas with low levels of agricultural modernization and high levels of unemployment or underemployment; and industrialized regions in rapid decline. The bulk of the spending is directed towards those regions with a gross domestic product (GDP) below 75% of the EU average. To secure the modernization or renewal of these regions, EU policy has three strands. In addition to providing aid for the development of poorer regions, the Commission seeks to co-ordinate the regional policies of member states and secure a co-ordinated approach to regional problems in all relevant EU policy concerns.

The principal element of regional policy is the financial programme, channelled primarily through the **European Regional Development Fund** (ERDF), which was established in 1975 and funded from the EC **budget**. The other **structural funds** of the EU are also required to maintain a strong regional focus in their own areas of concern. A number of further special regional programmes have been launched by the European Commission to deal with the problems of regions that are economically coherent, but divided politically between two or more member states, and several attempts have been made to ensure that the poorer regions benefit from, and participate in, technological developments and programmes. To ensure co-ordination across all these investment activities, the Commission monitors and reviews the socio-economic state of the regions on a regular basis, and undertakes analyses of the regional impact of all EU policies. With respect to the regional policies of the member states, the Commission is concerned to avoid duplication or waste of resources. Maximum limits have been established for the financial inducements that governments may offer to potential industrial investors in the poorer regions: the limits vary according to the nature of the particular regional problem. The resources of the structural funds have been directed more towards integrated programmes that link together various elements of a region's needs rather than isolated and discrete development projects. Financial resources are distributed under the terms of various agreements, or Community Support Frameworks (CSFs), between the Commission and the member states. Regional policy was formally recognized in the **Single European Act**, which identified it as a major element in developing the socio-economic cohesion of the EC. Its centrality was further emphasized by the **Treaty on European Union**, particularly by the establishment of a **Cohesion Fund** and the commitment to **Trans-European Networks**.

The EU has used its recent enlargements to re-examine its regional policy and to analyse where the monies are spent and whether they could be spent more effectively. Regional policy remains a commitment of the EU. In 2007–13 some 36% of the entire EU budget was allocated to this area, representing some €350,000m. over seven years, and regional policy is being targeted to tackle convergence, competitiveness and co-operation. These are known collectively as **cohesion** policy. Priority in terms of regional policy spending has shifted eastwards over the last decade and towards the countries of Central and Eastern Europe. Indeed, the 12 states that joined after 2003 have secured 51% of the overall receipts even though these countries make up only one-quarter of the entire EU population. The money available is divided into three separate funds: the ERDF to enhance infrastructure projects; the **European Social Fund** to help provide vocational training projects and other employment assistance initiatives; and the Cohesion Fund which targets environmental and transport projects.

REGIONAL POLICY COMMITTEE: See **European Regional Development Fund**

REGIONS: See **Cohesion Policy**; **Committee of the Regions**; **European Regional Development Fund**; **Nomenclature of Territorial Units for Statistics**; **Regional Policy**

REGULATIONS are one of three different types of **legal instrument** that the **European Commission** and **Council of the European Union** are empowered to issue. Regulations are the highest, most rigorous form of **legislation**. They are fairly detailed instructions, applicable throughout the European Union, and are directly binding upon all member states. (See also **decisions**; **directives**; **law**; **opinions**; **recommendations**; **resolutions**).

REGULATORY POLICIES are those policies of the European Union based on regulations designed to achieve specific, and generally **internal market**-orientated, policies. Most prominent among them are **competition policy** and **environmental policy** and measures to promote **health and safety**.

OLLI REHN (1962–) is one of the 27 European Commissioners in the **Barroso** II Commission (2010–14), within which he has responsibility for one of the most important aspects of European Union (EU) integration: economic and monetary affairs and the euro. Rehn was born in Mikkeli in eastern Finland, studied Political Science (he has an MA from the University of Helsinki) and successfully completed a doctorate on the theme of competitiveness and small European states. He was elected to the Finnish parliament in 1991 and in 1995 became a **Member of the European Parliament**. He has a strong background in EU affairs and for a time was the head of the Centre for European Studies at the University of Helsinki and advised several Finnish governments on economic policy. He was first appointed a Commissioner towards the end of the **Prodi** Commission in July 2004, before going on to serve in the first Barroso Commission as the Commissioner for Enlargement.

RESEARCH AND DEVELOPMENT IN ADVANCED COMMUNICATIONS TECHNOLOGIES IN EUROPE: See **RACE**

RESEARCH AND TECHNOLOGICAL DEVELOPMENT (RTD) POLICY and the application of new technologies, apart from the sponsoring of research in the nuclear area through the **European Atomic Energy Community** (EAEC or Euratom), received relatively little attention until the 1980s. They remained very much an issue, however, for the various member states. The lack of a European-level policy led to both duplication of effort and, often, missed opportunities. More importantly, high-level research is increasingly complex and costly. Observing that the majority of items such as microcomputers and video recorders used in the European Communities (EC) were imported, the **European Commission** intensified its efforts to encourage technological and collaborative research, to foster and promote research networks and teams at the European level in order to permit the EC to remain economically competitive.

The main objective of European Union (EU) research and development policy is to amalgamate the many projects and individuals conducting research in the member states into collaborative programmes that involve companies, universities and research institutes. The focus is not so much on basic research as on the development of new technologies that can more appropriately be co-ordinated at EU level, and that will provide products for existing and new markets. The **European Strategic Programme for Research in Information Technologies** (Esprit), adopted in 1984, marked a real turning point and was swiftly followed by the first framework for research and technological development. The **Single European Act** made science a Community responsibility. A second framework programme identifying several priority areas for research was adopted in 1987, and in 1988 a monitoring system was introduced in the form of Strategic Analysis, Forecasting and Evaluation in Matters of Research and Technology (MONITOR). The importance of research and development was confirmed by the **Treaty on European Union**, and further general framework programmes that extended the list of priority research areas were adopted in 1990, 1993 and 1998. In just over a decade the budgets for these programmes had grown substantially, from €3,250m. for the first programme to €13,215m. for the fourth (1994–98). Overall, the 1990s heralded the emergence and increasing salience of EU RTD policy and this ensured the inclusion of this theme on the agenda of a series of **European Council** summits. For example, the summit in Lisbon in March 2000 acknowledged that European research and development needed to develop before the EU could legitimately claim to be the most competitive and dynamic knowledge-based economy in the world.

The Sixth Framework Programme (FP6), for 2002–06, allocated €15,000m. in funds to RTD, and was much more ambitious in scope than its predecessors. It sought to integrate research in priority areas (through the creation of centres of excellence) and to create and structure a European Research Area. To maximize its impact, the framework programme focused its attention on a limited number of research areas—technological, economic, social and cultural, among others. These considered the quality of life; a user-friendly information society; competitive and sustainable growth; energy and the environment; improving human resource potential; and the promotion of innovation and growth of small and medium-sized enterprises. Since their launch in 1984 it is clear that the six framework programmes have played an instrumental role in producing multi-disciplinary research and forging cross-national research teams and networks across the EU and beyond. The Seventh Framework Programme (FP7), which covers the period 2007–13, is the biggest and most ambitious to date and RTD was allocated a budget of €53,000m. The five designated RTD themes within FP7 are: co-operation (ensuring greater collaboration between industry and the university sector as a means of providing leadership in key technologies); ideas (supporting and fostering scientific research); people (especially supporting mobility and career development for researchers); capacities (developing the necessary means to create and maintain a thriving knowledge-based economy); and, lastly, nuclear research (where it is hoped to advance Europe's nuclear fission and fusion programmes). This current programme also contains some significant differences from its predecessors. The budget has been increased substantially and is 63% higher than that for FP6. There is now also the first pan-European agency, the European Research Council, which takes responsibility for funding scientific research. In addition, a new risk-sharing finance facility has been created to assist private investors who seek to engage in research projects by providing them with greater access to loans from the **European Investment Bank**. Finally, a single helpdesk has been set up to serve as the first point of contact for anyone who wishes to find out more about the activities and operations of FP7. (See also **Biotech**; **BRITE-EURAM**; **EUREKA**; **European strategic programme for research and development in information technology**; **Research and development in advanced communications technologies in Europe**.)

RESEARCH FRAMEWORK PROGRAMMES are the principal means through which the European Union implements its **Research and Technological Development Policy**. Each programme consists of a variety of specific projects.

RESIDER is the acronym of a 1988 initiative by the **European Coal and Steel Community** to assist in the economic conversion and redevelopment of areas formerly heavily dependent upon the **steel** industry. It was later complemented by the **Rechar** and Renaval programmes. Resider II superseded the programme, and ran from 1994 to 1999.

RESOLUTIONS are statements of principle adopted by the **Council of the European Union** on the recommendation of the **European Commission**. While indicating governments' agreement or willingness to act, they have no basis in the **founding treaties** of the European Communities and are not legally binding upon the member states. (See also **opinions**; **recommendations**).

RESTITUTIONS form an essential part of the **common agricultural policy** (CAP). They are the export **subsidies** or refunds that allow European Union (EU) agricultural produce to be competitive on world markets, where prices are usually lower. EU exporters receive restitutions to make up the difference between what they must pay to CAP producers and the lower prices at which they must sell on the world markets. Restitutions have been one of the most controversial elements of the CAP, because in the past they have consumed up to 30% of the **expenditure** made through the Guarantee Section of the **European Agricultural Guidance and Guarantee Fund**. This figure has been reduced and currently stands at some 15% of expenditure.

REVENUE accrues to the European Union (EU) from a variety of sources. Initially, the European Communities (EC) were financed by contributions from member states based upon the gross national product (GNP) of each member state. The **European Commission** argument that the EC should have their own sources of revenue was one of the contributing factors to the 1965 **empty chair crisis**. In 1970 the member states agreed that a system of **own resources** should progressively replace that of national contributions, with the change to be completed by 1975. Today, the EU has its own resources to finance its **expenditure**. These form the basis of the EU's own tax revenues which automatically accrue to it without the need for any subsequent decision by national authorities. In other words, while the own resources would be collected by the member states, the revenue would belong as of right to the EU.

In terms of revenue, own resources consist of several elements. The first is levies and duties on imports, comprising customs duties on finished products and a levy on agricultural imports to raise their price to the level set by the **common agricultural policy** (CAP). The second, which soon became the most important source of revenue, was a proportion of the **value-added tax** (VAT) imposed by the member states. The VAT contributions that would accrue to the EC were set at a maximum of 1.0% of the final selling price of a common base of goods and services. By the early 1980s this revenue was proving insufficient to meet demands and, after much argument, the VAT maximum level was raised to 1.4% in 1986. This still proved to be insufficient, and annual deficits in the EC **budget** had to be covered by non-refundable contributions from the member states. The reform of the Community's finances took another step in June 1988 when a new category of revenue, which was based on GNP and was derived from the application of a rate to the sum of the GNPs of all the member states, was approved by the **European Council**. This new revenue source provided the necessary funds for the **Delors I** package in 1989. To contain the growth of the resources taken up by the Community, the European Council decision set an overall ceiling rising to

1.2% of total Community GNP in 1992. This figure was applied for both 1993 and 1994. From 1994 a new decision on the own resources raised the ceiling of the GNP contribution to 1.21% and, in stages, to 1.27% of GNP by 1999. During this period the uniform VAT rate was gradually reduced from 1.4% to 1.0%.

In terms of EU budgetary calculations and expectations, gross national income (GNI) has widely replaced GNP in Commission documentation as an indicator of income. This alteration took effect in 2002. In order to maintain unchanged the cash value of the ceiling of EU revenue, referred to as the 'own resources ceiling', it became necessary to recalculate it in percentage terms. It was established at 1.24% of GNI instead of the previous 1.27% of EU GNP. (By means of a definition, GNI at market prices represents total primary income receivable by resident institutional units: compensation of employees, taxes on production and imports less subsidies, property income (receivable less payable), operating surplus and mixed income. GNI equals GDP minus primary income payable by resident units to non-resident units plus primary income receivable by resident units from the rest of the world.)

Total revenue during the 1990s increased from ecu 47,000m. (see **ecu**) in 1990 to €93,000m. by 2002. With the prospect of **enlargement**, the estimated costs of admitting more member states ranged from €4,000m. to €38,000m. for the CAP alone, plus an estimated €30,000m. for the **structural funds**. There was an expectation that total revenue would have to rise significantly. Reluctance on the part of member states to increase contributions meant, however, that greater emphasis was placed on reforming policies. Hence, according to the budgetary perspective for 2000–06 agreed at the Berlin European Council in March 1999, revenue was set to remain at or below current levels. This summit reached a political consensus on the EU budget and own resources and the Council adopted a new own resources decision in September 2000 that became effective in January 2002. This saw further reduction of the VAT resource, which in 2004 stood at 0.5%, and a reduction of the GNI contribution to 1.24%. Agreement was reached on the next financial perspective (2007–13) at a meeting of the European Council in December 2005 and, significantly, it provided for a further diminution of the GNI contribution, to 1.05%.

The **RIGHT OF ESTABLISHMENT**, as laid down in the **Treaty of Rome**, confers on nationals of one member state the right to set up business operations in another member state. It is a key principle underpinning the **internal market** and the free movement of services.

The **RIGHT OF INITIATIVE** within the European Union (EU) has traditionally been the preserve of the **European Commission**, it being the only institution that could formally initiate **legislation**. Since the **Treaty on European Union**, however, this is no longer technically the case. The **European Central Bank** has a right of initiative in certain areas concerning **economic and monetary union**, and member states were to enjoy a right of initiative over measures concerning asylum, immigration and border controls until 2004. The right of initiative under the **common foreign and security policy** and **police and judicial co-operation in criminal matters pillars** of the EU is shared by the European Commission and the member states. The **European Parliament** has no formal right of initiative, but can request that the European Commission submit a proposal under the **Treaty of Rome**.

ROAD TRANSPORT is the area of European Union **transport policy** where the **European Commission** has been most active. Most initiatives have been concerned with conditions of employment and road safety. Rules covering, for example, training and minimum rest periods have existed since the 1970s, and the ensuing decade saw the introduction of a common standard for the weight and dimensions of commercial vehicles, maximum limits for the axle weights of articulated vehicles, and several **directives** concerning road safety. More recently, the focus of road transport measures has been the deregulation of national licensing and quota systems governing inter-state road freight. A transitional road freight system of *cabotage* (the right to ply for hire in another country) was agreed to in 1993 and was to begin by 1998, and a decision was taken to introduce a *vignette*, or freight licence, which would raise funds for distribution among the member states most affected by road transport, to be fully operative by 1998.

ROMANIA concluded a trade and economic **co-operation agreement** with the European Communities in 1990, and a **Europe agreement** was signed in 1993, coming into effect in 1995. Although Romania applied for membership of the European Union (EU) in the same year, the **European Commission** recommended in 1997 that **accession negotiations** be deferred, owing to the need primarily for further economic reform in Romania. Its report stated that 'a considerable amount of work is still needed on environment, transport, employment, social affairs, home affairs, justice, and agriculture, and substantial reform is essential to provide Romania with the structures it needs for effective application and enforcement of the full body of Community law'. Subsequent reports made similar calls for further reform so that Romania could meet all the **accession criteria**. All the same, in 1999 Romania was invited to start **accession negotiations**. Despite the public commitment of a new Government elected in 2000 to speed up integration with the EU, progress in the negotiations was the slowest of all **candidate countries** involved. By the end of 2003, only 22 of the 31 negotiating chapters had been closed. As a consequence, Romania did not join the EU as part of the 2004 **enlargement**. By the end of that year, however, it had concluded the outstanding chapters. An **Accession Treaty** followed in April 2005, which envisaged Romania joining the EU alongside Bulgaria on 1 January 2007. However, concerns persisted about the country's preparedness for membership. With this in mind, it was agreed that accession could be delayed, through a decision by a qualified majority of the member states, if Romania failed to address EU concerns, particularly regarding corruption, state aid (see **subsidies**) policy and border controls. Three monitoring reports followed before it was finally confirmed that accession would take place on 1 January 2007. Romania duly entered the EU on that date. The first five years of membership were characterized, however, by domestic political crises, post-accession monitoring by the Commission of progress in terms of compliance with judicial reform and anti-corruption measures, and further calls for action to be taken in these areas.

The **ROYAUMONT PROCESS** was launched in 1995 as a European Union-sponsored effort to promote stability and good neighbourliness in the **Western Balkans**. It has since been subsumed within the **stabilization and association process**.

RRF: See **European Rapid Reaction Force**

RRM: See **Rapid Reaction Mechanism**

RUSSIA'S relations with the European Union (EU) are based on a **partnership and co-operation agreement** (PCA) concluded in June 1994, which provides for closer political, cultural and economic relations and which entered into force in December 1997. This PCA followed an earlier agreement in 1993 on the establishment of regular political dialogue. This led to annual summits between the President of the **European Commission**, the EU's **High Representative for the Common Foreign and Security Policy** and the Russian President. The PCA was complemented by the adoption in 1999 by the **Council of the European Union** of a **common strategy** on EU-Russia relations. The strategy placed considerable emphasis on assisting with the promotion of political and economic stability within Russia and the development of a market-based economy, as well as addressing common challenges relating to the environment, crime and illegal immigration. To these ends, financial assistance was made available under the **Technical Assistance to the Commonwealth of Independent States** (Tacis) programme, although there were calls for such assistance and the PCA to be suspended over Russia's handling of the Chechnya conflict. The EU generally resisted these. Nevertheless, the relationship—as a Commission report in 2004 highlighted—has not developed as positively as envisaged. There have been major disagreements over whether negotiations should be opened on upgrading the EU-Russia trade relationship to a free trade area, over access in an enlarged EU for Russian citizens to the exclave of **Kaliningrad**, over **ratification** of the Kyoto Protocol, and over the extension of the PCA to the 10 **candidate countries** that joined the EU in 2004. Such differences threaten to undermine progress in achieving the strategic objective of EU–Russia relations as set out in St Petersburg in May 2003: a common economic space, a common space of freedom, security and justice, a common space of co-operation in the field of external security, and a common space of research and education, including culture. A set of Road Maps for the development of these common spaces was adopted in May 2005 at an EU-Russia summit in Moscow, but progress has been limited. Initial plans for a replacement for the PCA also progressed little, leaving the PCA, renewed annually on a rolling basis, to continue to provide an inadequate legal basis for relations. In fact, relations have become more tense, with various disagreements over energy supplies, **Kosovo**, **human rights** and missile defence providing an unfavourable backdrop to the six-monthly EU-Russia summits. The summits have nevertheless continued to be held and have provided regular and institutionalized opportunities for dialogue at head of state and government level. In 2011 Russia was the third largest trading partner of the **Twenty-Seven**. The value of EU exports to Russia in that year was €108,400m., having been only €22,700m. in 2000. Russia's exports to the EU in 2011 were worth €199,500m. (€130,000m. of which was oil and €24,000m. natural gas), leaving the EU with a trade deficit of €91,100m. A mandate for a new agreement covering trade and co-operation to replace the PCA was eventually agreed by EU member states in May 2008. Negotiations, expected to be protracted, began the following month. They were suspended, however, as a result of the Russia–Georgia conflict of 2008. Russia subsequently agreed to withdraw its troops from Georgia by mid-October. In November EU ministers of foreign affairs agreed to resume talks with Russia on the new EU-Russia agreement. By the end of 2010 12 full rounds of negotiations had taken place.

S

SAA: See **Stabilization and Association Agreements**

SAFETY: See **Health and Safety**

SANCTIONS and their collective imposition against specific countries were accepted by the member states as a valuable element of their collaboration on foreign policy under **European political co-operation**. European Union (EU) sanctions have been applied on numerous occasions over the years. However, it is debatable whether any had the desired effect upon the embargoed countries, or whether they were not much more than symbolic gestures of EU solidarity. In addition, not all member states are willing to participate in a collective imposition of sanctions against a named country. The most infamous example in recent years involved the imposition of sanctions against Austria in 2000 following the inclusion of the far-right Freedom Party under Jörg Haider in the Austrian Government. The sanctions were strongly resented in Austria and only helped to fuel anti-EU feeling; they were lifted within six months.

JACQUES SANTER (1937–) was Prime Minister of Luxembourg in 1994 when he was chosen as President of the **European Commission** after a contentious debate among the national governments of member states to find a successor to **Jacques Delors**. The United Kingdom had blocked the selection of Jean-Luc Dehaene, the Belgian Prime Minister at the time, even though his candidature was supported by the governments of the 11 other European Union member states. Santer was the compromise candidate and took up his appointment on 9 January 1995. He pursued a less ambitious programme than his immediate predecessor, a programme that was encapsulated in his phrase 'to do less but to do it better'. He was also responsible for introducing a series of internal reform initiatives within the Commission that encountered varying degrees of resistance. However, Santer's term in office is more associated with the scandal and malpractice that led to the resignation of the entire College of Commissioners. The resignation followed a report that was highly critical of parts of the Commission and in particular of two Commissioners. When the two individuals concerned refused to accept the blame for their alleged malpractices, Santer and the entire body of Commissioners assumed collective responsibility and resigned in March 1999 before the almost certain prospect of being censured by the **European Parliament**. This was the first time that the College had resigned in the history of the Commission. Santer and his team, however, remained in charge of the Commission until a new College was appointed under his proposed successor, **Romano Prodi**, in the latter half of 1999. In 2002 Santer was appointed the Luxembourg government representative to the **European Convention**.

SAPARD was the acronym of the Special Accession Programme for Agriculture and Rural Development, a programme of the European Union (EU) operating in the **candidate countries** of **Central and Eastern Europe** in order to prepare their agricultural sectors for membership of the EU. Following the **enlargement** of May 2004, when 10 candidate countries became members, **Sapard** continued with a budget of €225.2m. for Bulgaria and Romania in 2004. **Sapard** came under the remit of the Directorate-General for Agriculture, and covered 2000 to 2006. From 1 January 2007 **Sapard** was replaced by the **instrument for pre-accession assistance**.

NICOLAS SARKOZY (1955–) was elected as the sixth President of the French Fifth Republic (and also simultaneously became a Co-Prince of **Andorra**) in May 2007. Sarkozy is the son of a Hungarian immigrant whose family had fled first to Germany as the Soviet troops moved westward into Hungary in 1944. Once realizing that they had lost their property in Hungary, the Sarkozy family settled in France. Sarkozy studied law at university, but after a short legal career opted to enter the political arena. His political career began when he was 22 years of age, when he was elected in 1977 as a city councillor in the wealthy Paris suburb of Neuilly-sur-Seine. He became one of the youngest ever mayors of a French town in recent French history, and held this position from 1983 to 2002. He quickly became involved in national politics and served as the Minister for the Budget in 1993. It was at this point that he is deemed to have made a political miscalculation, when he opted to support Edouard Balladur's bid for the French presidency (to succeed **François Mitterrand**) at the expense of **Jacques Chirac**. Initially Sarkozy had been one of Chirac's protégés, but Sarkozy's decision to back Mitterand angered Chirac and severely damaged their personal relationship. Nevertheless, Chirac appointed Sarkozy as Minister of the Interior in 2002. Sarkozy briefly became Minister of Finance in 2004 and returned to the Interior Ministry in 2005. By this stage he had been elected as the leader of the UMP (Union pour un Mouvement Populaire), and was developing a growing reputation as a hard-hitting politician whose ideas were dividing French public opinion. Calls for a radical shake-up of France's economic and social policies, and for a tougher immigration policy to include greater tracking of immigrants, kept him in the media spotlight. He launched a successful bid to be selected as the UMP candidate for the presidency of France in January 2007 (winning 98% of the party representatives' votes). Interestingly, he received lukewarm support from Chirac. Sarkozy went on to top the poll in the first round of the presidential elections before defeating the Socialist Party's Ségolène Royal in the second round (where he polled 53% of the votes). He assumed office on 16 May 2007, and it proved interesting to observe how he projected French interests on both the European and the global stage. He has often been described as an 'Atlanticist', although he opposed the **Iraq war** and was expected to reforge the Franco-German friendship. Areas that brought him into direct conflict with his European partners include his continued opposition to **Turkey**'s bid to join the EU and his position on the reform of the **common agricultural policy**. Sarkozy appeared to have re-established very cordial relations with **Angela Merkel** and also adopted a much more positive attitude towards relations with the USA, with a keenness to court President Barack Obama. In a major change in French foreign policy, Sarkozy also reintegrated French forces into NATO command structures. Sarkozy stood for re-election as French President in April/May 2012, but was narrowly defeated in the second round of the poll by the candidate of the Socialist party, **François Hollande**. Hollande won 51.63% of the vote to Sarkozy's 48.37%.

SCADPLUS is the name of a European Union (EU) system for accessing documentation relating to EU **legislation**, official publications and articles. It is an internet information service, produced by the **European Commission**, which provides approximately 3,000 summaries of European legislation, divided into 32 subject areas corresponding to the activities of the EU. It is accessible through the Europa server on the Summaries of EU legislation website.

The **SCHENGEN AGREEMENT** is the name of a document originally signed by five founder members of the European Communities in the town of Schengen, Luxembourg, on 14 June 1985. The Schengen Convention was signed in June 1990. Under the Agreement, Belgium, France, the Federal Republic of Germany, Luxembourg and the Netherlands agreed in principle to work towards the formation of a border-free **Schengen Area**. The Agreement was implemented with effect from March 1995 by the original five signatories, along with Portugal and Spain. Frontier controls at airports on travellers between the countries were dismantled. However, France continued to impose border controls on countries other than Spain and Germany. Italy, Austria, Greece, Denmark, Finland and Sweden (along with non-member states **Norway** and **Iceland**) later became signatories. Of the then **Fifteen**, Ireland and the United Kingdom remained outside the Schengen Area.

Five years of negotiations were required before the Agreement was finalized in detail, but even then the increased worries of some member states over drugs-trafficking and illegal immigration led to doubts about its value and created further delays in its **ratification** and **implementation**. Although the Schengen Agreement began as an international agreement outside the framework of the

European Union (EU), it was incorporated into the **Treaty of Rome** and the **Treaty on European Union** following provisions contained in the **Treaty of Amsterdam** as part of moves to create a common area without frontiers. The United Kingdom and Ireland negotiated an **opt-out** and were allowed to retain jurisdiction over their borders and rules of asylum and immigration. Both states kept open the possibility of involvement, and in May 2000 the United Kingdom Government secured agreement in the **Council of the European Union** that enabled the country to participate in substantial parts of the Schengen *acquis,* particularly in relation to the creation and operation of the **Schengen Information System** (SIS); Ireland did likewise. Currently both the United Kingdom and Ireland are partial members of Schengen. It should also be noted that two non-EU states, Iceland and Norway, are officially classified as states associated with Schengen (and where Schengen rules apply) because of their involvement with the 1957 Nordic Passport Union, and also because of the lengthy land border between Norway and Sweden. Both non-EU states, however, remain uninvolved in decision-making within Schengen. In 2005 seven member states signed the **Prüm Convention**, known as Schengen III, on data exchange for the purpose of combating terrorism, cross-border crime and illegal migration. On 21 December 2007 the Schengen Area was enlarged to include nine of the member states that joined the EU in 2004: the Czech Republic, Estonia, Hungary, Latvia, Lithuania, Malta, Poland, Slovenia and Slovakia. Initially internal land and sea border controls were abolished, and the abolition of air border controls followed in March 2008. **Switzerland** gained the status of a country associated with the Schengen activities (like Iceland and Norway) in December 2008 following the approval in a referendum of Bern's bilateral agreement with the EU to abolish passport controls. This episode clearly illustrates the pull of EU governance on a non-member state, while the act of being associated with the Schengen Area offered the benefit to the Swiss authorities of access to a vast database on criminals, traffickers and stolen goods. Liechtenstein became the 26th member of the Schengen Area (as an associated state) in December 2011.

The **SCHENGEN AREA** is the area in Europe in which the free movement of people has been realized on the basis of the **Schengen Agreement**. Following the EU's most recent enlargement in December 2007, it covers all EU members, with the exception of Bulgaria, Cyprus, Ireland, Romania and the United Kingdom, and also includes four non-members, **Iceland**, Liechtenstein, **Norway** and **Switzerland**, which have the status of countries associated with Schengen (and subject to Schengen rules and regulations). The Schengen Area also, de facto, includes Monaco, San Marino and the Vatican. Although not members of the Schengen Area, the United Kingdom and Ireland participate in substantial parts of the Schengen *acquis*. Further expansion of the Schengen Area to include Bulgaria and Romania (both of which joined the EU in 2007) was anticipated in 2011, but this move was blocked in September of that year when Finland and the Netherlands vetoed their entry into the area amid ongoing concerns about corruption, organized crime and illegal immigration. It is also intended to extend the area to Cyprus, subject to progress in resolving the country's division.

The **SCHENGEN INFORMATION SYSTEM** (SIS), once also known as the European Information System (EIS), is a computer network that links the computer systems of immigration services and the police in signatory countries of the **Schengen Agreement**. A new network, SIS II, was expected to become functional in 2009, but is now scheduled to be in operation from 2013.

HELMUT SCHMIDT (1918–) was Chancellor of the Federal Republic of Germany (West Germany) from 1974 to 1982. During this period he exerted great influence on the operation of the European Communities (EC). Believing that many of the objectives and timetables set at previous **summit meetings** had been unrealistic, he was willing to support and advance initiatives for further integration only if they appeared to be both possible and practical. He was the principal supporter in the **European Council** of **Roy Jenkins**' proposal for a **European Monetary System**. At the same time, he firmly defended West German interests in the EC, and was particularly concerned about the costing of proposed programmes and initiatives. He collaborated closely with President **Valéry Giscard d'Estaing** of France and, acting in conjunction, the two men were often able decisively to influence the direction and **decisions** taken by the European Council. However, Schmidt's more pragmatic approach and scepticism perhaps caused the EC to operate in a particular way, accumulating issues, such as the question of the United Kingdom budgetary contributions, which had to be dealt with in the 1980s.

GERHARD SCHRÖDER (1944–) became Chancellor of Germany in September 1998, when he headed a coalition Government of Social Democrats and Greens that was returned to power in October 2002. Schröder's political career unfolded rather quickly within the left–of–centre Social Democratic Party (SPD) and he rose swiftly through the ranks. He was elected a member of parliament in 1980 and became the Minister-President of Lower Saxony in 1990. Before becoming a politician he had pursued a successful career as a lawyer. His reputation as German Chancellor was decidedly mixed, and he was often portrayed as changing his mind or his policies to reflect prevailing opinion. On the foreign policy front he spoke out strongly against the **Iraq War** during 2003, and refused to provide any military assistance to the US-led campaign. This was a very popular move at home but helped to foster tensions with the **USA**. He sought to cultivate closer relations with President **Jacques Chirac** of France and **Russia**'s President Vladimir Putin, and sometimes found himself at odds with the United Kingdom Prime Minister **Tony Blair**. On the domestic front he found it particularly difficult to push through a much-needed series of economic and social reforms, and besides being attacked from all sides for trying to do so, he damaged both his reputation and the fortunes of his party. Schröder requested a dissolution of parliament and hoped that new elections in late 2005 would bolster his authority. The elections in September 2005 brought a narrow victory for the Christian Democratic Union/Christian Social Union (CDU/CSU), which beat the SPD by only one percentage point. The arithmetic arising from the results was extremely complicated and left the CDU with no other real possibility but to push for a 'grand coalition' with the SPD. Negotiations were prolonged and difficult, but both parties eventually settled to participate in Germany's only second ever post-war grand coalition, under the leadership of **Angela Merkel**. Schröder did not participate in this Government.

MARTIN SCHULZ (1955–) was elected as President of the **European Parliament** (EP) in January 2012. Schulz was born in North Rhine-Westphalia, Germany, where, following high school, he trained to be a bookseller before entering politics. He has been a member of the German Social Democratic Party since the age of 19 years and became the youngest mayor in North Rhine-Westphalia's history when he was appointed to the mayoralty in 1987 (at the age of 31). He was first elected to the EP in June 1994 and in 2004 was appointed as Chairman of the **Group of the Party of European Socialists** (renamed the **Group of the Progressive Alliance of Socialists and Democrats in the European Parliament**—S&D—in 2009). On assuming the presidency of the EP, Schulz was replaced as Chairman of the S&D by Hannes Swoboda.

ROBERT SCHUMAN (1886–1963) was foreign minister of France from 1948 to 1953. He imposed continuity in French policy towards Europe, which in part reflected his own cosmopolitan background. Born in Luxembourg, he spent his formative years in Lorraine, at the time part of the German Empire. He was a firm believer in European integration and an ultimate political federation, and was convinced that this could be secured only through a lasting reconciliation between France and Germany. He was persuaded of the practicality of **sectoral integration** by **Jean Monnet** and, with his declaration of the **Schuman Plan** in May 1950, began a new era of European developments. Schuman's pioneering role was acknowledged by the first meeting of the **European Economic Community**, when its Parliamentary Assembly (that is, the **European Parliament**) elected him as its first President, rejecting the nominee of the **Six** foreign ministers. In 1986, the centenary of Schuman's birth, the European Communities (EC) declared 9 May, the day in 1950 on which he made the speech that led to the creation of the EC, to be **Europe Day**.

The **SCHUMAN PLAN**, named after **Robert Schuman**, was the original proposal for a consolidation of **coal** and **steel** resources that led to the **European Coal and Steel Community** (ECSC). In addition to the economic benefits, the Plan also argued that it would 'immediately provide for the establishment of common bases for economic development as a first step in the federation of Europe'; it went on to state explicitly that 'Europe must be organized on a federal basis'. The more specific political objective was to secure a rapprochement between France and the Federal Republic of Germany (FRG—West Germany). The Plan opened with the declaration that 'the French Government proposes that Franco-German coal and steel production should be placed under a common High Authority within the framework of an organization open to the participation of the other countries of Europe'. The Schuman Plan was first revealed at a press conference on 9 May 1950. It was immediately supported by West Germany and the **USA**. Only six countries entered the negotiations resulting in the **Treaty of Paris** of 18 April 1951, which formally established the ECSC.

The **SCIENTIFIC AND TECHNICAL RESEARCH COMMITTEE** (CREST) is an **advisory committee** to the **European Commission** composed of scientific experts. It is usually consulted on its opinions about proposals and funding for scientific research programmes. It meets on a regular basis, and also reviews progress reports on ongoing research programmes.

SCOTLAND EUROPA is an innovative alliance of public, private and civil society bodies networking Scotland in Europe. Its aim is to promote Scotland's interests to the key institutions of the European Union (EU) and to the regions of the EU and beyond. It is located in Scotland House alongside the EU Office of the **Scottish Executive**.

The **SCOTTISH EXECUTIVE** established a European Union (EU) Office in 1999 to support and promote both itself and its EU-related work and to help increase Scotland's influence in the EU. The office is co-located in Scotland House, in **Brussels**, with **Scotland Europa** and provides a focal point for Scottish interests in the EU. The Office works closely with the United Kingdom's Permanent Representation, UKREP, which remains responsible for representing the views of the United Kingdom as a whole to the EU institutions, and alongside the Office of the Northern Ireland Executive in Brussels (**ONIEB**) and the Welsh National Assembly Office.

SCREENING is an integral stage of the process leading to accession. In order to ensure as smooth a transition as possible into the European Union (EU) for the countries of **Central and Eastern Europe**, a 1995 **White Paper** drew up an initial list of EU **legislation** that had to be incorporated into the domestic legislation of all the applicant states before membership could be deemed possible. The negotiations on EU membership began formally in 1998 and have involved a careful examination of the compatibility of all existing legislation with current EU rules and the necessity of additional legislative action. This process conforms to a screening mechanism. It is conducted primarily by the **European Commission** and each of the **applicant countries**, which together analyse, sector by sector, the degrees of compatibility. The process has allowed outstanding measures to be identified and a timetable for their **implementation** to be drawn up.

SCRUTINY is the process whereby **national parliaments** monitor and try to influence **legislation** emanating from the European Union (EU). In the United Kingdom, for example, the procedure is centred on the 'scrutiny reserve', which prohibits a national minister from adopting any legislative proposal unless it has been examined by the House of Commons Select Committee on European Legislation. Scrutiny of the EU policy process and of the annual **budget** is performed by the **European Parliament** (EP). Members of the EP can put forward questions (orally and in writing) to both the **Council of the European Union** and the **European Commission**; they can, moreover, question individual Commissioners and national ministers in parliamentary committees. The EP also has the authority to draw up reports in particular policy areas and can pass **resolutions** on current themes. It can also hold public hearings and establish committees of inquiry. Ultimately, the EP can dismiss the Commission and can bring cases before the European courts.

SEA: See **Single European Act**

SEC DOCUMENTS are those produced by the **Secretariat-General** of the **European Commission**. Less formal than **COM Documents**, they consist of internal reports, discussion papers and draft **resolutions**.

SECRETARIAT-GENERAL is the name of the senior and central bureaucratic service of the **European Commission**. It sits alongside other services such as **Eurostat**, the **European Anti-fraud Office** and the **European Community Humanitarian Office**. It is answerable to the President of the Commission, and is the major administrative link between the President and the various **Directorates-General** and other agencies. It comprises some 450 officials and is headed by the Secretary-General of the Commission, the most senior official within the Commission, whose post should not be confused with that of the **Secretary-General of the Council of the European Union**. The Secretariat-General is a highly important part of the Commission's machinery and ensures that all parts of the Commission co-ordinate their activities, act in accordance with established procedures and liaise properly with the other **institutions**.

The **SECRETARY-GENERAL OF THE COUNCIL OF THE EUROPEAN UNION** heads the administration of the Council. The structure of the General Secretariat was changed in the late 1990s to make the Secretary-General also the European Union's **High Representative for the Common Foreign and Security Policy**. The Secretary-General is appointed by the Council (although in reality he or she is selected by the **European Council** operating under **unanimity**). The appointment of **Javier Solana** in 1999 marked a significant departure from previous practice, since, for the first time, a politician was selected instead of the more customary senior diplomat. Solana, who was the fifth Secretary-General, stepped down in November 2009 and was replaced by Pierre de Boissieu, his deputy, as Secretary-General, while Baroness **Catherine Ashton** took over as the new **High Representative for Foreign Affairs and Security Policy** (in accordance with the Treaty of Lisbon, the two posts were now separate). In June 2011 **Uwe Corsepius** replaced Boissieu as the new Secretary-General of the Council of the European Union. The Council's General Secretariat, which has about 3,200 employees, is divided into seven **Directorates-General** (the largest of which is responsible for administration), the Legal Service and five departments under the Secretary-General.

A **SECTION** is a subdivision of a **Chapter** within a European Union treaty.

SECTORAL INTEGRATION was the major alternative to the federalist approach to integration. **Jean Monnet** was the main proponent of the more gradualist sectoral approach. The strategy was to integrate national economies in stages, by taking one economic sector at a time. The process would be accelerated by '**spillover**', and would eventually create such an interlocking of national economies that a common political structure for their direction would be required and inevitable. Ultimately, the **European Coal and Steel Community** was the only successful example of sectoral integration, following which the **Six** directed their efforts instead to the development of a **common market**.

SEDOC: See **EURES**

MAROŠ ŠEFČOVIČ (1966–) is one of the Vice-Presidents of the second **Barroso** Commission of the European Union (EU) (2010–14). He is the Commissioner for Inter-institutional Relations and Administration and, in

2004–09, prior to assuming his current position, had been Slovakia's Permanent Representative to the EU.

SEM 2000 stands for Sound and Efficient Management and was one of the first initiatives launched by the **European Commission** as headed by **Jacques Santer** in 1995. The main aim of this project was to ensure that the Commission complied with the basic principles of sound financial management, and that issues such as financial controls, internal audits, public procurement and evaluation of resource management were assessed.

ALGIRDAS ŠEMETA (1962–) is one of the 27 European Commissioners in the **Barroso** II Commission (2010–14), within which he has responsibility for taxation and the customs union, audit and anti-fraud. He is a Lithuanian national and studied Economics at the University of Tallinn. He has twice served as the Minister of Finance of Lithuania and is affiliated to the **European People's Party** in the **European Parliament**.

SEPA: See **Single Euro Payments Area**

SERBIA emerged as an independent country from the former state of Serbia and Montenegro (which itself had previously been named the Federal Republic of **Yugoslavia**) in May 2006. For much of the 1990s, the former Federal Republic of Yugoslavia (FRY) underwent a process of disintegration, with Serbia, under Slobodan Milošević, being held responsible internationally for much of the ensuing conflict. After the departure from office of Milošević in October 2000, **sanctions** imposed by the European Union (EU) in the 1990s were lifted and the FRY was included in the EU's **stabilization and association process** and financial assistance programme for the **Western Balkans** (**CARDS**). Despite fears of the disintegration of the FRY, agreement was reached in 2002 on maintaining the republic and renaming the country Serbia and Montenegro. However, in April 2002 the coalition Government in Montenegro collapsed, as a result of opposition to the agreement, although this was subsequently ratified by the Federal Assembly in May. Within Serbia, the assassination of the Prime Minister, Zoran Djindjić, in March 2003 reinforced concerns about organized crime and political stability in the country. Such concerns, along with continued unrest in **Kosovo**, which remains under international civilian and military administration, initially prevented the EU from opening negotiations on a **stabilization and association agreement** (SAA) with Serbia and Montenegro. However, progress with political and economic reforms in 2004 led the **European Commission** to propose such negotiations in April 2005 and these were later opened in October. Seven months later the negotiations were suspended owing to Serbia's lack of co-operation with the International Criminal Tribunal for the Former Yugoslavia (ICTY), notably regarding the arrest and handing over of alleged war criminals such as Ratko Mladić. Also overshadowing relations was the prospect of Montenegrin independence—on which a referendum had been scheduled for April 2006—and the future of Kosovo. In the referendum a majority (55%) of Montenegrin voters opted for independence, and the union with Serbia was soon dissolved. Kosovo was also moving towards independence, a development Serbia utterly opposed.

Disagreement on the future of Kosovo cast a shadow over Serbia's relations with the EU. However, improved co-operation with the ICTY led the EU to resume SAA negotiations in June 2007, and these were concluded at the technical level three months later. A process of 'enhanced permanent dialogue' was now under way too and focused on monitoring and encouraging the reforms set out in the **European partnership**, first adopted in 2004 and subsequently revised. Visa facilitation and readmission agreements were signed in September 2007, and in its progress report on Serbia in November 2007 the Commission, while critical of reforms in many areas, did record encouraging progress in others. It also noted that Serbia was in receipt of financial assistance under the new **instrument for pre-accession assistance**. (Serbia was projected to receive €624m. during 2011–13.) Formal conclusion of the negotiations and signature of the SAA were still outstanding, however, and in early 2008 relations entered a new period of strain following Kosovo's declaration of independence and pledges of support for the new state from many—but not all—of the EU's member states. However, in a subsequent move designed to bolster the electoral prospects of pro-EU forces around the then Serbian President, Boris Tadić, member states, demanding that Serbia improve its co-operation with the ICTY (notably by tracking down Mladić), agreed to lift their veto on finally concluding the SAA, and the agreement was signed on 29 April 2008. The move was welcomed by supporters of integration in Serbia but widely criticized by nationalists and others as a cynical move to interfere with the election by manipulating public opinion. Victory for Tadić and his supporters led to a rapprochement with **Brussels** and, in December 2009, an application for EU membership. The Commission's **opinion** was published in October 2011 and, due in part to the arrest by the Serbian authorities of Mladić and his transfer to the ICTY in May of that year, was broadly positive. Conferral of **candidate status** followed in March 2012. When the EU will invite Serbia to open **accession negotiations** remains to be seen.

The **SET-ASIDE SCHEME** was adopted by the **Council of Ministers of the European Communities** in **Brussels** in 1988 as a means of improving the effectiveness of the **common agricultural policy** (CAP) through the elimination of surpluses of produce. Under the scheme, farmers receive financial compensation, on the condition that they undertake not to produce anything, leaving land uncultivated or destroying crops and livestock, on at least 15% (reduced to 10% in 1996) of their arable land for five years. The idea of set-aside became a fundamental part of the **Ray MacSharry** CAP reform package endorsed by the Council in 1992. In November 2008 the European Commission agreed to abolish the set-aside scheme completely as part of the CAP Health Check.

SEVESO DIRECTIVES are the name given to European Communities **directives** first issued in 1982 on requirements relating to the accident risks of several industrial activities, and to the supervision and control of the transportation between member states of hazardous waste. They are named after Seveso, the Italian site of a major chemicals accident in 1976.

SHIPPING has only recently been regulated by the European Union (EU), despite the fact that almost 90% of EU external trade is carried by sea, short sea shipping represents around 40% of intra-EU exchanges in terms of ton-kilometres, and land links between member states on the geographical fringes of the EU are relatively indirect. A common shipping policy was adopted in December 1986, consisting of four **regulations**. The first regulation made sea transport subject to EU **competition policy**, from which it had been exempted in 1962; certain shipping consortia, however, remained exempt from competition rules. The second endorsed the right of EU-based ships to ply freely for trade within and beyond the EU. This was reinforced by a 1992 regulation on the liberalization of coastal shipping within the EU. The other two regulations dealt with **discrimination**. One permitted the **European Commission** to take anti-**dumping** measures against third parties: where the case was proved by a complaints investigation procedure, duties could be imposed upon vessels from the country concerned. The other regulation permitted the EU to retaliate against countries that reserved a proportion of the trade between themselves and the EU for their own vessels: the Commission was authorized to impose loading or discharging permits and quotas, and/or to levy duties. To maintain an adequate shipping fleet, the EU has, since the 1970s, had guidelines for state **subsidies** to shipping, in order to help it combat world competition, and proposals have been made for an EU system of vessel registration. In January 2009 the Commission presented its new Maritime Transport Strategy 2018, the two main goals of which were: the ability of the maritime transport sector to provide cost-efficient maritime transport services adapted to the needs of sustainable economic growth in the EU and other world economies; and the long-term competitiveness of the EU shipping sector, enhancing its capacity to generate value and employment in the EU, both directly and indirectly, through the whole spectrum of maritime industries.

SIMMENTHAL SPA V COMMISSION is the title of an important case heard by the **Court of Justice**, which ruled that national governments must apply European Union **law** in full, and that, where this is not done, individuals have the right to appeal to the Court.

SIMPLIFICATION relates to efforts to simplify **legislation** in order to make it much easier to comprehend, and to ensure greater effectiveness. The notion dates back to the 1985 **White Paper** on the Completion of the **Internal Market** and was explicitly dealt with at the December 1992 meeting of the **European Council** in Edinburgh. Since the 1980s the pursuit of a genuine single market based on the free movement of people, capital, services and goods has produced a substantial amount of European Union (EU) **legislation**. Simplifying this is a necessity. A pilot programme (SLIM—Simpler Legislation for the Internal Market) was launched in 1996 (running until 2002) and this could be extended to other areas. Simplification is also used to describe the process undertaken via the **Treaty of Amsterdam** to repeal or amend obsolete **articles** in the **founding treaties**. The **Treaty establishing a Constitution for Europe** should also be read as an attempt to simplify EU machinery and EU decision-making. The same is true for the **Treaty of Lisbon**, which repealed or amended obsolete treaty provisions and saw the formal abandonment of the EU's **pillars** and the **European Community**.

The **SIMPLIFIED REVISION PROCEDURE** was introduced by the **Treaty of Lisbon** and allows the **European Council** to amend certain provisions of the **Treaty on the Functioning of the European Union** governing internal policies and how they are made, without recourse to a convention or an **intergovernmental conference**. Such amendments cannot involve any increase in the competences of the European Union and have to be ratified by **national parliaments** or by referendum.

SINGLE CURRENCY: See **Economic and Monetary Union**; **Euro**

The **SINGLE EUROPEAN ACT** (SEA) was an important amendment of the **founding treaties** of the European Communities (EC) that came into force in July 1987 after **ratification** by the national legislatures of the member states. The Act consisted of 34 Articles, divided into four sections. The first section (Articles 1–3) constituted the objective of the SEA—'making concrete progress towards European unity'—as well as legitimizing the status of the **European Council**. The second section (Articles 4–29) formed the greatest part of the SEA, dealing with the amendments to the founding treaties. The third section (Article 30) provided for a permanent secretariat for **European political co-operation** (EPC), while the final section (Articles 31–34) outlined the procedures necessary for the ratification and **implementation** of the Act.

The SEA had three main themes: the **internal market**, EPC and institutional reform. Its implications for the internal market were enormous. It obliged the EC to deal definitively with the whole range of national systems of **taxation** and law, national standards and **regulations** in a number of policy areas, and national social security and welfare systems. It specifically strengthened the role of the EC in several policy areas. It made the **European Commission** an equal partner in EPC, with the views of the **European Parliament** (EP) also needing to be taken into consideration; and it committed the EC to extending EPC to include collaboration on security policy issues. While its institutional reforms were limited, it provided for a more widespread use of **qualified majority voting** in the Council (see **Council of the European Union**), and required the latter to collaborate more with the EP in the legislative process according to a new **co-operation procedure**, whereby a rejection by the EP of a Council decision could be overturned only by unanimous agreement in the Council. A final amendment created a **Court of First Instance** to reduce the workload of the **Court of Justice**.

The **SINGLE EURO PAYMENTS AREA** (SEPA) is a private-sector initiative, launched in early 2008 and involving about 4,000 banks in Europe representing approximately 80% of transactions, which facilitates cross-border payments made electronically within the **eurozone**. At 2012 SEPA comprised 32 countries—all 27 European Union member states, the four EFTA member states and Monaco.

SINGLE MARKET: See **Internal Market**

SIS: See **Schengen Information System**

The **SIX**, or the Europe of the Six, is a popular way of referring to the membership of the European Communities from the **Schuman Plan** of 1950 until the first **enlargement** of 1973. It refers to the six founder members: Belgium, France, the Federal Republic of Germany, Italy, Luxembourg and the Netherlands.

SLOVAKIA applied for membership of the European Communities (EC) in early 1993, and subsequently signed a **Europe agreement** in October of that year. This agreement superseded the earlier Europe agreement signed between the EC and the former Czech and Slovak Federative Republic (Czechoslovakia) in 1991. The first Agreement had become obsolete in January 1993 with the creation of two separate states, the Czech Republic and Slovakia. Relations between Slovakia and the European Union (EU) can be divided into two periods. The early years of the new Slovak state under the authoritarian Prime Minister, Vladimír Mečiar, were characterized by a degree of friction between that country and the EU. The second period, since the election of a new Prime

Minister, Mikuláš Dzurinda, in October 1998, has constituted nothing less than a complete transformation in relations and contacts with the EU.

Despite the Europe agreement in force since the beginning of 1995, and Slovakia's application for EU membership, doubts about the country's potential membership persisted under the Mečiar regime because of reservations about the country's commitment to democracy. The **European Commission**'s 1997 report on Slovakia's membership application stated that the country's institutions were unstable and that there were shortcomings in the functioning of its democracy, a situation which was 'all the more regrettable as the country would be capable of meeting the economic criteria [for membership] in the medium term'. Considerable improvements were made under Dzurinda's leadership, particularly with regard to **minority rights**, but Slovakia continued to struggle on the economic front. Unemployment in the early 2000s stood at some 20%. However, progress was made in the **accession negotiations**, which were opened in 2000. By the end of 2002 Slovakia had closed all negotiating chapters. A national referendum in May 2003 then endorsed membership (92.46% of those who participated voted in favour), and paved the way for Slovakia to join the EU on 1 May 2004. The Slovakian parliament ratified the **Treaty establishing a Constitution for Europe** by 116 votes to 27, with four abstentions, in May 2005. Slovakia adopted the **euro** and thereby joined the **eurozone** in January 2009. It joined the EU's **Schengen Area** in December 2007. However, public support and interest in the EU seems low: Slovakia recorded the lowest turn-out figures for the European Parliament elections among the **Twenty-Seven** (EU27) in both 2004 and 2009 (both were less than 20%). In October 2011 the Slovakian legislature failed to support plans by the EU to enhance the powers of the **European Financial Stability Fund**; the proposals required ratification by each EU member state prior to their implementation. The Government of Iveta Radičová subsequently collapsed, owing to opposition to the plans of coalition partner the Freedom and Solidarity Party.

SLOVENIA was the first of the former Yugoslav republics to declare independence, in 1991. The country was recognized by the European Communities in 1992. Slovenia is a small nation with some 2.06m. citizens and was clearly the most economically advanced of the former Yugoslav republics. Moreover, Slovenia found the transition from a socialist to a market economy easier than most. Nevertheless, relations with the European Union (EU)—primarily the conclusion of a **Europe agreement**—were initially held up by difficulties with Italy, which demanded compensation for Italian nationals who in 1947 had left territory now held by Slovenia. Once a compromise solution had been found and a Europe agreement concluded in 1995, Slovenia applied for EU membership in June 1996. The country subsequently received praise from the **European Commission** for its economic endeavours and political stability and, with strong political support from both Austria and Germany, opened accession negotiations with the EU in early 1998. These were successfully concluded just under five years later and, following the successful outcome of a referendum on EU membership held in March 2003, when 89.61% of the electorate voted in favour of accession, Slovenia joined the EU on 1 May 2004. Slovenia's parliament voted overwhelmingly (79 votes for and four against) to ratify the **Treaty establishing a Constitution for Europe** in February 2005. Slovenia joined the **eurozone** and adopted the **euro** on 1 January 2007. In December of the same year it joined the EU's **Schengen Area** and the following month it became the first of the new members from the 2004 **enlargement** to hold the **Council presidency**.

The **'SLUICE-GATE' PRICE** is similar in its effect to the **threshold price**. It applies to pig meat and eggs and other poultry products. Imports of these products into the European Union are liable to a levy to raise them to the level of the sluice-gate price.

SMALL AND MEDIUM-SIZED ENTERPRISE TASK FORCE: See SME Task Force

SMALL AND MEDIUM-SIZED ENTERPRISES (SMEs) and their development in the **internal market** have been the subject of a number of European Union (EU) policies. In 1996 the **European Commission** agreed new guidelines for state assistance for SMEs: aid for the acquisition of licences, patents, etc., would be allowed at the same level as aid for tangible investment. SMEs have been financially assisted to invest in new technologies. **Euro Info Centres** were established primarily as a source of information for SMEs. The Commission has prioritized the simplification of the legislative, regulatory and administrative constraints on SMEs, and in 1997 a **European Council** meeting approved an action plan for the **European Investment Bank** to generate additional investments for SMEs. In November 1998 CREA (the French acronym for Risk Capital for Business Start-ups) was launched to offer investment to small businesses. Since 2009 the EU has also developed the **JEREMIE** (Joint European Resources for Micro to Medium Enterprises) initiative together with the European Investment Fund to support SMEs. JEREMIE promotes the use of financial engineering instruments to improve access to finance for SMEs via structural funds.

The **SME TASK FORCE** was an agency directed by the **European Commission**. It offered help and advice to **small and medium-sized enterprises** (SMEs) on **competition policy** and the **internal market**. It was later subsumed into the former **Directorate-General** XXIII. (See also **European Business and Innovation Centre Network**; **European Private Equity and Venture Capital Association**.)

SMES: See **Small and Medium-sized Enterprises**

SNAKE was the name given to an agreement in 1972 by several European states to establish a European system of exchange rates within the broader Smithsonian Agreement, with only one-half of the permissible fluctuation range of the latter. It proved to be ineffectual as an instrument of exchange-rate control. Many countries were forced to leave it because of their inability to stay within the prescribed parameters. The Snake was effectively abandoned by the mid-1970s, and its failure disappointed the European Communities' hope that it would enable them to achieve **economic and monetary union**.

SOCIAL ACTION PROGRAMME is the name of a document adopted by the European Communities (EC) in 1974 as a response to the severe economic problems of the time. It was an attempt to counter criticisms that the EC had not fulfilled their obligation to develop a **social policy**. Under the programme, the member states undertook to implement some 40 priority measures over the following three years in pursuance of the main principles of social policy: full and better employment, improved living and working conditions, and closer collaboration between employers and workers. Further social action programmes have included the 1995–97 medium-term programme and the 1998–2000 Social Action Programme, whose priority areas were promoting jobs, skills and mobility, the changing world of work, and developing an inclusive society. During 2006–10 the European Union (EU) developed a 'Social Policy Agenda', which sought to strengthen economic performance, create more and better jobs, and make the most of the opportunities offered by the knowledge-based society. It was based on a desire to ensure that economic, employment and social policies worked together in a mutually reinforcing way. The principal goals in the area of social policy of the Europe 2020 Strategy, which was launched in 2010, are: helping students and trainees to gain experience in other countries; improving the quality and attractiveness of education and training in Europe; giving fresh momentum to labour market reforms to help people gain the right skills for future jobs, to create new jobs and to overhaul EU employment legislation; and lifting at least 20m. people out of poverty and exclusion by 2020.

SOCIAL CHAPTER: See **Charter of Fundamental Social Rights of Workers**

SOCIAL CHARTER: See **Charter of Fundamental Social Rights of Workers**

The **SOCIAL DIMENSION** is a concept that gained increasing significance from the second half of the 1980s onward. It was promoted by left-of-centre politicians, most notably by the then French President, **François Mitterrand**, the Spanish Prime Minister, **Felipe González Márquez**, and the President of the **European Commission**, **Jacques Delors**. They argued for the development of a social dimension at the European Communities level to protect and advance matters relating to workers. This new policy commitment was regarded as an essential complement to the **internal market** programme, which contained benefits for the business community. Social issues emerged as one of a series of policies that culminated in the 1989 **Charter of Fundamental Social Rights of Workers** and the **Social Protocol**, part of the **Treaty on European Union**.

SOCIAL DUMPING is a phrase that has been used to describe the process whereby, taking advantage of the greater freedoms available under the **internal market**, manufacturers relocate their production sites within the European Union from high- to low-wage areas.

SOCIAL FUND COMMITTEE: See **European Social Fund**

SOCIAL PARTNERS refers to the organizations that the **European Commission** is obliged to consult when it wishes to pursue policy proposals in the field of **social policy**. This social dialogue takes place between the Commission and the following three main organizations that represent the social partners: the **European Trade Union Confederation** (ETUC), BUSINESSEUROPE (formerly called the **Union of Industrial and Employers' Confederations of Europe**, or UNICE) and the European Centre of Enterprises with Public Participation and of Enterprises of General Economic Interest (CEEP). The Commission encourages and facilitates discussion with each of these groups on issues relating primarily to the labour market. In addition, the Commission is also obliged, under the 1957 **Treaty of Rome**, to consult with the **European Economic and Social Committee** on a range of policy issues.

SOCIAL POLICY in the context of the European Union (EU) has a much narrower ambit than is usually implied by the phrase in the domestic context: it refers specifically to **employment** matters, education and vocational training, **health and safety** issues, equality matters and the part of social policy that relates to employer–worker relations. During the first decade of the European Communities' (EC) existence, social policy had a very low profile and priority. The **Treaty of Rome** contained very few references to a specific social policy. The provisions that did exist related to the free movement of workers and to the freedom of establishment and creation of a then-small **European Social Fund**. Social policy became much more important with the arrival of mass unemployment in the 1970s, and the EC adopted a **Social Action Programme** in 1974. From 1983, social policy had two priority areas: the training and employment of people aged 25 years or under, and the provision of training and employment in the most economically disadvantaged regions of the EC. Social policy is administered by the **European Commission** through the **European Social Fund** (ESF).

The United Kingdom under Prime Ministers **Margaret Thatcher** (1979–90) and **John Major** (1990–97) strongly resisted the development of EC **competences** in the field of social policy and was highly critical of the 1989 **Charter of Fundamental Social Rights of Workers**; the country, moreover, gained an **opt-out** at Maastricht from the new social policy **protocol** that was annexed to the **Treaty on European Union** (TEU). The UK opt-out caused a great deal of confusion and effectively meant the existence of two distinct legal bases for social policy measures: the TEU itself and a separate agreement (the **Social Protocol**) from which the United Kingdom was exempt. This situation only came to an end when the Government led by **Tony Blair** signed the Charter soon after coming to power in May 1997.

The **Treaty of Amsterdam** marked an important step forward in this particular policy area, as it promoted a series of social policy priorities at EU level, particularly in the area of employment, which has now been designated as an EU objective (under Article 2) and a matter of common concern. The aim is to reach a 'high level of employment' throughout the EU and to this end the EU is charged with developing a 'co-ordinated strategy' for employment that should complement the activities of the member states. A new title on employment (125–130) spells out EU priorities in this area and provides for the creation of an **Employment Committee**. Furthermore, a new provision refers to the adoption of provisions on non-discrimination and enables the Council, acting unanimously, to take appropriate action to tackle any **discrimination** that is based on sex, race, ethnic origin, religion or belief, disability, age or sexual orientation. Now, as a result of changes introduced by the **Treaty of Amsterdam**, all social policy measures can be adopted on the basis of a new Chapter within the treaty. This has effectively created a new legal base for **equal opportunities** and equal treatment of men and women at work. Indeed, the Treaty of Rome explicitly states that the EU must strive to eliminate all inequalities and to promote equality. As regards **decision-making**, the Council adopts **directives** by **qualified majority vote** and in conjunction with the **European Parliament** under the **co-decision procedure** in the following areas: workers' health and safety, working conditions, integration of persons excluded from the labour market, information and consultation of workers, and equality between men and women. **Unanimity** prevails, however, in relation to the following areas: social security and social protection of workers, conditions of employment for third-country nationals residing in the EU, and financial contributions for promotion of employment and job creation. It should be noted also that certain matters have not been brought into EU **competences**. These include pay issues, the right of association, the right to strike and the right to impose lockouts. Since the Treaty of Amsterdam, the **Charter of Fundamental Rights** has been drawn up. It restates many of the principles and goals underpinning social policy, including the aim of combating social exclusion.

More and better jobs as well as equal opportunities are the key watchwords of European employment and social policy. The EU wants to make sure that no one gets left behind as it strives to become the world's most competitive and dynamic knowledge-based economy. The framework of the Social Policy Agenda (2006–10) was designed to link economic, employment and social policies. The key strands of the agenda were: the **European Employment Strategy**; improving working conditions and standards; social inclusion and social protection; and equality of women and men.

The EU has long sought to protect workers' rights by reaching agreement on common minimum rules on working conditions and health and safety at work. It has also attempted to promote better relations and an improved dialogue between worker representatives and employers. More recently, the European Commission has been encouraging corporate social responsibility by promoting the concept that companies should include social and environmental concerns as an integral part of their business strategies.

Common EU rules establish the baseline standards in a wide range of areas. These include protection against specific health risks, such as **noise** or exposure to chemicals, or in specific circumstances, such as pregnancy or where workers are under 18 years old. They also cover workers' rights. Equal pay for equal work, and protection against sexual harassment and all forms of discrimination, are fundamental tenets of the EU. The fight against discrimination and xeno-phobia was stepped up through an action programme to combat discrimination covering 2001–06. Moreover, a Gender Equality Framework Strategy for the period 2001–05 sought to ensure that gender issues were taken into account in all EU policies.

Four agencies provide essential technical input into EU work on employ-ment, carry out research on social policy matters and disseminate best practice. They are the **European Agency for Safety and Health at Work** in Bilbao; the **European Foundation for the Improvement of Living and Working Conditions** in Dublin; the European Institute for Gender Equality (which was established in 2007 and is now located in Vilnius, Lithuania); and the **European Monitoring Centre on Racism and Xenophobia** in Vienna.

The **SOCIAL PROTOCOL** was an agreement, stemming from the **Charter of Fundamental Social Rights of Workers** (aiming to promote employ-ment, improve living and working conditions and combat exclusion), reached between 11 of the **Twelve** European Communities member state governments at a meeting of the **European Council** in December 1991 at Maastricht. The only hesitant state was the United Kingdom. On account of the United Kingdom's negotiated **opt-out**, the agreement was annexed to the **Treaty on**

European Union as a **protocol** and became part of the treaty only when the United Kingdom finally signed up to the social charter in 1997.

SOCIALIST GROUP IN THE EUROPEAN PARLIAMENT: See **Group of the Party of European Socialists**

SOCRATES, a European Union (EU) programme, was introduced in 1995 to bring language, education and learning programmes together in order to promote co-operation and the exchange of information between member states with regard to education, as well as the mobility of students, especially in higher education. The 10-year programme, based in **Brussels**, combined a number of educational programmes, including **Erasmus**, **Grundtvig**, **Lingua**, **Minerva** and **Comenius**. €383m. was provided by the EU in 2006 to assist mobility and co-operation networks. Around one-half of these funds were earmarked specifically for Erasmus. The overall budget for the second part of the programme—Socrates II (2000–06)—totalled €1,850m. According to the **European Commission**, nine out of 10 universities in Europe participated in this programme, with some 165,000 mobility scholarships being awarded each year. The Commission also encouraged the mobility of teachers, and some 23,000 received money in 2006 to enable them to benefit from cross-border educational exchanges. In 2007 the new **Lifelong Learning Programme** 2007–13 replaced the Socrates, **Leonardo** da Vinci, and eLearning programmes, which expired at the end of 2006.

SOFT LAWS are rules of conduct that in principle have no legally binding force, but which nevertheless may have practical effects in aiding policy development. This broad definition encompasses not only international agreements but also texts issued by the European Union (EU) **institutions**. In terms of the **European Commission**, soft law is usually equated with the following: codes of conduct, frameworks, **resolutions**, communications, **declarations**, guidance notes and circulars. Although the concept of soft law remains a highly problematic one for lawyers, it is generally regarded by policymakers as a useful instrument to encourage consistency in bureaucratic **decision-making**, to enable speedy resolution of issues that would otherwise demand **legislation**, and to allow for regulation where no regulation would otherwise be possible. However, the use of soft law has its detractors, who emphasize the dangers and the undemocratic and illegitimate situations that might arise from such informal policymaking. When soft law is utilized, parliaments are bypassed, which, as far as the public is concerned, leads to opaque decision-making, and the content of policies may often be vague, as well as possibly inconsistent with existing legislation. Moreover, it can be argued that because soft law is not legally binding, **implementation** must rest on the goodwill of those agreeing to it.

Nevertheless, soft law is a fundamental part of EU policymaking (e.g. state aid—see also **subsidies**).

JAVIER SOLANA (1942–) became **Secretary-General of the Council of the European Union** and the European Union's first **High Representative for the Common Foreign and Security Policy**. During his period in office (1999–2009), he was instrumental in overseeing the development of the **European security and defence policy**. He was also the author of the **European security strategy** adopted in late 2003. While in office he was also Secretary-General of the now essentially defunct **Western European Union**. Previously, Solana had been Secretary-General of the **North Atlantic Treaty Organization** (NATO) in 1995–99. During the earlier part of his career, Solana was a Socialist member of parliament and minister in Spain.

SOLEMN DECLARATION ON EUROPEAN UNION is the title of the general statement signed by the heads of government and foreign ministers at the conclusion of the meeting of the **European Council** held in Stuttgart, Federal Republic of Germany, in June 1983, which had discussed the **Genscher–Colombo Plan**. The Declaration reviewed the extent to which the potential of each institution of the European Communities (EC) had been implemented, and considered possibilities for their further co-ordination. It asserted a wish to work for further EC development as a nucleus of European union, to strengthen **European political co-operation** (EPC), to promote closer cultural co-operation, to launch a concerted action to deal with international problems of law and order, and to seek further **approximation** of the **legislation** of the member states. It also indicated the purpose of the Council and its relationship to the EC **institutions**. More a statement of belief than a plan of action, it nevertheless contributed to the movement in favour of change that developed during the 1980s.

SOUTH AFRICA over the last two decades or so has witnessed a transformation in its relations with the European Union (EU). For much of the 1980s it was the focus of **sanctions** adopted under **European political co-operation**, although a European Special Programme (ESP) was agreed to assist the victims of apartheid. Later, once the apartheid regime collapsed, the ESP was renamed the European Programme for Reconstruction and Development. This committed €500m. to South Africa for the period 1996–99. Further financial assistance has since been agreed. In addition, a trade, development and co-operation agreement was concluded in 1999. South Africa is now the EU's largest trading partner in Africa (with total trade between the two countries amounting to €47,100m. in 2011).

SOUTH AND CENTRAL AMERICA has not been, in general, the subject of a co-ordinated policy. However, the European Union (EU) has concluded economic and trade co-operation agreements with most of the countries in this area, which enable the latter to benefit from the EU **Generalized System of Preferences**. The arrangements allow duty-free access into the EU for some of their manufactured products. Moreover, regular ministerial meetings have been held with the so-called 'Rio Group' (Brazil, Colombia, Mexico, Panama, Peru, Uruguay and Venezuela) since 1987. Prior to 1999, the San José dialogue existed as the institutional forum between the EU and six countries of Central America (Costa Rica, El Salvador, Guatemala, Honduras, Nicaragua and Panama). In 1998 the **European Commission** proposed negotiating mandates for the creation of a free trade area with the countries of Mercosur (Argentina, Brazil, Paraguay and Uruguay) and Chile. This was followed by a first summit between heads of state and government of the EU and the six above-named Central American countries at Rio de Janeiro in June 1999. At this meeting (the first EU-Latin America and Caribbean—LAC summit), a highly ambitious action plan, with 54 priorities covering institutional dialogue, trade liberalization and investment, was agreed. Such multilateral co-operation supplements existing bilateral co-operation between the EU and countries in the region. In June 2012 the EU and six LAC countries signed a comprehensive **association agreement**, which included an ambitious trade component. In the same month the EU signed a trade agreement with Colombia and Peru.

SOUTH-EASTERN EUROPE is a term used by the European Union when referring to Bulgaria, Romania and the countries of the **Western Balkans** collectively. (See Stability pact for South-Eastern Europe.)

The **SOVEREIGNTY** of the member states has been significantly diminished by their acceptance of the principles of the **founding treaties** and their subsequent amendments. Encroachment on national sovereignty has further increased with the accumulation of the *acquis communautaire*. The net effect is that while the European Union (EU) may not be a sovereign body in the full political or legal sense, neither are the member states. The question of sovereignty has remained a contentious issue within the EU.

SOVIET UNION: See USSR

PAUL-HENRI SPAAK (1899–1972), head of government or foreign minister of Belgium on several occasions after 1945, became popularly known as 'Mr Europe'. He was one of the principal conceivers of **Benelux**, was involved in the 1948 **Congress of Europe** and the subsequent **European Movement**, and took the first initiative in the developments that led to the creation of the **Council of Europe**. Elected as the first President of its Assembly, he resigned in 1951 because of his disillusionment over its inability to achieve concrete progress towards integration. He supported the **sectoral integration** approach of the 1950s, and it was he who led the initiative that resulted in a draft plan for a **European Political Community**. As Belgian foreign minister, he attended the 1955 **Messina Conference**, where he was charged with chairing a committee that would consider, develop and report on the proposals made at Messina. The Spaak Report was accepted by the **Six**, after which Spaak and his committee went on to draft the treaties for the **European Economic Community** and the **European Atomic Energy Community**.

SPAAK REPORT: See **Messina Conference**; **Paul-Henri Spaak**

SPACE POLICY until recently has been barely considered by the European Union (EU). While some of the member states were involved in space research and development as early as the 1960s, the European Communities (EC) was slow in developing a collaborative approach to space, despite retaining links with the **European Space Agency** (ESA). A space policy document was produced by the **European Commission** in July 1988. It identified six 'action lines': the promotion of co-ordination and complementary action between space programmes and EC **research and technological development policy**; **telecommunications** and satellite technology; industrial development and the **internal market**; the development of observation of the Earth from space; the legal environment; and the development of space-related technology training programmes. Since 1988 the EC/EU has collaborated more closely with the ESA. The **Treaty of Lisbon**, following the abandoned **Treaty establishing a Constitution for Europe**, envisages the EU adopting a more focused engagement, with space policy as part of its activities in the area of **research and technological development policy**. In October 2009 the first EU-ESA International Conference on Human Space Exploration was held, in Prague, Czech Republic.

SPAIN first approached the European Communities (EC) in 1962, with a request for an **association agreement** that would, in time, permit full membership. The request was renewed in 1964. Negotiations on a **preferential trade agreement** began in 1967, and an agreement was signed in 1970. Full membership could not be considered by the EC as long as Spain continued to be governed by an authoritarian regime. Discussions on a new agreement for a free trade area were broken off by the EC in October 1975 in protest against executions in Spain that violated 'the principles of the rule of law and in particular the rights of the defence'. The new, democratic Spanish Government that emerged after General Francisco Franco's death in November 1975 submitted an application for full membership in July 1977, and negotiations began in February 1979. The negotiations proved to be difficult, particularly where agriculture and fishing were concerned, but were eventually concluded in March 1985, and Spain joined the EC the following January. A beneficiary of

EC **regional policy**, including the **Cohesion Fund**, and **social policy**, Spain has been a strong supporter of further economic and political integration, even though its determination to meet some of the economic and monetary criteria set by the EC placed enormous strains on the Spanish economy. Spain successfully entered stage three of **economic and monetary union** in 1999. Under the premiership of the conservative José María Aznar (1996–2004), Spain's economic boom continued. Little known outside Spain prior to his first election victory and appointment as Prime Minister in 1996, Aznar rapidly emerged as a leading figure on the European stage. His decision to support the **USA**-led invasion of Iraq in 2003 (see **Iraq War**) may have won both US and British plaudits, but it was not a popular move in Spain. Aznar's decision to stand down in 2004 may also have contributed to his determination to resist the proposals (which reduced Spain's position) outlined in the **Draft Constitution** on the new voting arrangements within the **Council of the European Union** after **enlargement**. This led to bitter recriminations from other European Union (EU) member states and the entire episode not only marginalized Spain but also helped to ensure that the 2003 Rome **intergovernmental conference** collapsed without agreement. A change in government in April 2004, when **José Luis Rodríguez Zapatero** became Prime Minister, brought a more accommodating Spanish approach to the EU and a swift decision to settle any outstanding differences. This approach helped the EU leaders to agree a treaty text in June 2004. Spain was the first EU member state to hold a referendum on the **Treaty establishing a Constitution for Europe** in February 2005 and a decisive majority (77%) approved the text. However, turn-out was low, at just 42%. No referendum was held on the **Treaty of Lisbon**, Spain opting instead for parliamentary **ratification**, and this was easily secured. The Spanish economy was severely hit by the 'credit crunch' that began in 2007 and the Zapatero Government introduced an austerity programme in April 2010 to ease the country's debt burden and to help stabilize the **euro**. However, the country's economic situation deteriorated further throughout 2011 and into 2012 as the growth rate fell, the housing market collapsed and unemployment climbed steadily. Amidst these economic problems an early general election was held on 20 November 2011. These elections saw the defeat (and worst ever electoral result since 1982) of the Socialist Party and the victory of the centre-right Peoples' Party. The new Spanish Prime Minister, **Mariano Rajoy**, assumed office on 22 December 2011. He participated in the negotiations with the EU that led to the signing of the **Fiscal Compact Treaty** (**Treaty on Stability, Co-ordination and Governance in the Economic and Monetary Union**) in March 2012 and supported the austerity agenda. By the spring of 2012 nearly 25% of the country's workforce was unemployed and opposition was growing towards the Government's stringent austerity measures. Large protest rallies were held, notably in Madrid. The Spanish Government was compelled to bail out a number of leading Spanish banks in May and in the following month the eurozone finance ministers agreed to provide Spain with up to €100,000m. in loans from euro-zone funds in an attempt to support the country's ailing banking sector.

SPECIAL COMMITTEE ON AGRICULTURE is the name of a specialist committee within the **Committee of Permanent Representatives** (COREPER). It is the only COREPER body that deals with all agricultural issues that come before the plenary Committee.

SPIERENBURG REPORT is the name of a document produced for the **European Commission** in 1979. A group of experts headed by a former Netherlands diplomat, Dirk Spierenburg, was asked to review the structure and organization of the European Communities. The Report recommended a rationalization of the Commission—including a reduction in the number of Commissioners—and of its system of personnel management. It was opposed by the Council of Ministers (see **Council of the European Union**), and was never implemented.

SPILLOVER was a term widely used in the 1950s to describe how **sectoral integration** would lead to full European union. It had two components. Functional spillover was based on the principle that modern economies were based on interrelated sectors. Once one economic sector had been integrated, this complexity would generate pressure for the integration of other sectors. Political spillover suggested that once European institutions had been established for one sector, economic interest groups would look to that political level for the realization of their demands, and the advantages provided would lead them also to press for further sectoral integration. The notion largely fell into disfavour after the late 1950s as an explanation of, and strategy for, integration.

ALTIERO SPINELLI (1907–86) was a life-long advocate of a federal United States of Europe. His views had first been expressed in the Ventotene Manifesto of 1941, which served as the basis of several documents prepared for international meetings of federalists and Resistance activists in 1944 and 1945. Spinelli drafted most of these documents, which envisaged a federal Europe with a written constitution, a judicial tribunal and a supranational government directly responsible to the people of Europe. Active in the federalist organizations of the late 1940s and 1950s, Spinelli, with his more populist approach, was out of tune with the élite-led economic approach to integration that came to dominate developments. He later served as a member of the **European Commission** from 1970 to 1976, but his greatest contribution to the development of the European Union (EU) came after 1979 when, as a **Member of the European Parliament**, he was the principal conceiver of the **draft Treaty establishing the European Union**, a document that influenced much of the later development of the EU.

SPORT was identified by the **Committee for a People's Europe** as an area where, because of the mass interest and loyalties it generates, the European Communities (EC) could seek to encourage a sense of European identity and awareness. The **European Commission** had already sought, on a modest scale, to involve the EC in sporting events, most prominently through its sponsorship since 1976 of the Sail for Europe Association, a group which has formed international crews of EC nationals to compete in round-the-world races and other sailing events. The Commission also sponsored the European Yacht Race in 1985, an event that now takes place on a biennial basis. Tennis and swimming championships have also been sponsored, along with a number of football, motor rally and walking events. The Eurathlon programme provides grants to sports projects. In 1997 the **European Parliament** passed a resolution requesting that a reference to sport be inserted into the **article** of the **Treaty of Rome** dealing with culture. This was not taken up, although the **Treaty of Lisbon**, following the abandoned **Treaty establishing a Constitution for Europe**, does envisage a greater role for the European Union (EU) in promoting European sporting issues as well as developing the European dimension in sport. This is to be done by 'promoting fairness and openness in sporting competitions and co-operation between bodies responsible for sports, and by protecting the physical and moral integrity of sportspeople'. The EU Sport Forum, which coincides with an informal meeting of EU Sport Ministers, is held annually, bringing together some 250 delegates, including leading figures from the international and European Olympic Committees, European federations, 'sport for all' organizations, and organizations of leagues, clubs and athletes.

The **STABILITY AND GROWTH PACT** (SGP) emerged as an essential aspect of the third stage of plans for **economic and monetary union** (EMU). It was realized that if EMU were ultimately going to be successful, budgetary discipline across all **eurozone** members would have to be maintained after EMU had been launched in 1999. This demand was principally led by Germany and resulted in a **European Council** resolution (adopted at the Amsterdam European Council in 1997) and two subsequent Council regulations. The pact established clear and detailed arrangements for the surveillance of budgetary positions and for the co-ordination of economic policies, and procedures for dealing with excessive deficits. All eurozone members pledged to pursue budgets close to balance or in surplus for the foreseeable future and to present both the **European Commission** and the **Council of the European Union** with annual reports on their economic situation.

The SGP allows the Council to penalize any participating member state that fails to take the necessary measures to end an excessive deficit. In the first instance the penalty is more likely to constitute a non-interest-bearing deposit with the European Union (EU), but it could be converted into a fine if the deficit is not corrected within two years. The Commission is charged with supervising the economic policies of the participating countries and with alerting the member states to potential problems. The situation with Germany, the prime architect of the pact, deteriorated in 2003 as both Berlin and Paris watched their economies remain locked in recession or stagnation. For the third year in a row, both states breached one of the keystones of the pact—maintaining budget deficits at less than 3% of gross domestic product (GDP), the total value of goods and services the economy produces. With their economies stagnant, tax receipts were down, while public spending in terms of unemployment benefits had gone up. In November 2003 the SGP was effectively suspended through the reluctance of France and Germany to accept the recommendations of the **European Central Bank** and the Commission to reduce their budget deficits to below 3% of GDP. According to the rules, both states were therefore liable to pay substantial fines. However, the **Economic and Financial Affairs Council of Ministers** (Ecofin) disregarded the Commission's recommendation and granted the eurozone's two largest economies an extra year's grace. France and Germany were therefore allowed to break the 3% rule again in 2004. The pact was thus severely undermined. Germany's wish at the time was to draw up additional EU fiscal rules that would lead to a 'better interpretation'—in other words, a less strict interpretation—of the pact, allowing more account to be taken of the economic situation, the impact of ageing on social security systems and the role played by public investment in modernizing the economy. The **eurozone** crisis of 2010–12 led to a stricter interpretation of the SGP generally being favoured. A revised pact, the Euro Plus Pact, was agreed in March 2011. It provides for more stringent commitments with emphasis on competitiveness, employment, sound public finances and financial stability.

The **STABILITY PACT FOR SOUTH EASTERN EUROPE** was launched in June 1999 following the **Kosovo** conflict to assist in the stabilization and reconstruction of the region, the European Union playing a lead role through its **stabilization and association process** and the implementation of the former **CARDS** programme of financial assistance and its successor the **instrument for pre-accession assistance** (IPA). In April 2008 the Stability Pact was replaced by a Regional Co-operation Council, based in Sarajevo, Bosnia and Herzegovina

STABILIZATION AND ASSOCIATION AGREEMENTS (SAAs) are the **association agreements** that the European Union (EU) has devised for countries in the **Western Balkans** as part of the **stabilization and association process**. The first was concluded with the **former Yugoslav republic of Macedonia** (FYRM) in 2001 and was soon followed by an agreement with **Croatia** and, later, one with **Albania** (2006). In March 2007 **Montenegro** concluded negotiations on an SAA. Agreements with **Bosnia and Herzegovina** and with **Serbia** followed in 2008. These, like the agreements with FYRM and Croatia, are modelled very much on **Europe agreements**, but place a much greater emphasis on the pursuit of regional co-operation as a prerequisite for closer collaboration with the EU. They also confirm the associate country's status as potential candidate for EU membership (see **potential candidate state**).

The **STABILIZATION AND ASSOCIATION PROCESS** (SAP) was launched by the European Union as its contribution to the **stability pact for South Eastern Europe** following the **Kosovo** conflict in 1999. Its key elements are the **stabilization and association agreements**, the **CARDS** programme of financial assistance and its successor the **instrument for pre-accession assistance** (IPA).

STABILIZERS were introduced into the **common agricultural policy** (CAP) in 1988. They are fixed ceilings, or upper limits, imposed on the production of several agricultural products. They involve production quotas, limits on both production and processing guarantees, and intervention ceilings, and have been supported by a system of **co-responsibility levies**. If the ceiling is exceeded, an automatic reduction in the level of price support provided by the CAP is triggered. The most significant effect, perhaps, has been upon cereal production.

The **STAFF** employed by the European Union (EU) numbers some 55,000, and about 33,000 of these work for the **European Commission**. The total is substantially lower than staff employed by national bureaucracies. Formally, there are no quotas for each of the member states; in practice, however, an unofficial system of national allocation is employed, to ensure that each member state is adequately represented in all areas and at all levels of the administration. In principle, officials must be EU nationals and adequately bilingual, and those appointed as translators or interpreters must be reasonably proficient in two EU **languages** other than their own. Apart from these qualifications, most posts are filled by open competition, having been advertised in the *Official Journal of the European Union*. In addition, several senior posts are filled by nomination from the member states.

STAGIAIRE is the name given to a short-term trainee, usually a recent graduate, attached to a **European Commission** office. The position provides the appointee with an apprenticeship and in-service training, but does not guarantee subsequent employment with the European Union.

STANDARDIZATION: See **CEN**; **CENELEC**

The **STANDING COMMITTEE ON EMPLOYMENT** was established in 1970 to act in an advisory capacity. In 1996 the **European Commission** invited interested parties to consider how the Standing Committee could be reformed in order to improve social dialogue. Two years later the Commission presented a draft decision for reform to the **Council of the European Union**. The document entitled *Adapting and promoting the social dialogue at Community level* was adopted by the Council in March 1999. The newly revised Committee was to serve as a European forum, in effect a tripartite dialogue, between the Council, the Commission and European Union-level employer and employee organizations (including the **European Trade Union Confederation**, the **Committee of Professional Agricultural Organizations in the European Union** (COPA), EUROCOMMERCE and the **Union of Industrial and Employers' Confederations of Europe**) to discuss **employment** strategy.

STATE AID: See **Subsidies**

STATISTICAL OFFICE OF THE EUROPEAN COMMUNITIES: See **Eurostat**

STOCKHOLM CONVENTION is the name of the document that in 1960 formally established the **European Free Trade Association**. The signatories accepted the economic aim of an elimination of tariffs on reciprocal trade in industrial goods, with special provisions for agriculture and fisheries. The Convention had no political implications.

The **STOCKHOLM PROGRAMME** is the latest initiative of the European Union (EU) to establish and develop its **area of freedom, security and justice**. Launched in 2009, it follows the Hague programme, and is designed 'to define the framework for EU police and customs co-operation, rescue services, criminal and civil law co-operation, asylum, migration and visa policy' for the period 2010–14.

STRASBOURG, France, is central to the theme of European unity because it is the home of the **Council of Europe**, and became the location of the plenary sessions of the **European Parliament** (EP) after 1958. Although the EP continues to meet in the city, many of its members would prefer it to be relocated in **Brussels**, where many EP committees meet. In recent years an absolute majority of members of the European Parliament (MEPs) have repeatedly voted in favour of a single seat (i.e. Brussels). However, any decision to move must be agreed by all European Union member states and France is adamantly opposed to a move. Indeed, **Nicolas Sarkozy**, the former French President, even claimed that the issue was 'non-negotiable'. The **Treaty of Amsterdam**, by means of a **protocol** on the location of the **institutions**, had tried to put an end to suggestions that the EP might relocate by confirming Strasbourg as its home and requiring that 12 plenary sessions be held in the city each year.

The **STRUCTURAL AND COHESION FUNDS** (see also the **Cohesion Fund**) have been designed to reduce the socio-economic gap between the richest and poorest member states, and between rich and poor regions within states, through a coherent redistribution of financial resources. The strategy of reducing regional disparities has always been central to the European Union (EU) because such disparities clearly undermine the integrity of the single market and also run contrary to the aims of solidarity and assistance advocated by the European integration project. The **Treaty of Rome** explicitly, although briefly, referred to regional disparities; however, the initial assumption was that the operation of the free market would help reduce these. Attention was originally focused upon southern Italy and was subsequently widened to cover other Mediterranean regions as well as Ireland. The decision to create an **internal market** made resolution of the disparities more urgent, and the term 'cohesion' was first employed in the **Single European Act**. The inclusion of the relevant paragraph (title V) owed much to the efforts of the four poorest states (Greece, Ireland, Portugal and Spain), but was also promoted by richer states (notably Germany) as a means of presenting financial support and inducements to those regions that would not necessarily or immediately reap benefits from the prompt completion of the single market.

The term cohesion encompassed notions of solidarity and harmonious economic development that could not be secured by the free market alone, and the following **structural funds** were established: the **European Regional Development Fund** (ERDF), which was set up in 1975 and finances infrastructure, productive investment to create jobs, local development projects and assistance to small and medium-sized enterprises (SMEs); and the **European Social Fund** (ESF), which was established in 1958 and is designed to help the workforce adapt to changes in the labour market. The term cohesion was further elaborated in the negotiations on the **European Economic Area** (EEA) and in the **Treaty on European Union**, which established a new structural fund, known as the Cohesion Fund, through which monies from the richer member states and the other members of the EEA would be directed to aid infrastructural developments in the poorer countries of the EU. The latter, in return, agreed to accept the provisions in the treaty relating to **economic and monetary union**. The major beneficiary of the Cohesion Fund has been Spain. Two other funds that contribute to regional development are the **European Agricultural Guarantee Fund** (EAGF), which finances rural development measures and provides assistance to farmers, and the **European Fisheries Fund**.

The financial assistance provided to counter regional disparities increased rapidly, from some 5% of the **budget** in 1975, and the structural and cohesion funds have accounted for over one-third of the EU budget since the late 1980s (see **Delors I** and **Delors II**). Spending in these areas has now more or less stabilized. Although politically successful, the funds themselves lack sufficient scope and scale to reduce the disparities completely.

The financial assistance for these programmes is calculated on a multi-annual basis, with the funds being used to tackle regional disparities and support regional development through actions including developing infrastructure and telecommunications, developing human resources and supporting research and development. They are subject to continuing change of emphasis.

To facilitate the provision of financial assistance to the most needy areas and to prepare the EU for **enlargement** (see **Agenda 2000**), the EU's structural policy was substantially reformed and now focuses on a number of objective areas. The declared aim of the particular reform initiative was to concentrate aid where it was most needed, that is, on those regions that were falling furthest behind. In the 2000–06 financial perspective there were three main areas. Objective 1 areas were those regions that were lagging behind the rest of the EU in terms of development, i.e. regions in which gross national product (GNP) per head was less than 75% of the EU average. These objective 1 areas consumed 70% of structural funds expenditure. Objective 2 areas were those areas with structural difficulties, such as areas undergoing economic change, rural areas in decline and areas dependent on fishing. The third objective area related to the development of human resources outside those regions eligible for objective 1 aid.

In addition, there have been four major structural funds initiatives. These are **Interreg** (1989–), which seeks to stimulate cross-border, transnational and inter-regional co-operation; **Leader** (1991–2006), which aimed to foster rural development through the initiatives of local action groups; EQUAL (2000–08), which provided assistance for the creation of new means to combat **discrimination** and inequalities in general; and **URBAN** (1994–2006), which promoted economic and social revitalization of cities and suburban areas in crisis.

As the **candidate** states moved closer to EU membership, it was decided to create two new funds to assist their progression for the period 2000–06. These funds (see **Agenda 2000**), namely the **instrument for structural policies for pre-accession** (ISPA) and the Special Accession Programme for Agriculture and Rural Development (**Sapard**), were designed to support infrastructure projects, industry, services, SMEs, agriculture and the environment. ISPA and **Sapard** were replaced in January 2007 by the **instrument for pre-accession assistance**.

At a **European Council** meeting in Berlin in March 1999, although the member states agreed to maintain their levels of spending on these funds, a general consensus emerged that such spending should be regarded as promoting short- and medium-term solutions, and that, in the longer term, market mechanisms would have to reduce the inequalities. The 2006 budget was heralded by the Commission as a decisive step towards reforming EU spending, in that it placed emphasis on investment in growth and the necessity to create more and better jobs. As part of this objective, the funds for cohesion policy were linked to a new drive for **competitiveness**. Together, the initiatives that fell under these headings amounted to 39% of the planned budgetary **expenditure**. The bulk of this remained earmarked for regional development.

Together the funds are intended to support integrated, rather than individual, projects and increasingly are expected to have a regional focus. They are allocated through Community Support Frameworks (CSFs) that are negotiated between the regions, the **European Commission** and the member states. For example, in the United Kingdom context, the **Scottish Executive**, the Welsh Assembly Government and the Northern Ireland Administration are responsible for **regional policy**, including delivering the structural and cohesion funds in their territories.

In December 2005 the European Council agreed a total structural and cohesion funds budget of €347,000m. (at 2007 prices) for 2007–13. As a result of the agreement, the United Kingdom is expected to receive a substantial €9,400m. (at 2004 prices) from the structural funds for 2007–13. Further changes have been made for the current financial perspective period. The available funds are going to be more tightly focused to help secure the targets laid down in the renewed Growth and Jobs (Lisbon) Agenda. It is also hoped to encourage and stimulate more ownership of the agenda at regional and local level. For instance, in the United Kingdom, 60% of expenditure for **convergence** regions and 75% of expenditure for regions under the regional competitiveness and **employment** objective were allocated to the **Lisbon agenda**. The new period also sees a simpler and more efficient operation of the funds. To this end, the number of instruments has been reduced from six to three, and a new 'proportionality' principle will provide for less bureaucracy.

The Commission has defined new objectives for the current financial perspective that covers the period 2007–13. The greatest emphasis is placed on the first objective, which targets **convergence**. The Commission seeks to accelerate the economic convergence of the least developed countries and regions of the EU, which are home to some 35% of the EU's population. This area consumes the lion's share of the money, some 82%. To this end, monies are available through the ERDF, the ESF and the Cohesion Fund. This objective is very much concerned with developing human and physical capital, innovation, knowledge society, environment and administrative efficiency. The budget allocated to this instrument is €251,300m. The second objective centres on regional competitiveness and employment (where some €55,000m. has been allocated for 2007–13). It applies to all parts of the EU and seeks to ensure greater competitiveness and boost employment opportunities. The main themes here are innovation, entrepreneurship and environmental protection. The third and final objective focuses on territorial co-operation. This builds directly upon the Interreg initiatives of the previous years, which were originally planned to be fully incorporated into the main objectives of the structural funds. There is some €7,750m. available under the ERDF for this objective, which covers three distinct strands: cross-border co-operation, transnational co-operation and interregional co-operation. In total, some 423 programmes are being financed by the structural and cohesion funds between 2007 and 2013.

STRUCTURAL POLICY: See **Structural and Cohesion Funds**

STUTTGART DECLARATION: See **Solemn Declaration on European Union**

SUBSIDIARITY is a term that was first used in the context of the European Communities (EC) in the 1970s, but it only became politically contentious in the period preceding the signing of the **Treaty on European Union**. As defined by the **Treaty of Rome**, the term embodies the principles that the European Union (EU) can act only when they possess the legal power to do so, that the EU should act only when an objective can be better achieved at the supranational level, and that the means employed by the EU when they do act should be proportional to the desired objective. It implies, therefore, that national powers are the norm, with EU action the exception. It remains, nevertheless, an ambiguous and controversial concept regarded by both those for and those against more intensive integration as supporting their own agenda. An attempt was made in a **protocol** introduced by the **Treaty of Amsterdam** to provide a clearer definition of subsidiarity. In the framework of the **intergovernmental conference** launched in February 2000, the **Committee of the Regions** asked for the principle of subsidiarity to be amended formally to recognize the role of the local and regional authorities. This did not happen at the Nice **summit meeting**. The **European Commission** produces, on an annual basis, a report (*Better Lawmaking*) that for the most part examines the application of the subsidiarity principle. The concept of subsidiarity was reaffirmed in the **Treaty establishing a Constitution for Europe** and more recently in the **Treaty of Lisbon**.

SUBSIDIES by the member states to either private companies or public enterprises are, in general, not permitted if the effect is likely to be contrary to the **competition policy** of the European Union (EU). **European Commission** guidelines permit subsidies for industries experiencing very severe economic difficulties, but in each instance the case should be demonstrated to be exceptional, the aid programme should be short-term only, and the objective should be the re-establishment of economic viability by a planned reduction in capacity. State aid is also permitted for natural disaster relief, depressed regions, and investment in new economic activities. In each instance, member states must inform the Commission of their intentions. Where member states have provided subsidies that do not conform to EU **regulations**, the Commission has the authority to demand their repayment and to levy fines on member states. Subsidies have always been controversial, and especially so in such sectors as agriculture and aircraft manufacture, and have led to ongoing disagreements within the EU and in relations with third states. The whole issue of subsidies became extremely controversial following the onset of the economic recession in 2008 and governments' subsequent moves to assist their respective banking sectors.

SUMMIT MEETINGS are gatherings of the heads of government of the member states. During the first decade of the three European Communities only three summits were held by the **Six**. Three further ad hoc summits were held between 1972 and 1974. In 1974 it was agreed to institutionalize summits with the establishment of the **European Council**, which was to meet three times a year. The frequency of summit meetings was reduced to twice yearly in 1985. Provisions also exist for the convocation of extraordinary or emergency sessions. Most summit meetings deal primarily with routine business and general reviews; a few, however, have been highly significant for European developments. (See, for example, **Essen summit**; **Fontainebleau summit**; **Hague summit**; **Maastricht summit**; **Milan summit**; **Tampere summit**.) It was traditionally the practice that summits were held in the country holding the presidency of the **Council of the European Union**. Since the second half of 2003, however, all scheduled summit meetings of the European Council have been held in **Brussels**.

SUPRANATIONALISM is the condition whereby the structures and **decisions** of the European Union are superior to and, some would claim, independent of national governments. Supranationalism is completely different from intergovernmental **co-operation**.

The **SUSPENSION CLAUSE** was written into the **Treaty on European Union** by the **Treaty of Amsterdam**. Under this clause, some of the rights of a member state (e.g. voting in the **Council of the European Union**) can be suspended if that particular member state consistently or seriously contravenes the principles on which the European Union has been constructed, such as liberty, democracy, respect for **human rights** and the rule of law.

SUSTAINABILITY is the quality that may be ascribed to a form of economic growth that is self-maintaining without exhausting natural resources.

The **SUTHERLAND REPORT** dates from 1992 and was produced by a former Commissioner responsible for competition, Peter Sutherland, at the request of the **European Commission**. He was charged with producing a report on how the European Commission could develop a strategy to ensure that the **internal market** functioned properly and efficiently. The Report advocated a series of initiatives to achieve this goal. These included the necessity for greater **transparency** and much more monitoring and enforcement of European Union **legislation** at the national level. It also placed an emphasis on

subsidiarity. The Commission responded to the report by promising to pursue many of the suggestions, particularly with regard to national enforcement. In addition, it promised to publish an annual report on the state of the single market and make more use of **Green Papers** to engage the wider public in suggestions on proposed legislation.

SWEDEN maintained a position of political and military **neutrality** after 1945, eschewing involvement in anything other than intergovernmental and economic co-operation. In 1961, it approached the European Communities (EC) for a form of economic association that did not imply full membership. Negotiations eventually began in 1970, and in 1971 Sweden ruled out full membership as being incompatible with its policy of neutrality. A **free trade agreement** was signed in 1972. Following the EC decision to implement the **internal market** by 1992, Sweden accepted the need for a closer economic relationship with the EC. This was eventually achieved through the **European Economic Area**. Before this was concluded, however, Sweden revised its view on membership, and in 1991 submitted a formal application to join the EC. Negotiations were completed in 1994 and, following approval in a popular referendum, Sweden joined the European Union (EU) on 1 January 1995. Sweden's transition to membership of the EU has been smooth, but the EU remains, according to **Eurobarometer**, less popular in the country than in other member states, and, like Denmark and the United Kingdom, Sweden opted not to enter **economic and monetary union** (EMU) in 1999. In a referendum held in September 2003 on joining EMU, a majority of those participating (56%) voted against replacing the krona with the **euro**.

SWITZERLAND has historically adopted a strict position of **neutrality**, but did, nevertheless, become a founder member of the **European Free Trade Association** (EFTA). It applied to the European Communities (EC) in 1961 for an economic association, but negotiations began only in 1970. A **free trade agreement** was signed in 1972 and subsequently ratified by a national referendum. In 1989 Switzerland accepted the need for EFTA to seek a new and closer relationship with the EC, and subsequently began examining the question of EC membership. However, in a referendum in December 1992, the Swiss rejected participation in the **European Economic Area**, thus forcing the Government to suspend the application for EC membership that had been submitted in the previous May. Since then, the Swiss have negotiated a series of sector-specific bilateral agreements with the European Union (EU) covering free movement of persons, air and land transport, agriculture, research, public procurement and the mutual recognition of conformity assessments; these were signed in June 1999 and entered into force two years later. In June 2002 negotiations on a further 10 bilateral agreements began. The negotiations lasted until 2003–04 and covered: pensions; trade in processed agricultural products; the environment; statistics; education, occupational training and youth; the media; taxation of savings; the fight against fraud; and co-operation in the fields of justice, police, asylum and migration. It remains to be seen whether these will provide the long-term basis for Switzerland's relations with the EU: during their negotiation and **ratification**, official government policy was to seek EU membership. In 2001, however, the Government advised the population against supporting a popular initiative to open negotiations for EU membership (since pre-conditions had not been met). In a referendum held in March 2001, 77% of voters voted against commencing membership negotiations. In 2005 Switzerland moved a step closer to the EU when its citizens voted in a referendum to join the **Schengen Agreement**. The decision meant that Switzerland would open its borders and become part of Europe's passport-free zone, and that the Swiss authorities would also share information with their EU colleagues on crime and on asylum applications. A year later, however, the Government, although it did not withdraw the 1992 membership application, dropped eventual EU membership from the objectives of its relations with the EU. Switzerland joined the **Schengen Area** in December 2008. By 2010 Switzerland had signed about 210 trade treaties with the EU. In September 2011 the Swiss Franc effectively switched to a euro peg: the franc had hitherto floated independently until its currency appreciation had become unsustainable during the eurozone debt crisis.

SYNERGY was the name of a programme introduced in 1997 to encourage international co-operation in the energy sector. It ended in 2002.

T

TAC: See **Total Allowable Catch**

TACIS: See **Technical Assistance to the Commonwealth of Independent States**

ANTONIO TAJANI (1953–) is one of the Vice-Presidents of the second **Barroso** Commission of the European Union (2010–14). He comes from Italy and first became a European Commissioner in 2008 following the election of the **Berlusconi** Government. He was re-appointed to the Barroso II team, where he took charge of industry and entrepreneurship.

The **TAMPERE SUMMIT** of the **European Council** in November 1999 represents a highly significant event in the development of European Union (EU) policy governing **justice and home affairs** (JHA). It was the first time that an area of loose intergovernmental co-operation had been propelled to the top of the political agenda. The origins of this agenda date back to early 1999 and a joint letter from the German Chancellor, **Gerhard Schröder**, and the Finnish Prime Minister, Paavo Lipponen, which called for European action in three broad areas. These all related to the then third pillar activities initiated by the **Treaty on European Union**, and covered **asylum** and **immigration policy**, the creation of a European **area of freedom, security and justice** and combating transnational crime. These became the main agenda items of the Tampere summit, where the heads of state and government reached agreement on the need for a 'common asylum system'. Tampere highlighted the expanding nature and position of the European Council as an agenda-setter and a driving force for EU integration. It led directly to a further extension of the EU's scope vis-à-vis policy-making in the field of JHA and resulted in several new initiatives and new bodies being set up in 2000, such as **Eurojust** and a European Police College.

With regard to the **European Commission**, Tampere was the first occasion for the post-**Jacques Santer** Commission to present itself as a credible and potent force to the leaders of the member states. However, the scandal surrounding the Santer regime and the growing determination of the European Council to control the policy agenda had already put the Commission on the defensive.

The changing relationships amongst the EU **institutions** were epitomized by the European Council's rejection of the Commission's report on the restructuring of the EU institutions.

TARGET, or Trans-European Automated Real-time Gross Settlement Express Transfer, is a system of inter-bank payments established on 1 January 1999, the start of the third stage of **economic and monetary union**, to regulate transactions between the **European Central Bank** and commercial banks of the participating member states. National central banks of non-participating member states also have some access to the settlement system. TARGET2 was launched in 2007. In 2011 TARGET2 processed a daily average of 348,505 payments, representing a daily average value of €2,385,000m.

The **TARGET PRICE** is the basic price set annually for each commodity covered by the **common agricultural policy**. The price support provided for farmers is calculated with reference to the target prices.

TARIC is the acronym for the Integrated community tariff established within the former Caddia (Co-operation in automation of data and documentation for imports/exports and agriculture) structure in 1988. It is similar to the **common external tariff**, but contains additional provisions relating to preferences and quotas. The tariff is published annually in the *Official Journal of the European Union*.

TARIFFS on intra-European Communities (EC) trade were removed by the **Six** by 1968, well within the time limit set by the **Treaty of Rome**. New member states have been given a transitional period in which to remove their tariffs, although increasingly, acceding states already participate in free trade arrangements with the European Union (EU). The EU **common external tariff** has been progressively reduced in line with decisions taken under the **General Agreement on Tariffs and Trade**, and now by the **World Trade Organization**.

TAX HARMONIZATION: See **Taxation**

TAXATION has, in general, been accepted by the European Union (EU) as a policy field that is the preserve of the member states and, normally, proposals relating to taxation that come before the **Council of the European Union** require unanimous approval. Despite the introduction of an **internal market** and **economic and monetary union**, an EU policy on taxation is still absent and this reflects the political sensitivity of fiscal policy and explains why the principle of unanimous **decision-making** in this area was maintained in the

Single European Act and beyond. The exceptions to the general rule are cases where national taxation policy is against EU **competition policy**, or where it discriminates against nationals of other member states. The problems of maintaining monetary union without economic and fiscal union were brought to the fore in early 2010, when the **euro** came under increasing strain on account of the financial difficulties throughout the EU and in particular in Greece, Spain and Portugal.

By contrast, the EU has an interest in indirect taxation and is bound to work for the **harmonization** of indirect taxation in order to enable the **internal market** to function properly. Currently, significant disparities exist in the levels of excise duty paid, for example, on alcohol and tobacco within the internal market. A code on corporate taxation was agreed in 1997 that would eliminate harmful tax competition between member states. Proposals made in December 1998 for the harmonization of taxes in the member states were rejected by the United Kingdom, which made it clear that a **veto** would be used to keep taxation within the realm of national governments. Such a position, shared by other member states, was emphatically restated during the **intergovernmental conference** in 2000. Consequently, the **Treaty of Nice** failed to extend **qualified majority voting** to tax harmonization. Nevertheless, it should be noted that the adoption of a single currency has intensified the pressure for a truly common rate of **value–added tax** (VAT) and for common rules in the area of corporate taxation in the EU. Moves in this direction continue to be strongly resisted by both the United Kingdom and Ireland.

TECHNICAL ASSISTANCE TO THE COMMONWEALTH OF INDEPENDENT STATES (Tacis) was an aid programme for the successor states of the **USSR**, often referred to as the **Commonwealth of Independent States**, and also Mongolia. Established in 1991, Tacis had as its objective to assess and aid economic reform and privatization in a range of economic sectors and to foster the development of democratic societies. In 1995 the **European Commission** extended the programme until 1999, when a revised programme to promote democracy and encourage investment was proposed. A **Phare** and Tacis Information Centre was opened in **Brussels** in 1998 to offer advice on the programmes. In the period 1991–99, the European Communities provided more than €4,000m. in assistance under the Tacis programme. A further €3,138m. was allocated for 2000–06. In January 2007 Tacis was replaced by the European Neighbourhood and Partnership Instrument (ENPI) (see **European neighbourhood policy**).

TED: See *Tenders Electronic Daily*

The **TELECOMMUNICATIONS** sector has been regarded by the **European Commission** as one of the real success stories of the single market and the

European Union (EU) regulatory framework. It has come a long way since the time of the traditional national telecommunications monopolies that controlled telecommunications, both voice and data, in the mid- to late 1980s. In order genuinely to compete with their major world rivals and to reap the emerging benefits of this new multi-million dollar industry, the EU member states were compelled to collaborate more closely.

Three factors propelled the Commission towards the liberalization of this sector. These were recognition of the radical changes in technology and the impact they would have on the industry, the shift towards globalized markets, and a growing trend towards greater liberalization and competition, especially in the **USA** and Scandinavia.

Several initiatives were launched in the fields of **media policy**, information networks, common standards and the **harmonization** of technical rules, and the development of satellite transmissions. Moreover, the telecommunications sector was targeted as part of efforts to develop **Trans-European Networks**. These initiatives, however, did not lead to an integrated policy. The push towards the creation of an **internal market** focused attention on the public monopolies, and, in particular, on telecommunications and energy. The former became a priority for the Commission (as identified in the Commission's 1987 **Green Paper** on the development of the common market for telecommunications services and equipment). This led to a 1988 directive which really marked the start of the transformation of telecommunications. This directive opened the telecommunications terminals market up to competition. It was supplemented by a directive relating to the liberalization of satellite telecommunications equipment and services, which came into force in late 1994, but allowed for deferment until 1 January 1996. Telecommunications infrastructures in the EU, which had been operated mainly by state monopolies, also faced the arrival of competition. In 1993 the **Council of the European Union** decided to liberalize voice telephony services fully by January 1998 (although some states, such as Ireland, Spain, Portugal and Greece, were given **derogations** until 2003). Agreement by member states on common rules in the form of the Open Network Provision framework effectively meant the full harmonization of an EU-wide telecommunications market. It allowed new entrants into the market, and the growing ethos of competition completed the drive to create a genuine single telecommunications market. Simultaneously, the Commission defined the concept of universal service, detailing the provision and quality of the service, the charging principles and the dispute settlement procedures.

By 1998 the EU had liberalized all telecommunications goods and services and, as a result, the number of operators doubled between 1998 and 2003, investment intensified and greater levels of competition brought better deals for consumers in terms of both product specification and lower prices.

Yet, more had to be done, as the sector was constantly undergoing new phases of modernization, notably the rise of the internet and the advance of digital technologies that can access any terminal. The sector also witnessed a series of huge mergers, for example between AOL and Time Warner. The potential impact of the internet revolution heralded the Commission's 1999 review of the sector. This review culminated with agreement in July 2000 on five directives and a new regulation that focused on electronic communications.

Commission statistics reveal that telecommunications services grew cheaper (on average some 30% cheaper) between 1996 and 2002. The Commission has also been keen to stress the high levels of new investment in this sector. In 2005 Europe's market for electronic communication services alone was deemed to be worth some €273,000m. Indeed, figures for 2005 reveal that European investment (€45,000m.) outstripped similar investments in both the USA and the Far East. It has also become increasingly clear that a pan-European tele-communications industry is emerging as companies seek economies of scale and adopt real European strategies. The Commission adopted the i2010 agenda—A European Information Society for Growth and Employment—in 2005 and laid out an ambitious scheme to create a single European Information Space in the field of electronic communications and media services by 2010. As an integral part of this drive, the Commission launched a review of the telecommunica-tions sector in 2006 to discuss, among other things, the realities of a wireless society and the need for better and simpler telecommunications regulations. In August 2010 the Commission launched a Digital Agenda for Europe, which highlighted the creation of a single market for content and telecommunications services as a vital tool to regain progress lost during the ongoing economic crisis. In particular, as part of the new agenda, the Commission aims to bring to near zero the difference between roaming and national tariffs by 2015. It has also set ambitious targets for fast and ultra-fast internet access in Europe.

TELEVISION: See **Media Policy**

TEMPUS stands for the Trans-European Mobility Scheme for University Studies, a European Communities programme introduced in 1990. Its objec-tives are to provide financial assistance for university education in, for the most part, the countries of the former **USSR** and the **Western Balkans**, and to facilitate courses taught in **Central and Eastern Europe** by European Union (EU) nationals, and student and staff exchanges with EU countries. Tempus has featured also as part of the programmes providing assistance for the economic and social reform of the countries of Central and Eastern Europe (see **Phare**) and the territories of the former USSR (see **Technical assistance to the Commonwealth of Independent States**—Tacis), where it operated as an EU aid scheme to assist the restructuring of higher education in these states and to facilitate their development towards a market economy. The Tempus pro-gramme, as well as being open to the eligible countries under the former **CARDS** and Tacis programmes, is also open to all EU member states, the EU **candidate countries**, and Australia, Canada, **Iceland**, **Japan**, **Liechtenstein**, New Zealand, **Norway**, **Switzerland** and the **USA**. Countries outside the

EU are able to participate only through co-financing projects. From 1990 to 1999 Tempus/**Phare** actions received €720.9m., and from 1993 to 1999 Tempus/Tacis actions amounted to approximately €130.2m. The third phase of Tempus expired on 31 December 2006; the programme was extended over the period 2007–13 under the name Tempus IV, financed partly under the European Neighbourhood and Partnership Instrument (ENPI). Tempus, which, in its current fourth phase, has an annual budget of some €50m., facilitates joint European projects in higher education that support joint teaching actions, the development of new courses, the promotion of links between universities and the wider community, and increasing the mobility of teachers and students. Some 120,000 teachers and 35,000 students from over 2,600 institutions states have directly benefited from the Tempus programme.

The **TEN**, or the Europe of the Ten, are terms sometimes used to describe the membership of the European Communities (EC) between January 1981, when Greece became the 10th member state, and January 1986, when EC membership rose to **Twelve**.

TENDERS ELECTRONIC DAILY (TED) is an electronic information service detailing those **public procurement** contracts awarded by national and local authorities where bidding for the contract is open to any supplier within the European Union. It is operated by the **Publications Office of the European Union**.

TENS: See **Trans-European Networks**

TESM: See **Treaty establishing the European Stability Mechanism**

TEU: See **Treaty on European Union**

TEXTILES: See **Multifibre Arrangement**

TFEU: See **Treaty on the Functioning of the European Union**

MARGARET THATCHER (1925–), now Baroness Thatcher of Kesteven, was Prime Minister of the United Kingdom from 1979 to 1990. Throughout much of the 1980s she was the most forceful personality on the **European Council**, even though she often adopted an isolated position. Her first major argument with the European Communities (EC) concerned the size of the United Kingdom's contribution to the EC **budget** and the fact that the United Kingdom, one of the poorer member states, was the second largest net contributor to the budget. The issue appeared on every European Council agenda between 1979 and 1984, and was related to what she saw as the profligacy of the **common agricultural policy**. The issue was resolved at the 1984 **Fontainebleau summit** with the acceptance of an adjustment mechanism that gave the United Kingdom a rebate.

Thatcher supported many of the economic goals of the EC, including liberalization and the completion of the **internal market**. Her political vision, however, was one of willing and positive co-operation between sovereign states, and she resisted all demands for political, economic and monetary union. She was a strong critic of anything that would increase the powers of the **European Commission**, which she regarded as overly bureaucratic and unrepresentative. In 1988 she denounced it for attempting to construct what she described as an 'identikit European personality' and a 'European superstate exercising dominance from **Brussels**'. Her views brought her into constant conflict with both the Commission and the other 11 member states. After resigning from the premiership, she continued her criticism of the EC, particularly over the **Treaty on European Union** and **economic and monetary union**. In her 2002 book *Statecraft* Thatcher called for the United Kingdom's **withdrawal** from the European Union.

GASTON THORN (1928–2007), a former Prime Minister of Luxembourg, served as President of the **European Commission** from 1981 to 1985. Widely perceived as a less dynamic figure than his predecessor, **Roy Jenkins**, he failed to maintain the momentum of previous years, and his Commission struggled without much success to deal with the accumulation of unresolved issues facing the European Communities.

THRESHOLD PRICE is the name of the minimum price fixed for cereals, milk products and sugar within the **common agricultural policy**. Cheaper imports into the European Union (EU) are subject to a levy to raise their price to the level of the threshold price, which, unlike the **target price**, includes internal transportation costs from the port of entry into the EU.

TINDEMANS REPORT is the name of a document that originated at the 1974 **summit meeting** in Paris, where the heads of government commissioned Leo Tindemans, the Prime Minister of Belgium, to undertake a series of consultations in the national capitals examining what might be achievable by political co-operation. The Tindemans Report was published in 1976. It proposed a common foreign policy and defence collaboration, economic and monetary union, the development of regional and social policies, a common industrial policy and a strengthened **European Commission** elected by, and accountable to, a popularly elected European legislature. It also advanced the notion of a 'two-speed' Europe, suggesting that the goals of the European

Communities (EC) might be more easily achieved if all member states were not expected to proceed at the same rate in all policy areas. Despite remaining on the agenda of all its sessions until 1978, the Report was never discussed by the **European Council**. It did, however, serve as a basis for the several reviews of the EC that occurred in subsequent years.

A **TITLE** is a sub-division of a **Part** within a European Union treaty. Titles can in turn be divided into **Chapters**. In the **Treaty on European Union**, titles form the main sub-division of the treaty.

The **TOTAL ALLOWABLE CATCH** (TAC) is a central element of the **common fisheries policy**. It relates to the conservation and management of fish stocks. TACs are overall quotas, fixed annually by the **Council of the European Union**, for each species of fish that is thought to be threatened by overfishing. Within each overall quota for the European Union, each member state is allocated its own quota. The documentation of catches and other surveillance measures are the responsibility of the member states. The scheme is supervised by a team of inspectors who report directly to the **European Commission**, which has the authority to impose penalties for infringements of the TAC quotas.

TOURISM is a major industry in the European Union (EU) and an important growth area for **employment**. However, **European Commission** efforts to gain member state approval of a multi-annual programme for European tourism (Philoxenia) in 1996 failed. The major emphasis since has been focused on tourism within the context of employment. The **Treaty of Lisbon**, like the abandoned **Treaty establishing a Constitution for Europe**, does, however, envisage EU action complementing that of the member states in promoting the **competitiveness** of undertakings in the tourism sector.

TOURS DE TABLE refers to the procedure where each national delegation at a meeting of the **Council of the European Union** is allowed to make an opening statement on its views of a particular proposal or subject. In the enlarged European Union of 27 states, such interventions could be problematic in terms of time. For example, assuming each member state took five minutes to make its statement, this would mean that more than two hours would elapse before any discussions proper could commence.

TOWN TWINNING was launched by the **European Commission** in 1989. Through carefully targeted grants it seeks to foster and develop further existing links between the populations of the member states. It aims to raise awareness of other European cultures and to promote an understanding, through meetings of twinned towns and municipalities, of what European integration has achieved to date and what challenges remain. The Commission's work under this programme is divided into two areas. Under 'Town Twinning' the Commission promotes exchanges between towns across the European Union and projects that involve towns in current member states and in **applicant countries**. To this end, it supports financially exchanges between citizens and towns that are twinned, conferences and meetings on European subjects, and training seminars for organizers of town-twinning schemes. The second area deals with the so-called 'golden stars of town twinning', which is essentially an annual award presented to the towns that are judged to have done the most in forging closer links between their respective citizens.

TRADE and its development between the member states was the initial economic objective of the European Communities (EC). By 1968 internal **tariff** barriers had been removed by the **Six**, and new member states have been given a short transitional period in which to eliminate their tariffs. The process of free trade was not completed until the implementation of the **internal market**. The European Union (EU) has become the world's largest trader, accounting for some 20% of world trade. The EU has agreements of various kinds—**association agreements**, **free trade agreements** and **trade and co-operation agreements**—with over 120 countries, as well as some 30 multilateral arrangements.

TRADE AND CO-OPERATION AGREEMENTS take various forms and have been concluded with a variety of states, notably those in **Central and Eastern Europe** before the negotiation of **Europe agreements**. Such trade and co-operation agreements form part of the **common commercial policy** and normally involve preferential access to the European Union's **internal market** and the eventual establishment of an industrial free trade area. This is supplemented by co-operation in areas of mutual interest, often focused on facilitating trade and the economic development of the signatory state.

TRADEMARKS are important as indicators of the origin and quality of goods, but companies have had to make separate applications in each member state to secure protection for their trademarks. Since 1980 the **European Commission** has pursued a policy of **harmonization** that envisaged a common European Union trademark that would exist alongside the national ones. (See also **Community Patent Convention**; **Office for Harmonization in the Internal Market**.)

The **TRANSATLANTIC DECLARATION** is the name of a document signed in November 1990 by the European Communities (EC) and the **USA**. It was intended, given the common heritage and the close historical, political, cultural and economic links between Europe and the USA, to form the basis of greater collaboration and co-operation between the two. The Declaration affirmed their desire for a partnership with specific goals and aspirations. These included openly supporting democracy and the rule of law and advancing respect for **human rights** and individual liberties. The signatories of the declaration sought to safeguard peace and promote international stability; to pursue policies that were targeted at advancing economic growth (such as greater liberalization and **competition policy**) and maintaining low inflation; to promote market principles; to reject all manner of protectionism; and to provide adequate support, in co-operation with other states and organizations, for the emerging liberal democracies of **Central and Eastern Europe**. The Declaration envisaged close consultation between the EC and the US Government on issues of mutual concern and common interest. For example, emphasis was placed on the need to strengthen the multilateral trading system and its organizations, on promoting liberalization and on pursuing bilateral dialogue in order to reduce and eventually eliminate other non-tariff barriers that impeded trade. Also within the Declaration, attention was focused on the need to develop joint scientific research projects in areas such as high-energy physics, space policy and environmental protection, as well as on extending youth and student exchanges. To facilitate such co-operation and networking the Declaration set up a regular system of biannual summits and ministerial meetings. (See also **New Transatlantic Agenda**.)

TRANS-EUROPEAN MOBILITY SCHEME FOR UNIVERSITY STUDIES: See **Tempus**

TRANS-EUROPEAN NETWORKS or TENs is a concept introduced by the Treaty on European Union, which commits the European Union (EU) to developing such networks in energy, telecommunications and transport through the interconnection and opening-up of national networks. The assumption is that such networks will aid both the **internal market** and social and economic cohesion within the EU. The EU is expected to develop common projects and provide financial assistance through, for example, the Cohesion Fund, while member states are expected to co-ordinate national infrastructure projects that are likely to have a trans-European effect. The priority transport projects for development include high-speed rail links, such as the British Maritime and Cork–Dublin–Belfast–Larne rail links, a rail and road tunnel through the Brenner Pass in Italy and a motorway linking Lisbon and Valladolid (Spain). The TENs scheme has since been extended into Central and Eastern Europe, using financial assistance from the **Phare** programme; projects include a motorway link between Berlin and Kiev.

TRANSPARENCY is a term now used widely in the context of the need for more **openness** in and easier public access to the working of the institutions of the European Union (EU). It is hoped that increased transparency and openness will improve the **legitimacy** and **accountability** of the EU.

TRANSPORT POLICY was particularly slow to develop in the European Communities (EC), despite being identified as an objective by the **Treaty of Rome**. The vested interests of the member states in the domain of transport—for example, road haulage quotas and licences, customs documentation, **subsidies** for **railways** and **shipping**, and the protection of national airlines—meant that little progress was made towards a common transport policy until 1982. The catalyst was an action brought by the **European Parliament** in the **Court of Justice** against the Council of Ministers (see **Council of the European Union**) for failing to fulfil the requirements of the Treaty of Rome. The Court upheld the complaint, arguing that the Council had an obligatory duty to liberalize international transport within the EC and to make it open to carriers of all member states, and recommended the establishment of a common transport policy. The Court ruling enabled the **European Commission** to act with more vigour. In 1983 the Commission formulated a list of policy objectives: a more effective integration of national transport policies; greater productivity and efficiency through reducing the number of bureaucratic constraints and the amount of documentation; greater competition within and between different modes of transport; and **harmonization** of rules relating to working conditions, **health and safety**, environmental protection and technical standards. However, because of the different problems and requirements of the various transport sectors, the Commission found it difficult to develop a common transport policy. Instead, it has sought common rules and harmonization within each major sector: **air transport**, **inland waterways**, **railways**, **road transport** and **shipping**. Common to all sectors is a programme of support for infrastructural developments and modernization. (See also *cabotage*; **Trans-European Networks**.)

The **TREATY ESTABLISHING A CONSTITUTION FOR EUROPE** was agreed in June 2004 and, had it been ratified, would have replaced the **Treaty of Rome** and the **Treaty on European Union** (TEU) as the formal legal basis of the European Union (EU). Often referred to as a **Constitutional Treaty** or the **European Constitution**, the treaty emerged out of the deliberations of the **European Convention** that adopted the **draft Treaty establishing a Constitution for Europe** and the negotiations that took place in the subsequent **intergovernmental conference** (IGC).

The Treaty establishing a Constitution for Europe envisaged a range of reforms to the EU and its institutions. These included abolishing the existing **pillar** structure and granting the EU **legal personality**. New posts of **Union Minister for Foreign Affairs** and **President of the European Council** were planned, as were a new system of **qualified majority voting** (QMV) and a revised range of **legal instruments**. **Ratification** of the treaty would also have resulted in the **Charter of Fundamental Rights** being made legally binding, and in increased use of QMV, the extension and a renaming of the **co-decision procedure** as the '**ordinary legislative procedure**', an eventual reduction in the size of the **European Commission** and changes in the rotation of the **Council presidency**. The rules governing use of **enhanced co-operation** would also have been eased and a **European Public Prosecutor's Office** provided for and, for the first time, a formal mechanism for **withdrawal** from the EU would have existed.

Unlike the **Single European Act** or the **Treaty on European Union**, no significant expansion of the EU's policy competences would have occurred with the Treaty establishing a Constitution for Europe. All the same, the list of areas in which the EU enjoys a formal **competence** to act would have been increased, mainly in recognition of existing practice. Such areas include administrative co-operation, energy, **humanitarian assistance**, intellectual property, **public health**, **space**, **sport**, and **tourism**. One new area of competence was **civil protection**. In addition, the Treaty establishing a Constitution for Europe envisaged reforms to the **common foreign and security policy**, the **European security and defence policy**, EU activities regarding **police and judicial co-operation in criminal matters** and the **area of freedom, security and justice**.

The entry into force of the Treaty establishing a Constitution for Europe was thrown into question in early summer 2005 when electorates in France and the Netherlands voted against its ratification. For some, such a dual rejection should have seen the immediate abandonment of the ratification process. Instead, it was agreed that member states could choose for themselves whether they wished to pause for 'reflection' as the **European Council** in June 2005 agreed or push ahead. Cyprus, Luxembourg, Malta and later Belgium, Estonia and Finland took the latter route, while others put on hold their ratification processes, pending clarification from the French and Dutch on how they intended to proceed. For states outside the EU seeking membership, the **ratification crisis** was worrying since it threatened to postpone or derail further **enlargement**. For others, there were concerns that it would lead to a period of introspection on the part of the EU as well as political weakness—two situations that the treaty had been designed to avoid. There were also concerns that the enlarged EU would not be able to function effectively without the reforms contained in the document. This led to suggestions that alternative mechanisms might be sought to allow key elements to enter into force. Any significant progress, it was widely held, would have to await the outcome of elections in France and the Netherlands in 2007. Following these, in June 2007 the European Council agreed a mandate for a new IGC that would subsequently adopt the **Treaty of Lisbon** incorporating key elements of the Treaty establishing a Constitution for Europe.

TREATY ESTABLISHING THE EUROPEAN ATOMIC ENERGY COMMUNITY: See **Treaty of Rome**; **European Atomic Energy Community**

TREATY ESTABLISHING THE EUROPEAN COAL AND STEEL COMMUNITY: See **Treaty of Paris**

TREATY ESTABLISHING THE EUROPEAN COMMUNITY: See **Treaty of Rome**

TREATY ESTABLISHING THE EUROPEAN ECONOMIC COMMUNITY: See **Treaty of Rome**

The **TREATY ESTABLISHING THE EUROPEAN STABILITY MECHANISM (TESM)** was signed by the 17 members of the **eurozone** on 11 July 2011 as part of their efforts to resolve the financial crisis in the euro area. With additional decisions to strengthen the ESM being adopted in July and December 2011, the treaty was subsequently revised and a new version signed on 2 February 2012. With the crisis in the euro area deepening, swift ratification was demanded. However, the scheduled date of 1 July 2012 for the entry into force of the treaty was not met, owing to delays in ratification in **Germany** and **Italy**.

A **TREATY OF ACCESSION** contains the legal instruments governing the accession of a state to the European Union (EU). Accession treaties have to be ratified by all existing member states as well as the acceding state or states. **Ratification** normally involves a referendum in the acceding country. Since the **Single European Act**, the approval of the **European Parliament** via the **consent procedure** has also been necessary. The most significant accession treaty of the past decade was signed in Athens, Greece, on 16 April 2003 between the EU's member states and 10 applicant states, mainly from **Central and Eastern Europe**: Cyprus, the Czech Republic, Estonia, Hungary, Latvia, Lithuania, Malta, Poland, Slovakia and Slovenia. With the exception of Cyprus, each of the applicant states held a referendum during 2003 on whether the country should join the EU. In each case, a majority of those voting voted in favour of membership. Successful ratification of the Accession Treaty in the member states ensured that **enlargement** took place, as planned, on 1 May 2004. An Accession Treaty was signed in Luxembourg on 25 April 2005, which governed the accession of Bulgaria and Romania to the EU. Neither country held a referendum to ratify the Accession Treaty. Its ratification was successfully completed in December 2006, allowing the two countries to accede to the EU on 1 January 2007. The most recent Accession Treaty was signed with Croatia on 9 December 2011 and membership was approved by a referendum held in Croatia on 22 January 2012. Croatia's accession to the EU was due to take place on 1 July 2013.

The **TREATY OF AMSTERDAM** was agreed in June 1997 by the **Fifteen** heads of state and government of the European Union (EU). The Treaty was signed in October 1997 and, following **ratification** by the member states, came into force on 1 May 1999. The measures it introduced were discussed during the 1996 **intergovernmental conference** (IGC) review of the **Treaty on European Union** (TEU), which sought to address changing circumstances in **Central and Eastern Europe** and the new arrangements that would be required on **enlargement** of the EU. The IGC also highlighted measures introduced by the TEU that had not proved effective, particularly in relation to closing the gap between national governments and the people, regarding the way the EU was developing (see **democratic deficit**). The new Treaty therefore amended and updated the TEU. It also amended the **founding treaties**, removed many obsolete provisions and renumbered the **articles** of these treaties.

High priority was given in the Treaty of Amsterdam to measures that combat high unemployment, extend citizens' rights and improve democratic **accountability** and participation in the institutions of the EU. In future, governments were to co-ordinate their employment strategies and a new **Employment Committee** was to be established to oversee the co-ordination process. Greater efforts were to be encouraged in the battle against **discrimination** on grounds of sex, race, ethnic origin, religion or belief, age, disability or sexual orientation. Member states were also required to address gender inequality, and to protect citizens against misuse of data stored in EU **institutions**. New and continued efforts in the fields of public health, the environment and sustainable development, and consumer protection were also to be encouraged. The **protocol** on social policy (see **Charter of Fundamental Social Rights of Workers**) was incorporated into the revised **Treaty of Rome**, following the decision of the British Labour Government to sign the Charter in 1997.

The **pillar**-based system brought in by the TEU was kept, although much of the province of the **justice and home affairs** pillar was transferred to the Treaty of Rome, thereby coming under the first, or Community pillar, leaving the third pillar to deal primarily with **police and judicial co-operation in criminal matters**.

In an attempt to improve public accountability, the treaty introduced measures to ensure greater **openness** and **transparency** by improving public access to documents originating from the institutions of the European Communities and to the voting results of legislative **decisions** taken by the **Council of the European Union**. Moreover, in an attempt to counter criticisms that a **democratic deficit** existed within EU institutions, members of **national parliaments** were to become more involved in the **decision-making** processes of the EU through **COSAC** (the Conference of European

Affairs Committees). This group was to be encouraged to voice its opinions in specific policy areas such as fundamental rights and freedoms, justice and security, and **subsidiarity**. National parliaments were also to be given more time to debate EU issues, as the treaty provided for a six-week interval between the tabling of legislative proposals and their placement on the Council agenda, thereby improving democratic participation.

Institutional reforms also featured in the treaty (see **Council of the European Union**; **European Commission**; **European Parliament**—EP), not only to improve democracy but for practical reasons as the EU prepared for expansion. The number of **Members of the European Parliament** (MEPs) elected to the EP was to be limited to 700, and decision-making procedures were simplified. **Qualified majority voting** was extended, although **unanimity** was required for constitutional matters and certain policy areas, such as **taxation**. The authority of the Commission's President was also enhanced prior to a review of that institution before enlargement.

Moreover, membership of the EU was made more explicitly conditional. This means that successful applicants have to agree to abide by the principles of **human rights** and fundamental freedoms, liberty and democracy in relation to their citizens, as set down by the EU, or face suspension of certain membership rights, including the right to vote.

The Treaty also focused on creating a safer and stronger Europe by introducing new internal security measures, as well as measures that were intended to promote greater co-operation in foreign policy. A timetable was set within which a series of common **immigration** and **asylum** rules was to be established. Improved co-operation between national police forces and the legal systems of the member states was also required, as was incorporation of the **Schengen Agreement** *acquis* into the treaties (although the United Kingdom and Ireland were allowed an **opt-out**). Strict anti-**fraud** measures were to be introduced. The position of the **Court of Auditors** was to be enhanced to assist in fraud prevention, and greater co-operation between customs authorities in the member states was to be developed. A stronger Europe in the world was also considered to be a priority, given the EU's failure to agree on a united policy during the 1990–91 hostilities in the Gulf, or in relation to the break-up of, and civil war in, the former **Yugoslavia**. The Secretary-General of the Council was simultaneously to hold the newly created post of **High Representative for the Common Foreign and Security Policy**. A new unit charged with early warning, planning and analysis in EU foreign affairs was also to be created. Closer co-operation between the EU and **Western European Union** (WEU) was called for, and the possibility of the integration of WEU into the EU was raised, but the **North Atlantic Treaty Organization** (NATO) was still seen by the EU to be the main security organization for Europe.

Despite its innovations and reforms, the treaty failed to introduce the institutional reforms necessary to prepare the EU for enlargement. Hence, even before it entered into force on 1 May 1999, preparations were being made for a further IGC that would lead to the **Treaty of Nice** in 2001.

The **TREATY OF BRUSSELS** was signed in March 1948 by the Governments of the United Kingdom, France and the **Benelux** countries. It was modelled on the 1947 **Treaty of Dunkirk** and, as such, was an agreement on mutual military assistance against military attack from either Germany or, more likely, the **USSR**. It also sought to foster greater economic, social and cultural issues between the five states. The Treaty was a precursor to the **North Atlantic Treaty Organization** (NATO) in 1949 and **Western European Union** in 1954. The Treaty was largely the creation of Ernest Bevin, the United Kingdom's Foreign Secretary. This initiative was endorsed warmly by the **USA** and by many Europeans who hoped that it promised greater British involvement in the construction of a new European order. However, the treaty was rendered almost meaningless with the creation of NATO under US hegemony in 1949.

TREATY OF DUNKIRK was the name of a document signed in 1947 by France and the United Kingdom. Although the pact called for bilateral economic assistance and co-operation, its justification was primarily military: a guarantee of mutual aid in the event of any future German aggression. It was superseded by the **Treaty of Brussels** in 1948.

TREATY OF FRIENDSHIP is the name of the pact, also known as the Elysée Treaty, signed by France and the Federal Republic of Germany (West Germany) on 22 January 1963. It was the only tangible result of the **Fouchet Plan** for greater political co-operation and integration, and provided for institutional co-operation between the two states in the four policy areas of defence, foreign affairs, education and culture. Strongly criticized at the time by the other members of the European Communities (EC), it became the basis of a considerable degree of liaison and regularized co-operation between the two states, and of a powerful Franco-German axis within the EC.

The **TREATY OF LISBON**, originally named the **Reform Treaty**, was agreed in October 2007 and signed on 13 December 2007. It was drawn up in an **intergovernmental conference** launched by the **European Council** in June 2007 and, having been ratified by all 27 member states, introduced a range of essentially institutional and political reforms originally contained in the abandoned **Treaty establishing a Constitution for Europe**. The Treaty of Lisbon was agreed with a view 'to enhancing the efficiency and democratic legitimacy' of the EU and 'to improving the coherence of its action'. To these ends, it provided for increased use of **qualified majority voting** (QMV), the eventual replacement of QMV with a **double majority voting** system, the extension and a renaming of the **co-decision procedure** as the '**ordinary legislative**

procedure', an eventual reduction in the size of the **European Commission** and changes in the rotation of the **Council presidency**. It also eased the rules governing use of **enhanced co-operation**. In terms of the coherence of what the EU does, particularly externally, the Treaty of Lisbon introduced a number of reforms to the **common foreign and security policy** and was more explicit about what the EU envisages as the form and purpose of its **European security and defence policy**. It also developed the position of the **High Representative for the Common Foreign and Security Policy**, now retitled **High Representative of the Union for Foreign Affairs and Security Policy**, created the post of **President of the European Council**, and allowed for **permanent structured co-operation** on military matters.

Drawing also on what was envisaged in the Treaty establishing a Constitution for Europe, the Treaty of Lisbon abolished the EU's existing **pillar** structure, granted the EU **legal personality**, made the **Charter of Fundamental Rights** legally binding, provided for the establishment of a **European Public Prosecutor's Office** and, for the first time, established a formal mechanism for **withdrawal** from the EU. There was also clarification of the EU's formal **competence** and formal legal bases in a number of areas of existing practice, notably administrative co-operation, energy, **humanitarian assistance**, intellectual property, public health, **space**, **sport**, and **tourism**. One new area of competence was **civil protection**. EU activities regarding **police and judicial co-operation in criminal matters** and the **area of freedom, security and justice** also saw some reforms.

With the exception of Ireland, all member states were scheduled to pursue **ratification** using purely parliamentary means. By the end of May 2008, the parliaments of 16 member states had endorsed the treaty. The remaining member states were due to complete ratification by the end of the year, thereby allowing the treaty to enter into force on 1 January 2009. In the first half of June 2008 a further three parliaments—those of Estonia, Finland and Greece—ratified the treaty before attention switched on 12 June to Ireland, the only member state to hold a referendum. The outcome was a seemingly decisive victory for opponents of the treaty. However, the Irish came under considerable pressure to hold a second vote. Agreement to do so came following a commitment from the European Council to agree various clarifications and guarantees concerning the impact of the treaty on Irish neutrality, taxation powers, the right to life, family and education, and workers' rights. A second referendum was held in October 2009, at which voters endorsed the treaty by a two-thirds' majority. Following some last-minute delays in the Czech Republic, ratification was completed in time for the Treaty of Lisbon to enter into force on 1 December 2009.

TREATY OF LUXEMBOURG is the name of a document signed by the member states in April 1970. An amendment to the **Treaty of Rome**, it incorporated the new budgetary system of **own resources** into the structure of the European Communities.

The **TREATY OF NICE** was agreed in December 2000 and signed in February 2001. **Ratification** took longer than expected after the process was thrown into doubt when, in June 2001, the Irish people rejected the treaty in a referendum. As had been the case following the **ratification crisis** in 1992, when the Danish people rejected the **Treaty on European Union** (TEU), a second referendum was scheduled. This took place in October 2002 and on this occasion the treaty was endorsed by 63% of those who voted. The Treaty was then successfully channelled through both Irish houses of parliament before finally coming into force on 1 February 2003.

The essential purpose of the treaty was explained in its preamble: to prepare the European Union (EU) for **enlargement**. It did this by introducing a series of staged reforms to the **institutions**, notably by: reducing the size of the **European Commission** to a maximum of one national from each member state; re-weighting votes within the **Council of the European Union**, essentially to the advantage of the larger member states; and re-allocating seats in the **European Parliament** (EP). Moreover, Council votes and EP seats were provisionally allocated to the **candidate countries** (albeit with the exception of **Turkey**), as were seats on the **Committee of the Regions** and the **Economic and Social Committee**. The **Court of Justice** and **Court of First Instance** were also to undergo some reform: innovations included the creation of **Grand Chambers** and **Judicial Panels** in an attempt to enable the courts to deal with an already large case-load. The existence and activities of **Eurojust**, established to enable member states to co-operate in the area of cross-border crime, were also formally recognized.

Beyond institutional reform, the Treaty of Nice introduced changes to the **common foreign and security policy** (CFSP), allowing for **enhanced co-operation** and essentially excising from the TEU references to **Western European Union**, a move that coincided with the establishment of the CFSP. More generally, enhanced co-operation was to be facilitated by reducing the number of member states needed to begin a project. Likewise, **decision-making** generally was also facilitated through the extension of **qualified majority voting** to more than 40 provisions, although **unanimity** was still retained for the most sensitive areas (e.g. tax **harmonization**).

Unlike earlier treaties such as the **Single European Act** and the **Treaty of Amsterdam**, the Treaty of Nice did little in the way of increasing the competences of the EU. Little was included beyond a slight extension of the treaty-making powers of the EU to include services and the insertion into the **Treaty of Rome** of a new **title** on economic, financial and technical co-operation with third countries. However, when adopting the treaty, the member states set in motion a process that could lead to significant increases in the activities of the EU. Equally, it could lead to limits being placed on them. The process in question was the debate on the future of Europe, which was later expanded in the **Laeken Declaration** and provided with a forum for expression in the **European Convention** launched in February 2002. Its conclusions informed a further **intergovernmental conference** that began work in October 2003.

TREATY OF PARIS is the commonly used name of the document, signed on 18 April 1951 and designated to remain in force for 50 years, which established the **European Coal and Steel Community**. This **founding treaty** committed the signatories to contribute to economic expansion through 'the development of employment and the improvement of the standard of living in the participating countries through the institution, in harmony with the general economy of the member states, of a common market'. Subsequent entrants to the European Communities and European Union had to accept the terms and obligations of the treaty, although after 2002 new members were no longer required to, as the Treaty of Paris expired in July 2002.

TREATY OF PRÜM: See **Prüm Convention**

TREATY OF ROME is the commonly used name of the document that established the **European Economic Community** (EEC). Signed on 25 March 1957, it is the most important of the **founding treaties** of the European Communities. It was concluded for an unlimited period of time and committed the signatories, 'by establishing a **common market** and progressively approximating the economic policies of member states, to promote throughout the Community a harmonious development of economic activities, a continuous and balanced expansion, an increase in stability, an accelerated raising of the standard of living, and closer relations between the States belonging to it'. The greater part of the treaty lists the actions and common policies to which the member states committed themselves, and the institutions of the new body. The Treaty has been amended on several occasions since 1957, most significantly by the **Single European Act**, the **Treaty on European Union**, the **Treaty of Amsterdam** (which renumbered the treaty's **articles**) and the **Treaty of Nice**. With the entry into force of the **Treaty of Lisbon**, the treaty was further amended and renamed the **Treaty on the Functioning of the European Union**. The **European Atomic Energy Community** was established by a separate document, also often referred to as the Treaty of Rome, which was signed at the same time. With the exception of its institutional provisions, this largely remains unamended, although there is currently support from some member states for a substantial revision.

TREATY OF ROME (EURATOM): See **European Atomic Energy Community**; **Treaty of Rome**

TREATY OF WESTMINSTER: See **Council of Europe**

The **TREATY ON EUROPEAN UNION** (TEU) is one of the main **European treaties**. Agreed at the **Maastricht summit** of the **European Council** in December 1991 and later signed by representatives of the member states of the European Communities (EC) on 7 February 1992, it formally established the European Union (EU), basing it on three **pillars**: the existing EC as the first pillar and two new pillars of intergovernmental co-operation covering a **common foreign and security policy** (CFSP) and **justice and home affairs**. In doing so, the TEU also brought about a significant revision of the **Treaty of Rome**, thereby increasing the powers of the EC. The member states, with the exception of the United Kingdom, agreed to further integration in social affairs in the form of a Social Chapter (see **Charter of Fundamental Social Rights of Workers**). Substantial institutional reforms to the EC were also introduced, as was the notion of EU **citizenship**. More significantly, the TEU laid down a detailed timetable and established **convergence criteria** for **economic and monetary union** (EMU), which was to be established by 1999 at the latest. Not all member states wished to be tied to the goal of EMU, however. Hence special **opt-outs** were agreed for Denmark and the United Kingdom, the latter also gaining an opt-out from the Social Chapter. The EMU opt-out did not assuage the concerns of the Danish people, however, who rejected the TEU in a referendum in June 1992. This led to a **ratification crisis** and the granting of further concessions to Denmark. In May 1993, the Danish people approved the TEU and it entered into force on 1 November 1993.

The Treaty was formally reviewed by an **intergovernmental conference** in 1996. The conference debated the measures required to address the shortfalls of the TEU, with the place of the EU in the world and its position vis-à-vis **enlargement** featuring prominently in debates. Measures required to move forward to a 'People's Europe' were also discussed and introduced via the **Treaty of Amsterdam**, which was signed in October 1997. Amendments to the TEU made in the Treaty of Amsterdam were soon to be followed by further revision via the **Treaty of Nice**. Had the **Treaty establishing a Constitution for Europe** been ratified, it would have replaced the TEU. Its replacement, the **Treaty of Lisbon**, further amended—and renumbered—the TEU's provisions.

TREATY ON STABILITY, CO-ORDINATION AND GOVERNANCE IN THE ECONOMIC AND MONETARY UNION: See **Fiscal Compact Treaty**

The **TREATY ON THE FUNCTIONING OF THE EUROPEAN UNION** (TFEU) is the new name of the **Treaty establishing the European Community**—the Treaty of Rome—following the entry into force of the

Treaty of Lisbon in December 2009. With this name change, all references to the **European Community** have been replaced with 'European Union' and the European Community has ceased to exist.

TREVI stands for Terrorisme, Radicalisme, Extrémisme, Violence Internationale. It was established in 1975 as a forum for intergovernmental co-operation by the member states on matters relating to internal security, organized crime, terrorism and drugs-trafficking. It also worked for the co-ordination of **asylum policy** and **immigration policy**. Its twice-yearly meetings of justice and home affairs ministers were held in secret. A more structured approach towards these policy areas was accepted as a consequence of the decision to establish an **internal market**, and in the late 1980s several more specialized subgroups were established within the **TREVI** framework. It formed the basis of the more formal **justice and home affairs pillar** of the European Union that was established by the **Treaty on European Union**.

JEAN-CLAUDE TRICHET (1942–) was the second President of the **European Central Bank** between July 2003 and October 2011. After obtaining a degree in economics from the University of Paris, Trichet studied at the prestigious Ecole Nationale d'Administration before pursuing a career in the French civil service, where he spent most of his time in the Treasury. In 1987 he became director of the Treasury Department and an alternate governor of the International Monetary Fund as well as an alternate governor of the World Bank. In 1993 he started his first term as Governor of the Bank of France and also in that year became a Governor of the World Bank. The choice of Trichet as ECB President was made in 1998, as part of a Franco-German power-sharing deal. During his eight-year tenure, Trichet's focus on controlling inflation gave rise to both praise and criticism, particularly given the onset of the European sovereign debt crisis in 2010–11, with some observers suggesting that his focus on inflation detracted attention from the accumulation of excessive credit. He was succeeded by **Mario Draghi** in November 2011.

TROIKA is a term that refers to the grouping that, prior to the **Treaty of Lisbon**, represented the European Union (EU) internationally as part of the **common foreign and security policy** (CFSP) and, previously, **European political co-operation**. Originally it comprised the member state occupying the presidency of the **Council of the European Union**, its immediate predecessor and its scheduled successor. The idea was that such a combination would achieve consistency in the activities and efforts of the EU and greater success in the attainment of their aims. Following the **Treaty of Amsterdam** the member state holding the presidency of the Council was accompanied by the **High Representative for the Common Foreign and Security Policy** and the member of the **European Commission** responsible for external relations. With the coming into force of the Treaty of Lisbon, representation now falls to the **High Representative of the Union for Foreign Affairs and Security Policy**.

TUNISIA: See **Maghreb States**

TURKEY, recognized by the European Communities (EC) as a European state, submitted an application for association in July 1959. Negotiations began in 1962 and concluded with an **association agreement** in 1963. This specified a transitional period of 22 years, commencing in 1970, that was designed to lead to a **customs union**. Further developments were delayed by European opposition to the Turkish military coup of September 1980. Talks were resumed in 1983, after the re-establishment of civilian government, and in 1987 Turkey submitted an application for full membership. The application did not progress within the European Union (EU) because of fears over Turkey's weak economy, doubts about its suitability in terms of democracy and **human rights**, and concern over the continuing partition of Cyprus. However, in March 1995 an agreement on a customs union was signed; it came into force in December 1995, following **ratification** by the **European Parliament**. In spite of persisting doubts over Turkey's progress in the economic, political and human rights fields and over the Cyprus issue, Turkey's eligibility for accession to the EU was confirmed in 1997: the country would be judged according to the same criteria as the other **applicant countries**. As a result, a number of measures were proposed by the **European Commission** in 1997 to assist the country in preparing for accession by extending its relations with the EU beyond the customs union. Turkey was not, however, invited to participate in the accession process launched in 1998.

This led to a further souring of relations before the **European Council** at Helsinki in December 1999 decided to recognize Turkey, alongside the applicant countries from **Central and Eastern Europe**, as a **candidate state**. At the same time, Turkey was invited to become part of the accession process. However, **accession negotiations** did not begin. Instead, further progress with economic and political reforms was deemed necessary before they could be opened. In 2002 the **European Council** agreed to address the question of whether to open accession negotiations in December 2004. Formal negotiations commenced on 3 October 2005, but progress proved to be slow. This was due in part to the state of Turkish preparedness, but reformist governments have made considerable progress in meeting EU benchmarks for the opening of negotiating chapters. However, by the end of 2007 only six chapters had been opened. Two further chapters were scheduled to be opened in June 2008. Although officially, in the eyes of the EU, progress was dependent on domestic reforms being undertaken in Turkey, the slow progress owed as much to the EU and the reluctance of some of its members to push forward towards Turkish accession. Acting as notable brakes were Cyprus and France, but the

Netherlands, Austria and Germany were also dragging their feet. For the most part, the lack of enthusiasm coincided with domestic popular opposition to or scepticism about Turkish accession. In some cases, national leaders were personally opposed to Turkish accession. Hence some, notably **Angela Merkel** and **Nicolas Sarkozy**, preferred to talk of Turkey being granted a 'privileged partnership' instead of membership. Little of this provided much encouragement to Turkey, even if some EU member states were vocal in their support of Turkey becoming an EU member.

Events since negotiations were launched clearly indicate that the road to Turkish membership of the EU will remain a bumpy one. In some member states there is evident popular disquiet at the prospect of Turkish membership. In the case of France, this has led to a constitutional change, subjecting future EU enlargements to a referendum. A number of other member states have indicated that they too might put the question to the people. Given such a context and Cyprus' determination to see Turkey fulfil its obligations towards the EU and open up access to its ports to Cypriot vessels, the accession negotiations have progressed only very slowly. To many, even the Commission's 2005 estimate that Turkey was unlikely to join the EU before 2014 seemed hopelessly optimistic. As of 1 July 2012, only 13 of the 35 negotiating chapters had been opened and only one had been closed. The snail-like progress with negotiations has led to consternation in Turkey and has undoubtedly contributed to a decline in domestic support for EU membership. Concerns exist that Turkey may ultimately abandon its membership ambitions, particularly as it becomes more successful in economic terms.

TV WITHOUT FRONTIERS: See **Cultural Policy**; **Media Policy**

TWELVE, or the Europe of the Twelve, are terms sometimes used to describe the membership of the European Communities after 1986, when the accession of Portugal and Spain increased the number of member states from **Ten** to Twelve, and before 1995, when the accession of Austria, Finland and Sweden made the number **Fifteen**.

TWENTY-FIVE (EU25), or Europe of the Twenty-Five, is a term used to describe the membership of the European Union after May 2004, when Cyprus, the Czech Republic, Estonia, Hungary, Latvia, Lithuania, Malta, Poland, Slovakia and Slovenia joined the existing **Fifteen** member states.

TWENTY-SEVEN (EU27), or Europe of the Twenty-Seven, is a term sometimes used to describe the membership of the European Union from 2007, when Bulgaria and Romania joined the **Twenty-Five** existing member states.

TWINNING is a programme directed at assisting the process of administrative reform in **candidate countries** in **Central and Eastern Europe**. The focus of the project is the development of the administrative capacity in these countries to implement effectively the *acquis communautaire*.

TWO-SPEED EUROPE is a more limited variant of **multi-speed Europe**.

U

UEN: See **Union for Europe of the Nations Group**

UK: See **United Kingdom**

UK CORRECTION: See **United Kingdom Budget Rebate**

UKRAINE gained its independence from the **USSR** in 1991. It concluded a **partnership and co-operation agreement** (PCA) with the European Union (EU), which entered into force in 1998. It is also a recipient of financial assistance from the EU under the **Technical assistance to the Commonwealth of Independent States** programme (now the **European neighbourhood policy**—ENP), and in 1999 was the focus of an EU **common strategy**. This is designed to support the democratic and economic transition process in Ukraine; to ensure co-operation in meeting common challenges in the areas of stability and security in Europe, the environment, energy and nuclear safety; to assist Ukraine's integration into the European and world economies; and to enhance co-operation in the field of **justice and home affairs**. To date, Ukraine's relations with the EU have not developed much beyond the PCA, despite the wishes of successive Ukrainian governments for a more advanced form of relationship. However, with **enlargement** in 2004 meaning that Ukraine now shares a border with the EU, further developments in relations have taken place primarily within the framework of the ENP. Westward-looking governments in Ukraine, under Viktor Yushchenko's (2005–10) presidency, expressed strong interest in EU membership sometime in the future. For the moment, however, the focus is on implementing the ENP Action Plan agreed in 2005 and completing negotiations on an **association agreement** to replace the PCA (which expired in 2008). The new agreement will involve more intense political dialogue, a **deep and comprehensive free trade area** and strengthened co-operation. Negotiations began in March 2007 and were eventually closed at the end of 2011 (without any agreement being signed). In the mean time, in May 2009 Ukraine became part of the EU's **Eastern partnership**. Elections in early 2010 saw the defeat of Yushchenko, his replacement by Viktor Yanukovych and the start of a new period of less ambitious engagement with the EU. In fact, relations soon deteriorated as the EU strongly criticized the Ukranian Government for its politicization of the country's judicial system. Particular criticism was reserved for the treatment of the imprisoned former Prime Minister, Yuliya Tymoshenko. The signing of the association agreement was consequently postponed.

UNANIMITY applies to certain types of decision taken by the **Council of the European Union**. Its use is laid down in the **founding treaties**. Policies that are subject to unanimity require the agreement of all member states before a proposal can be adopted. For much of the early history of the European Communities (EC), especially following the **Luxembourg Compromise**, unanimity was essential. Since the **Single European Act**, there has been a general shift away from unanimity towards greater use of **decisions** being taken under **qualified majority voting** (QMV). The **Treaty on European Union**, the **Treaty of Amsterdam** and the **Treaty of Nice** extended the use of QMV, and currently far fewer decisions are subject to unanimous agreement in the Council. This is particularly the case following the entry into force of the **Treaty of Lisbon**. For what were previously **pillar** I and pillar III matters— the pillars have since been abandoned—QMV became the general rule. By contrast, decisions relating to the **common foreign and security policy** are still generally subject to unanimity. However, even with QMV, the Council prefers to reach either unanimous agreement or consensus wherever possible.

UNICE: See **BUSINESSEUROPE**

UNIFORM ELECTORAL PROCEDURE relates to the method of elections to the **European Parliament** (EP). The idea that some form of uniform electoral procedure based on direct universal suffrage should be used across all member states dates back to the **Treaty of Paris** and can be found also in Article 190 of the **Treaty of Rome** (now Article 223 of the **Treaty on the Functioning of the European Union**). However, despite treaty commitments there has been little progress towards any uniform procedure. Elections in the member states and rules pertaining to them are decided at the national level. Elections to the EP first occurred in June 1979 but the procedures varied from state to state. Most countries opted for some form of proportional representation, while the United Kingdom maintained its 'first past the post' system that was used in elections to Parliament. The United Kingdom (with the exception of Northern Ireland, which was deemed a three-member constituency where the **Members of the European Parliament** (MEPs) are elected under the single transferable vote procedure) maintained this system until the Labour Government introduced legislation to use proportional representation in the European elections of June 1999. Currently there is no single electoral procedure throughout the member states, and voting continues to take place on different days (e.g. Thursday in the United Kingdom, Sunday in France and Germany and both Sunday and Monday in Italy).

The **UNION FOR EUROPE OF THE NATIONS GROUP** (UEN/UPE) is a former **party group** of the **European Parliament** (EP). It was formed in 1999 as a conservative force that was largely sceptical towards the issue of any deeper European integration, although some of its member parties, such as the Irish Fianna Fail, supported the Constitution for Europe. In stark contrast to the other EP groups, the UEN was a noticeably less cohesive force, reflecting the wide and often divergent views of its members. It grew gradually in membership following its establishment. In 2002 UEN had 21 members in the EP. After the 2004 elections it increased its representation in the parliament by securing 27 deputies, and its membership climbed to 35 immediately after the 2009 EP elections. However, the lack of internal cohesion not only ensured a lack of common purpose, but also created tensions. The group dissolved following the 2009 EP elections, as the representatives from the Polish Law and Conservative Party forged a new alliance (the **European Conservatives and Reformists Group**) with **David Cameron**'s British Conservatives, while Fianna Fail had already left the group's ranks to join the **Alliance of Liberals and Democrats for Europe** (ALDE) (in April 2009).

The **UNION FOR THE MEDITERRANEAN** is a relatively recent addition to the **Barcelona process**, hence its official title, Barcelona Process: Union for the Mediterranean. It was launched in July 2008 and follows from ideas promoted by **Nicolas Sarkozy**, the French President. Initially limited to littoral states of the Mediterranean, it now comprises all European Union (EU) member states plus **Albania**, Algeria, **Bosnia and Herzegovina**, **Croatia**, Egypt, Israel, Jordan, Lebanon, Libya (observer status only), Mauritania, Monaco, **Montenegro**, **Morocco**, the Palestinian Autonomous Areas, Syria, Tunisia and **Turkey**. In essence, the Union for the Mediterranean is a relaunch of the **Euro-Mediterranean partnership**, albeit with some additional elements, notably a dedicated Secretariat responsible for promoting co-operation projects in six designated areas: de-pollution of the Mediterranean Sea; the establishment of maritime and land highways; joint civil protection initiatives to combat natural and man-made disasters; a Mediterranean solar energy plan; the inauguration of the Euro-Mediterranean University in **Slovenia**; and the Mediterranean Business Development Initiative focusing on micro, **small and medium-sized enterprises**. The launch of the Union for the Mediterranean signalled a shift in the EU's approach to its immediate neighbours. Henceforth, as was underlined by the later launch in 2009 of the **Eastern partnership**, the **European neighbourhood policy** would essentially comprise distinct Mediterranean and Eastern elements.

A **UNION MINISTER FOR FOREIGN AFFAIRS** was envisaged in the **Treaty establishing a Constitution for Europe** and would have replaced the **High Representative for the Common Foreign and Security Policy**. Under the terms of the **Treaty of Lisbon**, which came into force in December 2009, many of the powers planned for the Union Minister for Foreign Affairs have been passed to the renamed **High Representative of the Union for Foreign Affairs and Security Policy**, currently **Catherine Ashton**.

UNION OF INDUSTRIAL AND EMPLOYERS' CONFEDERATIONS OF EUROPE (UNICE): See **BUSINESSEUROPE**

UNION OF SOVIET SOCIALIST REPUBLICS: See **USSR**

The **UNITED KINGDOM** (UK) plays an important role in European Union (EU) affairs. However, the United Kingdom has often had a troubled relationship with the EU in so far as it has found itself resisting further steps towards integration and often in opposition to **France** and **Germany**. In 1945 British prestige in Europe was very high, and in many states there was an expectation and hope that the United Kingdom would take the lead in developing European integration. However, British policy was to seek nothing more than intergovernmental co-operation, and the United Kingdom avoided involvement in any partnership that might diminish its own sovereignty and affect its relations with the **USA** and the Commonwealth. Europe was seen as an important issue, but it ranked behind both of these. Consequently, the United Kingdom dismissed the European initiatives contained within the **European Coal and Steel Community**, the **European Economic Community** (EEC) and the **European Atomic Energy Community**. The United Kingdom finally applied for membership of the EEC in 1961 and again in 1967, but both applications were effectively vetoed by France under President **Charles de Gaulle**. Negotiations recommenced in 1970, and the United Kingdom became a member of the European Communities (EC) in January 1973. Both major political parties, however, were divided over the merits of membership.

After 1973, the United Kingdom was often seen as only a partial member of the EC. It demanded and obtained a renegotiation of its terms of entry in 1975, and waged a campaign until 1984 for a reduction of what it regarded as its excessive contribution to the EC **budget**. Although the United Kingdom was at the forefront of plans for the **internal market**, its Prime Minister, **Margaret Thatcher**, grew increasingly hostile to the process of European integration by the late 1980s, and was particularly opposed to plans towards **economic and monetary union** (EMU). The United Kingdom has frequently maintained a position of complete isolation in the **European Council** and the Council of Ministers (now the **Council of the European Union**). For example, the United Kingdom declined full membership of the **European Monetary**

System until October 1990: even then, as a result of speculative pressure on sterling, it withdrew from the **exchange-rate mechanism** in September 1992. The United Kingdom also negotiated exemptions, or **opt-outs**, from parts of the **Treaty on European Union**, most notably from the Social Chapter (see **Charter of Fundamental Social Rights of Workers**), and from the **Treaty of Amsterdam**, which incorporated the **Schengen Agreement**. However, the Labour Government, which came to power in 1997, agreed to sign the Social Chapter shortly after coming into office, and hence the **protocol** on social policy was incorporated by the Treaty of Amsterdam into the revised **Treaty of Rome**. Although often hostile to moves towards political integration, the United Kingdom has been a strong advocate of economic reform, supporting **freedom of movement** and the internal market. It refused, however, to join EMU, which came into operation in January 1999. The United Kingdom strongly supported **European political co-operation** and its replacement, the **common foreign and security policy**, and it has a reasonably good record of compliance with EU **legislation**. The Government led by **Tony Blair** (1997–2007) was very pro-active at the start in pushing EU integration (e.g. promoting a **European rapid reaction force**), but in general the United Kingdom has adapted less easily to EU membership than most other EU member states. Public opinion in the country remains highly divided as to the desirability of membership of the EU and of joining EMU and adopting the **euro**. The UK Government pledged to hold a **referendum** on the **European Constitution**, and this was originally scheduled to take place in 2006. Opinion in the country was certainly divided, although most opinion polls predicted that in any referendum the **Treaty establishing a Constitution for Europe** would be rejected. This outcome seemed even more likely following events in France and the Netherlands, and in June 2005 the United Kingdom Government announced that it would shelve any such referendum, at least for the time being.

The UK took up the presidency of the Council of the European Union in the latter half of 2005, at a more troubled time than had been expected, and found itself trying to advance its arguments for more liberalization and economic reform while also having to deal with the issue of the budget, the reform of the **common agricultural policy** and the future direction and priorities of the EU itself. All were particularly controversial and achieving agreement was expected to prove difficult. This presidency sought to make the single market work better, but in retrospect never managed to escape the more pressing issues outlined above. These issues dominated the United Kingdom's discussions with the other member states as all participants prepared for the critical meeting to determine the budget in December 2005. Agreement on securing the commencement of **accession negotiations** with **Turkey** was clearly one of the highpoints of the British presidency, alongside the deal on the budget. Both were achieved after much internal bickering and disagreements, and this disharmony may be the lasting memory of that particular presidency for some time to come.

The UK's relationship with the EU has rarely been harmonious or without a degree of friction. This member state still holds the unenviable but often justified reputation as being one of the more awkward partners within the EU in terms of the integration process. **Gordon Brown**'s premiership was not expected to reverse recent trends. On the contrary, his apparently lukewarm approach to the EU after he succeeded Tony Blair in June 2007 reinforced the disengaged nature of the United Kingdom's attitude to European affairs. On a more positive note, Brown's stature among his European peers grew as he tried to lead a co-ordinated response to the economic downturn towards the end of 2008. However, Europe remained very much a secondary concern, and efforts were made to play down rather than tackle the meaning of European integration and its impact on the United Kingdom. There can be little doubt that minimal debate among politicians and scanty EU coverage from large sections of the popular media had a negative impact on voters in EP elections. This was reflected in another low turn-out (34.5%, down from 38.4% in 2004) in the United Kingdom at the EP elections in 2009 and ongoing apathy and resistance towards European integration amongst the general public and large sections of the British media. The Labour Government lost power in May 2010. A new Conservative/Liberal Democrat coalition Government was formed under **David Cameron**'s leadership. As expected, the Liberal Democrat members of the coalition arrangement were able to tone down the more Eurosceptic tendencies of their Conservative partners. This influence saw the replacement of the former Eurosceptic Conservative shadow Minister for Europe with the more pragmatic and moderate **David Lidington** as Minister for Europe. The coalition Government nevertheless proposed an 'EU Bill' which envisaged tighter parliamentary controls over transfers of power and competence from the United Kingdom to the EU and a referendum on the adoption of most future amending treaties as well as on key decisions concerning the United Kingdom's position within the EU (e.g. on adopting the euro and joining the **Schengen Area**). The bill was passed into law on receiving Royal Assent in July 2011. The issue of closer EU integration resurfaced amost immediately as members of the **eurozone** endeavoured to respond to the ongoing instability with the **euro** by searching for greater co-ordination. To this end, most of the EU member states agreed to sign the **Fiscal Compact Treaty (Treaty on Stability, Co-ordination and Governance in the Economic and Monetary Union)**. Neither the United Kingdom nor the **Czech Republic** signed this document, once again exemplifying the fact that these two countries appeared to be 'out of sync' with the majority of their counterparts.

The **UNITED KINGDOM BUDGET REBATE**, also known as the United Kingdom correction or the 'British budgetary question' (BBQ), resurfaced as a major and controversial issue in discussions over the future financing of the EU at a **European Council** summit in Luxembourg in June 2005. The issue had lain dormant for a number of years, but was now once more a major point of disagreement between the member states. President **Jacques Chirac** persistently questioned the need for the United Kingdom rebate, but **Tony Blair** stated that he was unwilling to consider its curtailment unless major reforms were made to how agriculture was financed. This stance opened up an immediate battle with France, the largest recipient of CAP spending, and relations between Chirac and Blair took an extremely frosty turn for most of the United Kingdom presidency of the Council of the European Union in the latter half of 2005. An agreement on the budget was finally reached in December 2005, whereby the United Kingdom gave back some of its rebate in return for the promise of a wholesale review of the CAP in 2008.

The British rebate had been negotiated by Prime Minister **Margaret Thatcher** after a long battle between 1979 and 1984. In the end, a deal had been reached, essentially between **François Mitterrand**, **Helmut Kohl** and Margaret Thatcher, at the **Fontainebleau summit** in 1984 to settle the BBQ and to allow the EU time to pursue the **single market** programme. The UK's annual rebate is currently worth about £5,000m., but it was only designed or agreed to as a temporary measure. The rebate was intended to make up the shortfall between what the United Kingdom paid into the EU **budget** and what it received back. The UK argued that the difference was significant because some 80% of the EU budget in the early 1980s went towards the **common agricultural policy**, a fund from which the United Kingdom was not a major recipient. Another issue that should be factored into understanding the United Kingdom arguments for the rebate was the much weaker economic position of the United Kingdom in the 1980s. The actuality and desirability of the United Kingdom rebate have appeared sporadically on the EU agenda over the course of the last 20 years or so—particularly whenever the member states have been considering the overall composition of the budget. It surfaced in March 1999 at the Berlin summit of the **European Council** and emerged again in the deliberations for the current financial period, which runs from 2007 to 2013. In December 2005 the Prime Minister Blair agreed to give up some 20% of the rebate for this period, on the condition that the funds did not contribute to CAP payments, were matched by contributions from other countries and were only for the new member states. Other member states, such as Germany and the Netherlands, have also in the past expressed an interest in achieving their own rebates.

The **UNITED NATIONS** (UN) is one arena where **European political co-operation** and the **common foreign and security policy** have generally been applied successfully. The permanent representatives to the UN of the European Union (EU) member states continue to meet regularly, to ensure that the member states vote together in as many divisions within the UN General Assembly as possible. In addition, the foreign minister of the member state currently holding the presidency of the **Council of the European Union** addresses the opening session of the General Assembly each September on behalf of the EU. In May 2011 the EU was granted an enhanced observer status at the UN. This means that the EU now has the right of reply, the right to speak in debates among representatives of major groups and before individual states, the right to submit proposals and amendments, and the right to raise points of order and to circulate documents. However, the EU does not have voting rights in the UN or the right to sit on the UN Security Council. In addition, the EU, which is the UN's largest financial contributor, holds an observer seat on the UN executive board for funds and programmes.

UNITED STATES OF AMERICA: See **USA**

UPE: See **Union for Europe of the Nations Group**

URBAN is the acronym of a 1994 initiative intended to promote the proliferation of innovative ideas and actions by means of their exchange between cities in the European Union, and to develop co-operative networks for the exchange of experience. Funded via the **European Regional Development Fund**, the subsequent initiative, URBAN II, covered the period 2000 until 2006. In the United Kingdom, Northern Ireland was a recipient of URBAN II funding, which was designed to assist urban regeneration of inner North Belfast.

URUGUAY ROUND is the name of a series of talks within the **General Agreement on Tariffs and Trade** (GATT). They began in 1986 and were initially due to be completed by the end of 1990. They were hindered by several disagreements over various aspects of the attempt to extend GATT rules beyond manufactured products to a variety of other areas, including services and intellectual copyright, and were eventually blocked by an impasse between the **USA** and the then European Communities (EC), primarily over agriculture (with France being the most vocal defender of the EC agricultural policy regime). Risking collapse on several occasions, the Round was eventually concluded in 1994, after France had agreed to accept the inclusion of agriculture in the agreement, resulting in a World Trade Agreement that led to the creation of a **World Trade Organization**.

The **US-EC DECLARATION** of 20 November 1990 was an attempt to place the relationship between the **USA** and the then European Communities (EC) on a more regularized base. Its major element was an agreement on the need for a framework within which consultations could be held on political and economic issues of interest to both sides, and since 1991 regular meetings have been held. (See **Transatlantic Declaration**.)

The **USA** (United States of America) made a major contribution to the development of European integration in the form of its strong involvement in European affairs after 1945, especially its provision of economic assistance (see **Marshall Plan**) and a defensive shield (see **North Atlantic Treaty Organization**), with the benefit of which the Western European states had the time to consider and explore ways of closer collaboration. Itself a federation, the USA encouraged efforts at integration until the 1960s, and did not seem to be averse to the notion of political union. After the 1960s, relations between the European Communities (EC) and the USA became more strained. While to some extent this was due to political arguments over foreign and defence policy, the major point of difference was economic. As the EC grew to be a more integrated economic entity, a conflict of interest developed with the USA, which was both a major economic rival and the EC's most important trading partner. Threats of action and retaliation from across the Atlantic, which reached their peak during the **Uruguay Round**, became commonplace, but disputes were usually resolved eventually by some form of compromise. (See **bananas**.)

During the 1990s, relations between the EC and the USA were institutionalized via a number of initiatives. The **Transatlantic Declaration** of 1990 provided a basis for greater collaboration and co-operation, and was followed in 1995 by the launch of a **New Transatlantic Agenda**. As a consequence of this, in May 1998 a Transatlantic Economic Partnership was initiated. In its draft Action Plan for the Partnership, the **European Commission** proposed that the European Union (EU) and the USA stimulate trade liberalization at worldwide level. Efforts to achieve such a goal have often been hindered by EU–US trade disputes. Equally, relations have often been soured as a consequence of major differences over, for example, the **Middle East** and the **Iraq War**. Annual summits nevertheless provide opportunities to stress the extent to which the EU and the USA do co-operate in an ever wider range of areas, including, for example, sharing information on **competition policy** cases.

The **USSR** (Union of Soviet Socialist Republics) was the major European military power after 1945 and unwittingly influenced the development of integration in Western Europe by arousing fears about its own power and intentions. Its actions in Eastern Europe between 1945 and 1948 and the dawning of the **Cold War** persuaded many Western states of the virtues of collaboration, at least in the form of a collective security system, and led them to urge greater involvement of the **USA** in Europe. The USSR remained hostile to Western European integration on both economic and political grounds, and only in 1988 did it declare a willingness to enter into discussions with the European Communities on a possible trading agreement. Since then, the USSR has disintegrated, with most of the successor states becoming members of the **Commonwealth of Independent States** and concluding **partnership and co-operation agreements** with the European Union (EU). The three Baltic States—Estonia, Latvia and Lithuania—are the main exceptions, having concluded **Europe agreements** and having now gained EU membership, which all three countries applied for in 1995.

V

V: See **Group of the Greens/European Free Alliance**

VAL DUCHESSE is a château on the outskirts of **Brussels** variously associated with the European Communities and the European Union. It was at Val Duchesse that the **Spaak Report** and the **Treaty of Rome** were drawn up in 1955–58. More recently, in 1985, the château gave its name to the process of social dialogue between the employers represented by the **Union of Industrial and Employers' Confederations of Europe** (UNICE—now renamed BUSINESSEUROPE), employees represented by the **European Trade Union Confederation** (ETUC), and the European Centre of Public Enterprises.

VALUE-ADDED TAX (VAT) is the second most important source of **revenue** for the European Union (EU), and represented 13.4% of the total revenue in the 2011 **budget**. (The most important source of revenue, based on gross national income (GNI), accounted for 75.6% of total EU revenue in that year.) Traditional **own resources** (TOR) comprise customs duties, agricultural duties and sugar levies. These own resources are levied on economic operators and collected by member states on behalf of the EU, and in 2011 represented 13.4% of the budget.

In 1967 two **directives** obliged all member states that had not already done so to introduce a system of VAT as the third major element of indirect **taxation** by 1970. New members have also had to introduce a VAT system. With the introduction of own resources to fund the budget, the European Communities (EC) were to receive up to a maximum of 1.0% of the VAT collected by the member states. In 1986 this was increased to 1.4%. By 2000 the percentage had been reduced to 1.0% and it fell back further, to 0.75%, in 2002 and to 0.50% in 2004.

A second dimension to VAT is the issue of **harmonization**. As part of the **internal market** programme, an attempt to introduce a greater degree of harmonization was made by Francis Cockfield in his **White Paper** (see **internal market**). This was only partially successful, and the member states continued to contribute moderately different VAT rates. In 1992, however, formal agreement was reached on a minimum standard rate of 15%. This was subsequently confirmed in 1996 when informal agreement was also reached on a maximum rate of 25%. Certain goods remain 'zero-rated' or appear on a special list subject to 'reduced rates' of VAT. Clearly, full harmonization is far from having been achieved. Moreover, the determination of several member states to make certain that the harmonization of VAT rates specifically, and indirect taxes in general, continues to be subject to voting by **unanimity** looks likely to ensure that it remains an elusive goal.

VAN GEND EN LOOS is the shortened name of a case, *Van Gend en Loos v Nederlandse Administratie der Belastingen*, which was heard by the **Court of Justice** in 1962. The Court ruled that European Communities **law** was a new legal order, directly applicable in the member states, and that individuals were required to be aware of this.

HERMAN VAN ROMPUY (1947–) was appointed as the first **President of the European Council** in November 2009 under the terms of the **Treaty of Lisbon**. He is an economist by profession. He studied philosophy at the University of Leuven, Belgium, before undertaking a Master's degree in applied economics at the same institution, working for the Belgian Central Bank, lecturing, and then pursuing a career in politics. Van Rompuy took up his post at the start of December 2009 when the Treaty of Lisbon entered into force. His appointment to the 30-month position, which will see him chair all meetings of the **European Council**, was something of a surprise given the number of more high-profile and immediately recognizable possibilities (such as **Tony Blair**). However, Van Rompuy had several factors in his favour: he had successfully led the Belgian Government (December 2008 to November 2009) through that country's recent phase of turmoil and political instability; as a fellow Christian Democrat, he secured the backing of both **Angela Merkel** and **Nicolas Sarkozy**, who also opposed the accession of **Turkey** to the European Union (EU); and, perhaps most importantly, he came from one of the smaller EU member states.

VARIABLE GEOMETRY is a phrase that was coined by **Jacques Delors** in the early 1980s and is widely used to refer to the possibility of common policies being developed and implemented at different rates by the member states, depending upon their degree of commitment to each policy. Reminiscent of the notion of a **two-speed Europe** raised by the 1976 **Tindemans Report**, it met with strong criticism from countries wary of political union. All the same, it has come to characterize aspects of the European Union's activities, notably **economic and monetary union** and the **area of freedom**, **security and justice** where certain member states enjoy **opt-outs**.

ANDROULLA VASSILIOU (1943–) is one of the 27 European Commissioners in the **Barroso** II Commission (2010–14), within which she has responsibility for education, culture, multilingualism and youth. She was first appointed to the Commission in 2008, when she held responsibility for health. She read law and later international affairs at the University of London in the 1960s, before pursuing a legal career until her partner became the President of Cyprus in 1988. Thereafter, she became more involved in the political arena and has had a distinguished career at home and abroad. She was particularly engaged in European Union issues as a member of the Cypriot parliament's European Affairs Committee and was its alternate member to the **Convention on the Future of Europe**.

VAT: See **Value-added Tax**

GÜNTHER VERHEUGEN (1944–) was born in Bad Kreuznach, Germany, and initially trained as a journalist before studying history, sociology and politics in Cologne and Bonn in the later 1960s. He worked as a civil servant in the German Federal Ministry of the Interior and then the Federal Foreign Office before being elected as a deputy for the Social Democratic Party in 1983. Thereafter he took a keen interest in foreign affairs, serving as a member of the Foreign Affairs committee from 1983 (and also chairing the parliament's European Union special committee in 1992) until he was appointed as Minister of State in the Foreign Office in 1998. He was appointed to the **Prodi** Commission in September 1999 and served his term as the Commissioner for Enlargement. He quickly emerged as a highly competent individual and was reappointed (as one of only three Commissioners from the Prodi team) to the new **Barroso** Commission by the German Government in 2004. In November 2004 he assumed responsibility for the Enterprise and Industry portfolio and was also made one of the five Vice-Presidents of the Commission. His portfolio was largely a new departure for someone who had specialized in, and was more familiar with, foreign affairs. He stepped down as the German Commissioner at the end of his term and was replaced by **Günther Oettinger**.

VERS: See **Voluntary Export Restraints**

VETO refers to the option available to each member state in the **Council of the European Union** to reject proposals put before it. Thanks to the **Luxembourg Compromise**, the option to veto survived almost unscathed until the mid-1980s. Since then, and owing mainly to the increased use and acceptance of **qualified majority voting**, the use of the veto is essentially restricted to areas (e.g. tax **harmonization**, the admission of new member states, treaty reform) where **unanimity** is still required under the treaties. In practice, the veto is rarely used.

A **VISA POLICY** was established by the **Treaty on European Union** (TEU), which declared the aim of developing such a policy, applicable throughout the

European Union (EU), for nationals from third countries. The TEU demanded the establishment of a common format for all visas before January 1996, by which time visa policy decisions would require only a **qualified majority vote** in the **Council of the European Union**. The visa policy does not prevent member states from pursuing their own policies with regard to internal security and the maintenance of law and order. The **Treaty of Amsterdam** was also concerned that there should be greater co-operation over visa policies. Today, all EU states, with the exception of **Ireland** and the **United Kingdom**, have a unified visa system as part of the **Schengen Area**. Even **Iceland**, **Norway**, **Liechtenstein** and **Switzerland** are part of this Schengen **Area** (with associated status). In April 2010 a new EU Visa Code (previously adopted in 2009 by the **Council** and the **European Parliament**) came into force. This code, which represented an attempt to harmonize EU visa law, collected into one document all legal provisions governing the decisions on visas for those states belonging to the Schengen **Area**. It is hoped that the conditions for issuing visas to third-country nationals will now be more straightforward, transparent and fair.

The **VISEGRAD GROUP** originally consisted of Czechoslovakia, Hungary and Poland when it was created in 1991–92 as a mechanism for the three states to support each other in efforts to pursue closer integration with Western European organizations, notably the European Communities. In 1993 membership rose to four countries when the Czech Republic and Slovakia replaced the now-disbanded Czechoslovakia. Among the activities of the Visegrad group was the establishment of the **Central European Free Trade Association** (CEFTA). The extension of CEFTA to include other countries from **Central and Eastern Europe** and Slovakia's slower progress towards European Union membership during the mid-1990s led to the effective demise of the Visegrad Group. Multilateral co-operation between the members has nevertheless continued.

VOLUNTARY EXPORT RESTRAINTS (VERs) are bilateral agreements reached by the European Union (EU) with other countries, whereby the latter voluntarily agree to limit exports of particular products to the EU. The restraints are not in fact truly voluntary, but have been accepted by the exporting countries in preference to other restrictions that might be imposed. The best-known VERs have related to trade in steel and cars. The **European Commission** has a mandate to negotiate VERs on behalf of the EU.

The **WARSAW PACT** was the name of the **Cold War** alliance of Eastern European countries led by the **USSR** that regarded itself as a mutual defence organization against the ambitions of the **North Atlantic Treaty Organization** (NATO). It derived its name from the Warsaw Treaty of Friendship, Co-operation and Mutual Assistance which was signed by the USSR, **Albania, Bulgaria**, Czechoslovakia, Hungary, Poland and Romania in May 1955. The Warsaw Pact was dissolved in 1991 following the fragmentation of the USSR.

WATER and its pollution are major European Union (EU) concerns, and a number of **European Commission directives** have been aimed at improving the quality and protection of water in all its aspects. High standards have been set for the quality of both drinking and bathing water, and member states risk punitive action if they do not meet the required standards within stipulated deadlines. Further directives relate to fish habitats and the discharge of pollutants. The EU has also signed several international conventions designed to reduce the level of water pollution. (See also **environmental policy**.)

The **WERNER REPORT** is the name of a 1970 plan for **economic and monetary union** (EMU) prepared by a committee, headed by Pierre Werner (1913–2000), then Prime Minister of Luxembourg, which was appointed by the 1969 **Hague summit**. The Report emphasized the need for the European Communities to proceed simultaneously in co-ordinating and harmonizing economic policy, narrowing exchange-rate margins, integrating capital markets and establishing a common currency and a **European Central Bank**. It presented a three-stage programme for the implementation of full EMU by 1980, the deadline imposed by its remit. Although its views were accepted in a modified format by the Council of Ministers (see **Council of the European Union**), the economic difficulties of the 1970s led to the programme's abandonment. The question of full EMU was not considered again fully until **Jacques Delors** was appointed by the Council in 1988 to consider the EMU question, and this led directly on that occasion to a specific title on EMU being inserted into the **Treaty of Rome** by the **Treaty on European Union**.

WEST GERMANY: See **Germany**

The **WESTERN BALKANS**, as far as the European Union (EU) is concerned, comprises **Albania**, **Bosnia and Herzegovina**, **Croatia**, **Kosovo**, **the former Yugoslav republic of Macedonia**, **Montenegro** and **Serbia**. Currently they are involved in a **stabilization and association process** with the EU. The EU continues to support political stabilization and economic development in this region, and provided more than €4,500m. to the above countries through the former **CARDS** programme in 2000–06 to anchor the democratization process and promote economic growth. Since early 2005 the Directorate-General for Enlargement has been responsible for managing all relations with the countries of the Western Balkans. Financial assistance is now provided via the **instrument for pre-accession assistance** and amounted to €2,900m. for 2009–11.

WESTERN ECONOMIC SUMMITS: See **G-8**

WESTERN EUROPEAN UNION (WEU) originated in the 1948 **Treaty of Brussels** and was designed to promote co-operation in the fields of defence and security. After the collapse of the **European Defence Community** (EDC) proposals in 1954, the treaty was used to establish a body 'to promote the unity and to encourage the progressive integration of Europe', which included the Federal Republic of Germany (West Germany) and Italy in addition to the original five signatories (Belgium, France, Luxembourg, the Netherlands and the United Kingdom). WEU had little infrastructure, and was only occasionally activated in the 1950s. Its military functions were more or less immediately absorbed by the **North Atlantic Treaty Organization** (NATO) after 1949, and it ceded its social and cultural responsibilities to the **Council of Europe** in 1960, in effect becoming moribund. Some attempts to revive it were made in the 1960s and 1970s, but it was not until 1984, partly as a result of the growing rapprochement between the **USA** and the **USSR**, that it was reactivated as a body that could provide a distinctive Western European voice on defence and security issues.

In 1987 it adopted a programme that called for the creation of a 'cohesive European defence identity', strengthening conventional capabilities while retaining nuclear potential, improving consultation and co-operative mechanisms, and establishing a common system of monitoring obligations. The **Treaty on European Union** made WEU an integral part of the European Union (EU), identifying it as a de facto constituent of the pillar of **common foreign and security policy** (CFSP). The EU was to 'foster closer institutional relations with the WEU with a view to the possibility of the integration of the WEU into the Union'. WEU moved its headquarters to Brussels, granted observer status to other Western European countries, and engaged in discussions on closer ties with countries from **Central and Eastern Europe**. Consequently, by 2002 28 countries enjoyed one of four different types of status with regard to WEU. These ranged from membership through associate membership and observer status to that of associate partner.

The pursuit of closer co-operation between the member states of the EU and WEU was further encouraged by the **Treaty of Amsterdam**. Moreover, the **Treaty of Nice** paved the way for the de facto incorporation of WEU into the EU by reducing the status of WEU and establishing a **European security and defence policy**. The Treaty effectively removed various references to WEU from the TEU, with the most visible representation of the incorporation of WEU into the EU being **Javier Solana** assuming the dual roles of Secretary-General of WEU and **Secretary-General of the Council of the European Union**. In December 2009 the entry into force of the **Treaty of Lisbon** transferred the mutual defence clause of WEU to the EU. WEU was formally dissolved in June 2011.

WEU: See **Western European Union**

WHITE PAPER is the term used to describe a **European Commission** document setting out proposed legislative initiatives, such as, for example, the 2001 White Paper on **Governance** or the 2006 White Paper on a European Communication Policy. In some cases it follows a **Green Paper**, which is used by the Commission to launch a full-scale public discussion on a proposal. The document produced in 1985 by Francis Cockfield for the European Commission on the measures required to implement the **internal market** by 1992 is still the most widely known example. Entitled *Completing the Internal Market*, it listed some 300 separate measures that would need to be taken, for each of which a target date and a timetable were set. The measures related to the removal of physical, technical and fiscal barriers to a single market. To facilitate their **implementation**, appropriate provisions were incorporated into the 1987 **Single European Act** and, by 1992 most of the measures had been introduced. When a White Paper has been endorsed enthusiastically by the **Council of the European Union**, it becomes the action programme for the European Union in that specific policy area.

WIDENING involves extending the membership of the European Union (EU) through the process of **enlargement**. For much of the history of the EU, widening has been subordinate to **deepening**.

HAROLD WILSON (1916–95), later Baron Wilson of Rievaulx, was Prime Minister of the United Kingdom from 1964 to 1970 and again from 1974 to 1976. He submitted the second UK application to join the European Communities (EC) in 1967, reversing Labour Party policy. However, after 1970 he attacked the terms of entry negotiated by the Conservative Government, and upon his return to office in 1974 sought their renegotiation. Talks with the EC were completed in January 1975, and the new terms were subsequently endorsed in a referendum on whether the United Kingdom should remain in the EC, held in June 1975. The result showed a clear majority in favour of continued membership (67.2%). However, the renegotiations and referendum deepened the divisions within the Labour Party over EC membership, and became one of the reasons why **Roy Jenkins** and others subsequently left the party.

WINE LAKE, like **butter mountain**, is a term, usually of derision, that has been employed to symbolize the consequences of the price guarantee and intervention elements of the **common agricultural policy**. It refers to the large surplus stocks of wine created by over-production.

WITHDRAWAL from the European Union (EU) has rarely been seriously contemplated by any member state, although **Greenland**, as part of Denmark, did withdraw in 1985. With increasing evidence of Euroscepticism and concerns among some member states over the future path of integration, the Treaty establishing a Constitution for Europe included a dedicated withdrawal clause. This clause, inserted into the **Treaty on European Union** by the **Treaty of Lisbon**, allows a member state to withdraw from the EU provided it notifies the **European Council** of its intention. An agreement setting out the arrangements for withdrawal is then to be concluded by the Council, acting by a two-thirds' majority and after obtaining the consent of the **European Parliament**. Withdrawal will take place two years at the latest after the notification to withdraw has been received by the European Council.

WITHDRAWAL PRICES: See **Common Fisheries Policy**

WOMEN'S RIGHTS have become an important European Union (EU) concern, based initially upon Article 141 of the **Treaty of Rome** (now Article 157 of the **Treaty on the Functioning of the European Union**). The Article, as amended by the **Treaty of Amsterdam**, committed the member states to ensuring that 'the principle of equal pay for male and female workers for equal work or work of equal value is applied'. Various **directives** require the member states to amend their laws to exclude any form of sex **discrimination** and to ensure equality in training, appointments, promotion and pay. Workers who believe they are the victims of discrimination have the right to take their case to a tribunal without fear of dismissal: the **Court of Justice** can act as the final arbiter as to whether national laws conflict with EU rules. Discrimination in social security systems was banned in 1978, and in 1986 it was decreed that discrimination in occupational pension schemes had to end by 1993. In 1997 the **Council of the European Union** adopted a directive on sex-discrimination cases, whereby the plaintiff and defendant were to share the burden of proof. The **European Commission** has also launched a number of special action schemes. In May 1998 the EU's first conference on women's **employment** was held in Belfast. (See also **Equal opportunities**.)

WORKER PARTICIPATION: See **Charter of Fundamental Social Rights of Workers**; **Fifth Directive**; **Workers' Rights**

WORKERS' RIGHTS were referred to in the **Treaty of Rome**, which obliged the member states to promote the improvement of living and working conditions for workers and required member states to collaborate on a number of questions relating to **employment**. Most European Communities/Union activity has been devoted to improving working conditions through the implementation of several **directives** on occupational **health and safety** (see **European Foundation for the Improvement of Living and Working Conditions**). Other directives relate to the principle of **freedom of movement**. Restrictions on free movement can be applied by the member states only on grounds of a risk to public order, safety or health, or where jobs are in a particular sector of public administration. Persistent efforts by the **European Commission** to establish worker participation in company decision-making (see **Fifth Directive**) first achieved success when all the member states, except the United Kingdom, decided to implement the **Charter of Fundamental Social Rights of Workers**; the United Kingdom eventually signed up to the Charter in 1997 after the election of a Labour Government. Workers' rights are also prominent in the **Charter of Fundamental Rights** proclaimed in December 2000.

The **WORKING TIME DIRECTIVE** (WTD) aims to protect the **health and safety** of workers against the adverse effects of working long hours without adequate breaks. It also addresses disrupted working patterns and sets a maximum working week of 48 hours within any four-month period. Guidelines relating to daily rest times, weekly rest periods, minimum holiday entitlements and night-shift working are also included. Certain categories of workers, including those employed in oil extraction and transport, and junior doctors in training, were initially excluded from the **directive**.

The 1993 Working Time Directive has a treaty basis under Article 138 of the **Treaty of Rome** (now Article 154 of the **Treaty on the Functioning of the European Union**), which was incorporated into the treaty as part of the **Single European Act** in 1986. Approval of measures is by **qualified majority voting**. The United Kingdom opposed the directive and was successful in obtaining an **opt-out**. This allows a member state not to apply the limit to working hours under certain conditions. Following the adoption of the **Charter of Fundamental Social Rights of Workers** by the Labour Government in 1997, however, the Working Time Directive became effective in the United Kingdom in September 1998. The original Working Time Directive (93/104/EC) covered all sectors of activity except transport, activities at sea and the activities of trainee doctors. The provisions of the WTD did not apply if other European Union (EU) law contained more specific provisions in a particular field or if national laws contained provisions that were more favourable to workers.

The WTD provided for: a maximum 48-hour working week averaged over a reference period; a minimum daily rest period of 11 consecutive hours a day; a rest break where the working day is longer than six hours; a minimum rest period of one day a week; and a statutory right to annual paid holiday of four weeks. Night working must not exceed eight hours a night on average. Normal hours of work for night workers must not exceed an average of eight hours in any 24-hour period. Workers are entitled to a free medical examination before being employed on night work and at regular intervals thereafter. Anyone suffering from health problems connected with night work must be transferred, wherever possible, to day work. The issue of the WTD remains highly topical and controversial. In 2000 the scope of the WTD was extended to include some previously excluded professions (doctors in training, transport workers, activities at sea) to cover some 5m. people. In 2003 the **European Commission** issued a Communication on the review of the directive which analysed the **opt-outs** and **derogations** in member states, and summarized recent case-law concerning the definition of working time. This consultation period ran until the end of March 2004 and fed into a new Commission proposal that still contained an opt-out, but one that made it more difficult for employers to press staff against their will to work for any longer than 48 hours. The sensitivities that working hours still cause for some member states, including especially the United Kingdom but also Germany, Malta, Poland, Slovakia and Slovenia, became apparent in early 2005 when the **European Parliament** voted in its first reading of the proposal to phase out the opt-out over a three-year period. The **European Trade Union Confederation** strongly supports the ending of the opt-out as do some of the United Kingdom's main trade unions, but **Tony Blair** consistently resisted any such moves and sought to garner enough support in other member states to form at least a blocking minority in the Council. In June 2005 the Council voted to maintain the opt-out.

The **WORLD TRADE ORGANIZATION** (WTO) was established on 1 January 1995 as the successor to the **General Agreement on Tariffs and Trade** (GATT). The origins of both GATT and the WTO can be traced back to the late 1940s and efforts to liberalize international trade by reducing the levels of tariffs. By the 1990s the agenda of international discourse on trade issues had widened considerably with a series of policy issues requiring consideration at a multilateral level. These included **competition policy, environmental policy** and approaches to labour market deregulation. GATT had been a fruitful exercise but was limited in its scope, and for this reason it was decided to establish a new organization that became the WTO. The WTO has a much broader scope than GATT. Whereas GATT regulated trade in merchandise goods, the WTO also covers trade in services, such as **telecommunications** and banking. The highest body of the WTO is the Ministerial Conference. This usually meets every two years and, among other things, elects the organization's chief executive—the director-general—and oversees the work of the General Council. The General Council is in charge of the day-to-day running of the WTO and is made up of ambassadors from member states who also serve on various subsidiary and specialist committees. The WTO has a crucial role to play in ensuring, promoting and protecting trade liberalization. It serves as a forum to settle disputes—these have occurred between the European Union (EU) and the **USA** over such issues as **bananas**, hormone-treated beef and hush kits (noise reduction devices) for aircraft—and may operate as the ideal body for settling cases on competition policy that involve European and North American companies.

Despite the apparent logic of such an international forum to resolve disputes, there has been growing unease and dissatisfaction among sections of the public about the democratic credentials of this body. Four main criticisms abound. These are: firstly, that the WTO is too powerful; secondly, that (it is believed) the WTO only serves the needs of the rich states and is largely indifferent to the needs of the economically less advanced states; thirdly, that the WTO is indifferent to the impact of free trade on workers' rights, child labour, the environment and health; and lastly, that this organization lacks democratic **accountability**. This discontent was, in the early 2000s, manifest in street protests and a series of violent confrontations between protesters and the police at meetings of the WTO in response to the perceived threat of **globalization**. In September 2002 a former Thai Deputy Prime Minister, Dr Supachai Panitchpakdi, began a three-year term as Director-General and was charged with pursuing the **Doha Round**. He was the first WTO head to come from a developing nation. As a respected economist, he played a key role in leading Thailand out of the Asian currency crisis. In September 2003 the world trade talks in Cancún, Mexico, collapsed after four days of wrangling over farm **subsidies** and access to markets. Many commentators maintained that the failure to reach agreement would hit the poorest nations hardest. Pessimism intensified when the WTO announced that there was little hope of restarting the collapsed world trade talks in December of that year because both the developing countries and the rich nations seemed unable to agree on the scope of trade negotiations and the need to reduce agricultural subsidies. Nevertheless, agreement was attained in Geneva in August 2004 when talks achieved consensus on a framework agreement on opening up global trade. The USA and the EU were to reduce agricultural subsidies, while developing nations would cut tariffs on manufactured goods. At mid-2012, however, the future of the Doha Round appeared uncertain, with disagreements over trade liberalization and protectionism remaining the major obstacles to progress.

The WTO had 157 members in 2012. In September 2005 the Frenchman Pascal Lamy became the fifth Director-General of the WTO, and he was re-elected to a new four-year term in 2009.

WTO: See **World Trade Organization**

XYZ

YAOUNDÉ CONVENTION is the name of an agreement signed in 1963 and renegotiated in 1969. Named after the capital of Cameroon, the Convention provided for the former colonial territories of the member states to be associated with the **European Economic Community**. Eighteen countries, known collectively as the Associated African States and Madagascar, were signatories of the Convention. They were permitted duty-free access to the European Communities for most of their products on a non-reciprocal basis and were eligible for grants from the **European Development Fund** and loans from the **European Investment Bank**. The Yaoundé Convention was superseded in 1975 by the **Lomé Convention**.

YOUTH FOR EUROPE was the name of a programme established in 1987 to promote a sense of European identity and understanding among young people. It was a scheme enabling young people not engaged in higher education to spend at least one week in another European Union country. Participants were expected to have already received some instruction about socio-cultural aspects of the country they wished to visit. The scheme was modelled on the successful bilateral youth exchange programme between France and the Federal Republic of Germany (West Germany), which began in the 1950s. Youth for Europe was renewed in 1991 for three years, and was subsequently extended until 1999. It was replaced by the Youth Programme in 2000, which was in turn succeeded by the **Youth in Action Programme**.

The **YOUTH IN ACTION PROGRAMME** superseded the Youth Programme in 2007, and targets young people aged between 13 and 25 years. The programme was to run until 2013 and was given financial resources of €885m. in order to contribute to the education of young people, particularly through exchange activities and European voluntary service. The scheme involves 31 countries: the 27 European Union member states, plus **Iceland**, **Liechtenstein**, **Norway** and **Turkey**. The programme focuses particularly on promoting co-operation in youth-related matters. The programme incorporates the **European Voluntary Service** programme and runs a Euro-Med partnership programme. The 2001 **White Paper** on Youth was the result of a wide-ranging consultation at national and European level, and seeks to engineer new mechanisms and ways to counter young people's strong disaffection with the traditional forms of participation in public life. At its core it calls on young Europeans to become active citizens.

YOUTH TRAINING: See **European Social Fund; Social Policy**

YUGOSLAVIA's disintegration in the 1990s was associated, as far as the European Union (EU) was concerned, with the early failure of efforts to develop an effective **common foreign and security policy** (CFSP). From the outset of the conflict in the Balkans (see **Western Balkans**), the European Communities (EC) were involved in efforts to try to avert war and the disintegration of the Yugoslav federation. Initially, the EC offered the prospect of an **association agreement**, but this failed to prevent the secession of **Slovenia** and **Croatia** in 1991. Indeed, under pressure from Germany, the EC effectively sealed the fate of Yugoslavia by recognizing the two countries. Soon after this, **Bosnia and Herzegovina** was recognized, although Greek objections delayed recognition of the former Yugoslav republic of **Macedonia** until 1995. All that was now left of Yugoslavia was **Serbia** and **Montenegro**, which existed as the Federal Republic of Yugoslavia until adopting the name 'Serbia and Montenegro' in 2003. The dissolution was completed in June 2006 when, following a referendum, Montenegro declared its independence, a move officially recognized by the Serbian Government 10 days later.

In the mean time, the EC sought to avert further conflict in Bosnia and Herzegovina by sponsoring a Conference on Yugoslavia in August 1992 and seeking a new mandate for **sanctions** from the **United Nations**. Sanctions and renewed attempts to broker ceasefires failed to have much impact, and a plan for a confederal solution in 1993 had to be abandoned for lack of support within Bosnia and Herzegovina. The plan was replaced by a proposal to, in effect, divide the new state, but this too was eventually rejected by the Bosnian Serbs in 1994. Soon the **USA** became more deeply involved and, with the backing of the **North Atlantic Treaty Organization**, secured a peace deal at Dayton in November 1995.

Post-Dayton, the role of the EU in the reconstruction of the former Yugoslavia was initially focused on the **Royaumont Process**, aimed at promoting stability and good neighbourliness between the successor states, and the administration of Mostar, a city divided between Croats and Muslims. In 1997 proposals on closer ties with the EU were put forward. In what was referred to as the 'regional approach', the EU required that the successor states co-operate with one another and commit themselves to respect minority and **human rights** as well as democratic principles as preconditions for financial aid and better trade access to the EU market. Following the **Kosovo** conflict in 1999, the need to promote stability in the region—now referred to as the **Western Balkans** and incorporating **Albania**—led to the creation of the **stabilization and association process**. As part of this process, countries of the former Yugoslavia gained the status of **potential candidate state** as well as access to a new programme of financial assistance, **CARDS** (replaced in 2007 by the **instrument for pre-accession assistance**, or IPA).

JOSÉ LUIS RODRÍGUEZ ZAPATERO (1960–) became Prime Minister of Spain in 2004 and was re-elected for a second term in 2008. Zapatero studied law at the Univerity of León and joined the Spanish Socialist Party in 1979. He entered politics and was first elected to the Spanish parliament in 1986. He was appointed as Secretary-General of the Spanish Socialist Workers' Party in 2000 and shortly afterwards launched a successful bid to take the leadership of the party. In office as Prime Minister, he placed greater emphasis on fostering ever better relations with his European counterparts and in so doing downgraded the Atlanticist direction of the previous governments of José María Aznar. Following his party's heavy defeat in an early general election held in November 2011, Zapatero was succeeded as Prime Minister by **Mariano Rajoy** of the People's Party.